CREATIVE HEALERS

A Collection of Essays, Reviews, and Poems from *The Pharos*
1938–1998

Compiled and Edited
by Edward Day Harris, Jr., M.D.
Alpha Omega Alpha Honor Medical Society
Menlo Park, California

The articles that comprise this book originally appeared in *The Pharos*,
the literary, non-technical quarterly of Alpha Omega Alpha Honor Medical Society.

Printed by The Ovid Bell Press
Design and composition by Laura Carter
Cover sketch by Jim M'Guinness

For information, write:
The Ovid Bell Press
1201-05 Bluff St.
Fulton, Missouri 65251

Printed in the United States of America

This anthology is dedicated
to the memory of
William Webster Root, M.D.,
who had the imagination and the energy
to found Alpha Omega Alpha in 1902,

to the many writers who have
contributed their work to *The Pharos*
from 1938 to the present,

and to Drs. Bob and Helen Glaser
who, together for so many years,
led AΩA and produced *The Pharos*.

CONTENTS

PREFACE

There was no need to write a separate introduction for this anthology because the following paper, published in the Centennial Issue of *The Pharos* (Autumn, 2002), provides in great detail the history of Alpha Omega Alpha honor medical society and folds in the chronicle of development of *The Pharos* as well. Appropriate for this preface, however, is a brief recounting of the process of compilation of selected essays and poems from the 60 years, 1938 to 1998. First, why the cut-off at 1998? The reason is that, in addition to the symmetry of 60 years existence, that year marked my first as editor, having taken over from Bob Glaser in the late spring of 1997. Bob is the first to admit that so many of the scholarly and well-written papers that are included in this anthology were reviewed, revised, and carefully edited by his partner, wife, and managing editor of *The Pharos,* Helen Glaser.

Intriguing to me is the unplanned way in which the papers I selected classified themselves without effort into 13 broad topics (not including poems), and they are presented in this order. This number, 13, intrigues me because it illustrates the breadth of interests that American physicians (and a few special non-physicians) embody as they take up their pens and write. The largest section is *III. History of Medicine and the Physicians Who Made History.* Other sections, given their own space and heading, could have been lumped in section III, but it seemed best to separate out scholarly papers on the ancient Egyptians, Greeks, and Romans; two accounts focusing on Sir William Osler; three papers with special attention given to the special challenges for women in both delivering and receiving care; and three papers describing physician involvement in the horrors of wars. Pure enjoyment for me was stumbling upon so many effective essays dealing with the doctor both as a writer of poetry and prose, and as a subject of others' writing.

The concept of "timelessness" is a vague one, but in choosing among the many papers that dealt with health policy and medical education, it was gratifying to find several that were written with prescient predictive powers, and although written as long ago as the 1980s, remain relevant to these early years of the 21st century.

Although it is unlikely that many medical students, with the pressures upon them to learn a geometrically expanding universe of medical science, will have time and desire to read through this compilation, there are many papers that we—their teachers, role models, and mentors—will find inspirational and, through the writing of these masters, be able to impart wise and helpful insights to our students.

Particularly enjoyable has been finding amidst the many pages of *The Pharos* over this long stretch of years, writings by men and women (mostly men, because until recently women have contributed papers less often than their male colleagues) who are readily recognized as leaders of American medicine, individuals who have shaped health policy, education and training, and clinical science. Some of these are Lewis Thomas, A. McGehee Harvey, Robert Zollinger, Helen Taussig, Max Finland, Francis D. Moore, Paul Beeson, Carleton Chapman, Bob Petersdorf, John Knowles, Faith Fitzgerald, and Denton Cooley. It also is a particular pleasure to introduce to many younger readers two essays of Alan Gregg; he writes with an easy grace and deep literary background common to few physicians.

It is striking to me how much the quality of poetry submitted to *The Pharos* has increased in the years since 1998. There is no logical reason for this, but it has happened. For that reason, only the best of poems published prior to that year were included here. Someday, it may be appropriate to publish a separate collection of poems from the pages of *The Pharos*.

I very much wanted to include the longest paper (by far) ever published in *The Pharos*, "The evolution of the right to health concept in the United States," a thoroughly scholarly and fully referenced historical treatise written by Carleton Chapman (then dean of Dartmouth Medical School), and a young apprentice, William Talbott. Alas, there were not enough pages to include this, but I commend it to you (*The Pharos*, Spring 1971) for an account of the struggles to achieve any form of universal health insurance in this country . . . a struggle that goes on.

Readers will note that I have made an attempt to summarize the professional lives of those whose papers are included but are no longer alive, and to track down those who are living for an account of their present activities. Some, still very much alive, I assume, have not been traced; I apologize to each of them in advance of their reading their work in this anthology.

I have made minimal attempts to standardize the format for references and, rather, have kept the reference format essentially as authors submitted their essays to *The Pharos*.

Edward D. Harris, Jr., MD (AΩA, Harvard, 1962)
Editor, *The Pharos*, 1997–present

ACKNOWLEDGMENTS

I am particularly indebted to my department and deans at Stanford University School of Medicine both for having an enlightened sabbatical program for faculty and for allowing me to take the months that I needed to read, compile, and edit this anthology. Laura Carter of Carter Document Services designed and composed the final version, and the loyal artist who has contributed to each issue of *The Pharos* for many years, Jim M'Guinness, generated the cover sketch and those preceding each section. John Bell, president of The Ovid Bell Press in Fulton, Missouri, has long been the printer of *The Pharos* and has been both willing and interested to take on printing and binding of the book. Finally, the authors of poetry and prose receive my thanks and, at the same time, my encouragement to continue sending manuscripts to *The Pharos* for review, inclusion in an upcoming issue, and—perhaps—inclusion in the next anthology of writings from *The Pharos*.

ALPHA OMEGA ALPHA: ENCOURAGING EXCELLENCE IN MEDICINE FOR MORE THAN A CENTURY

DAVID C. DALE, M.D., AND
EDWARD D. HARRIS, JR., M.D.
(Autumn 2002, pp. 4–21)

Dr. Dale (AΩA, Harvard Medical School, 1966) is the immediate past president of Alpha Omega Alpha, and Dr. Harris (AΩA, Harvard Medical School, 1962) is editor of The Pharos *and executive secretary of AΩA. This paper led off the Centennial issue of* The Pharos *in 2002. Dr. Dale found many useful papers for preparation of his part of the treatise in records of the society kept in the National Library of Medicine.*

"Worthy to Serve the Suffering"

ALPHA OMEGA ALPHA (AΩA) was founded by a small group of medical students at the College of Physicians and Surgeons of Chicago in 1902, at a time of critical transitions in American medical education. The sciences basic to medicine—microbiology, chemistry, and physiology—were blossoming, but only a few medical schools had faculty qualified to teach them. Hospitals were growing in size and numbers, but the modern relationships of teaching hospitals to medical schools were only beginning to emerge. The number of students in medical schools had increased dramatically. In 1880, the United States had about 100 medical schools with 12,000 students; this represented about one-tenth of all students in higher education. By 1900 there had been a 60 percent increase in the number of medical schools, to 160 schools, and the number of medical students in U.S. medical schools had doubled. Rapid expansion of the population and settling of the western states were important factors in this growth, but running a small medical school could also be an attractive and remunerative enterprise for some physicians.

In the 1890s, the Association of American Medical Colleges (AAMC) characterized schools as "regular," "homeopathic," "eclectic," "physiomedical,"

1

and "non-descript." The facilities, faculties, finances, and curricula, as well as the students in all schools of all classifications were very heterogeneous. In 1871, Charles Eliot, president of Harvard, stated that "the Harvard medical students were noticeably inferior . . . to students in other departments." He felt then that increasing entrance requirements and a three-year curriculum would improve the quality and dedication of students. By the late 1800s, many schools had introduced curricular changes as well as stricter admission standards. The most notable and influential curricular changes were at Johns Hopkins University, the University of Michigan, the University of Pennsylvania, and Harvard University.

Overall, at the turn of the century medical students were not well prepared for scientifically-oriented medical training; it was unusual if they had more than a high school education.

William W. Root and the founding of Alpha Omega Alpha

The founder of AΩA, William Webster Root, began his medical education at the National Medical School in Chicago in 1899. In 1900, he transferred to Harvey Medical College, and then enrolled at the College of Physicians and Surgeons of Chicago (later renamed the College of Medicine of the University of Illinois) in 1901. Root was born in Niagara Falls, New York, on August 19, 1867, the son of E. Volney and Amelia Emily Root. He was a descendant of Thomas Roote, who had emigrated from England to Hartford, Connecticut, about 1637. Root graduated from Cornell University with a Bachelor of Science degree in 1890. He then completed two years of graduate work in chemistry at Cornell while teaching chemistry, physics, and biology. Just before matriculating at medical school, Root taught at the Chicago Manual Training School and was enrolled as a graduate student at the University of Chicago. He was then 34 years old, married to a college classmate, Anna Bronson, and father of three children.

Undoubtedly, Root was one of the most mature and prepared students in his class. In an essay he wrote in 1909, Root stated that it was the lack of interest in scholarly attainments among medical students that led him to begin AΩA. A classmate, Ernest S. Moore, and one of the original members of AΩA, was more critical of his fellow students and the school. In describing the class, he said that "honesty was conspicuously absent" and that "behavior in the halls and classrooms was rough and boorish." He said that "articles of any value would be sure to remain where placed in the medical building only by nailing them securely." He also indicated that the faculty was only interested in training new practitioners and that "heads of departments at the school were selected by who could buy a substantial block of stock."

Root first discussed the idea of forming an "honor fraternity" with a few of his classmates in July 1902. Years later, Ernest Moore wrote, "In the summer of 1902, I was sitting on the steps of the old College building. It was almost time to start the grind when Dr. Root came out of the building and sat down beside me and began to tell me about a plan he had in mind to organize a medical honor fraternity, patterned after the lines of Phi Beta Kappa. When this conversation had ended, he had sold me his ideas and we had selected a list of men to be invited to membership." Root then presented his ideas to this group of students at a meeting on August 25, 1902. Plans moved quickly, and on September 27, 1902, twenty-eight students met for a dinner at the Bismarck Hotel in Chicago to ratify a constitution drafted by Root and to induct the society's original members. Today the name, emblem, motto, and goals of ΑΩΑ are the same ones presented at the early organizational meetings. ΑΩΑ still uses the motto proposed by Root — Ἄξιος ὠφελεῖν τοὺς ἀλγοῦντας — "Worthy to Serve the Suffering"—and emphasizes scholarship and appropriate professional demeanor as the basis for membership. Remarkably, the founders clearly stated from the beginning their intentions that race, color, creed, gender, and social standing should never be barriers to membership.

After the Alpha Chapter of ΑΩΑ was established at the College of Physicians and Surgeons at Illinois, plans developed quickly for other ΑΩΑ chapters, all orchestrated by the vision and leadership of William Root. Root first talked with students at the other Chicago medical schools. On December 13, 1902, a charter was granted for 14 senior students at Rush Medical College to become members of ΑΩΑ. On January 31, 1903, Root, with two other students, Thomas A. Bryan and Benjamin Thomas, filed with the State of Illinois the Articles of Incorporation for the Alpha Omega Alpha Medical Honor Fraternity. The original documents named John Eddy Haskell, Chairman; William Henry Moore, Director; and William Webster Root, Secretary. The fee for incorporation was ten dollars. Less than two months later, on February 7, 1903, thirteen senior students at Northwestern University Medical School were inducted. It is not clear how these original students from the Chicago schools were selected, and a few years later this became the subject of some controversy. It is very likely that Root himself identified like-minded students who then selected the other initial members.

In the February 2, 1903, minutes of the Committee on the Constitution and Extension, Root recorded, "Five present. [We discussed] whether to send a man east. Four moved in favor; I did not vote." Root then loaned the society $100 without interest and his fellow student, Burchard Hayes Roark, traveled to Cleveland and Philadelphia to help organize chapters at Western Reserve, Jefferson, and the University of Pennsylvania. Then, at the end of the 1903 academic year, Root transferred to Rush Medical College and graduated in 1904, along with 24 Rush classmates as members of the beta, or second chapter of ΑΩΑ in Illinois. His academic transcripts from the College of Physicians and Surgeons and from Rush show that Root was a good student. His best grades were in pediatrics (100 percent), surgery (95 percent), and obstetrics (95 percent), and his attendance record was excellent.

Dr. Root remained the secretary–treasurer of AΩA and the key person who maintained both the records and the cohesiveness of the organization until his death on April 23, 1932, after 30 years of leadership. Given his interest and training, it is surprising that Root did not enter academic medicine after medical school. However, at the time of graduation he was 37 years old with four children, a number that later swelled to six. Following graduation, Root practiced medicine in Parker, Indiana, for four years. From 1908 to 1911, he worked at the Parke Davis Company in Detroit in bacteriological research, and subsequently moved to the HK Mulford Laboratories in Philadelphia (from 1911 to 1912). Root then returned to the family home in the rural village of Slaterville Springs, New York, nine miles from Ithaca. From 1920 to 1921, he served as physician at the Utica, New York, State Hospital for the Insane, and was commissioned as First Lieutenant, M.R.C., U.S. Army (from 1912 to 1917). Root spent the rest of his professional life as a family physician in Slaterville Springs and as secretary-treasurer for AΩA.

William Webster Root died in 1932.

Anna Bronson Root

William Root's widow, Anna Bronson Root, continued to work on behalf of AΩA until her death in 1947, serving in the capacity of assistant secretary-treasurer and editor of *The Pharos*. An article in the May 1947 issue, written by one of her daughters, Hasseltine Root Brill, is excerpted here:

Anna Conant Bronson Root 1865–1947

It is with regret that we announce the death on February 15 of Mrs. Anna Conant Bronson Root, widow of the late Dr. William Webster Root, founder and lifetime secretary-treasurer of this Society. At Dr. Root's death in 1932, Dr. J. J. Moore became general secretary-treasurer and Mrs. Root was appointed assistant secretary-treasurer. She officiated in this capacity until her death, with the assistance of Mr. and Mrs. G. Meredith Brill, her daughter and son-in-law. In addition to ordering insignia, answering correspondence, keeping up-to-date membership card files for sixteen thousand members and other duties incidental to such an office, Mrs. Root became, in 1937, editor of *The Pharos*. She was happy to remain affiliated with the Society and was deeply grateful for the consistent cooperation of the national officers.

Born in Boston on June 6, 1865, she was the only daughter of Dr. Benjamin Franklin Bronson and Ann Hasseltine (Chaplin) Bronson, whose father, Jeremiah Chaplin, was the founder and first president of Colby College at Waterville, Maine. She was graduated from Abbot Academy in Andover,

Massachusetts, and from Cornell University in 1893 after which she taught French and German in secondary schools and at the Women's college of Brown University. A woman of scholarly aptitude, she relinquished a promising career in the teaching profession to marry William Webster Root, who was then a teacher of physics and chemistry in Chicago Manual Training School and at the University of Chicago. Mrs. Root encouraged his decision some years later to study medicine though it meant very frugal living for their growing family. It is well known that he conceived the idea of Alpha Omega Alpha as an effort to encourage among the students "personal honesty and the spirit of medical research," while yet an undergraduate at the University of Illinois School of Medicine in 1902. Rush Medical College awarded him the M.D. degree in 1904 and he proceeded to practice medicine in Indiana and in Slaterville Springs, N.Y.

... Mrs. Root helped her husband constantly with the ever-growing Society correspondence since his patients took much of his time. Indeed, Society work became so much a part of their family life that their children learned to say "Alpha Omega Alpha" as soon as they learned to talk at all. The Roots were unable to afford regular household help and Mrs. Root shuttled between kitchen and office. Many an address which Dr. Root gave was read first to his wife.

They collaborated on the wording of the constitution and other Society publications where Mrs. Root's unfailing excellence in phrase turning and use of English were a valuable asset. She proofread all publications then and later on.

The national Alpha Omega Alpha office was in the Root home until 1938 when the equipment necessary to carry on the work completely outgrew the home accommodations. During Dr. Root's lifetime, however, the office remained in their home and Mrs. Root always found time to counsel her husband on Society business and answer correspondence in his absence.

Dr. and Mrs. Root rest under a simple white marble stone. Under Dr. Root's name are these words, so engraved at his request—"Founder of AΩA."

— May 1947, pp. 3, 15

Root, Hall, Cannon and the Committee on Expansion

The year 1905 marked an important transition for the fledgling organization. Although started by students, Root and a few of his colleagues maintained leadership of the organization. They proved to be effective in recruiting exceptional leaders from academic medicine to join them in making AΩA a national organization. Dr. Root was clearly the person making this all happen. Ernest Moore wrote, "Root was a sturdy, sincere man. He was a crusader at heart and a quiet, persistent, efficient warrior when in action. His high ideals, his enthusiasm, and his earnestness gave us AΩA."

With a vision of building a national organization, Root first recruited Winfield Scott Hall to become the primarius or president. Thomas Bryan first suggested the title "Primarius" for the leaders of the organization at the Constitution and Extension Committee meeting in February 1903. Bryan also recommended that Root be the first primarius. Handwritten records of this meeting show that at first Root accepted the idea, signing the minutes for that meeting as "Dr. W. W. Root, Primarius, Alpha Omega Alpha." Root subsequently chose, instead, to become the organization's long-term secretary-treasurer.

Winfield Scott Hall served as primarius of AΩA with great dedication from 1904 to 1913. Hall was a European-trained physician and head of the Department of Physiology of the School of Medicine at Northwestern University. In this era, physiology was the cornerstone for basic science education for medical students. Hall had joined the faculty at Northwestern in 1885. He, like Root, was a crusader, determined to bring scientifically-minded teaching to Northwestern. He was captured by Root's idea that a medical honor fraternity could aid in bringing Northwestern to the forefront of U.S. medical schools, and he put all of his prestige and reputation as an educator to the use of the organization.

Hall then aided Root in recruiting another physiologist and a rising young star on the faculty at Harvard, Walter B. Cannon, to become associate primarius or vice-president of Alpha Omega Alpha, even before there was a chapter at Harvard. Cannon became famous as a teacher, researcher, and author of *The Wisdom of the Body*. He is best known for his research on the sympathetic nervous system, beginning with the first radiographic studies of gastrointestinal motility. Like Root and Hall, Cannon was an idealist who believed that good works could make a difference in society. Cannon served as associate primarius and the principal aide to Hall and Root from 1904 to 1913. More importantly, Cannon served until 1930 as chairman of AΩA's Committee on Extension, the group that reviewed applications and decided which medical schools were permitted to open AΩA chapters.

In his third annual report to Primarius Hall in 1906, Root noted with some pleasure that AΩA, for the first time, was no longer in debt, having a credit balance of $67.34. He wrote, "It is exceedingly gratifying to me, to whom the society when in the experimental stage owed some $200, to see a comfortable bank account with every assurance that it will be increased in the future." He then stated, "Our regular income for this coming fiscal year from keys, certificates, and chapter tax should be, not counting any increase in the chapter role, not less than $350." Root then added, "Considering the labor that will be necessary for the next year, which I think will be more than in either Phi Beta Kappa or Sigma Xi, and also considering our present financial condition and future prospects, I think it would not [be] out of place to respectfully ask the Primarius for the same salary that Dr. Voorhees, Secretary-Treasurer of Phi Beta Kappa receives, viz $100. If the Society could not afford any compensation, I should most willingly, even to the neglect of my practice, put the enormous amount of time on this work that I have in the past." He closed, "Congratulating you on the wonderful growth of this ethical order under your able leadership, I remain, William W. Root."

For the year ending August 31, 1906, the Society had receipts of $536.17, expenses of $486.83, with a credit balance at the Parker Bank Company in Parker, Indiana. Root recorded expenses for one trip, a trip to Ann Arbor to visit the University of Michigan, from October 20 to 24, 1905. The round-trip train fare was $15.60, shoe shine and shave $0.15, a newspaper, $0.05, and per diem requested was five days at $4 per day. Over the years, Root requested modest compensation for his time, and at one point requested a new typewriter to be paid for by AΩA. As secretary-treasurer, his careful stewardship, as well as his dedication to the organization, were very important.

It was fortunate for AΩA that Walter B. Cannon agreed to chair the Committee on Expansion. He served in this role 1905 to 1930, relinquishing it only after all of the American Medical Association (AMA) Class A medical schools had opened AΩA chapters. Cannon stepped down after developing papillary cancer of the bladder, which presented as hematuria on a trip in Europe, his first major health problem and one possibly caused by the radiation exposure he experienced early in his research career. Joining Cannon on the original committee were: John M. Dodson, dean of the Rush Medical School, then affiliated with the University of Chicago; William Pepper, dean of the University of Pennsylvania School of Medicine; and Nathan P. Colwell, secretary of the AMA Council on Medical Education. By 1905, national leadership of AΩA had clearly passed from the students to the medical establishment.

Under this able leadership, AΩA grew steadily. New chapters were added: in 1905, Washington University; in 1906, Harvard University, the University of California at San Francisco, Johns Hopkins University, and the University of Toronto; the University of Michigan in 1907; in 1908, the University of Minnesota; Cornell University in 1910; Syracuse University and McGill University in 1911. AΩA grew easily because William Root had drafted a good constitution in 1902. With revisions in 1904, 1909, 1911, and 1920 (and a few thereafter), AΩA had a reliable blueprint for the remaining years of the century. The constitution made it relatively easy for new schools to organize their chapters and gave considerable latitude to each school in selecting a councillor and student members and in organizing chapter activities.

Expansion was central to the development of AΩA, and Walter B. Cannon was the central figure in this process. Cannon was a Midwesterner from Wisconsin who went to Boston for medical school, but never forgot his rural roots and simple upbringing. Years after becoming an internationally recognized professor, he still enjoyed summers of physical labor on his small New Hampshire farm. At Harvard, Cannon rose from the position of instructor in physiology in 1900, to the George Higginson Professorship of Physiology in 1906. One of his biographers, Elin L. Wolfe, commented in a personal communication that there seemed never to be a medical organization Cannon would not join, and AΩA was one of them. As associate primarius and first AΩA councillor at Harvard, he helped the class of 1906 establish its chapter, both as a stimulus for better work among students and as the link binding Harvard with other important medical schools of the country. Root wrote to the senior class president, Channing Frothingham, on January 15, 1905, "Go ahead and pick out five men who can, with Cannon and Mallory [form a chapter]." At the end of the year Frothingham recorded, "The men are chosen solely from those of the highest rank. Besides scholarship, the character of the individual is taken into consideration and those men, given the preference, who appear destined for a successful medical career."

After Hall invited Cannon by telegram to become associate primarius, Cannon responded promptly on stationery from the Physiology Laboratory of the Harvard Medical School, "I should esteem it an honor to be Associate Primarius of the Alpha Omega Alpha fraternity." Only eight days later, he sent another note to Dr. Hall, on the new AΩA stationery that listed his name as the associate primarius, together with Primarius Hall and Secretary-Treasurer Root, writing, "I am much pleased with this new honor, and I shall be happy to promote the aims of the new fraternity as far as I can." And to show his interest, he added, "I have written to Dawson at Johns Hopkins about the Society, but have not yet received an answer." Primarius Hall then wrote Cannon after receiving the application for the Harvard chapter, "Through the leverage that we can get from Harvard, I hope that [we can] organize chapters at Columbia and Johns Hopkins." Later that year, Cannon invited Professor Barker of Johns Hopkins to speak at the AMA meeting in Boston so that they could discuss AΩA. He also wrote to Root about inviting other schools to have chapters: "I have no doubt in my mind as to the advisability of such possibilities as Columbia, McGill, Toronto, or any of the larger state university medical schools." He added, "What is meant by New York University? I do not know of it. I do not know the character of St. Louis University or Syracuse University. If you and Dr. Hall approve, however, I see no reason to differ from your opinion." In this same letter he added, "The two things needed in medicine, as I see it, are a high spirit of service and a searchingly thorough acquaintance with the methods of discovering disease and caring for diseased people. To support these two needs, the Society stands for moral uprightness and devotion."

Cannon's job in deciding which schools to recommend for chapters was sometimes difficult. On October 21, 1907, he wrote to Primarius Hall that he had inquired of members of the chapter at Western Reserve about the conditions of the medical school at the University of Cincinnati, and that their recommendation was against forming a chapter there. Cannon said, "I wrote as kindly a letter as I could to Dr. J. H. Shaw, of the University of Cincinnati, stating that for the present that there was likely to be opposition to opening a chapter there." Shaw responded to Root that he regarded Cincinnati as a "one-horse, low-down affair, not worthy of consideration" and imputing to Cannon a smug complacency because he was at Harvard. Cannon wrote to Hall, "Of course the first charge is ridiculous, but the second is rather serious. . . . I wrote to Dr. Shaw and now I hope that, so far as my attitude is concerned, he is informed." Cannon also favored establishing chapters in the Midwest (e.g., Iowa, Kansas, Minnesota), but met with substantial opposition, particularly from the chapter at the University of Pennsylvania.

Controversies and stories

As AΩA grew, not every school that applied was granted a chapter. If disagreement existed, delay ensued until a consensus was reached. Weaker schools, particularly those that got low marks from the AMA reviews, did not receive chapter charters. When there were problems, Cannon, with the support of the primarius and Root, managed to select only the best schools for new chapters. Consistently, however, there was candor in the evaluations and politeness in the correspondence with the schools.

There were also other interesting controversies. For example, on November 26, 1907, Root, always signing as the Founder and Secretary-Treasurer, wrote to Primarius Hall proposing that three officers, the primarius, the associate primarius, and the secretary-treasurer be appointed to their positions for life. Hall responded quickly in a letter November 29, 1907, stating, "Now, doctor, I cannot bring myself to affix my name to this document. I cannot feel that it is wise. I fully believe that you should be life-Secretary and through life a member of the board of directors. I believe it would be a grave and tactical blunder for me to retain the position of Primarius for much longer. Let us hold this in abeyance till we have had an opportunity to think it over." The wisdom of Hall prevailed. He later retired from AΩA activities, but Root remained secretary-treasurer and member of the board for the rest of his life

A more serious controversy arose in 1912 regarding the role of the chapters versus the board of directors in controlling the affairs of AΩA. The constitution stated that the general executive control of the society "shall be vested in the Primarius and the Board of three Directors." The primarius was designated to select his own successor and to remain on the board for six years after leaving office. As the number of chapters increased, the constitution was revised, and the board of directors expanded to five members, with three of the five chosen from the chapter councillors, with terms of three years.

F. C. Waite of Western Reserve had been appointed to the Committee on Expansion about 1908, and was then elected to the Board in 1909. Early in 1912, he wrote to Primarius Hall stating, "Now that the first 10 years have elapsed, the fraternity should be put in the control of its constituent chapters." He advocated that all of the directors should be elected, and he announced his resignation from the Board effective June 10, 1912. He implied that Hall, Cannon, and Root did not now have legitimate authority to lead the society and indicated that they had achieved their positions without competing for them. This angered Root. He quickly marshaled several resources in his defense. In a memorandum to the councillor and secretary of each chapter, he pointed out that Waite was "not a medical man." He noted that concessions had been made repeatedly to the Western Reserve chapter and that Waite's term on the board was expiring anyway. He consulted Baird, Cox and Scherr, a New York law firm. Raimond Baird replied on May 6, 1912, that the administration of the fraternity was in line with customary and proper procedures. Root made sure that chapter representatives supporting his views would be present or represented at the upcoming Atlantic City meeting of AΩA, in conjunction with the annual AMA meeting. The June meeting occurred. Root and Hall prevailed and continued to direct national affairs.

Another idea of potentially major impact surfaced in 1909, when Primarius Hall suggested to E. A. Schafer of the University of Edinburgh that AΩA might establish a chapter in Scotland as part of international expansion. On February 2, 1909, Schafer responded to Hall, indicating that the Royal Medical Society of Edinburgh had given the idea "prolonged consideration" but could not "see its way to take up formation of a branch in Edinburgh." He commented, "Medical ethics are very well looked after in Great Britain." He added, "The Royal Society was of the opinion that there was therefore no serious necessity for impressing the medical minds over here with the importance of the Hippocratic maxims." This response probably tempered Hall's enthusiasm to pursue this idea. Over the years that followed, many other discussions about forming AΩA chapters outside of the United States and Canada probably occurred. A chapter chartered at the American University at Beirut, Lebanon, in 1958 remains the sole exception to this decision to limit chapters to accredited schools in North America.

Another interesting controversy arose in the late 1920s, during the Prohibition era. Some AΩA students at Tulane were accused and convicted of prescribing alcohol for the families of their friends. It is not entirely clear who turned them in, but the AΩA councillor wrote asking Dr. Root to decide whether the students should be dismissed from AΩA. Root deferred to the local chapter for resolution of this politically charged issue.

The evaluation of medical schools

After the first few schools had established their chapters, the evaluation of schools for new chapters became more systematic and more stringent, greatly aided by Nathan Colwell of the AMA's Council on Medical Education. Schools petitioning for a chapter were required to provide detailed information on their facilities, faculty, finances, curricula, and students. At some schools, the initial inquiry about starting a chapter came from students; at others it came from the dean or a faculty member. Inquiries came to Root, Cannon, and Hall, who remained in remarkably close contact with each othter. The records suggest that Root was the first of these men to have a typewriter; most of the early correspondence from Cannon and Hall is in beautiful penmanship. Letters from the medical school dean often accompanied applications for a new AΩA chapter. If an application was promising, it was sent to the members of the Committee on Expansion. If the Committee approved, Cannon advised Hall, who in turn asked Root to obtain votes from current chapters on admitting a new chapter. This process worked well for well-known schools, but it was also cumbersome. As Hall pointed out to Root in a letter on December 7, 1905, it was difficult for the medical student members in one chapter to know enough about another school to give a meaningful evaluation.

Several tensions were at play in selecting schools for AΩA chapters. Root was particularly interested in having chapters at the best U.S. medical schools. The schools and their faculties and students often had difficulty in assessing their own quality. The best assessment of schools was information garnered through the AMA review process, to which the AΩA Committee on Expansion was closely linked because Dean Dodson of Rush chaired the Committee and Colwell was its executive secretary. Correspondence between Root and Hall indicated their belief that where there were multiple medical schools in a city or state, it would be better if the higher ranked school had an AΩA chapter first. Thus, Johns Hopkins was encouraged to open a chapter before the University of Maryland, Washington University before St. Louis University, and Columbia before the other New York schools. From one vantage point, this brought prestige to AΩA; from another, it served to raise medical school standards, as school leaders appreciated AΩA's expectations and saw themselves compared with other schools. It is clear from the correspondence that the officers and directors took their responsibilities very seriously, and they were thorough in their evaluations. When proprietary schools wrote to Root about a new chapter, he directly discouraged them from applying, politely pointing out deficiencies or reasons for the likelihood that their application would not be successful.

On August 29, 1909, Root sent out a list of schools without chapters to members of the Committee on New Chapters: Cannon, Hall, Dodson, and Waite.

Root favored chapters for Stanford, Colorado, Yale, Indiana, Drake, Iowa, Kansas, Tulane, Nebraska, Cornell, Syracuse, Texas, Virginia, and McGill. He included a "doubtful" list: St. Louis University, Dartmouth, Fordham, New York University, Cincinnati, Manitoba, Queens (Kingston-Ontario), and Laval (Quebec and Montreal). None of the small "proprietary" schools were on Root's list.

Over the next two decades, Root, Cannon, Hall, and Hall's successors corresponded actively with schools proposed for, and discouraged from, applying for AΩA chapters. For example, William Leavenworth, a student at the Bowdoin Medical School in Portland, Maine, wrote to Dr. Root about establishing a chapter at his school on February 6, 1916. Root replied on February 9, 1916, indicating that he had reviewed the facilities and information about the school provided to the AMA. He acknowledged hi interest in a school in Maine having an AΩA chapter because his mother-in-law had been born in Brunswick and her father had been the first president of Colby College there. He then indicated that before the application could be given serious consideration, a detailed review would be necessary by the Committee on Extension, composed then of Cannon, Dodson, Dean Heffron of Syracuse University, Colwell of the AMA, and Root. He also advised the student that if he personally wanted to be a member, "it will be necessary first to convince us that you are one of the ranking men of your class."

When students from Vanderbilt University inquired about a chapter, there was considerable correspondence about whether the Methodist-Episcopal bishops or a Board of Trustees controlled the institution. When the courts decided in favor of the Trustees, Root assured students at Vanderbilt that a chapter was possible there. However, it was several more years before the Vanderbilt chapter was actually approved. Root, Cannon, and members of the committee favored opening a chapter at Stanford in their review of 1909. There was a wealth of correspondence, but school officials were very slow in getting the application completed. The chapter finally opened in 1928 with much celebration, although in the late 1970s Stanford students decided that AΩA engendered a "competitive spirit" that was incompatible with the medical school and, in addition, all formal grades for students had been abolished; the chapter became inactive and eventually was dissolved.

AΩA was expanding, and it was evaluating schools at the same times as were several other organizations that had substantially larger budgets. AΩA benefited from their efforts. The AAMC, organized in 1876, was a relatively weak organization before 1900. In 1903, its new secretary-treasurer, Ted C. Zapffe, began visiting member schools, summarizing their plans of study, and making specific recommendations for conversion to four-year medical programs and higher entrance requirements. In 1904, the AMA Council on Medical Education had been formed with Arthur Dean Bevan, professor of surgery at Rush and colleague of

Dodson of the AΩA Committee on Extention, serving as its first chairman. In 1909, Abraham Flexner began his national review of medical schools under the sponsorship of the Carnegie Foundation. Flexner's status as an educator and the bite of his comments were very important in the closing of small, private, for-profit medical schools and raising the standards of medical education.

Councillors, students, and membership

The 1904 constitution of Alpha Omega Alpha set forth the standards for selection of medical student members to the society by each chapter. The constitution stated that

> the mission of AΩA is to encourage high ideals of thought and action in the schools of medicine and to promote that which is the highest in professional practice. As students, members are to avoid that which will make them unworthy of their calling and to further the same spirit among fellow students. As practitioners, members are to maintain and to encourage the lofty ideals set forth by the revered father of medicine, Hippocrates; to show respect for other members of their calling, to advocate high requirements for entrance to the course in Medicine and for graduation; in short, to do what they can to exalt and to ennoble the profession. A commercial spirit and all departures from medical ethics are to be avoided and the purely scientific, the philosophical and the poetic features of the profession are to be cultivated.

This early version of the constitution also stated that "junior and senior students in medical schools, possessing a chapter were eligible for election as active members, based on scholarship, strength of character; individuality and originality, and moral character; unselfishness, respect for one's self and for others, combined with lofty ideals." The total number of members in the senior class was not ever to exceed one-sixth of the class. At the first election for the junior class, no more than five candidates were to be selected. One negative vote was sufficient to exclude a candidate, but in such cases, the member so voting was responsible to state the reasons in full before the other members. Privileges of membership required payment of an initiation fee of $3. The constitution has since been revised several times, but the basic criteria for the selection of student members have not changed.

In the 1909 constitution, Article III, Section 11, stated,

> Graduate students and other physicians or investigators in subjects allied to medicine, who have gained wide recognition through original research, or in an administration, and who conform to the requirements demanded for undergraduates may be elected to active membership provided the number of living members thus elected in any chapter shall not at anytime exceed one-twelfth of the total number of living members elected in course.

The constitution also stated "physicians may also be elected from classes antedating the granting of the charter, not more than one-twelfth of any class being chosen."

Honorary members also were elected. This class of membership later became limited to distinguished individuals not eligible for membership by usual routes, i.e., those who did not attend a medical school that has an AΩA chapter, or are members of a medical school faculty that lacked an AΩA chapter. The first 1911 Harvard Medical School report lists six honorary members: Reginald Heber Fitz, Frederick Cheever Shattuck, Theobald Smith, Edward Hall Nichols, Richard Clarke Cabot, and Henry Asbury Christian.

At first, with only a few chapters and a few students, AΩA was a small organization. However since the number of chapters was increasing and election to membership was for life, membership has grown quite substantially. By 1922 there were 3780 members; in 1936 there were 10,125 members; and by 1956, 25,848 had been elected. In 2002, at the one-hundredth anniversary of its founding, there were more than 100,000 members of AΩA.

Changes in leadership

After Primarius Hall left office in 1913, the titles of president and vice-president were used for all subsequent officers. Burton Opitz of Columbia University was president from 1913 to 1918, and G. Carl Huber of the University of Michigan was vice-president during the same period, followed by Dean John L. Heffron of Syracuse University as president from 1918 to 1924 and John J. MacKenzie of Toronto University as vice-president from 1918 to 1922. While serving as vice-president, Mackenzie was killed in an accident en route to a meeting with Root on August 1, 1922.

Through the early years, a major factor for the success and stability of AΩA was the gradual transitions that occurred in its leadership. In 1930, with all of the AMA category A schools having chapters and with other changes in their lives, both Cannon and Colwell resigned from the Committee on Extension/Committee on New Chapters. Root became ill and died in 1932 from carcinoma of the stomach. John Dodson resigned from the Board and subsequently died in 1933, and new leadership was sorely needed. Fortunately for AΩA, Josiah J. Moore of Chicago was ready to assume the responsibilities of the secretary-treasurer, Elias P. Lyon became the chairman of the Committee for New Chapters, and Walter L. Bierring was then serving as AΩA's president.

Walter Bierring, president of AΩA from 1924–1960

After Root, Hall, and Cannon, Walter Lawrence Bierring was the next powerful force leading AΩA. Bierring was born in July 1868 in Davenport, Iowa, and graduated from the State University of Iowa College of Medicine. After graduation, Bierring spent two years absorbing the best of European science and medicine, including studies at the Pasteur Institute, where he learned to prepare diphtheria toxin. In 1903, he became professor of medicine at the University of Iowa and, in 1908, director of the University Hospital in Iowa City.

In 1909, Abraham Flexner visited Iowa. The visit was described as a whirlwind affair and, by many accounts, was superficial. Flexner's report was highly critical of the medical school. It was rebutted bitterly by the faculty at Iowa. The professor of surgery was livid: "The facts intended to be set forth [in Flexner's report] are so far removed from the truth that a relationship cannot even be recognized." The price for saving the school was the removal of Walter Bierring as chairman of the Department of Medicine. This occurred on June 24, 1910. Campbell Howard, a junior member of the McGill medical school faculty was hired in his place. In 1921, Bierring was elected to AΩA, and he became a member of the AΩA board of directors, following the death of John Mackenzie.

William Bean, former chairman of the University of Iowa Department of Medicine, wrote a fitting tribute to Walter Bierring for the July 1961 issue of *The Pharos*:

MEMORIAL TRIBUTES
Walter Lawrence Bierring, M.D., 1868–1961

Dr. Bierring, the grand old man of American medicine, is dead. He whose life seemed inextinguishable and who had risen more than once from a grave illness, is no longer among us. The plain fact of his mortality is set before us to contemplate. He, who seemed to have captured the well hidden secret of Ponce de Leon and embodied youthfulness in great antiquity has departed in the ninety-third year of his age. With his death one of America's strongest links with British and Continental medicine of the Nineteenth Century is broken. No longer do we have the beneficence of the urbane wisdom and humanity of this grand old man who managed to retain a young outlook, despite his venerable years which he wore with dignity but without solemnity.

Only when I came to Iowa thirteen years ago did I fall directly under his spell. He had been head of the Department of Internal Medicine of the College of Medicine, Iowa City from 1903 to 1910.

I think many undergraduate medical students shared my delight in the inspirational recollections Dr. Bierring was able to evoke of memorable days in the Pasteur Institute, of working in Koch's laboratory, visits and studying at the famous German schools and his visits to Britain. He was able to share with us intimate knowledge of many of medicine's heroic figures. Possessing as he did great natural advantages in mind and character, his habits and attitudes guaranteed for them full employment. He exemplified the rare phenomenon of productivity which increased rather than diminished with the years. Not for him was just the old man's dreaming of dreams but also the seeing of visions. Finally combining the zest of youth and the wisdom of years Dr. Bierring escaped the bane epitomized by La Rochefoucauld who said, "Old men are fond of giving good advice in order to console themselves for being no longer able to serve as bad examples."

Dr. Bierring can properly be called the father of Alpha Omega Alpha since, though he did not found it, it was through his thoughtful and constructive work that it reached its full stature as a symbol of distinguished excellence in medicine. As president of Alpha Omega Alpha for 36 years and editor of The Pharos Dr. Bierring saw the unprecedented growth of American medicine with great improvement in quality of research, scholarship and practice. Members of Alpha Omega Alpha may be proud that through his wise statesmanlike control this growth has been not only very extensive in scope but very fruitful in encouraging excellence.

Perhaps Dr. Bierring's character can be summed up best in a story which Dr. Peyton Rous once told me, which I have related elsewhere. "It occurred at the time when the cornerstone of the University Hospitals building was laid in Iowa City in the middle 1920's. The great ceremonial occasion was attended by representatives from many universities and institutions. As Dr. Bierring and Dr. Rous were being driven to the affair to hear the great speakers, they came upon the scene of an accident. A runaway horse had overturned a wagon and a young farmer lay injured. Dr. Bierring immediately got out and attended to the medical needs of the injured man, while the procession moved on without him. Only when the injured man was cared for did Dr. Bierring, unruffled and unaware of the impression he had made, move on to the pavilion of the elect where the speeches were in progress."

Others have listed the many marks of distinction, the numerous memberships, honors, and offices in the oustanding medical societies which came Dr.Bierring's way. He accepted them with good grace but without any notion that they conferred infallibility. The essence of Dr. Bierring's contributions was his vision of the larger aspects of medicine, its potential grandeur and the value of encouragement of scholarship, seeking out the best in learning, in teaching, in research and in practice. His several missions accomplished, Dr. Bierring died in the fullness of years, ripe in wisdom, mellow in the knowledge of history so much of which he himself had seen at first hand. American medicine may well take pride in a person whose accomplishments are worthy of the heroes of old. We all share with his family the sorrow inevitable with bereavement, and we sympathize with the members of his family who survive him, but this sorrow happily is tempered by our contemplation of his great achievements, his wisdom and his character.

— July 1961, pp. 184–87

While Bierring can be considered the father, if not the founder, of the society, it is appropriate to list here the presidents whose sequential vision and leadership have held AΩA together while advancing its programs and influence.

William W. Root, founder (1902, University of Illinois)	1902–1904
Winfield S. Hall (1903, Northwestern University)	1904–1913
Russel Burton-Opitz (1907, Columbia University)	1913–1918
John L. Heffron (1911, Syracuse University)	1918–1924
Walter L. Bierring (1921, University of Iowa)	1924–1960
Wilburt C. Davison (1931, Duke University)	1960–1963
Victor Johnson (1936, University of Chicago)	1963–1966
Donald G. Anderson (1938, Columbia University)	1966–1968
John Z. Bowers (1954, University of Maryland)	1968–1978
James A. Campbell (1944, Harvard Medical School)	1978–1980
Sherman M. Mellinkoff (1944, Stanford University)	1980–1984
James F. Glenn (1953, Duke University)	1984–1986
Carol J. Johns (1950, Johns Hopkins University)	1986–1987
Jeremiah A. Barondess (1949, Johns Hopkins University)	1987–1989
Leo M. Henikoff (1961, University of Illinois)	1989–1990
Stuart A. Schneck (1952, University of Pennsylvania)	1990–1993
William B. Deal (1974, University of Florida)	1993–1995
Frank C. Arnett (1968, University of Cincinnati)	1995–1996
David C. Dale (1966, Harvard Medical School)	1996–2002
Michael V. Drake (1989, UCSF)	2002–

The Pharos

One of Bierring's most noteworthy accomplishments was initiating the AΩA quarterly journal, *The Pharos*. When publication of *The Pharos* began in January 1938, forty-one chapters of Alpha Omega Alpha had been chartered. The list of the chapters, with the names of their secretaries or councillors, was published in this and subsequent issues. The first listing included the board of directors and the members of the single committee that had been organized and put in charge of developing interest in other medical schools to apply for charters. Initially, *The Pharos* served as a newsletter for the society, but gradually grew into a nontechnical medical quarterly with focus on medical history, ethics, and literary essays related to medicine.

The May 1938 issue of *The Pharos* noted that the 1937 annual dinner of AΩA was in Atlantic City, concurrent with the annual meeting of the AMA. Morris Fishbein, editor of the *Journal of the American Medical Association*,

Charles Heyd, president of the AMA, and John Upham, president-elect of the AMA, joined AΩA speakers and officers at the head table, reflecting the warm and natural association that existed then between the two organizations. The leadership of American medicine was supportive of AΩA and its members. This was a relationship that was to change in subsequent decades as academicians rejected what they believed to be the conservative and reactionary policies of the AMA.

For many years, beginning with the first issue, *The Pharos* published a section titled "Chapter News from Chapter Secretaries" that listed activities of each chapter during the preceding months. It appears that there were no limitations placed on the number of words that each secretary could submit! A "Necrology" section was included as well in each early issue. It is striking how many members died then at young ages, clear evidence of the extension of longevity achieved through medical science and practice since the 1930s.

In the 1950s another section, "AΩA Personals," was added. In that column, appointments of deans and chairpersons at academic medical centers were recorded. For example, the January 1960 issue of *The Pharos* announced that Dr. Robert J. Glaser had been named vice-president for medical affairs at the University of Colorado School of Medicine. In 1957, the first publication of a "Medical School News" section in *The Pharos* announced, "The facilities of Stanford University School of Medicine in San Francisco are to be replaced by a modern medical center on the University campus at Palo Alto." Thus, *The Pharos* provided a distributive news function that has since been assumed by national newspapers and the journal of the AAMC, *Academic Medicine*.

Over the years, but particularly under the editorship of Doctors Robert and Helen Glaser from 1962 to 1997, *The Pharos* became recognized as a leading publication on the social, ethical, and professional issues of medicine. Other features were subsequently added: book and movie reviews, student essays, illustrations, and poetry to enrich the experience of readers.

The Root lectureship

Several factors were responsible for the growth and flowering of AΩA in its early years, including social and professional fellowship. One of the high moments each year was the annual dinner held during the annual meeting of the AMA. From 1927 through 1954, the feature of the evening was the William W. Root lecture. In 1955, AΩA accepted an invitation to present the lecture at the annual session of the Student AMA, but this arrangement has not continued. The distinguished Root Lecturers were:

1927	Ray Lyman Wilbur	Washington, D.C.
1928	James B. Herrick	Minneapolis
1929	William S. Thayer	Portland, Oregon
1930	William J. Mayo	Detroit

1931	George E. de Schweinitz	Philadelphia
1932	Lafayette B. Mendel	New Orleans
1933	Charles F. Martin	Milwaukee
1934	Lewellyn F. Barker	Cleveland
1935	George R. Minot	Atlantic City
1936	Anton J. Carlson	Kansas City
1937	Walter B. Cannon	Atlantic City
1938	George Dock	San Francisco
1939	Ludvig Hektoen	St. Louis
1940	Irvin Abell	New York
1941	Howard T. Karsner	Cleveland
1942	Morris Fishbein	Atlantic City
1943	No session of the AMA was held in 1943	
1944	T. Clarence Routley	Chicago
1946	Robert A. Millikan	San Francisco
1947	Charles Hill (London)	Atlantic City
1948	R. Scott Stevenson (London)	Chicago
1949	Lord Horder (London)	Atlantic City
1950	Robert L. Stearns	San Francisco
1951	Alan Gregg (his speech is in this anthology)	Atlantic City
1952	Walter L. Bierring	Chicago
1953	Willard C. Rappleye	New York

After World War II: A celebration

In 1944, as the United States was deeply involved in World War II, fighting both the Axis powers and Japan, Alpha Omega Alpha had expanded to 47 chapters. Before the end of the war, more than 6,000 members of AΩA, representing 40 percent of the entire living membership, were in the armed services. In one issue of *The Pharos* from 1944, a list of 50 members killed in action was printed, with the promise of a complete list at the end of the war. That final list was never published.

In 1946, in commemoration of the founding of Alpha Omega Alpha at the University of Illinois in 1902, a drinking fountain surmounted by a statue of Apollo was erected in a courtyard there. The reasons for the choice of Apollo for the statue were addressed by David J. Davis, dean emeritus of the University of Illinois, and published in *The Pharos* in December 1946. After a long and convoluted introduction and recounting of Greek mythology, Dr. Davis concluded,

> In making these remarks I have presented only a few of Apollo's outstanding attributes, selecting those that may explain why this God of the ancients still appeals to us and why we should wish to preserve him in stone as we are doing here today. He had many virtues. In directing the pestilence it is evident he, in his vengence, was seeking a crude justice, it

is true, but perhaps the only kind that the Greeks at that time could understand. He, their God, had been defied and that meant defying Light and Life, indeed, the very Sun itself. And by this pestilence the Greeks were taught a lesson they could never forget.

Alpha Omega Alpha was created for the purpose of directing attention to the higher and finer things in medicine. Apollo stands here as the material embodiment of the higher and finer things not only in medicine, but also in the far wider range of human life itself.

—December 1946, pp. 3, 7–11

One more celebration at the University of Illinois

In 1955, a further dedicatory exercise to commemorate AΩA was held at the University of Illinois and recorded in *The Pharos*:

Through the active interest of the Medical Center Citizens Committee of Chicago, a bronze plaque with the following inscription in simple Gothic lettering was placed in Pasteur Park, Chicago Greater Medical Center on Tuesday afternoon, November 22, 1955:

"On August 25th, 1902, at this location which was the College of Physicians and Surgeons, later the University of Illinois College of Medicine, there was founded the Alpha Chapter of Alpha Omega Alpha, Honor Medical Society, dedicated to the improvement of scholastic standards in medicine and to the advancement of the profession. Since then its influence has grown and its chapters expanded throughout North America."

—February 1956, pp. 25–27

Relocation of Alpha Omega Alpha's offices

From the time of the society's founding, the administrative offices of AΩA had been in Dr. Root's home in Slaterville Springs, New York. In 1960, however, President Bierring was able to announce that the "change in the central office from Slaterville Springs, New York, to Chicago, Illinois, marks an important epoch in the future life of the Society." The space was granted by Dr. James A. Campbell, chairman of medicine at the University of Illinois, on behalf of the administration of Presbyterian-St. Luke Hospital at a "moderate" rent. It was noted that the new offices were "only fifteen minutes by taxi from the Palmer House" and within 100 yards of the "old Bacteriological Laboratory where the Society had its beginning on August 25, 1902." The challenge of moving the central office of the society was daunting, and it remained in Slaterville Springs under the auspices of Mr. G. Meredith Brill, assistant secretary-treasurer, until 1968. (Mr. Brill was the husband of Hazel Root Brill, daughter of William Root.) During this period, the office of the secretary-treasurer, Dr. James Campbell, was in Chicago, while the editorial office of *The Pharos* in 1962 was in Dr. Robert J. Glaser's office at the University of Colorado School of Medicine in Denver. Glaser succeeded Campbell as the secretary-treasurer, the position being renamed executive secretary. The editorial office traveled with Dr. Glaser to Boston in 1963, and then to Palo Alto, California, in 1965 when he became Dean of the Stanford University School of Medicine. It was not until 1980, upon the death of Dr. Campbell, that the administrative offices of AΩA and the editorial offices of *The Pharos* were combined in the Menlo Park, California, office complex where they remain. Dr. Glaser retired as executive secretary and editor of *The Pharos* in 1998. Through most of the years Dr. Glaser was involved in the direction of AΩA's national office and programs and *The Pharos*, he was ably assisted by AΩA's administrator, Carolyn Kuckein. Mrs. Kuckein retired from this important job at the end of 2002 and has been succeeded by Mrs. Ann Hill. Mrs. Kuckein died in 2004 from pancreatic carcinoma.

Funding and new initiatives

In its early years, AΩA could barely support keeping its own records and funding a few visits to evaluate schools for new chapters. Publishing *The Pharos* was expensive. Dues were $2 per year in the 1950s. This gradually changed under the Glaser leadership. By the 1970s, AΩA Visiting Professorships were available to chapters and production of the videotapes of "Leaders in American Medicine," a project initiated and funded by Drs. David and Beatrice Seegal of Columbia University, had begun.

In 1982, a broader range of programs were developed and presented to the board of directors by Dr. Jeremiah A. Barondess, chairman of the Committee on Program and Planning. These were recorded in the minutes of the annual meeting of the board held on October 7, 1982. Dr. Barondess reported on the implementation of the following recommendations presented at the September 29, 1981, board of directors' meeting.

1. The establishment of an AΩA Student Essay Award, beginning in the 1982–83 years.
2. The establishment of up to five AΩA Student Research Awards, beginning with the 1982–82 year.
3. A proposed amendment to the constitution to provide for the election of up to three members of the house staff at a medical school with an AΩA chapter.
4. A meeting of all chapter councillors or their designates, the first such meeting to be national in scope and to be held in 1983 in conjunction with the annual meeting of the Association of American Medical Colleges.

5. More vigorous promotion of the "Leaders in American Medicine" including: a) preparation of a catalog that includes a paragraph on each
subject, and b) samples of video tapes that will be sent to chapters to
familiarize them with the series.

6. Improved communication between the national office and AΩA chapters through a president's letter once or twice a year informing chapters
of AΩA issues and activities.

7. The continuation of the policy of electing as honorary members in AΩA
only those physicians or nonphysicians who have attained national or international recognition in teaching, research, patient care, or other areas
pertinent to medicine, and who are not otherwise eligible for election.

—Winter 1983, pp. 45–46

The recommendations of this committee were approved by the Board, and remain major programs of the national office to this day.

Alpha Omega Alpha, 1902 to 2002

AΩA is a successful organization and has lasted for a century because of several
key qualities. It was founded on the lofty goal of raising standards in medical
education with a spiritual motto—"Worthy to serve the suffering." It has benefited from stable and devoted leadership, William Root, Walter Cannon, Walter
Bierring, and Robert Glaser each having served AΩA for more than 25 years.
Anna Root, Hazel Root Brill and G. Meredith Brill, Helen Glaser, and Carolyn
Kuckein were the foundations of the society's infrastructure for many years.
AΩA's founder, W. W. Root, drafted a good constitution—clear and firm in its
principles, but allowing schools to organize chapters and elect students within
broad guidelines. AΩA developed *The Pharos* as a lasting way to showcase the
most important values of the medical profession and to add value to the life
and work of all members of the medical profession. The society managed its
fiscal resources well, and, as these have grown, it has continually returned them
to programs to enhance the quality of medical education. Election to membership has been appreciated and valued by members throughout their careers and
lifetime, with many participating in local chapter activities, contributing to *The
Pharos*, and becoming lifetime members.

Throughout its first hundred years, AΩA has often been criticized as being
just another fraternity, too secretive, too undemocratic, and too elitist. As some
medical schools have sought to decrease the pressures on students by developing pass/fail curriculums, it has become more difficult to identify the top academic students in the class. It is certainly more difficult than in Root's days or
in the days, even more recently, when letter or numerical grades were given.
Articles in *The Pharos* have addressed most of these issues. A paper in the Spring
1994 issue by Peter Dans, M.D., who currently writes the "Physician at the

Movies" column in the quarterly, summarized both the rationale and current need for AΩA.

Is Alpha Omega Alpha Still Relevant?

My answer, then to the question that I posed in the title of my paper is: Yes, Alpha Omega Alpha is still relevant today. Without reminders of the ideals to be striven for, we shall descend . . . into mediocrity and a least common denominator approach to character and scholarship. In fact, I believe that AΩA must reaffirm its commitment to Root's concern about character—not just on the pages of *The Pharos* but by chapters taking a leadership role on campus. . . . AΩA can play a major role in publicly rededicating the profession to its noble ideals. The advent of new health care reforms and the resultant attention being focused on medicine make this a most propitious moment to do so.

—Spring 1994, pp. 7–10

References

The quotations and much of the information on the early history of Alpha Omega Alpha are from the archives of AΩA now located at the National Library of Medicine, Bethesda, Maryland. Additional correspondence of Walter B. Cannon was reviewed from the Countway Library, Harvard Medical School, Boston, Massachusetts. Excerpts from *The Pharos* are noted in the text. Other sources of information are listed below.

Benison S, Barger AC, Wolfe EL. Walter B. Cannon: The Life and Time of a Young Scientist. Cambridge, MA: Belknap Press, 1987.

Cooper JAD. Undergraduate Medical Education. In Bowers JZ and Purcell EF. Advances in American Medicine: Essays at the Bicentennial. New York: Josiah Macy Jr Foundation, 1976. 1.

Crispell KP. Dr. W. W. Root: Family Physician in a Rural Area. Pharos, October 1977. 2–6.

Ludmerer KL. Time to Heal: American Medical Education from the Turn of the Century to the Era of Managed Care. New York: Oxford University Press, 1999.

Moore ES. The Early Days of Alpha Omega Alpha. Pharos, May 1944: 3–4.

Wolfe EL, Barger AC, and Benison S. Walter B. Cannon: Science and Society. Boston: Boston Medical Library, 2000.

PART I

SCHOLARSHIP AND INTELLECT... THE FIRM FOUNDATION OF MEDICINE

EMERGENT ABILITY

ALAN GREGG, M.D.

(November 1951, pp. 3–9, 23)

"Emergent Ability" was presented as the William W. Root Lecture
at the Alpha Omega Alpha Society Annual Dinner in Atlantic
City, New Jersey, on June 14, 1951, shortly after Gregg was elected
as an alumnus to the Harvard chapter of Alpha Omega Alpha.

IF LOOKING FOR WISDOM IN VERY UNLIKELY PLACES be occasionally wise, then for Dr. Walter Bierring to have invited me to speak to you was the beginning and end of wisdom—the alpha and omega of Alpha Omega Alpha. For up until March of this year I was not a member. It was not a case of abstention, nor of oversight. I just wasn't bright enough to qualify for Alpha Omega Alpha. Indeed, my feelings about this society during the past thirty-five years remind me of a Rumanian candidate for a traveling fellowship who wrote me years ago his convictions as to a career in clinical medicine. "I have so profound a respect," he wrote, "for clinical medicine that I have decided not to attempt to make a career in that field." This is the principle of self-knowledge raised to heroic proportions. But I must admit that together with such Spartan self-discipline my regard for Alpha Omega Alpha has always been mixed with the same wistful preoccupation that may be seen in men staring through the show windows of Abercrombie & Fitch one week before the hunting season opens. After thirty-five years of appropriate and thoroughly justified reluctance, the Harvard Chapter of Alpha Omega Alpha has given me a bootlegger's wink and I am one of you. From such an uncommon origin . . . I venture to submit to you . . . a few reflections on the early recognition of *early ability*—which I take to be one of the cardinal activities of Alpha Omega Alpha.

In the first place, we must remember that ability, like wisdom, may be of two sorts: recognized or unrecognized. Perhaps a further and more subtle distinction might be made by suggesting that ability may be of two more profound categories: recognizable or unrecognizable.

Such a distinction calls to mind the difference between the Greek idea of virtue and the Roman idea of morality. The Greek was virtuous if his conduct was consistent with his convictions; the Roman was moral if his conduct followed the mores of his station and his times. It is thus possible to be virtuous without being moral and to be moral without being virtuous. Similarly, it is possible to possess abilities that, like Greek virtue, may not be recognizable by one's fellows or, on the other hand, to show abilities that, like Roman morality, receive immediate recognition because they fit into the system of values in vogue at the time when such abilities emerge and become evident.

Recognizing ability: The task of AΩA

Alpha Omega Alpha sets itself the task of promptly recognizing early ability. This is easier than recognizing potentialities that will become realities only later in life, which is the task of supermen, fellowship boards, and college presidents, just as the late recognition of early ability is celebrated at college reunions. . . . Real ability, like true virtue, exists. And all too frequently for the comfort of us all, it exists independently, and at times unconcerned as to whether it be recognized or not. If we face that fact, we may well, with the alacrity of humility, betake ourselves to the consideration, not of ability, but of the recognition of ability.

The variable timing for recognition of ability

Let us first consider the timing of the appearance of the evidence of ability. From watching a number of careers in medicine I gather the impression that in point of timing, emergent ability is of four general types: the Rampart, the Plateau, the Slow Crescendo, and the Late Bloomer.

The **Rampart** type in its extreme form suggests the adjective *precocious*. It shows a rapid rise to an early maximum sometimes attained at about the time the M.D. is obtained. Similar to what the geologists call an escarpment, the Rampart type of career shows a gradual slope downward after the summit is reached. . . . But please note that the decline may be real or it may be fictitious, the deception often lying more in disappointed expectations of onlookers than in any actual decline in abilities. My witty and perceptive classmate George Hoyt Bigelow said to me a year or so after we had graduated, "Alan, I've made the greatest mistake a young man can make!" Impressed by such a tragic declaration, I asked him what he had done. "I've shown promise," he replied. "I haven't promised anything myself but, damn it, I've 'shown promise'—promise formulated by older men and now saddled on me."

I could have called the Rampart type by the invidious name *skyrocket*—up with a blaze of glory and down with a dull thud—but I hate the facile ignorance that passes such summary opinions on mere appearances.

A wise woman of my acquaintance says, "you never know the true inwardness of somebody else's marriage; you only know your own—in fact, you only know half of that." Much the same comment is usually applicable to somebody else's career. Many a kind of reason may lie behind an apparent failure to fulfill the expectations of onlookers, young or old. Illness borne in silent fortitude, some proudly concealed handicap, or just a turn of chance at a crucial time may explain the apparent diminuendo in the output of an individual example of the Rampart profile. And still, in a statistical sense the Rampart type exists, with its later years often marked by resignation, embitterment, self-pity or, as often, by patient self-acceptance.

The **Plateau** type of ability declares itself equally promptly but maintains itself with equanimity and steady continuity. They prove dependable, consistent performers, serene and solid, beautifully free from bad luck or bad management. I suspect that Alpha Omega Alpha catches a good many of these but misses some.

The **Slow Crescendo** shows steady, slow improvement throughout his professional life. Being a slow starter, he has created neither great expectations nor consequent disappointment. Usually the Slow Crescendo type has a singularly shrewd knowledge of the pitfalls of versatility and of all of what Bill Palmer used to call life's gilded lemons. In contrast to the almost monotonous dependability of the Plateau type, the Slow Crescendo creates a pervasive impression of growth, development, and increasing strength. The rest of us usually overload him with administrative duties—or try to—in our wonder and lazy admiration. It is a lethal sort of compliment we pay—distinction and extinction in one move. Let me add that ours is a big country now, equipped with such facilities for travel and communications as to exhaust the energies of many a man with duties so glibly described as being "at the national level." In smaller countries he can and does enjoy a less exhausting and better-balanced life.

Although the Slow Crescendo type is generally recognized in time to be exploited, the **Late Bloomer** type usually escapes attention and thus enjoys a freedom from importunities and demands that is, in many ways, enviable. He manages to mix surprise with success since his ability shows itself so unexpectedly and so late as to excite but little jealousy and few dependents to abuse his time. He is credited with a foresight in planning his life that I am not always sure he has possessed. He acquires an aura of mildly romantic appreciation and respect. Perhaps the singular distinction of the Late Bloomer is that he is accorded by his fellows a measure of neglect and so of a freedom that is given to no other type. We feel so ashamed of not having recognized his abilities earlier that we spare him from the demands we impose on other types of ability.

Such, then, are at least four familiar types of ability differing mainly in the time at which they appear. What has the recognition implied by election to Alpha Omega Alpha to do with such types?

Thoughts on continued personal development

I think election to an honor society when deferred to the last or nearly the last year in medical school carries a deceptive flavor of finality about it. It is in reality an early recognition of early ability—how very early we shall never realize until we stop accepting that remarkable make-believe that education and training for medicine is a four-year affair. We all know a decent medical education takes at least seven years. Indeed, one of the most helpful bits of advice I ever got on my way through medical school was from Richard Cabot:

> If you ever thought that the preparation for medicine is a hundred-yard dash and that what your record is in the medical school is all-important, just stop thinking that way. It is more like a two-mile race. I wouldn't think the time for estimating your abilities could sensibly come much before you are forty years old.

On any such time schedule as Cabot suggested, the award of Alpha Omega Alpha comes at the end of only the first sixth of a long period of growth and development. And recognition so early can hardly be expected to catch any of the Late Bloomers or even many of the Slow Crescendo boys.

Indeed, it has long seemed to me that there is a curious discrepancy between what human biologists believe and the usages they follow. They believe that the long period of pre-adult life not only is peculiar to man but is probably one of the principal factors in permitting man to develop a culture transmissible from one generation to the next. Julian Huxley points out that among litter-bearing animals, precocity of development is so heavily rewarded that mutants of higher potentialities but slower development may suffer the fate of the runt in being the victim of intra-uterine competition. Did our Alma Mater have any such struggles going on within her before she brought forth the June litter we belonged to? Precocity thus may succeed in the immediate competitive struggle but in the long run at the expense to the species of mutants having a slower rate of development but greater potentialities. Certainly the years spent in infancy and adolescence provide man with a disproportionate advantage over the animals whose learning period is relatively so much shorter.

Expectations are linked to chronologic age, unfortunately.

By being generous with time, yes, lavish with it, Nature allows man an extraordinary chance to learn. What gain can there be, then, in throwing away this natural advantage by rewarding precocity, as we certainly do when we gear the grades in school to chronological age by starting the first grade at age 6 and so college entrance for the vast majority at ~17 to 19? For once you have most of your students the same age, the academic rewards—from scholarships to internships and residencies—go to those who are uncommonly bright for their age. In other words, you have rewarded precocity, which may or may not be the precursor of later ability. So, in effect, you have unwittingly belittled man's cardinal educational capital—time to mature.

Such biological phenomena as precocity or slowness of development are not often deliberate or under the control of the will. Indeed, I doubt if they ever are. At any rate, such considerations when carried a little further, have helped me to understand one of the causes of ill-will and injustice in academic life—namely, the plight of an individual who happens to mature intellectually two to five years earlier than his fellow students. I can see his precocity not as the result of a deliberate and relentless determination to excel at any price. I no longer need suspect him of dishonesty or selfish competitiveness because his abilities already show what his fellows will achieve three or four years later. His brilliance may be of the Rampart or the Plateau type or, in quite exceptional cases, of the Slow Crescendo or Late Blooming type—but while he is still in medical school it is brilliance largely in terms of his chronological age. He can't help it. And there are some considerable consequences if we realize that he can't help it.

Now, I say to you in the earnest desire to do away with anti-Semitism in our medical schools forever that this concept of involuntary precocity could do much to help us all. If we insist in drawing the record of performance against an abscissa of chronological age and an ordinate of ability, we have scant grounds for resentment against an individual (or a group) if he matures early. Rather, it is we who have decided to ignore the greatest ally of education, which is time in which to mature.

I shall be criticized for mentioning such a subject as anti-Semitism. I can only reply that I am prepared to pay any price that may be demanded for trying among scientists to apply dispassionate analysis for the sake of relieving a troublesome form of human behavior. Whether a Jewish heritage involves precocity in the individual I do not know. But personal experience has taught me that living in a minority group hastens the appearance of maturity. When children grow up anywhere in a cultural minority—the children of American missionaries in China would serve perfectly as another example—they mature earlier than the children living in a uniform and homogeneous society. A Cambridge don, Geoffrey Young, made a similar observation to me. It was his conviction that boys going down to Cambridge from the public schools were less mature as a rule than boys coming from the board schools. The public school boys saw everything with the monocular vision, as it were, of their group, that is, of their sex, their age, and their school. The board school boys, having lived at home, had the analogue of binocular vision, for they could see things not only as boys of 18 but they could see things in some measure from the standpoint of their father, their mother, their sisters, or their older and younger brothers. I think such factors deserve consideration—a word whose "con" means together, and "sidera" means stars—"taking the stars together."

Turning back to the early recognition of early ability, I would suggest that in point of its effect on young men, much may depend upon who does the recognizing. A wise friend of mine once observed, "It's queer, isn't it, that praise from an elderly person almost never turns your head, whereas praise from contemporaries or juniors may very easily spoil you. When an older man lays it on a bit, you think, 'Well, the old boy doesn't know what he is talking about, but I'm not going to let him down if he thinks that way.' But with praise from contemporaries it is so different." Perhaps one feels that contemporaries are more grudging as well as better informed and, therefore, their praise if given at all may be relied upon as the truth. I remember asking President Eliot of Harvard, whose discrimination in picking faculty members was remarkable, what was the best criterion to follow in choosing a man for his ability? He replied that the best single criterion, though not infallible, is the judgment of his contemporaries.

From these two opinions, one could conclude that election to Alpha Omega Alpha is at once the most likely single evidence of future creditable output, and also an event more likely to corrupt the recipient than good marks, recognition, or praise from his elders. In this case one could use a metaphor to describe election to Alpha Omega Alpha that I got from a young Southerner whom I once asked what love at first sight was like. "Why, sir," he answered, "I felt just like a kitten around a saucer of hot milk!"

In short, the early recognition of early ability may run the risk of hurting the winners—which cannot have been the purpose of Alpha Omega Alpha, whose motto recommends helping the sufferers.

Is there a remedy for the defects of so early, so incomplete, so accurate, and so corrupting a recognition of early ability as Alpha Omega Alpha appears to be?

. . . When I made my first visit to Sweden, the Professor of Medicine at the Karolinska Institute, Israel Holmgren, asked me about the Rockefeller Foundation and what countries I had seen. He was obviously interested that anyone had had the opportunity to visit so many countries in the study of medical education and research.

"What books or monographs have you written on your experiences? I do not see all the American literature, I am afraid," he said. I shall never forget the expression of astonishment and disapproval in Holmgren's manner when I told him I had written nothing! Indeed, I saw what had been his interest fading so rapidly into what could have been boredom, if not disdain, that I played for the only chance I thought I had left and invited him to dinner at the hotel. No, he regretted, with chilling finality.

That night, dining alone, I pieced the whole experience together. It was clear that Holmgren believed that when you have remarkable opportunities, you have equally notable obligations. Or at least among those whose respect you want, your opportunities, if seized, create expectations. And if unusual experiences do not call forth your best abilities, then you forfeit the respect and interest of people who would have reacted to such experiences with the best they could summon. I had never experienced anything so near to a snub—certainly not in

America—for appearing to ignore the principle of noblesse oblige. Next day at his clinic I went in for a bit of self-defense. I explained that I had not written anything because my opinions had not been asked and because usually Foundation officers in the different medical schools we visit, sooner or later were taken so far behind the scenes in the hope of securing financial support that I had come to feel that all the needs, faults, and difficulties I was shown in confidence were best regarded almost as professional secrets. Holmgren, greatly to my relief, changed his attitude as soon as he understood my defense and asked me to dinner at his house that evening. But I had learned my lesson—or, rather, his lesson—that expectancy is one of the most powerful consequences of any deliberate effort or singular opportunity.

I remember that on graduation from college we were told that the degree admitted us "to the company of educated men." Looking about me at alumni in the various stages of class reunions, I suspected there was some trace of cant in that pronunciamento: with the passage of forty years the suspicion has hardened to the consistency of conviction. The reason, I think, is that honors and degrees carry too little expectancy—they have the general odor of receipted bills, certificates of past performance, or rewards, or honorable scars, or epitaphs.

And that brings me to my suggestion. Why not surround Alpha Omega Alpha membership with such privileges, such opportunities, and especially with such expectancies as to make it the early recognition of oncoming obligations? Get rid of thinking of ability in a mere chronological framework, for that leads to merely rewarding precocity. I would like to see in every medical school in this country at least one faculty meeting a year devoted to things of the mind— not mere administration. At such a meeting, or perhaps at two such faculty meetings a year, I'd like to see each professor in turn present to his colleagues and equals an hour's lecture entitled "Recent Advances in My Field." And to this company I'd like to invite the members of Alpha Omega Alpha, and thus actually as well as symbolically admit them to the company of scholars.

OUR ANABASIS

ALAN GREGG, M.D.

(February 1955, pp. 14–25)

This address was presented at the annual dinner of the Association of American Physicians, May 4, 1954. "Anabasis" is generally an obsolete term, defined by the Oxford English Dictionary *as "The course of a disease from the commencement to the climax."*

NOW THIS EVENING I SUGGEST THAT YOU CLOSE YOUR EYES or stare in an imaginary fire. For I have no graphs for you to look at, no facts to prove, no hopes to cultivate, nor preferences to exploit. It is in your own recollections that I shall find, or fail, of corroboration.

For my central theme concerns the profound power of experience in shaping us for the practice of medicine, the power of experience as contrasted with the mere acquisition of information. Surely we retain residues from the past more pervasive and long-lived than memorized facts. Edouard Herriot said that what the French call "formation" is what remains after one has forgotten everything. We are only speaking of different aspects of this same idea of "formation" when we refer to a man's turn of mind, his ways of thinking, his approach, or his attitude. I repeat then that out of the three forces that bind men together in effective and rewarding association—namely common experiences, agreed upon facts, and shared hopes—I shall deliberately choose to examine the role of what may be called shared experience.

Is this thing we call shared experience so powerful? I think it is. . . .The bonds of common experience require no verification and no renewal. It is not the areas of merely intellectual agreement that bind us to our colleagues of the past but the frustrations and predicaments both we and they have lived through, of ignorance and powerlessness, or sometimes a happier circumstance—the kinship of lucky survivors. We have thus something in common with the doctors of every age and every country, with the mediocre, obscure, and forgotten, as well as with the great and distinguished and famous. It is what our patients have made of us quite as much as what we have made of them, that forges for doctors a common bond. We all have played the same role to the rest of mankind. We had to meet their expectations, and had each our bit of that community of experience that all doctors share—and *only* doctors. For in the last analysis, human societies make their healers, and the healers then make the doctrine. And eventually if the makers of doctrine happen to espouse the scientific method a feed-back phenomenon begins: the doctrine, because it is true, begins to make true healers of the healers, and the healers, using the truth, begin to remake the society that made them. But until science has provided us with the complete explanation and control of every phenomenon that confronts us as doctors we shall have to accept, with a degree of modesty to match our ignorance, the traditional professional role that society has given us—its pleasures, its frustrations, its humor and its anguish, its rewards and its burdens.

. . . But still if a recognizable assortment of experiences characterizes the entrance to medicine whether or not they follow any pattern of sequence, then I would say that in sharp contrast to their apparent universality, these typical experiences have received astonishingly little attention, deliberate or inadvertent.

Except for those examples of young men going into medicine to please or to obey their parents, the earliest event of major importance on the way into Medicine relates to the choice of medicine as a career. An experienced schoolmaster of my acquaintance told me that boys decide in favor of medicine both earlier and with fewer subsequent changes of mind than they bring to the choice of any other calling.

* * * * *

You must have been about 11 years old when it happened. You had a very sore throat and after a night when the lamp never went out and your mother was at your side whenever you called for her, you awakened to see her anxiously scanning your face and heard her ask your father to call Dr. Lawrence. You used to see Dr. Lawrence go up Cascade Avenue in his new horseless carriage followed by his man driving the other older horseless carriage in case the new one broke down or blew out a pneumatic tire. When Dr. Lawrence came into your room he put his lighted cigar very carefully on the marble top of the dressing table. Your mother didn't seem to mind that at all. He smelled awfully strongly of tobacco when he leaned down and put his ear right on your bare chest. Then he asked your mother to get a pitcher of fresh water, turned to you and said, "Now watch!" He took a bottle out of his medicine bag, uncorked it deftly with one hand, and shook some shiny brown crystals into the water, which immediately turned a wonderful purple. "Let him" (he didn't say *"make* him") "let him gargle with this every two hours," and then turning to you, "but don't swallow it! Two pounds of this powder would turn all Prospect Lake purple! By the way did you hear the sicklebill curlews night before last? Asleep? Well I was coming home from the Malones at 3 o'clock in the morning," and turning to your mother he added, "8 and 1/2 pound boy . . . and the curlews' eerie crying was beautiful." Then he turned to your Mother and said, "Mrs. Bacon, you haven't a thing to worry about. I'll be back day after tomorrow and sooner if you want." Your mother suddenly looked very relieved and just after Dr. Lawrence had left you heard her say to your father, "Doctor Lawrence is so *faithful.*" That was her highest praise, as anyone could guess from her way of saying it.

Four days later, sitting in the swing in the bright September sun, an idea suddenly swept you through and through—"when I grow up I want to be a doctor." You rather thought that with anything as big as that you ought to tell God about it immediately—and not just casually standing up, either. But if you knelt down then and there somebody might see you and ask why—and you couldn't tell. So you ran upstairs to the only room in the house that could be locked—the bathroom—and there you knelt down under three towels, an empty hot water bottle, and your father's back-scratcher, and took the Almighty in on a decision that you never doubted nor regretted from that day to this.

After that day there came—some years later—a wonderful experience encouraging your hope or confirming your resolve to become a doctor. One Saturday afternoon you were down town shopping. You met your English teacher right in front of Eldon's book store. He had always seemed busy—too busy to talk to any of his students with any appearance of leisure. So you were surprised when he said with the air of an equal rather than a teacher, "Say, Raymond, have you a few minutes free?" Such a dignifying form for the question! On promptly saying yes, you were led the length of the book store back to a browsing room you had never seen before. Your English teacher reached down a volume of Wordsworth and read you the *Ode to Tintern Abbey*. That was all he did, but you walked home on air. It wasn't the beauty of the *Ode* that stirred you: you were moved beyond words and just because—for the first time in your life—you were treated as a grown-up presumably possessing freedom and tastes of your own. Then why not go to the university of your dreams instead of the nearby college? Right there in that book store you turned the corner.

Perhaps one further event reinforced the nascent conviction that you really were grown up and free to choose your own career. In your junior year in college you wanted to take an advanced course in Psychology without having taken the preliminary course. For this you had to get special permission. You explained that you were interested in Psychology, had read a good deal, and that your roommate who took the preliminary course the year before had mentioned nothing of it that was unfamiliar to you. Almost miraculously you were admitted to advanced standing on the basis of interest and independent reading instead of the usual requirement of "credit hours": that was a bracing and beautifully maturing thing to have happened—even though it came before the medical school. What it really suggested to you—though you may not have formulated it at the time—was simply that one can learn without having a teacher—an axiom that only the best teachers apparently can afford to identify themselves with at all generously.

These two types of experience are characteristic for the years before entering the medical school: the choice of medicine as a career and some form of reassurance that this choice has been better than a hope; a responsible personal decision rather than a dream. Nowadays in the United States such reassurance must frequently come only on the day the college student gets the letter of acceptance from a medical school admissions committee. Elsewhere in the world it is the students who decide whether or not they will enter the medical faculties since the only requirement is satisfactory graduation from secondary school.

. . . As you got well into the medical school there came slowly, or perhaps . . . in some sudden revelation an almost overwhelming sense of how much you ought to know to practice medicine. As an alternative to the cheap cynicism or truculent self assurance so often summoned to meet such worries I venture to record what Soma Weiss told me was his experience.

> I was inscribed as a first year student at the University of Budapest. We counted ourselves very fortunate to have the great Professor Eötvös as our Professor in Physics. He did not appear on time at his first lecture. This seemed to increase our interest in what he would prove to be like. Suddenly the side door to the platform swung open and a huge white-bearded man strode in carrying two large books. He must have been six feet two or three and in every way he met or surpassed my expectations. He slammed the two books on the lectern and then looked out over some three hundred of us students and in a deep booming voice he cried, "I know nothing!" We students were dumbfounded at such a fantastic statement. With some reason we could have said that—but not Professor Eötvös. He repeated it—"I know nothing!"—and then dramatically pointing to the books he shouted with a peculiar precision and emphasis, "But gentlemen, I have learned how to find out anything I want to know!" He stopped, and looked out over the class as though to let that idea sink in.
>
> Now I do not believe I have ever felt such a glorious sense of relief, of spiritual freedom, elation, almost ecstasy, in all my life before or since. I see why now, but I didn't then. The swiftly increasing sense of how much I would have to know in order to practice medicine had up till that moment all but overwhelmed me. And here was no less an authority than the great Professor Eötvös saying that finding out how to learn was what he relied on—not on knowing everything . . . or even anything. To me such a simple incisive attitude toward the vast accumulations of medical knowledge came as an astounding relief.

My essential thesis has been that what binds our profession together throughout the world is not so much the facts we agree upon or the knowledge we share, as the experiences we have all gone through and the way we understand them and fit them to the pattern of our values. Our fellow-feeling rests as much on the similarity of our relationships with patients as on the identity of our formulated knowledge or beliefs. And even more certain, the continuity of our professional heritage from the past cannot have come from the changelessness of either theory, practice, belief, or admitted fact. All these have changed too much for that to be possible. Our professional history hangs together because the cardinal experiences of the doctor with death, birth, responsibility and confidence, fear and courage, ignorance and learning, power and powerlessness, have remained so little changed through the centuries, and even through the last few decades.

* * * * *

The paragraphs below are reminiscences of his father by Alan Gregg's son, also a physician, and sent to us especially for this anthology.

Alan Gregg will be remembered in medicine as a physician, communicator, educator, philosopher, philanthropist, and humanitarian—although he never truly practiced medicine or taught in medical school. Remarkable, too, as a father, he practiced and demanded high standards; gave quiet, restrained support, and seldom used discipline.

A true "diamond in the rough" from Colorado Springs, Gregg attended Harvard College, its medical school, and interned at Massachusetts General Hospital. Following service in the British Medical Corps in World War I, he joined the Rockefeller Foundation, spent three years in Brazil, eight years in Europe, and over 20 years as director of medical sciences. Spanning nearly three decades, he knew more about medical schools, medical faculty, and medical education in the United States and the world than anyone. He promoted the incorporation of departments of psychiatry into medical schools; fostered the creation of schools of public health; and championed support for such persons as Alexander Fleming, Alfred Kinsey, and Wilder Penfield—while giving freely of his counsel and wisdom to faculties, deans, and ministries of health.

My earliest recollections of Dad centered about family walks, stamp collecting, and this large, barrel-chested, deep-voiced man who smelled of Grand Central Station. However, he traveled so much, he was almost a stranger to me—distant, unreachable. In Victorian tradition, he was really a father rather than a "dad."

By high school I began to feel his intellectual presence, his quick, perceptive, yet simple and compassionate personality. I saw him near tears only once: when he told the family of the handsome young Australian dying in his arms in World War I. I also felt his high expectations of me. He grilled me mercilessly in Julius Caesar, expected honor roll status from me, yet he showed great humor and understanding—all at a safe Victorian distance.

Dad philosophized by letter about my successes and failures in college and encouraged me to "just be yourself." Encouragement, yes, but seemingly not fully engaged; long, wonderfully rambling letters, supportive, anecdotal, but not very inquisitive. He was demonstratively very happy when I entered Western Reserve University's School of Medicine.

What did he want for me? The opportunity to observe, experience, and practice the best medicine possible. What did he share with me? The importance of simple and exact communication, a respect for, and a devotion to medicine, a desire to serve, and a passion for the truth. As he told me once, "The great thing about honesty is that it works." The greatest thing about Alan Gregg was that he cared.

— MICHAEL B. GREGG, M.D.
AΩA, Case Western Reserve University, 1955

THE MEANING OF SCIENCE IN MEDICINE

LEWIS THOMAS, M.D.

(July 1962, pp. 3–19)

The life of Lewis Thomas (1913–1993) spanned the golden age of American medicine, an era when—as Thomas put it—our oldest art became the youngest science. Thomas played a major role in that transformation as an innovative immunologist and medical educator (professor of pathology at Minnesota, Yale, and New York University; professor and chairman of medicine at New York University). He became far better known as a deft writer who turned the news of natural science into serious literature. Thomas was master of the informal essay, a literary form that accommodates many topics but always has the mind of its author as the subject. Witty, urbane, and skeptical, he may have been the only member of the National Academy of Sciences to have won both a National Book Award and an Albert Lasker Award. He is certainly the only medical school dean (of NYU and Yale) whose name survives on professorships at Harvard and Cornell, a prize at Rockefeller University, a laboratory at Princeton—and on the cover of a book that is eleventh on the Modern Library's list of the best 100 nonfiction books of the century (Lives of a Cell). Thomas made three important discoveries in immunopathology. He found that neutrophils were important mediators of fever and shock caused by bacterial endotoxins. He also made the novel observations that IV injections of papain caused rabbit ears to collapse, suggesting that endogenous proteases might break down connective tissue. But perhaps his most prescient suggestion was that our immune system constantly scans our body to find and destroy aberrant cancer-prone cells; we owe the principle of "immune surveillance" to Thomas. Those discoveries were made in a very intense period of bench research (1950–1965) at the University of Minnesota and at NYU before he turned his attention to broader issues of science and to his writing. But his years in the lab served him well on the page. His sense of trial and error at the bench and in nature, of how cells divide, microbes hurt, and creatures die, gave a tough edge to his writing. A number of his compositions stand up to essays by such other modern masters of the genre as A. J. Liebling, E. B. White, and John Updike. In a select few, Thomas reaches back to touch the mantle of Montaigne.

— GERALD WEISSMANN, M.D.
AΩA, New York University, 1965

Dr. Thomas also wrote "Biological Aspects of Death," which appeared in The Pharos *of July 1974, and is included in this anthology. "The Meaning of Science in Medicine" was delivered at the Annual Initiation Dinner of the New York University chapter (Delta) of Alpha Omega Alpha on March 2, 1962.*

I SHALL TRY TO DISCUSS THE PLACE OF SCIENCE IN MEDICINE and the place of medicine in science.

I hope to proceed in an orderly fashion. First . . . the place of science in medicine. My position on this is that there is plenty of room for it, a good deal more room than we are prepared to fill at the moment. We are, in this respect, still fair game for the skeptics, and it is possible to make a damaging case against us if those who wish to say that Medicine is not a Science are allowed to select their own items. Just to get this part of it out of the way, let us, at the outset, confess to a few of our sins.

Item: The ways in which we mislead ourselves, and allow the public to be misled, on matters of therapy. Here, if we were all-round, 24-hours a day, self-critical scientists, we would not permit ourselves to do a number of things that most of us actually do in practice as a matter of routine.

Medicine without science? Superstition

One best, or perhaps worst, specific, single example of this is in the field of cardiology, in which the public is continually being assured that we are making tremendous steps. In point of fact, the most tremendous step cited since the '30's is the introduction, and now routine use, of anticoagulant therapy for coronary disease. Perhaps this is a step, but only in the sense that walking is a series of interrupted falls. I doubt that it has taken us in any special direction, We have most certainly taken it without much guidance from the scientific method, and I am not yet persuaded that we would have come a shorter distance had we not taken it at all. If it should suddenly and unaccountably turn out that anticoagulants have a genuine, unmistakably beneficial effect on the final outcome in coronary disease, measured in numbers of lives or deaths—if this were to be proven, with all the double-blind controls necessary for such proof—I think that nobody would be more astonished than the cardiologists themselves.

Still, we go on with it, spending heaven knows how much of the public's money—most of this for the laboratory checks to make sure the patients don't bleed to death. Some of us observe a less committed ritual, we should now confess, and administer them in less than truly anticoagulant doses in order to avoid trouble. It may be good luck to give anticoagulants, we say, as though we were casting a spell. This is, I submit, a manifestation of the superstition which has always been a part of Medicine, and of which we can't seem to rid ourselves.

And now we're beginning some new ones, on equally flimsy grounds that bear no semblance to kinds of scientific evidence we would demand in a laboratory. The diet is the key to atherosclerosis; cholesterol is bad; no, cholesterol is all right, it's the fat; but not all kinds of fat, and so forth. And the television blathers on about polyunsaturated fats, about drugs that lower the blood cholesterol, and about the great strides being made by Medical Science. And so do the color print, fabulously expensive advertisements in the pages of our own scientific journals, even the best ones, even the *Journal of Clinical Investigation*. No one is to blame for the dissemination of this kind of claptrap but ourselves.

Item: We can treat malignant hypertension in a solitary patient with enough drugs to underwrite the full annual costs of the *Journal of Clinical Investigation* and the *American Journal of Medicine*, but all we can be really sure of producing are irrelevancies like fainting in elevators, the LE phenomenon, and impotence. As to hypertension itself, if these drugs are as effective in changing the natural course of the disease as they are claimed to be, it is remarkable, and disheartening, that the change is so obscure to so many of us. This kind of obscurity in interpreting results doesn't happen in other kinds of scientific enterprise. I do not think the difference can be accounted for by the greater difficulty involved in scientific studies on human patients. It goes deeper than this. Where therapy is concerned, we wish too hard for results, and scientists must not do this. It can only lead to trouble.

I shall say nothing whatever about steroids. Or, perhaps, just a word. It has taken us a full ten years to learn that they have no beneficial, long-range effect on rheumatic fever or rheumatoid arthritis, and now we are arguing mainly about the degree to which they make matters worse.

Item: The way we name things in order to make them less puzzling, or worse, in order to persuade ourselves that we understand them. Collagen disease, or connective tissue disease, for which we have as yet no real evidence that either collagen or connective tissue is in any meaningful sense the seat of disease, is an outstanding example of this. Congestive heart failure, about which we know nothing to speak of, but write endlessly, is another. In Neurology, there is still a state of affairs referred to, as though it meant something, as "toxicmetabolic" disease of the brain.

As for psychiatry, I cannot speak of it.

That will be enough to illustrate our bad side, and having confessed to it let us all forget about it again. Let us, from here on, look on our bright side as it is.

The bright side

There is, of course, very good science in medicine, and there is a great deal more to come in the near future. To be sure, we are not much better at coping with the important diseases today than we were 30 years ago—with notable exceptions, such as some of the bacterial infections—but the kind of information that will lead to a real understanding of disease is beginning to roll in in surging waves, and there is more to come. Some of it comes from our colleagues in the basic sciences, but a great deal of it has come, and continues to come, from physicians engaged in research.

Time is too short to attempt to document the role of physicians in modern medical science, and perhaps the best way to make the point is to use a few representative samples. The whole field of modern biochemical genetics had its beginning with the discovery, announced in 1941 from the Hospital of the Rockefeller Institute, that the transforming principle of pneumococci was DNA; this was the work of three physicians, Avery, MacLeod, and McCarty. Dr. William S. Tillett discovered the enzymes of streptococci, along with a fabulous number of other things, and had the daring and wit to apply them to human disease. Both of these elegant pieces of work can be used to illustrate both the role of science in medicine and that of medicine in science. The pneumococcus became the subject of major interest in Dr. Avery's laboratory at the Rockefeller Institute Hospital because of the magnitude of the problem of pneumococcal pneumonia during and after World War I. Avery began with studies on lobar pneumonia itself, and then became primarily interested in the capsular polysaccharide because of its role in pneumococcal immunity. In the course of these studies, which began with the human disease, he became diverted by the phenomenon of transformation, and thus DNA became the gene. Dr. Tillett, similarly, was interested in streptococcal infection, and somewhere along the way noticed the phenomenon of fibrinolysis by streptococci.

Much of the other research now going on in clinical departments, work still in progress and unfinished, has started out with the same orientation toward human disease. . . . Many clinical investigators have become interested in the physical chemistry of proteins and, by taking advantage of increasingly sophisticated techniques, not only find the disordered plasma proteins in human disease to be most convenient instruments for their work but have recently found interesting markers for genetic analyses among the proteins. Clinicians, beginning with a study of disseminated lupus, have learned that the LE factor is directed against nucleoprotein; later studies in many laboratories have shown that the LE phenomenon is a manifestation of anti-DNA antibody. The implications of this extraordinary phenomenon, not only for immunology itself but for all of biology, have hardly been grasped by any of us; I have a hunch that the new fact that a human being can, under pathological circumstances still obscure, actually manufacture an antibody against his own DNA—this solitary fact may one day become the basis for a new field in biology which we have not yet imagined.

It occurs to me, parenthetically, that there ought to exist, in some of our major universities, Departments of Human Biology, staffed in some part by borrowed members of the medical faculty, and with the responsibility to teach both undergraduate and graduate students the emerging facts relating to the state of man.

Bench to bedside—the expectation of scientists in medicine

The great difficulty for scientists in medicine is that something more is expected from them than from investigators in other fields. It is not enough to uncover fascinating new mechanisms at work in disease, or even to discover new principles. It is expected of us that we then turn back to the wards and do something useful with our information, and soon—in short, to treat disease.

The fact is that medicine, as a science, is just at its beginning. Our field, long after the basic biological sciences of other disciplines, is just beginning to emerge into the 20th century. There is an immense distance still to go. Time is needed, much more time, and many more minds. Up until now, progress has been extremely slow, in contrast to the dazzling new vistas that have opened up in biochemistry, microbiology, genetics, physiology, and cellular biology.

But medicine is, nevertheless, moving steadily ahead, and we must expect the same kind of rapid, transforming, revolutionary movement in our field to occur, in the near future, as has already begun in our sister fields in the other biological sciences. Once it really begins to accelerate, there will be no stopping it, and this, in my opinion, will be the greatest shock for physicians of the future to withstand. I am worried only a little about the changes that lie ahead in the economics or logistics of medicine; there will be important changes, I am sure, but I'm also sure that we will all make peace with them, whatever they may be. But the changes in medicine itself, in our concepts of disease, in what we think we know about human form and function, in the things we have become accustomed to doing in diagnosis and treatment—these will all change in the lifetime of most of us here so completely as to seem an absolute upheaval.

The medicine of 1962, learned to scholarly perfection, mastered by rote, may seem as remote a doctrine 10 years from now as the medicine of Galen seems to us. This, in my belief, is the pace at which we will soon begin to move.

Medical students and research

I think that it is partly for this reason, consciously or unconsciously, that there has come to be so much emphasis on research in undergraduate medical education. This is a new phenomenon, with its beginning less than a decade ago. It is not, I believe, explainable by any sudden urge on the part of medical school faculties to turn out whole classes of investigators. Everyone knows that this can't be done, and shouldn't be tried. Instead, it is an attempt to prepare students for the practice of a discipline which will change so constantly, and so rapidly, that they must learn early to change with it and to understand the sources of the change. Otherwise, we will have a profession in which young men become old men in a handful of years.

There is another reason which, I believe, underlies the phenomenal increase in our emphasis on research in medical education. We do need more investigators for the future. Even though we all will agree that the numbers of such people are limited by talent and inclination—we should be training more than we are.

Health and disease in 2000 A.D.

Let us consider, for a moment, the conditions ahead of us, in the year of our Lord 2000. This seems a great distance away in time, almost a matter for science fiction, but it really isn't far off.

What will it be like in the year 2000? In 1920, the year 1960 must have seemed a tremendous distance away, but here we are and already whistling past it. There are, in fact, more of us here now, in sheer numbers, than ever before in history. And if there is any certainty in human affairs today, it is the certainty that there will be still more of us, a staggering number of us, in 2000.

It seems to me that of all the vexing considerations posed by this expansion of humanity, the most alarming—from this distance—are the health problems of this huge population. If we are to drift along into the next century with the same diseases that confront us today, and with no better therapy and no greater knowledge of the conditions which we now find worrying, or puzzling, or expensive, then our lot will be almost intolerable. Things that are difficult for us now will be impossible then. Think of the frantic rate at which we are compelled to build new hospitals in 1962, and our concern over their lack of interns, and the recommendations by national committees that we create more medical schools and train more doctors forthwith. No one could have predicted in 1920 that we would have such a problem today, and perhaps nobody cared that much about 1960. But we, standing equidistant between 1920 and 2000, can predict what it will be like for our children, and for theirs.

The course of action that we must take to avoid an unbearable future is to undertake, now, on a vast scale, the elimination of chronic and incapacitating human disease. I do not mean that we will ever achieve a disease-free species, and I'm not sure it would be altogether good for us if we should do so. The common cold and lobar pneumonia may actually be good for the soul, as much as fresh air, hard exercise, cold water, and prayer. But I do believe that we ought to be able to prevent, or cure, the diseases that now make cripples out of so many human beings. This strikes me as reasonable, practical, realistic, and down to earth. To put it off in order to save money, to postpone it as a luxury, seems to me quite unsound, unrealistic, and impractical.

Whether it can be done by the year 2000 is unpredictable, but if we keep at it we should be able to finish crucial parts of the job. If we don't do it, the prospects for our public health facilities are entirely hopeless. No conceivable number of physicians will be able to cope with human disease if our methods are the same in 2000 as now, nor is it imaginable that we can have enough hospitals for the chronically ill of that population.

I do not believe in the inevitability of human disease. There is nothing preordained about senile psychosis, any more than there was about child-bed fever a century ago. Cancer is not a natural aspect of the human condition, nor is heart disease, nor epilepsy, nor heroin addiction, nor multiple sclerosis, nor insanity, nor blindness, nor any of the lists of maladies which plague us today. Ageing may be inevitable, and death is a part of nature, but disease is not, or needn't be, for humans. We have got to become a healthy species. This, it seems to me, is the task for medical research in the years that lie ahead, not for our own comfort, not for our remote posterity, but for the people who are the same distance from us in time as we are from 1920.

Medical education: The only path to understanding form and function of human beings

I have suggested that medicine, as a scientific discipline, is beginning to move ahead and the pace is now beginning to accelerate. Soon, I believe, we will see advances as unexpected and breathtaking as those that have occurred in biochemistry since the war. When this begins to happen, Medicine will enter a new role among the Sciences as the major discipline of Human Biology. The study of the form and function of human beings is the proper bailiwick of medicine, and medical education is by all odds the best—and perhaps the only—preparation for this field. As advances are made in the medicine of the future, they will have meaning far beyond their implications for the management of disease. It may well be that in the second half of this century we are in for changes in our views of ourselves, and of the human situation in general, that will be quite as drastic and shattering to our equanimity as have been the advances in the physical sciences in the past 50 years.

If biology, including human biology, accomplishes what it should accomplish, and begins to match the scope and grandeur of the physical sciences—or if, as seems to me a likely thing, the two come together—what effects will this have on mankind? I haven't a shadow of doubt but that man is capable of learning all there is to be known about himself and his environment, but I tend to drift at the thought of what he will do with his knowledge.

Will he control his environment more successfully (I think he will), and will that be enough to content him? I doubt it. Will he improve the human species with his new information about genetics? I suppose he will be able to, but I hope this chancey business will be deferred for several hundred years or forever. Will he have a longer life, and a merrier one? Yes, and no. What is he going to do about religion?

Well, I should like to finish with a kind of footnote on this problem.

The meaning of human existence

For many or us, religion in the old sense, the clear idea of God and His involvement with human beings, the accepted protocols for dealing with Him, and the daily concern with His Health and His Ear—these have already disappeared behind us like scenes from a train.

To have a religion requires, demands, a feeling of solid conviction about the nature of the universe, first of all, and about the meaning of human existence, second. In our terms, as if we were writing a conventional paper, the first is the Method, the second the Result. Any comprehensive idea about the meaning of existence, formed on whatever premises, is a religion, but it is always based, and has to be, on a set of clear assumptions concerning the nature of the world, and in these days, the whole universe, whether they are in fact valid or not.

Until recently, the nature of the universe was easy to come by. Anybody could see it by just looking up, the whole thing, plain as day, and arguments about what it meant to mankind, if anything, were matters of opinion. Since the interpretation of the nature of things was, as it turned out, the purest fantasy, the extrapolation to meaning, or religion, was also largely fantasy.

In our time, or in the past hundred years or so, we have had to learn that the universe makes no more sense than a clock without hands. It will make sense eventually, of course, but from our observatory, here in the provinces, it will take a long time and a lot of unimagined data, and probably a new kind of thinking, before it has been figured out. Nevertheless, we have begun on it, and having come this far, enough to know our ignorance, we are bound to go the whole distance before we can expect to find any meaning, ever again. We are now committed.

Humanity: No longer the center of the universe

Another tremendous difficulty is the new idea we have developed about ourselves in the past century, strengthened to the stature of a philosophy in the last thirty years. As people, we are not the fixed, stable, eternal thing at the center of all the whirl. We are a part of all biology; there are things about us that are always mutable. We tend to change, like all biological forms. We have changed before, many times, from one form to the next, and we shall probably keep at it. The latest and most drastic change, as important in biological terms as if we had suddenly given birth to a mutant generation with wings and fins, is information, never before available to human beings, which is now streaming into the recording and computing centers of our brains. This will affect our behavior as a species more surely than the sensing of distant sugar affects bees, although not as predictably.

We are being influenced by information, and are in the process of change. The change is not under our control, nor can we predict the outcome for ourselves. What causes biological change, and to what purpose? This is a question about God, but it cannot have the kind of answer that awoke our fathers at dawn in the twelfth century and sent them out to build, just for the record, Notre Dame. Ours, if it comes, will be a long, slow answer, fragment after fragment, all in code, with the key at the very end.

We are living between religions, between believable ideas about meaning. Up to now, we have made do with grossly mistaken notions about ourselves and our setting, but we believed them and found meaning in them. Now they are gone, and most of the meaning with them. The convictions of three decades ago seem to me as antique, as quaint with good intentions, as the ideas of three centuries ago, or for that matter three millennia.

Increasing knowledge will solve the mysteries of life

It is the mounting torrent of new information, the learning of new facts every day, the massive changes in the recognizable structure of the universe, and most of all, the increasingly formidable dimensions of the unknown, that unnerve us today. We cannot stop short in the middle of any morning and say: this is as far as we go; let us now decide what it means. We are swept along.

We are the generation, or, more likely, the set of generations, between the truth and the revelation. The truth will be a long time coming in all in pieces and requiring somehow to be re-assembled, and only then can we sit and contemplate the revelation.

The human mind is no longer as simple as a mystery. It has become a problem to be solved. Mysteries are oversimplifications of the problems that seem insoluble. We must begin to give them up, all of them, for we have entered a time when we must undertake, whether we like it or not, to solve all problems and answer all questions, over the long haul.

If we are to believe, as many of us now do in our hearts, that there can no longer be any mysteries, what then? It is, at first sight, a bleak and terrifying prospect. Every religion has been based and centered on a mystery, of one sort or another, with the meaning hidden somewhere inside. Must we look forward to an age of Science, stretching ahead of us a thousand years in helical coils, with no religion and no awareness of God?

It is, I believe, both better and worse than this, and more demanding of courage than any time that has ever confronted mankind. Eventually we may reach an understanding of our source and purpose, of the core and activator of our being, the designer, the controller, the inner meaning. But it may not be a mystical experience when it happens. Instead, it may be the plainest and hardest of facts of life, and there will be no talking our way out or deciding on a different church.

Will God be seen by man?

Like it or not, if man continues, as he will, his ceaseless and, on balance, almost infallible inquiry about everything related to himself, he may eventually, a thousand years or more from now, see God as whole and clear as Augustine hoped to. It may not look like God, and perhaps other names will at first be given to Him, or a Number, or a Code. But everything will have derived from Him, and He will contain all the meaning of things.

When this discovery is made, I have a hunch that nobody will like it much. They will at first be far less happy with this kind of truth than this generation is without it, and perhaps they will turn on us in our graves and shout at us angrily. There will be muttering, but no music, no chorales, not even plainsong. The ultimate religion will be no easier to adjust to at the beginning than any of the symbolic tragedies that were its predecessors. No matter how much we will have learned by that distant time, understanding and wisdom in such a totally new situation will, I think, come no more quickly to the human mind than now.

Well then, what will happen then? Perhaps, and this will please those who like the idea of intellectual continuity, and dislike any end of the long affair, it will all begin again, all over again.

The new truth may not turn out to be enough, and, after a few years or a few hundred, men will set out to search again for a different answer and a better one. Or, conceivably, they may at long last settle down.

We can only hope for them, as for ourselves, that they will turn to each other. For there is another kind of meaning, less deep but easier on the soul, and it exists in all human beings. Its name is goodness, and it can be relied upon. It is not the full face of God, but we can hope that it will always be an aspect, and, for what it is worth, it will help us now, then, and long afterward.

SCHOLARSHIP IN MEDICINE

HENRY A. CHRISTIAN, M.D.
(December 1940, pp. 4–5)

This paper, "Scholarship in Medicine," was published in the sec-
ond volume of The Pharos *on the occasion of the first annual*
meeting of the chapter of AΩA at Tufts University School of
Medicine. Dr. Christian was a true scholar and teacher. He was born
in Virginia and graduated from Randolph-Mason College in 1895.
He received his M.D. from Johns Hopkins University in 1900.
In 1908 he became the first Physician-in-Chief at the Peter Bent
Brigham Hospital, retiring 31 years later. His name is forever at-
tached to Hand-Schuller-Christian disease and to a form of re-
lapsing febrile nodular nonsuppurative panniculitis. Perhaps his
finest achievement was serving a mentor and guide for many
young people as they entered what was then known as academic
medicine. He was elected, along with others, to AΩA in 1909,
shortly after establishment of a chapter at Harvard. Only a por-
tion of his essay is reprinted here.

Today, December 2, 1940, is a significant date for Tufts College Medical School because it marks a national recognition of the high quality of scholarship that may be attained by its diligent students working under wise guidance of a stimulating faculty, itself richly endowed in the realm of scholarship. On such an occasion thought turns to answering the questions:

What constitutes scholarship in the learned profession of medicine?

How may it be attained?

What practical value has scholarship for the individual physician and for his profession?

* * * * *

I rather like a dictionary definition of scholarship that I have seen lately: "the character and qualities of a scholar; attainment in science or literature; learning; erudition." Scholarship is not a static condition; it is kinetic; it grows; it advances, but it can recede if its cultivation relaxes; it is not acquired for life, but once attained, its continuation ever grows easier. Continuation in its cultivation is imperative for the maintenance of scholarship.

Scholarship thrives best in an atmosphere of inquiry, of investigation, of exploration. It is nurtured on books and journals and their contents. Scholarship requires reading over a range of topics and texts. The narrow fields of specialism are consonant with scholarship, but he who restricts himself to such a narrow field is not a scholar. The scholar projects his interests, his studies, his investigations in all directions beyond the boundaries of his specialty.

Scholarship can be developed in the classroom, in the library, in the laboratory, in the clinic, in the office of the practitioner. Several of these various places, rather than but one, furnish a setting in which scholarship thrives most luxuriantly. Scholarship is stimulated by leadership and the influence of other scholars, but scholarship cannot be passively absorbed. Its attainment requires work, effort, study, denial of diverting calls hither and yon, resistance to the distractions and the seductions of ephemeral pleasures. Scholarship requires persistence in its quest and devotion to its demands.

Work: the master-word

The primal foundation of scholarship in medicine lies in work: diligent, absorbing, persistent work. He who does not work long hours never can attain to scholarship. The laggard and the lazy never become scholars. Osler delightfully in one of his essays says,

> It seems a bounden duty on such occasion to be honest and frank, so I propose to tell you the secret of life as I have seen the game played, and as I have tried to play it myself. You remember in one of the "Jungle Stories," that when Mowgli wished to be avenged on the villagers he could only get the help of Hathi and his sons by sending them the master-word. This I propose to give you in the hope, yes, the full assurance, that some of you at least will lay hold upon it to your profit. Though a little one, the master-word looms large in meaning. It is the open sesame to every portal, the great equalizer in the world, the true philosopher's stone which transmutes all the base metal of humanity into gold. The stupid man among you it will make bright, the bright man brilliant, and the brilliant student steady. With the magic word in your heart all things are possible, and without it all study is vanity and vexation. The miracles of life are with it; the blind see by touch, the deaf hear with eyes, the dumb speak with fingers. To the youth it brings hope, to the middle-aged confidence, to the aged repose. True balm of hurt minds, in its presence the heart of the sorrowful is lightened and consoled. It is directly responsible for all advances in medicine during the past twenty-five centuries. Laying hold upon it, Hippocrates made observation and science the warp and woof of our art. Galen so read its meaning that fifteen centuries stopped thinking, and slept until awakened by the De Fabrica of Vesalius, which is the very incarnation of the master-word. With its inspiration Harvey gave an impulse to a larger circulation than he knew of, an impulse which we feel today. Hunter sounded all its heights and depths, and stands out in our history as one of the great exemplars of its virtues. With it Virchow smote the

rock and the waters of progress gushed out; while in the hands of Pasteur it proved a very talisman to open to us a new heaven in medicine and a new earth in surgery. Not only has it been the touchstone of progress, but it is the measure of success in everyday life. Not a man before you but is beholden to it for his position here, while he who addresses you has that honour directly in consequence of having had it graven on his heart when he was as you are to-day. And the Master-Word is Work, a little one, as I have said, but fraught with momentous consequences if you can but write it on the tables of your heart, and bind it upon your forehead. But there is a serious difficulty in getting you to understand the paramount importance of the work-habit as part of your organization. You are not far from the Tom Sawyer stage with its philosophy that "work consists of whatever a body is obliged to do, and play consists of whatever a body is not obliged to do."

If the master word, "Work," is the key to unlock the way to scholarship in medicine, it must be applied in large measure in reading. If, as I have just said, the primal foundation of scholarship in medicine lies in work, then much of the structure of scholarship above the foundation is to be builded of bricks and stones, gathered from the writings of past and present men of the medical profession. . . . Early in his student days and throughout his professional life, the medical man should read something almost daily. It is a habit, which once cultivated, continues and is one of the roads toward scholarship easy to follow and lined with pleasant impressions innumerable. The medical student should spend part of each day in reading, and his work week can be no labor union maximum of 40 hours, if he has any expectation whatsoever of attaining to scholarship. The student reads mostly in text books, but he should read also some things in current journals. . . . The most effective text book reading is to peruse the description of some disease suffered by a patient seen by you a short time previously. Here you compare your personal observations with those of the author of the book; the clinical case helps to fix in your mind the text book discussion of the disease; you have begun in this way to acquire clinical experience in relation to the understanding of a disease.

INTELLECTUAL CURIOSITY AND THE PHYSICIAN'S RESPONSIBILITIES

WILLIAM B. CASTLE, M.D.

(January 1959, pp. 24–30)

Bill Castle died on August 9, 1990, at the age of 92. He was born in Cambridge, Massachusetts, and did not have far to travel to attend Harvard College, matriculating in 1914. After medical school at Harvard (election to AΩA in 1921) he served as a "house pupil" at the Massachusetts General Hospital. He received research training from Cecil Drinker, but in 1925 Francis Peabody attracted him back to clinical medicine at the Thorndike Memorial Laboratory at the Boston City Hospital. After the discovery that lightly cooked liver could cure patients with pernicious anemia, Castle set about to find out why. He and Thomas Hale Ham found, after nine years of clinical studies, that " . . . if beef muscle and gastric juice are administered without opportunity for contact, they are not effective. It is obvious, therefore, that the activity of mixtures of beef muscle and gastric juice cannot be due to the simple addition of two sub-threshold substances but requires an interaction between them." The investigators called the essential gastric secretion "intrinsic factor." In 1948 Castle and associates showed conclusively that "extrinsic factor" was identical to the B vitamin now known as cobalamin. It is very clear that his clinical experiments would not have passed human experimentation review boards in 2003!

This paper was presented as an Alpha Omega Alpha Lecture at Jefferson Medical College in Philadelphia on March 21. 1958.

ODAY, ACCORDING TO JAMES B. CONANT,[1] formerly President of Harvard University, "A modern, industrialized, highly urbanized country can prosper only if the professions are full of capable, imaginative, forward-looking men."

A succinct modern definition of the fundamental privileges and responsibilities of the physician appears in Harrison's *Principles of Internal Medicine* in a single paragraph as follows:

No greater opportunity, responsibility, or obligation can fall to the lot of a human being than to become a physician. In the care of the suffering, he needs technical skill, scientific knowledge, and human understanding. He who uses these with courage, with humility, and with wisdom will provide a unique service for his fellow man and will build an enduring edifice of character within himself. The physician should ask of his destiny no more than this; he should be content with no less.

Moreover, there are at the roots of our professional life things that keep men together in happy and effective association. These, according to the late Doctor Alan Gregg[2] are "shared experiences of the past, present beliefs generally agreed upon, and common hopes and desires for the future." The first of these, so marvelously enhanced in modern civilization by the many means of communication, begins in the process of formal education with learning to read. Its relevance to a particular set of historical experiences is intensified during the years in medical school. After graduation, the intern and resident, the physician in practice, and even the academic doctor live very much in the frothy and fascinating present. Indeed, only as they advance to professional maturity do an especially vigorous and generous-minded few catch up with time and begin to dream for the future of their profession.

But to return to the individual physician, what then are the qualities of heart, hand, and head that characterize the good physician? In view of the many ways in which modern doctors function, various abilities of special kinds are needed for different types of professional activity; but the good doctor is not one who possesses only particular skills with special tools. He is a man who understands the basic principles of his job and its relation to the contributions and needs of others. Thus, it seems to me that there are three qualities that the doctor must exhibit if he is to be worthy in the eyes of the community, of his fellows, and according to his inmost self-appraisal. I shall, for convenience, define them with alliteration as *conscientiousness*, *competence*, and *curiosity*. Among these, it is difficult to choose. But of curiosity in its best intellectual sense, it is possible to say much, for it serves not only to bring its own rich rewards but it also sustains and enhances those other desirable qualities, conscientiousness and competence.

Some years ago, Doctor Samuel A. Levine addressed the Alumni of the Harvard Medical School on the topic of "Worry, Where Does It Get You?" As I sat in the audience, knowing full well his pre-eminence in the field of cardiovascular disease, I foolishly expected to hear that worry would get *you,* if it didn't get your coronaries first. But, of course, I completely underestimated the speaker's wisdom and sense of values as a physician. What Dr. Levine did say in effect was that worry—by which he meant thoughtful concern for the patient—often leads to recognition of the early signs of complicating clinical circumstances. He illustrated this from his own broad experience and he also made the point that what is usually known in the trade as a high index of suspicion could lead, through reflection and consultation, to appropriate diagnostic or therapeutic measures. He explained that thought-provoking concern for the patient may do much to solve the dilemma of the present-day physician whose fund of knowledge must inevitably be inadequate in the face of the constantly increasing body of specialized information. He was not advocating the substitution of conscientiousness for competence but rather he was illustrating how competence may be extended through conscientiousness.

Conscientiousness can thus aid the physician in the care of the patient, and it can save him the most agonizing of experiences: the feeling of vain regret that he has neglected something. The mistakes of surgeons are more likely to be positive and perhaps, therefore, conscientiousness with them comes more in the form of the self-imposed injunction, "do no harm." But for the physician, there is special need for the positive exercise of conscientiousness. A telephone call in the night about a child is more often a false alarm than an emergency; but how to be sure—only by going and taking a look and a loss of sleep. And going the next time, too! Conscientiousness may even have to be exerted against the natural inclination of patient or family in the interests of good medicine. Familiar enough is the importance of self-imposed imperatives to biopsy, not simply to "watch" the lump in the neck; to refrain from blunting the edge of a good antibiotic on a cold; or, despite the inconvenience, to examine carefully the apparently well members of a family in which tuberculosis has appeared. Then, there is the undemanding patient who follows directions so well that she scarcely stimulates even the occasional review of the clinical status that is required for good medical care. Restudied as a new patient, instead of as an old story, the mass in her left upper quadrant would have been obvious. Surely it is conscientiousness that supports the physician in the care of the aged with their small and varying or monotonous complaints that loom so large in a tapering vision of life. What quality but compassion, the warmer word for conscientiousness, enables the physician to buoy up the hopeless and to stand by his patient until ultimately death defeats him in whom the patient has placed his last best hope?

Happily, conscientiousness has its cheerful employments far more often than when the patient is in the valley of the shadow. A high empathic index defined by Doctor Sidney Burwell,[3] formerly Dean of the Harvard Medical School, as "a lovely term for the imaginative capacity for putting oneself in other people's situations," is an important asset for the good physician to possess. Patients enjoy a visit to such a one and tell their friends; and even specialists agree that the symptoms of half of their patients are attributable to emotional disturbances. But to understand is often to listen to a long recital of a private experience of undue importance to the patient. If the definition of a bore is a person who, on being asked casually, "How are you?", tells you, then the experience of listening unsympathetically to the neurotic patient is indeed social torture to the Nth power. But this *is* his illness. An audition can be borne cheerfully only for the sake of good medicine, and unless he possesses the wisdom and humanity of the good physician, the expert, cynically described as "one who knows more and more about less and less," may not listen. Whereas the patient, thinking himself the victim of heart disease, may have chosen wisely a recognized specialist in such disorders, there is no board that certifies that the heart of the diplomate is in the right place. Nor do such higher qualifications show, to quote the immortal words of Doctor Francis Peabody,[4] that the physician has also learned that "the secret of the care of the patient is in caring for the patient."

The famous painting by Luke Fildes of "The Doctor" depicts the devotion of a night-long vigil at the bedside of a sick child. In our mid-twentieth century, the beholder admires the sense of responsibility of the Victorian doctor so displayed but considers that, perhaps, there was then little else that a doctor could offer. Remember that this tired, bearded man had at his disposal perhaps only twelve drugs of proved effectiveness. More readily, perhaps, recall those that he did possessed no antitoxin, no insulin, no liver extract, no antibiotics, no wonder drugs, and especially no hospital with its modern marvels of equipment and service. Today, although not every x-ray examination or every laboratory test leads to a diagnosis, and although the measure of our therapeutic advance is not best reckoned by the *Physician's Desk Reference, the increase of knowledge* potentially useful to the physician in practice is truly vast. Neither he nor any other doctor can alone encompass more than a fraction of it. A doctor's competence by today's standards then means ability to recognize what he can perform and what he must leave to the special skills of others.

A professor of philosophy at Harvard, in response to a question by a student, once defined Heaven as for himself "a state of being in which he would understand completely what he was doing." For the physician, this world will never provide such an earthly paradise. To understand even partially some of the many problems that beset him in his daily rounds, the mind of the physician would be required to hold available for recall not the facts contained in many volumes but rather those of a whole medical library, to say nothing of the necessary accumulated experience and ability to apply them in practice to a variety of poorly indexed clinical circumstances. Obviously, no solution can be wholly satisfactory; but still something can be offered with which to confront a situation that would otherwise be a cause of despair.

. . . *Competence*, then, is not necessarily ready in advance for a particular clinical situation; but the right kind of knowledge knows how to become competent for almost any situation. This is the unfolding thesis of sound education and of the growth of knowledge: that if the principle is understood, the appropriate practice can be determined. The best premedical education is then simply the best education; and knowledge of medical science is the best general guide to the understanding of future clinical experiences. After graduation, the principle still holds good. I have been impressed that the best diagnosticians are usually those who are able to resolve clinical problems into their underlying aberrations of function or of form. The explorer in medicine, whether in the laboratory or at the bedside, must travel light. His ability to meet new circumstances successfully depends upon a knowledge of general principles and of where to find the details of what more he may need to know.

The third quality of the good physician that I shall discuss is *curiosity*. Only in the age of science has intellectual curiosity become respectable rather than a somewhat simian and irreverent quality of the mind tending to heresy. Greek mythology leaves us the legend of Pandora's Box. The Bible speaks of the forbidden fruit of the Tree of Knowledge. No doubt the ancients took some comfort in the fact that both episodes with their resultant misfortunes to mankind were the result of feminine curiosity. However, the later Greeks, whose minds were as open and clear as any that the world has produced, must have understood that curiosity leads to or arises from reflectiveness. At any rate, Plato espouses this collateral virtue of curiosity with the statement that "the unexamined life is not worth living." In modem literature, *insatiable curiosity* was the obtrusive characteristic of Kipling's *Elephant's Child*. This habit of mind annoyed his aunts and uncles, but it took him places and evolved for him an improved proboscis with better technological possibilities. This caused him to reexamine his position in life, an exercise of great importance to the progress of mankind. Indeed, it may be said that the chief benefit of civilization—or at least of such civilizations as preceded the immediate present—was the leisure they afforded to some men for the exercise of curiosity and reflection. In all ages, the time available in which to think has probably been largely wasted by most; but the few men and women who have employed it well are the great; and their excellent use of leisure has paid off handsomely for the rest of us. This is why the deans of some medical schools insist on free time for their students even though it displaces some of the courses offered by eager professors!

It is readily understood that a primary responsibility of teachers of undergraduate medical students is to stimulate their curiosity. Less well appreciated is the importance of the process in reverse. But we find Dr. L. G. Welt[5] pointing out to the first year medical students at the University of North Carolina that it is their privilege, nay duty, to ask questions that will help to prompt the imagination of their professors! Actually, this is a long-established experience of those who toil in academies. I am told that in the *Talmud* appears the statement by an elder scholar somewhat to this effect, "Much have I learned from my teachers, and much too from my colleagues, but most of all from my students." Now, my own experience as a teacher would specify this as likely to occur in the form of questions by students even following a lecture that has left things to be desired, possibly including unanswered promptings to curiosity.

. . . Medical students are acutely aware of their state of uncompleted experience. Curiosity among them during some centuries has led to many significant discoveries in medicine or the natural sciences.[6] Thus, Harvey was a pupil of Fabricius in Padua around 1600 when he first saw the beating of the embryo chick heart. Black, a student at Edinburgh, reported in his doctor's thesis the discovery of "fixed air" (carbon dioxide) in magnesium carbonate and later became the father of quantitative chemical analysis. . . .Too numerous to mention are all but the most important discoveries of other medical students. In the first half of the nineteenth century, Humphry Davy and W. T. G. Morton, on opposite sides of the Atlantic, laid the foundations of modern anesthesia while still in medical school. Thomas Young first saw as a medical student in London that compression of the lens of the eye on an ox was the mechanism of its accommodation, and went on to the wave theory of light and to decipher the Rosetta Stone. Claude Bernard, the father of experimental medicine, also began his studies when in medical school. Walter Cannon[7] who, while a medical student, first applied x-ray to the study of the digestive tract, later defined curiosity as the mainspring of the initiation and persistent industry of the investigator.

Others famous for discoveries begun as medical students are Ehrlich, Einthoven, Freud, Helmholtz, Hopkins, Jenner, Laennec, Langerhans, Poiseuille, Purkinje, Sherrington, and Stenson. John Shaw Billings was an undergraduate in a sleepy American college whose library was open only on Saturdays. He made a key that gave him quiet access to its collection of six thousand volumes on the other six days. Small wonder that with this advantage he successfully became a medical student! But soon, interested in the treatment of epilepsy, he found that the libraries of Cincinnati provided no help although his professors thought that those of Philadelphia, or of far-away Europe, might do so. These frustrating experiences led to a life-long crusade against ignorance which resulted in the founding of the Surgeon General's Library—among the greatest of all American contributions to Medicine.

But you may ask, "Of what special value is curiosity to the majority of medical students who do not intend to follow the way of an investigator or to spend much time in the medical library?" The answer is not difficult, for the habit of curiosity and its gratification are enduring and, best of all, enjoyable. For the physician, they are independent of such spurs to effort as a medical school diploma, the will to survive as an over-worked medical resident, or the certification by a specialty board, professional prestige, and economic success that may come later. Moreover, curiosity is an autocatalytic process. More facts come to the attention of the curious observer, and so more and often unexpected data accumulate to be contemplated in search of significant relations. Now, the most difficult problem in medical education is not how to become, but how to remain educated in a rapidly changing scientific world. I can think of nothing more likely than intellectual curiosity to provide the necessary growth and development of the individual's knowledge and effectiveness. Indeed, if every patient is regarded as a fresh exercise in the detection of disease and its treatment, the challenge to the curiosity of the modern practitioner is not so very different from that of the clinical investigator. Certainly, both are well supplied with analytical methods. The modern doctor has at hand the resources of the biochemical, microbiological, and radiological laboratories of the hospital. He may explore every orifice of the body by endoscopy, sample many organs by needle biopsy, and inspect others by operative procedure when necessary. A variety of effective drugs is available to him, and therapeutic measures beyond enumeration are his to command. However, as with the modern clinical investigator, a hazard run by the busy physician is that he will forget the basic orientation value of his senses. Complex apparatus is not without its disadvantages to the mental activity of the clinical investigator; and without a clear history, a careful physical examination, and simple laboratory studies, the physician may also become lost in a wood in which he sees only the trees; worse, he may lose the curiosity that urges him onward to a better understanding of disease and of his patients. This is the danger when the dizzy round of the immediate and the urgent becomes too pressing. Then is the occasion for time out for a refresher course or for the preparation of a case report with the help of the medical library where there is sanctuary and sustenance for the hard-pressed mind. Even the doctor who systematically takes time for the medical literature, if he only follows the advice of the late Dr. Henry Christian to read for at least a half hour a day without fail, keeps a salutary awareness of medical events beyond his horizon.

Such personal impressions of the continuing value of intellectual curiosity in the life of the good doctor receive some support from the findings of a recent survey[8] sponsored by the Rockefeller Foundation concerning the competence of general practitioners in North Carolina. It was found that men under thirty-six who had been in the upper third of their medical school classes, those who had had more than eight months of hospital training in internal medicine, and those who currently read the most medical journals were the best family doctors. On the other hand, the occupations of their fathers, the medical schools they attended, their hospital training other than in internal medicine, and the number of refresher courses taken made little difference in the average professional performance. Of course, there were striking individual exceptions; but I would like to read into these findings the implication that native intelligence, fostered by practical experience with major systemic disease, and followed by a self-activated system of postgraduate medical education were the successful ingredients.

In concluding, I would remind you that the basic assumption of western culture, and in a small way of these remarks, is the great importance of the individual to society. To me, the performance of the medical profession is best measured as the aggregate of the performance of its individual members.

I have spoken not so much of the nature of the responsibilities of the doctor to his profession and to the community as of the means by which the individual may best insure his own development and stature as a good physician. It is my belief that in this way he will best serve his profession, notable from the days of Hippocrates for its humanity and high purpose, and in the last century for its increasing scientific knowledge as well. I have set conscientiousness, competence, and especially curiosity before you as qualities essential for the good doctor to have and to hold. I regard curiosity as invaluable for the maintenance of the other two qualities and as the intellectual characteristic most likely to enable the physician to discharge with satisfaction his responsibilities to society throughout his professional life.

References

1. Conant JB. Education for a Divided World. Harvard University Press, 1948.
2. Gregg A. Our Anabasis. Trans. Assoc. Amer. Physicians, 1954; 67:47.
3. Burwell CS. Class Day Address. Harvard Med Alumni Bull, 1952; 27:176.
4. Peabody F. The Care of the Patient. JAMA, 1927; 88:877.
5. Welt LG. The Contribution of the Student to Education. Yale J Biol and Med, 1955; 27:279.
6. Gibson WC. Significant Scientific Discoveries by Medical Students. Scientific Monthly, 1955; 81:2.
7. Cannon WB. The Way of an Investigator. W. W. Norton and Co., New York, 1945.
8. Peterson OL, Andrews LP, Spain RS, Greenberg BG. An Analytical Study of North Carolina General Practice, 1953-1954. J Med Education, 1956; 31:Dec., Part 2.

A SALUTE TO SCHOLARSHIP

WILLIAM J. KERR, M.D.

Professor of Medicine

University of California Medical School, San Francisco, California

(April 1950, pp. 14–17)

Born in 1889, William Kerr was an undergraduate at UC Berkeley, and went east to earn his M.D. at Harvard Medical School, graduating in 1915 and being elected to AΩA in that year. He returned to San Francisco and in 1927 was appointed the first full-time Chair of the Department of Medicine. He had a special interest in cardiology, but is perhaps best known for his persuasive and keen political acumen. He convinced the California legislature to fund a floor for cardiovascular research at Moffitt Hospital and engineered founding of the renowned Cardiovascular Research Institute, funded primarily by NIH dollars. Julius Comroe was his choice to direct this center, one of the first that demonstrated the value of interdisciplinary, interdepartmental research. This address was presented at the Installation of the Gamma Chapter, California, of Alpha Omega Alpha at the University of Southern California School of Medicine, Los Angeles, California, on November 14, 1949.

IT IS A GREAT HONOR for me to be included in this select company this evening and to bring to the new Gamma Chapter of Alpha Omega Alpha the greetings of the Alpha Chapter at the University of California Medical School. Because of my great respect and admiration for your distinguished leader, Dean Raulston, and the many worthy scholars on your faculty, I find it a pleasure to take part in this ceremony. And it is an added pleasure to participate with Dr. Walter L. Bierring, who has done so much to advance the standards of medical scholarship and practice in this era. He also has made notable contributions in the field of public health throughout the country, including the State of Iowa where I was born. I wish to pay my respects to Dr. Josiah H. Moore who has promoted the scholarly interests of medicine throughout his life. His influence upon a long succession of classes of students has been notable. He has labored many years in behalf of the profession. Each of these worthy gentlemen has inspired me to strive for greater achievement. The affairs of our organization are secure in their hands.

The University of Southern California School of Medicine, like most of our American schools, has a history of irregular and often interrupted growth. At last your school, like my own, has reached a more favorable state of stability and security. During the past fifty years most of the proprietary schools have fortunately gone out of existence. The few which have survived are showing healthy growth as integral parts of universities where the theoretical and practical knowledge necessary for modern medicine may be acquired and taught.

During the lifetime of the medical students who are here tonight, we have witnessed a general letdown of ethical and moral standards. Many people say the two World Wars are to blame for loss of faith in God, nations, and each other. The sanctity of the home has been shattered to an appalling degree; it has become a favorite pastime to discredit our national heroes and to destroy our personal idols; it has been popular to abhor virtue in public and to imagine ourselves as "men of distinction" when we "bend the elbow." At such a time it is refreshing to see a fine young matron such as Princess Elizabeth of Great Britain speak up for the cardinal virtues. Parenthetically, Bonnie Prince Charlie is one year old today.

In the field of education during the past generation, it has not been "smart" to appear bright in class, to be seen going to call upon the professor, or to present an introductory letter to a member of the faculty. This attitude on the part of students has deprived them of the benefit of close association and acquaintance with their teachers, which, in my experience, may be as stimulating to the teacher as to the student. I believe that fortunately the tide is turning. We should make no apology for scholarship. We should promote mutual trust and friendly relations between student and teachers.

The rewards of the scholar are great. Many of them are personal, through satisfaction in a job well done. Some scholars are undeniably wedded to their work and care nothing for the application of their knowledge or the approbation of others. Most scholars, however, derive great satisfaction if their efforts bring benefits or pleasure to others; they still believe in rewards and fairies. The growing list of prizes, awards, honorary degrees, and other forms of recognition serve as constant reminders that talents and achievements are honored and respected. The Alpha Omega Alpha membership is in recognition of a student's scholarly talents. You, as students, have given promise of achievement in the field of learning. In wearing the key you are in hostage to your councilor and teachers who have shown faith in your future careers. It may well be that some of you have already lighted your torches at the altar of inspiration. It is our hope that all of you may do so.

The elements of success are many and complex, but the master word, as expressed so well by the great physician, William Osler, whose centenary we celebrate this year, is Work. The catalyst for success is inspiration. This may come from unexpected quarters. It may well be that the spark will come from an upper classman, an intern or resident, or some younger member of the faculty or profession who is in close contact with the student. It may come from a sweetheart or wife. Sometimes those of us who direct the affairs of departments wish to think we are the ones who guard the sacred fires.

The teacher's prime function: Recognizing talent

I have always held in great respect the late William H. Welch, who is credited with developing many notable pathologists. He modestly explained that his only claim to fame in this regard was the ability to recognize promising talent when he saw it. I would agree that this is the most important function of the teacher. Once this selection is made, it is the solemn duty of the teacher to push the assistant, if need be, into situations calling for industry, accuracy, evaluation, and judgment, and at the same time to set an example of performance of high order. . . . One of the greatest moments of my life is to witness the eruption . . . of inspiration in a student or assistant. He may have been prodded and encouraged without apparent results, and then one day he comes to discuss a problem which to him has now become the most important thing in the world. There is a new light in his eyes. He is impatient to be off on the quest, like a bird dog on a hot scent. Now he is a "self-starter" and doesn't need to be "cranked up." Thereafter the teacher needs only to provide the facilities and opportunities to make his dreams come true.

I cannot close this discourse without discussing the key we hope you will wear with distinction. The honor society key is a carry-over from the days when key-winding watches were worn. Some of the early honor society keys had a square hole in the tip for winding or tightening the spring. Then came the stem-winding watches. In my medical school days, the honor society keys were worn with some pride on a long watch chain swung across the chest from vest pocket to vest pocket. A key student with Phi Beta Kappa, Sigma Xi, and Alpha Omega Alpha keys over the "weskit" was a sight to envy! In those days the appelation of "stem-winder" to a person was a term of distinction. Now we witness the passing of the stem-winder. Recently I had to have repaired the stem of my Longine stem-winder, which I had carried for many years and from the chain of which were suspended my keys. The watch needed cleaning, which would cost a tidy sum. I said, "No, I guess not. I don't care whether it keeps time or not. I use it only with my dress suit and to display my keys." And then I reflected, sadly this time, "My dinner jacket is doubled breasted, and I don't even wear a 'weskit.' Thus, how am I to wear my Alpha Omega Alpha and other keys?" And how will you? I am hopeful that our officers will find some new and modern way for us to display our key. Perhaps a lapel button or a miniature key on the dial of the wrist watch might serve the purpose. The women who may be elected to membership might choose to wear the key on a charm bracelet, until fashion dictates that charm bracelets are passé.

May your chapter prosper and may your example be a continuing stimulus to scholarship in your medical school. It is not enough to be admired. You must constantly strive to promote respect for learning and whenever possible to provide the catalyst—inspiration.

PART II

THE ANCIENTS: EGYPTIANS, GREEKS, ROMANS, AND CHINESE

HEALTH CARE DELIVERY SYSTEMS IN ANCIENT GREECE AND ROME

WARREN L. KUMP, M.D.

(April 1973, pp. 42–48)

Dr. Kump was elected to AΩA in 1950 at the University of Kansas. Remaining in the Midwest for his professional career, he is now retired as chief of radiology at North Memorial Medical Center in Minneapolis where he also served as chief of the medical staff and later as chair of the Board of Trustees.

MEDICAL HISTORY IS USUALLY WRITTEN BY PHYSICIANS or other health professionals. Consequently the emphasis is on the evolution of scientific knowledge and theory, on the circumstances attending various medical discoveries, or on biographical detail relating to important practitioners of the healing arts. In this day of consumerism and the rising influence of third parties it is appropriate to attempt a more general perspective, one in which the sick or injured patient occupies the center, and the physician is relegated to a supporting position as one of society's several major health resources.

When the more general consideration of health care is undertaken, the relative value of the contributions made by various cultures is subject to revision. One example is in the case of ancient Greece and Rome. Traditionally Greece has been given the credit, and rightfully, for the development of rational or scientific medicine. Rome adopted rational medicine along with many other intellectual and scientific contributions of the Greek civilization, but added comparatively little of its own to the body of medical knowledge. In the field of total health care, however, the performance of Rome was more creditable.

A differentiated medical profession was recognizable in Greek society as early as the siege of Troy in the 12th century, B.C. Its practitioners, if they attempted to gain their entire livelihood by the treatment of wounds and sickness, were dependent upon the wealth and good will of their patients. The idea that a patient's access to such treatment depended upon his ability to pay for it could not have become widespread until the position of medicine had become much more secure. It was not until the sixth century, B.C., that the Greeks considered the importance of the medical profession great enough to warrant official notice by a unit of government. In 526 B.C. the celebrated practitioner Democedes was appointed public physician of Aegina. The following year he was attracted to Athens and still later to Samos by offers of higher salaries. By the fourth century the practice of engaging public physicians or *demosieuontes* was widespread in Greece, with cities or districts contracting to pay them out of public funds.

Evolution of public, as opposed to personal, health

The responsibilities to the community of the public physicians has long been a matter for study. Cohn-Haft, in the most extensive modern investigation, has concluded that, contrary to previous impressions, the demosieuontes were not engaged to provide free medical care for the poor, but rather to insure the availability of medical service in the community on a dependable and stable basis. In his view the rather small salary offered by the municipalities was considered in the nature of a bonus or retainer, obligating a popular or highly regarded physician to practice in the city, but not to give his services free of charge. He practiced medicine as did any other physician, collecting his fees according to convention and the ability of his patients to pay, and with no more obligation to treat the poor free of charge than was felt by any other practitioner.[5]

Such an arrangement, more similar to the modern attempts to attract physicians to rural communities through scholarships, grants, and other financial inducements than to the free care offered in charity hospitals and the military, would have been in accordance with the early Greek conception of public welfare. In the classical view a public expenditure should be made to promote the interests of all citizens directly and equally, not to provide exclusive aid to any special segment of society such as the poor. In the case of the retention of a physician at public expense, however, the equal benefit would have seemed more theoretical than real to those unable to afford his services.

If public welfare programs were rudimentary, large scale private philanthropy was also limited. This was largely because of the lack of a legal concept of the corporation or foundation in classical times. . . . The result was a discontinuous or sporadic approach to poor relief, consisting of isolated and occasional giving and dependent on the personal fortunes and inclinations of the wealthy. The absence of the idea of a foundation also made it impractical for men of modest means to join in raising funds for purposes of mutual aid.

The milieu of individualism makes the socio-economic policy of Hippocrates understandable. Various Hippocratic maxims advised selflessness on the part of physicians, such as one urging doctors to take into account the resources of the patient, and sometimes to be ready to give treatment without fee. Inscriptional evidence makes it clear that some physicians were indeed ready to regard remuneration as of secondary importance. Free service by doctors acting in a private capacity, however, was optional and not required by any moral or legal code. Plato's *Republic* includes evidence of separate standards of medical care for poor and rich; the carpenter was expected to recover or die with minimal medical care and loss of time from work, while the rich man could continue to live, supported by his wealth and protracted medical attention.

The individualist position was not embraced unanimously, however, as evidenced by Socrates' belief that a man, whether rich or poor, should not be encouraged to live if unable to contribute to his own welfare and that of the state. Other egalitarian sentiments, although not encountered very frequently, are manifested occasionally among the official actions of the Greek city-states. An example is the direct payment of two obols a day to the crippled and disabled of Athens whose property assessment was less than three hundred drachmae. This allowance, originally limited to injured war veterans but soon extended to all the physically-handicapped, represents a rare example of the application of a "means test" in classical times.[9]

Asklepios can help?

There existed in Greek society besides the medical profession yet another health resource in the presence of temple medicine. While Apollo and the goddess Athena were renowned healers, the most important institution in the field of faith healing was the Cult of Asklepios. Its influence by the fourth century, B.C., was widespread, offering the people an attractive alternative to the rational or natural approach to health care. Matters of relative effectiveness aside . . . the Cult was more appealing to the poor than was the medical profession. The physicians who practiced among the poor were not the most skilled and highly educated, but rather those who could not hope to attain a following among the rich. The open-air stands in the city streets from which they dispensed their first-aid and counsel were no match for the pastoral surroundings and the richly ornamented edifices of the Asklepieia. Neither were their simple ministrations as impressive as the solemn ceremonies to be observed at the temples of healing. The allegiance of the masses therefore went mainly to the Asklepieia.[16]

The temples made provisions for the many ailing visitors who were unable to pay. There were inns or hostels nearby for the accommodation of the sick and their friends or relatives; these were open to rich and poor alike. Asklepios himself was a compassionate god and socially aware, widely known to be satisfied with small offerings. A cock was the most common sacrificial gift of the poor, while the rich were expected to give generously.[6] In fact the temple practice of putting whatever was necessary at the disposal of those supplicants who were unable to pay amounted to a considerable subsidy of the poor, since the masses tended to patronize the Asklepieia while the more wealthy and sophisticated consulted physicians.

Thus with public physicians who did not necessarily treat the poor, and Hippocratic physicians who charged according to opportunity and conscience, there was a clear contrast with Asklepieia and sliding scales of suggested donations. The Greeks developed not only an early model of the non-system, but a pluralistic non-system.

Social planning among expatriate Greeks

Ptolemy's Greek enclave in Egypt, on the other hand, with its tightly organized totalitarian state, represented another extreme of social planning. Here was developed the *iatrikon*, a tax levied on the Greek settlers which entitled all of them to free medical care. The treatment was provided by physicians who were in the royal service, receiving their income from the king and giving their services as directed. Undoubtedly the state medical service was under the strong influence and quality control of the prestigious medical faculty of Alexandria, itself under royal patronage and regulation. Of special interest here is the fact that, in a prophetic protofascist spirit (Ptolemy was once a general in the armies of Alexander the Great), neither the tax nor the free medical service was applied to the far larger indigenous population, which made do with second-class citizenship or no citizenship at all.[9,16]

Roman approaches to public health

Despite a reputation for having a word for every need, the Greeks were remiss in developing a jargon applicable to community health care. The Romans at first were little better; although they did come up with the S.A.C. (stationes arcariorum Caesarianorum), the official name of Rome's welfare offices. In the early days of the Republic, however, the Romans showed little promise in the field of medical bureaucracy. Their society lacked even a formal medical profession. Instead they relied on a system of popular or folk medicine, treating themselves and their families according to tradition and under the direction of the head of the family. The paterfamilias presided over a small collection of household remedies which were administered in time-honored ways, a particular combination and ritual for each affliction. Many households had their own specifics: Cato's cure-all was cabbage. The central theme of this fiercely private medicine was a strict consumer control that opposed the development of medical professionalism and refused, as Pliny records, "to give payment to profiteers to preserve their lives."[16]

The practical Romans first approached the problem of community health in a characteristic way, utilizing one of their leading technological resources, civil engineering, in conformity with the classical philanthropic ideal of equal and direct benefit to all. The long range program was a series of public works projects to provide for an adequate supply of healthful water and a system of drainage. The results of the program are well known: The first of the aqueducts was built in 312 B.C.; by 96 A.D., there were ten aqueducts capable of supplying Rome with 250,000,000 gallons of water daily. About half of this torrent flowed through the immense system of public baths. The remainder was enough to provide an average of more than 100 gallons per capita daily for a population of one million.[12,13] The same provision for a plentiful supply of pure water was made in the other cities of the empire, with good examples remaining to this day in Turkey, Spain, and France.

The problem of the disposal of human wastes was mingled with that of the drainage of ground water, as both were recognized as threats to public health. The Roman author Varro anticipated the germ theory of disease in a tentative way: "in the neighborhood of swamps . . . there are bred certain minute creatures which cannot be seen by the eyes, which float through the air and enter the body through the mouth and the nose and there cause serious diseases." Although the existence of these "minute creatures" was mere speculation, we do know that as early as the sixth century B.C., the Roman Forum was drained by the Cloaca maxima, receiving the wastes from public urinals and water-closets flushed by running water. The Cloaca maxima, as the aqueducts, was copied widely throughout the Roman Empire.[12,16]

The achievement in public hygiene accomplished through engineering clearly exceeded in importance any contribution which could have been made by the medicine of the day. In well planned and well executed bursts of technological creativity the Romans provided general and more or less permanent solutions to some of the most basic of public health problems. However as a community they managed a less imaginative response to the need for individual care of the sick: they imported the Greek dichotomy of temple medicine and Hippocratic medical science.

The first major Greek import by the Romans in the health field was the Cult of Asklepios. An epidemic ravaging Rome in 295 B.C. seemed to require more effective measures than were available at home, so the Romans called upon the greatest of the Greek gods of healing, whose fame was by then widespread. According to tradition a deputation of Romans applied for help at Epidauros and induced some of the temple personnel to return with them to Rome. As the homeward-bound ship proceeded up the Tiber toward the city, an Asklepian snake swam ashore on the Tiber Island, providing a miraculous and supernatural selection of the site for the transplanted healing temple. A less romantic, though more credible version of the location on the Isola Tiberina rests with the Roman official suspicion of foreign gods, which probably dictated the site outside the city proper for caution's sake.[16]

The island, cut into the shape of a ship 300 yards in length, 80 yards in beam, and complete with mast, prow, and stern, resembled a huge vessel at anchor in the river. Near the "stern" was erected the main temple dedicated to the Great One, whose name was now latinized to Aesculapius. The site of the temple is presently occupied by the Basilica of St. Bartholomew, and fourteen of the church's columns survive from the original Aesculapian structure. Beside the main temple there were smaller satellite temples, shelters for the sick, and medicinal baths.[1,11]

The Roman epidemic subsided, and Aesculapius shared in the credit. The popularity of the cult was assured as accounts of miraculous cures, once only vague tales circulated by travelers, were now recounted first hand. The influence of Aesculapius increased steadily until the end of the second century, A.D.; hundreds of temples were built and dedicated to him, and his popularity was comparable to that of any of the other transplanted Greek gods. In general the rites of the Roman Cult of Aesculapius were borrowed from the Greek ritual, with an occasional cultural modification (such as the practice of praying with the head covered) to the Roman fashion. Devotion to the god came from all classes of Roman society from the lowliest dwellers of the crowded apartment houses to the wealthy land owners and public officials.[6]

The importation of Greek temple healing to Rome was eventually followed by that of its parallel natural counterpart, "rational" or theoretical medicine. The first Greek physician known to practice in Rome was Archagathos of Sparta, who arrived in 219 B.C. Archagathos, like many of the Greek physicians who came soon afterward, was probably a marginal practitioner who saw in the expanding western city an opportunity for greater success and acclaim than were likely to be his among his more talented colleagues at home. He was granted the right of free citizenship in Rome and was provided with an office at public expense. In spite of the generous welcome, however, his practice did not go well. His cruelty in cutting and searing his patients earned for him the nickname "The Butcher," and he was eventually expelled from Rome.[8,12]

Besides the bad impression made by the earliest Greek practitioners, there was another more culturally related reason why the Romans were reluctant to accept theoretical medicine. They were above all a practical people, disinterested in abstractions, distrustful of lofty intellectual processes, and impressed only by useful results. Hellenistic medicine made its greatest inroads in the upper strata of Roman society; the best and most highly educated of the Greek physicians found acceptance among the rich and the powerful, among intellectuals and emperors. Their role, however, was more akin to consultant or confidant than to authoritarian practitioner. They discussed theories of disease and health and suggested possibilities for treatment, but the Roman patient or his family made the final decisions about therapy.[16]

Among Rome's poor and ignorant, Greek medicine fared even worse. Only the physicians of lesser repute served the masses, and they lacked true skill and learning. The poor often resorted to another class of healers, the *pharmocopolae*, or drug sellers. Until the middle of the second century these were free of any kind of supervision or regulation and were usually fraudulent. Evidence of general dissatisfaction with all these practitioners is so abundant that there is small wonder that reliance on traditional folk remedies and the Cult of Aesculapius persisted for centuries.[1,14,16]

In discussions of the availability of physicians' services in Rome, reference is often made to the well publicized and obviously well organized "house of the surgeon" unearthed at Pompeii. The building would seem to be a suitable model for a modern clinic, and its presence at Pompeii suggests that doctors' offices must have existed and functioned in ancient Rome much as they do in modern society. But it would be a mistake to consider Pompeii as representative, for it was a resort town. As a haven for the rich it was probably no more representative of Roman society than are Carmel or Miami Beach of ours. Most Romans lived in apartment buildings; because of the population density the streets were narrow and the apartment buildings dark, poorly ventilated and tall, averaging five or six stories. The ground floors were used for shops and taverns or as home for the wealthy. The masses lived upstairs in descending order of social station, the poorest reaching their humble attic rooms by ladders. In the days of the Empire a sturdy and numerous middle class still survived in the provinces and in rural areas, but in urban Rome their ranks grew ever thinner until there were few left between the plutocracy of the court and masses too poor to exist without the doles of the emperor and the charity of the rich.

During the 100s, half the population on the dole

In the second century, A.D., more than half a million persons, possibly half the population of the city, lived on public charity, and this figure does not include the slaves, who were not eligible. Permanent offices of public assistance (*stationes arcariorum Caesarianorum*) were set up in the halls of Trajans market, and from the second century on public distributions of food or money were made from them.[3]

The provision of physicians' services for the poor was not the serious problem one might suppose; in the minds of the poor such services were superfluous and not even necessarily desirable. They had their folk medicine, which was free, and in the case of more serious ailments there was ready access to the shrines of Aesculapius. Shrines dotted the empire and were available to citizens everywhere. The temple on the Tiber Island was the most popular at Rome, widely used and trusted by the ordinary people. Sick and worn-out slaves were brought there, sometimes to spare their masters the trouble of caring for them. The Emperor Claudius freed such slaves and decreed that if they recovered, they should not be returned to the control of their masters. The Island of Aesculapius thus became a place of refuge for the sick poor.[16,18]

The emperors, because they had a higher opinion of physicians than did the masses, occasionally took measures to increase their availability. Doctors were provided with an indirect subsidy through the offer of immunity from taxes, first by Vespasian and then on a larger scale by Hadrian. This may have been intended to place a moral obligation in favor of those unable to afford a physician's fee. It was not until the fourth century, A.D., however, that Valentinian I appointed *archiatri* for each of the fourteen regiones of Rome with the admonition, "honestly to attend to the poor rather than basely to serve the rich." While the Emperor had never heard the term "third party," he was obviously aware of the concept.[9,14]

In Greece and early Rome there was little provision for individual health care beyond the services of the physician. Nursing and other supportive care were usually undertaken in the home by members of the patient's family. In the case of those without home or family, arrangements had to be individualized, if possible, and according to no particular system.

Valetudinaria: Providing hospital and nursing home facilities

The growth of slavery in the Roman Empire overtaxed the non-system of supportive care and eventually necessitated an institutional approach. In the case of the enormous households of the wealthy where slaves might number in the hundreds or even in the thousands, medical and nursing care became a need of such magnitude as to require specialized facilities and personnel. The buildings outfitted for such use were the *valetudinaria*, and references to them, especially after the first century, A.D., are numerous. They existed both in the city and on the large country estates. Columella, in his treatise on agriculture about 60 AD., pointed out the need for providing valetudinaria for slaves as places where they could rest and recuperate when ill. He suggested that at slack times the buildings be well aired and cleansed so that everything should be well arranged, decorated, and wholesome for the patients. He further urged that particular attention be given to the quality of the provisions and cookery.[1]

The personnel of the larger valetudinaria undoubtedly included slaves assigned to cooking, cleaning, and assisting the sick. If the household was an especially large or wealthy one there might be a Greek philosopher-physician attached to it who would provide consultation to the valetudinarium. Otherwise the only skilled care was provided by a *medicus*, who was the counterpart of the street physician or drug seller, a man of uncertain education or training and ranked socially as a tradesman. In many instances he might be himself a slave, and in any case the final authority in medical matters as well as in all others was the head of the household.[16]

As a private household infirmary, the valetudinarium was not reserved for slaves alone, but was utilized by all classes. Seneca himself refers in one of his writings to "lying in a valetudinarium." In addition to the immediate family of the master, the valetudinarium might also provide care and comfort to friends and clients of the family, but scarcely in any instance where no such personal relationship existed. Galen makes mention of general hospitals in the provinces, especially the Greek provinces, under public control and with doctors officially appointed to them. Such hospitals, if they were truly public institutions, must have been few or short-lived, since there is so little evidence, either literary or archeological, for their existence. There is abundant evidence, however, for the fact that the Romans did develop a well organized system of hospitals for the military.[1,9]

In the days of the Republic there was little medical care of any kind for sick or wounded soldiers, and what crude care existed was practiced by them on one another. A seriously wounded soldier was left to fend for himself or, if particularly fortunate, might be left in a friendly town to the ministrations of well-intentioned townspeople. As long as the military campaigns were conducted within the Italian peninsula it was often possible to return the sick and injured to their homes for treatment and recuperation.

The *medici*: medics in combat

In the later days of the Republic, the Hellenistic influence infiltrated the army and Greek physicians began to accompany the ranking officers in the field. Their functions seem to have been limited to medical care of officers only and to consultation in matters involving the health of the troops. Among the common soldiers there developed a category of those judged by their fellow legionaries to be experienced and especially adept at wound-dressing: the *medici*. A *medicus* held a position of respect among his fellows, but he was first a soldier in his duties; his quasi-medical function was secondary. His medical knowledge, such as it was, had been obtained through observation and trial and error or gained through contact with senior medici; his knowledge of anatomy was learned from the wounds of the soldiers. He wore the same uniform as did his "patients," shared their chain of command, and enjoyed little privilege by virtue of his special skill.[15,16]

The function and deployment of the army changed markedly during the early years of the Empire with the recognition by Augustus that there must be an eventual limit to the extension of Roman authority. The concept of a frontier where the area of undisputed Roman control came in contact with barbarian lands called for a system of forts, supply bases, and communications. The complex of fortified defensive boundaries, known as the *limes* (pl. *limites*), moved with changing Roman fortunes, but henceforth until the fall of the Empire required the permanent stationing of troops far from home.

The establishment of these more or less permanent military installations so far from Rome meant that soldiers no longer returned to their homes at the

ends of military campaigns and that the services for which they had once returned to Rome had now to be provided along the limes. The distances also
meant that sick or wounded soldiers could no longer be sent home for treatment, and the need for a more effective army medical service was apparent, including facilities for the complete care of the temporarily disabled.

Most of the military valetudinaria were built in the first century, A.D., when
the system of frontier fortifications was being developed. The major valetudinaria were located in the legionary fortresses, so named because they were designed to accommodate an entire legion or division, numbering usually
6,500–7,000 men.[18] Most of them appear to have had a capacity of 300–400
patients or about 5 per cent of the camp's population, a ratio similar to that of
modern military base hospitals.

The "ward" concept for care of hospital patients

One characteristic feature of the valetudinaria, found almost as consistently as
the basic quadrangular plan, was the arrangement of paired small wards. The
wards usually measured about 12 × 15 feet and accommodated five to eight
patients each. Typically two such wards shared a small anteroom by which they
communicated with the circulation corridor. The indirect access from corridor
to wards provided not only quiet and privacy, but freedom from drafts. A third
room, intermediate in size between the anteroom and the wards, communicated with the anteroom and lay between the two wards. The function of this
room has been the subject of some conjecture. Jetter[10] states that it was used
by the personnel of the valetudinarium as a sort of nursing station; Webster[19]
identifies it as a latrine; Simonett[17] believed it to be a storeroom for the patients'
belongings. Whatever the function of the intermediate room, The Romans
seemed to have been pleased with the basic arrangement, for they repeated it in
legionary hospitals from Austria and Switzerland to the Rhineland and Scotland.

It is safe to assume that medical care in the military valetudinaria proceeded
at a low level. Galen, critical of Roman military medicine, once described being summoned to the scene of a battle to give proper medical treatment where,
in his opinion, little such treatment existed. He noted caustically that many
doctors "talk" medicine without proving their skill.[15] Galen's comment doubtless could also have been applied to a large segment of the civilian profession
of his day.

The Greeks created, the Romans followed and refined

In summation, there can be no doubt that the first important steps toward the
development of scientific medicine were taken by the early Greeks and were
merely followed by the Romans. What is less appreciated is the contribution
to total health care and maintenance made by the Romans. Their technologi-

cal approaches to the provision of healthful water supplies and sanitation and their development of the world's first hospital system were probably more important contributions to the solution of the health problems of their increasingly complex society than was the medical progress made by the Greeks. The appointment and official support of public physicians, the *archiatri*, for the express purpose of proving free medical care to the poor represented social progress, considering the ambiguous position of the Greek demosieuontes.

If there was no public clamor for better health facilities and a more equitable distribution, it was because the quality of the care available had stimulated little demand. As long as the masses preferred supernatural medicine to the natural, the competition for physicians' services was negligible. In a day when supportive care in the home was approximately as good as that available in the best valetudinaria there was a limited need for the specialized institutions.

References

1. Allbutt TC. Greek Medicine in Rome. London, Macmillan and Co., 1921.
2. Bawra CM. Classical Greece. New York, Time, Inc., 1965.
3. Carcopino J. Daily Life in Ancient Rome. New Haven, Yale University Press, 1940.
4. Cavvadias AP. From Epidauros to Galenos. Ann. Med. Hist. N.S. III, 501, 1931.
5. Cohn-Haft L. The Public Physicians of Ancient Greece. Smith College Studies in History. XLII, 1956.
6. Edelstein E and Edelstein L. Asclepius, A Collection and Interpretation of the Testimonies II. Baltimore, Johns Hopkins Press, 1945.
7. Gask GE. The Cult of Aesculapius and the Origin of Hippocratic Medicine. Ann. Med. Hist. N. S. III, 128, 1939.
8. Gask GE and Todd J. The Origin of Hospitals in Science, Medicine and History. (E. Ashworth Underwood, ed.) I. Oxford University Press, 1953.
9. Hands AR. Charities and Social Aid in Greece and Rome. Ithaca, Cornell University Press, 1968.
10. Jetter D. Geschicitte Das Hospitals I. Wiesbaden, Franz Steiner Verlag, 1966.
11. Leake CD. Roman Architectural Hygiene. Ann. Med. Hist. N.S. It, 135, 1930.
12. Major RH. A History of Medicine. Springfield, Charles C. Thomas, 1954.
13. Packer JE. Housing and Population in Imperial Ostia and Rome. J. Roman Studies, 57, 80, 1967.
14. Paoli UE. Rome, Its People and Customs. Trans. by RD Macnaghten. London, Longmans Green & Co., Ltd., 1963.
15. Scarborough J. Roman Medicine and the Legions: A Reconsideration. Med. Hist. 12, 254, 1968.
16. Scarborough J. Roman Medicine. Ithaca, Cornell University Press, 1969.
17. Simonett C. The Roman Military Hospitals at Vindonissa. Ciba Symposia I., 292, 1939.
18. Singer C. The Legacy of Rome (Cyril Bailey, ed.).Oxford, Clarendon Press, 1923.
19. Webster G. The Roman Imperial Army of the First and Second Centuries A.D. London, Adam and Chas. Black, 1969.

ANCIENT EGYPTIAN ATTITUDES TOWARD DEATH AND SUICIDE

L. D. HANKOFF, M.D.

(April 1975, pp. 60–64)

Dr. Hankoff (AΩA, University of Maryland School of Medicine, 1951) is retired as chairman of Psychiatry at Elizabeth General Medical Center in Elizabeth, New Jersey. He wrote this paper as an extension of his work and interest in suicide. Following his internship and psychiatric residency at Kings County Hospital Center, he established there the first suicide prevention service in New York City. His interests in these areas led in 1968 to one of the first textbooks in the then-emerging area of emergency psychiatry. Dr. Hankoff's research publications in various areas included psychopharmacology, community psychiatry, and the history of medicine and psychiatry. One other article in The Pharos, *"Poetry, Adolescence, and Suicide," was published in Spring 1984 and also is included in this anthology.*

STUDY OF THE PSYCHOLOGY AND PSYCHOPATHOLOGY of the ancient Egyptians reveals an enormous concern with death and afterlife. Of all ancient peoples they were the most preoccupied with funerals, funerary preparations, and death monuments.[1,2] Their greatest works, the sphinx and the pyramids, were tombstones. Their finest sculptures were statues of deceased individuals. One finds a vast portion of Egyptian culture centered around the world of the dead and a surprisingly large amount of extant writings by the Egyptians on death and suicide.

In evaluating the attitudes and concepts of ancient Egyptians one must obviously proceed cautiously. To begin with, ancient Egypt covers a time span of 3,000 years and contains a range of evolving attitudes, cultural currents, and events. Another difficult and confusing aspect of Egyptian attitudes towards death and suicide lies in the fact that we are dealing with a different man, a basically different mentality. In his thinking about fundamental matters the ancient Egyptian accepted and utilized what we might consider conflicting and incompatible explanations or formulations.[3] Whereas the modern mind consciously pursues matters logically and applies only one or at least compatible scientific explanations for a given issue, such would not appear to be the mentality of the Egyptians. The Egyptian simultaneously described and explained the afterlife, for example, in several different ways and applied all of these explanations to his practices.

H. Frankfort calls this mechanism "a multiplicity of approaches" and views the Egyptian mentality as being able to apply a variety of partial solutions to a difficult and complex problem.[4]

The Egyptian personality. A perspective on the attitudes toward death and the dead may be gained from a brief look at some features of Egyptian personality. The ancient Egyptians, it is written by many, had certain well defined characteristics culturally and personality-wise, much of it related to the fact that Egypt was a country of great fertility and reliability,[3,4] "the gift of the Nile," as Herodotus called it.[5] It was a nation and country with a strong sense of symmetry, balance, order, and predictability.

A comparison in the ancient Near East is often made between Egypt and Mesopotamia.[3,4] Egypt's River Nile rose and fell, bringing with it the yearly inundation, sprouting seeds, growth, harvesting, and the undeniable evidences of a preordained life cycle. By contrast, the Tigris and Euphrates Rivers in Mesopotamia produced an entirely different situation with a tumultous, unpredictable environment and a markedly contrasting culture.

Egypt is fortified on all sides by nature: the delta, the cataracts, and the desert. There was regularity, protection and a remarkable kind of constancy. Mesopotamia, on the other hand, was subject to invasion by nature and outsiders alike.

The Egyptians considered themselves to be the most advanced, the most cultured people in the world. They loved and enjoyed life and hoped to live an ideal one of 110 years.[6] They were contemptuous of foreigners, self-aggrandizing, logical, stylistic, and committed to order, justice, righteousness, and truth. One interesting historical sidelight is that in its long history there never was a popular revolution in Egypt.[4] Throughout the inevitable turns of history this quality of solidity and regularity in the life of Egypt is consistent.

The Egyptian religion. In their basic beliefs, the Egyptians regarded the three states of life, death, and divinity as having basically similar characteristics.[6–8] Most important for the present inquiry is the fact that they conceived of all three beings, the living, the dead, and the gods, as having the same physical and personal needs. All three needed to be fed, clothed, and otherwise physically satisfied; they all had personal and emotional needs. There were, for instance, gods in the Egyptian pantheon who were at times petty or jealous, who squabbled and sometimes got drunk. They were very much like people, even to the point of having longevity.

The same applied to the dead. An individual who passed from the state of the living into the state of the dead continued to have all the same needs and the same sort of personal involvement with day-to-day affairs. Since the three states of aging were so closely, so analogously viewed, it is valuable to look at the Egyptian concept of health and physiology, which also applied equally to all three.

Egyptian physiology and medical belief. A central concern of the Egyptian with putrefaction and bodily decay was described by the Greeks, Herodotus and Diodorus, but also in many Egyptian medical writings.[5,6,9,10] The Egyptian believed that if he were not careful about his gastrointestinal tract, particularly the lower end of it, trouble would ensue from advancing intestinal putrefaction. Rot would cause gas, decaying products, and foul odors. Fever would be produced as the gases rose in the abdomen, into the hypochondrium from the lower intestines, and then to the blood, the head, and the rest of the body.[10] The Egyptians rigorously applied this theory to daily living, as reflected in their practice, according to Herodotus, of purging themselves for three successive days every month with emetics and clysters.[5] Prevention, then, of putrefaction became a core theme throughout Egyptian medical belief and practice. The ancient Greek clyster physician, whose specialities were enemas, was probably a legacy from Egyptian medicine.[10]

The Egyptian concern for putrefaction and the dangers of intestinal decay and spreading odors throughout the body applied to both the living and the dead body. In the case of the dead, however, an additional important physiological consideration entered in. The dead were viewed as inhabiting a netherworld under the surface of the visible earth. In this existence the individual might find himself walking upside down with his feet applied to the surface of the earth's disk and his head pointed downward.[6] Such an unhappy circumstance might reverse the movements of the contents of the digestive tract and result in excrement and putrefactive products arriving in his mouth. Indeed, the dead person's mouth might come to serve as his anus. Spells were composed to avert such unfortunate developments. The coffin inscriptions of ancient Egyptians included spells designed to prevent the individual from eating his excrement or drinking urine, and directing that he conduct his afterlife in a normal alimentary condition, e.g. that he eat only normal food.[6] Other related spells were intended to keep the individual from going about upside down.[6]

In general, excrement was thought to cause impurity through any kind of direct contact, and spells were designed to prevent the dead individual from touching excrement with his hands or feet. The undesirability of eating excrement is further illustrated in descriptions of demons of the netherworld who ate products of digestion. The executioners of Osiris were described as eating excrement.[6]

The Egyptians feared that putrefaction and loss of effective internal body functioning would endanger the important organs of emotion and intellect, thought to be housed within the torso and particularly vulnerable to spreading gases. The heart was seen as the organ that mediated understanding and intellectuality. The belly was the seat of desire or passion and was particularly potent in terms of magical powers.

The development of a physiology that applied equally to the dead and to the living is entirely consistent with the general attitude of the Egyptians toward the dead, namely, that they existed in a state in every way similar to that of the living. This concept contributed to an emphasis on embalming, which obviously was dedicated, and with considerable success, to preventing putrefaction. The detailed writings of Diodorus and Herodotus described three forms of embalming, based on economic considerations.[5,9]

Regardless of the price, the technique was always concerned with emptying out the lower gastrointestinal tract and avoiding putrefaction. Any Egyptian could be embalmed if he could pay for it, and funerary practices were progressively extended to include more and more of the citizenry.[11] H. J. Breasted has labeled this trend, which emerged fully in the Middle Kingdom, as "the democratization of the Hereafter."[12]

The cheapest form of embalming involved simply introducing spices and preservatives into the body through an enema. In the more familiar or classical form, an operator incised the flank and removed the contents of the abdomen; the heart was left in place. The operator also quite often removed the brain with a hook up through the nostril. According to Diodorus, the embalmers took out the intestines, the liver, and the spleen, and preserved them separately.

It has been observed that the dry climate of Egypt leads to the natural preservation of dead bodies. On the other hand, the ongoing enzymatic processes at death will very rapidly cause some degree of decomposition, especially at warm temperatures. An interesting side note in relation to this fact is mentioned by Herodotus. Embalming ordinarily proceeded quickly after death. However, in the case of a beautiful woman, the family would hold the body for three days, with the idea that the body would become repulsive and discourage necrophilic designs on the part of the embalmer.

Attitudes toward the dead. The dead themselves were held in little awe or dread by the ancient Egyptians, being co-equal with the living and with the gods. They had their definite place, their needs, and their limitations. There was no ancestor worship. The dead were assumed to be around, but basically they had their own domain, as did the living.

The dead needed, above all, to be protected from putrefaction. They also needed nourishment, attention, and loving, much like the living. To arrange for these necessities the Egyptians developed contracts of service by the living for the dead.[7] The dead man, perhaps during his life time, arranged a contract with the survivors by which he would be fed and attended to regularly. In addition, the elaborate tomb settings had inscriptions on them asking that the living pay attention, offer a prayer, and otherwise consider the emotional needs of the dead. This arrangement was not entirely one-sided, however, since one also finds letters from the living to the dead asking the dead for favors. Messages were left in tombs asking that the dead stop bothering a living individual or that a dead relative intervene to keep another dead relative from haunting the living.[7] Another possible indication of the relative lack of fear that the Egyptians had for the dead is the fact that all of the tombs were regularly opened and vandalized. The dead by and large did not fare very well.

Attitudes toward death. How might the Egyptian have regarded his own death, in light of this neutral attitude toward the dead? J. Zandee has distinguished between monistic and dualistic Egyptian attitudes toward death.[6] The monistic or traditional religious view is one in which the state of life is merely premonitory to existence among the dead. The dualistic view posed death as the enemy of life, bringing to an end the pleasures and joys of life on earth. The dualistic view is embodied in the many inscriptions from Middle Kingdom tombs that address the reader: "O ye who love life and hate death."[6,7] The dualistic view feared and hated death and wished for a long and good life on earth.[6] Herodotus has described the coffin, which was kept in preparation and displayed on festive occasions to remind the merrymakers of their inevitable future.[5]

The monistic or religious view was not completely free of fears, either. Being among the dead involved a test of one's mortal worth, a perilous journey to the afterworld, and the continuing adventures of the transfigured dead. Being dead also meant having a body in danger of putrefaction and in need of continuing supplies from external sources.

The Egyptian attitude toward death must not be oversimplified. Their "multiplicity of approaches" toward the afterlife probably allowed for the inclusion of doubts and ambivalence on the subject. In all, however, the Egyptians seem to have been relatively free of the intense fear of death that is usually attributed to the ancient Greeks.[13–15] Reincarnation is never mentioned in Egyptian literature.

Suicide accounts and references. An impression of attitudes toward suicide may be obtained from the literature of ancient Egypt that mentions suicidal acts and ideation. Following are references to six pieces of ancient Egyptian literature containing suicidal themes, presented in approximate chronological order.

The first three references are attributed to the First Intermediate Period (Dynasties VII–X, c. 2181–2040 B.C.), an era following the collapse of the Old Kingdom of turbulence and transition preceding the establishment of the stable Middle Kingdom.[1]

The first of these three references regards the famous debate or dialogue of a man with his soul (in Egyptian, *bi* or *ba*)[1,2,16–20] It is the soliloquy of an embittered man pondering whether or not to take his own life. Life is unpleasant, he states, not worth living, and without honor or respect. The soul offers various rejoinders. The poem has been carefully studied, with differing opinions about the nature of the two disputants. It is variously suggested that the pair represent a) the self or ego versus the soul or spirit; b) the personifications of a skeptical attitude versus a traditionalist attitude; and c) the Osirian belief of the *ba* versus the anti-Osirian belief of the self.[17] The specific reference to self-destruction by burning has also been alternately interpreted as referring to earthly suffering as a metaphorical rather than physical burning.[17] Regardless of nuances of meaning, the poem clearly portrays a man serious about giving up his life. In his discussion on this point there is no sense of religious fear or feeling of sin in relation to an act of suicide.

The second reference to suicide is to be found in *The Admonitions of a Sage*,[1,16,21] a long discourse between the king and a sage, Ipuwer, who dramatically describes the decline of Egypt in their time. Following the Old Kingdom, with its great heights of attainment of Egyptian culture and society, a period of disorder and decline sets in, which the sage bemoans. Thoughts of death and suicide are common, he indicates. The river is filled with corpses; the crocodiles are glutted as the despairing people throw themselves into the river. Various interpreters of the work agree with the impression that during this period of social decay and disorganization, suicide and suicidal thoughts were extremely common.

The third reference from the First Intermediate period contains a suicidal threat. The narrative called *The Eloquent Peasant*[1,2] or *The Complaints of the Peasant*,[16] a papyrus dated near the end of the third millennium B.C., gives an account of a peasant who petitions a nobleman concerning social injustices afflicted upon him. He appeals repeatedly to the nobleman for redress. In desperation, on his ninth appeal he states that he may take his case to Anubis, the god of the dead, meaning he is contemplating suicide.[2] Following this threat the peasant receives proper attention, and justice is done. In the peasant's speech the mention of suicide is brief and metaphorical but obviously an important element. The mention of suicide occurs at the climactic appeal and drives home the peasant's extreme state of mind.

The backdrop of the fourth reference is a much later era in Egyptian history. A suicidal act is described in *Against Apion*, a propagandistic work of Flavius Josephus (30–100 A.D.). The quotations from Manetho's history given in Against Apion by Josephus are an important source of the Egyptian historian, who lived about 300 B.C.[22,23] Josephus quotes Manetho on events involving Pharaoh Amenophis III or IV (the latter is the famous Iknaton (c. 1394–1362 B.C.), the monotheistic or monolatrous Egyptian Pharaoh). A seer and advisor to the Pharaoh, also named Amenophis, had predicted dire results in the wake of advice he had given to the Pharaoh. Fearing the consequences, Amenophis writes a farewell note to the Pharaoh about his forebodings and then takes his life. Since Josephus' work is twice removed from the alleged event, this account is an obscure and difficult bit of literature to assess. Josephus had been strongly aroused by Manetho's criticism of the Jews and was writing to rebut Manetho and to expose Egyptian shortcomings. It is noteworthy as the first example in history of a suicide note.

The fifth reference is closely dated by an hieratic papyrus manuscript of about 1225 B.C., in the XIX Dynasty. It is the colloquial *Tale of the Two Brothers* and bears resemblances to Greek, Armenian, Norwegian, and Hottentot folk tales as well as to the Biblical story of Joseph and the wife of Potiphar.[16,24,25] The story contains two suicidal allusions. It involves two brothers and the wife of the older. When the younger brother, Bata, is at home and the older brother, Anubis, is out working, the latter's wife tries to seduce Bata, but fails. In anger she reports to her husband that she has been assaulted by Bata, demands justice, and announces that she will kill herself if not avenged. She does not need to act on her suicidal threat, as her husband attempts to do violence against Bata. Bata retreats and from a distance cuts off his phallus with a reed knife and throws it into the river, where it is eaten by the fish. His demonstration brings Anubis to realize his innocence, and Bata has the opportunity to explain fully. It is not completely clear from what follows if Bata dies from his self-mutilation. Bata announces that his heart is to be placed at the top of a tree, and that he will reside in the Valley of the Cedars. He subsequently has a wife fashioned for him by the gods and experiences other adventures, presumably in the afterlife. This is entirely consistent with our understanding of the Egyptian attitude toward death. It is my impression that his intention was suicidal and that the younger brother did indeed die from his act, but it is not completely clear. Another possibility is that the younger brother performed self-circumcision, an equally dramatic demonstration, to shock his older brother into hearing him out.

The sixth example of suicidal behavior is found in an account of a harem conspiracy against Rameses III (c. 1175–1144 B.C.).[26,27] This example is important for the attitude toward suicide that it portrays. From the record, it appears that there had been a conspiracy in the harem of the Pharaoh with the goal of a palace revolt. The perpetrators were uncovered, brought to trial, and judged. The account then states that after each guilty verdict, "he was condemned and he took his own life," a score of guilty individuals being named. Whether it happened as described, of course, is not critical for our understanding. The names are most probably fictitious, but the important point is that condemnation to death by suicide or suicide among condemned prisoners apparently was a usual course of events, and the description is a plausible one. In this connection, it is to be noted that societies in which execution by condemnation to suicide is found are highly accepting of suicide. The Romans, of course, used suicide by condemnation quite liberally.[28]

Suicidal prohibitions. We associate the development of formal religious law with the ancients. Was there a formal legal or religious Egyptian prohibition on suicide? From the above examples and our knowledge of Egyptian society and culture it appears that there was no clear-cut Egyptian prohibition. The Egyptians were not, however, lacking in direct legal commandments. Among the Egyptians a particular form of prohibition has survived in the ritualistic formula known as the *Negative Confession*, or *Declaration of Innocence*,[29–31] a series of forty-two questions regarding sinful acts that were put to the dead person.

In the netherworld the newly dead was tested and his organs weighed. In the process, the gods watched as the heart of the deceased was weighed against the white ostrich feather of justice and truth. If they did not balance, the heart was thrown to the awaiting crocodile and the deceased might wander forever in limbo. In the many illustrations of this weighing process, the scale is invariably pictured as felicitously balanced. The self-confident Egyptian personality manifested itself in death as well as life. The heart was the seat of the intellect or understanding and vital for mental functions in both life and death. While the ceremony is portrayed in the world of the dead, it was probably begun by the survivors in the funeral rites. The embalmed body may have been present at a ceremony in which the forty-two questions were asked and answered in the negative as a magical prelude to the important ceremony in the afterlife. Here forty-two divine judges each asked a question, "Are you guilty of murder?", "Are you guilty of slander?", "Are you guilty of covetousness?", etc. The person said "no," to each, thus guaranteeing his entry into the more desirable form of afterlife. It has been labeled the *Negative Confession* because everyone answered "no" to all questions, indicating that they had not done any of those awful things. A review of the forty-two questions (there are several versions) reveals no prohibition on suicide, although there are prohibitions against violence, maiming, bloodshed, and vicious or cruel acts.

The Egyptian religious attitude of neutrality is in marked contrast to the stringent (but implied) Biblical prohibition on suicide. This is a particularly important contrast, because the Israelite attitude was not a later religious development but is related specifically to the Pentateuch. Historically, Egyptian and Hebrew were closely involved for several hundred years in the second millennium B.C. The formative period of Israelite ethics, and the momentous giving of the Torah, are closely related to the stay of the Hebrews in Egypt. Mutual influences between the two cultures are widely evident.[32–35] Might there have been a relationship between the two attitudes toward suicide?

Among the ancient Israelites the prohibition on suicide was very closely related to their prohibition on bloodshed. The spilling of the blood of a tribal member involved awesome feelings and serious consequences.[36,37] Suicide was an act that violated these deep taboos and was such an unauthorized spilling of the tribal blood. By way of contrast, tribal integrity was of no concern to the Egyptians. As the national majority, urbanely self-assured and stable, the

Egyptians did not have the concern that a tiny isolated foreign nomadic tribe such as the Hebrews may have experienced. It is the smaller tribal group in contrast to the larger national group that is concerned about the intactness, imperviousness, and vulnerability of the social group. The death of one Hebrew by suicide may have threatened the tribe whereas among the Egyptians, the loss of the single individual was of little concern.

The attitudes toward blood *per se* were in marked contrast. The Hebrews, along with other ancient Semites, were enormously concerned with the power and meaning of blood and had a great fear of its misuse and contaminating or taboo qualities.[36,37] Blood was explicitly and repeatedly forbidden as a food. The Egyptians, in contrast, used blood for therapeutic and magical purposes. A. S. Yahuda has suggested that the Biblical attitude toward blood may have been a reaction to Egyptian practices just as the Pentateuch reacts against other Egyptian practices.[35,38]

As discussed above, the Egyptians were greatly concerned about being cared for in the afterlife. Might this have been a consideration in relation to suicide? While there may have been no religious prohibition, might the suicide victim have been in danger of becoming an unattended and putrefying corpse? Insight into this problem may be gained from what we know was done with a corpse discovered in the open field, perhaps the result of a murder. The Egyptians were extremely concerned about such an occurrence, just as Biblical law is very exact and stringent on attending to the discovered corpse, which was an object of extreme taboo.[36,37]

When a corpse was discovered in the open by the Egyptians they immediately went to a priest, who took responsibility for the burial.[5] Specifically, if the body was found drowned or mauled by a crocodile, it was given the most elaborate and consecrated burial. Thus, the Egyptian suicide may not have been concerned about his remains in the afterlife, because he expected that the townspeople would attend to a proper disposal of his body. Indeed, the body might fare better as a suicide than as a natural death in a family with little means for paying for embalming.

Another point of interest is that Herodotus specifies the priest of the Egyptians as attending to the corpse. This is the reverse of the practice of the Israelites, among whom the priests were forbidden to have contact with dead bodies (Leviticus XXI. 1).

The matter of the disposal of the body of the suicide is to be found in the Bible in the suicide of Achitophel, advisor to Absalom in the revolt against King David (II Samuel XVII.23). Following a setback he comes home, tells his family of his predicament, and makes his final arrangements. He then hangs himself and his family buries him. It is possible that an Egyptian suicide might similarly have planned and arranged his demise and the care of his remains.

Conclusion

From their history, literature, and artifacts, a set of attitudes toward death and suicide among the ancient Egyptians may be discerned: a) a great concern about the welfare of the dead person, his body, and his continuing needs in the after-life; b) an awareness of the transitoriness and pleasures of life; and c) a relative acceptance of suicide. In contrast to the Hebrews who sojourned in Egypt in the second millennium B.C. and evolved a stringent religious prohibition on suicide, the ancient Egyptian did not appear to view suicide as a violation of his religious or legal code.

The attitude toward suicide may even have been tempered by a certain de-sirability of the tranquil state of death. As suggested by the debate of the man with his *ba*, there were arguments on both sides of the issue of continuing to live or to die in times of overwhelming discomfort and disorder. And, finally, someone suggested that writing a book might be one way of accomplishing immortality.[7]

References

1. Albright WF. From the Stone Age to Christianity, 2nd ed. Garden City, Doubleday and Co., Inc., 1957.
2. Breasted JH. The Dawn of Conscience. New York, Charles Scribner's Sons, 1933.
3. Frankfort H, Frankfort HA, Wilson JA, Jacobsen T, and Irwin WA. The Intellectual Adventure of Ancient Man. Chicago, University of Chicago Press, 1946.
4. Frankfort H. Kingship and the Gods. Chicago, University of Chicago Press, 1955.
5. Herodotus. Translated by AD Godley. Cambridge, Mass., Harvard University Press (Loeb Classical Library), 1966, Vol. I, pp. 273–385.
6. Zandee I. Death as an Enemy According to Ancient Egyptian Conceptions. Leiden EJ, Brill, 1960.
7. Gardiner AH. The Attitude of the Ancient Egyptians to Death and the Dead. Cambridge, University Press, 1935.
8. Sigerist HE. A History of Medicine. Vol. 1, Primitive and Archaic Medicine. New York, Oxford University Press, 1951.
9. Diodorus of Sicily. Translated by CH Oldfather. Cambridge, Mass., Harvard University Press (Loeb Classical Library), 1962, Vol. 1, pp. 1–341.
10. Saunders JB deCM. The Transitions From Ancient Egyptian to Greek Medicine. Lawrence, Kans., University of Kansas Press, 1963.
11. Hayes WC. The Middle Kingdom in Egypt. In The Cambridge Ancient History, Vol. 1, Pt. 2.
12. Breasted HJ. Development of Religion and Thought in Ancient Egypt. New York, Harper and Brothers Publishers, 1959.
13. Dietrich BC. Death, Fate and the Gods. Glasgow, The Athlone Press, 1967.
14. Gouldner AW. Enter Plato. New York, Basic Books, 1965, p. 115.
15. Nilsson MP. A History of the Greek Religion, 2nd ed. Oxford, Clarendon Press, 1956, p. 169.
16. Erman A. The Ancient Egyptians: A Sourcebook of Their Writings. New York, Harper and Row, 1966.

17. Goedicke H. The Report About the Dispute of a Man With His "Ba." Baltimore, Johns Hopkins Press, 1970.

18. Faulkner RO. The Man Who Was Tired of Life. J. Egyptian Archaeology 42:21, 1956.

19. Thacker TW. A Dispute Over Suicide. In Documents From Old Testament Times, edited by DW Thomas. London, Thomas Nelson & Sons, 1958, pp. 162–167.

20. Wilson JA. A Dispute Over Suicide. In Ancient Near Eastern Texts Relating to the Old Testament, edited by JB Pritchard. Princeton, Princeton University Press, 1955, p. 405.

21. Gardiner AH. The Admonitions of an Egyptian Sage. Hildeshein, Germany, Georg Olms, 1969.

22. Josephus. Against Apion, Vol. 1. Translated by H. St. J. Thackeray. Cambridge, Mass., Harvard University Press (Loeb Classical Library), 1966, pp. 162–411.

23. Manetho. Translated by WG Waddell. Cambridge, Mass., Harvard University Press (Loeb Classical Library). 1964.

24. Wilson JA. The Story of Two Brothers. In Pritchard. op. cit., pp. 23–25.

25. Astour MC. Hellenosemitica. Leiden, EJ, Brill, 1967, pp. 186–187, 258–259.

26. Breasted JH. Ancient Records of Egypt. New York. Russell and Russell, 1962, Vol. IV, pp. 208–211.

27. DeBuck A. The Judicial Papyrus of Turin. J. Egyptian Archaeology 23(2):152, 1937.

28. Hastings J, ed. Encyclopaedia of Religion and Ethics. Vol. XII, Suicide. New York, Charles Scribner's Sons, 1955, pp. 21–40.

29. Budge EAW. The Book of the Dead: The Chapters of Coming Forth by Day. London, Kegan Paul, Trench, Trubner & Co., 1898, pp. 192–195.

30. Kamal H. Dictionary of Pharaonic Medicine. Cairo, National Publication House, 1967, pp. 339–379.

31. Maystre C. Les Declarations d'Innocence: Livre des Morts, Chapitre 125. Cairo, Institut Francais D'Archeologie Orientale, 1937.

32. Gordon CH. The Common Background of Greek and Hebrew Civilizations. New York, W. W. Norton and Co., 1965.

33. Montet P. Egypt and the Bible. Philadelphia, Fortress Press, 1948.

34. Petrie WMF. Egypt and Israel, New York, Macmillan, 1931.

35. Yahuda AS. Medical and Anatomical Terms in the Pentateuch in the Light of Egyptian Medical Papyri. J. Hist. Med 2:549, 1947.

36. Oesterley WDE. Sacrifices in Ancient Israel. London, Hodder and Stoughton, 1937.

37. Smith WR. The Religion of the Semites: The Fundamental Institutions. New York, Meridian Books, 1956.

38. Wright GE. How Did Early Israel Differ from Her Neighbors? Biblical Archaeologist 6:1, 1943.

GALEN AND THE GREATEST MEDICAL BOOK

NATHAN HIATT, M.D., AND JONATHAN R. HIATT, M.D.
(Winter 1989, pp. 24–26)

Dr. Nathan Hiatt (AΩA, New York University, 1935) is on the emeritus staff of the Department of Surgery at the Cedars-Sinai Medical Center in Los Angeles, California. Dr. Jonathan Hiatt (AΩA, University of Southern California, 1976) was a faculty member in the Department of Surgery at the University of California at Los Angeles and subsequently moved to Cedars-Sinai Medical Center, where he was vice chairman of the Department of Surgery until 1999, director of the Surgical Residency Program and Trauma Services, and professor of Surgery at the UCLA School of Medicine. He is now a working television writer in Hollywood and a member of the affiliate staff at Cedar-Sinai Medical Center. Drs. Hiatt also wrote "A History of Life Expectancy in Two Developed Countries," which appeared in the Spring 1992 issue of The Pharos.

WHAT IS THE MOST IMPORTANT MEDICAL BOOK ever written? This question has long been a subject of debate among medical scholars. Some would choose the first modern anatomy text, *De Humani Corporis Fabrica* of Andreas Vesalius, which appeared in 1543.[1] Others award the distinction to a book completed some seventy-five years later: *Exercitatio Anatomica de Motu Cordis et Sanguinis in Animalibus* of William Harvey.[2] These are the only contenders.[3,4]

On two facts there is agreement: (1) Vesalius struck the first blow at medical thought and practice then current, and (2) Harvey's blow was far more devastating. Their blows were dealt to a man who, it was believed, had so perfected medicine that further advances could only be trivial. That man was Galen, the "perfect physician," who dominated medical thought and practice in much of Europe and all of Islam for 1300 years. To understand what Vesalius and Harvey did, one must know something of Galen.

Galen: Imaginative ideas, free from factual support

Galen was a Greek from Asia Minor. Between 160 and 180 A.D., he practiced medicine intermittently in Rome among patients of the highest society, including the emperor himself, Marcus Aurelius. At the same time, he produced an astonishing number of books on all aspects of medicine, most of them written in Greek. In one, *On Anatomical Procedures*,[5] he nowhere stated or denied that he was describing human anatomy; until Vesalius, it simply was assumed to be human anatomy. (In fact, in 1300 a monk named Mondino dei Luzzi dissected a human cadaver in Bologna and reported that everything was exactly as Galen said. His text, *Anatomia*, was a Latin version of Galenic anatomy, which became a standard work for centuries.)

Galen taught that good health reflected the correct combination of four humors: **phlegm**, secreted into the nose by the pituitary; **yellow bile**, secreted into the duodenum by the gallbladder; **black bile**, secreted into the stomach by the spleen; and **blood**. Hypersecretory states also were described: too much phlegm, phlegmatic; too much yellow bile, bilious; too much black bile, melancholy; too much blood, sanguine. Humors had additional properties as well. Phlegm was cold and wet; yellow bile was hot and dry; blood was hot and wet; black bile was cold and dry. Since the humoral balance differed in different people, their diseases differed accordingly, and treatment had to be individualized. Plant extracts, excreta, and other medicaments were available, each with properties to combat the humoral imbalance.

Galen's physiology was, at once, simple and complex.[6] He knew, as did others, that the dead body was cold; that suffocation was fatal in minutes and left the body unchanged; that starvation was fatal in months and changed the body profoundly; that, in dead animals, thick-walled vessels were empty while thin-walled ones running parallel were filled with blood; that cutting certain large nerves defunctionalized the extremities; and that injuries of the brain could be fatal. He alone knew that, in life, the thick-walled vessels contained blood, since he opened the radial artery of a living dog between a proximal and distal ligature. He also recognized that nerves controlled function, as he stopped a pig's squealing by cutting the recurrent laryngeal nerve.

To Galen, all living creatures were surrounded by *pneuma*, a world principle essential to life.[7] It was thought that, after being inhaled, pneuma passed via the finest ramifications of the trachea to the left pulmonary artery and thence to the left side of the heart, where ultimately it was converted to vital spirit. Food was concocted (cooked) in the stomach and passed into the small intestine; there it was absorbed by venules and passed via the portal vein to the liver, where it was manufactured into blood and endowed with natural spirit. By sloshing about in the superior and inferior vena cavae, this natural spirit-enriched blood supplied nutrition to the body. Galen considered the right and left ventricles to comprise the heart; the right atrium was a diverticulum of the superior vena cava and the left an expansion of the pulmonary vein. Blood entering the right ventricle mixed with pneuma, a portion of it reaching the trachea by way of the pulmonary artery, with impurities being exhaled as "smoky vapours." The remainder passed through an opening in the interventricular septum, where the beating of the heart warmed it, mixed it with pneuma, and elaborated vital spirit. The vital spirit was distributed by the thick-walled vessels and supplied the warmth of living bodies. Some of the vital spirit-charged blood ascended to the base of the skull, where it spread out in a thin-walled network of vessels, the rete mirabile. There, animal spirit was added; the animal spirit ascended to the brain by way of the internal carotid artery, was distributed throughout the body by hollow nerves, and supplied the body with movement and sensation. The spinal cord had a function similar to the brain.

These principles endured unchallenged for thirteen centuries. Before medical thought could progress, they had to be put to rest.

Vesalius: A careful observer accused of heresy

Vesalius was born in Brussels in 1514. One of the wars between Francis I and Charles V forced him to transfer from the medical school of Paris to that of Padua in 1536. In Paris, he learned and helped to teach the anatomy of Galen. When Johannes Guinterius of Andernach planned publication of the complete works of Galen, Vesalius had a hand in bringing up to date the section on anatomy. At Padua in 1539, he and an affluent artist named Jan Stephan van Calcar published *Tabulae Anatomicae Sex*, six anatomical figures suitable for preexamination cramming—pure Galen. Yet, it appears that Vesalius soon concluded that Galen's anatomy, except for a brief description of the shoulder, was animal anatomy, most of it that of barbary apes, which were common in Southern Europe in Galen's time. He found that the human liver had two lobes (not five, as in the dog) and that there was neither a rete mirabile at the base of the brain nor a gross opening in the interventricular septum for passage of blood between the right and left sides of the heart. He also found that many bony protuberances described by Galen were absent in humans and that some protuberances present in humans were not described by Galen.

Based upon these observations, much of the Fabrica's text amounts to an immoderate denunciation of Galen, and in 1543 denouncing Galen was heresy. Criticism of the book was so violent as to drive Vesalius from academia to the court of Charles V. But the book continued to circulate and to demonstrate, for the first time, that Galen was wrong. It represented a signal to others to look for Galenic errors. It was Harvey who found a large one.

William Harvey: Extending anatomy to physiology in a hesitant fashion

Harvey studied medicine at Padua, some fifty years after Vesalius. His anatomy teacher was Hieronymus Fabricius of Aquapendente, discoveror of venous valves. The single illustration in De Motu is exactly like one in De Venarum Ostiolis, except for two small hands that demonstrate that the direction of blood flow in the veins of the forearm is toward the heart. When Harvey returned to England, he opened the left ventricles of dogs and found that one-half ounce of blood was ejected with each heartbeat. The liver could not conceivably manufacture 40 ounces per minute, 2400 ounces per hour, more than 50,000 ounces per day. It had to be the same blood going round and round, circulating. This experiment gave a quantitative basis to Harvey's argument, heretofore lacking in challenges to Galenic physiology.[8] Harvey also suggested that the radial pulse was not due to intrinsic expansion and collapse of the vessel, as Galen taught, but rather that it reflected the pumping action of the heart.

Harvey was less bold than Vesalius; he waited fifteen years before daring to publish his conclusions. His book elicited less violent criticism than that which greeted Vesalius, and soon he was honored as a prophet the world around and immortalized by the work of his successors.[8]

Vesalius' book did little to change medical thought and practice. To sixteenth century doctors, the fine details of human anatomy were unimportant, and the presence of a rete mirabile and the actual number of lobes in the liver really did not matter. Harvey's book brought radical change. New Galenic errors were found; a system of vessels (lymphatics) totally unknown to him was discovered; and new avenues were explored in search of the cause and to explain the course of disease. Once Galen was challenged, modern medical inquiry was born.

Vesalius showed that there was something to be found out, that medicine was not perfected by Galen. Harvey, and others who followed, showed that much of Galen was all wrong.

But the question remains: Whose book was greater?

References

1. Vesalius A. De Humani corporis Fabrica. Basel, 1543. Facsimile ed., Brussels, culture et civilisation, 1964.
2. Harvey W. Exercitatio Anatomica de Motu cordis et Sanguinis in Animalibus. Facsimile of 1628 Francofurti ed., together with the Keynes English translation of 1928. Birmingham, Alabama, Classics of Medicine Library, 1978.
3. Castiglioni A. A History of Medicine. Krumbhaar EB, trans. and ed. New York, Alfred A. Knopf, 1941, P. 418.
4. Cushing H. The Life of Sir William Osler, Vol. 2. Oxford, Clarendon Press, 1925, pp. 357, 431, 617.
5. Ouckworth WLH., trans.: Galen: On Anatomical Procedures: The Later Books, Lyons, MC, and Towers, B, eds., Cambridge, University Press, 1962.
6. Siegel RE. Galen's System of Physiology and Medicine. Basel and New York, S. Karger, 1968.
7. Singer C. A Short History of Anatomy from the Greeks to Harvey. New York, Dover Publications, 1943.
8. Frank RG, Jr. Harvey and the Oxford Physiologists: A Study of Scientific Ideas and Social Interaction. Berkeley, University of California Press, 1980.

EARLY GREEK THEORIES OF COGNITION: HOMER TO HIPPOCRATES

WILLIAM B. NASO, M.D.

(Summer 1990, pp. 23–28)

Dr. Naso received his M.D. degree from the University of North Carolina School of Medicine, Chapel Hill, North Carolina, in May 1990, and was trained in neurosurgery at the Medical University of South Carolina in Charleston, South Carolina. Another essay written jointly with Thomas H. Woolen, Jr., "Holistic Medicine in Ancient Greece: The Medical Model of Alcmaeon and Plato," was published in the Summer 1989 issue of The Pharos. *As a student, he was awarded first prize for this paper in the 1990 AΩA Student Essay Competition.*

HEARKEN TO ME, Trojans and well-greaved Achaians, that I may speak what my mind within my breast biddeth me.

Homer, The Iliad, Bk. VII[1p.118]

I therefore assert that the brain is the interpreter of comprehension. Accident and convention have falsely ascribed that function to the diaphragm which does not and could not possess it. . . . It is no quicker in perception than any other part of the body, and its name and associations are quite unwarranted, just as parts of the heart are called auricles though they make no contribution to hearing. Some say too that we think with our hearts and it is the heart which suffers pain and feels anxiety. There is no truth in this. . . . Neither of these organs takes any part in mental operations, which are completely undertaken by the brain.

Hippocrates, The Sacred Disease (20)[2pp.250–51]

Hippocrates (460–357 B.C.) wrote at the end of a long and bitter controversy. Since the time of Homer, the Greeks had been fascinated by the question of what constitutes man's central processor. They were forever seeking the physical basis for intelligence and emotion. What organ, what fluid, they asked, enables us to see, to think, to grieve, to rejoice; to do all those things that make us what we are—human beings? They wondered what it is that lets us know that the fire is hot and the ice cold. Where lies the seat of sensation? of thought? of emotion? of soul?

The author of *The Sacred Disease* clearly placed that seat in the brain. Yet even within the Hippocratic Corpus we discover conflicting opinions. One writer unapologetically asserted that blood is the medium of thought,[3] while another identified the left ventricle as the seat of man's intelligence.[4] In Homer's *Iliad*, we find little mention of the brain but do see the diaphragm and heart alternately invoked as the seats of the mind.

Between the times of Homer and Hippocrates flourished two physicians of the Sicilian school—Alcmaeon of Croton and Empedocles of Acragas. Whereas Alcmaeon argued that the brain contained the "governing faculty,"[5, p. 1044] Empedocles followed the Homeric tradition and insisted that the heart was central to cognition, regarding the blood as "the organ of understanding,"[6p191] Plato, a younger contemporary of Hippocrates, accepted the Alcmaeonian contention and placed both mind and soul within the brain. He also claimed some cognitive and psychological functions for the heart and other organs.

This essay traces ancient Greek theories of cognition from Homer, the earliest surviving example of Greek literature, to Hippocrates, the culmination of classical Greek medicine. These models represent some of man's earliest efforts to understand himself. They are answers to questions that, to a certain extent, confront us even today. Moreover, they reflect a critical advance in Western thought: man's growing rejection of superstition and embracement of science.

Homer (c. 900 B.C.)

Writing about events that took place around 1200 B.C., Homer was the first and arguably greatest Greek poet. Within his *Iliad* one finds several different viewpoints about the physical location of man's intellect or soul. In certain passages the poet unequivocally named the diaphragm as the organ of the soul. Elsewhere, however, he implied that it is the heart or breast that contains the cognitive element.

In Book XVI Homer related how the Greek warrior Patroklos took the field in Achilles' armour and fought to the death. But before his own ultimate demise, Patroklos killed many men, among them King Sarpedon:

> Even as he spake thus, the end of death veiled over his eyes and his nostrils, but Patroklos, setting foot on his breast, drew the spear out of his flesh, and the midriff [diaphragm] followed with the spear, so that he drew forth together the spear point, and the soul of Sarpedon.[1pp303–04]

The Greek word for diaphragm, *phrenes*, from which we derive the adjective phrenic, can also be rendered as "mind." This second meaning survives in such words as *phrenopathy* (any emotional or mental disorder) and *phrenology* (the doctrine that proposes that mental capacities can be gauged by palpating the external contours of the skull). The author of *The Sacred Disease* considered this relationship to be an etymological coincidence, arguing that "accident and convention have falsely ascribed that function [comprehension] to the diaphragm which does not and could not possess it."[2p250]

Elsewhere in the *Iliad* Homer's speakers place the mind not in the diaphragm, but in the heart. After Achilles had refused the entreaties of the Achaians in Book IX, the elderly knight Phoinix laments:

> If indeed thou ponderest departure in thy heart, glorious Achilles, and has no mind at all to save the fleet ships from consuming fire, because that wrath hath entered thy heart; how can I be left of thee, dear son, alone thereafter?[1p159]

Here Phoinix attributes to the heart both cognitive and emotional capacities. Later, he speaks of "my soul . . . within my breast,"[1p159] and elsewhere Aias informs Achilles that "the gods have put within thy breast a spirit implacable and evil."[1p164]

Why Homer placed emotion, mind, and soul within man's breast, we will never know. Perhaps the early Greeks had observed that men in battle died most quickly when a spear penetrated the thorax and punctured the heart itself. Conceivably, they could have observed the beating heart of a mortally wounded soldier. Or more likely, the Greeks might have felt the sudden palpitation at a moment of decision or the chest's fierce pounding at the height of anger and simply assumed that fear and rage and the other emotions must emanate from the heart. One can give only likely explanations. But perhaps even more perplexing is what first led the Greeks to question this supposition altogether and suggest that mind and soul might not reside within man's breast but rather exist within his brain.

Alcmaeon of Croton (fl. 500 B.C.)

The first serious expression of this latter theory was made by Alcmaeon of Croton, a physician who flourished at the end of the sixth century B.C. Variously styled the father of anatomy, of embryology, and even of medicine itself,[7] Alcmaeon was purportedly "the first to undertake dissection."[5p1044] Through dissection he identified what probably were the optic nerves, calling them the two "light-bearing paths" that connect the eyes to the brain, supporting his contention by noting the synchronous movement of the two eyes.[8] Aristotle's comment that "Alcmaeon is incorrect in his belief that goats breathe through the ears"[5p1045] suggests that Alcmaeon may well have discovered the auditory canals some two thousand years before Eustachio.[7] The Crotonian's remark that "we smell through the nostrils by drawing up the air to the brain during inspiration"[5p1044] could be interpreted to imply that Alcmaeon had discovered the perforations in the cribiform plate.[7p122]

Regardless of whether Alcmaeon did in fact delineate these anatomic structures, his underlying proposition is clear, "that all senses are connected somehow with the brain."[5p1045] He further supported this concept with a clinical observation, noting that "when the brain is agitated and displaced, maiming (of limbs or senses) follows."[5p1045] He then offered a pathophysiologic mechanism for cerebral dysfunction when the brain is moved or displaced: "the passages through which the sensations pass, are occupied."[5p1045]

Alcmaeon went even further. He maintained that the brain is not only the seat of sensation but of thought itself. He identified the brain as "the governing faculty."[8p137] He also distinguished between perception and understanding, arguing that it is the capacity to both process and comprehend incoming sensory data that separates humans from animals. This distinction was elucidated by Theophrastus, thus:

> Alcmaeon, one of those who do not regard sense perception as similar (to thinking), first points out the difference from animals. He says that man differs from other animals, because he alone comprehends, while the other animals perceive but do not understand, because understanding and perception are different things, contrary to what Empedocles states.[5p1042]

Interestingly, Alcmaeon attributed a third function to the brain, beyond its sensorial and cognitive capacities. He also considered the brain to be a procreative organ, identifying it as the source of semen.[5p1043] We shall meet this reproductive theory again in the works of Plato and a fourth-century B.C. Hippocratic writer.

Empedocles of Acragas (c. 495–435 B.C.)

Empedocles rejected Alcmaeon's contention and held that soul emanated from the heart, being carried by the medium of the blood. Empedocles wrote:

> Nourished in a sea of churning blood where what men call thought is especially found—for the blood about the heart is thought for men.[6p191]

More fundamentally, Empedocles believed that all entities emit invisible "effluences" that enable one to perceive that a thing exists:

> Know that effluences are given off from everything that comes into being. . . . Not only animals and plants and earth and sea, but even stones and brass and iron continually emit streams [of them].[9pp169–70]

These effluences enter a sentient being through "channels" and are transmitted through the blood stream. A predatory animal, for example, knows that his dinner is close at hand because he perceives the "effluences" emanating from his prey. The animal is "searching out with its nostrils the fragments of the wild limbs [of the hunted thing]—the living parts which it shed from its feet in the soft grass."[9p170]

Empedocles also proposed that different sensory modalities exist within a person, suggesting that they are limited by the physical channels that transmit the effluences. An individual cannot hear with his eyes, for instance, because sound cannot enter the channels of vision.

> This is why one sense cannot judge of the objects of another; for the passages of some are too wide and of other objects too narrow for the object perceived, so that some [effluences] go straight through without touching whereas others are unable to enter at all.[9p170]

Once the effluences enter the proper channel, they then find their way to the blood stream and ultimately to the blood around the heart, where cognition takes place. Yet, perception and cognition are not purely mechanical phenomena. A person's intellectual ability also depends on his emotional lability. If an individual is of good character and a receptive mind, the effluences may lodge deeply within his calm heart. Conversely, if he has an undisciplined mind, the effluences will not take root, and his understanding will be but momentary:

> But if your thought is for other things—the countless wretchednesses which arise among men and blunt the edge of their careful thought, these will desert you quickly when the time comes round; for they long to return to their own kind. For be assured that all things have intelligence and a share of thought.[9p171]

In all the surviving fragments, Empedocles did not address the brain. Instead, he subscribed to a purely hematologic theory of cognition. Yet, if interpreted with an appreciation for the anatomical knowledge base of the fifth-century physician, this theory might not seem so unreasonable. No clear description of nerves existed in Empedocles' era and would not until some 150 years later. Although Alcmaeon had described the optic nerves, his "passages" through which sensory data travelled were similar to the Empedoclean "channels." Physicians subscribed to what E.D. Phillips aptly called a "vascular neurology."[10p377] In other words, the ancient Greeks thought that perceptual data were transmitted by way of the blood stream to the organ of cognition. For Empedocles that organ was the blood around the heart; for Alcmaeon and, as we shall soon see, for Plato and Hippocrates as well, that organ was the brain.

Plato (427–347 B.C.)

Although Plato wrote mostly about spiritual and political matters, many of his dialogues touch on medicine and natural philosophy. He frequently described what he thought constituted the true physician and employed his model of the good doctor as a paradigm for the true philosopher. Plato also explored anatomic questions. He was particularly interested in cognition and emotions vis-à-vis anatomical structures. He addressed the possible cognitive, psychological, and inspirational roles of various organs.

Our richest source for the Platonic position is his great work *Timaeus*, really a creation hymn. Plato's main interest is the soul, its divisions, and their physical analogues. The Platonic soul is tripartite. Plato first divided the soul into its divine (immortal) and mortal elements. The divine element resides within the skull, which is a sphere, and reflects the spherical unity of the spiritual universe. This element contains mind or reason, and its physical analogue is the brain.[11]

The mortal or inferior aspect of soul is physically separate from the divine element:

> [T]hey gave to the mortal nature a separate habitation in another part of the body, placing the neck between them to be the isthmus and boundary, which they constructed between the head and breast, to keep them apart. And in the breast, and in what is termed the thorax, they incased the mortal soul; and as the one part of this was superior and the other inferior they divided the cavity of the thorax into two parts, as the women's and men's apartments are divided in houses, and placed the midriff to be a wall partition between them.[11p48]

The diaphragm physically separates the two parts of the inferior soul. Although the mortal soul does not participate directly in cognition, it is critical to a person's psychological or emotional makeup:

> That part of the inferior soul which is endowed with courage and passion and loves contention, they settled nearer the head, midway between the midriff and the neck, in order that it might be under the rule of reason and might join with it in controlling and restraining the desires when they are no longer willing of their own accord to obey the word of command issuing from the citadel.[11p48]

In a soul that would be well ordered, "reason" elicits "passion" to control "desire." Plato placed the "spirited" or "passionate" element of his tripartite soul within the breast. "Passion," however, implies not carnal urges but virtues and emotions such as courage, honor, and love. It must be contrasted to blind physical desire, the lowest element of mortal soul. This appetitive element Plato placed within the abdomen:

> The part of the soul which desires meats and drinks and the other things which it has need by reason of the bodily nature, they placed between the midriff and the boundary of the navel, contriving in all this region a sort of manger for the food of the body; and there they bound it down like a wild animal which was chained up with man, and must be nourished if man was to exist.[11p49]

In order that it might not too easily influence divine reason, the "lower creation" was situated "as far as might be from the council-chamber."[11p49] Yet, this inferior part of the mortal soul was not completely isolated from the divine. According to Plato, the creators, "knowing that this lower principle in man would not comprehend reason," placed the liver "in the house of the lower nature." Within the liver resides "the seat of divination" and thus the inferior soul, although it is truly divorced from reason, may at least "attain a measure of truth"[11p49] "And herein is a proof," Plato maintained, "that God has given the art of divination not to wisdom, but to the foolishness of man."[11p50]

Although Plato placed the two parts of the mortal soul within discrete regions of the body, he never proposed that the thoracic or abdominal organs (for example, heart, lungs, intestines) themselves were the resting place for the soul. True, the heart "was set in the place of guard,"[11p48] but Plato never actually said that soul itself resides within the heart. Instead, he proposed something radically different:

> That which, like a field, was to receive the divine seed, he made round every way, and called that portion of the marrow, brain, intending that, when an animal was perfected, the vessel containing this substance should be the head; but that which was intended to contain the remaining and mortal part of the soul he distributed into figures at once round and elongated, and he called them all by the name 'marrow'; and to these. . . he proceeded to fashion around them the entire framework of our body, constructing for the marrow, first of all, a complete covering of bone.[11pp51–52]

Plato thought that the divine soul rests within the brain while the two parts of the mortal soul (even though they are in fact within the thorax and abdomen) each reside within distinct parts of the spinal marrow. The heart and other organs had definite roles in cognition and especially in emotional variability, but they were not soul itself, as Homer and Empedocles maintained.

Plato not only accepted Alcmaeon's contention regarding the brain's supremacy, but he similarly suggested that semen originates from the brain. He proposed that "the seed" is transported through the marrow ("which passes from the head along the neck and through the back") and somehow arrives at "the organ of generation."[11p67] Because the "seed" originates from the divine soul within the brain it is alive and, "having life, and becoming endowed with respiration, produces in that part in which it respires a lively desire of emission, and thus creates in us the love of procreation."[11p67] Thus the brain and marrow are truly possessed of life, for therein rest both soul and the "seed" that breeds new life.

Hippocrates (460–357 B.C.)

Like Alcmaeon, Hippocrates was an experimentalist and an observationalist. He based his theories on what he learned at both the bedside and the dissection table. In his great treatise on epilepsy, Hippocrates argued that "this disease is not in the least more divine than any other [disease],"[2p240] but that it has identifiable and natural causes.

> When the disease has been present from childhood, a habit develops of attacks occurring at any change of wind and specially when it is southerly. This is hard to cure because the brain has become more moist than normal and is flooded with phlegm. This renders discharges more frequent. The phlegm can no longer be completely separated out; neither can the brain, which remains wet and soaked, be dried up. This observation results specially from a study of animals, particularly of goats which are liable to this disease. Indeed, they are peculiarly susceptible to it. If you cut open the head you will find that the brain is wet, full of fluid and foul-smelling, convincing proof that disease and not the the deity is harming the body.[2pp246–47]

Hippocrates wrote: "Personally, I believe that human bodies cannot be polluted by a god; the basest object by the most pure,"[2p240] and that no external deity would cause epilepsy. He maintained that "like other diseases it is hereditary"[2p240] and went on further to characterize the disease, propose pathophysiologic mechanisms, describe onset, causes, and prognosis, and, of particular interest to us, discuss the anatomical and functional characteristics of "the seat of this disease"[2p241]—the brain.

Hippocrates described the brain as "double" with a "thin membrane [that] runs down the middle and divides it."[2p241] Like Alcmaeon, he placed the cognitive element within the brain. But the physician of Cos did not stop there. He maintained that the brain is the seat of sensation, intellect, and emotion:

> It ought to be generally known that the source of our pleasure, merriment, laughter and amusement, as of our grief, pain, anxiety and tears, is none other than the brain. It is specially the organ which enables us to think, see and hear, and to distinguish the ugly and the beautiful, the bad and the good, pleasant and unpleasant.[2p248]

Hippocrates identified the brain as the focus for both physical and psychiatric diseases. He argued that the brain is

> . . . the seat of madness and delirium of the fears and frights which assail us, often by night, but sometimes even by day; it is there where lies the cause of insomnia and sleep-walking, of thoughts that will not come, forgotten duties and eccentricities. All such things result from an unhealthy condition of the brain.[2pp248–49]

Hippocrates called the brain "the most potent organ in the body" and maintained that "so long as it is healthy," the brain functions as the interpreter of sensations, the seat of consciousness, and "the organ of comprehension."[2pp249–50] And because of the brain's supremacy and complexity "the diseases which attack the brain are the most acute, most serious and most fatal, and the hardest problem in diagnosis for the unskilled practitioner."[2p251]

The author of *The Sacred Disease* (whom I have identified as Hippocrates himself) clearly made the brain the source and seat of man's thought. Other medical writers, whose works have been included in the Hippocratic Corpus, argued differently. The author of *Breaths* followed the Empedoclean tradition and maintained that understanding resides within the blood:

> Now I hold that no constituent of the body in anyone contributes more to intelligence than does blood. So long as the blood remains in its normal condition, intelligence too remains normal; but when the blood alters, the intelligence also changes. (*Breaths xiv*)[3p249]

This writer ascribed the dreams of sleep and the delusions of drunkenness to changes in a person's blood. He also dismissed epilepsy and its signs and symptoms as secondary to a simple dyscrasia.

The author of *The Heart*, probably writing over a hundred years after the historical Hippocrates died, also reflected the Homeric belief and placed the cognitive element within man's heart: "man's intelligence, the principle which rules over the rest of the soul, is situated in the left chamber."[4p351] He made no mention of the brain.

Like Alcmaeon and Plato, certain Hippocratic writers also claimed a procreative function for the brain. The author of *The Seed* expanded on the Platonic argument when he wrote of the sperm's origin in the brain and transportation through the spinal marrow:

> [Sperm] is diffused from the brain into the loins and the whole body, but in particular into the spinal marrow: for passages extend into this from the whole body, which enable the fluid to pass to and from the spinal marrow. Once the sperm has entered the spinal marrow it passes in its course through the veins along the kidneys (sometimes if there is a lesion of the kidneys, blood is carried along with the sperm). From the kidneys it passes via the testicles into the penis—not however by the urinary tract, since it has a passage of its own which is next to the urinary tract.[12pp317–18]

Although they agreed with the positions of many of their predecessors, the Hippocratic writers revealed a deeper appreciation for anatomical and physiologic principles. The author of *The Sacred Disease* cited anatomical, clinical, and experimental data to support his theories. Similarly, the authors of *The Heart* and *The Seed* described anatomical relationships that Homer, Alcmaeon, Empedocles, and Plato probably never recognized.

Comment

At first glance the early Greek theories of cognition appear to have evolved from the primitive and superstitious Homeric beliefs to the more scientific

Hippocratic contentions. And to a certain extent, this impression is accurate. Yet, the Homeric beliefs were never fully abandoned. They found expression in the works of Empedocles, Plato, and even some of the Hippocratic writers. *The Sacred Disease*, however, by no means settled the issue. Writing two generations after Hippocrates, Aristotle vehemently defended the claim that the heart was central to cognition, citing animal dissections that traced the blood vessels and nerves back to the heart to prove his point.[13] It was not until Herophilus carefully described the brain and spinal cord, distinguishing between motor and sensory nerves, that "vascular neurology" was disproved, and scientists recognized the brain as the center of the nervous system.[14,15]

Herophilus' anatomic discoveries, however, did not convince everyone. Physicians and philosophers have grappled with and continue to question what ultimately controls cognition. Even as late as the nineteenth century, eminent scientists suggested that organs such as the liver and spleen, although admittedly uninvolved with sensation, were in fact sources for emotions. They proposed, for example, that from the liver comes anger and from the stomach fear.[16] Even today our language reflects history's confusion. We speak of the courageous man's heart, the impudent child's gall, and the capricious person's spleen.

With the recent advent of transplantation surgery, there has been a reconsideration of these issues. Physicians are now discussing the psychological ramifications of organ transplantation. The psychiatric sequelae of cardiac, hepatic, and renal transplantation are well documented in the literature.[17] And although investigators can suggest many likely causes for the emotional and cognitive dysfunctions in the posttransplantation patient, some of the "less likely" explanations are a bit more thought provoking.

References

1. Lang A, Leaf W, and Meyers E., trans. The Iliad of Homer. New York, The Modern Library, 1950.
2. Chadwick J and Mann WN, trans.: The sacred disease. In: Lloyd, GER, ed. Hippocratic Writings, pp. 237–50. New York, Penguin Books, 1987.
3. Jones WHS, trans. Breaths. In Hippocrates, pp. 219–53. Cambridge, Massachusetts, Harvard University Press, 1981.
4. Lonie IM, trans. The heart. In Lloyd, GER, ed., Hippocratic Writings, pp. 347–51. New York, Penguin Books, 1987.
5. Codellas PS. Alcmaeon of Croton: His life, work, and fragments. Proc R Soc Med 25:1041-46, 1932.
6. Barnes J. Early Greek Philosophy. New York, Penguin Books, 1987.
7. Lloyd G. Alcmaeon and the early history of dissection. Sudhoffs Arch (5912): 113–47, 1975.
8. Freeman K. The Pre-Socratic Philosophers, A companion To Diels, Fragmenfe der Vorsokratiker. Oxford, Basil Blackwell,1946.
9. Robinson JM. An Introduction to Early Greek Philosophy. Boston, Houghton Mifflin Co., 1968.

10. Phillips ED. The brain and nervous phenomena in the Hippocratic writings. Irish J Med Science 6(381):377–90, 1957.
11. Jowett B, trans. Timaeus. In The Dialogues of Plato, vol. 2, pp. 3–68. New York, Random House. 1920.
12. Lonie IM, trans. The seed. In Lloyd, GER, ed., Hippocratic Writings, pp. 3 17–23. New York, Penguin Books, 1987.
13. Gordon BL. Medicine throughout Antiquity. Philadelphia, F.A. Davis Co., 1949.
14. Dobson JF. Herophilus of Alexandria. Proc R Soc Med, Section of the History of Medicine 18:19–32, 1925.
15. Potter P. Herophilus of Chalcedon: An assessment of his place in the history of anatomy. Bull Hist Med 50:45–60, 1976.
16. Walker AE. The dawn of neurosurgery. Clin Neurosurg 6:1–38, 1959.
17. Berenson CK and Grosser BI. Total artificial heart implantation. Arch Gen Psychiatry 41:910–16, 1984.

ACKNOWLEDGEMENT: Special thanks to James A. Bryan II, M.D., professor of medicine, University of North Carolina School of Medicine, for his advice and encouragement, and to Nicolette B. Naso, M.D., for her continued support.

TAOISM AND THE QUEST FOR IMMORTALITY

EDWARD JIN YOON
(Fall 1991, pp. 30–33)

Edward Yoon was a second-year student at the Northwestern University Medical School when he wrote this piece. He received his undergraduate degree with honors at Stanford University, where he majored in religious studies. This paper was awarded honorable mention in the 1991 Alpha Omega Alpha Student Essay competition.

WHILE THE FAINT STIRRINGS OF EMPIRICAL SCIENCE began to be felt in the medical landscape of ancient Greece, an equally dynamic exchange of ideas concerning the nature of health and disease was occurring thousands of miles removed from Athens in the diverse empire of China. By the third century B.C., a multitude of therapies and theories, some of them already centuries old, attempted to account for and alleviate the existence of human illness. The emergence of Taoism during this period would leave an indelible imprint on the practice of Chinese medicine and would significantly shape the history of East Asian philosophical thought.

One must be aware that the term *Taoism* has come to embrace many different schools of thought and figures in Chinese history; it does not represent a single discrete school of philosophy throughout the ages, like "Kantianism" or "Neo-Platonism." One reason for this diffusivity may lie, as we shall see, in its gnostic, mystical approach and its disinterest in employing linear and rationalistic discourse that establishes its philosophical claims. The two paradigmatic expositions of classical philosophic Taoism, the *Tao Te Ching* and the *Chuang Tzu*, are not philosophical texts in the style of traditional Western philosophy. They each employ humor, anecdote, and poetic device rather than a discursive argumentative style to make points.

Another reason for Taoism's diffuseness may lie in its extensive appropriation of terms and concepts that are not so much unique Taoist formulations as they are elements belonging to a common fund of Chinese ideas.

The Tao

What is this tao that the Taoist philosophers speak of? An ancient word that predates its appropriation by Taoism, tao literally refers to a way or road, a definition that was expanded to mean the way of nature, or the way of the universe.[1, p. 62] The Confucians employed the word tao to refer to the orderly nature of the universe and often associated it with the term *t'ien,* or Heaven. For the Confucian, the way of Heaven was a moral way, and that which went against the tao was an affront, a disruptive deviation from the proper and harmonious path that characterized the workings of the world. The Confucian universe was vaguely Newtonian in that for every action there was a reaction, a law that applied to moral actions as well. Although the tao lacked the highly anthropomorphic features common to Western religious deities, it did possess an unfailing moral regularity. Thus, because the tao represented the principles of all the world's processes, a lack of moral order on the part of the emperor could spell disaster for the entire kingdom.

Crops might wither, rebellions and social chaos could arise, and upheavals within the natural world could occur.[1, pp. 62–63] Just as removing a few strands of an intricately woven mat can compromise its entire integrity, a violation of the moral tao could produce ramifications that would reverberate throughout the natural world.

The Confucian concept of the tao reveals an intimate association between the natural world and the human world, one that can reflect the moral fortitude or decay of a ruling dynasty. In what way did the use of tao by the Taoists differ? In the classic texts of philosophical Taoism, the tao assumes a significantly less providential tone. Whereas the Confucians saw the tao bringing disaster on the wicked and fortune to the just, the authors of the *Tao Te Ching* and the *Chuang Tzu* viewed the universe as rather devoid of such moralistic leanings. The *Tao Te Ching* states: "Heaven and earth are ruthless, and treat the myriad creatures as straw dogs."[2] This view of an impersonal universe contrasted sharply with the human-centered outlook of Confucianism, a difference that explains why Chuang Tzu (369–286 B.C.), the Taoist sage, consistently ridiculed the Confucianists as useless bureaucrats who wasted their efforts in trying to impose a false social order and a false conception of what constitutes proper human relations. Such meddling only served to heap more suffering on the people of the nation:

> The corpses of the executed lie about in great numbers; the chained and bound crowd [the streets], and when someone is sentenced to flogging, he must first watch and wait his turn. And the Confucians and Moists stand on their toes and wave their arms among the hordes in chains and bonds. Oh, what an enormous affront to mankind! Oh why have they not recognized that all this sacredness and wisdom caused these chains and that all the benevolence and righteousness created these bonds!

Life and death in the Taoist matrix

The philosophical conflict between the Taoists and Confucians in the several centuries before the birth of Christ may become clearer in light of their shared historical context. Established circa 1100 B.C., the Chou dynasty enjoyed relative peace and stability for approximately two centuries, but then fell into a period of decay known as the Spring and Autumn Period (770–464 B.C.) and then a time of unprecedented strife known as the Warring States (463–222 B.C.).[1, pp. 56–57] The two-and-a-half centuries of the Warring States were characterized by a complete collapse of central authority and a Machiavellian viciousness that knew little restrain. This loss of political order "was exacerbated by countless cases of patricide, uxoricide, and fratricide within the many ruling families; this moral decay marks the decline of the Chou Empire as one of the bloodiest periods in Chinese history."[4, p. 31]

Thus, in a period marked by political chaos, Confucianism advocated centralized authority and statecraft practiced according to moral principles. In fact, Confucius considered his philosophy to be an earnest attempt to return China to the glorious days of righteousness and stability that prevailed during the Chou Dynasty.[1, p. 64] But the suffering and brutality inflicted by the regimes of the time led many to reject the ideas of influence-seeking political advisers and escape to the philosophy of Taoism. Yet, this flight must not be considered as a conscious escape from reality, but rather as an escape from the illusory world of human affairs to the higher reality embodied by the tao.

The realization that the tao transcended the petty aspects of human existence was neither nihilistic nor a cause of despair. Instead, there was a sense of mystical rapture and wonder that human language simply could not convey. It was a rapture that involved an appreciation of nature and the simplicity of a rustic life. A poem by Tu Fu* (A. D. 712–790), perhaps China's most celebrated poet, illustrates this.

> Sounding cold dawn skies, steady winds
> Tatter visions of cloud over the river.
> Ducks take refuge along the island. Among
> Thickets, swallows find shelter from rain.
> Huang and Ch'i both refused an emperor,
> Ch'ao and Yu an empire. A cup of wine,
> A thatched home—that l am here as today's
> Flawless morning passes gathers me in joy[5, p. 59]

For many Confucian scholars weary of the constant competition for honors and position in the imperial court, Taoism often represented a welcome respite from the noisome affairs of politics. Many Confucian scholars, such as Tu Fu, were

---

* The poems "Jade Blossom Palace" and "Morning Rain" by Tu Fu are used with permission of New Directions Publishing Corporation.

enamoured of Taoist themes in their poetry and admired the chance to cast away the artificial trappings of bureaucratic life.[5, p. 158] Few, however, were able to do so as easily and as categorically as the hermits Tu Fu describes in his poem.

The Taoist attitude towards life can be considered as an existential response to a universe that was both wondrous and mysterious, yet seemingly impersonal and indifferent to human affairs. For those philosophically minded Taoists, the person who had devoted his life to contemplation of the tao was called *chen-jen*, or "true man," a sage. A sage in harmony with the tao would be undisturbed by its inevitable process of change and would display an equanimity and a vitality that those ignorant of the tao lacked. In a extraordinary passage from the *Chuang Tzu*, which reflects a kind of Taoist ecology, four sages view their impending deaths not with fear and denial, but as events that are parts of a larger whole—a wholeness embodied by the tao. As one sage stated:

> Soon I will be dissolved. My left shoulder will become a cock announcing the morning, my right shoulder a cross bow with which I can hunt ducks to eat. My buttocks will serve as a pair of wheels, and with my soul for a horse to pull them, I will drive along in my own chariot. . . . I am simply hanging in the air, as they said in antiquity, incapable of freeing myself, tied by the thread of things.[6, p. 329]

And another said:

> And Yin and Yang are the parents of man. If they suggest I die, and I rebel against it that merely means that I have no piety—how could one reproach them for that?

> When it is time, I will fall asleep, and when the right time comes, I will wake up again.[6, p. 39]

In both of these passages the idea of change and evanescence is accepted as part of the tao. Only by melding with the tao, rather than resisting it, can true peace be attained and the wonder of living be realized. Thus, in a sense, mortality has been redefined: death is not perceived as an abrupt ending, but as a transition. True, the original individual self passes away, but for the Taoist sage there is a continuation, a sense of immortality, that comes with according one's life with the tao.

Taoism and the search for immortality

For many scholars, the Taoist expression of an impersonal universe created a ready environment for protoscientific investigations, and an appreciation of the natural world and stories concerning the purported life-enhancing powers of Taoist sages provided a fertile environment for research into the use of herbs and natural substances that could possibly prolong life.[7] The *Huang-ti nei-ching, The Yellow Emperor's Inner Classic,* the most renowned text of Chinese traditional medicine, representing a heterogeneous collection of medical writings dating as far back as the second century B.C., reveals significant debts to Taoist thinking. The text of the *Chuang Tzu* is quoted extensively, and the idea of the Taoist sage, *chen-jen*, as a model of human health, is consistently repeated.[4, pp. 56, 107] The structure of the *Huang-ti nei-ching* partly consists of conversations between the legendary Yellow Emperor, Huang-ti, and his advisors concerning the cause of various illnesses and their proper treatment, while in other sections formal treatises address similar medical issues. One passage that displays Taoist influences advocates the practice of preventive medicine:

> To live in harmony with yin and yang [influences] means life; to act contrary to them means death. To follow signifies order, contrary conduct means chaos. To oppose what is appropriate means contrary action, that is, inner opposition. This is the reason the sages do not treat those who have already fallen ill, but rather those who are not yet ill. They do not put [their state] in order when revolt [is underway], but before an insurrection occurs. This is what is meant. When medicinal therapy is initiated only after someone has fallen ill, when there is an attempt to restore order only after unrest has broken out, it is as though someone has waited to dig a well until he is already weak with thirst, or as if someone begins to forge a spear when the battle is already underway. Is this not too late?[8]

For many Taoists the search for immortality soon became their primary and all-consuming task, a practice that Chuang Tzu denounced even in his own day.[4, p. 106] Nevertheless, numerous sexual techniques, breathing techniques, and physical exercises designed to increase one's vitality, longevity, and perhaps achieve the status of an immortal became the subjects of avid research among many Taoist practitioners.[4, p. 110] For them, the philosophical aspects of Chuang Tzu were not as important as the few passages that seemed to promise the immortality that would allow one to "ascend to the cloudy heavens," like the Yellow Emperor himself."[1, p. 254]

For some, this path led to the extensive investigation of natural substances. Ko Hung (A.D. 283–343), perhaps the most famous of such Taoist alchemists, was said to have discovered the elixir of immortality, which combined esoteric substances such as dew, cinnabar (a mercuric compound), and a host of other ingredients that often had the effect of an early death on those few who could afford to have such costly mixtures prepared.[5, p. 134] While many of these investigations made little progress beyond the level of alchemcal magic, their empirical observations helped stimulate the studied practice of herbal medicine. The *Huai-nan tzu*, the first text to compile the therapeutic efficacy of various medicinal herbs, was named after the philosopher Liu An (179–122 B.C.), a Taoist-oriented philospher who rose to prominence among the Confucian literati of his time.[4, p. 113]

That the quest for immortality in China was indeed compelling is evidenced by the imperial records of Emperor Ch'in Shih Huang-ti, China's first and ruthless emperor, who was apparently obsessed with living forever. Excited by tales of a magical plant that no one had actually observed, he personally combed the mountains to find the legendary herb, *chih,* and then embarked on an expedition to the legendary island of Immortals in the East when his initial attempt at immortality failed.[4, p. 112] It has been theorized that the object of Emperor Chin's desires may have arisen from stories concerning the *soma,* a toadstool that occupied a prominent role in Indian religion.[4, p. 112] In any event, although it is clear that the Taoist "researchers" who sought the secret of immortality had departed from the philosophical vision of Lao Tzu and Chuang Tzu, they obviously lacked no audience for their efforts—either in the halls of the aristocrat or the commoner—and they continue to enjoy a vigorous and extensive following today, even in this country.

Taoism and modern medicine

The Taoist sage is oblivious to change. The sage flows with the tao and does not attempt to resist or deny its course. The four sages view death as a manifestation of the tao, as part of a mystery that is larger than even life itself. Rather than experiencing fear or bitterness, they seem to exult in the opportunity to participate in the endless possibilities that the tao represents.

While few people, if any, are capable of attaining the level of selflessness that a Taoist sage displays—and whether such selflessness should be emulated is an open question as well—it is undoubtedly true that for the patient afflicted with a serious illness and the physician who treats that patient, the issues of change and death are crucial ones. The tension between knowing when to accept those conditions of life that, despite our efforts, transcend our contrary will and desires, and the characteristic human desire to seek every opportunity to push beyond them is one that is powerfully expressed by Taoism; it is a tension poignantly displayed in another poem, again by Tu Fu, contrasting the haunting, beautiful, and enduring music of the tao with the tragic evanescence of human life.

> Below long pine winds, a stream twists.
> Gray rats scuttle across spent roof-tiles.
> Bequeathed now beneath cliffs to ruin—who
> knows which prince's palace this once was?
> Azure ghost flames flood shadow-filled rooms.
> Erosion guts manicured paths. Earth's
> ten thousand airs are the enduring music,
> autumn colors the height of indifference.
> All brown earth now—the exquisite women
> gracing his golden carriage have all become
> their rouge and mascara sham. Of those

stately affairs, one stone horse remains.
Sitting grief-stricken in the grasses,
I sing wildly, wiping away tears for life
scarcely passes into old age, and no one
ever finds anything more of immortality[5, p. 30]

Humanity's quest for immortality has assumed numerous forms. Some of us hold hopes in the possibility of life after death, or failing that, at least attempt to bequeath a legacy that will continue after we are gone. Taoism's long-standing concern with the issue of immortality has assumed a variety of responses and philosophies, ranging from attempts to extend the earthly life that all of us know to a radical redefinition of the nature of mortality and inexorable change. Its impact has helped shape the progress of Asia's medical systems and her views concerning the role of humanity in a fundamentally mysterious universe. Understanding its history not only helps elucidate the nature of medicine that has developed in that part of the globe, but also offers unique perspectives on philosophical questions that are universal and enduring.

References

1. Schwartz BI. The World of Thought in Ancient China. Cambridge, Massachusetts, Harvard University Press, 1985.
2. Lau DC, trans. Lao tzu: Tao Te Ching. London, Penguin Books, 1963, p. 61.
3. Wilhelm R. Dschuang Dsi. Das wahre Buch vom Siidlichen Blutenland: Nanhau Dschenging. Jena, Germany, Eugen Diederichs, 1920, p. 76. As translated and modified by Unschuld, PU: Medicine in China: A History of Ideas. Berkeley, University of California Press, 1985, p. 103.
4. Unschuld PU. Medicine in China: A History of Ideas. Berkeley, University of California Press, 1985.
5. Hinton D, trans. The Selected Poems of Tu Fu. New York, New Directions Books, 1988, p. 59.
6. Bauer W. China and the Search for Happiness: Recurring Themes in Four Thousand Years of Chinese Cultural History, Shaw, M, trans. New York, Seabury Press, 1976.
7. Needham I. Science and Civilisation in China, vol. 2, History of Scientific Thought. Cambridge University Press, 1956, p. 40.
8. Huang ti nei-ching su-wen, as translated in Unschuld, PU: Medicine in China: A History of Ideas. Berkeley, University of California Press, 1985, p. 283.

PART III

SOME HISTORY OF MEDICINE, AND PHYSICIANS WHO MADE HISTORY

"CHANCE FAVORS ONLY THE MIND WHICH IS PREPARED"— (PASTEUR 1854)

WALTER L. BIERRING, M.D.
(October 1958, pp. 39–45)

Dr. Bierring (AΩA, University of Iowa College of Medicine, 1921) was president of Alpha Omega Alpha from 1924 until 1960 and editor of The Pharos *from its inception in 1938 until 1960. After graduating from the University of Iowa College of Medicine in 1892, Dr. Bierring spent two years in Europe, where he studied in Heidelberg in Koch's laboratory, in Vienna with Billroth, and at the Pasteur Institute with Louis Pasteur and Emile Roux. Upon his return to Iowa, he worked in the departments of pathology and bacteriology, and in 1903 he was named Professor of the Theory and Practice of Medicine. In 1908 he took on the responsibilities of being director of University Hospital. Bierring took particular pride in the teaching of diagnostic skills, from simple patient histories to more complex diagnostic procedures and laboratory tests. In April 1909, Abraham Flexner visited the University of Iowa College of Medicine during his tour of American medical schools. He recommended that the school be closed. The school was saved at the price of Bierring's forced resignation, and he moved to Drake University Medical School in Des Moines. Bierring served as president of the American Medical Association in 1934 through 1935. He was active in the American College of Physicians and held certificate number one from the newborn American Board of Internal Medicine. Walter Bierring died in 1961 at the age of 92. He wrote many articles for* The Pharos, *among them "Medical Echos," which appeared in April 1950; "A Golden Epoch in American Medicine," published in November 1952, and "The Founder's Dream Comes True," in the April 1960 issue. This address was presented at installation of Alpha University of Beirut (the only AΩA chapter outside of North America) on May 12, 1958. Only the editorial portion of this long paper is presented here. Dr. Bierring was instrumental in establishing the National Board of Medical Examiners and influential in the introduction of practical bedside examination of patients as part of the requirement for certification by the National Board of Medical Examiners.*

Louis Pasteur

L OUIS PASTEUR, IN HIS INAUGURAL ADDRESS as Dean of the Faculty of
Sciences, University of Lille, on December 27, 1854, spoke these words:
"In the field of observation, chance favors only the mind which is pre-
pared." He was then only 32 years old, already a dean and a professor.

In speaking to students and faculty, the evident purpose of this adage was
to uphold the value, on the one hand, of practical laboratory instruction as an
aid to the solution of industrial problems, and, on the other, the importance of
investigation in pure science, even though the resulting discoveries might have
no immediate application.

It may be of interest to quote a few passages from Pasteur's address:

> Where will you find a young man whose curiosity and interest will not
> immediately be awakened when you put in his hands a potato, when with
> the potato he may produce sugar, with that sugar alcohol, with that al-
> cohol, ether and vinegar? Where is he that will not be happy to tell his
> family in the evening that he had just been working out an electric tele-
> graph? Such studies are seldom forgotten. It is somehow as if geography
> were to be taught by traveling; such geography is remembered because
> one has seen the places. In the same way the student will not forget what
> the air we breathe contains, when he has once analyzed it, when in his
> hands and under his eyes the admirable properties of its elements have
> been resolved.[1]

Pasteur was a chemist, a physical chemist, and his illustrations were drawn
from the realms of physics and chemistry, but the principle of the present method
of medical laboratory and clinical training is embodied in his argument. He
further upheld investigation for its own sake, as contained in another interesting passage:

> Without theory, practice is but routine born by habit. Theory alone can bring
> forth and develop the spirit of invention. It is to you specially that it will
> belong, not to share the opinion of those narrow minds who disdain every-
> thing in science which has not immediate application. You know [Benjamin]
> Franklin's charming saying? He was witnessing the first demonstration of
> a purely scientific discovery and people around said, "But what is the use
> of it?" Franklin answered them, "What is the use of a new born child?"

These arguments may seem trite, but it should be remembered that when
Pasteur made these statements, modern medical investigation was just beginning. . . . We can not say just what Pasteur meant by "chance" and a "prepared
mind." His meaning is evident in some of the examples given. A mind which is
trained to observe the details of natural phenomena, and to reason concerning
the bearing of known laws on such phenomena is the "prepared mind." A class
of mind which, because it is endowed with a peculiar faculty, best described as

scientific imagination, in that it grasps the significance of a new observation, or of a variation from a known sequence of events and thus establishes a new law or invents a new practical procedure. It may be referred to as the spirit of research and investigation. Goethe spoke of it as "Der Innere Geist" or the "spirit within."

To no one is this adage more applicable than Pasteur himself. It was his work in chemistry and crystallography that gave him the "prepared mind" for those fundamental observations which established the principles of fermentation, which as the result of work on alcoholic, acetic, lactic and butyric fermentation led to Pasteur's final dictum:

> The chemical act of fermentation is essentially a correlative phenomenon of a vital-living-act beginning and ending with it.

It was but a short step for the mind thoroughly familiar with the principles of fermentation and putrefaction to embrace the opportunity offered by the study of the etiology of the infectious diseases, and through all his work, as that in connection with silkworm diseases, vaccination against chicken cholera, anthrax, and rabies, the problem of wound infection and the treatment of rabies, the "prepared mind" of this great Master saw and appreciated the significance of every observation and every opportunity which presented itself.

In February 1874 came the historic letter from Dr. Joseph Lister of Edinburgh, prominent Scottish surgeon, that brought to Pasteur these words of homage:

> Allow me to take this opportunity to tender you my most cordial thanks for having demonstrated to me by your brilliant researches, the truth of the germ theory of putrefaction and thus furnished me with the principle upon which alone the antiseptic system of treatment can be carried out, and which I have been labouring for the last nine years to bring to perfection. Should you at any time visit Edinburgh, it would, I believe, give you sincere gratification to see at our hospital how largely mankind is being benefited by your labors. I need hardly add that it would afford me the highest gratification to show you how greatly surgery is indebted to you

Reference

1. Vallery-Radot. The Life of Pasteur. 1902.

OUR MEDICAL HERITAGE: SOME EXAMPLES OF CREATIVE SCHOLARSHIP

A. McGEHEE HARVEY, M.D.

(October 1973, pp. 122–128)

This paper was based on the lecture Dr. Harvey (AΩA, Johns Hopkins, 1934) delivered at the Mount Sinai School of Medicine in March 1973, when he served as Alpha Omega Alpha Visiting Professor. He also wrote for The Pharos *"Francis Weld Peabody: The Blending of General Internal Medicine and Clinical Science," which appeared in Summer 1981, and "Medical Mission to Moscow," published in Fall 1982. "Mac" Harvey was born in Arkansas in 1911. After graduating from Washington and Lee in 1930, he earned his M.D. at Johns Hopkins. After residency training, a faculty appointment at Vanderbilt, and service in the U.S. Army Medical Corps, he returned to Hopkins in 1946 at age 34 as the youngest physician-in-chief at that institution and served in that position until 1973. In 1973 he took on a new role as director of the Department of the History of Medicine and became Hopkins' chief historian and archivist. Victor McKusick wrote at the time of Harvey's death, "He is in the firmament of stars in American medicine. He was a sage of medicine, whose wisdom and insight were profound."*

A S ONE MARVELS AT THE ACCOMPLISHMENTS of the Golden Age of Medicine we live in, it is natural to wonder how they came about. Who were the physicians of the past with the creative spirit and drive to bring this Golden Age into being? Most of us have either never known about or have forgotten those whose contributions have over the years enriched medicine with new tools and new outlooks. The total pool of medical knowledge has been accumulated by the energies of many. Their work has not only established the major principles of clinical medical science, but has accumulated an enormous mass of information about the natural history and mechanisms of disease, the basic heritage of every physician. Many of the most important clinical tools that we make use of in our daily practice were discovered by men who had only the simplest of facilities to work with, and who had to overcome centuries of medical tradition, which made the introduction of new ideas difficult.

The contributions of the great physicians to be portrayed in this essay are clear evidence that creative scholarship in our everyday professional life can be productive of important new knowledge. The accomplishments of Sydenham, Laennec, Auenbrugger, Louis, Wünderlich, Billings, Osler, and Peabody should encourage each of us to rise above the routines of the daily ward rounds and clinics and to see in every patient an opportunity not only to serve mankind in the best tradition of medical excellence, but to add to the store of medical knowledge as these creative masters did.

Out of the dark ages: The births of modern medical science

The seventeenth century found medicine in an ambivalent state. Practitioners clearly sensed that the traditional Galenic concepts were inadequate, but as yet no practical substitute had been provided for them.[3] Most centers of learning still remained true to the old Classical and Arabian authors and their theories were still stoutly defended. Medical practice was in a confused state, but progress, while it may be impeded by human failings, can never be completely arrested. Fortunately, every patient is to the dedicated physician a stimulus to improve his capacity to aid the sick, and the impetus for change came from the simple efforts of a practitioner imbued with this drive to creative scholarship:

Thomas Sydenham. Born in 1624 in Dorset, where his family had been settled since the reign of Henry VIII, Thomas Sydenham was sent to Oxford at the age of 18. When the Great Rebellion broke out, his family all served in the Parliamentary Army. After the Civil War was over, he took up medicine as a profession and was granted his bachelor of medicine degree from Oxford in 1648. He rejoined the militia during Oliver Cromwell's campaign in Scotland against Charles II, not as a surgeon but as a captain in the cavalry. After the death of Cromwell and the coming of the Restoration in 1660 his political ties were ended. He had no resource other than a serious devotion to the practice of medicine, an event with important benefits to all succeeding generations of physicians. He went for a "brush-up" period to Montpellier, and, returning to London in 1661, he entered the practice of medicine, after passing with considerable difficulty in 1663 the examination of the Royal College of Physicians.[3]

Sydenham confined himself to the immediate observation of clinical phenomena. He was a close friend of the philosopher, John Locke, as well as an admirer of Francis Bacon. Bacon, in his book, *Advancement of Learning*, had noted two ways in which he thought medical science might be enhanced. First, he suggested a revival of Hippocrates' ancient method of recording an account of the various cases with their course towards recovery or death so that through such observations the description of diseases might be amplified and extended. Second, he emphasized that the pathological changes in the organs, the "footsteps of diseases," should be studied by anatomical investigations and the findings compared with the manifestations of disease during life. Many had begun to plough the anatomical-pathological field, but the fertile field of bedside observation remained almost virgin soil. It was Thomas Sydenham who first gave clinical observation its place of honor as a scientific method. His great contribution was that he turned attention toward particular illnesses.

Sydenham emphasized the importance of special pathology. He concentrated on the study of specific diseases and tried to discern how they make themselves perceptible to the physician in the individual patient. Where Hippocrates wrote the histories of sick people, Sydenham wrote the history of individual diseases. Thus, it was simple observation by a mind steeped in creative scholarship that put medicine back on the rails at this critical juncture in its long history.[3]

Sydenham improved the existing nosology by reviving and developing two taxonomic concepts, which are today referred to as cluster and temporal correlation. In the concept of cluster, often used medically to designate a syndrome, several individual manifestations are combined to form a single entity or disease. In the concept of temporal correlation, a "disease" is named not just according to its immediate manifestations but according to the correlated pattern of its evolving clinical course, or natural history. As examples, Sydenham descriptively separated the clustered temporal pattern of gout with its self-limited episodes from the individual entities that had been called rheumatism, and the cluster of measles with its non-repetitive transiency from what had been called exanthemata. A disease had become recognized for the first time as an entity in which specific clinical manifestations caused by specific anatomic abnormalities could evolve in a specific course and might be cured by a specific therapeutic agent.[3] As well summarized by his friend, John Locke:

> I wonder that after the pattern Dr. Sydenham has set them of a better way, men should return again to that romance way of Physick. But I see it is easier and more natural for men to build castles in the air of their own, than to survey well those that are to be found standing. Nicely to observe the history of diseases, in all these changes and circumstances, is a work of time, accurateness, attention and judgement.

In 1745, **Gerhard Van Swieten** was summoned from Leyden by the Empress Maria Teresa to revitalize medical studies in Vienna, and he proceeded to establish clinical teaching on a sound basis of observation. Van Swieten was strongly influenced by the precepts of Sydenham and of Hermann Boerhaave, who had fostered bedside teaching. The Vienna School prospered during the next half century, but its most important product was **Leopold Auenbrugger**. As it became more obvious that diseases have an organic basis and that anatomical changes are a decisive feature of disease processes, the interest grew in ways of recognizing these changes not just by the pathological anatomist, but in the living patient.[6] Invention being the offspring of necessity, it was the common practice in those days simply to tap a barrel with one's finger when there was need to know how much wine was in it. Auenbrugger, the son of an innkeeper, had seen his father perform this procedure on many occasions. The human thorax in certain respects resembles a wine barrel; normally the lungs are filled with air but in certain disease states they are filled with denser material. When the barrel is full of wine the note on tapping is dull or low pitched while when empty it is resonant or high pitched. Similarly, the lung is normally high pitched. When fluid or consolidation is present, the percussive sound is low pitched. Auenbrugger studied under Van Swieten and from 1751 to 1762 worked at the Spanish Hospital in Vienna. While there he began his experiments with percussion and soon was able to distinguish three chief percussion tones: normal pulmonary resonance, a dullness on percussion associated with consolidation or fluid, and the higher pitched tone produced by percussion over the larynx.[6]

He revealed his discovery on New Year's Eve, 1760, after seven years of patient work, by the publication of his *Inventum Novum ex Percussione*. In the preface he stated:

> Convinced by personal experience, I contend that the sign about which this book treats is of the utmost importance, not only for diagnosis, but also for the treatment of diseases, so that it ranks in value immediately after the examination of the pulse and the breathing. I contend that an abnormal tone in the thorax is, in every disease, a certain sign of the existence of serious danger.

In the next year, 1761, **Giovanni Morgagni's** great treatise on pathological anatomy was published. These two contributions were both important to rapidly advancing anatomical concepts of disease. Morgagni laid the foundations of pathological anatomy and Auenbrugger those of anatomical diagnosis. It was not, however, until the beginning of the nineteenth century that the true importance of his discovery was realized.

The great French physician, **J. N. Corvisart**, learned of Auenbrugger's great discovery when he translated Stoll's Aphorisms. [*Stoll's Aphorisms*. Translated by Jean Nicholas Corvisart (dedicated to Lepreux). Paris, 1797.] For the next twenty years he practiced percussion, and from that time on it formed an inseparable part of the clinical examination. In 1808 Corvisart made a fresh translation of Auenbrugger's booklet, expanding it from 95 to 440 pages. He made it possible for this imaginative but simple discovery to bear rich fruit.[6]

Centuries before this, the Hippocratic school had pointed out that certain ill people had strange noises that could be heard in their chests. These early Greek physicians vividly described instances in which "it bubbles like boiled vinegar" or "it creaks like a new leather strap." However, these observations were forgotten until physicians began to think of disease in anatomical terms. In the nineteenth century in France, when imaginative efforts were being made to discern anatomical changes in the living patient, such sounds became of great interest. Doctors found that by applying an ear to the front of the chest, they could hear the heart sounds.[6]

René Théophile Hyacinthe Laënnec, a pupil of Corvisart, enthusiastically pursued this manner of listening to the sounds within the thorax. By 1816, when he was appointed physician-in-chief to the Necker Hospital, he had developed a special interest in diseases of the chest. He well knew the great disadvantages of direct auscultation in the uncleansed or obese patient! On his way one day to visit a very obese lady with heart disease in whom, try as he might, he could not hear the heart sounds, he was crossing the courtyard of the Louvre. Children were playing on a heap of old timber stored in a corner of the yard. One of the pieces of wood was a long beam. One youngster had his ear at one end of it, and another was signaling to him by tapping the other end. It is said that the idea came in a flash. Laënnec hastened to the ward and obtained a piece of letter paper. Rolling this into a cylinder, he applied one end to the site of the cardiac impulse and listened at the other. The result was beyond all expectation. Then he listened over other parts of the thorax, and the intensity of the breath sounds astounded him. A new technique of physical examination had been discovered and he proceeded to devote all his energies to its development.

For the next three years he worked continuously making clinical observations and checking the results by autopsy. In 1819 the results were published in two large volumes—his *Traite de L'Auscultation Mediate et des Maladies des Poumons et du Coeur*.[6] Thus, in a dramatic way Laënnec brought to fruition the prophetic prediction made by Robert Hook in 1705:

> Who knows but that one may discover the works performed in the several offices and shops of a man's body by the sound they make, and thereby discover what instrument or engine is out of order.

The School of Medicine that flourished in Paris in the first half of the nineteenth century has usually been referred to as the pathologico-anatomical school. Its contributions to pathological anatomy were great, but it was most importantly a hospital-based school in which anatomy was used effectively to establish clinical advances. . . .Teaching and research were transplanted from the lecture room to the hospital ward and clinical observation with anatomical correlation reached its peak. . . .The opportunity for making careful observations at the bedside and at the postmortem tables caused hospital work to quickly gain a new significance.[1]

In the first half of the nineteenth century this mecca in Paris was a stellar attraction for young American students of medicine who received their greatest inspiration and stimulus from **Pierre-Charles-Alexander Louis**. It was Louis who first effectively applied the statistical method to clinical investigation. Louis was born on April 11, 1787. After finishing his medical course he spent three restless years in Russia and then settled in Odessa. Three years later, experience with an epidemic of diphtheria emphasized his shortcomings to him and he returned to Paris for further study. His classmate, Chomel, offered him the facilities of two of his wards in La Charito, a famous Paris hospital, as well as the privilege of performing autopsies. For the next six years he worked incessantly. The methods of approach that Louis employed and that entitled him to be designated perhaps as the first full-time clinical investigator were five in number:

(1) When the patient fell ill, an endeavor was made to find what state of health he was in previously . . . his age, occupation, residence, and manner of living. He was also questioned as to previous accidents that might have influenced his present disease, and his family history was thoroughly investigated.

(2) The history of the present illness was sought, its initial and later symptoms, and the order of their occurrence as well as all symptoms, no matter of what importance, and their degree and severity.

(3) The findings in the disease were then carefully sought from the patient's statements and the doctor's examination.

(4) A careful observation and record of the patient's clinical manifestations was made until he was restored to health or until his death.

(5) In fatal cases an autopsy was secured and the facts there found were carefully observed and recorded.

Thus, we see the extension of the approach initiated by Sydenham and the outlines of our present day technique of clinical examination.

Louis was the first to apply statistics to the evaluation of therapy, showing that blood letting did not cure acute diseases, especially pneumonia. This led not just to reform but to a real revolution in medical practice. Oliver Wendell Holmes reminisced in later years of his experiences with Louis as a young student:

> He especially taught us two things: 1) Always make sure that you form a distinct and clear idea of the matter you are considering. 2) Always avoid vague approximations where exact estimates are possible. Louis taught us who followed him the love of truth, the habit of passionless listenings to the teachings of nature, the most careful and searching methods of observation, and the sure means of getting at the results to be obtained from them in the constant employment of accurate tabulation. He was a man of lofty and admirable scientific character, and his work will endure in its influence long after his name is lost sight of save to the faded eyes of the student of medical literature.

Louis's contributions have not received the credit they deserve as subsequent evaluation of them has centered on his use of the "numerical method." However, it was Louis who developed the systematic approach to the accumulation of clinical evidence that forms the base of our present clinical procedures.[1,5]

Sanctorius, with a very primitive instrument, was the first to make measurements of body temperature. Boerhaave and Anton de Haen used the thermometer in their respective clinics and Andral, one of the older members of the Paris School, advocated clinical thermometry in 1841. An American, Elisa North, in his book on cerebrospinal fever published in 1811, had recommended the use of the clinical thermometer in the study of fevers. However, it was **Carl August Wünderlich** who first studied the fever curves in various diseases and noted that each of the specific infections had its characteristic pattern on the temperature chart. Born in 1815, Wünderlich was the son of a physician. In 1850 he became the head of the Leipzig Medical Clinic. It was here that he began his observations in clinical thermometry. He published many papers on the subject, and in 1868 his book entitled *Ueber Das Verhalten Der Eigen Warme in Krankheiten* appeared. He was an admirable teacher and a man of vision who made a fundamental contribution to the objective recording of the clinical evidence of disease.[6]

In this country, the development of the Johns Hopkins University and Hospital at Baltimore played a unique role in the evolution of medicine. As far as the construction of the medical faculty was concerned, something entirely new was to be created. It was to be a "focus of medical research, and clinical instruction and laboratory work were to be the important activities rather than attendance at lectures." It was appreciated that the future of the institution depended largely on the selection of the medical staff, and when they successfully recruited **William Osler**, the future of Johns Hopkins and medicine in the United States was secured.

. . . Those early years at Johns Hopkins were unique in medical history. All the workers were young and enthusiastic, and the chief had the knowledge and appreciation of the fundamental heritage represented by those basic contributions already described. For the first time, they were all put together as the complete goals of a medical clinic and the results were revolutionary.[2,5,6]

The formal opening of the Johns Hopkins Hospital took place on May 7, 1889, a time of flood tide in the natural sciences. Biology, physics, and chemistry had participated in the great rise. Medicine was beginning to apply to its own development the fruits of knowledge from the fundamental sciences. A number of special medical sciences were already in being, such as as anatomy, embryology, physiology, physiological chemistry, pharmacology, and pathology. These sciences were ready to serve as the base upon which the edifice of clinical science could be built. For the first time there was in the United States a well-endowed hospital as an integral part of the medical school of an endowed university. Furthermore, in all of its departments, top priority was given to an interest in original research. The hospital offered better facilities for the organization and conduct of clinical work than had ever before been available in America. Thus, the opportunity was unique, and William Osler was equal to the task. The medical clinic that he organized revolutionized medical teaching. For Osler, the welfare of the patients who came to the clinic for diagnosis and treatment had the highest priority; next came into consideration how undergraduate and graduate students could best be taught; and finally, came solicitude that every opportunity for contributing to the advancement of our knowledge of internal medicine should be eagerly seized. The principles he fixed upon and the methods he chose to illustrate them were derived from many sources including most importantly those which have already been alluded to. He synthesized many diverse elements into a harmonious and productive whole; revolutionary in its own time and yet plastic enough to adapt to the new needs of future development.

What was this magnificent plan of organization and how was it managed?

"One important element of success in the new clinic was the arrangement for a graded staff."[2] Out of this evolved the system of residency training, which has perhaps contributed more to the success story of American medicine than any other single factor. The basic feature was a whole-time resident staff among the members of which the responsibilities of the work were divided. The resident physician and the assistant resident physicians as well as the interns lived in the hospital and were thus available around the clock. The physician-in-chief as well as the other members of the faculty lived out but were available for teaching and consultation on a daily basis. The resident staff consisted of two groups:

(1) a lower resident staff constituted by the medical interns appointed for a single year, usually on graduation with high standing from the medical school; and

(2) an upper resident staff made up of the resident physician and several assistant resident physicians, usually men of exceptional promise. These were men who had served as hospital interns and who were willing to enter upon a more or less prolonged resident service often of several years' duration, in order to secure the best possible training for the "higher walks" of internal medicine. The upper staff was chosen partly from the lower staff; with the remainder, in order to prevent in-breeding, from other hospitals.

It was in November 1926, after he knew that he had cancer, that **Francis Peabody** added a significant contribution to our medical heritage—a lecture to the students at the Harvard Medical School entitled "The Care of the Patient." This penetrating description of the human qualities, which are just as important as all of the medical knowledge needed by the doctor, should be on every physician's desk. Peabody's place in American medicine is supported by many important contributions but none more important than this superb message about the hospital practice of medicine.[7]

The concluding paragraph epitomized the creed of Francis Peabody as well as an essential commandment of the complete physician:

> The good physician knows his patients through and through, and his knowledge is bought dearly. Time, sympathy, and understanding must be lavishly dispensed, but the reward is to be found in that personal bond which forms the greatest satisfaction of the practice of medicine. One of the essential qualities of the clinician is interest in humanity, for the secret of the care of the patient is in caring for the patient.

I believe that the basic tools and concepts that we use in the pursuit of scientifically oriented medical practice stand out more vividly for us when cloaked in the robes of their historical origins. I hope this essay will serve in some measure to stimulate future physicians to sample the "joy and satisfaction of seeking new truths." It has been correctly emphasized that chance may present to the most obscure practitioner, remote from a University Medical Center, an opportunity for observation that the greatest master may never meet.

References

In the preparation of this lecture generous use was made of the following source material:

1. Ackerknect EH. Medicine at the Paris Hospital, 1794-1848. Baltimore, The Johns Hopkins Press, 1967.
2. Barker LF. Osler as Chief of a Medical Clinic. Bull. J. Hopkins Hospital XXX: 189, 1919.
3. Dewhurst K. Dr. Thomas Sydenham (1624–1689), His Life and Original Writings. London, The Weilcome Historical Medical Library, 1966.
4. Garrison FH. John Shaw Billings, a Memoir. New York and London, G. P. Putnam's Sons, 1915.
5. Greenwood M. The Medical Dictator and other Biographical Studies. London, Williams and Norgate, Ltd., 1936.
6. Sigerist HE. Great Doctors, a Biographical History of Medicine. London, George Allen and Unwin, Ltd., 1933.
7. Williams TF. Cabot, Peabody, and the Care of the Patient. Bull. Hist. Med. 24:462–81, 1950.

PIERRE CHARLES-ALEXANDRE LOUIS: THE IMPACT OF A CLINICAL TRIAL

ALFRED YANKAUER, M.D., M.P.H.
(Spring 1996, pp. 15–19)

The author (AΩA, Harvard Medical School, 1938) is professor of Family and Community Medicine and Pediatrics at the University of Massachusetts Medical Center. After college at Dartmouth, he received his medical training at Harvard and the College of Physicians and Surgeons of Columbia University. A prior contributor to The Pharos, *he served as director of maternal and child health for the New York State Health Department from 1952 to 1961 and as an advisor to the World Health Organization, prior to assuming his present responsibilities. Among his literary achievements is translation of poetry from Spanish to English. One of the first properties in the West Virginia Conservancy was donated by Dr. Yankauer and his family.*

Let us bestow upon observation the care and time which it demands; let the facts be rigorously analyzed in order to a just appreciation of them; and it is impossible to attain this without classifying and counting them; and then therapeutics will advance not less steadily than other branches of science.[1, pp. 64–65]

Let those, who engage hereafter in the study of therapeutics, . . . labor to demonstrate, rigorously, the influence and the degree of influence of any therapeutic agent on the duration, progress, and termination of a particular disease. Let them not forget that nothing is more difficult, than to verify a fact of this nature; that it can be effected only by means of an extensive series of observations, collected with exactness.[1, pp. 96–97]

A T THE FIRST ANNUAL MEETING OF the American Medical Association, in 1848, Oliver Wendell Holmes, one of its founders, presented the report of the Committee on Medical Literature.[2] Dr. Holmes was chairman of the committee, and the wit and clarity of the report suggest that he wrote it as well. The committee noted that many articles reappeared in the same form in different journals: "The ring of editors sit in each other's laps, with perfect propriety, and great convenience it is true, but with a wonderful saving in the article of furniture."[2, p.50] The committee also noted that the paucity of original studies by American authors, and that "translations . . . are with few exceptions from the French and have naturalized many of the best practical authors of that country."[2, p. 53]

Holmes, like many of his American contemporaries, had spent two years in Paris as a young man. One of the French physicians frequently translated and quoted in the American medical literature during the first half of the nineteenth century was Pierre Charles-Alexandre Louis. There are frequent references to and letters about the writings of Louis in the two oldest extant American medical journals, the *Boston Medical and Surgical Journal* (now the *New England Journal of Medicine*) and the *American Journal of the Medical Sciences*.[3, p. 96]

Louis was one of the several French physicians responsible for what Richard H. Shryock has termed the emergence of modern medicine.[4] The French Revolution had swept away past privileges and beliefs and abolished the curriculum of medical schools of the *ancien regime* with its lectures in Latin commenting on Hippocrates and Galen.[5, pp. 115–20] The new curriculum emphasized clinical teaching and hospital experience that combined medicine and surgery for the first time. The advent of surgery led naturally to an interest in anatomy and pathological anatomy. Observation, rather than theory, the basis for this new approach, attempted to classify diseases by relating symptoms to gross anatomical changes.

Jean Nicolas Corvisart, who became Napoleon's personal physician, translated Leopold Auenbrugger's neglected 1761 discovery of percussion and popularized the method. A few years later René Théophile Hyacinthe Laënnec, a pupil of Corvisart, invented the stethoscope. Physical examination findings added to medical history taking and greatly enhanced the ability to relate observations in life to those in death. The basis of modern clinical medicine was established.

The classification of disease reflected a broader philosophic change in what it meant to have a disease. In the older tradition (with few exceptions, such as smallpox) all illness was explained as a constitutional problem, a loss of vitality, with symptoms varying because of individual susceptibilities or living conditions rather than caused by a specific identifiable disease. The excitement of a new and different approach to medicine drew physicians from all over continental Europe, England, and America to study in Paris; its influence carried over into related fields as well. William Farr, England's legendary medical statistician, drew on his Parisian experience to classify causes of death as specific disease entities, thus establishing the basis of modern vital statistics.[6]

The new movement in France was fortunate in the institutional structure that supported it. The Industrial Revolution and its accompanying urban migration had led to the growth of hospitals. The French revolutionary reform had converted hospitals from places to care for paupers, orphans, the elderly, and the infirm to places for the practice of medicine and surgery. The thirty hospitals of Paris with their 20,000 patients in 1830 provided a rich source of material for the practice of the new clinical medicine.[5, pp. 15–24] Thus, the hospital became the teaching center for medicine, and has remained so for the last century and a half.

Pierre Charles-Alexandre Louis was born in 1787 in Aix on the Marne river. He began the study of law, but abandoned it for medicine. After initial study in Rheims he completed his medical studies in the newly oriented Parisian medical school, where one of his mentors was Laennec. He received a Doctor of Medicine degree in 1817, and shortly thereafter was persuaded to go to Russia, settling in Odessa, where he received an honorary title of physician to the czar for that region. In the last year of his stay in Odessa, a diphtheria epidemic with a high mortality rate in children apparently convinced him of his lack of knowledge. He returned to Paris, determined to continue his studies.[7]

In Paris, at the age of thirty-four, Louis became what is probably the first full-time medical resident physician. For nearly seven years he eschewed private practice and worked full time in the wards of *l'Hopital de la Charite* and *l'Hopital de la Pitie*. He was his own teacher, examining hospital patients, performing his own autopsies (virtually all hospital deaths were autopsied), and recording all the details in a form that could be summarized statistically. He remained a hospital physician the rest of his professional life, never becoming a medical school faculty member. Nevertheless, he was an immensely popular medical teacher. American students particularly were drawn to him.[8]

During these seven years, Louis published several articles statistically summarizing the symptoms, signs, and pathological findings of various clinical entities. His first book (1825) collecting several such articles dealt with phthisis (tuberculosis), clearly establishing that its diverse symptoms and signs were all part of a single disease manifested by the presence of tubercles.[9] Seventy years later William Osler recommended the book as still of great value.[8] Although his skill as a pathologist (microscopes were not used) was recognized by all his contemporaries, even those who disagreed with his views, Louis must also have been an excellent clinician. In his preface to his book *Researches on Phthisis*, Louis wrote:

> . . . . [I]f we wish to discover whether the patient experienced pain . . . on either side of the chest, we mentioned first the side where we supposed the pain did not exist; if he then indicated the other side . . . we regarded the fact as certain. . . .

> For the determination of dates . . . we [asked] the patient not if he had experienced such a symptom from such a time, but how long he had experienced it.[9, p. 28]

His next major publication, in 1829, dealt with the disase known by many names: "gastroenteritis, putrid fever, adynamic atoxic typhoid, etc."[10] He differentiated typhoid fever from the other fevers with which it was confused by the inevitable presence of Peyer's patches and the frequent presence of rose spots.

In these two books, Louis developed what he termed the numerical method *(méthode numerique)*, an essentially Baconian approach to medicine, skeptical of all theories, ignoring hypotheses, and basing practice on the results of a series of observations that could be grouped and analyzed statistically. He had applied this method to studies detailing the characteristics of a series of cases of two of the most important diseases of the time. In describing the rationale of the numerical method, Charles Cowan, the translator of Louis's book on phthisis, wrote:

> Hitherto we have satisfied ourselves with the authority of experience, and its currency in medicine is such, that any distinct definition of its value has scarcely been attempted.[9, p. 28]

Probably the most disastrous therapy in the history of medicine was the practice of bloodletting, sometimes administered to such an extent that patients fainted; the practice was based on nothing more than tradition and "experience." Louis's next important contribution was the application of his numerical method to assessing the effect of bleeding on the outcome of cases of pneumonia, a disease in which bleeding was believed to be particularly efficacious. In doing so, Louis took on the leading figure of Parisian medicine, Francois Joseph Broussais, an ardent champion of bleeding.[12]

Broussais was the last of the great systematizers, expounders of the traditional constitutional view of disease. He attempted to reduce all diseases to a single factor, to make order out of chaos, as Isaac Newton had done. He had termed his system "physiological medicine" and placed the cause of all fevers in lesions of the gastrointestinal tract. Hence, all fevers were to be treated by bleeding to reduce the capillary engorgement and by a liquid diet that would not irritate the gastrointestinal lesions. This prescription is exactly the one followed by Honore de Balzac's community-minded "country doctor" in 1829.[13] In 1833, France is reported to have imported 41,654,300 leeches.[14]

In the elegant words of Oliver Wendell Holmes:

> At the time when Broussais erected his system, the characters of inflammation, especially as affecting the mucous tissues, were so little comprehended, that the whole fabric of our science tottered for a time before his audacious statements. A few vascular arborizations, . . . a little redness from cadaveric changes, were enough to demonstrate the existence of gastritis or gastro-enteritis, and all the dogmas, and all the practical inferences belonging to the so-called physiological system, followed in the wake of this error in observation. The subtlety of his reasoning and the hissing vehemence of his style, effervescent as acids upon marble, aided the temporary triumph of his doctrine. Whatever others have done for its downfall, the deathblow came from the scalpel of Louis . . . , and from that

moment the empire of Broussais began to dissolve. . . . The physiological system, as a whole, passed away, and with it a mode of practice founded upon false principles, and often leading to dangerous practical conclusions.[15, pp. 290–291]

The place bleeding held in the therapeutic armamentarium of the time can also be judged by the words of James Jackson, Sr., in his preface to Louis's book on bloodletting:

If any thing may be regarded as settled in the treatment of diseases, it is that bloodletting is useful in the class of diseases called inflammatory; and especially in inflammations of the thoracic viscera.[16, p. 5]

Louis's own words introducing his studies reflect the same thoughts:

The results of my researches on the effects of bloodletting in inflammation, are so little in accordance with the general opinion, that it is not without a degree of hesitation I have decided to publish them.[1, p. 1]

In his first publication on bloodletting, Louis reported on seventy-eight cases of pneumonia, twenty-eight of which were fatal, thirty-three cases of erysipelas, and thirty-six cases of tonsillitis. He later repeated the studies in another hospital, recording results of thirty-three cases of pneumonia with four deaths, and eleven cases of erysipelas. The book, whose English translation Dr. Jackson introduced, contains the reports of the two sets of cases and Louis's rebuttal of theoretical objections raised to the numerical method. An appendix contains Dr. Jackson's retrospective and less than satisfactory review of thirty-four cases of pneumonitis from the casebooks of the Massachusetts General Hospital.[16]

In all his cases, Louis had carefully recorded and tallied the age and sex of patients, the day of onset of the disease, the day patient was bled, the amount bled, the treatments given, the symptoms and signs each day, the duration of the illness, and its outcome. He defined each of these variables carefully.

In the cases of erysipelas and tonsillitis, bloodletting had no effect on symptoms, signs, or duration of disease, no matter when the patient was bled. In the cases of pneumonia, Louis concluded that mild bleeding (a pint or less) early in the disease may have shortened its duration but had no effect on symptoms, signs, or mortality. Bleeding later in the course of disease had no effect on duration. He ruled out the effects of confounding variables after finding that they were present in similar proportions in the two groups being compared (exceptions noted below):

Indeed what was to be done in order to know whether bloodletting had any favorable influence on pneumonitis, and the extent of that influence? Evidently to ascertain whether, other things being equal, the patients who were bled on the first, second, third or fourth day, recovered more readily or in greater numbers, then those bled at a later period.[1, p. 55]

Louis's conclusions would not stand up to today's peer review. They were based on data dredging, and *post hoc* viewing of proportions bled on the first two days of disease in one data set and the first four days of disease in the second set. If he had combined the two series there would have been little difference in disease duration regardless of day bled. Case fatality rates were higher in those bled early, a finding Louis noted and explained by the substantially older ages of those who died. He explained the differences in the case fatality rates of the two series by the fact that survivors in the second series were treated with antimony. Almost all of the differences in proportion on which his conclusions were based have wide confidence intervals with lower bounds below one and fail to meet conventional statistical significance. Louis was aware of the importance of adequate numbers, however, and never claimed that his conclusions were the last words of scientific truth. Even today the data in his major opus make out a strong case against bloodletting as a useful therapy.

Inevitably, Louis's method as well as the conclusions he drew from his analyses were controversial. They were challenged at meetings of the French Academy of Sciences and Academy of Medicine.[17] In 1837, Louis and two of his colleagues had reported that purgation was superior to bleeding in cases of typhoid fever. This observation precipitated a heated debated in which the numerical method was attacked as unsuited to the "art" of medicine, which depended on treating each patient as a unique individual rather than following a rigid regimen set by statistics; this argument against fixed protocols of diagnosis or therapy can still be heard today.

Louis's only son developed tuberculosis in 1853 and died the following year. His son's loss affected him deeply; perhaps he even blamed himself. In any case, he retired from his prestigious hospital position in 1854, although remaining active as a consultant. He died in 1872 at the age of eighty-five.

Louis's contributions to the advance of medicine lie in establishing the value of statistics in the study of disease and in his disproof of the therapeutic value of bleeding, leeches, and vesication (blistering) still widely practiced at the time. The effect of these contributions was summarized in 1862 by Austin Flint, the dean of American internists, who knew Louis only through his published writings:

> If we were to specify circumstances which have more especially been instrumental in leading to the principle of conservatism, we would mention, first, the abandonment of the attempt to found a system or theory of medicine after the decline and fall of Brunonianism and Broussaisism, and second, the study of diseases after the numerical method with reference to their natural history and law.[18, p. 137]

Flint's paper was aptly titled "Conservative Medicine." It summarized the vast changes that had occurred in the practice of medicine during the preceding quarter of a century, and extolled the value of the healing processes of nature and the conservative physician's maxim to do no harm. Indeed, there were few drugs other than opium and quinine (for malaria) whose value could stand up under scrutiny. Skepticism had become the order of the day; therapeutic nihilism on the one hand and homeopathic medicine on the other hand soon followed.

The nimble wit of Oliver Wendell Holmes characterized the prevailing attitude of mainstream medicine for a good part of the rest of the century:

> I firmly believe that if all the whole materia medica, as now used, could be sunk to the bottom of the sea, it would be all the better for mankind— and all the worse for the fishes.[15, p. 39]

Louis's influence was particularly felt in the United States. Not only were his publications translated and widely read, but the American physicians who studied under his direction became the leaders of American medicine for a good part of the nineteenth century. In 1897, William Osler described Louis's contributions and his enormous influence on the Americans who studied in Paris.[8] Osler was able to list the names of thirty-seven Americans who had studied in Paris between 1830 and 1840. They included seven from Boston, seven from New York, and fifteen from Philadelphia, the three leading medical centers in the United States. In addition to Holmes, many of the names (James Jackson, Henry I. Bowditch, George C. Shattuck, John Collins Warren, in Boston; Casper W. Pennock, Alfred Still & William W. Gerhard, William Pepper, in Philadelphia) are still familiar to us.

In addition to disposing of harmful therapies, Louis, in the last chapter of his book on bloodletting, answered his critics in a brilliant and often sarcastic fashion. In doing so he laid down many of the principles that govern the modern clinical trial. In recognizing the tentative nature of his conclusions and the need for a large number of cases, even the concept of multisite, multiauthored trials was foretold by James Jackson, Sr., at the end of his appendix to Louis's studies of bloodletting: "Ten hospitals, under the care of honest physicians, may settle the questions discussed in this work within five years."[16, p. 171]

Blinding, randomization, and placebo controls were not available to Louis. Even if feasible, an imagined institutional review board of the time would have deemed randomization and placebos unethical. "Blinding is sometimes impossible in clinical trials, and its absence need not negate valid results."[19]

The clinical trial, in its broadest sense, was not a new phenomenon in Louis's day. Examples abound in the Ancient and Renaissance world. An interesting account with a distinctly modern flavor is chronicled in the Book of Daniel. Daniel persuaded the steward of Nebuchadnezzar's chief eunuch to allow him and his companions, Shadrach (Hananiah), Meshack (Mishael), and Abednego (Azariah), to shun the king's "rich food" for ten days and subsist on vegetables. At the end of this time, Daniel and his three vegetarian companions were "better in appearance and fatter in flesh" than the other youths who had eaten the kings "rich food" (Dan. 1.1–16 RSV). James Lind's approach to the treatment of scurvy in 1747 involved only three patients fed lemons and oranges compared to nine others on varied regimens; yet, it clearly established the benefits of citrus fruits.[20] Louis, however, described, defended and promoted the method of comparative statistics as a way of advancing knowledge in the field of medical practice, although he had never considered it as a philosophy. Indeed, as also for his teacher Laënnec, theories and philosophizing were an abomination. It took one of Louis's many American proteges, Elisha Bartlett, to conceptualize and systematize Louis's approach in two books, both dedicated to his teacher: *An Essay on the Philosophy of Medical Science*, and *The History, Diagnosis and Treatment of Typhoid and Typhus Fever*. Bartlett's first exposition asserts, in a nutshell, that all medical science consists of facts ascertained by observation, independent of theory, doctrines, or induction; facts alone may yield themselves to relationships and to classification, the basis of the numerical method.[21]

This focus on observable clinical and gross pathological phenomena with its avoidance of theory was a necessary step in the overthrow of unproven theories that had dominated medicine for so long, and that now seem so absurd. In its neglect of hypotheses and causality, its insistence on purely clinical and autopsy observation, and its failure to admit microscopy and chemistry into its lexicon, however, the numerical method sowed the seeds of its own destruction. With a few notable French exceptions (Francois Magendie, his pupil Claude Bernard, and Louis Pasteur and his followers, who emerged later), laboratory medicine succeeded simple clinical medicine as the next stage in the advance to modern medicine, and the initiative passed from France to Germany.

Nevertheless, Louis's application of his numerical method to clinical trials may have had a more profound effect on medical therapeutics than has any clinical trial since that time. As the prolix but inimitable Oliver Wendell Holmes stated in his farewell address to Harvard Medical School students in 1882:

> You young men who are following the hospitals hardly know how much you are indebted to Louis. I say nothing of his Researches on Phthisis or his great work on Typhoid Fever. But I consider his modest and brief Essay on Bleeding in some Inflammatory Diseases, based on cases carefully observed and numerically analyzed, one of the most important written contributions to practical medicine, to the treatment of internal disease, of this century, if not since the day of Sydenham.[22, p. 432]

References

1. Louis PC-A. Researches on the Effects of Bloodletting in Some Inflammatory Diseases,

and on the Influence of Tartarized Antimony and Vesication in Pneumonitis, Putnam, CG, trans. Boston, Hilliard, Gray & Co., 1836.

2. Holmes OW. Report of the Committee on Medical Literature. In Brieger, GH, ed.: Medical America in the Nineteenth Century: Readings from the Literature, pp. 45–54. Baltimore, Johns Hopkins Press, 1972.

3. Bollet AJ. Pierre Louis: The numerical method and the foundation of quantitative medicine. Am J Med Sci 266:92–101, 1973.

4. Shryock RH. Chap. 9: The emergence of modern medicine 1800–1850. In The Development of Modern Medicine, pp. 151–69. New York, Alfred A. Knopf, 1947.

5. Ackerknecht EH. Medicine at the Paris Hospital. 1794–1848. Baltimore, Johns Hopkins Press, 1967.

6. Hamlin C. Could you starve to death in England in 1839? The Chadwick-Farr controversy and the loss of "social" in public health. Am J Public Health 85:856–66, 1995.

7. Steiner WR. Dr. Pierre-Charles-Alexander Louis, a distinguished Parisian teacher of American medical students. Ann Med Hist, 3rd ser. 2:451–60. 1940.

8. Osler W. Influence of Louis on American medicine. Bull Johns Hopkins Hosp 8:161–67, 1897.

9. Louis PC-A. Pathological Researches on Phthisis. Cowan C, trans. Washington, Duff Green, 1836.

10. Louis P. Anatomic, pathologic, and therapeutic research on the disease known by the name of gastroenteritis, putrid fever, adynamic atoxic typhoid, etc. Am J Med Sci 4:403, 1829.

11. Cowan C. Translator's introduction. In Lous, Pathological Researches, pp. 9–26.

12. Ackerknecht EH. Broussais, or a forgotten medical revolution. Bull Hist Med 27:320–43, 1953.

13. de Balzac H. The Country Doctor, Marriage, F, trans. New York, A.L. Burt Co., 1920, p. 115.

14. Kratzmann E. Die neure Medizin in Frankreich, nach Theorie und Praxis. Leipzig, 1846, p. 52. Cited in Ackernecht, Medicine at the Paris Hospital, p. 62.

15. Holmes OW. Currents and Counter-Currents in Medical Science with Other Addresses and Essays. Boston, Ticknor & Fields, 1861.

16. Jackson J, Sr. Preface and Appendix. In Louis, Researches on the Effects of Bloodletting, pp. I–xxvii, and pp. 99–171.

17. Murphy TD. Medical knowledge and statistical methods in early nineteenth-century France. Med Hist 25:301–19, 1981.

18. Flint A. Conservative medicine. In Brieger GH, ed.: Medical America in the Nineteenth Century. Readings from the Literature, pp. 134–42. Baltimore, Johns Hopkins Press, 1972.

19. Blinded by science. Editorial. Lancet 343:553–54, 1994.

20. Lilienfeld AM. Ceteris paribus: The evolution of the clinical trial. Bull Hist Med 56:1–18, 1982.

21. Ackerknecht EH. Elisha Bartlett and the philosophy of the Paris clinical school. Bull Hist Med 24:43–60, 1950.

22. Holmes OW. Some of my early teachers. In Medical Essays 1842–1882, pp. 420–40. Boston, Houghton, Muffin & Co., 1892, pp. 431–32.

CLOSURE

AUDREY SHAFER, M.D.
(Winter 1996, p. 33)

Stabbing crosswise at green stripes
I began to lengthen the gash when the watermelon cracked
the halves split apart
rocked and
tipped off the cutting board.
Red flesh gaped ragged at me.

So I knew when the surgeons opened Mr. W's belly
and his body could no longer contain itself
but spilled, disgorged over the edematous walls
That Mr. W
would die

Is it immoral to compare his abdomen to a
ripe ready watermelon?
If I had ever seen him
without blood welling around tubes and catheters
without the disfiguring kilos of fluid
mounding him
puffing his eyelids to permanent closure
If I had ever head him speak
blow his nose
tease a grandchild—
Would I stitch dermis to rind?

Once I saw the sky turn a blue
so unnaturally slick
it was the color of the suture
laced through plastic stents and
tied wide across Mr. W.

The next morning, silent monitors
reflected grey.
His bed
crisply made
was ineffably
flat.

PANDEMIC, MEDICINE, AND PUBLIC HEALTH: *Yersinia pestis* and Fourteenth-Century European Culture

SCOTT TENNER, M.D., M.P.H.,
AND ANDREW SCHAMESS, M.D.
(Fall 1993, pp. 6–10)

Scott Tenner graduated from George Washington Medical School in 1991 where he was president of the AΩA Chapter. He served as resident in medicine at George Washington University until 1994. As a Clinical Fellow in the Gastroenterology Division at Brigham and Women's Hospital, Harvard Medical School, Dr. Tenner performed clinical and basic science research in diseases of the pancreas. He has authored over 50 publications, including several texts and the State of the Art review on Acute Pancreatitis published in the New England Journal of Medicine. *He is married with 5 children, lives in Roslyn, New York. Currently, Dr. Tenner is Program Director, Division of Gastroenterology, and an Associate Professor of Medicine at Downstate Medical Center, SUNY.*

Andrew Schamess is in private practice in the rural community of Dalton, Massachusetts. He teaches students from the University of Massachusetts Medical School and residents at the Berkshire Medical Center. Prior to that he served as the senior deputy director for primary care, Prevention and Planning for the District of Columbia; and before that spent four years as the medical director of La Clinica del Pueblo, a community clinic serving the Latino population in Washington, DC.

War and pestilence

The year was 1346. The Mongol army on a raid from the East had surrounded the Genoese trading post of Caffa on the Black Sea. The siege was faltering. The troops of the invading army were falling prey to a mysterious disease. In desperation, the Mongol Khan ordered that the bodies of the dead be catapulted over the walls into Caffa. The city held firm. The Mongols retreated, and after a period, trading resumed.[1, p. 810]

Historian Barbara W. Tuchman, in her vivid portrayal of this period, has described how shortly after the fall of Calais, in the fall of 1347, Genoese trading ships sailed into the harbor of Messina in Sicily with men dying at their oars. The ships had come on a trading voyage from the Crimea. The dead and dying sailors showed black swellings about the size of an egg in the axillae and groin. The swellings oozed blood and pus, and ecchymotic lesions covered the bodies as hemorrhage spread internally. Some of the sailors died in less than twenty-four hours, spitting up blood while in torrents of fever. Their affliction was horrific in its appearance and its implications.[2, p. 92]

"Woe is me of the shilling in the armpit!" So went a Welsh lament.[2 p. 93] Rumors of an epidemic plague arising in China and spreading through central Asia into India, then Asia minor, had circulated in Europe by 1346.[2] By the summer of 1348, maritime trade had spread the pestilence throughout Europe. The continent was consumed in eighteen months. At least a third of the European population, 20 million people, would suffer the fate of rapidly progressive *Yersinia pestis* septicemia.[2, p. 94]

It was said that in crowded Avignon, the papal seat, 400 people died per day; 7,000 houses were emptied; and a town graveyard received 11,000 corpses in six weeks.[2, p. 94] When the graveyards were full, the pope consecrated the Rhone river so that the bodies could be thrown into it.[3, p. 17] An English bishop gave permission to laymen to make confession to each other, even to a woman.[2, p. 94]

Among the clergy and doctors, the mortality was naturally high due to the nature of their professions. Twenty of the twenty-four university-trained physicians of Venice lost their lives in the first month of the pestilence. At Montpellier, the leading medieval medical school, the physician Simon de Covino reported that "hardly one of them escaped."[2, p. 100]

To understand the dreadful impact of *Yersinia pestis* on the society of Europe, resulting in the name "The Black Death," one must examine the health and society of the thirteenth and fourteenth centuries. A religious and feudalistic society, centered around the church, had enjoyed two centuries of relative health. It saw itself progressing toward Augustine's City of God "with no ills." European agriculture had become well developed in the tenth through fourteenth centuries. The fruition of Europe's rural economy helped give rise to an urban revolution. The combination of food surplus and resultant population increase meant that fewer people had to live off the land. The period we call the Renaissance was beginning, as many individuals entered into travel, exploration, and discovery. Trade flourished, and new and old routes were becoming busy lanes of commerce.[2]

Centuries of isolation had resulted in a stable European disease pool. Smallpox, measles, malaria, and leprosy had established a tentative equilibrium within Europe's population. With the increase in trade, however, came the potential for the introduction of new pathogens. The urbanization of the masses created fertile ground for disease spread. To these elements were added unexpected climatic changes, which began to alter the insect and rodent ecology of Eurasia.[4, pp. 22–24]

By the late twelfth century, four hundred years of optimum weather were drawing to a close. During the period immediately prior to the plague, 1250–1350, the weather became severe. The glaciers advanced. Besides altering the environment for insects and rodents, the "Little Ice Age," as it is called, had an effect on agriculture. Fruits and vegetables, rich in vitamins C and A, were less plentiful. Hunger and malnutrition became more common. By 1347, resistance to infection was at a low point for middle-aged Europe. The stage was set for contagion, disease, and epidemic.[4, pp. 23–27]

Yersinia pestis is native to particular parts of the world. There are currently, and probably have always been, permanent reservoirs of invetebrate foci.[4, p. 19] One such location is at the foothills between India and Tibet. Mongol tribesmen began their conquest of central Asia in the early 1330s. The wars and trade routes set the stage for disease and pandemic. Urbanization with failure of crops created widespread poverty. Poverty made a virulent mix with the introduction of a rodent species, the black rat, host to a flea carrying the pest bacillus.[5, 6]

Although of no noticeable importance to an urban or agricultural sodety, this Asian rodent *(Rattus rattus)* had certain characteristics that favored the introduction into Europe of *Xenopsylla cheopis,* the flea that carries the pest bacillus. These included a low body temperature, a habitat in close proximity to humans, and good ship-climbing ability.[5, p. 200; 6, p. 123]

These seemingly minor population dynamics changed the course of history. The brown rat *(Rattus norvegicus),* also from the East and also a plague vector, did not enter Western Europe until the eighteenth century, but has now largely displaced its Asian cousin.[5, p. 201; 6, p. 123]

Although bubonic plague, with *Yersinia* transmitted via flea bites, is by far the most common form of the disease, plague in the pneumonic form can be spread among humans by a simple cough. Pneumonic plague is unique in that it can be transmitted thus from person to person, without intervention by the flea. It is far more virulent, almost always fatal. The incubation period of plague to the appearance of the first symptoms is generally about six days. In bubonic plague, the initial blackish, gangrenous pustule at the point of the flea bite is followed by adenopathy in the groin and axilla. Pneumonia may develop secondarily. In the droplet-transmitted form, a pneumonitis appears as the primary infection. The person is overcome by hemorrhaging from cell necrosis and disseminated intravascular coagulation (DIC). In the fourteenth century, the plague spread across Europe in both forms, following the trade routes.

The medical world of the fourteenth century

Modern epidemiologists explain a phenomenon such as the plague by establishing its causative agent, its vectors, the factors predisposing to an outbreak.

If we ask the question of why it affected the people of Europe in the fourteenth century, we are inclined to answer it materialistically by examining a chain of events occurring in the physical world.

Medieval Europeans answered the question differently. For them the issue was moral, not physical. Their notions of health and disease seem far removed from those of the twentieth century. Nonetheless, the roots of our own beliefs are found in theirs, and interesting parallels exist between the bubonic plague and modern epidemics.

Medieval medicine had its basis in Hippocratic doctrine. Hippocrates eschewed supernatural theories and taught that the job of the physician is to aid the natural healing processes of the body. Physicians' behavior during the Black Death is revealing. A large number took the Greek, Galen's advice that if a plague were in the vicinity, the doctor should leave as quickly as possible.[1, p. 816] For those physicians who stayed, Guy de Chauliac noted that "it was useless and shameful . . . since they did not visit the sick for fear of being infected; and when they visited them, they did not make them well, and gained nothing; for all the sick died."[7, p. 75] De Chauliac, physician to the pope, stayed in Avignon in 1348 ("to avoid infamy, not daring to absent [him]self"). He was infected, and suffered six weeks of severe illness, but recovered "by the will of God."[7, p. 76]

A few others also made the heroic choice to stay in plague cities and care for the dying. Gentilis of Foligno probably saved some lives in Perugia by recommending that all contaminated items be burned, before he himself died of plague in 1348.[3, p. 24] Paracelsus, a physician of the sixteenth century, hurried to the Brenner Pass, between Austria and Italy, to attend an outbreak of plague, only to be chased away by the inhabitants for the severity of his cures: he used extensive sweating, bleeding, and burning of the skin.[8]

Overall, physicians played a disappointingly minor role in the course of events during the plague years. Medieval therapeutics could not be brought to bear effectively in plague sufferers. Since their remedies proved useless, doctors were dismissed as quacks, or as well-intentioned men helpless in the face of disaster. As Giovanni Boccaccio put it, "Against these maladies, it seemed that all the advice of physicians and all the power of medicine were profitless and unavailing. Perhaps the nature of the illness was such that it allowed no remedy: or perhaps those people who were treating the illness, . . . being ignorant of its causes, were not prescribing the appropriate cure."[9, p. 51]

In any case, the people of the fourteenth century did not think of the plague primarily as a physical disturbance of the individual. They saw it as a collective affliction. The sickness was not located in the body, but in the city, the country, in fact, in the whole world of Europe. The soil and the air had putrefied; the pestilence found expression in unnatural events as well as in the disfigurement and death of those who encountered it.

These beliefs are reflected in the medical writings of the time. The most scholarly doctors (who were often also the furthest removed from the ravages of the disease) offered miasma as an explanation. The theory was that a body of air had been corrupted and moved through towns as an atmospheric front, causing illness in all who breathed it.

Popular views of the plague were quite diverse. Some people, as Boccaccio observed, "maintained that an infallible way of warding off this appalling evil was to drink heavily, enjoy life to the full, go round singing and merrymaking, gratify all of one's cravings whenever the opportunity offered, and shrug the whole thing off as one enormous joke."[9, p. 52] A majority, however, saw the plague as a religious visitation. Several cults flourished around figures such as Saint Sebastian, who was cured from the wounds of Diocletian's arrows, and Saint Roch, who after a severe illness devoted himself to curing the sick. Saint Roch was always pictured with a prominent bubo on his left thigh.[10, p. 113] Popular artworks represented the plague as a rain of arrows from the sky. The faithful are protected under the mantle of the Virgin or one of the saints.[10, p. 113]

Disease caused fear, fear allowed religious fervor, which meant that non-Christians suffered the blame. In Neustadt, Switzerland, in the wake of the 1348 plague outbreak, a Jewish physician named Balavignus was arrested on suspicion of poisoning the wells. According to the account of his confession forwarded to Strasbourg by the city's officials:

> He was put for a short time to the rack, and on being taken down, confessed, after much hesitation, that, about ten weeks before, the Rabbi Jacob of Toledo . . . sent him, by a Jewish boy, some poison in the mummy of an egg, . . . commanding him on penalty of excommunication, and by his required obedience to the law, to throw this poison into the larger and more frequented wells of Thonon, to poison those who drew water there."[3, p. 45]

Confessions were elicited in similar fashion from several other Jews. The plague was determined to have been caused by this poisoning of the water supply. A public trial was held and the Jewish population of Neustadt condemned by popular assent for complicity. "I must add," the letter concludes, "that all the Jews of Neustadt were burnt according to the just sentence of the Law." The exile or massacre of the Jewish population followed in many cities of the Netherlands, Germany, and France.[3, p. 47]

The final medieval conception of plague arose less from scholarly reasoning or religious belief than from experience. The contagious nature of the disease was noted by almost all who observed it. Boccaccio stated that "what made this pestilence even more severe was that whenever those suffering from it mixed with people who were still unaffected, it would rush upon these with the speed of a fire racing through dry or oily substances."[9, p. 51] This aspect of the disease was particularly terrifying because it caused people to shun one another for fear of contamination. As De Chauliac stated, "The father did not visit his son, nor the son his father. Charity was dead and hope destroyed.[7, p. 75]

The medieval notion of contagion stood with one foot in the fourteenth century and one foot in the twentieth. It did indeed anticipate our understanding of infectious disease. It also coexisted, however, with the conceptions of divine wrath, miasma, and poison described above, and was not necessarily seen as incompatible with them. Europe had not yet given rise to Sir Isaac Newton or René Descartes, and was not ready to accept a materialist causality of disease. Boccaccio, who clearly observed the contagious nature of the plague, criticized those nobles who tried to flee to unaffected areas: "It was as though they imagined that the wrath of God would not unleash this plague against men for their iniquities irrespective of where they happened to be."[9, p. 53]

The contagion that passed from one person to another was a hybrid of material and moral corruption. Contagion was closely linked in the medieval mind with decay. Several of the diseases known to be contagious—leprosy, plague, and later syphilis—had dermatologic manifestations that were quite disfiguring. Medieval observers saw an obvious similarity between these changes and the decomposition of the body after death. The interposition of contagion, decay, and social condemnation can be seen in the treatment of lepers. Their banishment from society, ostensibly for the common good, nonetheless had punitive overtones. Prior to expulsion, the leper underwent a symbolic burial ritual. The afflicted was brought to a cemetery in a funeral procession, and stooped in an open grave while a priest recited burial prayers.[8]

Are our own ideas of infection of the body really derived from these primitive notions of contagion? We need only look at the popular reaction to the modern epidemic of AIDS. Despite clear knowledge of its modes of transmission, schools continue to refuse admission to infected children; families fear infection if they share silverware with HIV-positive members; and nurses and doctors glove before shaking hands with such patients. Could this be because we associate AIDS with such stigmatized behavior as homosexual intercourse and intravenous drug use? Does the virus carry, in our minds, a taint of moral corruption that goes beyond its infective potential?[11]

Epidemiology and public health at the time of the plague were based on Galen's *Book of Fevers,* which was a thousand years old by 1337. It is of little wonder that in 1348, the advice given to King Philip VI of France by the medical faculty of the University of Paris was virtually useless.[1,2] Not surprisingly, none of the medical treatises of the mid-fourteenth century correctly described the plague's cause.[2, pp. 102–103]

That contagion, however primitively conceived, won out over other theories nonetheless represented a major triumph of modem science over medieval fatalism. Of all the theories, only contagion provided the basis for effective action.

In the wake of the first outbreak, cities, many of which were walled, started to bar the entrance of plague sufferers. Those who had been exposed in other cities were held outside the walls for forty days, a quarantine. The number forty was chosen based on numerology. Forty days had significance as the duration of the Biblical flood, and of Christ's fast in the wilderness.[8]

In Venice, the dead were removed outside the city on barges, and a plague council was appointed in 1348 to supervise this and other hygienic measures.[8] In Vienna, the bath houses and brothels were closed, and the dead were required to be buried outside city walls, although the populace initially paid little attention to either law.[1] The first public health board was created in Florence in 1347. Its duties were to "give full authority . . . for a period of three months to make provisions and issue ordinances."[4, p. 123] In Milan, the board was composed of one university-trained physician, one surgeon, one notary, one barber-surgeon, two horsemen (messengers), and two gravediggers.[4, p. 123] In many Italian cities, the board of health enforced moral as well as physical hygiene.[12, p. 83]

These interventions undoubtedly did prevent some plague outbreaks and reduce mortality. Over time, hygienic measures became more widely accepted and practiced. For medieval society, this was an early illustration of man's power to act on his own behalf, to protect himself from the forces of nature. In this sense, the plague laid the groundwork for future medical advances.

A new type of medicine

The plague had other effects, which brought medicine closer to its modern form. As scholastic medicine failed, the prestige of surgery rose. Chauliac's *Surgery* and John Ardeme's *Practica* were among the most widely read of all post-plague medical books. In 1348, the rulers of Florence allowed surgeons to do postmortem examinations on plague victims. Montpellier and Venice followed suit.[4, p. 118]

Another change related to the fall of academic medicine and rise of surgery was the growth of vernacular medical texts. Until the 1340s all texts were written in Latin, the language of medicine. The laymen demanded information, and like Martin Luther's translation of the Bible, texts were simplified and translated into local language.

The rise of hospitals was accelerated by the Black Death. They had begun as charitable institutions, founded by religious orders for the care of the suffering and disabled. During the plague years, they came to be seen by public authorities as potential isolation centers for plague victims. In many cities new hospitals were built, or leprosariums converted.[12, p. 87] Physicians were brought in to staff the hospitals, and these institutions remained after the plague subsided.

The *Danse Macabre*

Europe underwent an important transformation in the aftermath of the plague. The initial effect was devastating. The shock of survivors at the apparent crumbling of established order, as well as the personal loss of friends and family, must have been profound. The shattering of old institutions, however, and the rise of hygiene and its implicit social activism may have freed a creative spirit repressed by centuries of stability. A prosperous society emerged as survivors inherited the wealth of the deceased.[6, p. 121] In a sense, the plague helped to destroy the medieval world and open the door to the Renaissance.

A psychological transition can be traced in the art of the post-plague period. As noted above, the sight of corruption and decay of the flesh exercised a powerful influence on the medieval imagination. An image began to appear in paintings and illustrations early in the plague years, in which a certain number of the living, depicted as young gallants or beautiful women, encounter an equal number of the dead. In a representative fresco, *Triumph of Death,* found in the Campo Santo in Pisa, three mounted noblemen stare in disgust at three corpses in varying states of explicit decomposition.[10, p. 109] The message is clear: the dead are their doubles, a castigation of their vanity. What is mortal perishes and only the soul devoted to God achieves eternity.

As the plague accelerated, a new image gained popularity: the *Danse macabre* or Dance of Death.[10, p. 116] Many woodcuts and paintings depicted a procession of figures, representing the stages of life or the ranks of society, led by a grotesque dancing skeleton or corpse. Variations on the theme showed death peering over the shoulders of the living as they engaged in various activities. Death here had become the seer, exposing the hypocrisy behind social mores.

A third type of image arose later. In 1402, the plague revisited Florence. As an offering, in the hope that God would spare the city the devastation that had occurred in 1347, the governing council voted to build new doors for the San Giovanni Baptistry. They gave the commission to Lorenzo Ghiberti. Fifty-four years later he completed the series of bronze panels in front of which Michelangelo would stand transfixed, exclaiming that they were "fit to be the gates of Paradise."[13, p. 71] The central panel showed Abraham, knife poised to sacrifice Isaac. Ghiberti's Isaac is no medieval waif. He is a full-bodied youth, with a muscular chest and a beautiful, gentle face; a fully human figure. His virility is celebrated, not shamed. He is a harbinger of the Renaissance in art, and also, perhaps, a tribute to the millions of anonymous, unrepresented lives sacrificed in the prior dark century.

References

1. Velimirvoc B and Velimirovic H. Plague in Vienna. Rev Infect Dis 11 (5):808–26, 1989.
2. Tuchman BW. A Distant Mirror: The Calamitous 14th Century. New York. Alfred A. Knopf. 1989.
3. Hecker JFC. The Black Death: An Account of the Deadly Pestilence of the Fourteenth Century. Babington, BG, trans. New York. Humboldt Publishing Company. 1885, 386–433.

4. Gottfried RS. The Black Death: Natural and Human Disaster in Medieval Europe. New York. Free Press, 1983.

5. Zinsser H. Rats, Lice and History. New York. Blue Ribbon Books, 1935.

6. McEvedy C. The bubonic plague. Sci Am 258 (2):118–23, 1988.

7. De Chauliac G. LaGrande Chirurgie. Toumon. Laurens Joubert, 1619, p. 172. As cited in: Major RH. Classic Descriptions of Disease. Springfield, Illinois. Charles C. Thomas, 1932.

8. Riesman D. The Story of Medicine in the Middle Ages. New York, Paul Hoeber, 1935.

9. Boccaccio G. The Decameron, McWilham, GH. trans. London. Penguin Books. 1972, pp. 49–88.

10. Polzer J. Aspects of the fourteenth-century iconography of death and the plague. In Williman. R. ed.: The Black Death: The Impact of the Fourteenth-Century Plague, pp. 107–59. Binghamton. New York. Center for Medieval and Early Renaissance Studies, 1982.

11. Zuger A and Miles SH. Physicians. AIDS, and occupational risk: Historic traditions and ethical obligations. JAMA 258:1924–28, 1987.

12. Park K. Medicine and society in medieval Europe, 500-1500. In Wear A, ed.: Medicine in Society: Historical Essays. pp. 59–90. Cambridge. Cambridge University Press. 1992.

13. Hibbert C. The House of Medici: Its Rise and Fall. New York. William Morrow & Co., 1975.

SICKNESS AND SETTLEMENT: DISEASE AS A FACTOR IN THE EARLY COLONIZATION OF NEW ENGLAND

PETER H. WOOD, Ph.D.

(October 1964, pp. 98–101)

Peter H. Wood grew up in St. Louis, where his father, Dr. William Barry Wood, Jr., served as the Professor of Medicine at Washington University. Through this link to the Barnes Hospital, he knew and admired Doctors Robert and Helen Glaser, former editors of The Pharos. *In 1964, when he completed an undergraduate honors paper at Harvard concerning Indian-English relations in early New England, the Glasers invited him to prepare an essay for* The Pharos *on the medical issues involved. This was Wood's first published article, at age 21. It appeared well before Native American history and the decimating epidemics in post-Columbian America had become common topics for research. The author went on to a Rhodes Scholarship, a Harvard Ph.D. in colonial American history, and a scholarly career focusing on early contacts between Europeans and non-Europeans. Many other articles and books have followed this initial publication, including a new American History textbook from Longman entitled* Created Equal. *Professor Wood is married to Elizabeth A. Fenn, author of the recent volume,* Pox Americana: The Great North American Small-pox Epidemic of 1775–1781. *Both Wood and Fenn teach American History at Duke University.*

RUGGEDNESS—MORAL AND PHYSICAL—characterized the first settlers in New England. They were robust in body and spirit, as their demanding mission required. Generations of scholars have discussed the religious well-being of these colonists and have debated the role of Puritan morality in our heritage. Less well-known but no less interesting is the settlers' physical bill of health. Source materials provide scattered comments—freely spelled—on the medical aspects of settlement. Physical sickness ranked among their foremost enemies, but it also served them, unexpectedly, as a powerful ally. In our own secure age of advanced and massive medical care, it is sometimes difficult to acknowledge that contagion can help determine the course of human affairs. Almost three hundred and fifty years ago, along the rocky coast of Massachusetts, seeds of new life and seeds of death were being sown simultaneously. And there the patterns of disease left their indelible mark upon an early chapter of American history.

Migration

Typhoid and typhus, measles and syphilis, influenza and plague: these diseases crept, in some mysterious way, through the teeming streets of Shakespeare's London. The variola virus was endemic in England's bustling coastal cities, and periodically it swept the countryside, leaving pock-marks as common facial features. Repeated exposure to these sicknesses produced widespread immunity during the seventeenth century. But in the crowded seaports any group of migrants large enough to fill a ship was sure to include carriers of contagion. The ships sailing for New England in the sixteen-twenties and thirties invariably contained those "whose natures were so borne downe with Disease, that they could hardly craule up the Ships-side, yet ventured their weake Vessells to this Westurne World."[1]

Typical of these ships was the Talbot, which weighed anchor at Gravesend, April 25, 1629. Her flock of one hundred Puritans, shepherded by the Reverend Francis Higginson, formed part of the vanguard of the Massachusetts Bay Colony. Higginson kept a journal of the voyage, and on the fourth sabbath he recorded, with solemn constraint:

> This day my 2 children Samuel & Mary began to be sicke of ye small-pockes & purples together, which was brought into ye ship by one Mr. Browne which was sick of ye same at Graves End, whom it pleased God to make ye first occasion of bringing that contagious sicknes among us wherewith many were after afflicted.[2]

On the third day of fever, Mary, a sickly four-year-old, showed the punctate hemorrhages of purpuric smallpox (purpura variolosa), and her condition worsened. The minister wrote, "towards night my daughter grew sicker & many blew Spots were seene upon her breast, which aifrighted us. At ye first wee thought they had been ye plague tokens; but we found afterwards that it was onely a high measure of ye infection of ye pockes." Before morning the girl died, "being ye first in our shipp that was buried in the bowells of ye great Atlanticke Sea; . . . a sorrow to all ye rest as being ye beginning of a contagious disease & mortality. . . ."[3]

The fears aroused by one death were well-founded, for all knew stories of shipboard epidemics that had destroyed colonies before they could begin. Tossing in crowded loneliness on the North Atlantic, exposure to the diseases at hand was virtually unavoidable. Some passengers were able to strengthen their prior immunities, but others succumbed to viruses they had escaped at home. And all were threatened equally with scurvy due to poor rations. Wretched food, in cramped quarters, on an ever-rolling sea: for six to twelve weeks these harsh conditions tested the fitness of young and old. By the time land appeared in the west, the arduous passage had often winnowed the sickly from the strong. During the Talbot's seventh week at sea one poignant entry reads: "This day a child of goodman Blacke which had a consumption before it came to shipp, dyed. This day we had all a cleare and comfortable sight of America. . . ."[4]

But the comforting sight of New England cured only their seasickness; it was no assurance of health and success. For the Pilgrims in 1620, and for the Massachusetts Bay colonists in the following decade, the first year of settlement was the most trying. The Pilgrims, who had lost one life and added one during ten weeks at sea, saw more than half their company die in the first winter months at Plymouth. Influenza took some fifty souls as they huddled, homeless, aboard the Mayflower. The rigors of the voyage, the novel extremities of climate, plus the inadequacies of food and shelter, left physical resistance at a low ebb. "Head-aches are frequent, Palsies, Dropsies, Worms, noli-me-tangeres, Cancers, pestilent Feavers."[5] Thomas Dudley put the causes of sickness among migrants in "the want of warm lodging and good diet to which Englishmen are habituated at home, and in the sudden increase of heat which they endure that are landed here in the summer, the salt meats at sea having prepared their bodies thereto."[6] According to another settler, "Scurvies, the body corrupted with Sea-diet, Beef and Pork tainted, Butter and Cheese corrupted, fish rotten, a long voyage, coming into the searching sharpness of a purer climate, causeth death and sickness amongst them."[7]

Settlement

Physical conditions improved rapidly, and the level of health rose accordingly. Permanent houses soon replaced huts of bark or canvas, reducing the danger of exposure and congestion. As for food, Englishmen raised on meat and beer at first had little more than shellfish and springwater. But in time they were growing enough Indian corn and pressing too much apple cider. Though it took the Pilgrims several years to establish a sufficient food supply, the task became easier for each successive settlement. During the "great migration" of the sixteen-thirties, hundreds of early settlers sold supplies to thousands of newcomers. And the purer, harsher New England climate, if not overcome, was soon accepted and even appreciated. Salem's first minister claimed, "Many that have beene weake and sickly in old England, by comming hither have beene thoroughly healed and growne healthfull strong . . . a sup of New-England's Aire is better than a whole draught of of old England's Ale."[8]

Their voyage to America put the wide Atlantic between the colonists and the epidemic infections of England. And in Massachusetts (unlike west Africa and other colonies) they found no new diseases to jeopardize their health. The various "fluxes and fevers" which persisted among them were accepted stoically and described poorly. Any medical appraisal of the situation is complicated, not only by virtue of Puritan reticence, but by the fact that diagnostic medicine in old England and new remained strikingly imprecise in the seventeenth century. People still confused such distinctive diseases as measles and smallpox, and they had frequent trouble identifying syphilis ("large pox"). Terminology remained vague, with such terms as "plague" and "fever" having broad, non-medical connotations. Often individual symptoms were not carefully observed, nor, more importantly, were they grouped so as to define a specific disease. The imprecise statements in early New England documents suggest influenza, smallpox, and probably typhus as the primary contagions. But no disease approached major epidemic proportions among established New England settlers until 1666, when smallpox claimed forty "second generation" lives in the growing seaport of Boston.[9] In that same year, their remoteness saved them from the Great Plague that was ravaging London.

The actual practice of medicine was not highly regarded among these religious colonists, and some physicians had to look for better ways to earn a living. "I am strongly sett upon to studye divinitie," wrote Giles Firmin, a doctor more interested in anatomy; "my studyes else must be lost: for physick is but a meene help."[10] One malcontent claimed that Samuel Fuller, Plymouth's well-meaning deacon and physician, "cured John Endicott of that disease known as a wife."[11] And in 1630, Massachusetts Bay colonists made sure that the new Court of Assistants fined Nicholas Knapp the stiff sum of five pounds "for takeing upon him to cure the scurvey by a water of noe worth nor value, which hee solde at a very deare rate."[12]

In general these colonists considered ministers more worthy than doctors "to serve the suffering." For they believed that the causes and the cures of illness, like all else, rested in God's hands. Through disease the Lord purposefully tested, rebuked, or assisted His people, and they struggled to interpret His signs. On board the Mayflower, the swarthy seaman who chided the sickly believers was soon smitten "with a greevous disease, of which he died in a desparate maner, and so was him selfe ye first that was throwne overbord."[13] God's lesson seemed obvious, as it did also aboard the Tatbot. On June 18, 1629, Higginson recorded, with righteousness:

> This day a notorious wicked fellow that was given to swearing & boasting of his former wickedness bragged that hee had got a wench with child before hee came this voyage & mocked at or daies of fast railing & jesting against puritans, this fellow fell sicke of ye pockes & died.[14]

Such incidents readily affirmed their belief that sickness served God's scheme. But the most sweeping proof of all lay in the decimation of the coastal Indians: "God hath provided this country for our Nation, destroying the natives by the plague, it not touching one Englishman though many traded and were conversant amongst them. . . ."[15]

The Indians

For several decades prior to 1620, the Algonquin Indians of coastal New England had had increasing contact with foreign fishermen, traders, even would-be settlers. There was one drastic though unintended effect: novel diseases spread rapidly and repeatedly through this highly susceptible native population. "At our first discovery of those coasts," wrote an early trader, "we found it very populous, the inhabitants stout and warlike. . . ."[16] But soon sailors reported areas, "not long since populous now utterly void; in other places a remnant remaines, but not free of sicknesse."[17] No arrow could defend against the unseen and unscrupulous diseases of the English. The most devastating epidemic (probably smallpox) raged from 1617 to 1619 and killed almost nine-tenths of the Indians along the Massachusetts coast. Captain John Smith, who had stretched his stories of Virginia when necessary, was unable to exaggerate: "Where I have seene two or three hundred, within three yeares after remained scarce thirty, but what disease it was the Savages knew not till the English told them, never having seene, nor heard of the like before."[18] When the Pilgrims arrived the following winter, "skulls and bones were found in many places lying still above ground. . . ."[19] The surviving natives, now too weak to force the English out, befriended them and provided crucial assistance.

Desolation caused by infectious disease was a *sine qua non* of successful settlement. It allowed the English to secure a permanent foothold on new shores, and it advanced before them into the wilderness. The unknown sicknesses ravaged whole tribes, bringing utter fear, cruel suffering, and awesome mortality. Roger Williams, the dissenter who lived among the Indians, wrote sympathetically of their plight: "They commonly abound with children, and increase mightily; except the plague fall against them, or other lesser sicknesses, and then having no meanes of recovery, they perish wonderfully."[20] According to William Bradford, smallpox was their worst enemy: "a sorer disease cannot befall them; they fear it more than ye plague; for usualy they that have this disease have them in abundance, and for wante of bedding & lining and other helps, they fall into a lamentable condition, as they lye on their matts, ye poxe breaking and mattering, and runing one into another. . . ."[21]

During these virulent epidemics the English found themselves remarkably immune. In 1617, for example, some traders were forced to spend the winter with a tribe ravaged by the general "plague." Although the men "lay in the cabins of those people that died . . . not one of them ever felt their heads to ache while they stayed there."[22] Later Squanto, the famous native interpreter, felt confident in telling his people that the Pilgrims kept "the plague" hidden in their storehouse and could send it out at will on missions of destruction. When doubting tribesmen questioned this tale, the English had to admit that their own arsenal contained no such weapon. But they nurtured Indian fears by stating, as they themselves believed, that their God held disease in store and destroyed his enemies with it.[23]

The course of events lent stature to their claim. More than one Indian was converted to their faith simply by noting how the pale foreigners could enter a decimated encampment confident of God's protection. If the native leaders fled their stricken tribesmen, the English often showed compassion "and dayly fetched them wood & water, and made them fires, gott them victualls whilst they lived, and buried them when they dyed. For very few of them escaped. . . ." When "not one of ye English was so much as sicke, or in ye least measure tainted" at such times, then God's goodness was proclaimed.[24] Had they known, credit might better have gone to the antibodies which were in all probability directly responsible for immunity.

Conclusion

With shiploads of new recruits arriving yearly from England, the colonies expanded rapidly. By 1636 there were roughly five thousand settlers in Massachusetts, and a small college had been established to further their beliefs. Besides sharing similar beliefs, these people also had their physical experience in common. All but the youngest had had contact with the diseases of England and had endured the arduous Atlantic passage. They had overcome the trials of food and climate imposed by their adventure. Though initial hardships took a heavy toll, there soon resulted a sturdy and growing population, for the movement from the old England to the new one required strength, built immunities, and imposed isolation.

The American Indians, whose presence would dominate every thrust of the moving frontier, lost an early battle to these sturdy Englishmen. Utterly susceptible and unprotected, they surrendered to the ravages of foreign contagion. Disease drastically reduced their numbers and weakened their spirits along the Massachusetts coast. It precluded strong resistance, dictated meek cooperation, and made possible permanent English settlement.

References

1. Johnson E. Wonder-Working Providence. J. Franklin Jameson, ed. (New York, 1959), 63.
2. Higginson F. New-Englands Plantation (London, 1630) (reprinted, Salem, 1908). 65.
3. Ibid., 66.

4. Ibid., 76.

5. Josselyn J. An Account of Two Voyages to New-England (second edition, London, 1675). Reprinted in Massachusetts Historical Society, Collections, ser. 3, III, 334.

6. Dudley T. Chronicles of the First Planters of the Colony of Massachusetts Bay. Alexander Young, ed. (Boston, 1846), 325.

7. Josselyn, op. cit., 334.

8. Higginson, op. cit., 99–100.

9. Thacher T. A Brief Rule to Guide the Common-People of New-England How to Order Themselves and Theirs in the Small Pocks, or Measels. Henry R. Viets, ed. (Baltimore, 1937), xxxiv.

10. A letter to Governor Winthrop. ibid., xxxiv.

11. Coleman RV. The First Frontier. (New York, 1948), 179.

12. Massachusetts Bay Colony, Court of Assistants, Records, 1630–1692 (Boston, 1901–1928), II, 11. quoted in John B. Blake, Public Health in the Town of Boston, 1630–1822 (Cambridge, 1959), 9.

13. Bradford W. History Of Plimoth Plantation. Commonwealth edition (Boston, 1898), 91.

14. Higginson, op. cit., 75.

15. Smith J. Mass. Hist. Soc., Collections, ser. 3, III, 16.

16. Gorges F. Mass. Hist. Soc., Collections, ser. 3, VI, 89.

17. A letter to Samuel Purchas in London, 1619, quoted in Herbert U. Williams, The Epidemic of the Indians of New England, 1616–1620. Johns Hopkins Hospital Bulletin, XX (1909), 344.

18. Smith, op. cit., 16.

19. Bradford, op. cit., 123.

20. Williams R. A Key into the Language of America (London, 1643). Rhode Island Hist. Soc., Collections, vol. I (Providence, 1827), 125.

21. Bradford, op. cit., 388.

22. Gorges, Mass. Hist. Soc., Collections, ser. 3, VI,

23. Winslow E. Good News from New England. Mass. Hist. Soc., Collections, ser. 1, VIII, 239.

24. Bradford, op. cit., 389.

THOMAS JEFFERSON AND ACADEMIC MEDICINE

OSCAR A. THORUP, JR., M.D.

(April 1977, pp. 16–23)

Oscar Thorup is recognized as one of the team of three (he joined Monte Duval and Philip Krutsch) who planned the founding and growth of the University of Arizona College of Medicine. Thorup was chosen to be the first chair of the Department of Medicine. DuVal wrote, "I've seen him disappointed, but never angry; frustrated but never intemperate, anguished but never depressed. When he entered a room he lit it up in a way that General Electric would envy." During his nine-year tenure at Arizona, he continued his writings and research in hematology. After his Arizona days he returned to his beloved University of Virginia in Charlottesville, serving there as professor of medicine and an associate dean. He died recently, on October 21, 2002.

THE CONTRIBUTIONS OF THOMAS JEFFERSON to the political development of this country were many, as one can note by reading Jefferson's own modest account of his offices, written late in his life.

> I came of age in 1764, and was soon put into the nomination of justice of the county in which I live; and at the first election following I became one of its representatives in the Legislature. I was thence sent to the old Congress. Then employed two years with Mr. Pendleton and Mr. Wythe, on the revisal and reduction to a single code of the whole body of British statutes, the acts of our Assembly, and certain parts of the common law. Then elected Governor. Next, to the Legislature and Congress again. Sent to Europe as Minister Plenipotentiary. Appointed Secretary of State to the new Government. Elected Vice-President, and President. And lastly, a Visitor and Rector of the University.
>
> In these different offices, with scarcely any interval between them, I have been in public office now sixty-one years. . . . [1]

Recent history has been appropriately generous in praise of Jefferson, for his concepts of democracy relating to the rights of man and religious freedom, for his authorship of the Declaration of Independence, and for his role as founder of the University of Virginia. Jefferson's influence on the teaching of medicine is not so widely recognized.

Academic medicine was first established in the state of Virginia by Jefferson after he took office as Governor in 1779.

> I effected, during my residence in Williamsburg that year, a change in the organization of that institution by abolishing the Grammar School, and the two professorships of Divinity & Oriental Languages, and substituting a professorship of Law & Police, one of Anatomy Medicine and Chemistry, and one of Modern languages; and the charter confining us to six professorships, we added the law of Nature & Nations, and the Fine Arts to the duties of the Moral professor, and Natural History to those of the professor of Mathematics and Natural philosophy.[2]

The School of Medicine at William and Mary was established three years prior to that of Harvard College.[3] James McClurg was selected to be the first professor of medicine and served in that capacity for four years before he retired and moved to Richmond, the new state capital. His short tenure was occasioned by the significant disturbances of that time. The Revolutionary War lasted from 19 April 1775 until the surrender of Cornwallis on 19 October 1781. The College of William and Mary had had close cultural ties with Oxford University in England and had enjoyed considerable royal patronage. The loss of royal patronage, the move of the state capital to Richmond late in 1779, and significant physical damage during the Yorktown Campaign of 1781 all contributed to the misfortunes of the College, and the Chair of Medicine was allowed to remain empty.[4]

Jefferson had a remarkable interest in science, which he regarded as the surest means of advancing social progress and human happiness. The dominant aspect of his mind was an insatiable desire to learn. Not content with hearing about some new invention or technique, he was compelled to see it for himself. Everywhere he traveled, he found something of interest. He insisted on careful observation and throughout his life recorded in meticulous detail the data he collected. On board ship for Paris he recorded daily temperatures and observations of birds and marine life, and while on horseback during the British invasion of Richmond he recorded notes on scraps of paper kept in his boots. He once commented that it was truly unfortunate that so few public figures make notes, without which history becomes fable instead of fact.

By the turn of the century, Jefferson's knowledge of the world of culture and learning had grown enormously. He had spent five years in Paris, where he had, among his other duties, served several American universities by reviewing and often sending home the latest scientific journals as well as books and mechanical devices. He was well aware of the important advances made by science in the seventeenth and eighteenth centuries.

Jefferson's interest in the practice and teaching of medicine had continued unabated after he left Williamsburg, but on the whole he distrusted physicians, saying that he "would rather trust to the unaided, or rather uninterfered with efforts of nature than to physicians in general."[5] The wide disagreement among the physicians of that day as to the significance of the new scientific concepts and their "visionary theories" made him uncomfortable.[6]

Jefferson's distrust of physicians is perhaps nowhere better indicated than in a letter he wrote in June 1807, while serving his second term in the White House. The letter was written to Dr. Casper Wistar, requesting that he care for his grandson, who was to study in Philadelphia in the Schools of Botany, Natural History, Anatomy, and perhaps Surgery, but not Medicine. His reasons for not wanting his grandson to study medicine were given in part as follows:

> We know, from what we see and feel, that the animal body is in its organs and functions subject to derangement inducing pain, and tending to its destruction. In this disordered state, we observe nature providing for the re-establishment of order, by exciting some salutary evacuation of the morbilic matter or by some other operation which escapes our imperfect senses and researches. . . . Experience has taught us, also, that there are certain substances, by which, applied to the living body, internally or externally, we can at will produce these same evacuations, and thus do, in a short time, what nature would do but slowly, and do effectually, what perhaps she would not have the strength to accomplish. . . .

> So far, I bow to the utility of medicine. It goes to the well-defined forms of disease, and happily, to those the most frequent. But the disorders of the animal body, and the symptoms indicating them, are as various as the elements of which the body is composed. The combinations, too, of these symptoms are so infinitely diversified, that many associations of them appear too rarely to establish a definite disease; and to an unknown disease there cannot be a known remedy. Here then, the judicious, the moral, the humane physician should stop.

> Or, if the appearance of doing something be necessary to keep alive the hope and spirits of the patient, it should be of the most innocent character.[7]

President Jefferson continued:

> But the adventurous physician goes on, and substitutes presumption for knowledge. From the scanty field of what is known, he launches into the boundless region of what is unknown. He establishes for his guide some fanciful theory, . . . which lets him into all nature's secrets at short hand. On the principle which he thus assumes, he forms his table of nosology, arrays his disease into families, and extends his curative treatment, by analogy, to all the cases he has thus arbitrarily marshaled together.

> The patient, treated on the fashionable theory, sometimes gets well in spite of the medicine. The medicine, therefore, restored him, and the young doctor receives new courage to proceed in his bold experiments on the

lives of his fellow-creatures. I believe we may safely affirm, that the inexperienced and presumptuous band of medical tyros let loose upon the
world, destroys more of human life in one year, than all the Robinhoods,
Cartouches and Macheaths do in a century. It is on this part of medicine
that I wish to see a reform, an abandonment of hypothesis for sober facts,
the first degree of value set on clinical observation, and the lowest on visionary theories.

I would wish the young practitioner, especially, to have deeply impressed
on his mind, the real limits of his art, and that when the state of his patient
gets beyond these, his office is to be a watchful, but quiet spectator of the
operations of nature, giving them fair play by a well-regulated regimen, and
by all the aid they can derive from the excitement of good spirits and hope
in the patient.

The only sure foundations of medicine are, an intimate knowledge of the
human body, and observation on the effects of medicinal substances on
that. The anatomical and clinical schools, therefore, are those in which
the young physician should be formed. If he enters with innocence that of
the theory of medicine, it is scarcely possible he should come out untainted
with error. His mind must be strong indeed, if, rising above juvenile
credulity, it can maintain a wise infidelity against the authority of his in-
structors, and the bewitching delusions of their theories.[7]

Following his retirement from the presidency, Jefferson began his efforts to
establish the state university in Charlottesville, Virginia. He aided in the revival
of the Albemarle Academy, originally chartered in 1803 and converted by Act
of the Assembly into Central College in February 1816. The cornerstone of the
first building was laid on 6 October 1817, but before a single student could be
admitted, the bill for the establishment of a state university received final approval,
and Jefferson worked to assure that Central College would become the University
of Virginia.[8]

In February, 1818 the General Assembly of Virginia appropriated $15,000
to found the state university and appointed a commission with Jefferson as its
chairman to select a site, choose plans, and organize the administration. The
commission met 1 August 1818 at Rockfish Gap in the Blue Ridge Mountains.
The adoption of the Rockfish Gap Report by the General Assembly (25 February
1819), despite vigorous opposition from representatives of other counties, was
a great triumph for Jefferson; his county was chosen as the site, his designs were
accepted, and he was elected to the board of visitors and later made its rector.
From this position he would supervise the building, the selection of faculty, the
contents of the library, and courses of study.

The Rockfish Gap Report contains the following statement prepared by a committee headed by Thomas Jefferson:

Medicine, where fully taught, is usually subdivided into several professorships, but this cannot well be without the accessory of an hospital, where the student can have the benefit of attending clinical lectures, and of assisting at operations of surgery. With this accessory, the seat of our University is not yet prepared, either by its population or by the numbers of poor who would leave their own houses, and accept of the charities of an hospital. For the present, therefore, we propose but a single professor for both medicine and anatomy. By him the medical science may be taught with a history and explanations of all its successive theories from Hippocrates to the present day; and anatomy may be fully treated. Vegetable pharmacy will make a part of the botanical course and mineral and chemical pharmacy of those of mineralogy and chemistry. This degree of medical information is such as the mass of scientific students would wish to possess, as enabling them in their course through life, to estimate with satisfaction the extent and limits of the aid of human life and health, which they may understandingly expect from that art; and it constitutes such a foundation for those intended for the profession, that the finishing course of practice at the bed-sides of the sick, and at the operations of surgery in a hospital, can neither be long nor expensive. To seek this finishing elsewhere, therefore, must be submitted to for a while.[9]

A two-year medical school was developed, because there was no hospital available at the time.

By 1824, construction of the university was nearing completion, and the anticipated date of the first session was March 1825. Jefferson, then eighty-one years old, was dismayed to hear from Joseph Cabell, a member of the legislature, of the proposal by John Augustine Smith, the president of William and Mary College, to move that college to the state capital at Richmond and re-found a great university with schools of theology and medicine. Cabell first warned Jefferson of these efforts by letter 5 May 1824.

The clergy, the Federal party, the metropolis, and probably the faculty of medicine throughout the State, will advocate the removal. . . . The medical faculty, too, may say, the State wants a medical school, and there can be no hospitals at the University. Let us turn the college into a medical school at Richmond, where we can give clinical lectures. [10]

The forces favoring the move of the College of William and Mary to Richmond argued that clinical facilities would be more readily available in Richmond than in Charlottesville. During the exchange of letters with Cabell, Jefferson reflected the attitude of the times toward hospitals and recognized the benefit that might accrue from an association with the federal government in the education of medical students. In a letter dated 16 May 1824, he noted:

And I will ask how many families in Richmond would send their husbands, wives, or children to a hospital, in sickness, to be attended by nurses hardened by habit against the feelings of pity, to lie in public rooms harassed by the cries and sufferings of disease under every form, alarmed by the groans of the dying, exposed as a corpse to be lectured over by a clinical professor, to be crowded and handled by his students to hear their case learnedly explained to them, its threatening symptoms developed, and its probable termination foreboded? In vindication of Richmond, I may surely answer that there is not in the place a family so heartless, as, relinquishing their own tender cares of a child or parent, to abandon them in sickness to this last resource of poverty; for it is poverty alone which peoples hospitals, and those alone who are on the charities of their parish would go to their hospital.[7]

Jefferson continued:

I have always had Norfolk in view for this purpose. The climate and pontine country around Norfolk render it truly sickly in itself. It is, moreover, the rendezvous not only of the shipping of commerce, but of the vessels of the public navy. The United States have there a hospital already established, and supplied with subjects from these local circumstances. I had thought and have mentioned to yourself and our colleagues, that when our medical school has got well under way, we should propose to the federal government the association with that establishment, and at our own expense, of the clinical branch of our medical school, so that our students, after qualifying themselves with the other branches of the science here, might complete their course of preparation by attending clinical lectures for six or twelve months at Norfolk.[7]

The controversy continued, and by the end of the year Cabell wrote to Jefferson from Richmond of his increasing concern.

The hostile party in Richmond and the college aim decidedly at a great institution connected with a medical school.[10]

And further:

A powerful weapon used by the President of the College [William and Mary] is that of a medical college at this place by the voluntary annexation of a medical faculty to William & Mary on its removal. He says it is as impossible to make doctors at the University of Virginia as it is to have ships without sails or waves; and asserts that he will teach here what cannot be taught there.[10]

Mr. Jefferson replied on 22 December 1824:

The proposition to remove William and Mary College to Richmond with all its present funds, and to add to it a medical school is nothing more or less than to remove the University also to that place. Because, if both remain, there will not be students enough to make either worthy the acceptance of men of the first order of science.[7]

The skillful and vigorous opposition led by Mr. Jefferson was enough finally to defeat the proposition that William and Mary College be moved to Richmond. The University of Virginia remained in Charlottesville.

Mr. Jefferson brought the twenty-six-year-old Robley Dunglison from England in 1825 to serve as first professor of medicine. Not only was he the first professor of medicine, he was the sole professor of medicine, and was responsible for Anatomy, Surgery, the History of the Progress and Theories of Medicine, Physiology, Materia Medica, and Pharmacy.

Rules were strict and devotion to academic life total. The board of visitors determined on 7 April 1824 that:

> The collegiate duties of a professor, if discharged conscientiously, with industry and zeal, being sufficient to engross all his hours of business, he shall engage in no other pursuits of emolument unconnected with the service of the University without the consent of the Visitors.[7]

Dr. Dunglison was apparently able to convince the board of visitors that the professor of medicine should be treated in a different fashion. An important administrative change was made by the visitors and recorded by Jefferson 3 October 1825.

> The Board, considering that it will be for the benefit of the school of medicine that its professor should have opportunities of keeping in mind, to a certain degree, the practical part of his profession, and of acquiring moreover a knowledge of the peculiarities of disease incident to our climate and country, are of opinion that, besides the habitual practice within the precincts of the University, allowed by a former resolution, he be permitted also to act as a consulting physician elsewhere, so timing those avocations however, as not to interrupt the regular business of his school.[7]

Dr. Dunglison was thus not permitted to practice his profession outside of the university except in consultation. He was the first full-time professor of medicine in this country.[5]

Classes were conducted in Pavilion X on the Lawn until completion of the first medical building, the anatomical Theater, in 1827. This building, designed by Mr. Jefferson, was not completed until after his death. It served the medical school until 1924, when it was declared unsafe, and it was demolished in 1938 as part of the site preparation for the Alderman Library.

That response to the potential of "outside funding" of medical education is not new, can be noted from a letter Mr. Jefferson wrote to Joseph C. Cabell 3 February 1825, regarding the anatomical theater.

> I mentioned to you formerly our want of an anatomical hall for dissection. But if we get the fifty thousand dollars from Congress, we can charge to that as the library fund, the six thousand dollars of the building fund

which we have advanced for it in books and apparatus, and re-paying from the former the six thousand dollars due to the latter, apply so much of it as is necessary to the anatomical building. No application on the subject need, therefore, be made to our Legislature . . . .[10]

From the wording of that letter it is apparent that Mr. Jefferson could still hold his own in bureaucratic Washington, and from the intent, it is clear that he would have made an outstanding medical school dean!

In his waning years Mr. Jefferson was attended by Dr. Dunglison, and an interesting series of letters passed between them. One of those, which follows, has reference to the refusal of Dr. Dunglison to tender a bill for his services to Mr. Jefferson, who, as rector of the University, was his employer.

Monticello, November 26, 1825

Dear Doctor

Your letter of the 18th [which contained Dunglison's refusal of compensation] places me under great embarrassment. The fragment of life remaining to me is likely to be passed in sickness and suffering. The young physicians in our neighborhood will probably be good ones in time. But time & experience as well as science are necessary to make a skilful physician, and Nature is preferable to an unskillful one. I had therefore made up my mind to trust to her altogether, until your arrival gave me better prospects. But these again seem likely to be disappointed by a refusal on your part to receive a just compensation for your services, without which it is impossible for me to consent to the trouble of your rendering them. I thought we had settled it otherwise; and I still hope you will relieve me by receding from this scruple and permitting me to avail myself of your skill and cares, on the footing of others; in which confidence, I enclose you an order on Mr. Raphael (who holds my little bank here) for a sum which I have been obliged to name by guess, being entirely ignorant of what it should be. I am sure it is not too much, and if too little say so with freedom and it shall be immediately corrected. Grant me this favor, dear Doctor as an assurance that I may freely expect your aid on the only condition on which I can possible reconcile to myself to ask it.

Ever and affectionately yours:

Th. Jefferson.[11]

For the young who take umbrage at Mr. Jefferson's emphasis on the need of time to insure the appropriate ripening of a physician, remember that Dunglison was himself but twenty-seven years old at that time. Those who find Mr. Jefferson's desire to pay for services rendered to him consonant with their own will be pleased to know that Dunglison did accept this single payment of $50.00.

In a second letter of 26 November 1825, Jefferson sought further comment from Dunglison on their plans for a dispensary at the university.[11] By the time of the April meeting of the board of visitors in 1826, these plans were far enough along for the following resolution to be adopted:

> At a meeting of the Visitors of the University of Virginia, held at the said University, on Monday the 3d and Tuesday the 4th of April, 1826, at which were present, Thomas Jefferson, Joseph C. Cabell, John H. Cocke, Chapman Johnson and James Madison, the following proceedings were had:

> There shall be established in the University a dispensary, which shall be attached to the medical school, and shall be under the sole direction and government of the professor of medicine, who shall attend personally at the anatomical theatre, or such other place as he shall notify, from half after one to two o'clock on every Tuesday, Thursday and Saturday, for the purpose of dispensing medical advice, vaccination, and aid in surgical cases of ordinary occurrence, to applicants needing them.

> All poor, free persons, disordered in body, topically or generally, and applying for advice, shall receive it gratis; all others, bond or free, shall receive it on payment of half a dollar at each attendance, for the use of the institution, and all persons shall be vaccinated gratis, and the students particularly shall be encouraged to be so, as a protection to the institution against the malady of the small-pox.

> The students of the medical school shall be permitted to attend with the professor, to examine the patients by the pulse, and other indications of disease, ask of them such questions as the professor shall think pertinent and shall permit, and to acquire practical knowledge of the processes of pharmacy by taking a part in the preparation of medicines.[7]

With this resolution the first clinic was established at the university. Medical students were urged to attend and assist the professor in the care of the patients. The poor received all care without charge. Vaccination against smallpox was offered free to rich and poor alike, and reflects Mr. Jefferson's extraordinary interest in and advocation of vaccination.[6]

Thomas Jefferson's influence on the teaching of medicine has extended beyond his own long life, even to modern times. The very first words in the introduction to the Arizona Medical School Study, undertaken to determine the need of a medical school in Arizona, were his.

> With your talents and industry, with science, and that steadfast honesty which eternally pursues right, regardless of consequences, you may promise yourself everything—but health, without which there is no happiness. An attention to health, then, should take place of every other object.[7]

These words, originally written by Jefferson in a letter to T. M. Randolph, Jr., 6 July 1787, were offered as a maxim for the citizens of Arizona in 1962 by the Study Committee headed by Joseph F. Volker.[12]

Jefferson's scientific knowledge was not always exhaustive; his facts and his conclusions not always right. But, for a man who devoted his life to politics in the service of his country, his scientific attainments were truly remarkable.

The concluding paragraph of the Wistar letter provides additional evidence of his personal sense of identification with science.

> I dare say, that by this time, you are sufficiently sensible that old heads as well as young, may sometimes be charged with ignorance and presumption. The natural course of the human mind is certainly from credulity to scepticism; and this is perhaps the most favorable apology I can make for venturing so far out of my depth. . . . At any rate, it has permitted me, for a moment, to abstract myself from the dry and dreary waste of politics, into which I have been impressed by the times on which I happened, and to indulge in the rich fields of nature, where alone I should have served as a volunteer, if left to my natural inclinations and partialities.[7]

References

1. Randolph SN. The Domestic Life of Thomas Jefferson. New York, Frederick Ungar Publ. Co., 1958, pp 410–411.
2. Ford PL, ed. The Works of Thomas Jefferson. New York, G. P. Putnam and Sons, 1904, vol. I, p.78.
3. Moore TC and Shield JA. Medical education at America's first university. J. Med. Educ. 44:241, 1969.
4. Shield JA. Jefferson's School of Medicine at the College of William and Mary in Virginia. Va. Med. Mon. 95:88, 1968.
5. Radbill SX. The autobiographical ana of Robley Dunglison, M.D. Trans. Am. Phil. Soc. N. 5. 53:3, 1963.
6. Hall CR. Jefferson on the medical theory and practice of his day. Bull. Hist. Med. 3 1:235, 1957.
7. Lipscomb AA, ed. The Writings of Thomas Jefferson. Washington, D.C., Thomas Jefferson Memorial Association of the United States, 1904, vol. VI, p.168; vol. XI, pp.242-248; vol. XVI, pp.37–39, 84; vol. XIX, pp.435–436, 470–471, and 488–489.
8. Hart AD, Jr. Thomas Jefferson's influence on the foundation of medical instruction at the University of Virginia. Ann. Med. Hist. N. 5. 10:58, 1938.
9. Lee GC, ed. Crusade Against Ignorance: Thomas Jefferson on Education. New York, Teachers College Press, Columbia University, 1961, pp.125–126.
10. Cabell NF, ed. Early Ilistory of the University of Virginia as Contained in the Letters of Thomas Jefferson and Joseph C. Cabell. Richmond, J. W. Randolph, 1856, pp.305, 317, 319, and 340.
11. Dorsey JM. The Jefferson-Dunglison Letters. Charlottesville, University of Virginia Press, 1960, pp.44–45, and 47.
12. Volker JF, dir. The Arizona Medical School Study, Tucson, Arizona, University of Arizona Press. 1962, p.xv.

ALEXIS ST. MARTIN, 1794–1880

EDWARD J. VAN LIERE, M.D.
(October 1963, pp. 105–108)

Ed Van Liere was born in Kenosha, Wisconsin, in 1895 and he died in Morgantown, West Virginia, in 1979. He earned his M.D. from Harvard Medical School and was elected to AΩA in 1920. As many in his era at that school, he was stimulated to do research by Walter B. Cannon, M.D., who also was one of the early faculty leaders of AΩA nationally, stirring interest in many medical schools to seek charters. One year after medical school, he arrived at West Virginia University as chair (and only faculty member) of the Department of Physiology. Hypoxia was the theme of his research throughout his career. In 1935, after West Virginia University School of Medicine had lost its accreditation, Van Liere was asked to re-establish the credibility of the school . . . and he did! He then served as Dean for a total of 25 years. At his retirement the president of the University characterized him as " . . . not only a gentleman but a gentle man, but with a hard core of absolute integrity. . . ."

PRESUMABLY EVERY PHYSICIAN, and indeed, nearly everyone who has studied physiology is familiar with the name of Alexis St. Martin, patient of the physician and renowned pioneer physiologist, William Beaumont. The scientific contributions and magnetic personality of this physician make him tower over Alexis St. Martin, the humble Canadian voyageur. There is, however, a glory of the moon as well as a glory of the sun. It is fitting that we pay tribute to one who, after all, made it possible for Dr. Beaumont to make his notable contributions to gastric physiology and gastroenterology.

Alexis St. Martin was born April 18, 1794 at Berthier, Lower Canada (now the Province of Quebec, near Montreal). His full name was Alexis Bidagan dit St. Martin. Virtually nothing is known of him except that he was a voyageur employed by the American Fur Company, until the day he received his grievous wound. Parenthetically, a voyageur is defined in the dictionary as an expert woodsman and boatman, but especially one employed by a fur company as a guide.

It was on June 6, 1822 that Alexis, then 28 years old, was accidentally shot when standing in the company store of John Jacob Astor's American Fur Company on Mackinac Island in northern Michigan. He had received a whole charge of powder, duck shot, and wadding in his left upper abdomen. He fell to the floor, and since he was only a couple of feet away from the muzzle of the gun, his clothes caught fire.

Fortunately, Dr. William Beaumont, 37-year-old United States Army surgeon, who was stationed at Fort Mackinac, was immediately available and he promptly attended St. Martin. As an army surgeon, Dr. Beaumont had had wide experience in treating battle wounds, and when he saw Alexis he did not think the man would live.

Dr. Beaumont wrote a vivid description of the wound:

> The whole charge . . . was received in the left side . . . in a posterior direction, obliquely forward and outwards, carrying away by its force the integuments more than the size of the palm of a man's hand; blowing off and fracturing the sixth rib from about the middle anteriorly, fracturing the fifth, rupturing the lower portion of the left lobe of the lungs, and lacerating the stomach by a spicula of the rib that was blown through its coat, lodging the charge, wadding, and fire in among the fractured ribs and lacerated muscles and integuments, and burning the clothing and flesh to a crisp. . . .

Dr. Beaumont cleansed the wound, but when he attempted to reduce the protruding stomach, he found that the membrane of the lung had caught on the sharp point of a fractured rib. He had, therefore, not only to reduce the stomach, but the lung as well, indicating the severity of the wound. The young surgeon placed a poultice (made up of flour, hot water, charcoal and yeast) on the wound to slough off the damaged tissue, and bathed the surrounding parts with a solution of muriate of ammonia "in spirits of vinegar." Much to Dr. Beaumont's surprise his patient lived.

The wound did not heal rapidly. Successive abscesses developed, fragments of bone and cartilage sloughed off as did portions of the lung and stomach. Beaumont found it necessary to remove the sixth rib. Eventually the muscles and integuments contracted around the wound and slowly began to cicatrize. A gastric fistula developed, and in order to prevent food from oozing out of the fistula, it was necessary for a while to apply a dressing over that portion of the abdomen. The aperture was closed after the fourth week by partial inversion, but not sealed, and a finger could be inserted into the cavity. A small fold, composed of the coats of the stomach and filling the aperture, appeared 18 months after the accident. This acted as a natural valve in retaining food and drink in the stomach.

Dr. Beaumont was quick to take advantage of the fact that there was an aperture in St. Martin's stomach, and began his studies on gastric digestion. Since this essay deals principally with Alexis St. Martin I will not dwell on the many noteworthy scientific contributions Beaumont made. Suffice it to say that his researches, many of which were performed with meager equipment, added greatly to our knowledge of gastric physiology. Dr. Beaumont is still recognized as one of the great American physiologists.

Following St. Martin's accident, public funds were provided for his care, but after ten months the governmental fathers announced that further money would not be forthcoming. He was declared a pauper upon the town and county of Mackinac. They proposed to send the young voyageur to Montreal in an open boat, a distance of about 1,500 miles. Dr. Beaumont, of course, complained bitterly that such a journey would kill his patient. The officials were, however, quite adamant despite the physician's objections.

Dr. Beaumont then did a kind deed. He took Alexis into his home, and made him a member of his growing family. He remained in Beaumont's household for about two years and during all this time received free medical care, which included having his wound dressed at least daily. After about two years Alexis was able to walk.

In June 1825, Beaumont was ordered to Fort Niagara. His family and Alexis accompanied him. The surgeon then went on furlough to visit his family in Plattsburgh and again he took St. Martin along. Beaumont had probably planned to exhibit his unusual patient to the prominent scientists of the day. Be that as it may, the voyageur finding that he was so close to the Canadian border, much to Beaumont's surprise and chagrin took "French leave."

Most scientists—and I have been one of them—instinctively censure St. Martin for running away, but perhaps we should assume a somewhat more charitable attitude toward him. Here was a man who had led the gay, roving, care-free life of a voyageur, and according to song and legend it would be difficult to imagine a more untrammeled existence.

After he received the gunshot wound his entire life was changed. He had to suffer the inconveniences and indignities of having someone constantly prodding him in the stomach, and placing both digestible and indigestible materials in it. When he became surly or depressed, his physician would study St. Martin's gastric mucosa, and when he drank too much liquor (and for a while he did) he was again minutely studied. Although Dr. Beaumont was kind and patient, St. Martin could not call his soul his own. He had to suffer further traumatic experiences, as people began to point him out as a man, "with a lid on his stomach." All in all, his life surely was not a pleasant one. It must have been difficult for an unlearned and uncultured person to appreciate the necessity of the endless, and to him pointless, experiments to which he was continually subjected.

Following St. Martin's disappearance, Dr. Beaumont made desperate efforts to locate him, but could find no clues. Actually, Alexis had acquired a wife and children, and supported them by working as a voyageur for the Hudson Bay Fur Company. It is known that he went to Indian country during 1827–28. He was living in a small Canadian village, and there is evidence that he was "poor and miserable beyond description." He remained in Canada for four years.

Finally, in 1829 Beaumont tracked him down, but after he got in touch with him it took about two years to induce Alexis to return to the United States. By using influential friends he had Alexis hired by the American Fur Company and sent to Fort Crawford where Beaumont was located. Fort Crawford was situated at Prairie du Chien, Wisconsin.

As soon as Alexis arrived with his wife and two children Beaumont launched upon a new series of experiments. This went on for about two years. In 1831 the voyageur's wife became extremely homesick and Beaumont allowed the entire family to return to their homeland. Alexis agreed that he would return within a year, and to Beaumont's surprise he fulfilled his agreement. Dr. Beaumont promptly drew up a most unusual legal contract with Alexis. In essence, the contract allowed Beaumont to "reasonably and properly" use St. Martin's fistula and stomach for experimentation and exhibition for a period of a year. Alexis in turn was to receive food, clothing, lodging and a certain amount of money.

In 1832, Beaumont went to Plattsburgh on furlough, but he spent most of his time in Washington, D. C. Alexis was with him. Surgeon General Loveil of the United States Army was a good friend of Beaumont and was sympathetic with his researches. Alexis was made a sergeant of a detachment of orderlies stationed at the War Department on December 1, 1832. This relieved Beaumont from a considerable financial burden. Presumably this shrewd move also prevented Alexis from running away, since it would now be a military offense.

In the year 1833 Beaumont published his famous work, *Experiments and Observations on the Gastric Juice and the Physiology of Digestion*. The book was well received indeed, and was heralded by no less a scientist than the great German physiologist, Johannes Müller. Following the publication of this book there was a lull in Beaumont's experiments.

In the spring of 1834 Beaumont and Alexis separated. Beaumont had completed a trip to Boston and other areas where he exhibited Alexis. The voyageur went to Canada, and promised to return, but never did. From 1834 to 1852, that is, for 18 years, attempts were made to persuade Alexis to return. Beaumont tried to bribe him in an effort to bring him back but to no avail. Alexis would write: "Money here is very scarce. . . ."

Beaumont then would send him money and complain about that "old fistulous Alexis." Beaumont even sent one of his own sons to bargain with the wiley Canadian, but the middle-aged voyageur stayed well out of reach.

Surgeon General Lovell died in 1836, and the new Surgeon General, a stickier for form, did not entirely see eye to eye with Dr. Beaumont and his experiments on Alexis St. Martin. Beaumont resigned from the army and developed a large practice in St. Louis, Missouri. Even a few months before his death

Beaumont still tried to entice his old patient to come to St. Louis. Dr. Beaumont died in March 1853, at the age of 68.

Alexis is more difficult to trace after Beaumont's death. It is known that in 1856 he was exhibiting himself in some of the eastern medical schools. In 1870 he lived in Cavendish, Vermont, with his wife and four married children, making his living by chopping wood. From 1876 to 1879 the family lived in Oakdale, Massachusetts, where several of his children worked in a cotton mill. In the early part of 1879 he returned to St. Thomas in Canada and went to live with one of his children. His other children and wife stayed in Oakdale.

On June 24, 1880 Alexis died at the age of 86. He was buried in the cemetery of the Roman Catholic Parish church at St. Thomas on June 28. It was said that the body was left to decompose for four days in the hot weather before burial so the coffin had to be left outside the church during the funeral services. He was buried in an unmarked grave. Presumably this was done purposefully for fear the body would be disinterred. It was said further that the grave was eight feet in depth and that stones were piled on the coffin to prevent grave robbing. Dr. William Osler was most anxious to obtain an autopsy, but he was warned to stay away, and was told that the grave was guarded every night by riflemen.

It is fitting that at last Alexis St. Martin has been commemorated. The Canadian Physiological Society has placed a tablet near the place of his burial. It is of more than passing interest to give some details concerning the incident. In 1957 a committee of the Canadian Physiological Society was formed to locate the grave of Alexis St. Martin and mark it with a commemorative stone or plaque.

It was known that St. Martin had died in 1880 at St. Thomas. At the Parish of St. Thomas there was a record of his burial on June 28, 1880, but his grave was unmarked. Finally, the members of the committee were able to get in touch with a granddaughter of St. Martin who lived in Montreal. This lady was seven years old when her grandfather died. She graciously consented to visit St. Thomas with members of the committee. She confided that there was a common agreement within the family on the site of the grave of her grandfather and pointed out the spot. The committee then placed the tablet in that area.

The inscription of the plaque reads:

In Memory of
Alexis Bidagan dit St. Martin

Born April 18, 1794 at Berthier. Died June 24, 1880 at St. Thomas Buried June 28, 1880 in an unmarked grave close by this tablet. Grievously injured by the accidental discharge of a shotgun on June 6, 1882 at Michillimackinac, Michigan, he made a miraculous recovery under the care of Dr. William Beaumont, Surgeon in the United States Army. After his wounds had healed, he was left with an opening into the stomach and became the subject of Dr. Beaumont's pioneering work on the physiology of digestion.

Through his affliction he served all humanity.

Erected by the Canadian Physiological Society.

June 1962

The unveiling of the tablet on the afternoon of June 9, 1962, was witnessed by a large group of people. Besides members of the Canadian Physiological Society there were in attendance many parishioners of St. Thomas, and a large number of the St. Martin family—all descendants of Alexis St. Martin, some of whom had come from the United States for the occasion.

In the group there were a number of distinguished visitors, among them a representative of the Surgeon General of the United States Army, the Dean of the faculty of the University of Ottawa, a representative of the Medical Research Council of Canada, and the curator of the medical library of Yale University. The tablet was unveiled by Dr. Alan C. Burton, professor of biophysics at the University of Western Ontario, and president of the Canadian Physiological Society. He delivered a brief address in French.

The Committee of Commemoration of Alexis Bidagan dit St. Martin of the Canadian Physiological Society wrote the following fitting tribute, not only to honor Alexis St. Martin, but to honor all those individuals, who have in one way or another, contributed to the growth and development of science by serving as volunteers:

> In recalling the memory of Alexis St. Martin the Canadian Physiological Society wished to encompass in its tribute all the passive collaborators of science, all the patients who without prospect of immediate benefit contribute nonetheless to the growth and development of science. But most of all the society wishes to pay homage to Alexis, this uneducated man who consented to make the long trips of several months' duration in the great canoes, to be separated from his family for years on end, and to endure who knows many other forgotten discomforts, in order to be of service to that pioneer of physiology, William Beaumont.

The Committee of Commemoration of Alexis Bidagan dit St. Martin
of the Canadian Physiological Society.

References

1. Alexis St. Martin Commemorated, The Physiologist, 6:63–65, No. 1 (Feb.) 1963.
2. Beaumont W. Experiments and Observations on the Gastric Juice and the Physiology of Digestion. (1883) Dover Publications, New York, 1959.
3. Bensley EH. Alexis St. Martin, J. Mich. Med. Soc., S8:738-741 (May) 1959.
4. Editorial: William Beaumont and Alexis St. Martin, JAMA, 182:863–865, No. 8 (Nov. 24) 1962.

5. Medical Milestones. Shot Heard Around the World, Wis. Med. Alumni J., 1:2–4 No. 1 (May) 1956.
6. Myers JS. Life and Letters of Dr. William Beaumont, C. V. Mosby Co., St. Louis, 1939.
7. Podolsky E. William Beaumont and the Mysteries of Digestion, W. Va. Med. J., 56:345–348 (Sept.) 1960.

THE LEGACIES OF WILLIAM BEAUMONT, PIONEER INVESTIGATOR

ROBERT M. ZOLLINGER, M.D.

(Winter 1983, pp. 20–23)

Dr. Zollinger (AΩA, Ohio State University, 1934) was professor and chairman emeritus of the Department of Surgery, Ohio State University College of Medicine. This paper is based on Dr. Zollinger's Alpha Omega Alpha lecture at the Northwestern University Medical School in Chicago in April 1982.

A NINETEENTH-CENTURY UNITED STATES ARMY SURGEON, William Beaumont, is known as a pioneer investigator of human gastric physiology. His studies of gastric digestion with his subject Alexis St. Martin, who had a permanent gastrostomy resulting from an accidental gunshot wound in June 1822, are recognized throughout the scientific world. He documented the presence of hydrochloric acid in human digestion and made man aware of gastric acidity.[1]

Few investigators have duplicated their experiments so frequently over such a long period of time. After the first report of 4 experiments in 1825, Dr. Beaumont did not publish the remaining 234 experiments until 1833. Beaumont believed that his observations constituted incontrovertible facts that could not be disproved and that they might lead other investigators astray. It is amazing that his fundamental observations were withheld from publication for so long.

Although Beaumont had no special training in chemistry or physiology, he must be credited with seeking the collaboration of basic scientists to support his studies of gastric juice. Perhaps General Joseph Lovell, the first surgeon general of the American army and Beaumont's benefactor, should also be given recognition, since it was he who placed Beaumont on detached duty as a recruiter for six months in Washington, D.C., to enable him to make further scientific observations on the gastric secretion of Alexis St. Martin. Lovell also arranged for St. Martin to be inducted into the U.S. Army as a sergeant at $12.00 a month, thus relieving Beaumont from the heavy personal expenses of supporting his subject.[2, p. 152]

At the same time, General Lovell extended an invitation to Professor Robley Dunglison of the University of Virginia to travel to Washington to aid Beaumont in his experiments on St. Martin's gastric juice. Dr. Dunglison had been brought to the United States by Thomas Jefferson of the University of Virginia as the first full-time professor of medicine in the United States, and he had also served as Jefferson's personal physician. Physiology was his chief scientific interest, and he had written a book on this subject. At a meeting in Washington, during the winter of 1832–33, Beaumont submitted a quantity of gastric juice to Professor Dunglison, and on February 6, 1833, Dunglison reported:

> We have found it to contain free Muriatic and Acetic acid, Phosphates and Muriates, with bases of Potassa, Soda, Magnesiam and Lime, and an animal matter, soluble in cold water, but insoluble in hot. We were satisfied, you recollect, in Washington, that free muriatic acid was present, but I had no conception it existed to the amount met with in our experiments here.[1, p. 78]

Beaumont had long been convinced of the presence of free muriatic acid in the gastric fluids, since it seemed quite obvious to taste. Beaumont stated:

> It is to be hoped that no one will be so disingenuous as to attribute to Professor Dunglison the design of finding the existence of certain chemical agents in the gastric juice, with the view of propping the theory of chemical action of this fluid, which he has maintained in his work on "Human Physiology"—or, in other words, to say, that he had determined to find certain results; and that he had accordingly found them. Those who are acquainted with him, know that his candour and fairness are above the reach of suspicion; and that he would be equally willing to retract a false opinion as to maintain a correct one. [1, p. 79]

Professor Dunglison had suggested the presence of a second important substance in the gastric juice. Within three years, Theodor Schwann identified this as a pepsin.[3] Beaumont expressed his high regard and gratitude to Dunglison for his kind and valuable assistance and the lively interest taken in the conduct of his gastric experiment.

Professor Dunglison observed, however, that Beaumont "avoided proper reference" to him in the publication of the experiments. Beaumont replied that he did not think Dunglison would care to be associated with so humble an individual as himself. Dunglison eventually gave Beaumont three dollars for a copy of the book *Experiments and Observations on the Gastric Juice, and the Physiology of Digestion,* which Beaumont had had published at his own expense in 1833.[1]

A final trenchant comment on the matter of collaboration appeared in the article "Beaumont and Dunglison: Who Was Dunglison?" by Kenneth Crispell in a verse he composed.

THE JUICE FEUD:
PUBLISH OR PERISH
Beaumont was wise to rush into press,
Leaving his colleagues in dire distress.
Beaumont gets credit for collecting the juice,
But Dunglison discovered
the "acid" truth.[4, p. 197]

In addition to seeking the aid of Dunglison, Beaumont had delivered a sample of gastric juice to Professor Benjamin Silliman, professor of chemistry at Yale, who suggested that a sample be sent through the Swedish consul in New York to the chemist, Professor Jacob Berzelius of Stockholm. Beaumont received a detailed report on August 2, 1833 from Professor Silliman, but other reports were received too late to be included in his book. Beaumont was a pioneer in seeking the assistance of basic scientists to solve a clinical problem. Such cooperation between clinician and basic scientist remains today a fundamental concept in the solution of clinical research problems.

One of the major legacies of Beaumont was the stimulation of physiologists to adopt a more direct method of studying gastric physiology. A Russian, Bassow (1843) and a Frenchman, Blondlot (1843), were credited with being the first physiologists to fashion permanent artificial gastric fistulas in dogs in an effort to pursue in animals the observations that Beaumont had made in man. Like the Italian naturalist, Spallanzani, Beaumont believed that the secretion of gastric juice was evoked by contact of any substance with the gastric mucosa. The "psychic secretion" of gastric juice was reported by Bidder and Schmidt in 1852;[5] Beaumont, however, had reported that irritation by a gastric tube or the stem of a thermometer stimulated a much smaller secretion than did food.[4] Babkin mentioned that Pavlov recognized his debt to his predecessors, Blondlot and Heidenhain,[6] and one could speculate whether the observations of Pavlov and others would have been made when they were, had it not been for the previous years of study and the observations made by Beaumont.

That Beaumont made such a magnificent contribution to the physiology of digestion after meager preparation of only two years of study in a physician's office might be used as an argument for a shortened present-day medical curriculum. Beaumont had read medicine for three or four years, however, while he taught school before beginning a preceptorship with Benjamin Chandler of Plattsburgh, New York, and his two years of active war experience in the War of 1812 had added much to his basic education. Beaumont's contributions clearly challenge present-day physicians to exceed routine commitments.

Beaumont's aptitude for self-education and his desire to keep abreast of the literature concerning the physiology of disease command admiration. He was a physician ahead of his time. As Connors stated:

It is abundantly clear from these documents that Beaumont had an un-
usually extensive background in general and medical literature and was
capable of conducting a sophisticated literature review in the most advanced medical libraries of the time.[7, p. 23]

Beaumont's general medical capabilities have been too little recognized because of the emphasis on his experimental observations on Alexis St. Martin.

Other Beaumont legacies are less well known. One of these was the securing of official sanction shortly after his arrival at the army post at Mackinac
Island in Michigan in 1820 to "moonlight" in order to provide private care to
civilians. Nonmilitary personnel commonly sought treatment from medical officers, who were either the only or the most outstanding physicians in the area,
and Beaumont wanted to be of service to the community. Possibly, he was loath
to sever completely his private practice ties, which he had enjoyed for several
years after his military service in the War of 1812. But it is also likely that he
wished to increase his income, since he planned to marry a widow, Deborah
Green Platt of Plattsburgh, as soon as he was established in his new post.

Beaumont made his unusual request in 1820 to his old friend of the War of
1812, General Lovell, who later recruited Beaumont back into military service. Official permission was granted, with the following limitation:

> The Secretary of War has no objection to your giving your professional serv-
> ices to the sick of Mackinac, provided it does not interfere with your offi-
> cial duties. They cannot, however, be furnished from the public chest.[2, p. 82]

The army's favorable response to Beaumont's request might well be considered the first official sanction of moonlighting. The limitation or prohibition of such activities by those in government and university services has remained
a controversial issue, and the medical profession has been slow to recognize
this practice. It has become obvious in recent years, however, that an ever-increasing
number of house staff at all levels are being compensated for activities outside
their own hospitals. In 1974, the House of Delegates of the American Medical
Association affirmed the right of house staff to use off-duty time as they choose,
provided that such activities not violate contract provisions.[8] More than 150 years
passed after Beaumont gained official permission to moonlight before this activity was officially recognized by organized medicine.

Beaumont's contribution as a diarist to record keeping constitutes another
legacy. Already a confirmed diarist, he was further stimulated by the influence
of his fine preceptor, Dr. Chandler, and by Jedidiah Morse, father of Samuel B.
Morse, the inventor of the telegraph. Dr. Morse traveled with Beaumont to his
post at Mackinac. The scholarly Morse was elderly and in such poor health
that he required considerable medical attention from Beaumont. Beaumont de-

rived much "benefit and instruction" from his association with Morse and later sent Morse a "specimen of composition. [9, p. xiv]

Morse, in his notes, paid great tribute to Beaumont as a physician:

> In the feeble state of my health, I felt it to be a peculiar smile of Providence, to be favored, as we were, from Canandaigua to Mackinaw, and during our stay at the latter place with the company of Dr. Beaumont, Post Surgeon of the 3rd Regiment of the U.S. Army, a gentleman of much skill in his profession, and of most amiable and kind dispositions. To him, by means of his medical prescriptions and attentions, I feel indebted, under Providence, for the degree of health, which enabled me to fulfill my duties to the Government, probably even for my life. [9, p. 78]

Being a compulsive diarist enhanced Beaumont's relationship with his old friend, Lovell. Beaumont continued to record extensive notes on many subjects in addition to those required by the surgeon general, which included a daily record of climatic conditions. Lovell embraced the theory that meteorologic conditions affected health, and he required every physician to provide daily detailed weather reports in addition to clinical notes. Out of these reports grew the U.S. Weather Bureau. Beaumont continued throughout his life to record careful and detailed clinical notes, even while he was on detached duty in Washington and his family had returned to Plattsburgh. Among his major concerns were proper and detailed recording of his patients' complaints and clinical progress, in addition to painstaking documentation of his own experimental observations.

Certainly, fewer medicolegal problems might have arisen over the years if physicians had adhered to Beaumont's principle of keeping detailed written diaries of events concerning patients. Beaumont could well be designated the godfather of the ideal progress note. Written documentation of the patient's complaints, the treatment given, and the physician's evaluation have been reemphasized in recent years.

Yet another legacy is Beaumont's intellectual curiosity and his zeal in educating himself, exemplified in his treatment of malaria. Known as intermittent fever, or ague, malaria was a serious disease in frontier life on the Mississippi River. Beaumont had made some observations on malaria in 1830 and used quinine regularly in the treatment of this disorder, although quinine was quite expensive and was not generally given until after 1840. He had become interested in vaccination as a preventative for smallpox while he was in Green Bay, Wisconsin, in 1827. His friend Lovell made sufficient living virus available to Beaumont to enable him to inoculate many Green Bay inhabitants as well as many local Indian residents. Vaccination had not been universally accepted at that time and was not generally adopted until after the Civil War. As Connors observed:

There is no question that Beaumont took great interest in these various epidemic diseases, and in some instances was in advance of his time in theory, and in the matter of treatment and presentation.[7, p. 24]

Throughout his military career, Beaumont received the support and encouragement of General Lovell, who made special concessions over the years. He permitted Beaumont to engage in "private practice" as a medical officer; he published his early experiments; and he arranged a six-month period of detached service so that the experiments could continue. Although he was unsuccessful in obtaining financial support for Beaumont from Congress, he was of invaluable assistance. He opened the way for Professor Dunglison to provide basic science documentation of the experiments. He encouraged the printing of Beaumont's book in 1833. He made Beaumont's military assignments as comfortable and lasting as possible, with a prolonged period in St. Louis, where Beaumont was offered the chair of surgery in the new St. Louis University, the first medical school west of the Mississippi River. Beaumont accepted the appointment, though he never gave lectures or acted as chairman.

With Lovell's death in 1835, the special consideration given Beaumont came to an end. He resigned from the army after twenty-five years of service on December 31, 1839, following a conflict with the new surgeon general, General Thomas Lawson. A brilliant captain of engineers, Robert E. Lee, who had lived with the Beaumonts in St. Louis, tried in vain to keep Beaumont in the army. Beaumont remained in St. Louis, where the family had a comfortable country home. He continued his busy practice and became interested in various business ventures, especially speculative land investments, many in Wisconsin, where land he purchased in 1834 became the heart of downtown Green Bay. Beaumont's practice continued to grow, and he had several different associates for varying periods. He was a respected member of the medical community and served in 1840 as president of the Missouri Medical Society. He died in 1853.

The scientific community continues to admire William Beaumont, the army surgeon of our frontier days. As our first and most outstanding clinical investigator, he commanded the respect and admiration of investigators throughout the world.[10] He was memorialized by Sir William Osler on the occasion of the XIII International Physiological Congress in 1929,[11] as well as on many other occasions.[12] His observations on human digestion, made without the aid of a modern laboratory, assistants, or special funds, clearly show what can be accomplished when there is a will to achieve. His enormous capacity for broadening his own education should serve as a stimulus for the current emphasis on continuing education for all physicians.

Beaumont led the full life of a physician with diversified interests in his profession, his family, and his fellowman. He can be described as a fine soldier, master physician and surgeon, pioneer dietitian, investigator of the physiology of digestion, superb diarist, medical politician, and teacher. While his contributions to gastric physiology are the most memorable of his accomplishments, he made many others. His dynamic life is an example for all of us. He clearly showed the three essential qualifications for success: intelligence, industry, and integrity.

References

1. Beaumont W. Experiments and Observations on the Gastric Juice, and the Physiology of Digestion. Plattsburgh, Printed by F. P. Allen, 1833.
2. Myer JS. Life and Letters of Dr. William Beaumont. St. Louis, C. V. Mosby Co., 1912.
3. Cushing H. William Beaumont's rendezvous with fame. Yale J. Biol. Med. 8:113–26, 1935.
4. Crispell KR. Beaumont and Dunglison: Who was Dunglison? Trans. Am. Clin. Climatol. Assoc. 92:194–98, 1980.
5. Bidder F and Schmidt C. Die Verdauungssaefte und der stoffwechsel. Eine physiologisch-chemische Untersuchung. Mittau und Leipzig, G. A. Reyher, 1852.
6. Babkin BP. Pavlov, a Biography. Chicago, University of Chicago Press, 1949.
7. Connors DM. William Beaumont, M.D., a Wisconsin legacy. Wis. Med. J. 76:22–26, October 1977.
8. Proceedings of the House of Delegates, American Medical Association, 28th Clinical Congress in Portland, Oregon., Resolution 53, December 1974, p. 318.
9. Miller G. William Beaumont's Formative Years. New York, Henry Schuman, 1946.
10. Rosen G. The Reception of William Beaumont's Discovery in Europe. New York, Schuman's, 1942.
11. Osler W. William Beaumont. Experiments and Observations on the Gastric Juice, and the Physiology of Digestion. A Pioneer American Physiologist. Reprinted on the occasion of the XIII International Physiological Congress, Boston, 1929.
12. Zollinger RM and Coleman DW. The Influences of Pancreatic Tumors on the Stomach. Fiftieth Annual Beaumont Lecture. Springfield, Illinois, Charles C. Thomas, 1974.

WALTER REED
AND THE CONQUEST
OF YELLOW FEVER

PHILIP S. HENCH, M.D.

(May 1948, pp. 8–14)

Philip Hench was born in Pittsburgh, Pennsylvania, in 1896. He graduated from Lafayette College, and after a stint in the U.S. Army Medical Corps, he matriculated at the University of Pittsburgh School of Medicine, graduating in 1920. He was elected as an emeritus member of AΩA. At the Mayo Clinic, which he joined in 1923, he rose to be Head of the Department of Rheumatic Diseases in 1926. His interest in pathophysiology and the response of the body to stress led him to the conclusion that a steroid might be involved in the alleviation of rheumatic symptoms during pregnancy. A colleague in Rochester, E. C. Kendall, had been isolating several steroids from the cortex of the adrenal gland, and in 1948, the decision was made to try the effects of one of these (compound F., cortisone) on arthritis patients. A moving picture of the "before and after" when the first patient rose from her bed after the therapy astonished physicians at the clinical meetings, and it was no surprise when Kendall and Hench were awarded the Nobel Prize in Physiology or Medicine in 1950. Dr. Hench died in 1965. His son, Kahler Hench, M.D. is a Master of the American College of Rheumatology.

This talk was given before the University of Virginia chapter at Charlottesville on November 17, 1947.

At THE END OF THE CIVIL WAR, IN THE FALL OF 1865, a circuit-riding Methodist minister and his wife moved to Charlottesville so that their sons might improve their education. Their 14 year old boy first went to the Charlottesville Institute, a boys day school here. Then, just 80 years ago, in the fall of 1867, he tried to enter the Academic Department of this University. Although he was only 16 years old and under the required age, the faculty admitted Walter Reed, hoping for the best that he would make good. After one year in the undergraduate school, Walter Reed entered the medical school and promptly accomplished one of his first unusual feats. He completed the medical course in a single year, and on July 1, 1869, as the youngest man ever to earn a medical degree here, he received his diploma.

Had there been at that time a chapter of the Alpha Omega Alpha Honorary Medical Society here, Walter Reed would certainly have qualified for membership (Of course he might not have been elected!). At this later date you are honoring him by listening today to the story of "Walter Reed and the Conquest of Yellow Fever." My story might well be entitled "The University of Virginia and the Conquest of Yellow Fever," because as we shall see, three other University of Virginia men also played important roles in this drama.

At the close of the Spanish-American War, thousands of American soldiers returned home to be received like conquering heroes. But others returned home not so gloriously. Some returned in hospital ships, soldiers whose bodies had been weakened by fever. Some were in coffins, soldiers who had met death at the hands of an enemy more powerful than any Spaniard. Disease, especially yellow fever, had killed more soldiers than had the bullets of the enemy. Day after day, strong young men became hot with fever and wracked with pain; then they turned yellow, suffered with the dreaded "black vomit," and died at the rate of as many as 100 each day.

"We'll stop that," said the United States Government, and with its Army of Occupation it sent physicians whose duty it was to control yellow fever which had been endemic in Havana for more than 200 years. Among these physicians were Major Gorgas, who was responsible for the health of the soldiers and civilians in the city of Havana, and Major Jefferson R. Kean, chief surgeon of the Department of Western Cuba, a graduate of the University of Virginia, whose chief responsibility was the health of the American Soldiers at Columbia Barracks on the outskirts of Havana in the little suburban town of Quemados de Marianao, near the famous bathing beach, La Playa.

Despite the vigorous sanitary methods which were instituted, yellow fever continued to spread, and in May and June, 1900, Major Kean, a worried man, compiled a tragic list of the names of soldiers and civilians, of fellow-officers and their wives, all living in the neighboring streets of Quemados and all victims of yellow fever. The mortality rate among the officers on the headquarters staff of Generals Wood and Lee was alarming. The clerks in General Wood's office burned on their desks sulfur candles as a prophylactic measure, but the candles burned in vain, and in the officers' mess they drank a gruesome toast, "Here's to the ones who have gone. Here's to the next one to go!"

One of the earliest to go was Major Edmunds, a friend of Major Kean. Because General Lee had already lost so many officers and men he ordered all those not immediately in charge of the sick to stay away from the sickrooms of those with yellow fever. Thus Major Kean could not visit Major Edmunds who lay sick unto death in the front room of this little house. But on the last dawn that Major Edmunds was to see, Major Kean, torn between the conflicting obligations of obedience to his commanding officer and of loyalty to his dying friend, rose about 4 a.m. and went to this little porch where, technically not in the patient's room, he spent a last few minutes. During that short visit Major Kean was bitten by mosquitoes from the sick room but thought little of it. A few days later on June 11 Major Kean suddenly developed yellow fever.

As if to ridicule the puny efforts of the army medical corps, the disease was now striking down the physicians themselves! Could nobody stop this evil thing? What was its cause, anyhow? One of the commonest ideas was that the mysterious cause of yellow fever arose like an evil spirit, a miasma from the tropical swamps. An Italian physician, Sanarelli, insisted it was due to a special germ which he had discovered. But nobody really knew the cause, and when a person died of yellow fever his home was often purified by fire to destroy his presumably infected furniture, clothing, and other personal belongings, called "fomites." Thus hundreds of thousands of dollars worth of military and civilian equipment went up in smoke in an attempt to control the disease. But it was all in vain.

On June 15, the fourth day of Major Kean's illness, another army physician arrived in Havana, rushed to the bedside of his friend, the major, and exemplified in him saw his first case of yellow fever. Later that day this man, Major Walter Reed, met with three others on the veranda of the officers' quarters at Columbia Barracks Post Hospital. The three others were Drs. James Carroll, Aristides Agramonte, and Jesse W. Lazear, and the four men thus ended their first day's work as the members of the United States Army Special Yellow Fever Board.

They first attempted to find Sanarelli's germ in the bodies of those sick or dead of yellow fever, but this search soon ended in failure. Perhaps, after all, no germ was responsible for the disease. Why in Quemados had the disease progressed so erratically down the streets, striking first in one house, skipping the next few houses, then hopping around the corner, rather than crossing the affected street? Another curious fact was noted when Reed, Agramonte, and Lazear went to study an epidemic which broke out among the soldiers at Pinar del Rio. A soldier in a prison cell fell sick and died of yellow fever but his cell mates, exposed to the same food and atmosphere, remained well. Could something have entered between the bats of the open window, struck one man down and gone away? Could yellow fever be caused by a winged agent? Could Dr. Carlos Finlay be right after all?

For nineteen years this kindly old Havana physician had been trying to convince his medical colleagues that yellow fever was caused by a common house mosquito. But nobody believed him, simply because, although he had inoculated over 100 volunteers with mosquitoes, he hadn't produced a single case of the disease, which other physicians regarded as unquestionably induced or experimental rather than probably spontaneous. The volunteers were not quarantined and those few who later developed yellow fever undoubtedly got it in the ordinary way.

When Reed, Agramonte, and Lazear returned from Pinar del Rio the Board decided on August 1st to try to prove or disprove Finlay's theory once and for all. They visited Dr. Finlay who graciously gave all the help he could, including a supply of mosquito larvae of the suspected species. Thereupon a momentous and heroic decision had to be made because no animal was then known to be susceptible to yellow fever. Human volunteers were required. Unwilling to ask others to do what they themselves would not do, the Board decided to inoculate each other among the first. At this juncture Reed was unfortunately ordered to Washington to finish an important medical report. Carroll and Agramonte continued respectively their bacteriologic and pathologic studies and it fell to Lazear's lot to begin the mosquito work. This was fortunate because he of all the Board was most sympathetic to the Finlay theory. Indeed, for some time Lazear had been trying (so far unsuccessfully) to prove a relationship between mosquitoes and yellow fever. Thus on the very day the Army Board was officially named in Washington, Lazear in Quemados, Cuba, was catching mosquitoes in the room of a patient with yellow fever and (as shown from notes in his laboratory notebook) was examining their bodies for agents responsible for the disease.

Lazear began to breed Finlay's mosquitoes in their little camp laboratory and then tried to infect them by allowing them to bite yellow fever patients at Las Animas Hospital. Between August 11 and 25 these presumably infected mosquitoes were applied to nine American soldiers including Drs. Lazear and Pinto, but nothing happened. They all remained well.

Two days later, on August 27th, discouraged and doubting, Carroll permitted Lazear to inoculate him again. In a few days Carroll developed a severe and almost fatal attack of yellow fever. On the way from Carroll's bedside, Lazear (without the knowledge of his colleagues) inoculated a scoffing volunteer soldier who "wasn't afraid of any little old gnat." When yellow fever hit him six days later this soldier became a very surprised hero whose widow later received his Congressional Medal, and a memorial bridge in Grand Rapids, Michigan, was named for him.

Having accomplished two very successful inoculations Lazear wrote his wife (September 8). "I rather think I am on the track of the real germ. But nothing must be said as yet, not even a hint. I have not mentioned it to a soul." How right he was, was tragically proven by what happened ten days later, when he himself developed the dreaded disease. During his illness Dr. Lazear told two visitors, Drs. Carroll and Gorgas, that a few days before, while feeding his mosquitoes on yellow fever patients (in this room) at Las Animas Hospital, a stray mosquito had alighted on his hand. Lazear had allowed it to take its fill of his own blood. From the first he was very ill and died September 25, 1900, officially listed as a victim of "accidental yellow fever" but none the less a true martyr to science. Such is the official version of this tragic incident.

But I am about to tell you another version of the affair, one which was kept secret for forty years, and which was not even known to Dr. Lazear's widow until I was permitted to tell her of it in 1940 through the courtesy of those who revealed it to me: Walter Reed's colleagues, Generals Truby and Kean, and Dr. Agramonte's daughter.

Reed hastened back to Havana (October 4) filled with mingled emotions. He was greatly depressed at Lazear's death, yet elated that success at last seemed at hand. But he was also confused. Why did the first nine inoculations fail and the next ones succeed? The second successful case seemed incontrovertible: having been quarantined at the otherwise fever-free Post Hospital the scoffing private (Private Dean—"case XY") had had no other conceivable source of infection than via the applied infected mosquito. But could one be sure that Carroll's disease had come from the experimental mosquito bite and not from some other source to which he might have exposed himself while going about town? And how could Lazear's tragic case be used to prove anything unless somebody knew what kind of a mosquito had bitten him?

In the side pocket of the uniform blouse which Lazear had recently worn, Lieutenant Truby, at that time commanding officer of the Columbia Barracks Post Hospital, had found a small notebook containing entries about Lazear's experiments. Reed eagerly studied these and other notes. Herein was the solution of the age-old mystery, a solution which became crystal clear to the brilliant mind of Walter Reed. Finlay's mosquito (the *Culex fasciatus* or *Aedes Aegypti*) could indeed cause yellow fever but only under certain special conditions. By carefully noting the relative timings of each step in the successful and unsuccessful experiments it became obvious that patients with yellow fever have the agent or virus of their disease circulating in their blood only during the first three days of their illness. Later, when they are sicker, even sick unto death, the agent has strangely disappeared from the blood. Therefore, a mosquito to become "infected" must bite a yellow fever victim during these first three days. But even then that "infected mosquito" cannot transmit its deadly load or infect another person until the virus has had a chance to develop or "ripen," within the mosquito's body for at least twelve days.

All of the failures of Finlay and of the Board were thus explained: those volunteers who had *not* developed yellow fever either had been bitten by mosquitoes which had really never been infected (having bitten patients too late) or had been bitten by "infected mosquitoes" which were still temporarily harmless because they had not been allowed to "ripen."

Thus Lazear's little notebook was vitally useful in solving one mystery but it posed another mystery, for in it Reed found some incomplete entries which appeared to indicate that Lazear had secretly submitted himself to other experimental inoculations. Reed pondered long over these entries and then concluded that when Lazear was taken sick he must have worried lest his life insurance become forfeited if it became known that he had deliberately infected himself with a fatal disease. (Actually, this explanation was incorrect; Mrs. Lazear told me Dr. Lazear left no life insurance.) But did he for some other reason at the last fateful hour withhold facts to protect his loved ones? Was this why he had told Gorgas and Carroll that he had been bitten by a stray mosquito at Las Animas? Reed believed that it was. Having produced two cases of yellow fever and knowing the danger, Lazear would surely never have allowed a mongrel mosquito to bite him and vitiate or interrupt his experiments. Reed confided his supicions only to two or three colleagues and then decided to permit the official records to read that Lazear had become accidentally infected while in the performance of duty. Having made his quiet and heroic gesture Lazear had sought to carry his secret to a better world. Our of respect for the unspoken wishes of their friend, Lazear's colleagues have kept that secret all these years, Reed and others having carried it to their graves.

In so doing, they eminently proved their loyalty to him. But it apparently disturbed them to deprive Lazear of a greater fame and in the following unpublished remarks of Agramonte, I sense a wistful desire to rectify matters. At a Havana banquet in honor of Drs. Gorgas and Kean in June 1902, Agramonre's speech contained this tribute: "The one of us who from the very inception of our work so strenuously believed in the mosquito theory in connection with the propagation of yellow fever, the one of us who was best fitted by his training in the line of our investigation to successfully carry out the work, who in fact performed the first successful inoculation unknown to his co-workers, Jesse W. Lazear, gave up his life in the pursuit of knowledge which shall immortalize his name. May he in the Regions of the Unknown find the glory that is his due which so unjustly has been witheld by man on earth."

Knowing that a skeptical world would demand more proof than that afforded by these three successful but relatively uncontrolled inoculations, Reed now conceived, and with Carroll and Agramonte, executed a series of brilliant experiments that were to write the final chapter of this story. On the advice of Major Kean, Reed asked General Leonard Wood, Governor General of Cuba, for money with which to set up an experimental camp and to pay what Americans and Spanish volunteers might be secured. To the lasting credit of General Wood, who had himself been a physician, he promptly granted Reed's request and threw behind Reed all the authority of the governor's high office.

Yellow fever was to be given away free with premiums of $200. The victims could spend the money any way they wanted to—if they survived; a rather large *if*, considering that the mortality rate of epidemic yellow fever was about 40 per cent. But before any paid volunteers were secured, two American soldiers, John R. Kissinger and John J. Moran (who later was to be student at the

Medical School of the University of Virginia), volunteered their services only on condition that they could do so without pay and in the interests of science. Legend has it that Major Reed, profoundly affected, rose and said, "Gentlemen, I salute you." Both Kissinger and Moran told me that actually, the legend is not true, which Reed's widow and children were sorry to learn from me a few years ago. But as one writer has penned, "If Reed didn't salute them he should have!" The world is still saluting them with many honors.

A specially guarded and quarantined experimental station named Camp Lazear was set up in a secluded spot a mile from Camp Columbia. There John Kissinger bared his arm in this manner for the bites of five infected mosquitoes and promptly developed the first case of deliberately accepted and completely controlled experimental yellow fever in history. Of this Reed wrote, "In my opinion this exhibition of moral courage has never been surpassed in the annals of the Army of the United States."

Then two small specially constructed wooden buildings were erected. The first was called Building Number One or the "Infected Clothing and Bedding Building." It comprised one room, 14×20 feet, had only two small windows, and was heated by a stove to a tropical temperature. Three cots were set up and into this sweltering room were brought the soiled and foul-smelling bed clothes of yellow fever victims. Night after night Dr. Robert Cooke (U. of Va. Med. Sch., 1897) and other soldier-volunteers (Folk, Jernegan, Hanberry, Weatherwalks, Hildebrand, and England) hung these offensive clothes around the walls and on their beds, and then lay down to try to sleep on stinking pillows and sheets soiled with blood and vomitus. Stomachs rebelled, but spirits remained firm and not one of these volunteers developed yellow fever, simply because there were no mosquitoes in the room. Thus was exploded the notion that "fomites" carried the disease.

The second building of similar size (Building Number Two or the "Infected Mosquito Building") was divided into two parts separated merely by a wire screen. On a cot in one side of this room, John Moran exposed his body to the bites of fifteen loaded mosquitoes let loose in the room. He was in the room only a little over an hour in all, but promptly developed yellow fever, while other volunteers who stayed long hours on the other side of the screen where there were no mosquitoes remained well.

Moran took sick on Christmas day. His yellow fever was a wonderful Christmas gift to Walter Reed and to all the world. A few days later on New Year's Eve, Reed in a mood of exaltation and humble gratitude to God, wrote his family a much quoted letter which has become famous: "11:50 p.m., December 31, 1900—only 10 minutes of the old century remain. Here I have been sitting reading that most wonderful work—La Roche on yellow fever, written in 1853. Forty-seven years later it has been permitted to me and my assistants to lift the impenetrable veil that has surrounded the causation of this most dreadful pest of humanity and to put it on a rational and scientific basis. I thank God that this has been accomplished during the latter days of the old century.

"...The prayer that has been mine for twenty or more years, that I might be permitted in some way or some time to do something to alleviate human suffering, has been answered..

"Twelve midnight—Hark! There go the 2.4 buglers, all in concert, sounding 'Taps' for the old year! How beautiful it floats on the midnight air—."

In the bodies of twelve more American and Spanish volunteers (Benigno, Fernandez, Presedo, Martinez, Jernegan, Olson, Folk, Forbes, Andrus, West, Hanberry, and Sonnrag) yellow fever was produced at will, either through the medium of mosquito bites or by injections of infected blood or serum. Fortunately all these volunteers survived, thanks to the excellent care of Dr. Roger Post Ames. Their problem solved after just eight months of work, the Board disbanded Camp Lazear on March 1, 1901. Now armed with precise knowledge, Gorgas within three months freed Havana of its age old scourge. Later, with this and other knowledge, he made safe the Isthmus of Panama for the passage of the commerce of the world.

PRESIDENT CLEVELAND'S SECRET OPERATION: THE EFFECT OF THE OFFICE UPON THE CARE OF THE PRESIDENT

LUDWIG M. DEPPISCH, M.D.

(Summer 1995, pp. 11–16)

Dr. Deppisch continues to be on the clinical faculty of the University of Arizona School of Medicine, although he is "mostly" retired from the practice of pathology. His interests in medical history are expanding, and—relevant to the article presented here—he teaches an elective course, Health of Presidents *for medical students. In his spare time he is progressing steadily towards completion of all the requirements for a masters degree in history. He was elected to AΩA at Northeastern Ohio University College of Medicine.*

THERE HAS BEEN SIGNIFICANT RECENT INTEREST in the effects of presidential illness upon the conduct of foreign and domestic policy, wherein health is a determinant of presidential decision making.[1] Franklin Roosevelt's illness at the superpower meeting at Yalta, and Woodrow Wilson's cerebrovascular accident, and the failure of the U.S. Senate to ratify the League of Nations are two prominent examples of this theme. In this paper I propose to assess this dynamic from a different perspective—to examine the effect of the presidency upon the health care received by the incumbent.

Grover Cleveland, the only U.S. president to serve two nonconsecutive terms, is a suitable subject for such an evaluation. On July 1, 1893, during a severe financial crisis (the Panic of 1893), the president underwent the secretive and successful removal of one-third of his hard palate, for cancer, while on a yacht cruising the East River of New York City.

In 1892, Grover Cleveland had stymied President Benjamin Harrison's reelection bid. Cleveland, a conservative Democrat with significant (for a Democrat) business support was able to unify his party only by the selection of a free-silver advocate, former Assistant Postmaster General Adlai Stevenson, as his vice-presidential nominee. At that time the Democratic Party was vehemently divided between the conservative probusiness gold standard faction led by Cleveland and the inflationary prosilver faction led by William Jennings Bryan. The latter, consisting of heavily indebted farmers and small businessmen, advocated the unrestricted coinage of silver, which in turn would lower the value of the United States currency and consequently the monetary burden of their debt. They would then be able to redeem their indebtedness by paying their bills with cheaper silver-backed dollars. This view had been legalized by the passage of the Sherman Silver Purchase Act of 1890, which mandated that the U.S. Treasury purchase 4.5 million ounces of silver monthly.

The year 1893 witnessed the onset of one of the most severe economic downturns in United States history (the Panic of 1893) which included the following: the failure of many of the nation's railroads, the failure of 642 banks, severe labor strife, and the unemployment of millions of American workers. European bankers started a run on U.S. gold reserves. It was in this setting that Grover Cleveland was inaugurated on March 4, 1893, to his second, but nonconsecutive, term. The business community was confident in Cleveland's monetary judgment and was willing to support the country's economy during this difficult time. Business, however, retained significant doubts about Cleveland's vice-president and possible successor, Stevenson. *The Nation* magazine editorialized, "A great deal is staked upon the continuance of a single life."[2, p. 254] Cleveland's proposed solution to this economic crisis was a call for a special session of Congress to repeal the Sherman Silver Purchase Act in order to restore confidence in the stability of the nation's money.[2]

It was in this context that on May 5, 1893, the president noted a rough spot on the roof of his mouth. This lesion gave him increasing discomfort, and on June 18, he was examined by the White House physician, Major Robert Maitland O'Reilly. Dr. O'Reilly discovered "a malignant growth as large as a quarter of a dollar, extending from the molar teeth to within a third of an inch of the middle line, encroaching on the soft palate, and accompanied by some diseased bone."[3, p. 528] A physical examination would have also revealed Grover Cleveland to be a massive, hulking figure—at 250 pounds the heaviest president up to that time. He stood at 5 feet 11 inches and had a great bull neck, strong jaw, double chin, and ham-like fists. His health was generally good, although he suffered from gouty arthritis.

Selection of the physician to the president

Who was Dr. Robert O'Reilly, and how was he chosen to provide the medical treatment of the president? He was a graduate of the University of Pennsylvania School of Medicine, and in 1867 he was commissioned Assistant Surgeon in the U.S. Army. Remaining in the army, in 1882 he was assigned as attending surgeon in Washington. "This duty he performed during the two administrations of President Cleveland, with whom his relations were most intimate and agreeable."[4, p. 339] Selection of a military physician as the president's doctor was customary during that period. O'Reilly was apparently capable, and subsequent to his White House service, he was appointed Surgeon General with the rank of brigadier general. His tenure as surgeon general was successful, with the introduction of antityphoid vaccinations to the military and a progressive reorganization of the medical corps. . . .[6]

The choice of the physician to the president has never been systematized to assure that the most competent and appropriate person be selected. The first military practitioner to attend a president was Arnold Elzey, who cared for President James Madison. This selection method has been attractive, first, because of availability (the proximity of Bethesda Naval Hospital and Walter Reed Army Hospital) and, secondly, because of cost. A perquisite of this responsibility may have been the title of Surgeon General, since many presidents' physicians, especially during the 1850–1950 period, either held this title or were promoted to this office shortly afterward.[5] This manner of selection, however, has been criticized, since the most talented medical professionals have usually chosen a civilian rather than a military practice, and the results of such medical recruitment have not always been salutary either to the president or to the country.[7]

A second method of selection has been the transplantation of a president's previous personal or family physician to the White House. Examples indude Dr. Janet Travell, who treated John F. Kennedy's back with a great variety of strong medicines, and Dr. Charles F. Sawyer, a homeopathic physician from Marion, Ohio, who was the physician for the Warren C. Harding family. Sawyer was rewarded for any personal sacrifice in relocation by appointment as a brigadier general in the army. Occasionally, in the earlier years of the republic, presidents might choose in Washington a prominent civilian doctor with whom they had established a prior relationship during previous service in the government. James Polk's selection of Dr. James Hall represents such an example.[5]

A third option has been the selection of a prominent, usually senior physician from outside of Washington. Dr. Daniel Ruge at age 63 was a neurosurgeon chosen for Ronald Reagan because of his former position as partner to Dr. Loyal Davis, Nancy Reagan's stepfather. President Reagan gave his father-in-law *carte blanche* in the appointment of the White House doctor. According to Herbert L. Abrams, Ruge was appointed because he would not "let anybody do foolish things to Ronnie."[8, p. 233]

A critical responsibility of the president's physician is the provision of the highest quality care through the timely selection of the most qualified and appropriate medical consultants. O'Reilly wisely discharged this responsibility by consulting with the eminent New York surgeon Joseph Decatur Bryant.[9,10]

The selection of medical consultants

The office of the presidency affects the selection of medical consultants in a predictable way. Presidential illness attracts the most eminent and qualified medical specialists of the period once their consultation is requested. . . . In the annals of presidential illness the best available have been summoned: Samuel Bard (George Washington), Roswell Park (William McKinley), Frank Lahey (Franklin D. Roosevelt), and Paul Dudley White (Dwight D. Eisenhower).[5] One reason for the solicitation of such expert opinion is a necessity to reassure the public that the president is the recipient of the best available medical care. Paul Dudley White, the most prominent cardiologist of his era, was consulted during Eisenhower's myocardial infarction to demonstrate to the electorate that a highly respected civilian doctor concurred with the military physicians' handling of this case.[11, 12]

Another characteristic of presidential medical consultation is a multiplicity of experts. During crisis situations the presence of a number of medical egos may lead to confusion in diagnosis, delay in therapy, or inappropriate, even harmful, treatment of the patient. An example was the lack of defined treatment goals and faulty diagnosis during James Garfield's protracted convalescence from an assassin's wounding. This problem was exaggerated by conflict between the allopathic and the homeopathic physicians who attended Garfield. In the first forty-eight hours after the shooting, as many as fifteen doctors examined Garfield and probed his bullet wound. Being in the preantibiotic era, this repeated examination produced sepsis, and the death of the president.[13]

Fortunately, Joseph Bryant exercised strong leadership in the medical care of Grover Cleveland. He was able to exert direction in part because of his medical competence, but principally because of his close personal ties to the president.[14] Bryant had been Cleveland's personal physician prior to his election; he had previously treated Cleveland for gout; and he would subsequently deliver the second of the Cleveland children.

The slides of Cleveland's palate biopsy had been read without identification of their source by the "expert" at the Army Medical Museum, who reported a "probable . . . case of epithelioma," the term then used for an epithelial malignancy.[15] After an examination of the lesion by Bryant, Cleveland asked, "What do you think it is doctor?" to which Bryant responded, "It is a bad looking tenant. Were it in my mouth, I would have it removed at once."[9, p. 543] With Cleveland's assent to surgical removal of the lesion, Bryant commenced his plans for surgery.

Although the selection of Bryant as the principal medical consultant was inevitable, it was also extremely fortuitous. Three years previously, Bryant had addressed the Medical Society of the State of New York on "A History of Two Hundred and Fifty Cases of Excision of the Superior Maxilla," of which two cases were his own. He reported a 14 percent operative mortality risk associated with this operation.[16] Bryant was widely recognized as an accomplished surgeon and had held many teaching appointments at Bellevue Hospital Medical School in New York, serving at various times as professor of general, descriptive, and surgical anatomy, professor of anatomy and clinical surgery, and associate professor of orthopedic surgery. He later wrote a textbook of surgery. He was also active in medical politics, serving later as president of the American Medical Association.[14] Possibly because of this ability to network, Bryant was able to assemble quickly and secretly a superb team of medical consultants who consented to assist in the president's surgery.

Bryant chose as his surgical assistant Dr. John Frederick Erdmann, who contemporaneously was clinical professor of surgery at Bellevue. Erdmann subsequently became professor of surgery at the New York Postgraduate Medical School and was one of the founders of the American College of Surgeons.[17] For his surgical consultant, Bryant selected the highly respected Dr. William Williams Keen, perhaps the preeminent surgeon of the day, who in 1893 was professor of surgery at Jefferson Medical College, Philadelphia. Keen subsequently was president of the American Medical Association and edited the eight-volume *Surgery, Its Principles and Practices*.[18] Since Cleveland's weight and corpulent neck together posed a significant medical risk during surgery, Bryant enlisted as medical consultant Dr. Edward Gamaliel Janeway, the foremost diagnostician in New York. Janeway at various times was professor of pathology and practical anatomy, professor of diseases of the mind and nervous system, professor of medicine, and dean at Bellevue Medical College. He wrote the earliest adequate description of leukemia in the American literature and was the first to call attention to the fever of tertiary syphilis.[19] In 1893, dentists were the most proficient medical practitioners in delivering anesthesia, and Bryant secured the services of Dr. Ferdinand Hasbrouck to provide nitrous oxide anesthesia. The aforementioned Dr. O'Reilly, who would administer the ether anesthetic, completed the medical team.[9,10]

The circumstances and nature of treatment

The office of the presidency has at times affected the location, the timing, the circumstances, and even the type of treatment received by the presidential patient. All of these factors influenced President Cleveland's surgical episode, as he would not under any circumstances consent to a time or place for surgery that would allow even the slightest possibility for disclosure. . . . Therefore, it was decided that the president's left palate would be removed under general anesthesia in the converted salon of the private yacht *Oneida* as it sailed the East River of New York City toward the president's summer home on Buzzards Bay, Massachusetts, where he could convalesce in private. On June 30, just prior to his departure for New York City and his operation, the president called for a special session of Congress to convene August 7, 1893, for the sole purpose of repealing the Sherman Silver Purchase Act.[2,9,10,20]

Although the scheduling of Cleveland's surgery was expeditious, the requirement of secrecy determined both its venue and its circumstances. . . . Since it was deemed essential that knowledge of this operation be limited, no nurses were present, with their functions accomplished by the presence of extra physicians or possibly by one of the crew members. In this case, however, the presidency did not affect the type of surgery, operational details such as the type of anesthetic, or the duration of convalescence. A combination nitrous oxide and ether anesthesia was employed. At that time "for long-continued operations this combination was one of the best."[21]

Medical necessity merged with political expediency to result in the expeditious treatment of this president's lesion. On occasion, however, the special nature of the presidential office has had a temporal effect upon presidential treatment. President Ronald Reagan's diagnostic colonoscopy in July 1985, which led to the discovery of a cecal adenocarcinoma, may have been delayed. Reagan had flexible sigmoidoscopies both in May 1984 and in March 1985, with the discovery on both occasions of a single benign polyp. A complete examination was delayed, however, until a later date because of "administrative and political considerations."[22, p. 91]

Political requirements also played a role in President Eisenhower's convalescence from a myocardial infarct suffered in Denver, Colorado, a year prior to his reelection bid for a second presidential term. He remained hospitalized at Fitzsimmons Army Hospital in Denver for nearly seven weeks subsequent to his heart attack, before he returned to Washington, D.C. "The return was delayed a month so that Eisenhower did not have to be seen wheeled to the plane in a chair and lifted on board."[12, p. 118]

The incumbent of the presidential office may be susceptible to either overtreatment or undertreatment. William Henry Harrison, the ninth U.S. president, contracted bronchopneumonia very early in his term. His position attracted a swarm of doctors, who employed all the elements then current in their therapeutic armamentarium, including suction cups, blistering agents, calomel, castor oil, ipecac, opium, brandy, and, finally, remedies of the Seneca Indian medicine men. These ministrations had the predictable but undesired result, the president's death.[2] A less frequent occurrence is the underutilization of available medical resources. It is possible, in the current climate of cost control, that the care of the president might be considered an example of cost containment. It might be speculated that Dr. Burton Lee's opposition to routine blood chemistry screening (including for thyroid function) of George Bush, might have been grounded in this philosophy. Consequently, Mr. Bush's hyperthyroidism was not diagnosed until he developed atrial fibrillation and a syncopal attack. Lee opined that medical resources should be rationed, especially unnecessary laboratory tests and surgical procedures: "We're never going to get a handle on medical costs unless we take the piecework out of medicine."[23, p. 2742]

President Cleveland recovered completely from his surgery. A vulcanized rubber prosthesis was fitted expertly into his upper jaw, permitting him to articulate normally and to appear physically robust. After a convalescence at his summer home, he returned to Washington. With his political leadership undiminished by his illness, the Sherman Silver Purchase Act was repealed by Congress in the latter part of 1893.[2,13,14] Its repeal, however, was not the solution to the nation's economic difficulties. Economic difficulties remained unabated, and labor strife intensified. Cleveland was so unpopular in 1896 that he declined to run for reelection, and in that year the presidency reverted to the Republicans.

The behavior of the president's physician

Jerrold M. Post and Robert S. Robins have discussed the value of the appointment as caregiver to the president upon the physicians selected.[11] Great prestige is attached to this appointment. . . . Moreover, there may be material as well as symbolic rewards intrinsic to this appointment. These might include the writing of books and articles about the experience, increased numbers of consultations, and, as has been noted, appointment as Surgeon General of the United States. Conversely, dismissal for any reason could lead to loss of professional status and material reward. The success of the presidential patient's political agenda becomes intertwined with the success of the physician. As a result, secrecy and misdirection can exaggerate and distort the traditional confidentiality of the doctor-patient relationship. A reading of the historical record discloses that the probity and honesty of presidents' physicians have frequently been compromised.

Dr. Bryant stage-managed Cleveland's operation to ensure the greatest possible degree of secrecy, so that the public would be misled regarding the president's medical condition. The members of the surgical team concocted cover stories to mask their presence on the *Oneida* and remained below deck to conceal their presence. Moreover, Bryant acquiesced in the false report that Cleveland's illness was merely a tooth extraction, after a remarkably factual description of the surgery appeared in the *Philadelphia Press* in August 1893.[9, 10] Later, when Bryant was asked his opinion regarding an operation on the president, he replied, "I am sick and tired of being asked about alleged operations on the President. This story is unworthy of the dignity of a denial."[9, p. 550] The overall deception was so successful that the details of Cleveland's surgery were not made public until one of the consultants, W. W. Keen, published a narrative of the operation in the *Saturday Evening Post* in 1917, twenty-four years after the event and nine years subsequent to Cleveland's death.[20]

A reading of the biographies of American presidents will disclose many additional examples of deception by the president's physician in order to protect both the policies and, especially, the political standing of the presidential patient. Selected examples include Cary Grayson, M.D., the physician to President Woodrow Wilson, who deliberately underplayed the seriousness of Wilson's cerebrovascular accident. Grayson's twice daily medical bulletins gave the public no hint that Wilson had suffered a severe stroke, describing his illness as the result of overwork and exhaustion.[1] Janet Travell, M.D., physician to John F. Kennedy before and during his presidency, issued artfully written medical reports whose sole purpose were to mislead the electorate regarding JFK's Addison's disease. Kennedy had been surreptitiously treated for Addison's disease for many years, but Travell attempted to explain his symptoms on the basis of malaria, war injuries, or other causes.[1]

The relationship between the president and his personal physician is likely to be one of extraordinary intimacy and can affect the physician's judgment.[11] The office of the presidency requires that medical attention be constantly available; consequently, the president's physician's care is focused almost exclusively upon the president and the president's family. Continual oversight and interaction might lead to an excessive closeness to the president with unfortunate effects upon the physician's objectivity. Cary Grayson and Ross McIntire were the long-term physicians to presidents Woodrow Wilson and Franklin Roosevelt. Both were friends and intimates of their respective presidents, and Grayson was best man for Wilson's remarriage during his presidency. It can be argued that their intimacy with their respective patients was a factor in the misdiagnosis and delayed treatment of the significant cardiovascular disease that chronically affected both leaders.

Joseph Bryant's medical judgment was not adversely affected by his long-term friendship with Grover Cleveland, a relationship that predated Cleveland's presidency. The treatment applied to the president's neoplasm was the most appropriate therapy, even today. Cleveland survived for fifteen years and died in New Jersey in 1908. There was no recurrence of his cancer. Through medical skill and more than a little luck, his risky surgery had been successful. In retrospect, the office of the presidency both hindered and abetted his medical care. Brooks et al. have described the fate of Cleveland's surgical specimen.[10] His resected palate was deposited at the Mutter Medical Museum in Philadelphia, where it resided for many years. In the late 1970s, subsequent to the death of Cleveland's surviving son, a gross examination was performed, and selected tissue sections were taken for examination. Microscopic examination proved conclusively that the president had developed a verrucous squamous cell carcinoma of the palate, an indolent low-grade malignancy. The appropriate treatment for this neoplasm then and now is exactly that carried out by James Bryant and colleagues in 1893, that is, wide local excision without lymph node dissection, radiation therapy, or chemotherapy. Interestingly, the natural history of this cancer was not recognized until many years later.[10]

References

1. Crispell KR and Gomez CF. Hidden Illness in the White House. Durham, North Carolina, Duke University Press, 1988.
2. Marx R. The Health of the Presidents. New York, C. P. Putnam's Sons, 1960.
3. Nevins A. Grover Cleveland: A Study in Courage. New York, Dodd, Mead & Co., 1948.
4. Pitcher JE. The Surgeon Generals of the Army of the United States of America. Caruse, Pennsylvania, Association of Military Surgeons, 1905, p. 90. As quoted in Roos CA. Physicians to the presidents and their patients: A biobibliography. Bull Med Library Assoc 49(3):291–360, 1961.
5. Roos CA. Physicians to the presidents and their patients: A biobibliography. Bull Med Library Assoc 49(3):291–360, 1961.
6. Deaths: Major-General Robert Maitland O'Reilly. JAMA 19:1731, 1912.
7. Weigele TC. Presidential physicians and presidential health care: Some theoretical and operational considerations related to political decision making. Presidential Studies Quarterly 20(1):71–89, 1990.
8. Abrams HL. The President Has Been Shot. Confusion, Disability and the 25th Amendment in the Aftermath of the Attempted Assassination of Ronald Reagan. New York, W. W. Norton & Co., 1992.
9. Morreels CL, Jr. New historical information on the Cleveland operations. Surgery 62:542–51, 1967.
10. Brooks JJ, Enterline HI, and Aponte GE. The final diagnosis of President Cleveland's lesion. Trans Stud Coll Physicians Philadelphia. 2:1–25, 1980.
11. Post JM and Robins RS. When Illness Strikes the Leader: The Dilemma of the Captive King. New Haven, Yale University Press, 1993.
12. Kucharski A. Medical management of political patients: The case of Dwight D. Eisenhower. Perspect Biol Med 22:115–26, Autumn 1978.
13. Clark JC. The Murder of James A. Garfield: The President's Last Days and the Trial and Execution of His Assassin. Jefferson, North Carolina, McFarland & Co., 1993.
14. Deaths: Joseph Decatur Bryant. JAMA, 62:1185, 1914.
15. Keen Scrapbook: Letter of R. M. O'Reilly to J. D. Bryant, June 19, 1893. As quoted in Morreels, New Historical Information, p. 543.
16. Bryant JD. A history of two hundred and fifty cases of excision of the superior maxilla. Trans Med Soc State NY, 1890, pp. 63–76.
17. Deaths: John Frederick Erdmann. JAMA, 155:296, 1954.
18. Deaths: William Williams Keen. JAMA, 98:2228, 1932.
19. Kelly HA and Burrage WL. American Medical Biographies. Baltimore, The Norman, Remington Co. 1920, pp. 610–14.
20. Keen WW. The surgical operations on President Cleveland in 1893. Saturday Evening Post, September 22, 1917, pp. 24–55.
21. Willard de F and Adler LH. Artificial Anaesthesia and Anaesthetics. Detroit, Michigan, George S. Davis, 1891, p. 103.
22. Beahrs OH. The medical history of President Ronald Reagan. J Am Coll Surg 178:86–96, 1994.
23. Breo DL. Tough talk from the President's physician. JAMA 262:2742–745, 1989.

THE OTHER FLEXNER REPORT: HOW ABRAHAM FLEXNER WAS DIVERTED FROM MEDICAL SCHOOLS TO BROTHELS

HORTON A. JOHNSON, M.D.
(Spring 1986, pp. 9–12)

Horton Johnson's abridged bio precedes his other paper in this anthology, "Osler Recommends Chloroform at Sixty."

HE DECADE BEFORE WORLD WAR I WAS A ROWDY TIME in adolescent New York City. It was a time of trust busters and Wall Street robber barons, of political reformers and corrupt machine politics, of moral crusaders and rampant vice. It was all of these intrigues that converged upon Abraham Flexner to turn him from his well-known study of medical education to his rather similar but less well-known study of prostitution.

In the year 1911, Flexner was out of a job. After a classical education at Johns Hopkins University, he had returned to Louisville, Kentucky, his boyhood home, where he taught in the public high school for four years and then in his own private preparatory school for another 15 years. In 1908 his first book, *The American College*, caught the attention of Carnegie Foundation President Henry S. Pritchett, who asked him to evaluate, as a layman, the medical schools of the United States, Canada, and Europe. In the course of these projects Flexner developed the style he would later use in his study of prostitution: the whirlwind tours, the firsthand observations, the countless face-to-face interviews. The publication of the last of his reports on medical education completed his specific commission undertaken for the Carnegie Foundation. At age forty-five and living in a Manhattan apartment with his wife and two children, Flexner faced an uncertain future.

In the year 1911, following his father's retirement, John D. Rockefeller, Jr., took over the active management of the family's vast financial interests. These were stormy times for the Rockefeller family. Since the turn of the century the senior Rockefeller had been denounced in the press, the pulpit, and the courts as a paradigm of capitalist ruthlessness and greed. Court action had, in 1892, dissolved the Standard Oil Trust, and in 1907 Judge Kenesaw Mountain Landis fined the Standard Oil Company of Indiana some $30 million for forcing rebates on the railroads. In 1911, the year of the elder Rockefeller's retirement, the Supreme Court called for the dissolution of his holding company, the Standard Oil Company of New Jersey. There were frequent references to his "tainted money" in sermons and editorials. He was attacked repeatedly and bitterly by the newspapers, which even questioned the motives behind his considerable philanthropic enterprises. The public had, by and large, come to view Rockefeller very much as Diego Rivera portrayed him years later in the quickly whitewashed murals of Rockefeller Center: as an evil villain. John D., Junior, his father's only son, was not only heir to the throne but also heir to the ridicule, often libelous, being heaped upon the family. He was a deeply religious man with a strong social conscience, and it was no doubt his desire to reverse the family's public image as well as his growing disillusionment with business that forced his decision to resign his directorships of the Standard Oil Company and U.S. Steel and to devote his life to spending his money for the betterment of society. In 1911 John D. Rockefeller, Jr., age 37, was, like Flexner, looking for new directions in which to turn his energies and resources.

In 1911, New York City's cantankerous Tammany mayor, William Jay Gaynor, was not only besieged by political opponents, but was receiving the brunt of scathing editorials and cartoons in nearly all of the city's newspapers and was the subject of abusive sermons by some of the city's most prominent clergymen. The clerical attack was led by the most notorious reformer of the time, Dr. C. H. Parkhurst, minister of the Madison Avenue Presbyterian Church. Parkhurst was famous for his tours of underworld haunts in search of material for his sermons. Gaynor was accused of moral laxity in his failure to control saloons, gambling, and prostitution. He did, in fact, seem to have a "live and let live" attitude. A few years before, while justice of the New York Supreme Court, Gaynor had ruled that any regulation of automobile or carriage traffic on New York City streets would be a curtailment of the constitutional liberty of the individual. He felt that prostitution could not be stifled by law, saying that prostitutes "were in the world at the beginning of history. . . .They will continue to be here until by the aid of moral teaching the hearts and propensities of men shall be subdued and made better."[1] But prostitution had become a traditional issue for the opponents of Tammany Hall. When Tammany's George B. McClellan, Jr., ran against incumbent Seth Low in 1903, Low supporters distributed leaflets saying, "A vote for Low is a vote for the home, a vote for McClellan is a vote for the brothel."[2] This topic emerged again as a partisan issue during William Randolph Hearst's unsuccessful campaigns against McClellan in 1905 and Gaynor in 1909. There were implications that prostitution and the "white slave traffic" were part of organized crime, which was, in turn, receiving protection from Tammany Hall.

Soon after he took office in 1910, Mayor Gaynor had attempted to put the matter to rest by requesting that Tammany's Judge Thomas O'Sullivan impanel a special grand jury to probe, not too deeply, into the question of organized prostitution. For the foreman of the jury, the judge needed a man with a proper image. He sought a man who was above politics, a man who could not be bought, a man long known to the public at large as the leader of the Men's Bible Class of the Fifth Avenue Baptist Church. He called upon John D. Rockefeller, Jr.

Understandably, this proposal did not appeal to Rockefeller at first blush, but under pressure from O'Sullivan he accepted the assignment.[3] Once turned on to the task, however, he attacked it with a vengeance that actually began to frighten Judge O'Sullivan. The grand jury returned some fifty-four individual indictments, but it presented no evidence to link Tammany with organized prostitution. The grand jury also recommended that the mayor appoint a permanent commission to carry on the work begun by the grand jury. Mayor Gaynor, by now thoroughly exasperated by Parkhurst and other moral zealots, had no enthusiasm for such a commission and dismissed the proposal out of hand.

By this time Rockefeller had become thoroughly engrossed in the problem and was not to be put off the track by such a small obstacle as City Hall. He would go it alone by establishing and supporting, with more than $5 million, the very innovative and farsighted Bureau of Social Hygiene. As one of its first projects after its establishment in 1911, the Bureau decided to undertake a survey of prostitution in Europe, its extent, its modes of operation, and the laws and methods used by government agencies to control it. Rockefeller looked about for the right person to conduct such an unusual survey. His good friend at the Rockefeller Institute, Simon Flexner, had a younger brother who had experience in European fact finding. It just so happened that this younger brother had recently conducted a survey of medical education in Europe for the Carnegie Foundation. And it just so happened that at that very moment this younger brother was looking for a job.

Abraham Flexner viewed prostitution as an object of study with about as much enthusiasm as Rockefeller had shown initially. At first he declined, but he was eventually persuaded by his brother to commit the next two years to this field of study. In the winter of 1911, Flexner left for England.

The grand tour began in London and ended in Budapest. All in all Flexner visited twenty-eight major cities in twelve countries. At each stop he talked with government officials, police officers, and physicians; he studied the laws and regulations pertaining to prostitution; he visited venereal disease clinics; and he carefully reviewed the local attitudes and social histories of this ancient profession. In this way he gathered more than enough data to fill the 450-page book he would eventually write on the subject.

To most itinerant investigators the completion of this assignment would have seemed to be a job well done, but Mr. Flexner had learned during his survey of conditions in medical schools that second-hand or official versions often have little to do with reality. He had to see things for himself. To do so, of course, demanded a drastic adjustment of life-style from that of a scholar who rarely retired after eleven to that of a habitue of red-light districts and brothels at three and four in the morning. He was evidently a persuasive conversationalist, this Louisville schoolteacher, as adept at extracting inside information from a streetwalker as at inspiring the generosity of a millionaire. In a sympathetic and naively charming way his report recounts a number of casual but revealing encounters with prostitutes in various European cities.[4]

In Paris he developed a close and trusting friendship with a prostitute who became his guide through the streets, cafes, and brothels of the city. In his biography he tells of taking this woman to dinner the night after their first meeting.[5] Afterward they went to her flat in Montmartre, where they talked for an hour or so. Rising to leave, he gave her several gold coins in payment for her time. "Is this all?" she asked, taken by surprise. When he replied that nothing more was to be asked of her, she said, "Why, then you are not a man; you are an angel." "No," he protested, "I am a man all right." In their jaunts through the Paris underworld Flexner had a chance to see many things that the police had chosen not to see. Months later, as he passed through Paris on his way home he took the woman out to dinner. As he said goodnight, he asked if there was anything he could do for her before he sailed for the United States. She replied that there were two things she would like very much: to dine with him some evening like a lady and then to go to the opera. Flexner saw to it that she got her wish. On the appointed evening they dined at the Cafe de Paris on the Avenue de l'Opera, he in his formal dinner jacket and she in the height of fashion. After dinner they went to the opera.

So it went in the other cities of Europe. Seeking out mercenary, unofficial guides, he saw far more than the police had been instructed to show him.

Mr. Flexner was primarily interested in estimating in some way the relationship between the extent of prostitution and the local methods of dealing with it. There were two general methods in operation: regulation with licensing of prostitutes, as in Paris, Berlin, and Vienna; and abolition of regulatory laws and licensing, as in England and Scandinavia. In trying to compare the relative intensities of prostitution under different systems of regulation, he needed quantitative data. Being of the opinion that police data were generally gross underestimates and of little value, he resorted at times to standing on street corners at night doing head counts of "unmistakable women." In Paris, for example, where the police had registered some six thousand prostitutes, Flexner reckoned the number to be closer to fifty thousand. It is interesting to recall that at that time the total population of Paris was under three million. If half of these people were female, and half of the females were between fifteen and forty-five years of age, one out of every fifteen young Parisian women was, according to Flexner's estimate, a practicing prostitute.

Flexner returned home in 1913 to write his report, which, with an introduction by John D. Rockefeller, Jr., was published by the Century Company in the following year.[4] He concluded that, at least in Europe, repression of prostitution by laws and law enforcement agencies had little to offer beyond superficial tidying up and that police regulation had probably even had a harmful effect on the spread of venereal disease. In general, prostitution was bound to follow the laws of supply and demand: as long as there is a demand for it there would always be prostitution. "Prostitutes," he said, "are manufactured by unschooled human nature and imperfect social institutions."[4, p. 397] Flexner's judgment pretty well paraphrased the position of Mayor Gaynor, which when stated earlier had so enraged New York's moral reformers, namely, that prostitution is basically not a matter of inadequate laws or insufficient police action, but is part of a much larger social problem.

Whatever use this report may have been to students of prostitution in Europe before the First World War, its significance to us now lies in the fact that it marked the beginning of the long and productive association of Abraham Flexner with John D. Rockefeller, Jr., and the men around him. While still in London, nearing the end of his unusual field trip, Flexner was invited to become a member of Rockefeller's General Education Board, which, during the fourteen years of his tenure, would invest many millions of dollars in educational projects in this country and abroad. Building upon the experience and contacts gained from his years on the General Education Board, Flexner would then conceive of and bring into being his crowning achievement, the Institute for Advanced Studies at Princeton. So it happened that in the chain of events that led Flexner to the Institute for Advanced Studies, the first link—the Rockefeller connection—was hinged upon the embarrassment of Tammany Hall over flagrant prostitution in New York City.

Time leaves in its wake many curious little eddies, but surely one of the most bizarre of these is the picture of the man who has influenced education in the United States as much as anyone in this century, the man who brought Albert Einstein to these shores, standing on a street corner somewhere in Europe, in the wee hours of the morning, dutifully surveying the ladies of the night.

References

1. Smith M. William Jay Gaynor: Mayor of New York. Chicago, Henry Regnery Co., 1951, pp. 137–38.

2. Syrett HC. The Gentlemen and the Tiger: The Autobiography of George B. McClellan, Jr. Philadelphia, J. B. Lippincott Co., 1956, p. 173.
3. Fosdick RB. John D. Rockefeller, Jr.: A Portrait. New York, Harper & Brothers, Publishers, 1956.
4. Flexner A. Prostitution in Europe. New York, The Century Co., 1914.
5. Flexner A. I Remember: The Autobiography of Abraham Flexner. New York, Simon & Schuster, 1940, p. 193.

DIFFICULTIES, DIAPPOINTMENTS, AND DELIGHTS IN MEDICINE

HELEN B. TAUSSIG, M.D.

(Spring 1979, pp. 6–8)

Helen was born in 1898 in Cambridge, Massachusetts. She had a tough childhood, suffering from tuberculosis and, to make matters worse, she had dyslexia. She overcame this handicap and graduated from Radcliff College. After being refused admission to Harvard Medical School because she was a woman, she was accepted at Johns Hopkins University School of Medicine and received her M.D. in 1927. Another difficulty for her to overcome was deafness. Instead of listening to her pediatric cardiology patients with a stethoscope, she "listened with my fingers." It was her idea, suggested to Alfred Blaylock when he arrived at Hopkins in 1941, that construction of a patent ductus could provide a solution to the hypoxemia of patients with tetralogy of Fallot. In 1944 the first of these operations was done. Less appreciated by most people was her leadership in recognizing in 1962 that it probably was the drug thalidomide that was causing phocomelia in babies being born in England and Germany. The FDA listened to her, and use of the drug in this country was outlawed. Among her many honors was the United States of America Medal of Freedom given to her by President Lyndon B. Johnson, and the receipt in 1970 of the Elizabeth Blackwell Award. She was killed in a car accident three days before her 88th birthday. This paper is based on her address at the Baylor College of Medicine, where Dr. Taussig served as Alpha Omega Alpha Visiting Professor in April 1978.

∞

A GOOD DEAL IS EXPECTED OF US WHO ENTER MEDICINE. We choose a very swift-flowing stream and we have to swim hard to keep up with the advances of knowledge. All of medicine and all of our work is not a bed of roses. It has its difficulties and its disappointments. My former chief said to me once, "That which is a disappointment at the beginning often proves to be your good fortune in the end." We should not be too discouraged in meeting disappointment; we all have met it before, and many times it has turned out to be good fortune.

198

I was disappointed when I first got to Hopkins. I couldn't work in physiology. Then Dr. Carter took me into the heart station, and thus began my career in pediatric cardiology. I was very disappointed when I didn't get my medical internship, but Dr. Carter offered me a fellowship in the heart station; and that really gave me my start. My friends said at the time, "That insignificant branch of pediatrics. . . why do you go into that?" And then, above all, what could be so foolish as to write a book on congenital malformations of the heart? I responded to them then what I would say now: If you are in academic medicine and if you learn anything, you are morally obligated to make that knowledge available to other people. That is what academic work really means.

Emerson once said, and I've remembered it always: "When ye shall say, 'As others do, so must I. I must eat the good meat of the land. I renounce I am sorry for it, my earlier visions. I must let learning and romantic expectation go until a more convenient season,' then dies the man in you; then once more perish the buds of art and science and poetry, as they have died already in a thousand, thousand men." Yes, I think learning and hard study and romantic expectation are the essential ingredients of art and science and poetry. To these ingredients I would add observation and deduction. Then one has to prove that one's deduction is right; that is a long, hard task. In academic medicine, by the time you have proved your point, written it, and published it, you are way ahead working on something else.

Medicine—the hybrid product of science and art

Medicine now is founded on science. We learn a great deal. We run our tests, and we figure out what is the acid/base and what is right and what is wrong with our patients; but young physicians are becoming too dependent on the laboratory. In my own field, new cardiologists feel that they have to do a catheterization, they have to see an angiocardiogram, they have to take an echocardiogram. Yes, they improve and they learn from the laboratory. Their computers help them to sort out their material, but the computers are only as good as the material put into them. If you don't put in the right material and you don't punch the right keys, you won't get the right answer. Statistics are valuable; but they, again, are only good for proving and verifying facts. They don't produce original work. It comes down to one's own experience and observation and deduction.

Then, on the other side of it, there is the art of medicine. We don't want to forget that after we've got all the laboratory data together we are taking care of patients or the health of the community. We are dedicated to making life better for humanity. I always did think that the highest form of art by man is the music of Beethoven, who could know how a thing sounded, know what he wanted to do to produce the sound, know what instruments to play and which notes to play, produce a perfectly beautiful symphony, and never be able to hear it with the ordinary external ear! He heard it in his mind, and the rest of us enjoy it with our ears. Sculpture is another very tremendous art. The sculptor can take a solid piece of marble, know the grain and cut, and produce something that is perfectly beautiful. Our art in medicine is quite a different thing. Our essential ingredients are kindness and compassion and human understanding; and we all strive for it. We all make mistakes; we can't help it. We all sometimes say the wrong thing at the wrong time.

How can we truly inform to achieve consent?

We talk a great deal today about informed consent. Informed consent, I think, is a fictitious thing. We must try to inform patients, try to be honest; but none of us knows all the possible dangers, as well as the benefits. We must put things in a way that is meaningful to patients. They must understand some risks, but we cannot possibly list every single possible untoward reaction. Nobody would consent to anything! In one of the recent federal pediatric regulations, it was forbidden to do anything on a child over seven years old without informed consent from the child. I wrote and said I did not think I could possibly explain enough to a child. I ended in saying that when the children went to high school he ought to be able to understand; but I did not expect a seven-year-old child to understand everything that I was saying.

. . .Then we come down to the question of operations and consent for them. We should not fool ourselves for one instant that the patient's answer does not depend on how we put the question. We really are influencing his decision a great deal. We are not just explaining a cold fact, but should try to consider the best course for the patient. At medical meetings we hear the best people in the field discuss situations and present their best results. That does not mean that a particular patient, with his particular surgeon, in his particular place, is going to get the same result or that his chances are the same. We must try to tell him what we think his chances really are.

. . . If a patient comes in and says, "Well, if I've got to have the operation, I will; but I know I'm going to die," we should not operate. Dr. Alfred Blalock and I, thirty years ago, operated on our last patient who was scared of operation. I did not know she was so scared, or I would have thought twice before proceeding. She died at anesthesia. Dr. Blalock said to me afterwards, "Why did she die?" I said, "I don't know, but her family told me she was scared of operation." He said, "Maybe that's just the reason she died." The patient was scared of leaving her house; she was scared of coming to Baltimore; she was scared of coming into the clinic; and she was scared, scared, scared.

I was asked recently what I thought was the most exciting thing in all my career. I said I supposed nothing would ever give me as much delight as seeing the first patient change from blue to pink in the operating room. Our first operations were on very, very severely incapacitated children. The first one was a little tiny baby with a match stick of a subclavian. The child did manage to live out of oxygen and to go home for Christmas. He did not maintain his improvement for a year, but very few of our ten-pound, year-old babies did. The second was an eleven-year-old child who could not have walked the length of a room without squatting, and she was beginning to lose consciousness for half an hour at a time. She had a right aortic arch. I told Dr. Blalock, "I don't know where the vessels are." Dr. Blalock replied, "Oh, I don't think it makes much difference. I'll just go in on the left just the same." Dr. Blalock reached up, hunting for the large vessel, and brought down the innominate artery. After anastomosis he got a beautiful thrill, but we did not see any significant change in color. The third child was a little six-year old who was miserably unhappy, crying and screaming. He had learned to walk once, but his pulmonary stenosis had progressed so that he could not walk. He was terribly unhappy. He had a left aortic arch. Dr. Blalock went in on the right deliberately to get the innominate artery. When he released the clamps, there was as bad a hemorrhage as I have seen in the operating room. My heart sank. I thought everything was over and I was going to have to go down and face his parents. But Dr. Blalock, with all his skill, got his finger on the bleeding point, got the clamps on, and sewed up the tiny hole. When he released the clamps again he said, "I've got a beautiful thrill." Almost simultaneously, the anesthesiologist called out, "A lovely color now." And there the little patient was, with bright pink cheeks and bright lips. Oh, what a lovely color! Anesthesia was light; and, as Dr. Blalock put the last bandages on the chest, the child woke up, looked at Dr. Blalock, blinked his eyes a little, and said, "Is the operation over? May I get up now?"

"No, please lie still a little longer," Dr. Blalock answered.

"Can I have a drink of water?"

"Just as soon as you get to your room."

And, from that day on, he was raring to go; and we realized we had won.

DOTING: MY EARLY EXPERIENCES AT BOSTON CITY HOSPITAL

MAXWELL FINLAND, M.D.
(Summer 1982, pp. 17–22)

Max Finland was a giant among those in the field of Infectious Diseases, although he stood only a few inches over five feet tall. He was born in a small town in the Ukraine in 1902, and his family moved to Boston when he was four years old. After Harvard College, he entered Harvard Medical School in 1922. His days as a house officer at Boston City Hospital are chronicled in his article re-published here. He worked at the BCH for most of his career, and those who were his fellows in the Thorndike laboratories there remember that it was not unusual for him to sleep in the hospital, even in his later years. After retirement and becoming the Minot professor emeritus he took the past of many HMS luminaries by accepting a position at the West Roxbury VA hospital. The National Foundation for Infectious Diseases has awarded a The Maxwell Finland Award for Scientific Achievement for the past 13 years. Finland died at age 85, never having married.
At the time this essay was published, Dr. Finland (AΩA, Harvard University, 1942) was George Richards Minot Professor of Medicine Emeritus at the Harvard Medical School, and Distinguished Physician, U.S. Veterans Administration. Dr. Finland also wrote for The Pharos *"Teaching and Learning in Government-Supported Hospitals," which appeared in October 1976. This paper was based on the Seventh Aaron Thurman Memorial Lecture, delivered by Dr. Finland at the Beth Israel Hospital in Boston in November 1981.*

∞

HAVING BEEN GIVEN AN OPPORTUNITY TO REMINISCE about infectious diseases and some of my early experiences at Boston City Hospital,[1] I found myself beginning to dote on those memorable days. Consulting my Webster's dictionary for the definitions of dote, I found most of them very unflattering. The first definition included the archaic meanings: (a) "to be or become foolish or imbecilic," and (b) "to be weak-minded or mentally deficient by reason of old age"; well, at least the age seemed appropriate. The second definition was "to show strong, excessive or felicitous fondness or affection," and that seemed to fit. Thus, I decided to use doting in the title of this paper.

202

Charles Wilinsky, Finland's early role model

I begin with my earliest medical experiences as a child in the West End of Boston. Like most Jewish families at that time we had a "Lodge Doctor," who was none other than the late Charles F. Wilinsky. His office then was on Green Street near the corner of Chambers Street. We lived at the foot of Chambers Street and later nearby on Charles Street. Dr. Wilinsky was the busiest doctor I have ever known. I'm not sure how many lodges he served. His office was always full, and he would be there long past his stated visiting hours, but he never failed to respond promptly when called to see a patient who was sick at home.

My first encounter with him was at age five or six, when I was run over by a horse-drawn American Express wagon. I probably suffered no sign of significant injury, but he was there to make sure.

My next visit from Dr. Wilinsky was several years later when he came to my home and made a quick examination. Within the hour I was at the Boston City Hospital being operated on for acute appendicitis. My surgeon, I later learned, was Allan Davis, who was then the chief resident at the hospital. His was a most important position at City Hospital, because he could perform any emergency operation he chose.

Dr. Wilinsky was probably the most popular physician in town. He later was instrumental in establishing and heading the first of Boston's health clinics, the one on Chambers Street, not far from his home. He became Boston's deputy health commissioner in charge of all of Boston's health centers and still held that post in 1928 when the new Beth Israel Hospital was opened here and he was chosen to be its first director. Herrman Blumgart, who had served at the Peter Bent Brigham Hospital and was one of Francis Peabody's early appointees to the staff of the Thorndike Memorial Laboratory at Boston City Hospital, was brought over to head up medical research and the teaching of Harvard medical students at the hospital. At first, the conduct of Harvard's interests at the Beth Israel was under the jurisdiction of the Department of Medicine at the Peter Bent Brigham Hospital, but Dr. Blumgart was soon promoted to a full professorship and made head of an independent medical school department on a par with those at the Brigham, Massachusetts General, and Boston City Hospital.

Harvard Medical School, its quotas, and tough internships

. . . A few words about Harvard Medical School. At the turn of the century President Charles Eliot recommended to the Faculty of Medicine that all candidates for admission be required to have Bachelor of Arts degrees and show evidence of knowledge of physics and chemistry, a new departure in the United States, and so there were few applicants. The new buildings could accommodate 125 students, but only about half that number applied at first, so that in 1908, when George Minot and his cousin Francis Rackemann were graduated from Harvard College, they merely went to the medical school and enrolled the day before classes began.[2] Tuition then was low (perhaps $150) and had risen to $400 per year by 1922, when I entered. Tuition has been climbing steadily since then, and now runs into five figures.

Soon, however, increasing numbers of candidates began to apply, and by 1922, many well-qualified students were denied admission. Abbott Lawrence Lowell was then president of the university, and he admitted to setting a rigid *numerus clausus*, limiting Jewish applicants to 10 percent of all admissions in the college and in all the professional schools. As I recall, however, neither I nor any of my classmates ever felt any discrimination, once we passed the interview under the keen nose and critical eye of the associate dean, Worth Hale, who made sure that the proper students were admitted and suggested to many others that they would surely do better in law school. I was fortunate, perhaps because I applied late and was not asked to appear for an interview. In fact, I didn't set foot in the hallowed precincts of the dean's office until my last year as a medical student.

Examinations for internships at Boston's teaching hospitals were held after many of the other desirable hospitals elsewhere had already held theirs and committed most, or all, of their places. Thus, the applicants for internship in Boston were at a disadvantage and often took the risk of turning down good offers before taking the Boston examinations. The applicants for more than one position listed the hospitals and services in order of their preference, and the hospitals listed their preferences. Representatives of the Boston hospitals then met and matched these lists, giving preference to the candidate's choice in every instance. This was essentially the "matching plan" later adopted nationally, permitting announcements of appointments in all American residency programs simultaneously.

The medical internship in my day at Boston City Hospital was a grueling experience. There were only five interns on each service, which had fifty to sixty beds, and up to 100 patients on the wards during several months of the year. The service was arranged in a "progressive system," one intern starting every four months. This meant that two of the three interns appointed on each service every year had to wait four or eight months after graduation before starting his service. . . . Some of my classmates and I spent the interval as residents at Boston Sanatorium (now the Mattapan Chronic Disease Hospital). This provided valuable experience in observing and caring for patients with tuberculosis in all stages, and work at a leisurely pace. In addition, it paid a salary of $100/month as well as providing room, laundry, and excellent meals. It offered an opportunity for the graduate to save a few dollars for the lean internship period, when there would be no financial reward at all.

During the first four months, the intern was called "junior" but was better known as "pup." He did all the errands and the "scut work," which included gathering up supplies, collecting blood for hematologic and chemical tests, then carrying out those tests and all urinalyses, and examining smears of sputum for tubercle bacilli, and feces for blood, ova, and parasites, on specimens that were generally left in the laboratory by the ward nurse. On the Harvard medical service, he also carried out the blood chemical tests for glucose and nitrogen, but on other services these and other special tests were done in the hospital's general chemistry laboratory. The results of all those tests had to be entered into the records and be available early in the morning before interns' rounds, which preceded the formal visiting rounds. The house officer served the second four months as "extern," spending each morning, Monday through Saturday, in the outpatient department from 8 a.m. until all patients were seen. This often meant rushing out for a quick lunch and returning to care for the remaining patients, and that often took until the middle of the afternoon. During the rest of the day the extern carried out "procedures," which were lined up for him during work rounds and attending rounds; these included, among others, lumbar punctures, thoracenteses, abdominal paracenteses, catheterizations, and epidermoclyses. Intravenous fluids were generally not given then as they were often associated with moderate or severe thermal reactions. On his "nights on," the extern also shared with his cohort the admission of new patients and carried out the necessary laboratory work on them.

The third and fourth segments were spent in the South Department, across Massachusetts Avenue from the main hospital, where patients with contagious diseases were housed. This rotation provided an exposure to pediatrics and a welcomed leisurely pace, with time for rest, reading, or recreation. But mostly, it offered an intensive experience in the diagnosis and management of the common contagious diseases. The only excitement was during the rotation on the diphtheria wards, where children with laryngeal involvement were kept in the "tube room," a room full of potentially obstructed patients, where the nurse in charge would sound a loud gong whenever a child became obstructed and would rush him or her to the special operating room, while the interns and the resident would drop everything and vie with each other to be the first to arrive there in order to intubate the patient and relieve the obstruction. Most often the resident would insert the tube through a special laryngoscope after applying suction to dislodge and remove any laryngeal or tracheal membrane, a procedure that often was lifesaving.

The rotation on the scarlet fever wards offered interns an opportunity to observe cases of varying severity and with all types of complications, including relapses that kept patients in the hospital for many weeks. In 1945, my colleagues and I were able to confirm British studies showing that relapses actually

were reinfections with streptococci of serologic types different from those causing their original infections and were acquired from patients in a neighboring
bed.[3] Otitis media requiring tympanocentesis was common, as was mastoiditis
requiring operation. Tonsillectomies were done on patients by the dozen before discharge by an otolaryngologist in an operating room on one of the scarlet fever wards. On the isolation pavilion, the house officers cared for patients
with measles, whooping cough, mumps, and other communicable diseases.

After finishing the rotation through the South Department, the intern had
two weeks for vacation before returning to the main hospital for four months as
"senior" and the final four months as house physician, the latter being equivalent to resident, or chief resident nowadays. (The surgical services had assistant
residents and chief residents, but the medical services did not.) The senior and
house physician admitted new patients on alternate days, nights, and weekends;
when they found time, they worked on their records, wrote follow-up notes,
and made rounds to assure that all patients were comfortable and to exchange
notes with the ward nurses before retiring on their nights on duty. They also supervised the work of the pup, extern, and students who served as clinical clerks.

The house physician conducted rounds with the house staff early in the
morning and took the visiting physician on rounds the latter part of the morning. Lists of laboratory work and "procedures" were drawn up at these rounds
to be carried out by the junior and extern. He also answered consultations on
other services.

Ward rounds on the Harvard Medical Services of the Boston City Hospital,
as at the other Boston teaching hospitals, were quite formal in those days. The
nurses made sure that everything on the ward was spick and span, the patients
having been bathed and fed and the bed linen changed. The doors to the ward
were kept shut and the head nurse accompanied the visiting physician and his
retinue of house staff and clinical clerks as they stopped at the bedside of each
patient, where the intern presented a summary of each new case and any progress
or change in condition of the others. The clinical clerks presented cases that
they had worked up after being instructed and rehearsed to be brief and concise without omitting relevant details. After every patient on the wards had
been seen and most of them briefly examined by "the visit," the house physician
accompanied the visit as he went to see private patients, if any, and others he
had been asked to see in consultation on other services.

Following the afternoon visiting hour on the wards, the house physician
made himself available to see relatives and friends of patients to answer any of
their questions. He also met with the social service worker to arrange for placement of patients in convalescent or long-term care facilities or to help provide
special services or materials for needy patients, of which there were all too
many.

Patients who were seriously ill and were not expected to survive were placed on the "Danger List"; this permitted relatives and friends to visit them at all hours of the day or night. It also allowed the house physician and senior to develop a good rapport with the relatives. If they did not come in and the patient looked moribund, they were called by the intern to be there and available when the patient died; the nearest relative could be induced to sign permission for an autopsy, an important teaching experience. The house physician or senior would solicit the permission on the ward, but if the nearest relative was not there or did not come in when called, one of the house staff would go to the patient's home and try to persuade the nearest relative to sign. The various services vied with each other in attempts to achieve the highest autopsy percentage when the scores were posted at the end of each month.

Time off—Rare for the BCH intern

Each intern was off duty every other night and every other weekend from Saturday noon until early Monday morning. Time off actually began whenever he could break away, but much of that time was utilized in catching up on records and follow-up notes on patients still in the hospital and writing summaries and posting final diagnoses on those who were recently discharged. Most of the time off, however, was spent catching up on sleep. Many an intern was found fast asleep at the bedside of a new patient he was admitting at night while taking the history.

I always tried to get home for Friday evening dinner on my night off. My family lived then in Roxbury near Franklin Park, and I would take the elevated train to get off at Egleston Square. Generally, however, I dozed off and was nudged by the conductor and told that I was at Forest Hills, the end of the line, and I then had to ride back to my station on the return run.

Little wonder then that there was a good deal of sickness among the house staff, mostly acute respiratory infections. Also, since they admitted and cared for many patients with active, and sometimes open, far advanced cavitary tuberculosis before they could be transferred to a sanatorium, some interns developed tuberculosis and had to be hospitalized, most of them in Trudeau Sanatorium at Saranac Lake. One-third of them, at the time of my internship, acquired the disease, and one died.

"Strikers," the first sub-interns

Fourth-year clinical clerks on the ward at the time would volunteer or be pressed into duty to take the place of sick interns; these "strikers," as they were called, lived in the hospital and performed all the duties of the junior intern or the extern. . . . Many years later Charles Davidson instituted the "night float" system, in which all duties throughout the night, including admissions and emergency calls, were given to a single intern, permitting the others uninterrupted sleep unless the night float was overwhelmed with urgent work and had to call the one on duty for help.[4]

Room, laundry, no salary, but great food!

. . . For all these labors and hazardous exposures the interns, as I already intimated, received no monetary compensation. At Boston City Hospital, as in other Boston teaching hospitals, they were provided uniforms, room, board, and laundry. Meals at Boston City Hospital were copious, varied, and of high quality and were served by jolly, mostly elderly Irish waitresses at tables covered with clean white tablecloths. Roasts, steaks, chops, chicken, fish, and sometimes even lobsters were served at one or two meals each day, and some hearty eaters would consume two, or even three full meals at one sitting. Desserts included large servings of freshly baked pies and cakes, and ice cream. Meals were also served late at night for those on duty and for any others who wished to partake, and many did. Little wonder that some interns gained weight in spite of their heavy work load. Evenings and weekends, interns often invited their friends, including interns from other Boston hospitals to visit them at the City and fill up on those fine meals, because the food at the other hospitals was both drab and skimpy.

It was not until quite a few years later that the City Hospital began to provide a stipend to interns. It first happened after a reporter on one of Boston's newspapers learned that interns were offering their blood at $25 a pint for ward patients and $50 a pint for private patients at the Massachusetts General Hospital. He reported this under banner headlines: "CITY HOSPITAL INTERNS SELL THEIR BLOOD TO BUY SHOES." James Michael Curley, who was mayor at the time, was embarrassed, called representatives of the house staff to his office, and by the next month the hospital began paying a stipend of $25 a month. The other hospitals in Boston and elsewhere soon followed suit.

In those days it was quite unusual for a medical student to be married, and very few got married before finishing an internship. Indeed, some hospitals, notably the Peter Bent Brigham under Henry Christian, refused to accept interns who admitted to being married. One of my classmates, who started eight months ahead of me on the same service, took his two weeks of vacation at the end of his stint at the South Department, and before returning as "the senior," to get married and go off on his honeymoon. I came on as the "pup" when he returned and we were generally on and off duty together. Since he always seemed anxious to get home, and I sympathized with him, I agreed to assume his duties after mid-day and, although he asked me to be sure to call him if I needed help, I never did. . . .

And for those who have not had enough of doting, I refer you to the recent cascade of letters from physicians in response to Norman Cousins's critique of the internship[4] and leave you with this bit by a physician with long service at Boston City Hospital, who predated me by many years. He put it in verse:

Refuge of sufferers! Conqueror of pain!
Healer of wounds, and woes and misery!
Bleeding or sick, the people turn to thee,
Seeking thy touch to make them whole again!
Standing within the city's southern gate,
Stretching wide open arms to all who need;
Sleepless, thou welcom'st every race and creed,
Spring time or autumn, early hour or late.
We are thy sons; each one in his own way
Gave of his best to thine abundant store,
And in thy service found, as children may,
Knowledge, strength, skill they knew not of before,
Loving, we watch thee grow from day to day,
Knowing thy name is blessed evermore![5]

References and Annotations

1. This paper is based on a lecture presented as one of the series in memory of Aaron Thurman (1897–1974), M.D. Harvard 1921. Dr. Thurman was a popular and respected surgeon who had served on the house staff of Boston City Hospital and its satellites, Boston Sanatorium and Long Island Hospital, and then for many years as surgeon-in-chief of Jewish Memorial Hospital and on the staffs of Boston City, Beth Israel, Mount Auburn, Faulkner, and Newton-Wellesley Hospitals, and on the faculty of Tufts Medical School.
2. Rackemann FM. The Inquisitive Physician, The Life and Times of George Richards Minot. Cambridge, Massachusetts, Harvard University Press, 1956, pp. 32–33.
3. Meads M, Flipse ME, Jr., Barnes MW, and Finland M. Penicillin treatment of scarlet fever: Bacteriologic study of the nose and throat of patients treated intramuscularly or by spray with penicillin and a comparison with sulfadiazine. JAMA. 129:785–89, 1945.
4. Leitzell JD, Turkewitz L J, Ratnoff OD, et al. Internship: Physicians respond to Norman Cousins. JAMA. 246:2141–43, 1981.
5. Blake JB. The Municipal History of the Boston City Hospital. In A History of the Boston City Hospital from Its Foundation until 1904. Edited by David W. Cheever, George W. Gay, A. Lawrence Mason, and J. Bapst Blake, Boston, Massachusetts, Municipal Printing Office, 1906, p. 126.

PART IV

STORIES FOCUSED UPON SIR WILLIAM OSLER

An anthologist of The Pharos *could fill a majority of pages in his collection with writings about or related to Osler. Many of the references to him by authors are of the third hand variety, suggesting familiarity but in reality drawing conclusions about the man from the writings of those who knew him personally. I have selected only two pieces from the many that focus upon different parts of this man, his career, and contributions to medicine.*

Sir William Osler was rarely criticized, but the exception was in 1905 when he gave his address, "The Fixed Period" to medical students and nurses at Johns Hopkins University School of Medicine, during which he suggested that it might benefit society if men over the age of 60 were euthanized. Horton Johnson describes this and the events surrounding it. Emile Holman presents the contrasts between Osler and Halsted, who converged in Baltimore for important segments of their careers.

"OSLER RECOMMENDS CHLOROFORM AT SIXTY"

HORTON A. JOHNSON, M.D.

(Winter 1996, pp. 24–26)

Dr. Johnson (AΩA, Tulane University School of Medicine, 1979), formerly director of pathology at St. Luke's-Roosevelt Hospital and professor of pathology at Columbia University College of Physicians and Surgeons, is presently a docent at the Metropolitan Museum of Art. Dr. Johnson has also written for The Pharos *"The Other Flexner Report: How Abraham Flexner Was Diverted from Medical Schools to Brothels," published in Spring 1986 (republished in this anthology) and "On the Accumulation of Small Insults," which appeared in Spring 2000.*

"OSLER RECOMMENDS CHLOROFORM AT SIXTY." That is what the newspaper headlines said.[1 p. 669] The leading spokesman for the medical profession throughout the English-speaking world had said in a public address that men (he specifically excluded women) over the age of sixty were useless, and that at the age of sixty "peaceful departure by chloroform" might lead to "incalculable benefits."[2 p. 382]

That was in the year 1905. Had it been made in 1995, ninety years later, Sir William's whimsical and tongue-in-cheek remark would have been taken literally by the media and would have been denounced on editorial pages, analyzed by pundit panels on television, and ridiculed on radio talk shows. Victim groups would have cried out for his immediate removal from any positions of influence.

In fact, in 1905 things were much the same! The media and special interest groups were every bit as humorless and predatory then as now. Newspaper headlines announced the shocking words, and, according to Harvey Cushing,

> . . . for days and weeks there followed pages of discussion, with cartoons and comments, caustic, abusive, and worse, with only an occasional word in his [Osler's] behalf lost in the uproar. Day by day there were columns of letters contributed by newspaper readers, . . . until to "Oslerize" became a byword for mirth and opprobrium. . . . [T]he public at large felt that it was the heartless view of a cold scientist who would condemn man as a productive machine. . . . [A]busive and threatening letters . . . by the wagonload poured into 1 West Franklin Street from all over the country."[1 p. 669]

213

The following day reporters interviewed elderly faculty members at Johns Hopkins, who were reported by the *New York Times* to be in disagreement with Osler. One of them, the distinguished professor of Greek and Latin, Basil Gildersleeve, was quoted on the front page of the *Times* as saying, "I have no right to express an opinion on the subject, because I am seventy-three years old. I may say, however, that I am very glad nobody thought to chloroform me thirteen years ago."[3] The *Times* was having its fun (and selling papers) at the expense of both Osler and his colleague, Professor Gildersleeve.

The Baltimore Sun, on its editorial page, saw fit to report abusive excerpts from newspapers around the country. From the *New York Evening Telegram* (regarding chloroform): "Will good, kind, old Dr. Osler do us one more favor and recommend a good, reliable brand?" From the *Washington Times*: "Dr. William Osler declares that men are old at 40 and worthless at 60. There must be an age at which a man is an ass. What is the Doctor's age, anyhow?" The *Sun's* editorial concluded: "Dr. Osler is 'off his base.'"[4]

And there were Osler jokes printed in the *Sun*: "Son—Father, what do S.P.C.A. stand for? Father (at age 61)—My son, they should stand for the Society for the Prevention of the Chloroforming of the Aged!" (*New York Herald*)[5]

The *Sun* published just a small fraction of the letters that poured into the editor's office. One advocated setting up chloroform stations in convenient locations. One said, "A doctrine more brutalizing in its effects on the youth of the country . . . can hardly be imagined." The word "brutalizing" was used in the headline.[6] This about a man who had given the best years of his life to teaching medical students. The *Sun* then went on to present a long inventory of accomplishments by people in their seventh and eighth decades.

The New York Times was in the vanguard of the attack. Its editorial on February 24, two days after the address, said that,

> . . . whoever examines his [Osler's] remarks will find them empty. They will make their appeal only to the hustling youth who pursue the 'jobs' of their seniors. It is extremely unlikely that they will lead to a reversion to the practice of those savage tribes whose custom it is to knock their elders on the head whenever the juniors find their elders in their own way.[7]

But Osler stood firm, and told the *Times*, "I meant just what I said, but it's disgraceful, this fuss that the newspapers are making about it."[8] The *Times* kept a running account of the affair, mostly on the front page. "Dr. Osler Sticks to Views," proclaimed a front-page headline on February 27.[9] Another front-page article, entitled "Suicide Had Osler Speech," told of a civil war veteran in Baltimore who had shot and killed himself and who was found to have a clipping of the Osler address in his desk. The implication was clear, although the article did go on to say that the old man lived alone, was physically debilitated, and was losing his vision.[10] Only on the 28th, six days after the address, was the Osler story relegated from the front page to farther back in the paper, with a few wise-cracking letters to the editor.

Osler was advised to refute his statement, but he refused, having decided to avoid any further involvement. Writing to a friend, he said,

> Such a torrent of abuse and misunderstanding began to flow in that I took my old Master, Plato's advice and crept under the shelter of a wall until the storm blew over—working hard and reading nothing about it.[1 p. 672]

Recovering from a bout of influenza several weeks later, he "crept under the shelter of a wall" by taking refuge in an obscure Atlantic City hotel under an assumed name. He maintained a stoic silence, but one can sense how deeply hurt Osler must have been by the avalanche of public ridicule and lampoonery.

* * * * *

February 22, 1905, was the birthday of both George Washington and the Johns Hopkins University. It had been decided to use that celebration for the public announcement of Osler's retirement from the university and for his farewell address to the faculty. Osler was leaving later that spring to accept the Regius Professorship at Oxford University. A few days before the occasion he fled from Baltimore to the library of the University Club in New York City, where he put his difficult address into final form. It would stress, among other things, a life planned according to fixed periods. The title would be "The Fixed Period."[2]

"The Fixed Period": The address

Although he did not say it in so many words, Osler apparently wanted to make the point in his valedictory address that he was not being lured away from Hopkins, away from the place where he had done his most productive work, away from his dearest friends and colleagues, by the prestige of the Oxford position. His leaving was a part of a plan that he had thought out long before the call to Oxford. He had planned all along to retire at the age of sixty from the rigors of direct patient care and teaching students on ward rounds. He saw the chair at Oxford, though not really retirement, as a much more peaceful, leisurely, and contemplative way of life. Then, as now, academics showed a tendency to ignore the decline of old age and to hang on as long as possible, to the disadvantage of the young and promising. Osler would have none of it. He was approaching age fifty-six and without a gray hair on his head when he wrote in a letter to a colleague,

> I am on the down grade, the pace of the last three winters has been such that I knew I was riding for a fall. Better to get out decently in time, and leave while there is still a little elasticity in the rubber. . . . I shall only cut off 4 years as I had firmly decided to chuck everything at 60. We can have

a last good winter's work together, I hope, before I lapse into a quiet academic life." [1] pp. 650–51

Although Osler advised students to live in "Day-Tight Compartments." [11] in the long run he believed strongly in a life planned according to a rational scheme. His own scheme for a teacher was study until age twenty-five, investigation until forty, profession until sixty, and retirement after sixty.

In his address, he unfortunately suggested the two cut-off ages, forty and sixty, in a way that sounded too precise to a literal-minded and unbending public. He pointed to the

> . . . comparative uselessness of men above forty years of age. . . . Take the sum of human achievement in action, in science, in art, in literature—subtract the work of the men above forty, and while we should miss great treasures, even priceless treasures, we would practically be where we are today. . . . In the science and art of medicine young or comparatively young men have made every advance of the first rank. [2] p. 381

He also pointed to

> . . . the uselessness of men above sixty years of age, and the incalculable benefit it would be in commercial, political, and in professional life if, as a matter of course, men stopped work at this age. . . . As it can be maintained that all the great advances have come from men under forty, so the history of the world shows that a very large proportion of the evils may be traced to sexagenarians—nearly all the great mistakes politically and socially, all of the worst poems, most of the bad pictures, a majority of the bad novels, not a few of the bad sermons and speeches. [2] pp. 382–83

It was to add a bit of levity to what was otherwise a serious and even painful farewell that Osler referred to a humorous novel that advocated "peaceful departure by chloroform at sixty." That novel, *The Fixed Period*, by Anthony Trollope, [12] was the one from which he had taken the title of his address.

The Fixed Period: The novel

Osler was a great reader, and in lighter moments he enjoyed the Victorian writer Trollope. There was little danger of running out of material—Trollope wrote forty-seven novels in addition to biographies, histories, travel books, sketches, and five collections of short stories. Trollope poked barbed humor at the proud and the morally correct, exposing flawed natures beneath fraudulent exteriors. Finished in 1882, his forty-seventh and last novel, *The Fixed Period*, made fun of the fact that the most reasonable of social programs are apt to collapse because of that unaccountable factor, human nature.

His fanciful tale takes place one hundred years in the future, in the latter part of the twentieth century. The Parliament of the small, imaginary Pacific island of Britannula has passed a bill that would lead to national happiness and prosperity by lege for twelve months of preparation for euthanasia by chloroform. They would depart this earth just before their sixty-eighth birthdays.

It may have been more than a coincidence that Trollope chose the age of sixty-seven for departure to the terminal college. He was sixty-seven when he wrote the novel. Ironically, he died in his sixty-eighth year, the age at which citizens of Britannula were scheduled for euthanasia. (Osler misquoted Trollope in giving sixty years as the age for euthanasia in Britannula. He had evidently revised Trollope's fixed period downward to fit his own scheme.)

But back to our novel. Two of the most enthusiastic supporters of the "Fixed-Period" law are the president of the island, Jack Neverbend, and his dear friend, Gabriel Crasweller. The fun begins when Crasweller, a robust and successful business man who has never had so much as a headache in his life, approaches age sixty-seven and is about to take his honored place in history as the first to enter the college. As it begins to dawn on Crasweller that he will be first in line, second thoughts begin to drift into his mind. Neverbend struggles to try to prop up his friend's former enthusiasm for the principle of "The Fixed Period." Eventually, Neverbend is removed from the scene by a British gunboat. The novel is a charming and timeless satire—timely in Osler's day and timely in our own era of "senior entitlement programs."

"The Fixed Period" address had an unfortunate long-lasting effect. Plans to build, by popular subscription, an academy of medicine in Baltimore, to be named for Osler, had to be scrapped because so many subscriptions were withdrawn.[1 p. 677] What a dreadful price Sir William Osler paid for sharing his idea of a planned life, and making his good-natured reference to the novel, *The Fixed Period*. But the news media needed a story.

References

1. Cushing H. The Life of Sir William Osler, vol. 1. London, Oxford University Press, 1925.
2. Osler W. The fixed period. In Aequanimitas: With other Addresses to Medical Students, Nurses and Practitioners of Medicine. 3rd ed., pp. 375–93. Philadelphia, Blakiston Co., 1943.
3. Don't agree with Osler. New York Times, February 24, 1905, p. 1.
4. Dr. Osler is not joking. Baltimore Sun. February 25, 1905, p. 8.
5. Caustic comments pour in. Baltimore Sun, February 27, 1905, p. 12.
6. Calls it brutalizing, letter to the editor. Baltimore Sun, February 28, 1905, p. 7.
7. Old men at forty. New York Times, February 24, 1905, p. 6.
8. Osler writing essay on man's crisis at 40. New York Times, February 25, 1905, p. 5.
9. Dr. Osler sticks to views. New York Times, February 27, 1905, p. 1.
10. Suicide had Osler speech. New York Times, February 26, 1905, p. 1.
11. Osler W. A Way of Life. New York, Paul B. Hoeber, 1937, p. 21.
12. Trollope A. The Fixed Period (1882). London, Penguin Books, 1993.

SIR WILLIAM OSLER AND WILLIAM STEWART HALSTED — TWO CONTRASTING PERSONALITIES

EMILE HOLMAN, M.D.
(October 1971, pp. 134–139, 144)

Emile Holman was born into the family of a Methodist minister in 1890. After graduating from Stanford University in 1911, he won a Rhodes Scholarship and studied with Sir William Osler. Stimulated by Osler to apply to Johns Hopkins University School of Medicine, he received his M.D. in 1918. His surgical training was at Hopkins under William Halsted. He finished his surgical training in Boston with Harvey Cushing and then realized his goal of returning to California as the first Chair of Surgery at Stanford in 1926, where he was elected as a faculty member to ΑΩΑ. His surgical research was focused upon arteriovenous fistulae, and his love of teaching was a prominent part of his professional life. Although an ardent opponent of war from 1919 until his death in 1977, he served willingly as a Navy surgeon in the South Pacific during World War II. One of his sons, Halsted, was chair of medicine at Stanford from 1960 to 1970, and still is an active faculty member there.

Prologue

PATIENT CARE TODAY IS UNDERGOING A DRASTIC CHANGE, whether for better or for worse is not fully established. In the process, the patient is in danger of being alienated by the technical straightjacket into which his doctors have thrust him. The doctor, in turn, is in danger of being viewed as a sophisticated technician concerned primarily with complex machines, with electronic devices, with innumerable chemical tests, and with an impersonal catechism that frequently obscures the all-important details of the patient's illness. Meanwhile, the doctor may lose his role as a sympathetic healer.

Should the present trend continue, patient care will become increasingly depersonalized and dehumanized. But humanism has been declared an indispensable and integral part of a patient's care! What is "Humanism"? In Medicine it connotes compassion, benevolence, and charity. It implies human understanding, a social conscience and a sympathetic attitude toward those in distress.

Sir William Osler so enriched the lives of patients and of society in general with his deeply humanistic approach to human ills, that he was recognized early as a prototype of what the ideal physician should be. I would like here to explore further the meaning of Humanism and to seek ways of re-infusing patient care with kindness, compassion, and sympathy.

Osler

Sir William Osler is universally credited with having been the leading physician and medical teacher of his day. Today he is recognized also as the leading medical humanist of his time. Wrote Sir Frederic Kenyon, one of Britain's great classical scholars: "Osler was a well nigh perfect example of the union of science and the humanities."[6]

In an introduction to Osler's presidential address before the British Classical Association on "The Old Humanities and the New Science," Harvey Cushing wrote:

> Sir William Osler was a man first—a physician and scholar afterward; and beneath his high spirits, his love of fun, lay an infinite compassion and tenderness toward his human kind.[6]

William Welch said of Osler's presidency of this Association: "I felt it to be the triumphant culmination of a great career, throughout which, amid professional activities, high achievements, and useful services of extraordinary diversity, the humanistic spirit was a quickening, delightful, and pervasive influence."[9]

How and whence came this ardent humanist, this universally revered scientist? A brief review of the salient features of his life provides important clues.[3]

He was born in 1849 at Bond Head at the then edge of Ontario's wilderness, twenty-five miles from Toronto, the youngest boy of nine children of an Anglican missionary who served numerous parishes in twenty townships, travelling always on horseback. The mother of these nine children, born under the primitive conditions of the frontier, lived not only to celebrate her one hundredth birthday, but also to see three of her sons attain international fame, one as lawyer, one as banker, and one as physician. Here one detects Osler's key possession: superior genes!

Young Willie early came under the salutary guidance of a Reverend Johnson who introduced him to the wonderful world to be seen under a microscope, and before the age of twenty this lad had written three papers on the diatomaceae, the infusoria, and the polyzoa found in Canadian waters. Although originally directed toward the clergy, he graduated from McGill Medical School in 1872 and spent the next two years in Europe studying under Virchow, Rokitansky, Jenner, and Burdon Sanderson. On his return at the ripe age of twenty-five, he was made professor of medical institutes at McGill which involved the teaching of physiology, pathology and histology. The students dubbed him the "Baby Professor."

A pathologist in Montreal

A year later he was made pathologist to the Montreal General Hospital and in the next nine years he performed over nine hundred autopsies, the protocols of which filled five volumes, written in his own hand, carefully correlating the clinical picture with his own observations at the autopsy table. On the title page of one of these volumes he wrote: "Pathology is the basis for all true instruction in clinical medicine." These exacting and instructive experiences in the post-mortem room, many times repeated, undoubtedly provided the basis for the uncanny clinical sense that he displayed in later years.

In 1884 at the age of thirty-five he was made professor of medicine at the University of Pennsylvania, then considered the highest post in medicine in this hemisphere. In the meantime Johns Hopkins of Baltimore, a Quaker who was not unwilling to make a dollar in the selling and bartering of liquor, had left his seven million-dollar fortune for the founding of a university and a hospital.[8] (Seven million dollars at that time bought what 130 million dollars buy today.) A bachelor, he sought advice how best to perpetuate his name. He was advised by a friend to found a university—there would always be students; by another friend to found a hospital—there would always be sick people; and so he founded both, each with its own endowment and its own board of trustees.

The construction of the hospital was begun in 1877, but was not completed until twelve years later, only the income of the endowment being used. This unique tactic was stipulated in Mr. Hopkins' will. The medical school itself did not open until 1893, four years later, and then only through the fortuitous interest of a group of prominent Baltimore women who offered the $500,000 necessary to finish the school on one condition: that women be admitted on the same basis as men. Dr. Welch, the dean, shied at the word "same" and wanted to change it to "equal," but the ladies would have none of it. The offer was accepted, and, not long after, Osler was recruited.

A second distinctive feature of Hopkins was the requirement of a bachelor of arts degree for admission to the medical school. Harvard followed suit eight years later. Such high standards of admission to the new school were set that Osler once remarked to Welch, the dean: "It's good you and I entered this school as professors—we never would have made it as students."

A third unusual, and, at that time unique feature, was extension of the medical curriculum to four years beyond the degree of bachelor of arts.

The dominant influence in the new school besides Welch was Osler. These two impresarios were a great team, working harmoniously and effectively together, with much amusing repartee between them. "Welch has a three-story intellect with an attic on top!" commented Osler on one occasion.

Osler laid the greatest emphasis, first on the patient, and second on the student. He abolished didactic lectures and made the student an integral part of the hospital organization. Said he modestly: "I hope my gravestone will bear only the statement: 'He brought medical students into the wards for bedside teaching.'" In addition, he made the students responsible for the history of the patient's illness, for a complete physical examination, and for the simpler laboratory examinations. To us, now, all this seems quite commonplace, but at that time it took vision, courage, and faith to assign such important tasks to "mere" students. Osler himself was beset by the haunting fear that these innovations would be fought by the public and spurned by the medical profession. To his genuine relief, their acceptance by both was immediate and general, and they survive today as important keystones in medical education.

Osler was known as a therapeutic nihilist. He had no sympathy with random polypharmacy and relied a great deal on Mother Rest and Father Time. He was fond of quoting Oliver Wendell Holmes that if the entire pharmacopoeia were dumped into the ocean it would be good for the patients but very bad for the fishes!

He was an inspiring teacher of students for he himself remained a student to the very end. As MacCallum once wrote, " . . . he made frequent visits to the autopsy room, studying in death the puzzles he had helped solve, or failed to explain, during life." His influence on Johns Hopkins was incalculable. He set a pattern that is still an intimate part of the Hopkins of today.

It was at Oxford that I knew him, a gracious and generous host—especially to American doctors and students—a fascinating teacher, a profound student of the classics, and an enthusiastic medical historian and bibliophile, who in his lifetime collected 7,600 volumes, including 104 incunabula.

These manifold interests made his teaching a delight, replete with literary and historical allusions, and apt quotations. To him a patient was not a drunkard, he was a "disciple of Bacchus"; he was not a laborer but a "follower of Vulcan." If a victim of syphilis or gonorrhea, he was referred to in bedside conversation as "a devotee of Eros or Venus."

On ward rounds, his diagnostic acumen was a constant cause for surprise and admiration. One Sunday morning, as he entered the ward, his eye had rested only momentarily on the first patient when he exclaimed: "Hello, where did you get this luetic encephalitis?" "Why do you call it that?" asked the incredulous house physician, Dr. Mosse. Said Sir William: "A completely unilateral paralysis, including face and extremities on the same side, in a young man who is a sailor (he was widely and visibly tattooed) is most likely due to lues," and so it was!

On another Sunday morning as he walked down the ward he noted a chart with a high, septic fever, and inquired the diagnosis. "Sciatica" was the house physician's reply. "Sciatica, and that fever?" remarked Sir William as he turned down the covers, rolled the patient over and demonstrated a previously un-noted loss of the lumbar lordosis, a beginning kyphosis. He then embarked on a detailed exposition of Pott's disease of the spine with paravertebral abscess and pressure irritation of the lumbar nerve roots, producing sciatic pain. He called for X-ray studies and, as he predicted. they disclosed tuberculous destruction of two lumbar vertebrae.

On another occasion a patient with unexplained diarrhea was presented with the casual statement that amoebic dysentery had been ruled out on the basis of negative smears. "And how were the smears made?" "Stools were sent to the laboratory." "That's no good,"and he called for a glove, a rectal tube, a slide, and a microscope. In no time at all he had passed the tube, placed a bit of mucus from the end of the tube on the slide and under the microscope. To the great delight of his audience he demonstrated live, motile, *amoeba histolytica*.

The rare failure of diagnosis

Despite his fantastic medical knowledge, he too "came a cropper" on rare oc-casions. A young man with a lower midline abdominal tumor, the size of a large grapefruit, was operated upon with the diagnosis of urachal cyst, a diagnosis in which he had concurred after examination and discussion at Sunday rounds. At operation it proved to be solid. A week later the pathologic diagnosis re-ceived by the house surgeon, Dr. McDonald, as we were having afternoon tea, read: "Sarcoma, probably of ovarian origin." Without a word, McDonald jumped up and, dragging me with him, ran down the hall into the ward and to the young man's bed, pulled back the covers to find only one testicle in the scro-tum. The obvious diagnosis was sarcoma of an undescended testicle.

The next Sunday morning as the facts were being related to Sir William, his face gradually fell in crestfallen silence. When the sad tale was ended, incrimi-nating so sharply both house staff and consultant, his only comment was: "Gentlemen, these cases are sent to keep us in proper diagnostic humility," and he hurriedly went on to the next case. To his great chagrin, as he revealed later, he had failed to observe two of his own well-worn aphorisms:

"The abdomen extends from the neck to the knee."

"It is the duty of the consultant to do a rectal examination."

He loved children, and rounds usually ended on the pediatric ward. Children would listen for his coming and regret his parting step. A favorite trick was to put a large English penny on the umbilicus of a bedridden youngster with the promise that "if you keep it there until next Sunday, there'll be two." After Sir William's departure a nurse with farseeing compassion would fix the penny in place with adhesive. Another trick of his informality was to tiptoe into the pediatric ward where the head nurse or sister would be seated at her desk, put his hands before her eyes, saying in a gruff voice: "Guess who's here!" to the great delight of the youngsters in the ward.

He had a ready wit and an ever-present sense of humor, much given to practical jokes. When two of his young trainees opened an office next to his on Charles Street in Baltimore they returned one day to find a sign on their lawn reading: "These young fellows are novices—come next door."

He was frequently heard to whistle as he walked along the hospital corridors. Once when asked why he whistled, he replied: "I whistle that I may not weep." What a deeply compassionate nature lies hidden in that simple remark!

During his long last illness, extending over several months of pneumonia, pulmonary abscess, and empyema, he once said in a humorously pathetic vein: "How I regret I cannot attend my own post mortem. I've watched the case so long it would be most interesting."

His ashes and magnificent library are now housed in the Osler Library at McGill, thus fulfilling a long-cherished hope:

> I like to think of my books in an alcove of a fireproof library in some institution that I love; at the back of the alcove an open fireplace and a few easy chairs, and on the mantelpiece in an urn with my ashes, through which my astral self could peek at the books I have loved, and enjoy the delight with which kindred souls still in the flesh would handle them.

His many aphorisms reflect the flair of a schoolmaster as well as the heart of a humanist:

> "Above everything, gentlemen, come to the study of the diagnosis of disease with all the modesty at your command."

> "Positiveness and dogmatism are inevitable associates of superficial knowledge in medicine."

> "Care more for the individual patient than for the special features of the disease."

> "The motto of each of you as you undertake the examination and treatment of a case should be: put yourself in his place. Realize so far as you can the mental state of the patient, enter into his feelings-scan gently his faults. The kindly word, the cheerful greeting, the sympathetic look-these the patient understands."

> "Keep a looking glass in your own heart, and the more carefully you scan your own frailties, the more tender you are for those of your fellow creatures. In Charity we of the medical profession must live and move and have our being."

"A little old-fashioned courtesy which makes a man shrink from wounding the feelings of a brother practitioner leaves no room for envy, hatred, malice, or any uncharitableness."

"If you can't see good in people, see nothing."

"A physician may possess the science of Harvey and the art of Sydenham and yet there may be lacking in him those finer qualities of heart and head which count for so much in life. . . . While doctors continue to practice medicine with their hearts as well as their heads, so long will there be a heavy balance in their favor in the bank of Heaven."[2]

This, in brief, was the art of medicine as practised by Osler. Wrote Welch: "He was in the broadest sense a humanist," but he promptly added Osler's own perceptive comments:

The so-called humanists have not enough science, and science sadly lacks the humanities. . . . Twin berries on one stem, grievous damage has been done to both in regarding them in any other light than complemental.

Osler the scientific physician was perhaps over-complemented by Osler the humanist. All his writings, all his actions, bespeak his intensely humanistic qualities.

Halsted

A contrasting personality heavily weighted on the scientific side was that of Osler's good friend and longtime medical colleague, William Stewart Halsted. A thumbnail sketch by Harvey Cushing presented at the time of Halsted's death (1922) is without parallel in its apt epitome of the man:

Professor Halsted, one of the most cultivated and regarded by many as the most eminent surgeon of his time, was a man of unique personality, shy, something of a recluse, fastidious in his tastes and in his friendships, an aristocrat in his breeding, scholarly in his habits, the victim for many years of indifferent health. Nevertheless, he was one of the few American surgeons who may be considered to have established a school of surgery, comparable, in a sense, to the school of Billroth in Vienna. He had few of the qualities supposed to accompany what the world regards as a successful surgeon. Over-modest about his work, indifferent to matters of priority, caring little for the gregarious gatherings of medical men, unassuming, having little interest in private practice, he spent his medical life avoiding patients—even students, when this was possible—and, when health permitted, working in clinic and laboratory at the solution of a succession of problems which aroused his interest. Many of his contributions, not only to his craft but to the science of medicine in general, were fundamental in character and of enduring importance.

Directly emanating from these predominantly non-humanistic traits, and from the abundant and valuable free time they provided to follow his own pursuits, were numerous original surgical procedures, expertly developed in the laboratory or tested in the clinic, and the many original scientific treatises[4] which flowed from his pen to win world-wide acclaim. To mention a few:

- his introduction of rubber gloves into operating room techniques;
- his concepts of complete hemostasis and of reducing traumatized tissue in the operative wound to a minimum;
- his discovery of local anesthesia and its application to dentistry and surgery;
- his operative techniques for hernia; for carcinoma of the breast with skin grafting;
- for resection of the thyroid with preservation of the parathyroids;
- his results of the open air treatment of surgical tuberculosis;
- his treatment without drainage of a suppurating compound comminuted fracture of the ankle joint;
- his observations on the training of the surgeon.

His presentations were models of lucid style and diction. Witness the following paragraph (1920):

> In a delightful discourse on arterio-venous aneurysm Osler takes a swift flight into a vibrant domain of surgery, tracing into and out of the dark ages steps of the few surgeons who blazed the way. Well he knew and loved the crystal springs and sources bearing their tiny freights of knowledge to the flood. . . .

It is quite apparent that Halsted labored painstakingly over his writing, weighing carefully vocabulary, construction, and meaning. He sought diligently for perfection in the written word, achieved by many revisions—frequently eight to ten—and by consulting ever so diligently his much-thumbed Century dictionary.

A letter to Fielding Garrison (dated November 27, 1920, less than two years before his death), reveals his striking preoccupation with style:[5]

> We heartily welcome your kindly touches and masterful calligraphic strokes. They recall the pleasure I found, a few years ago, in reading in manuscript a long letter of Swinburne caressingly repolished. You may have noticed that in one of the volumes of Henry James' letters there is reproduced, as a sample of his method, a slice of page proof devoutly slaughtered by his fastidious pencil. How interesting it would be to gather for publication some of the piously revised galley proofs of great writers of poetry and prose. Doubtless you know of such a collection. I have in mind its value to me and to medical men plunging feet first into print, blissfully ignorant of the existence of such a thing as the art of expression or helpless in their search for it.

Brilliance masking addiction

But these beguiling literary and scientific activities, conducted up to three months before his death, were not sufficiently engrossing to forestall another quite unsuspected activity. Wilder Penfield's fascinating disclosures from Osler's diary[7] revealed that at the very time these original and fundamental advances in surgery were being initiated, developed, and described, Halsted by his own admissions was taking large doses of morphia.

Osler's diary as presented by Penfield records the following important items:

> The proneness to seclusion, the slight peculiarities, amounting to eccentricities at times, were the only outward traces of the daily battle through which this brave fellow lived for years. When we recommended him as full surgeon to the Hospital in 1890, I believed, and Welch did too, that be was no longer addicted to morphia. He had worked so well and so energetically that it did not seem possible that he could take the drug and do so much.

> About six months after the full position (as Professor of Surgery) had been given, I saw him in a severe chill, and this was the first intimation I had that he was still taking morphia. Subsequently I had many talks about it and gained his full confidence. He had never been able to reduce the amount to less than three grains daily; on this he could do his work comfortably and maintain his excellent physical vigor (for he was a very muscular fellow). I do not think that anyone suspected him, not even Welch.

> Subsequently, 10 Jan. 1898, he got the amount down to 1.5 grains, and of late years (1912) has possibly got on without it.

However, important information to the contrary was presented later by Welch. While a patient at Johns Hopkins Hospital for 14 months preceding his death on April 30, 1934, Welch was under the temporary care of a young house officer named David Sprong, now Professor of Urology at the University of California in Los Angeles. In a letter to me dated May 29, 1968, Dr. Sprong recalls the following statement by Welch:

> Although it has been widely reported that Halsted conquered his addiction, this is not entirely true. As long as he lived he would occasionally have a relapse and go back on the drug. He would always go out of town for this and when he returned he would come to me, very contrite and apologetic, to confess. He had an idea that I could tell what he had done. I couldn't, but I let him go on thinking so because I felt it was good for him to have someone to talk it over with.

Dr. Sprong continued:

> I do not remember that Dr. Welch mentioned how long these relapses might last, or how often they occurred, but he felt pretty strongly that the facts should be on the record.

Thus, at long last, through Osler's diary as presented by Penfield, and through Welch's reminiscences as disclosed by Sprong, the probable course of events may be reconstructed:

> The early period of addiction (1885–1898) characterized at first by heartrending attempts at control including a futile sea voyage with Welch, and two incarcerations at a Rhode Island hospital, from which he emerged presumably, though actually not, cured; a second period of less demanding addiction (1898–1908), and the last ten years of his life of semicontrolled addiction characterized by occasional lapses from grace.

We may now hope that the controversy which beguiled both friend and foe for over 38 years is resolved. . . . As Margaret Boise, his long-time anesthetist, so perceptively wrote in 1952 for the Halsted Centenary:[1]

> There was the perennial question as to which road the Professor pursued: the courageous and victorious fight against the enemy, or the equally courageous thirty years of fruitful activity with the haunting enemy always at hand.

Miraculously, despite the long duration of the addiction, there was no deterioration of self, of health, or of mentality. In confirmation of this providential course, the following evidence is presented: Two years before his death there appeared the impressive volume of "The Operative Story of Goitre,"[4] adjudged to be the most complete and most scholarly study of the subject available.

In the same year appeared his valued monograph on "Ligation of the Left Subclavian Artery in Its First Portion."[4] On April 20, 1920, he, with the assistance of Drs. Heuer and Reid, operated successfully for the second time upon Alexander Miller for the excision of a large left subclavian aneurysm, the subclavian artery having been ligated two years previously, by him, in its first portion proximal to the aneurysm.

In the academic year of 1921–22, the year of his death, I, as resident surgeon, assisted him on a number of occasions in the conduct of the Friday Noon Surgical Clinics at which he discussed surgical problems in a most lucid manner. I have vivid memories, for example, of his discussion of the healing that follows the ligation of a large artery. Said he to the students:

> John B. Murphy, the Chicago surgeon, claims that intima adheres to intima. Not so, when an artery is ligated sufficiently tightly to close its lumen, it also closes the vasa vasorum and the tissue included in the ligature dies, to be replaced by fibrous tissue, as proven in the experimental animal.

Turning from the students to me, he continued: "Isn't it a pity Murphy died before knowing this?"

In the concluding remarks of his scholarly Harvey Lecture given on March, 1914, on "The Significance of the Thymus Gland in Grave's Disease," he said,

> I have touched my subject only very lightly at some of the higher points.

Hardly enough has been said even to make it clear that an enormous amount of work underlies the facts which we at present possess. It must be evident to everyone, however, that there reigns the greatest confusion on the subject of the function of the glands of internal secretion.

Fortunately, the ardor for research on our globe is not diminished by the conviction that we are laboring in the wake of workers infinite in numbers on countless worlds who have carried their investigations millions of years beyond the stage reached by us, and are rapidly progressing towards an ultimate solution which may never be reached.

In his last years none suspected his continuing addiction, not even his two secretaries, nor his intimate friends, Sam Crowe, Mont Reid, and George Heuer.

In the meantime, a second enemy had appeared. In 1919 his gallbladder had been removed for numerous stones, long held responsible for frequent attacks of abdominal pain. Little improvement followed this operation, and in August, 1922, while at his mountain home in North Carolina, he again suffered a severe attack of abdominal pain accompanied by jaundice. After many annoying delays, he set out on a three-day journey to Baltimore by wagon, rail, and ambulance. He arrived at Johns Hopkins Hospital delirious, deeply jaundiced, severely dehydrated and greatly undernourished.

After massive infusions of normal salt solution he became conscious, entirely lucid, and requested an operation by Drs. Heuer and Reid. This disclosed in the common duct a single stone the size and shape of a large olive. For a few days his condition promised well, but, alas, a wound infection developed, accompanied by an aphthous stomatitis, repeated bleeding from rarely encountered aphthous ulcerations of the esophagus and stomach, and finally by a lobar pneumonia of the right upper lobe, which ended in death on September 7, 1922.

In reviewing Halsted's enigmatic though fruitful life, one stands in awe and veneration of this unique and solitary figure, beset through long years by a fearful enemy against which his courage and a strong will repeatedly prevailed to build a life of remarkable achievement. His original conceptions embellished in many areas the art and science of surgery. A valuable legacy to his pupils lay in the inspiration of his dedication to thoughtful inquiry, to the pursuit of perfection, and to the scientific search for truth. In the history of surgery, Halsted clearly and uniquely embodied the role of an original and productive thinker, to whom all surgeons the world over are deeply indebted, now, and in the limitless future. Has there ever been a saga of more poignant miseries, of more dramatic recoveries, of more magnificent triumphs?

The contrast between these two giants in medicine

This brief and incomplete study of two contrasting personalities should not detract from the great inspiration and influence each provided in his day. How fortunate that two such vital personalities simultaneously left their permanent mark on the great institution they helped to found and develop. Each complemented the other, and each left a thoroughly individualistic but deep impression on his and subsequent generations.

May the light of these two brilliant stars never be dimmed.

References

1. Boise M. Dr. Halsted as an anesthetist knew him. Surgery, 32:498, 1952.
2. Camac CNB. Counsels and Ideals from the Writings of William Osler. Boston and New York, Houghton Milton Co., 1905.
3. Cushing H. The Life of Sir William Osler, Oxford, The Clarendon Press, 1925.
4. Halsted WS. Surgical Papers. Baltimore, The Johns Hopkins Press, 1924.
5. Holman E. William Stewart Halsted as revealed in his letters. Stanford Med. Bull., 10: 137, 1952.
6. Osler W. The Old Humanities and the New Science. Boston, Houghton Muffin Co., 1920. Also: New York, The Riverside Press, 1920.
7. Penfield W. Halsted of Johns Hopkins. JAMA, 210: 2214, Dec. 22, 1969.
8. Thom HH. Johns Hopkins, A Silhouette. Baltimore, The Johns Hopkins Press, 1929. Also: London, Oxford University Press, 1929.
9. Welch WH. Foreword: Appreciations and Reminiscences of Sir William Osler. Edited by Maude E. Abbott, M.D. Bulletin No. IX, International Assn. Med. Museums, Toronto, Murray Printing Co., 1926.

PART V

THE PHYSICIAN
AND
WARTIME

COMING TOGETHER DURING WORLD WAR I: MEDICINE'S RESPONSE TO THE CHALLENGES OF TRENCH WARFARE

ERIC DAVID SCHWARTZ, M.D.
(Fall 1995, pp. 5–9)

Eric D. Schwartz earned a B.A. in History, Phi Beta Kappa, from Dartmouth College in 1991 and his M.D. from The Johns Hopkins University School of Medicine in 1995. He completed his residency in Diagnostic Radiology at the University of Miami in 1999 and his fellowship in Neuroradiology at the University of Pennsylvania School of Medicine in 2001. Dr. Schwartz has stayed on as a faculty member in the Radiology Department at the University of Pennsylvania School of Medicine, and his research focuses on the development of a non-invasive MRI technique for imaging axon regeneration and neuroprotection in the spinal cord following injury. He is also working to develop and evaluate transplants designed to help cure spinal cord injury, and has received funding from the NIH and the American Society of Neuroradiology. This paper was accorded Honorable Mention in the 1995 Alpha Omega Alpha Student Essay Competition.

O N AUGUST 20, 1914, THE BRITISH EXPEDITIONARY FORCE (BEF) marched toward Mons for its first encounter with the Germans. The war, Britain declared, would be "over by Christmas." By August 30, the French and British were beaten back, and one of every six members of the BEF was wounded.[1, p. 25] And by Christmas, 90 percent of the BEF were casualties in a war that had become deadlocked from "Switzerland to the sea."[2, p. 4] The character of warfare had changed. No longer were battles going to be decided by swift maneuvering. Instead, each army was "entrenched in a fixed position which, give or take a mile or so, would hardly alter for the next three years and a half."[1, p. 25] The trench warfare, which characterized the First World War, brought with it new challenges to medicine, such as gas gangrene, gas warfare, and trench fever. The medical community responded, however, by organizing its clinical, bacteriological, and administrative branches, and, by 1918, many of these problems had been nearly conquered.

When the wounded began to arrive from the first battles, doctors and nurses realized that their war was not against the Germans but against infection. Sir Wilmot Herringham, a consulting physician to the British forces, wrote that all the lessons of warfare learned in the Boer War had to be unlearned, as the battles in South Africa were fought in a clean desert in pure air, while in France, the fighting occurred "over some of the richest and therefore the filthiest land in the world."[3, p. 79] When doctors saw the first casualties of the war, they were shocked that nearly all the wounds were severe, lacerated and were suppurating.[4, p. 209] The infection that caused the most death and disability was gas gangrene. Captain Geoffrey Keynes, of the Royal Army Medical Corps, (R.A.M.C.) recalled the hopelessness of this infection during the first few months of the war:

> We knew nothing about it at all. . . .You got this appalling infection with anaerobic bacteria and the men just died like flies. We got the causalities straight from Mons and the infection had usually been set in by the time they got to us and, if the men had been several days on the way, as most of them had, the wound was simply a mass of putrid muscle rotting with gas gangrene. . . . We simply didn't know how to treat it. We'd never come across it before. Of course, there were no antibiotics. No effective disinfectants. We would cut away as much of the diseased tissue as we could. On a leg or an arm we would remove the limb, but that didn't stop it. It just went on up, and still the men would die from the toxic effects.[1, p. 24]

Surgeons found that the aseptic operating conditions used in civilian practice were ineffective in a theatre of war with grossly contaminated wounds.[5, p. 174] Medicine's initial failure to deal with these problems led to finger pointing, and "there was a disposition to blame either the military administration for delay in collecting the wounded, or the surgeons near the front for inefficient methods of treatment."[6, p.v] As Sir Wilmot pointed out, however, "all such criticism was due to ignorance of the conditions under which the work was done."[3, p. 95]

Explosive shells, trench conditions, and the problems of evacuation were much to blame for the poor presenting condition of the wounded at field hospitals. Explosive shells released shrapnel that caused ragged wounds, and bullets from high-powered rifles fired at short range left gaping exit wounds.[2, p. 5; 7, p. 268] One observer, Sir Philip Gibbs, at a casualty clearing station, described the viciousness of the wounds when he wrote of:

> men with chunks of steel in their lungs and bowels vomiting great gobs of blood, men with legs and arms torn from their trunk, men without noses, and their brains throbbing through open scalps, men without faces.[4, p. 224]

Sister K. Luard of Queen Alexandra's Imperial Military Nursing Service called the shrapnel wounds "more ghastly than anything I have ever seen or smelt; . . . wounds of the Boer War were pinpricks compared with them."[1, p. 48] In addition to causing extensive lacerations, shrapnel and explosions drove contaminated mud and mud-encrusted clothing deep into the wounds.[5, p. 175; 8, p. 6] Evacuation from the trenches was difficult because of constant bombardment, and sometimes the wounded had to wait for days in the mud and cold.[2, p. 6; 4, p. 218]

These characteristics of trench warfare all contributed to the problem of infected wounds. The British responded quickly, however, and began to solve the problem of sepsis from administrative, clinical, and bacteriological standpoints.

The rapid mobilization of research may be credited to "the insight of a single individual, Mr. Lloyd George."[3, p. 149] In 1911, Lloyd George pushed legislation through Parliament that provided funds for the formation of a Medical Research Committee. When the war started, the administration of this committee was firmly established, and it could instantly concentrate its resources on solving the medical problems arising from the war.[6, p. vi]

For the first time ever, bacteriological laboratories were brought to the front lines of a war.[3, p. 115; 10, p. 9] Sidney Rowland, a pathologist from the Lister Institute, made the first mobile laboratory from a motor touring caravan in October 1914. Within a year, several more mobile labs were sent to France[3, p. 115] with three basic objectives: bacteriologists would examine pathological specimens to aid in diagnosis, determine how infectious diseases spread and search for carriers, and investigate new diseases in order to discover causes and means of prevention.[10, p. 9] Gas gangrene fell under the category of new diseases, and bacteriologists endeavored to find the responsible organism. The responsible microorganisms turned out to be a variety of gas-producing anaerobic bacteria.

The list included *Bacillus welchii*, *Bacillus sporogenes*, *Bacillus edematiens*, *Bacillus histolyticum*, and *Bacillus hibier*, with *Bacillus welchii* being the most common causative microorganism.[2, p. 36]

Researchers also focused on the gross and microscopic changes that occurred in gangrene in order to improve diagnosis at the front. Gas gangrene was "essentially a muscle disease,"[11, p. 52] but changes could be seen early by looking for changes in skin color. Colonel Cuthbert Wallace, a consulting surgeon for the British Armies in France, described the gross changes in skin and the correlating clinical prognoses. According to him, if the skin was swollen with a dirty cream tint, and crepitation and resonance were just perceptible, local excision of the affected area might be all that was necessary for treatment. When purple-staining areas coalesced and were surrounded by a greyish-white border, the gangrene probably had spread far enough as to require amputation of the limb.[12, pp. 50–51]

Captains J. W. McNee and J. Shaw Dunn outlined the microscopic changes in muscle that occurred from gangrene in a report they sent from a mobile laboratory in France. The series of colored plates accompanying the article show the atrophy of muscle fibers occurring before the arrival of bacteria, suggesting that a toxic fluid preceded the arrival of bacteria; the fluid filled the spaces between the degenerating muscle fibers and interstitial tissues. McNee and Dunn proposed that the bacilli spread down the muscle, producing a vicious cycle. The anaerobic bacilli live on dead tissue, breaking down sugars and producing large amounts of gas and toxic fluid. The toxic fluid produced by the bacilli moves down the fibers, providing the bacilli with the proper environment to infect and produce more toxic fluid.[1, p. 53] Even at the front lines in a war, McNee and Dunn followed Koch's postulates concerning infectious diseases by using large rabbits with long hind legs for reproducing the disease, using pure cultures of bacilli.

At the start of the war, surgeons treated the casualties as they would in peacetime, by cleansing the wound and then immediately sewing the wound closed.[5, p. 176] The potential for infection in war conditions, however, required a more aggressive approach to prevent infections such as gas gangrene. In July 1915, a French surgeon named R. LeMaitre introduced the technique of completely excising all wounded flesh, followed by delayed suture.[7, p. 268] LeMaitre based this treatment on the concept that bacteria would not multiply or spread to any great extent during the first twelve hours following a wound.[7, p. 216] Richard Derby, a physician for the American Army, recalled how LeMaitre was warned that the method had to be proved clinically before being divulged, else he would be considered a "mad man."[13, pp. 27–28] By 1917, however, surgeons were singing this method's praises, calling the routine excision of damaged tissues "the most important alteration in treatment since the early days of the war."[9, p. 33]

An article by three surgeons in the R.A.M.C. demonstrates how bacteriological and clinical advances could be merged to prevent gas gangrene. C. H. S. Frankau, Hamilton Drummond, and G. E. Neligan described surgical methods designed to remove as much of the infected tissue through resection of muscle, based on principles supplied by the mobile laboratories. Researchers, such as Colonel Cuthbert Wallace, had shown that gas gangrene spread longitudinally and did not generally spread from one muscle bundle to another. This knowledge helped explain why amputation stumps would often contain one gangrenous muscle, while adjacent muscles would be healthy. The surgeons realized that resection should include all the muscle that might be infected, while any good muscles or parts of muscles could be spared. Clinical experience and laboratory research helped define what constituted a healthy muscle: the tissue had to have unchanged color, normal contractility, and a good blood supply, as indicated by bleeding.[14, p. 54] The excision of diseased muscle in this fashion could arrest the disease without recourse to amputation.

The problems of evacuation, however, prevented many wounded from reaching a surgeon during the crucial few hours, and often the patient presented with an already suppurating wound. In the search for an effective antiseptic agent, "every day produced a new compound."[2, p. 11] Finally, English chemist Henry Dakin and Frenchman Alexis Carrel collaborated in creating a system of antisepsis that may have been one of the greatest contributions made to surgery during the war.

A few months into the war, Dr. Harvey Cushing visited Dakin in his laboratory and observed:

> The lines along which they [Carrel and Dakin] have started to work include the suction treatment of suppurating wounds without dressings; the employment of irrigation with bactericidal fluids.[1, p. 66]

After testing nearly 200 substances,[5, p. 176] Dakin and Carrel determined that the most suitable antiseptic was sodium hypochlorite, neutralized with boric acid.[2, p. 16] In an article written for the British Medical Association, Dakin outlined the thought behind the creation of the antiseptic. Early in the war, Dakin noted, the goal was to find a rapidly sterilizing antiseptic that could be applied to a badly infected wound just once. This method was rarely successful, however, and the corrosive antiseptic solutions often caused damage to living tissue, an effect that outweighed any positive ones. Consequently, "attention was turned to the repeated or even continuous application of relatively mild antiseptic solutions."[15, p. 12] Hypochlorites had been known to have germicidal properties, but the free alkali present in such solutions was extremely irritating. To combat the alkaline nature of the solution, Dakin used boric acid, producing a buffered solution that could maintain neutrality. Other advantages of Dakin's solution included the ability to dissolve necrotic tissue and keep lymph tracts from clotting, thereby keeping wound surfaces moist and allowing the solution to reach bacteria protected by masses of dead tissue. The strong oxidizing strength of the solution also worked to prevent toxemia by reacting strongly with bacterial toxins.

Carrel's contribution was the invention of an irrigation system composed of "bifurcated rubber tubes that would keep the wounds continuously bathed and drained."[13, p. 18] A flask of solution was suspended above the patient and, by a series of tubes, drained into the wound, which was packed with a sterile gauze dressing; nurses changed the solution and dressing every two hours, day and night. Secondary suture was undertaken after a bacteria count showed one bacterium for five microscope fields for two successive days.[2, pp. 26–28]

The British took no time in implementing this new clinical discovery, and by 1915, nurses on the front were making up the solution by the gallon. The Carrel-Dakin method's greatest impact was on the wounded who could not get to a hospital within the window of twelve hours that LeMaitre had established. As British Surgeon-General Sir George H. Makins wrote in an article concerning the military hospitals in France:

The best results that are being attained in all forms of wound treatment are undoubtedly those in which the Carrel-Dakin method is employed. This method has not only shown itself successful in the early treatment, but also in the later treatment of septic wounds, even in the stage of chronic established suppuration.[16, p. 60]

The first few battles of the war brought out the problems with evacuation of wounded, and the British and French responded to create an efficient system of transport. After the battle of Mons, it became obvious that horse transport would be unfeasible if casualties were heavy, and so, by mid-October of 1914, convoys of motor ambulances were arriving in France.[9, p. 30] A railway system of hospital trains had to be set up, as the majority of patients admitted to general hospitals were transported by rail. A series of "luxuriously appointed hospital trains"[16, p. 58] were produced, allowing for better care of the wounded during transport. The extraordinary advances in surgical wound treatment, as well as improvements in evacuation, were extremely successful.

On April 22, 1915, during the Second Battle of Ypres, the Germans surprised British, French, and Canadian troops by releasing a strange gas from cylinders near the allied trenches.[4, p. 222] Gas warfare had begun. In retrospect, it seems surprising that the allies were not prepared to deal with this threat. Despite the Hague Conference of 1907, which prohibited the use of chemical or gas warfare, both sides had most likely already developed and stockpiled weapons of this nature. The doctors responded as quickly as possible, however, and, copying protective pads discovered on captured German soldiers, created crude masks by wrapping hypochlorite-soaked cotton in muslin containers.[8, p. 8] Within sixty hours from the first attack, the army distributed 90,000 of these hand-held protective pads.

Soon, however, the wards were full of men with acute bronchitis, slowly drowning from pulmonary edema. Many were also blinded by the gas, which only served to increase the horror.

Four days after the first gas attack, Dr. J. S. Haldane visited the casualties and, after examining the blue-faced soldiers gasping for breath, definitively stated for the world that "the symptoms and the other facts so ascertained point to the use by the German troops of chlorine or bromine for purposes of asphyxiation."[1, p. 85] As with sepsis, the allies responded quickly to counter this new threat. The British set up a committee of ten persons to examine the effects of gas as seen by the naked eye and by microscope, as well as to determine how gas affects the blood and respiration.[3, p. 143] In France, the R.A.M.C. set up two laboratories dedicated to developing protection and treatment to gas warfare. The urgency of the situation often required personal sacrifices from the researchers, and Sister Luard wrote in her diary about a doctor who had to be admitted for gas inhalation:

This afternoon the medical staffs of both divisions have been trying experiments in a barn with chlorine gas, with and without different kinds of masks soaked with some antidote, such as lime.

[T]hey found the [doctor] getting blue and suffocated. . . . But they found out what they wanted to know—that if you put on this mask, you can go to the assistance of men overpowered by the gas, with less chance of finding yourself dead when you get there.[1, p. 85]

The Germans, however, did not stop with chlorine; they soon used more lethal gases, such as phosgene ($COCl_2$) and mustard gas (dichloroethyl sulphide). Phosgene caused mortality rates twice those of chlorine, and irritated eyes so intensely that, according to United States surgeon Richard Derby, exposed soldiers just "sat there with their faces buried in their hands, rocking to and fro in an agony that was dreadful to witness."[13, p. 31] Mustard gas burned the skin, causing blistering and "in some cases, stripping a man's entire body of skin."[4, p. 222]

Clothing retained the gases, and consequently, men needed to bathe as soon as possible with soap and water. The Red Cross managed to obtain showers from the French government and installed them at hospitals located nearest to the front lines. Dr. Haldane invented an apparatus designed to give oxygen to as many men as possible at the correct dosage for each patient; a reducing valve, connected to the oxygen cylinder, allowed oxygen to be released at a low pressure to four distributing valves and rubber masks.[3, p. 144] In addition to these clinical improvements, gas masks continued to improve, and by the end of the war, almost 27 million masks were made and distributed to soldiers on the front.

Early in May 1915, doctors faced another complication of trench warfare. Soldiers from the front were presenting with a form of fever which struck every one as novel Colonel Herringham described the disease as starting with faintness, leading to severe headaches and leg pain so intense that the pressure of bedclothes caused severe pain; there were also relapsing cycles of fever that lasted about five days.[17, p. 10] The doctors dubbed these symptoms "trench fever," and the British created a Trench Fever Committee, under Sir David Bruce, to organize the attack on this baffling disease.

Sir Wilmot, in an article to the British Medical Association and in his memoirs of the war, described the bacteriological approach taken to combat this disease. The symptom of relapsing fever appeared similar to malaria, and so researchers concentrated on blood. Bacteriologists injected blood from patients to volunteers, and the resulting infections led researchers to look for microorganisms in the blood. No organism unique to trench fever patients could be found. At the same time, researchers wondered whether trench fever was only a variant of enteric fever or influenza. The former was ruled out, however, after hundreds of comparisons, and the lack of mucus secretions. The relative confinement of trench fever to those at the front or to medical personnel ruled out the latter. By 1917, the clinical features had been well defined, but no cause or cure had been found. A breakthrough occurred, however, when teams of U.S. and British researchers transmitted the disease through previously sterile lice. The results of these experiments would lead to hygienic changes for the soldiers.

The number of cases of trench fever had diminished substantially by 1918, as better hygiene became available. Huge cylinders, mounted on truck chassis, provided clothing with a steam bath, fifteen minutes of which would "kill not only all lice but their eggs as well"[13, p. 43] In addition to being supplied more of these disinfection units, troops bathed more often, and had their clothes and equipment disinfected at the same time. The British Medical Association, in its preface to a collection of articles taken from the *British Medical Journal* during 1917, wrote that the medical advances made during a three-year period "stand out among the wastage of war as benefits of permanent value for the future."[6, p. vi] Perhaps, however, the extraordinary partnership of clinical, administrative, and bacteriological branches was more important than the actual discoveries.

References

1. Macdonald L. The Roses of No Man's Land. New York, Atheneum, 1989.
2. Rice AG. Surgical Lessons of the Great War. Providence, E.A. Johnson & Co., 1920.
3. Herringham W. A Physician in France. London, Edward Arnold, 1919.
4. Laffin J. Surgeons in the Field. London, JM Dent & Sons, 1970.
5. Richardson RG. The Story of Modern Surgery, new revised ed. New York, Collier Books, 1964.
6. British Medicine in the War, 1914-1917: Being Essays on Problems of Medicine, Surgery, and Pathology Arising among the British Armed Forces Engaged in This War and the Manner of Their Solution. Collected out of the British Medical Journal, April-October, 1917. London, British Medical Association, 1917.
7. Maltz M. Evolution of Plastic Surgery. New York, Froben Press, 1946.
8. Poynter FNL, ed. Medicine and Surgery in the Great War (1914–1918). London, Wellcome Institute of the History of Medicine, 1968.
9. Bowlby A and Wallace C. The development of British surgery at the front. In: British Medicine in the War, 1914–1917, pp. 30–50.
10. Herringham WP. Bacteriology at the front. In: British Medicine in the War, 1914–1917, pp. 9–10.
11. McNee JW and Dunn JS. The method of spread of gas gangrene into living muscle. In: British Medicine in the War, 1914–1917, pp. 52–54.
12. Wallace C. The colour changes seen in skin and muscle in gas gangrene. In: British Medicine in the War, 1914–1917, pp. 50–52.
13. Derby R. "Wade In, Sanitary!" The Story of a Division Surgeon in France. New York and London, G.P. Putnam's Sons, 1919.
14. Frankau CHS, Drummond H and Neligan GE. The successful conservative treatment of early gas gangrene in limbs by the resection of infected muscles. In: British Medicine in the War, 1914–1917, pp. 54–57.

15. Dakin HD. Biochemistry and war problems. In: British Medicine in the War, 1914–1917, pp. 11–14.
16. Makins GM. The development of British surgery in the hospitals on the lines of communication in France. In British Medicine in the War, 1914–1917, pp. 58–75.
17. Herringham WP. Trench fever and its allies. In British Medicine in the War, 1914–1917, pp. 10–11.

DOCTORS IN WARTIME: JOHAN SCHARFFENBERG, PROPHET IN HIS OWN COUNTRY

MAYNARD M. COHEN, M.D., AND DORIS VIDAVER-COHEN
(Spring 1988, pp. 28–30)

Dr. Cohen (AΩA, Wayne State University School of Medicine, 1944) was chairman and Jean Schweppe Armour professor emeritus of the Department of Neurological Sciences at the Rush Medical College. He was a president of the American Academy of Neurology and co-director with Doris Vidaver-Cohen of the Humanities in Medicine Program at Rush Medical College. The authors received a National Endowment for the Humanities Project Award for work on literature and medicine.

FOR JOHAN SCHARFFENBERG IT WAS BUT A SHORT STEP from his life's work as psychiatrist, criminologist, and journalist to sparking the Norwegian Resistance movement into being during the Nazi occupation of his country. With a mixture of repugnance and fascination, he had been drawn to study Hitler's rise as self-proclaimed "prophet" of an evil, almost mystical, quasi-religious movement, even before the tyrant seized power in Germany. As early as the summer of 1933 Dr. Scharffenberg's incisive article in the widely read daily journal *Arbeiderbladet,* "Hitler—Saviour or Madman?" described the German dictator as a paranoid psychopath who adopted his "prophetic" role as a manifestation of mental illness.[1, p. 191]

The article resulted in a protest by the German minister in Oslo to the Norwegian foreign ministry denouncing Scharffenberg's defamation of the chief of state of a *friendly foreign country*, even to the point of demanding prosecution. After investigation, however, the Norwegian attorney general found no cause to proceed, and the Germans withdrew their charges. When that particular Norwegian government later fell to a vote of no confidence, the German diplomat renewed his complaint against Scharffenberg, again demanding prosecution. A newly appointed foreign minister diplomatically agreed, at the same time pointing out that Norwegian law afforded Dr. Scharffenberg the opportunity to prove the accuracy of his assertions.

At the time, Dr. Scharffenberg was director of the Oslo Asylum for the criminally insane. Recognizing the psychiatrist to be both qualified and respected, and to have been meticulous in documenting his psychiatric evaluation of Hitler, the German minister felt it wisest to withdraw his accusations a second time. Yet the diplomat's report to his own foreign office claimed Scharffenberg to be acknowledged as a psychopath in official Norwegian circles and depicted as a great villain by the press. False and inaccurate as these statements were, they would prove helpful to Johan Scharffenberg when the Germans invaded his country in 1940.

Scharffenberg, himself of distant German extraction, became deeply devoted to the cause of all those fleeing Hitler's tyranny. He proposed that the Norwegian government permit entry and resettlement of 5000 fugitive Jews in 1937. Among other things, he believed a greater Jewish presence could only enrich a country that contained but 1500 Jews at the time. He regretted that he himself had not a drop of Jewish blood in his veins.

By 1937, the Norwegian psychiatrist considered a second world war inevitable; he had become intensely concerned with the dangers posed by Hitler's fanatic obsessions. Although he assumed Denmark to be in a hopeless position, he continued to believe that maintenance of vigorous armed forces could protect Norway's and Sweden's neutrality. He repeatedly pressed the country's ruling party to strengthen Norway's defenses. Early in 1939 he recommended that the general staff assign permanent guards at each Norwegian fortress to forestall any Nazi attempt at invasion.

Dr. Scharffenberg was as alarmed by other instances of armed aggression as he was by Nazi military expansionism. Indignant at the unprovoked Soviet attack on Finland late in 1939, he castigated the Russians and defended his fellow Scandinavians in strident newspaper articles and in fiery speeches. If ever right were on a single side in wartime, he declared, it was with the Finns. Finland nourished every value the Soviets abhorred—freedom, truth, justice, and human rights. Scharffenberg urged his own government to allow the Norwegian unemployed to work as civilians in Finland, thus freeing young Finns to enter military service.

Just three days before the Nazi invasion of his own country Johan Scharffenberg published his long review of Rauschning's *Conversations with Hitler,* a book highly uncomplimentary to the German dictator. Dr. Scharffenberg concluded his article with an old Roman quotation: "Those whom God will destroy, He first makes mad."[1, pp. 191–192] Scharffenberg's earlier jousts with the German legation led him to expect immediate arrest once the Nazis had overrun his country on April 9, 1940. Yet, he continued calmly with his psychiatric duties at the prison and on the service for the criminally insane, and freely expressed his anti-Nazi sentiments in newspaper columns. He was extremely critical of the ruling Labor government, blaming their disregard of military preparedness for "Norway's greatest shame and misfortune." On Norway's traditional Independence Day, May 17, he concluded his column: "Only free citizens in a free Norway can bring the 17th of May to its full realization."[1, p. 199]

Initially, the occupying Nazis chose to ignore Dr. Johan Scharffenberg, but his defiant defense of free speech and a free press incensed the Germans. His challenging *Arbeiderbladet* articles of May 25 and 28, 1940, began with anecdotes from Plutarch and biblical quotations, as he stressed the need for protection of principles and country—even in the face of physical violence and threat to life:

> More dangerous and effective than physical violence is the intellectual assault through censorship, one-sided propaganda, or direct lies. . . . Suppressing opposing criticism does not bear witness to strength, but to cowardice. . . . When freedom of the press is so greatly restricted remaining silent about subjects that have been termed "taboo" deserves greater consideration than my personal safety.

> That there is an intellectual guardianship by people who are hardly my superior, I feel as a slow suffocation. If that be the condition in Norway, for long, then, as often before, the words "Vivere non estnecesse" lie before me."[1, pp. 200–201]

Infuriated by Scharffenberg's references to "people who are hardly my superior" and to the challenging tone, the Nazis forbade Johan Scharffenberg from publishing further. Yet, unaccountably, he remained free to move about Oslo. He shifted his attack from the newspapers to the speaker's podium, calling upon his own "prophetic persuasion" to stir his countrymen to defend freedom and human rights.

His climactic speech to the University of Oslo students' association on September 21, 1940, enlisted his young audience in the battle against tyranny. At the time tens of thousands of German soldiers occupied Norway, and SS troops patrolled the streets of Oslo. The Nazi Command threatened to depose the king. Dr. Scharffenberg spoke with pride of the freedom the Norwegian Parliament had exerted in choosing the Danish Prince Carl as Norway's King Haakon in 1905, contrasting that open and free choice with Nazi attempts to press a puppet Quisling government on an unwilling people.

The University Aula reverbrated with the students' shouting acclaim, forcing Scharffenberg to return to the podium with a final warning; "Be clear about the obligations that go with this approval," he admonished his enthusiastic audience. "Let them know that Norway's youth will defend freedom and independence no matter the cost to us all."[1, pp. 205–206] In many Norwegian eyes, the

Resistance movement was born at that instant. The noted journalist Arne Skouen was to write in the Oslo newspaper *Dagbladet* thirty years later:

> [It was] a stroke of genius, professionally executed at exactly the right second. A front was formed by the stroke of a hand and these words. "Husk! En slik tilslutning forplikter." (Remember, such an approval carries the obligation to act.)[1, p. 206]

The furious Nazi *Reichkommissariat,* unable to tolerate taunts and exhortations to resist, soon arrested Dr. Scharffenberg. His countrymen rose to honor him, delivering masses of flowers to his cell in the infamous prison at Mollergate 19. The Norwegian psychiatrist was treated correctly and courteously during his imprisonment—not due, however, to any generosity of his usually brutal captors. The German cleric, V. H. Gunther, while on a Nazi mission to Oslo, had spent many hours in conversation with Scharffenberg and convinced the Gestapo of the seventy-year-old doctor's "senility." The earlier report of the German minister in Oslo, Scharffenberg's public attacks on the occupying Nazis, and the fearlessness of his responses all led his captors to accept Gunther's contention. In response to questioning, the Norwegian psychiatrist insisted that his diagnosis of Hitler's mental illness was not an accusation *(beskylding),* but an excuse *(unnskylding),* for the hallucinating German dictator was insane, and therefore not responsible for his actions. Besides, Scharffenberg continued, he preferred to discuss Hitler's mental status with colleagues qualified to understand the diagnosis.

The Gestapo had no desire to convert a Norwegian folk hero into a martyr and released Johan Scharffenberg after six weeks at Mollergate 19. He could no longer speak in public, however, and subsequently was removed from his position as director at the Oslo asylum.

The Resistance movement Dr. Scharffenberg had spawned remained vital throughout the occupation—salvaging lives of Jews and Resistance workers threatened by the Nazis, actively combating the German propaganda assault, circulating the underground publications that evaded censorship, and preparing to assist the Allies in the ultimate German defeat. The figure who had inflamed his countrymen in their darkest days, however, could no longer play an active role. The very qualities that led Johan Scharffenberg to call forth the Resistance made him a liability to the underground—complete openness, unwavering honesty, fearless speech, and carelessness about his own safety. He was under constant Nazi surveillance and interrogated repeatedly, but never again imprisoned. No matter their admiration, the Home Front leadership could not safely include him in underground deliberations—and the exclusion embittered the zealous doctor.

Scharffenberg was now forced into the "illegal" press for his publications— an activity that had begun even during his imprisonment, when he aided in the formation of *Nittentitten (Looking in at 19),* referring to the jail at Mollergate 19. He contributed articles to the clandestine press throughout the war and devoted further efforts to aiding refugees escape across the Swedish border.

Dr. Scharffenberg's old popularity surged to the surface once again on the liberation of Norway, May, 1945, as his countrymen turned to him to welcome a king returning from war-long exile in London. Johan Scharffenberg spoke before the Royal Palace with all his warmth and his characteristic dignity. He thanked King Haakon on behalf of the Norwegian people for his unwavering defense of Norwegian sovereignty, and for his two great and resounding "no's"— first, an unyielding refusal to appoint a Quisling government, and then for adamantly standing firm against German demands that he abdicate.

Suppressing his emotion, Dr. Johan Scharffenberg, whose own loyal efforts had been instrumental in the continued existence of a free nation, beckoned to the enormous procession behind him to join in uttering to the King and his household the simple words, "Welcome home to Norway."

Reference

1. Sundet O. Johan Scharffenberg (1869–1965). Oslo, Norway, Tanum-Norli, 1977. (English translations by the authors)

Additional readings

Vokso P. Krigens Dagbok: Norge 1940–1945. Oslo, Norway, Forlaget Det Beste, 1984.

Andenaes J, Riste O and Skodvin M. Norway and the Second World War. Oslo, Norway, Johan Grundt Tanum, 1966.

Riste O and Nokleby B. Norway 1940–1945: The Resistance Movement, 2nd ed. Oslo, Norway, Johan Grundt Tanum, 1973.

IMPRESSIONS OF
OPERATION CROSSROADS

HAROLD C. HODGE
(December 1947, pp. 11–12)

*Born in 1904 in Chicago, Harold Hodge grew up in the midwest
and earned his masters and doctorate in Pharmacology at the
State University of Iowa. He had a long and fruitful academic career at the University of Rochester School of Medicine and
Dentistry. His seminal paper published in 1950 established that
fluoride in drinking water could prevent dental caries with minimal if any side effects . . . a work of enormous significance for public health. His reputation grew through his career and he was
regarded as the "dean of American toxicology." His appointment
to the Manhattan Project and Atomic Energy Commission led to
his being in attendance at the tests in the Pacific of the atomic
bomb. He died in Boston in 1990.*

UNDER THE ABLE LEADERSHIP OF VICE ADMIRAL WIN. P. BLANDY, the
organization of Joint Task Force 1 was entirely comparable in magnitude to one of the amphibious operations of the war. However, in addition to the customary problems of supply, operations, and security, the work
anticipated at Bikini lagoon involved a major problem of safety. This problem
was of such magnitude and so unusual that a special section, the Radiological
Safety Section, was set up under the direction of Col. Stafford L. Warren of the
Army and Captain George Lyon of the Navy. This section is proud of the summary which can be made of its activities; not one man is known to have been
injured by the special hazards of the atom bomb test.

Able Day

On ABLE DAY the bomb was dropped from a bomber high in the air, as were
the bombs dropped at Hiroshima and Nagasaki. The bomb exploded high in the
air over the target fleet. From this height the bomb exhibited a maximum of
concussion force (blast effect) and of heat destruction—but a minimum of radioactivity left on the surface. By "maximum blast effect" is meant the force
which reduced the heart of the city of Hiroshima and of Nagasaki to rubble, with
the exception of certain modern earthquake proof buildings still standing, but

in which walls and floors were so disturbed and twisted that demolition may be necessary. At Bikini, the blast effect accounted for the immediate sinking of several big ships. By "a maximum of heat destruction" is meant the kind of heat that left a shadow of a Japanese pedestrian on the pavement some 3/10th of a mile from the zero-point over Nagasaki. The shadow was used to help fix the exact point of explosion by having a soldier stand in the footprints of the Japanese pedestrian, and sighting from the apex of the shadow over the head of the soldier to the point where the bomb exploded. The shadow was the unburned part of the pavement. By a "minimum of radioactivity" is meant so little radioactivity that when our forces entered Hiroshima and Nagasaki, some six weeks after the bomb drops, nowhere on the surface of the ground was there an amount of radioactivity even remotely comparable with the amount present on the dial of a luminous-faced watch. I wish to repeat—when the bomb exploded high in the air the blast effect was maximal, heat effect was maximal—but the radioactivity remaining was minimal.

The reason the radioactivity was minimal should be made clear: At the instant of the detonation, the upper half of the explosion went immediately toward the stratosphere, carrying with it a large share of the radioactivity. This half of the explosion formed the puff ball at the top of the famous mushroom cloud. The lower half of the explosion drove with enormous velocity toward the surface of the water, struck with terrific force, and rebounded to form the lower part, the pillar, of the mushroom cloud. Most of the radioactivity in this part of the explosion was therefore also carried up into the stratosphere. At greater heights, the total radioactive matter was mixed with air, diluted, and dispersed. Carried by the air currents, it may have encircled the globe. Only traces remained on the surface of the lagoon.

From the air, Bikini was a long, narrow expanse of green, surmounted on the eastern aspect by the white coral reef. This tiny island, roughly one mile by one-quarter, was the only substantial piece of land for many miles in any direction. In the lagoon off the island of Bikini was the impressive array of the target fleet at anchor. The battleship *Nevada*, center of the target fleet, was painted a brilliant orange-red, except for the top of the ship and the installations. This color made it a striking target for the bombardier high in the air. Ironically, there was enough overcast so that the bombardier could not see it on ABLE DAY.

Army material of all sorts was placed on the decks of the target ships to be exposed to the effects of the atom bomb; it was a veritable museum of Army equipment. There was a huge 47-ton tank, an amphibious vehicle, a jeep, a seemingly endless array of guns—from giant howitzers to BAR. Some experimental animals were also distributed in strategically chosen locations throughout the target fleet to obtain maximum information about the effects of the atom bomb on living creatures.

Just before 9:00 o'clock on the morning of ABLE DAY, a group of specialists under Capt. Fred Bryan, M.C., assigned to a gun boat, were gathered amidships at the command of "All hands on deck." At the direction of the skipper we turned our backs to the Bikini lagoon, 18 miles west of us, and faced the midmorning sun. We closed our eyes and covered them with one arm. Standing in this position we heard over the radio, through much static, the bombardier call, "Bomb away," and the metronome ticking off the last seconds. Suddenly there was the sensation of a flash of light. We distrusted this sensation because one sometimes gets "flashes of light" by closing the eyes in broad daylight; but a second later, when it felt as if someone slowly brought a hot iron up behind our heads and slowly removed it, we were no longer in any doubt as to whether the bomb had exploded. There was a clearly-discernible heat wave at a distance of 18 miles! We turned then and watched the mushroom cloud start to ascend. It was full of color, especially browns and yellows, from the nitrogen oxides produced by the extraordinary heat and radiation. (The ball of fire has a temperature estimated to be of the order of 100 million degrees Centigrade.) A sound like that of a distant blasting came over the water. In a few minutes the cloud reached a height of about 25,000 feet, at which point a lovely scarf cloud of ice crystals seemed to grow out over the top of the ball. In a minute or two more the cloud had reached its final height of approximately 40,000 feet; the ball part of the cloud, at that time about five miles across, still retained a yellow tint.

In a few minutes, as we watched, the mist and smoke at the base of the cloud cleared sufficiently for us to see the red painted mast of the *Nevada*. The target ship was still afloat. We felt a sort of disappointment, because, from our position, it was impossible to tell that *any* ships had disappeared from the target fleet. In the succeeding two hours long steamers of black smoke from the burning vessels drifted across the lagoon. We watched these evidences of damage with a great interest. Another extraordinary sight went on overhead—mother airplanes guided radio-controlled drone aircraft through various parts of the cloud to collect radioactive dust in special filters.

As we entered the lagoon, we were first aware of the effects of the heat: blackened, charred paint; vessels afire. Then we became aware of the curious pattern of the bent and twisted masts; many masts were bent nearly at right angles, and on the various ships around the center of the target area, masts were always bent away from the center. Some of the ships' funnels appeared crumpled. In skirting the target fleet, we passed one ship capsized, hull awash, that sank a few hours later. On ABLE DAY afternoon we watched the aircraft carrier *Independence* burn fiercely; explosions aboard sent gigantic white smoke rings hurtling into the air. A dull glow of fire came from the stern of the ship. The Japanese cruiser, *Segawa*, which sank on the morning of ABLE plus one, seemed crushed and twisted. The enormity of the damage awed us.

Baker Day

There was an important difference in events after the BAKER DAY explosion. This bomb was exploded by radio signals sent from a ship (the *Cumberland Sound*) several miles away. When the bomb went off, a substantial part of the radioactive materials were caught in the seawater; and, in addition, the neutron emission converted some salt of the sea water into radioactive sodium and radioactive chlorine. The water, containing various radioactive materials and, incidentally, powdered coral, was thrown high in the air, turned and cascaded down over the ships in the center of the target fleet.

I would like to emphasize the magnitude of the radioactivity in this sea water. In our hospital clinic, we have a few milligrams of radium. These few thousandths of a gram are treated with great respect; many health rules are laid down for the safety of those whose work includes the handling of this material. Special, long-handled instruments are provided. The workers carry pieces of film in the pockets of their laboratory coats. Blood counts are made at frequent intervals; and the workers are required to take four weeks of vacation each year. Such precautions are taken with a few milligrams of radium. There are a thousand milligrams in a gram, one million grams in a ton. The water on BAKER DAY contained the equivalent (in gamma radiation) of several thousand tons of radium. Man has never seen before such a stupendous radioactive hazard.

As the BAKER DAY bomb exploded, a column of water was driven skyward in a twinkling, and then the spreading pressure wave with its attendant fog obscured the scene. When the fog evaporated, the water column, one-half mile across, was still ascending. The column of water extended more than two miles in the air, and the top was nearly three miles across—twenty million tons of water. As the column of water began to descend, a tremendous breaker, a wave 600 feet high arose. It subsided as it traveled toward the island so that it was only a few feet high when it reached the shore. A tremendous mist cloud full of radioactivity drifted along the surface of the lagoon, permeated the ships, and was carried downwind, dropping radioactivity onto the surface of the ocean in an area nearly twenty miles wide and forty miles long. In this area, dangerous radioactivity existed for many hours.

The mighty *Saratoga* sank on BAKER DAY afternoon before anyone could get aboard. Tugs sent to tow her into shallow water could not approach close enough to get hold of her anchor chain because the radioactivity was so intense.

After periods of hours or days the ship-washing processes started; and in due time boarding parties were permitted to inspect the damage. Always a "geigerman" from the Radiological Safety Section accompanied or preceded such a party and decided whether it was safe for man to stay aboard for ten minutes, one hour, or all day.

Some of the precautions might be mentioned. Shoes became so heavily contaminated that they were dangerous and, when cleaning was impossible, they had to be discarded—fifty thousand pairs were thrown away. Rust in pipes inside ships became contaminated; bunks near these pipes were evacuated. If the rust and paint on the sides of ships became sufficiently contaminated, the outermost bunks next to the hull were evacuated. The big evaporators, which prepare drinking water, accumulated such large amounts of radioactivity in some ships that engineers could only work a fraction of their working day. Everywhere, all possible hazards were anticipated and checked. Some of the ships, even after the most diligent washing, could not be rendered safe. A few of these were taken out into the ocean and sunk. Others were towed to Kwajalein, to our own coast, or elsewhere where disposition has not yet been decided.

A brief comparison might make the problem growing out of BAKER DAY test more easily appreciated. The water on BAKER DAY contained the equivalent of several thousands of tons of radium. This figure should be contrasted with the amounts of radium remaining in the bodies of some of the women employed during World War I as radium dial painters. These women, despite all safeguards, persisted in tipping on their tongues the brushes they were using to apply radium paint to airplane dials. Those unfortunate enough to retain lethal amounts of radioactive material died of cancer from radium deposited in the bones. Deaths were recorded five, ten, and even fifteen years later. One of the women who died nearly fifteen years after exposure had in her body at that time only one-millionth of a gram of radium. Contrast these two quantities: the equivalent of several thousands of tons of radium in the water vs. one-millionth of a gram of radium retained in the body producing death by cancer in fifteen years. No wonder the medical men in charge of the Bikini tests have repeatedly given us warning. The frightening possibilities must not be ignored.

A Committee headed by Dr. Albert Einstein has given us six statements of fact:
(1) Atom bombs can now be made cheaply and in large numbers. They will become more destructive.
(2) There is no known defense against atom bombs, and none is to be expected.
(3) Other nations can rediscover our secret processes by themselves.
(4) An atomic armament race is futile, and if attempted will ruin the structure of our social order.
(5) If war breaks out, atom bombs will be used and they will surely destroy our civilization.
(6) There is no solution to this problem except the international control of atomic energy and, ultimately, the elimination of war.

PART VI

A SAD ERROR
IN JUDGMENT
IN AMERICAN
MEDICINE

A HISTORY OF LOBOTOMY
IN THE UNITED STATES

MARY ELLEN FORD, M.D.

(Summer 1987, pp. 7–11)

The author was a member of the Class of 1989 at the Johns Hopkins University School of Medicine. This paper won the 1987 AΩA Student Essay Competition.

ROM 1935 TO 1954, LOBOTOMY BECAME ONE OF THE MOST POPULAR treatments for mental disorders. It may seem shocking that this method, in which portions of the frontal lobes were cut and destroyed as a "cure" for psychoses, became widespread in the United States and remained popular until medical opposition finally suppressed its use. Perhaps a closer look at the history of lobotomy and the context in which it developed will allow greater understanding of how lobotomy was established within an era of "modern medicine."

The origins of psychosurgery extend as far back as the 1800s, when Gottlieb Burckhardt, a Swiss psychiatrist, excised portions of cortical matter in an attempt to "extract from the brain mechanism the emotional and impulsive element in order to bring back the patient to calm."[1] Nonetheless, Egas Moniz, a Portuguese neurologist, is generally considered to be the inventor of psychosurgery. In 1935, he directed the first prefrontal leucotomy performed on a mental patient.

The operation consisted of removing cores of skull and injecting alcohol or inserting an instrument called a leucotome into the frontal lobes to crush or cut nerve fibers. Moniz believed that serious mental disorders were the result of "fixed thoughts . . . maintained by nerve pathways in the frontal lobes which have become pathologically 'fixed' or 'stabilized.'"[2, p. 84] By destroying these fixed neural patterns, one cures the patient.

Moniz ignored the available evidence that damage to the frontal lobes resulted in serious impairment. In 1848, Phineas Gage, a capable young construction foreman for a railroad, was injured when an accidental explosion drove an iron rod through his left cheek and into the frontal lobes of his brain. Although Gage survived, he was reported to have the intellectual capacity of a child, as well as emotional changes giving him animal passions. The effects of frontal lobe damage were also studied in patients who were operated on for cerebral tumors. These patients were reported to have intellectual impairment—especially in problem solving and abstract thinking—as well as emotional changes including "juvenile or puerile behavior; lowered moral standards and tactlessness; inappropriate affect . . . ; restlessness; unrestrained talkativeness (loquacity); apathy; a decrease in motivation, initiative, and will . . . ; and irritability."[2, p. 90]

Moniz was quite optimistic about this procedure and concluded: "Prefrontal leucotomy is a simple operation, always safe, which may prove to be an effective surgical treatment in certain cases of mental disorder."[3] He performed no preliminary animal experiments to test his method but immediately began to operate on mental patients.

Moniz, who had earlier made important contributions to the field of cerebral angiography, was also a distinguished politician and diplomat. His methods were accepted without much question, and his reports on the "success" of these operations, presented as little as eleven days to two months after the surgery, received little criticism. In 1936, Moniz published several articles and a monograph about his new technique—"psychosurgery."

Walter Freeman, a neurologist at George Washington University in Washington, DC, read Moniz's first article on prefrontal leucotomy. Familiar with Moniz's work in cerebral angiography, he immediately became interested in this new technique. On September 14, 1936, Freeman and James W. Watts, a neurosurgeon, performed the first prefrontal leucotomy in the United States.

Freeman renamed the operation "lobotomy" because he believed that nerve cell bodies and fibers were being cut, whereas "leucotomy" implied that only nerve fibers are cut. He developed a "standard" lobotomy procedure, which involved inserting the leucotome into the frontal lobes through a hole on each side of the skull, then swinging the leucotome back and forth to cut the white matter.

According to Freeman, in severing the connections between the frontal cortex (considered responsible for ideation) and the thalamus (considered responsible for emotional charge): "It is as if the 'sting' of the psychosis [is] drawn"[4, p. 23] In an article summarizing twenty years of experience in leucotomy, Freeman stated: "Leucotomy achieves its most satisfactory results in patients who are distressed by feelings of anxiety, obsessive thinking and what may be termed anguish or tortured self-concern. The operation reduces the emotional tension to a point where it no longer disables the patient."[5]

Freeman reported that lobotomy produced no impairment of intelligence or personality. Thelma Hunt, an associate professor of psychology at George Washington University, tested patients before and after the operation and concluded that "there is no impairment of intelligence following prefrontal lobotomy."[6] Hunt suggested that following lobotomy, the personality was more "constricted." In his first report on prefrontal lobotomy, Freeman included the warning: "Prefrontal lobotomy should at present be reserved for a small group of specially selected cases in which conservative methods of treatment have not yielded satisfactory results."[4, p. 30]

TIME magazine reported that by 1942, 300 lobotomies had been performed in the United States.[7] The publication in 1942 of the Freeman and Watts text, *Psychosurgery: Intelligence, Emotion, and Social Behavior following Prefrontal Lobotomy for Mental Disorders,*[6] greatly extended interest in lobotomy. This book was filled with reports of "successful" cases of lobotomy, complete with before and after photos of patients. Lobotomies were performed in many state hospitals, but were also tried by neurosurgeons affiliated with well-known universities and hospitals, such as the Massachusetts General Hospital, the University of Pennsylvania, and the Mayo Clinic.

Although Freeman received some criticism from other physicians, most of it was not published. Some psychoanalysts complained that lobotomy only provided symptomatic relief and ignored the underlying cause of the mental disorder; but without any effective alternatives to offer, their arguments seemed weak. When Freeman presented his first report on prefrontal lobotomy at the meeting of the Southern Medical Association in November 1936, some physicians began to object to the procedure. A comment, however, made by Adolf Meyer, a highly influential figure in the field of psychiatry, seemed almost sympathetic to Freeman:

> I am not antagonistic to this work but find it very interesting. I have some of those hesitations about it that are mentioned by other discussants, but I am inclined to think that there are more possibilities in this operation than appear on the surface. . . .The available facts are sufficient to justify the procedure in the hands of responsible persons.[8]

This comment by Meyer helped to subdue the criticism of lobotomy.

Prefrontal lobotomy required a neurosurgeon and staff to give supportive care during the long recovery period. Because these were not easily available in state mental hospitals, Freeman developed a modified lobotomy procedure that would be more adaptable to the resources of mental institutions. He adopted ideas from a lobotomy procedure that had been established in 1937 by Amarro Fiamberti, an Italian psychiatrist.

In the new procedure, called transorbital lobotomy, a sharp-pointed instrument was driven through the bony orbit behind the eyeball, then swung from side to side to cut nerve fibers in the frontal lobes. Freeman practiced this procedure on cadavers, using an ice pick. In January 1946, he performed the first transorbital lobotomy in his office, using electroconvulsive shock as an anesthetic, and an ice pick as a leucotome. This procedure was essentially a "blind" attack on the brain and involved great risk of rupturing cerebral arteries. Watts, a trained neurosurgeon, strongly objected to the brain surgery being done as an office procedure by Freeman, who was not certified in surgery. The conflict between Freeman and Watts over this procedure was evident in an excerpt from the preface in the second edition of their text *Psychosurgery,* published in 1950:

> The authors regret to announce that they have been unable to reach an agreement on the subject of transorbital lobotomy. Freeman believes that he has proved the method to be simple, quick, effective, and safe to entrust to the psychiatrist. Watts believes that any procedure involving cutting of brain tissue is a major operation and should remain in the hands of a neurological surgeon. In all other respects the authors are in complete and cordial agreement and they continue as co-heads of the Department of Neurology and Neurological Surgery of George Washington University.[9]

Eventually, Watts moved out of the office he shared with Freeman in Washington.

In 1948, Freeman introduced a modified transorbital lobotomy, which not only involved medial and lateral swings of the leucotome, but also included forcing the handle of the leucotome upward to drive the tip into the deep parts of the frontal lobe. After several accidents in which the leucotome tip snapped off while Freeman was making the deep frontal cut, he designed a stronger instrument, which he called an "orbitoclast."

Freeman set out on a one-man crusade to promote the transorbital lobotomy. He traveled to state mental hospitals across the United States to demonstrate the new procedure on patients. Following lectures on the technique, he then taught psychiatrists how to perform the operation on their own, using electroshock as an anesthetic in order to avoid the need for an anesthesiologist.

The introduction of transorbital lobotomy created new interest in lobotomy, and Freeman recommended this procedure as preferable to the standard Freeman-Watts lobotomy.

In 1949, Egas Moniz was awarded the Nobel Prize in Physiology or Medicine for his contributions to the development of lobotomy. This recognition helped to increase the respectability of lobotomy in general. During the procedure's peak, from 1949 to 1952, about 5,000 lobotomies were performed per year in the United States; one out of three operations was a transorbital lobotomy.[2, p. 229]

Freeman's intrusion into the domain of surgery by training psychiatrists how to perform transorbital lobotomies was a step out of bounds that drew violent opposition from neurosurgeons. In 1949, *Newsweek* published an article containing comments by Nolan D. C. Lewis, director of the New York State Psychiatric Institute of Columbia-Presbyterian Medical Center.

> Lobotomy is now being used much too indiscriminately. Some doctors have shown an utter lack of respect for the human brain. . . .There are probably a great many failures that aren't ever reported. . . .The information supporting psychosurgery simply is not available. . . . All the ma-

jor lobotomies produce some personality damage. . . . It does disturb me to see the number of zombies that these operations turn out.[10]

In 1954, chlorpromazine and other psychoactive drugs were introduced as simple, inexpensive alternatives to brain operations. By 1960, the number of lobotomies being performed was drastically reduced.

In the 1980s, psychosurgery has survived in the form of stereotactic placement of lesions in the brain, most often by electrocoagulation. The forms of psychosurgery practiced by Freeman—prefrontal lobotomy and transorbital lobotomy—have been abandoned as therapeutic technique.

This treatment continues to be highly controversial.[11,12] In Oregon and California, specific legislation concerning the practice of psychosurgery was enacted in 1973 and 1976, respectively.[2, p. 289] Other states are also considering such legislation to regulate the practice of psychosurgery.

Lobotomy was never proven to be either a success or a failure.[2, p. 242] Some patients were sent home, but they were not self-sufficient and were a heavy burden on their families. Other patients remained institutionalized, but they no longer had to be restrained in locked wards. The results of lobotomy involved many side effects. Freeman himself admitted that "every patient probably loses something by this operation, some spontaneity, some sparkle, some flavor of the personality,"[4, p. 30] although he felt this loss was justified in preventing the further degeneration of the patient.

Why did lobotomy—always a highly controversial procedure—become so successful in the United States? Within the medical profession itself, the tradition of not criticizing one's fellow physicians in public helped subdue the opposition to lobotomy. In an atmosphere not yet permeated by legal checks, such as malpractice suits and review boards, physicians relied mostly on their own judgment and the consent of the patient's family (if available) to decide who would receive a lobotomy. Moniz performed operations on mental patients without testing his procedures first through animal experimentation. Freeman described the success or failure of his operations by subjective observations of the patients without the use of controls as a standard for comparison. Today, stringent controls on medical practice and research do not allow such haphazard methods.

The values emphasized by society in the 1940s and 1950s also facilitated the success of lobotomy. Much emphasis was placed on the family unit, in contrast to the "me" generation and focus on the individual that prevailed in the 1970s and continues in the 1980s. Sending the patient back to the home was interpreted as success. Since many of the lobotomy patients were women and returned to a more "sheltered" life in the home, the lack of self-sufficiency in lobotomized patients was not considered to be too debilitating. Also important was the atmosphere of desperation among the families of patients and their doctors as well. When other alternatives, such as shock therapy or institution-alization, did not seem to be working, lobotomy offered the opportunity for a "cure" that everyone had been hoping for.

The majority of lobotomies were performed on patients in state mental in-stitutions. If one considers the conditions of state mental hospitals at the time, it may be easier to understand why lobotomy became so popular. In a dramatic expose of the Byberry mental hospital in Philadelphia published in 1946, *LIFE* magazine revealed the shocking conditions representative of most mental hos-pitals at the time:

> Institutions that would be seriously undermanned even if not overcrowded find themselves swamped with 30%, 50%, and even 100% more patients than they were built to hold. . . . Restraints, seclusion, and constant drug-ging of patients become essential in wards where one attendant must herd as many as 400 mentally deranged charges.

> Thus thousands who might be restored to society linger in man-made hells for a release that comes more quickly only because death comes faster to the abused, the beaten, the drugged, the starved and the neglected.[13]

In a setting such as this, lobotomy offered an appealing release from the nightmare of confinement in mental hospitals.

Not all lobotomies, however, were performed on poor or abandoned pa-tients in state mental hospitals. Some patients were confined to private institu-tions and university hospitals and had ample funds to provide for their care. The popular press had a tremendous influence on promoting the cause of lobotomy to the public. In dramatic articles about the success of lobotomy, magazines and newspapers made the procedure appear to be a miracle cure for the men-tally ill. An article in *TIME* magazine in 1942 stated that in a "drastic method of rescuing psychotic patients from complete insanity," "[t]he surgeon's knife can reach into the brain to sever the tensions which underlie a psychopathic personality."[7, p. 48] In 1947, an article in *LIFE* magazine, "Psychosurgery. Operation to Cure Sick Minds Turns Surgeon's Blade into an Instrument of Mental Therapy," reported:

> The surgeon's blade, slicing through the connections between the pre-frontal area (the location of the superego) and the rest of the brain, frees the tortured mind from its tyrannical ruler. . . . Intelligence is not affected (patients have done well in college and business).[14]

In response to these articles, people brought in family members who were mentally disturbed and requested lobotomy as a "cure." These individuals hardly fit the role of end-stage patients for whom lobotomy was used as a last resort.

Freeman peformed transorbital lobotomies on private patients who were often referrals from out of town. These operations were usually done within twenty-four hours of the patient's arrival. Most patients were not even admitted to the hospital but left within a couple of hours of the operation in order to defray the expenses of hospitalization. Freeman sent off the patient and his family with a recommendation to provide the patient with a pair of sunglasses to cover up the black eyes that would appear later as a result of the transorbital lobotomy.

In a few cases, lobotomy was attempted as a cure for criminal tendencies, although this idea was blocked by the legal difficulties involved. The developments in these cases were closely followed by the media.

In his quest to make a medical breakthrough in the treatment of mentally ill patients, Walter Freeman lost his professional objectivity about lobotomy. Beginning with a cautionary approach, Freeman's opinion of psychosurgery evolved from prefrontal lobotomy as a "last resort" intervention into transorbital lobotomy as a "starting point" in effective therapy. With his stubborn resistance to opposition and obsessive mission to promote lobotomy, Walter Freeman was "the person most responsible for the acceptance of psychosurgery around the world."[2, p. 244]

All of these factors combined—a limited knowledge of the brain and its functions, a medical profession that protected its own, a society that was desperate and ready for a cure, deplorable mental institutions, lack of other effective alternative therapies, popular articles by the press, and extremely ambitious individuals—provided the stage upon which lobotomy was performed and applauded, despite its controversial nature. Lobotomy—right or wrong? Was lobotomy a failure that should be swept into the shadows of the past and forgotten?

Perhaps the ultimate failure would be hiding the truth about lobotomy, since much can be learned from this experience in the history of medicine.

References

1. Mueller C. Gottlieb Burckhardt, the father of topectomy. Am J Psychiatry 117:461–63, 1960, p. 462.
2. Valenstein ES. Great and Desperate cures: The Rise and Decline of Psychosurgery and other Radical Treatments for Mental Illness. New York, Basic Books, 1986.
3. Moniz E. Prefrontal ieucotomy in the treatment of mental disorders. Am J Psychiatry 93:1379–85, 1937, p. 1385.
4. Freeman W and Watts JW. Prefrontal lobotomy in the treatment of mental disorders. South Med J 30:23–30, 1937.
5. Freeman W. Twenty years of leucotomy. Proc R Soc Med 50:79–84, 1957, p. 79.
6. Freeman W and Watts JW. Psychosurgery. Intelligence, Emotion and Social Behavior Following Prefrontal Lobotomy for Mental Disorders. Springfield, Illinois, Charles C Thomas, 1942, p. 154.
7. Psychosurgery. TIME, November 30,1942, pp. 48–50, p. 48.
8. Meyer A. Discussion, after Freeman, W, and Watts, JW. Prefrontal lobotomy in the treatment of mental disorders. South Med J. 30:31, 1937.

9. Freeman W and Watts JW. Psychosurgery: In the Treatment of Mental Disorders and Intractable Pain, 2nd ed. Springfield, Illinois, Charles C Thomas, 1950, p. x.

10. Lobotomy disappointment. Newsweek, December 12, 1949, p. 51.

11. Bridges PK and Bartlett JR. Psychosurgery: Yesterday and today. Br J Psychiatry 131:249–60, 1977, p. 255.

12. Breggin PR. What cost leukotomy? (letter) Am J Psychiatry 140:1101, 1983.

13. Maisel AQ. Bedlam 1946. LIFE, May 6,1946, pp. 102–3, p. 103.
   Psychosurgery: Operation to cure sick minds turns surgeons blade into an instrument of mental therapy. LIFE, March 3, 1947, pp. 93–97, p. 95.

LOBOTOMY:
A PERSONAL MEMOIR

LAURENCE M. WEINBERGER, M.D.

(Spring 1988, pp. 17–18)

The author (AΩA, 1933, Ohio State University College of Medicine)
was trained and certified in both neurological surgery and in neu-
rology and psychiatry.

THE ESSAY BY MARY ELLEN FORD in the summer 1987 issue of *The Pharos* stirred long dormant memories of my introduction to lobotomy and to its passionate proponent, Walter Freeman.[1] I can add little to her excellent historical account except a personal reminiscence of long ago, which may substantiate her judgments of events and personalities that existed before she came on the scene.

In the spring of 1938 I was a second-year fellow in neurological surgery in the Hospital of the University of Pennsylvania. Francis Grant, my chief, asked me one day to accompany him to the Delaware State Hospital to meet Dr. Freeman so that we could learn from him how to select patients for lobotomy. I think Dr. Grant's interest in the new and novel procedure was spurred by his confidence and respect for James W. Watts, Freeman's co-worker, who had been a neuro-surgical fellow under the tutelage of Professor Charles H. Frazier and Dr. Grant a few years earlier. Dr. Grant and I set out one late spring morning for Wilmington, where we were to meet Dr. Freeman, who was coming up from Washington.

We arrived mid-day and were met by the director, who turned out to be a tall, dark, White Russian emigre with a charming accent and urbane, continental manners suitable for a grand duke. His conversation clearly indicated that he wanted added prestige for his institution, which, I think, he hoped would be among the first to exploit the new treatment of mental disorder. Only two years had passed since Egas Moniz and Almeida Lima had published their original paper.[2] Dr. Freeman was waiting for us in a small demonstration theater. My first impression of him fit in with my preconception of a Svengali. He was tall, dark, and balding, having characteristics that, together with a mustache and a pointed Van Dyke beard, gave him a distinctly Mephistophelian cast. His physical features were emphasized by his air of arrogance and authority, which made him somewhat intimidating. In those days he did not have the reputation of being a prominent psychiatrist; indeed, he was known largely through his publication of a primer in neuropathology, the first in the United States. In the early 1930s neuropathology was an arcane discipline practiced by a handful of eccentric scholars in a few large cities. Dr. Freeman's career had been different; his excursion into neuropathology was a passing one, and now his chief interest was psychiatry, albeit of a distinctly nontraditional kind. Dr. Freeman's personality, his intensity, his air of profundity and of absolute certainty, was impressive and may explain in part his enormous worldwide influence, which for a time so altered the practice of psychiatary as to convert subjects with psychological problems into candidates for frontal lobe surgery.

Led in, one by one, the patients were introduced and questioned by the director. Watching intently, Dr. Freeman signaled that some patients were suitable for surgery but that others were not. Possessing the elementaries of medical psychology acquired during three years of neurological residencies in New York and being puzzled by his purely observational method, I took it upon myself to ask him—because no one else spoke up, "What are your criteria for selection?" My question, coming from a young man in training, was evidently regarded as an impertinence. It was answered with a prolonged silent stare and finally one word: "Experience!" Squelched, I said no more.

There was, however, a spirited discussion with Dr. Grant about the precise location of the burr holes to be made, the depth the instrument should be inserted into the frontal lobes, and the extent of the sweep of the "leucotome." Dr. Freeman seemed to include all the details of the surgical procedure within the scope of his expertise; he had not brought along his neurosurgical colleague, Dr. Watts.

Mulling over the sparse information we had obtained from our tutorial session, Dr. Grant decided that he would let psychiatrists pick his patients in the future, but that we would do the procedure on those selected by Dr. Freeman. We took it on faith that he was reliable, in spite of the nonchalant way the selection had been made.

Plans were made to travel to Wilmington one day each week until we had worked through those selected. These trips required taking our scrub nurse, a nurse anesthetist (medical anesthesiologists were unknown then), packs of sterile instruments, dressings, and supplies, and a Bovie unit and suction machine, to be hauled in a truck. The operating room at the Delaware State Hospital was old-fashioned, ill-equipped, poorly lighted, and used only for in-house emergencies.

We had to give our own anesthesias, which consisted of rectal Avertin supplemented by local procaine injection. The state hospital staff was to provide the aftercare. It was a poor arrangement and kept covert because Dr. Grant was not only dubious about the operation itself, but also because of the circumstances under which we were doing the procedures. It was against the surgical ethos to leave postoperative patients miles away in another state. In spite of these misgivings, we were encouraged enough by Dr. Freeman's optimism to proceed with performing the operations. Bifrontal lobotomy was technically simple, although it made a surgeon cringe to sweep a thin instrument blindly through the frontal lobes. Our postoperative results were discomfiting. There was one death, one hemiplegia, and aphasic defects in two patients. As for the other patients, the director thought they were improved, although this impression may have been the triumph of hope over reality. The surgical directions given to us by Dr. Freeman appeared to have been flawed, although we attempted to follow his directions exactly. After this experience a few more patients were operated upon at a local psychiatric hospital, but Dr. Grant became disenchanted, lost interest, and never spoke more about it. He remained indifferent to the many modifications and alterations of approach later introduced to make the procedure more controllable and less dangerous.

Lobotomy was actively discussed at neurological meetings, although the numerous complications that were occurring were played down, since they might, if admitted, suggest that the surgeon was inexperienced or his technique poor. The notion of informed consent lay many years in the future, before lawyers sensed the legal possibilities of suit for untoward results and for uninformed consent. In those days operative consent was signed by the responsible relative, who was told of the possible benefits, although not always of the possible complications, nor of the peculiar personality that might emerge later on.

Each year Freeman extravagantly propagandized the treatment of mental disorder by lobotomy in an annual review: *Progress in Neurology and Psychiatry.*[3] The yearly chapter, "Psychosurgery," increased in pages and in enthusiasm from 1946 onward. Dr. Watts dropped out after 1952, but Dr. Freeman carried on with undiminished zealotry. As time passed, he was convincing fewer and fewer people, so by 1962 the chapter was anemic and only four pages long. Then it expired.

In that last final chapter, however, Dr. Freeman celebrated "The Ten Thousand," referring to "10,365 patients subjected to a single operation on the frontal lobes for mental disorder," reported on in England in 1961.[4] Dr. Freeman's infatuation with lobotomy is suggested by his publication of 48 cases in 1939,[5] and by a monograph reporting 242 cases in 1942.[6] By January 1946 the number had grown to 331 patients,[7] and by June of that year to 400,[8] although there had been a long war going on that had involved most physicians in the effort.

In later years Dr. Freeman adopted a new technique—transorbital leucotomy—which required a single operator. He toured the country, visiting state hospitals for the mentally ill where he performed the procedures for $25 each if the hospital could muster up at least ten patients. He taught his method to their staffs. The "ice-pick" was now made of stainless steel and weighted at the proximal end, although it could be carried in the pocket.

Our paths nearly crossed again when he came through Akron, Ohio, where I was practicing. He performed "leucotomies" at our local county receiving hospital, which, incidentally, treated the "acute" psychopathies. The hospital superintendent invited me to watch the demonstration in hopes that I might then be willing to do the procedure in the future. I demurred, as I had long come to believe that there was little sense in attempting to improve the operations of a complex instrument by wrecking a part of it.

Mary Ellen Ford offers cogent explanations as to why lobotomy took such a hold on the medical profession and on the public mind. Dr. Freeman was certainly the driving force. He brushed aside the opposing voices here and abroad, some of them very vociferous, using such perjorative terms as "Jack, the Brain Slasher."[9] They did not slow the torrent of lobotomies.

Dr. Freeman was a brilliant man with fixed and unshakable ideas that, in retrospect, were naive and jeopardizing. Even though intellectualized and systematized in the language of anatomy, the deeper moral issues received scant consideration. He not only rejected criticism but gained strength for his views through it. His relentless insistence on the merits of disconnecting the frontal lobe fibers from the thalamus now seems artless, but then his voice was so strong, unwavering, and compelling that he swept asid doubting, ambivalent, or irresolute colleagues. It was not the first time, nor will it be the last, that the medical profession is stampeded by a prophet of false therapies.

References

1. Ford ME. A history of lobotomy in the United States. Pharos 50(3):7–11, 1987.
2. Moniz E and Lima A. Premier essais de psycho-chirurgie: Techniques et resultants. Lisboa Med 13:152–61, 1936.
3. Spiegel EA, ed. Progress in Neuroiogy and Psychiatry—An Annual Review, vols. 1–17. New York, Grune & Stratton, 1946–62.
4. Freeman W. Psychosurgery. In: Spiegel, EA, ed. Progress in Neurology and Psychiatary, vol. 17, pp. 386–89, New York, Grune & Stratton, 1962, p. 386.
5. Freeman W and Watts JW. Interpretation of the functions of the frontal lobe based upon the observations in 48 cases of prefrontal lobotomy. Yale J Biol Med 11:527–39, 1939.
6. Freeman W and Watts JW. Psychosurgery. Intelligence, Emotional and Social Behavior Following Prefrontal Lobotomy for Mental Disorders. Springfield, Illinois, C.C.Thomas, 1942.
7. Freeman W and Watts JW. Prefrontal lobotomy: Survey of 331 cases. Am J Med Sci. 211:1–8, 1946.
8. Freeman W and Watts JW. Pain of organic disease relieved by prefrontal lobotomy. Lancet 1:953–55, 1946.
10. Freeman W and Watts JW. Psychosurgery. In Spiegel, EA, ed. Progress in Neurology and Psychiatry, vol. 2, pp. 461–72. New York, Grune & Stratton, 1947, p. 461.

PART VII

THE DOCTOR AS WRITER AND SUBJECT IN POETRY AND PROSE

HALLUCINOSIS

PAUL RODENHAUSER, M.D.
(Summer 1995, p. 7)

This numbness thaws to unleash
familiar who-am-I question mark
creatures when a phantom from the past
whispers final instructions into the wind.

Climbing to the edge of my absence,
they dismantle the abstraction
I call existence. They devour
all glimpses of once feeling

at least momentarily alive.
They incite shapeless cravings
to stampede the vacant corridors
of my never mind, hammering,

clamoring for something—
anything—to penetrate, anything
to mutilate, while this sapless flesh
prays for a quisling matador.

The better for burning, the better
for carving in the code, I say,
so rage can soar again
at the expense of nothingness.

Thus the cage that otherwise
restrains its flight melts
into the dark disturbance
or another orgastic delirium.

And as that faceless fearmonger
profits from another sweet victory,
I celebrate our secret in a season
quietly known as emptiness.

THE POET-PHYSICIAN:
MEDICINE'S IMPACT
ON THE LIVES AND WORKS
OF JOHN KEATS AND
ROBERT BRIDGES

ROBERT P. LABORDE, M.D.
(Winter 1986, pp. 8–11)

SINCE THE TIME OF HIPPOCRATES, countless physicians have engaged sporadically in the art of writing poetry. In recent history, notable examples of poet-physicians include Sir Thomas Browne, John Keats, Silas Weir Mitchell, Robert Bridges, Oliver Wendell Holmes, and William Carlos Williams. While most of these men devoted most of their careers to medicine and engaged in poetry as a secondary endeavor, two of them, John Keats and Robert Bridges, diverged from this pattern. Keats and Bridges shared the striking similarity of having abruptly terminated their allegiances to Aesculapius in favor of lives devoted to poetry. Even though Keats and Bridges wholeheartedly terminated their medical careers, their works and letters illustrate the inseparable bond between creativity and the healing process.

Much has been written, mostly by nonphysicians, of the relationship between medicine and the creative arts. Most commonly considered is the need for empathy on the parts of healer and artist alike. While sensitivity and empathy are certainly essential to both artist and physician, several other important shared qualities exist.

Poetry, perhaps more so than any other art form, demands many of the exact skills required in medicine. The poet must detect, perceive, and manipulate the subtlest nuances of language. The poem is constructed much in the same way that a diagnosis is achieved, with the poet constantly ruling in and ruling out choices of words based on their appropriateness in an ever more clarified picture. For the poet, a poem is conceived as starkly as a patient's first clinical presentation. The poet and physician must carefully sense and observe their subjects. Both artists organize newly gathered information and weigh new data against prior experience to achieve a logical arrangement that will transform a bulk of sensation into a whole, final product. Denise Levertov has stated:

> The great power of art is to transform, renovate, activate. If there is a re-
> lationship between art and healing it is that.[1]

While numerous physicians have engaged in both arts simultaneously, Keats and Bridges, whose lives we shall now examine, were accomplished in both, separately and distinctly.

John Keats

John Keats (1795–1821) was born two months prematurely, the eldest son of a livery-stable keeper in Moorsfield, England. Author of "Ode on a Grecian Urn," "Endymion," "The Eve of St. Agnes," "La Belle Dame Sans Merci," and many other poems, Keats led a short but immensely productive life.

Keats's early years were marred by serial tragedy. Keats was enrolled at age eight in a boarding school in Enfield. Within one year his father died after being thrown from a horse. Three years later his uncle, whom Keats admired as a substitute father, died of tuberculosis. Soon thereafter his mother also contracted tuberculosis and maintained a chronic, feeble course. At the age of thirteen, Keats was the eldest male member of a family that consisted of a bedridden mother and three younger siblings. In Keats's time, tuberculosis claimed the life of one in every four Londoners. As tuberculosis was thought then to be a hereditary ailment, Keats doubtless felt that he was destined to contract this dreaded disease. Before his death at age twenty-five, Keats would also witness consumption put its death grip on his beloved younger brother.

While it would be ludicrous to claim that Keats's early exposure to death and tragedy caused him to become a poet, it is reasonable to propose that these early events constituted a "burden of emotion" that might later seek an outlet.[2] These events, coupled with subsequent experiences in the medical arena, would have profound effects on Keats's perception and appreciation of his surroundings.

Inevitably, Keats's mother died of consumption in the spring of 1810. Shortly afterwards, his grandmother, concerned for the boy's future, obtained a deed that transferred guardianship of Keats to a prosperous London tea merchant, Richard Abbey. Early in Abbey's guardianship came considerations of career plans for young Keats. Brief consideration was given to the clergy; the cost of lengthy university training, however, was prohibitive.

For reasons that remain unclear to Keats's biographers, Abbey settled on surgery as a career for the bright and sensitive adolescent. Keats entered into a five-year indentured apprenticeship to Thomas Hammond, a surgeon of Edmonton. He withdrew from John Clarke's school in Enfield where he had just begun to develop an interest in poetry and literature. Hammond and Abbey planned for Keats a career as a country doctor: pulling teeth, setting bones, amputating limbs, and draining abscesses.

As for the duties of the young apprentice, Keats's role was that of Hammond's man-on-the-side. He accompanied the surgeon on house calls and, when necessary, assisted in the restraint of patients. Except for changing dressings, Keats had little actual clinical responsibility, but his role offered much exposure to medical practice.

Throughout his apprenticeship at Edmonton, Keats maintained his scholastic acquaintances in Enfield. On free days he would return to Clarke's school and pursue his burgeoning interest in poetry. While apprenticed to Hammond, Keats completed a translation of the *Aeneid*. Keats's concomitant exposure to classic literature and daily horrors such as surgery without anesthesia may well have ignited the flames of creativity in this imaginative and resourceful adolescent.

During 1814, the third year of Keats's apprenticeship, he became increasingly interested in the poetic works of Sir Edmund Spenser. It was during this year that Keats authored his first known poem, "Imitation of Spenser." A few months later, deeply moved by the death of his grandmother, he authored "On Death."

For Keats, who planned a career as a combination apothecary-surgeon, the recently enacted Apothecaries Act provided perfect reason for breaking his apprenticeship to Hammond so that he might depart for more formal studies in London. In September of 1815 he enrolled in London's United Hospital of Guy's and St. Thomas's. Here, Keats was an autonomous medical student, free from the supervision of Hammond and, more importantly, free to pursue his own interests more fully. Early in his days at Guy's, perhaps because of past surgical training, Keats drew the favorable attention of faculty member and eminent surgeon Astley Cooper. Cooper took a special liking to Keats and assigned one of his house officers to "look over" the new student.[3] Cooper was at that time personal surgeon to George III. Although London was the seat of state-of-the-art medicine, Keats's surgical experience was still in the pre-anesthesia and pre-antisepsis era. Patients were given a bottle of alcohol and then strapped to the operating table to endure the procedure as best they could.

Keats's first-year studies at Guy's bore some similarity to today's preclinical curriculum—two courses in anatomy and physiology, two on theory and practice of medicine, two on chemistry, and one on "material medica." During his first year Keats found time to broaden his appreciation of English poetry, developing his taste for Wordsworth, Milton, Burns, and Byron. A first-year classmate wrote of Keats:

> Poetry was to his mind the zenith of all his aspirations.

> Whilst attending lectures he would sit and, instead of copying out the lecture, would often scribble doggerel rhymes among the notes of Lecture.[4, p.87]

An example of one of these "doggerel rhymes" taken from a Keats chemistry notebook speaks lightly to the timelessness of medical student life.

Give me women, wine and snuff
Until I cry out, "hold! enough."
You may do so sans objection
Until the day of resurrection.[4, p. 88]

Despite his classmate's implication that Keats was not wholeheartedly attentive, he nonetheless clipped through two years of medical school and easily passed his licensure examination.

The year 1816 saw John Keats performing a combined dresser/intern role at Guy's Hospital. Busily absorbed by being solely in charge of several wards of postoperative patients, Keats had difficulty managing his other responsibilities, including attending surgeries and outpatient clinics. This overwhelming load, coupled with his growing interest in poetry, led to disillusionment with his hospital-based existence. His poem "Solitude" reveals this conflict as he rejects the hospital setting as "the jumbled heap/Of murky buildings."[5, p. 41] Douglas Bush has likened Keats's final days as a medical student to those of a seeker of refuge through poetry.[6]

While Keats's precise reasons for abandoning medicine were never clearly stated in his letters, there is little doubt that he was certain in his decision. In a letter written two years after leaving Guy's, he wrote:

In no period of my life have I acted with any self will, but in throwing up the apothecary profession.[7]

The few references in Keats's letters to medicine also suggests the degree of certainty with which Keats adopted a new life. John Keats embarked in 1817 on a short but phenomenal career. Having just completed six years of exposure to agony, hopelessness, joy, and every imaginable breadth of human experience, Keats would devote his final five years to the praise of nature, beauty, and truth. His works reveal an intense sense of compassion as well as keen powers of natural observation.

Keats's death at age twenty-five from pulmonary tuberculosis marked a major loss to the world of literature. No other poet in the history of English literature has achieved, at so young an age, his remarkable mastery of the language.

Robert Bridges

Although not a meteoric literary figure of the order of Keats, Robert Bridges is a second example of a poet-physician who rejected his medical vows in favor of a life devoted to poetry.

Robert Seymour Bridges (1844–1930), a classical poet of the late Victorian period, was a medical student and practicing physician for nearly thirteen years. Born on October 23, 1844, Robert Bridges was the eighth in a family of nine children. Like Keats, Bridges lost his father at a young age; unlike Keats, however,

Bridges was born into an affluent family. He spent eight years at Eton, where he received a superb classical education. He made the most of his opportunities and later finished at Corpus Christi College, Oxford, in 1867. Like Keats, he initially considered a career in the clergy. After traveling widely to Egypt, Syria, and Germany, he settled on a medical career. He entered St. Bartholomew's Hospital as a student on November 6, 1869, at the age of twenty-five.

Of Bridges's years in London, little written record remains. He did, however, maintain a lively correspondence with his lifelong friend Lionel Muirhead. In a letter to Muirhead he stated that he was busy "reading medicine" and was "only at home in the evenings."[8, pp. 111,113]

Although Bridges scorned the poetic cult, he did enjoy literary exchanges with friends and began developing his own poetry even as a medical student. His first volume, *Poems,* was published in 1873, just one year before he took the post of casualty physician at St. Bartholomew's Hospital. Despite being tied to many responsibilities in London, he often managed to get away to the seaside. As he put it, "Complete idleness is the root of all energy."[8, p. 114]

Like Keats, Bridges wrote his earliest works as a medical student. While these works are certainly not his greatest, most Bridges critics agree that his earliest poetry shows "delicate mastery of rhythmical variety."

After becoming a house officer, Bridges wrote several letters to Muirhead from the hospital library. In his letter of December 13, 1875, Bridges wrote, "I am very busy with my medical work and get on well." In the same letter he mentioned, "My sonnets are nearly ready."[8, p. 123] Unlike Keats, Bridges seemed to have been able to assemble his poetic works while in the hospital environs. While Keats required absolute separation from medicine, Bridges was able for some years to merge the two endeavors.

Bridges was certainly influenced and impressed by Keats's works. Whether this impact was related to their common medical backgrounds is uncertain; it is clear from Bridges's letters, however, that he was very fond of Keats's poetry. In 1894 Bridges undertook to write an introduction to a collection of Keats's poetry. He considered his essay a "stiff job" and took great pains with it. On July 16, 1894, in a letter to a physician friend, Bridges wrote a humorous differential diagnosis of possible causes of Keats's death.

Bridges suffered a near fatal bout of pneumonia in 1881. Within a year he retired from medicine and brought to a close his brief twelve-year medical career. Bridges's retirement at age thirty-seven marked the beginning of a comfortable, serene life devoted to poetry at his country home in Yattendon. Donald E. Stanford has stated:

> At Yattendon, Bridges wrote some of the most beautiful lyrics in the language: it was his great period.[9]

Bridges was appointed Poet Laureate in 1913. He died in 1930 at the age of eighty-six.

Discussion

Armed with an understanding of Keats's and Bridges's background, we may now examine the impact of medical experience on a few examples of their works. Themes of beauty, imagination, love, melancholy, and the enjoyment of nature are common in both men's poems. Both poets, understandably, treated the subjects of death and disease. Keats, shortly after the death of his younger brother, in his 1819 poem "Ode to a Nightingale," described the world of reality:

> The weariness, the fever, and the fret.
> Here where men sit and hear each other groan;
> Where palsy shakes a few, sad, last gray hairs,
> Where youth grows pale and spectre-thin, and dies;
> Where but to think is to be full of sorrow
> And leaden-eyed despairs.[5, p. 82]

In the poem he often alludes to fits of melancholy and despair, when the wish for death comes upon him. Only poetry has any healing effect upon him, and even it, he says, "cannot cheat so well/As she is fam'd to do."[5, p. 83]

Robert Bridges's poem "On a Dead Child" is clearly a recollection of a clinical experience:

> Perfect little body, without fault or stain on thee,
> With promise of strength and manhood full and fair!
> Though cold and stark and bare,
> The bloom and charm of life doth awhile remain on thee.[10, p. 267]

Keats and Bridges often treated death as a symbol of refuge. In "Elegy Among the Tombs" Bridges wrote:

> From death, still death, still would a comfort come:
> Since of this world the essential joy must fall.[10, p. 259]

Similarly, Keats wrote in "Ode to a Nightingale":

> . . . for many a time
> I have been half in love with easeful Death,
> Call'd him soft names in many a muséd rhyme.[5, p. 83]

Medicine's principal impact on these poet-physicians is not found in their specific allusions to death and disease, but rather in their remarkable capacities for observation and description of natural beauty. "To Autumn," one of Keats's most famous odes, shows his talent for detail and description:

> While barred clouds bloom the soft-dying day,
> And touch the stubble-plains with rosy hue;
> Then in a wailful choir the small gnats mourn

Among the river sallows, borne aloft
Or sinking as the light wind lives or dies;[5, p. 87]

Their love of beauty and dedication to poetry allowed both Bridges and Keats to bring a studied yet imaginative style to their art.

Just as Bridges felt the impact of Keats's work, other poet-physicians have also expressed the influence of poetry on their careers. William Carlos Williams, this century's most notable poet-physician, stated in his autobiography:

Keats, during my years at medical school, was my God. Endymion really woke me up. I copied Keats's style religiously.[11]

Anton Chekov described the relationship between medical training and his writings.

[Medicine] significantly extended the area of my observations, enriched my knowledge, and only one who is himself a physician can understand the value of this for me as a writer.[12]

The literary world remembers and honors John Keats and Robert Bridges for their remarkable powers of observation, organization, description, and transformation. Because these are the precise skills that every medical curriculum strives to cultivate, Keats and Bridges must also be remembered as great men of medical history.

References

1. Levertov D. Literature and medicine. In Trautmann, J, ed. Healing Arts in Dialogue: Medicine and Literature. Carbondale, Illinois, Southern Illinois University Press, 1981, p.153.
2. Ward A. John Keats; The Making of a Poet. New York, Viking Press, 1963, p. 17.
3. Bate WJ. John Keats. Cambridge, Massachusetts, Belknap Press of Harvard University Press, 1963, p. 47.
4. Lowell A. John Keats, vol. 1. Cambridge, Massachusetts, Riverside Press, 1925.
5. Baker C, ed. Keats: Poems and Selected Letters. New York, Charles Scribner's Sons, 1962.
6. Bush D. John Keats: His Life and Writings. New York, MacMillan Co., 1966, pp. 27-29.
7. Gittings R, ed. Letters of John Keats: A New Selection. London, Oxford University Press, 1970, p. 299.
8. Stanford DE, ed. The Selected Letters of Robert Bridges, vol. 1. Newark, New Jersey, Associated University Presses, 1983.
9. Stanford DE, ed. Robert Bridges: Selected Poems. Cheadle, England, Carcanet Press, 1974, p. 10.
10. Bridges R. Poetical Works. London, Oxford University Press, 1953.
11. Williams WC. Autobiography. New York, Random House, 1951, p. 53.
12. Sandblom P. Creativity and Disease. Philadelphia, George F. Stickley Co., 1982, p. 102.

BABY

PHILLIP J. COZZI, M.D.
(Fall 1994, p. 13)

Into the great big toy box of death,
death dolls, death blocks, xylophone of death,
pop-up death, toy trucks on a highway of lies
where life toddles across lanes and death approaches

on eighteen wheels, the one-piece flannel sleeper
of death, the battery-run three-keyed piano
of death, the dangling strings of nucleotides,
the laugh and lullaby of death,

what does it matter if she could spell
the word, the puberty she might have known,
piece of meat thrown to ravenous cats,
to know the sovereignty of death, the wind-up

teddy muted, the future pecked away,
her body a cloud steadily passing out of sight,
a trace of pure white forehead vanishing
as a thought, to feast upon firm peaches

of her thought, to climb her body to the snowline
and turn back suddenly finding the canyon
opened, a deer-travelled footpath spread apart
to swallow us, our lifelong goals burst into jewels

of light, a thumb-smeared memory obliterated
in firework ashes on lawns, the braided whip
of snake sucked her dignity into a plastic bag
hung on a hospital wall, the trap door on the timber

scaffold where she toddled, condemned, and nothing
was left of her, the inflatable frog, the miniature
shopping cart, we plunged into the ravine and there
at the bottom of the pit we found her stare.

LOST SOUL

ALFRED P. INGEGNO, M.D.
(Fall 1995, p. 12)

Was he the only one so unaware?
He lived life's definition, breathed and walked;
he fornicated, loved, and talked,
reacted without care, amorally,
to those whose lives, on blood's or friendship's ground
or merest chance, to him were bound, and not
till late did he and others sense
the awful truth that deep within
and long ago, unnoticed, he had died.

ATHEROBLOSSOMS

MICHAEL B. GRAVANIS, M.D.
(Fall 1995, p. 12)

Like the shy April rose
that unfolds one petal at a time
my beginning is also subtle
'til I reach my full bloom
with colorful labyrinthine caves
and craters that Enkelados will envy
full of factors and mediators
but most of all full of junk
memories of sinful indulgence
of a lovely undisciplined past.

GRAHAM GREENE'S DOCTORS

JOHN H. DIRCKX, M.D.

(Spring 1983, pp. 27–29)

I can hardly remember a time in my childhood when I didn't look forward eagerly to a medical career, or when I wasn't utterly enraptured by the notion of acquiring, reading, and writing books. Nothing has changed.

In 1968, after four years in solo family practice including obstetrics, with sidelines in emergency and occupational medicine, I accepted a full-time salaried position in college health so as to have more time for my family and leisure to pursue literary and linguistic studies and to indulge my cacoëthes scribendi.

Among the fruits of my leisure activities have been books and articles on medical terminology and medical writing, and articles in The Pharos *and other journals exploring the humanistic dimensions of medicine as reflected in history, language, and literature.*

During the past decade, I've enjoyed providing editorial support and doing consulting work on various Stedman's medical dictionaries published by Lippincott Williams & Wilkins. A longer and even more rewarding collaboration has been with the American Association for Medical Transcription. My medical language column has appeared in every issue of the Association's journal published in the last 18 years. In addition, I've written several books and dozens of articles intended specifically for these highly professional and dedicated but seldom-appreciated members of the health care team.

My paper on the mad doctor grew out of a lifetime fascination with literary works pertaining to physicians and medicine. Other interpretations than mine of the enduring appeal of that stereotypic figure of popular literature, the mad scientist, are surely possible, but I'm satisfied that mine contains more than a grain of truth.

I first became interested in the work of the late Graham Greene when I was in high school. As a medical student, I once wrote to Greene to inquire about some technical details in his latest novel, A Burnt-Out Case, *and was gratified to receive a courteous and thoughtful reply. As I continue to collect materials by and about him, my conviction keeps growing the Greene the man was as complex and haunted as any character ever created by Greene the writer.*

JOHN H. DIRCKX, M.D.
August, 2003
AΩA, Marquette University, 1961

279

IN THE JUDGMENT OF MANY COMPETENT CRITICS, Graham Greene is the greatest living novelist. Born in 1904 at Berkhamsted, England, the son of a schoolmaster, Greene published his first novel, *The Man Within,* at the age of twenty-five, and won international acclaim with *Brighton Rock* (1938) and *The Power and the Glory* (1940). His most recent book, *Dr. Fischer of Geneva or The Bomb Party* (1980), shows that his impressive literary powers are unimpaired by age.

Besides twenty-three novels, Greene has published short stories, biography, and criticism. Many of his novels have been made into films, often with screenplays written by himself. The most memorable of his films, *The Third Man* (1950), was made before the novel was written. Greene has traveled extensively as a journalist and on diplomatic missions for the British government.

The novels of Graham Greene fall naturally into groups. He has used the term "entertainments" for a series of action-filled tales of crime and espionage beginning with *Orient Express* (1932). All of these have been filmed. Their influence can be clearly seen in the Cold-War espionage fiction of LeCarré, Deighton, and Fleming.

A group of novels with deeper psychological themes, starting with *Brighton Rock,* have been called Greene's Catholic novels, because each explores the moral predicament of a Catholic character trapped in a web of guilt. (Greene converted to Roman Catholicism in his twenties.) In the Catholic novels many readers have found evidences of the "sin mysticism" characteristic of the novels of François Mauriac, with whom Greene is often compared.

Like *The Power and the Glory,* that takes place in war-torn Mexico, most of his novels written in the 1950s and 1960s are melodramas set against a background of political and social upheaval: in Vietnam *(The Quiet American,* 1955), in Cuba (*Our Man in Havana,* 1958), and in Haiti *(The Comedians,* 1966).

Sin, neurosis, frustration, and failure are recurring themes in Greene's major novels. Even in the "entertainments" he typically builds characters and events around moral conflicts or social problems. In his autobiography, *A Sort of Life* (1971), he said that if he were to choose an epigraph for all of his novels, it would be this passage from "Bishop Blougram's Apology" by Robert Browning:

> Our interest's on the dangerous edge of things.
> The honest thief, the tender murderer,
> The superstitious atheist, demirep
> That loves and saves her soul in new French books—
> We watch while these in equilibrium keep
> The giddy line midway.

As these lines suggest, Greene's characters often embody contradictions. His amoral and immoral villains are seldom so steeped in vice that they lack even a spark of goodness, while his protagonists, for all their rigid principlesand stifling qualms of conscience, are morally flawed, damned, and lost.

In four novels published in succession between 1958 and 1973, Greene cast physicians in important roles.

Our Man in Havana marked a new departure in technique for Greene. A parody of spy novels, including his own, the book taps a rich vein of irony and caricature reminiscent of the work of Greene's contemporary, Evelyn Waugh. Jim Wormold, the Havana representative of a vacuum cleaner manufacturer, is recruited by the British Secret Service to collect and transmit information about local politics. Endowed with a fertile imagination and a bizarre sense of humor, Wormold simply invents the information that he sends back to his principals in London. After coming into conflict with the police and narrowly escaping assassination, he is recalled to England and given a training assignment at the ministry.

Wormold's only close friend is Hasselbacher, an old German doctor. The two spend lazy afternoons drinking together at the Wonder Bar. In the end, Hasselbacher falls victim to Wormold's fictions. Threatened by the Cuban authorities with deportation, the doctor reveals "secrets" that Wormold has manufactured. Not long after saving Wormold's life by warning him that he is going to be poisoned, Hasselbacher is gunned down in the Wonder Bar by an unidentified assassin.

In *A Burnt-Out Case* (1961), Greene traces the decline and fall of Querry, a famous architect who has traveled to the Congo in search of something that civilization and success have not been able to supply. When he arrives for an indefinite stay at a mission clinic for lepers, he is befriended by Cohn, the mission doctor. Cohn assigns Deo Gratias, a native disabled by a burnt-out case of leprosy, as Querry's servant and tries to persuade the architect to design a proper hospital for the mission. At the end of the novel Querry is murdered by a local factory manager.

Brown, the narrator of *The Comedians*, tells how he returns to Haiti and assumes possession of a hotel left to him by his long-estranged and recently deceased mother. He does well for a time, but after Papa Doc Duvalier comes to power the hotel fails, because tourists are scared off by the secret police, and Brown ends up becoming an undertaker. Along the way he is befriended by Dr. Magiot, a native heart specialist who attended his mother during her last illness. Magiot, a Communist, is murdered by the secret police, who hope thus to curry favor with the CIA.

Dr. Eduardo Plarr is a pivotal character in *The Honorary Consul* (1973)—indeed almost the central character. The son of an English father and a South American mother, he lives in Pilares, Argentina, where he has an extensive practice among the poor. A gang of Paraguayan terrorists, some of whom were his schoolmates, trick him into supplying them with information that will enable them to kidnap the American ambassador. By mistake they kidnap Charley Fortnum instead, an old alcoholic of English ancestry who has been named "honorary" consul in Pilares for some trifling services to the British government. After Fortnum is shot in the foot while trying to escape, the terrorists summon Plarr to treat him. The doctor becomes their prisoner also, and when troops arrive to rescue Fortnum, they shoot Plarr as one of the terrorists. Fortnum survives.

To explore the personalities and review the activities of the protagonists in these four novels would lead us far afield. Suffice it to say that each is endowed with the full complement of the neurosis, self-doubt, self-pity, and moral confusion that one expects in Greene's major characters. But whereas in most of his other serious work Greene has created tension and conflict by joining disparate and incompatible elements in one and the same personality, in each of these novels he has introduced a second character as a sort of alter ego to the principal one. The second is usually complementary, compensatory, and in some measure, contradictory.

Each of these alter egos is a male physician without wife or family, of basically the same temperament as the protagonist, so that a bond of friendship inevitably unites them—even, as in A Burnt-Out Case and The Comedians, after short acquaintances. But whereas Wormold, Querry, Brown, and Fortnum are restless, unruly, unstable elements, their physician counterparts are passive, disciplined, and resigned, supplying in each case what Jung called the female principle or *anima* that is lacking in the principal character.

In each novel the physician acts as an advisor or mentor to the main character, often with unfortunate results. It is Hasselbacher who advises Wormold to fabricate information and invent other agents. But he also suggests the stratagem of the checker game played with miniature whiskey bottles, by which Wormold succeeds in overpowering the police chief. Cohn helps Querry to understand himself better and gives him a new sense of purpose in life. After Querry's death, only the doctor believes him innocent of the supposed adultery for which he was shot. When Brown inherits his mother's hotel, Magiot offers him sound and disinterested personal and business advice, and later provides behind-the-scenes support for his revolutionist dabblings. Plarr tries to arrange for Fortnum's release before his own capture. Afterwards, he comforts the honorary consul, who he thinks is about to be murdered.

All of these physicians are outcasts or exiles, with roots in cultures other than those in which they live. Hasselbacher is an ex-officer in the German army who now and then, for sentiment's sake, dons his old uniform, complete with spiked helmet, breastplate, and white gloves. He is superstitious about lottery numbers and conducts elaborate experiments on the blueness of cheese. Cohn is a Belgian who has buried himself in the Congo, faithful to his medical vocation, though he had lost his religious convictions even before leaving Europe. Magiot was trained in Paris, and his home is full of old French books and furniture. Though most of his colleagues have bought exit permits, he remains behind. Like Cohn, he is a lapsed Catholic in an essentially Catholic milieu, and a Marxist as well. Plarr, yet another fallen-away Catholic, is a native of Paraguay whose English father sent him across the border into Argentina when he was still a child. Shortly afterward, his father became a political prisoner, and it is in hope of effecting his release that Plarr cooperates with the terrorists.

Greene's physicians are all exemplary members of their profession—competent, compassionate, and self-sacrificing. Asked whether a phone call that upset him was about a patient, Hasselbacher replies, "Who is not a patient?" He laments that he has never grown used to death, and concludes from that that he is not a good doctor. Cohn is an effective healer despite the enormous difficulties under which he functions. He is impatient with leprophils—neurotics who love leprosy rather than lepers—and assures Querry that, unlike Fr. Damien of Molokai, he has no death-wish. Though Magiot is a cardiologist—the best in Haiti—he practices general medicine among the poor. When the secret police decide to murder him, they lure him into the open with a false summons to a patient, knowing that he will not refuse. Plarr also has an extensive practice among the poor of the *barrio popular,* from whom he collects no fees. He risks his own life to attend Fortnum, a man from whose death he stands to benefit in various ways.

Greene's entertainments generally have "happy" endings. That is, the good guys survive—and in most of his straight novels any deaths that occur along the way are inevitable adjuncts of the plot line. Even Querry's death might be viewed as the logical culmination of an existence without meaning. But the deaths of Hasselbacher, Magiot, and Plarr are sheer wastes of human life, from petty, absurd political motives, they are not the inevitable consequences of plot development, unless we view them as sacrifices or immolations. In this perspective, the unremitting servitude of Cohn, trapped in his own frustrating world without faith or spiritual commitment, can also be viewed as a kind of immolation.

Consciously or not, a novelist gives expression and form to the attitudes and values of his culture and his times. In the characters of Hasselbacher, Cohn, Magiot, and Plarr, we have the recurring image of a kind and compassionate physician who, though himself a misfit and an agnostic, provides guidance and support to the protagonist, and ends by being sacrificed for obscure or trivial reasons.

Graham Greene's sympathetic, eccentric, heroic, tragic physicians are cast in the same mold as Dr. Ragin in "Ward No. 6" by Anton Chekhov, Dr. Gottlieb in *Arrowsmith* by Sinclair Lewis, and Dr. Abelman in *The Last Angry Man* by Gerald Green. Through these characters, perceptive and articulate writers of differing cultures and periods have illuminated the role that modern man has assigned to his doctors.

Like the medicine man or shaman of primitive cultures, the Western physician of today is expected to fulfill both medical and priestly functions. Modern man has rejected the notion of a divine Savior and replaced Him with human ones, weak and fallible like himself, from whom he demands not only the cure of physical ills but also spiritual succor, guidance, and even the supreme sacrifice of life.

It is not by mere chance that modern society has chosen members of the medical profession to shoulder these superhuman duties and responsibilities. In the relations between Greene's protagonists and their physician doubles, we can see an extension and refinement of the love-hate relationship that subsists between many patients and their doctors. The patient loves the doctor because the doctor shares the burden of his pain—physical, mental, and spiritual— and promises to make it go away. But the patient resents having to place himself in the power and control of a fellow man, to whom he must expose not only his body but his soul, and for this he punishes the doctor by alienating him through mistrust and noncompliance, and crushing him beneath an intolerable burden of responsibility, killing him symbolically if not in fact.

Whether the conception of the physician presented in the novels of Graham Greene and other modern works of fiction is fantasy or allegory, an invented or a reflected view, each reader must judge for himself.

THE MAD DOCTOR IN FICTION

JOHN H. DIRCKX, M.D.

(Summer 1992, pp. 27–31)

THE NIGHT IS DARK AND STORMY. *In an underground laboratory, far from the haunts of men, a grisly experiment is in progress. The human subject, drugged and strapped to an operating table, is about to undergo a surgical procedure in which his brain will be replaced with that of a gangster whose bullet-riddled corpse has just been purloined from the county morgue.*

All is ready. Razor-sharp instruments of stainless steel and curiously shaped glass vessels gleam in the operating lights. The surgeon, his features distorted by a grin of maniacal glee, prepares to make the first incision.

Again and again this scene is reenacted in cheap novels and comic books, in ludicrously dated horror movies on cable television channels that specialize in such antiques as well as in the latest "buckets-of-blood" feature film now showing at a theater near you. The details vary from story to story. For example, instead of performing surgery, the doctor may be found in a chemical laboratory hunched over a retort full of boiling fluid, or surrounded by the hum and crackle of an electric dynamo. His goal may be to restore the dead to life, to achieve immortality, or to avenge himself on colleagues who have ostracized him for his unorthodox visions and methods. He may have at his disposal Satanic or supernatural resources. He may be his own experimental subject. He may be a she.

But in all his incarnations, the central figure of such scenarios commands instant recognition as that stock character of modern sensational literature and the entertainment media, the mad doctor. The purpose of this paper is to trace the literary origins of the mad doctor of modem fiction and to offer a sociologic interpretation of his enduring popularity.

At the outset it is necessary to define precisely the persona whose sources and popular appeal are under investigation. The mad doctor is nearly always portrayed as a physician. He may, however, be a biologist, chemist, or practitioner of some unspecified branch of "science" who has a knowledge of medicine and facilities for carrying out medical or surgical procedures or experiments—hence the alternative and more comprehensive term, "mad scientist."

The mad doctor is generally a person of superior intelligence, perhaps even a genius, with both creative and analytic gifts that enable him to see further than his fellows and to invent methods or unleash forces that have eluded others. But he is also mentally unbalanced, displaying evidence of egocentrism, fanaticism, a distorted view of reality, and faulty judgment. The ultimate motivation for his actions may lie in misguided altruism or psychotic delusions, but because he violates societal norms of behavior he is typically credited with evil intent. Often his unique vision or his daring experiments have made him a misfit or an outcast from society, and this alienation may foster ideas of persecution and supply further reasons for antisocial behavior. Not in-frequently, he appears as the tool of criminals, who exploit his talents (and flexible conscience) for their own ends.

The mad doctor typically performs experiments in an unknown or forbidden branch of medical science, playing God by seeking to control the forces of nature, conquer disease and death, restore youth, prolong or even create life. His methods are untried, unorthodox, hazardous, and illegal; often they are also frankly fantastic or supernatural.

As a footnote to this profile of the mad doctor it may be remarked that, once he begins his experiments, things always go wrong. Through the inexorable operation of Murphy's Law, the experiments have unexpected, horrifying, and uncontrollable consequences. And as the plot runs on to its inevitable conclusion, poetic justice eventually catches up with the mad doctor and makes him the final victim of his own twisted vision and misdirected genius.

The mad doctor is uniquely a product of the twentieth century, with its stupendous advances in biology, medicine, and technology. Exactly when he came into being is impossible to say, but certainly the 1931 film version of Mary Shelley's novel *Frankenstein,* made by Universal Pictures and directed by James Whale, was a crucial step in his genesis. (Just for the record, the Frankenstein in this film was a medical-school dropout, not a doctor.) In any event, he reached his full development in the many sequels, imitations, and offshoots of this film made by Universal and other studios during the 1930s and 1940s.

The character of the mad doctor represents a fusion of three older literary strains or traditions, to one of which the novel *Frankenstein* belongs. (Shelley's Frankenstein was neither mad nor a doctor.) After reviewing these three traditions, I propose to seek an explanation for the esthetic appeal of the mad doctor by exploring its psychosocial content and value for a nonmedical audience.

The first literary stereotype that has supplied material for the standard image of the mad doctor is the medical villain, the physician who is a criminal. The physician-murderer is an ideal character for the mystery writer to manipulate. Hiding behind a façade of professional respectability, he can easily abuse the powers and prerogatives attached to his social position. Moreover, he possesses special skills and resources for both taking human life and eluding detection.

Examples of the medical murderer abound in classical detective literature.

One of Arthur Conan Doyle's most sinister creations was Dr. Grimesby Roylott in *The Adventure of the Speckled Band* (1892). In order to prevent his step-daughter from marrying and inheriting money over which he will lose control, Roylott kills her by sending a poisonous snake into her room at night through a ventilator in the wall.

The villain of Dorothy L. Sayers's first mystery novel, *Whose Body?* (1923), is Sir Julian Freke, a neurologist who has written a book to prove that conscience is purely a matter of deranged physiology. When the amateur detective Lord Peter Wimsey visits Sir Julian, in the guise of a patient, to gather evidence that he has committed a murder, he narrowly escapes becoming the next victim. Dr. James Sheppard, general practitioner of King's Abbot, is the murderer in Agatha Christie's whodunit *The Murder of Roger Ackroyd* (1926). By an auctorial feint that created an uproar at the time, Christie made Dr. Sheppard the narrator of the novel.

Somewhat different from these fictional physicians who turn casually, as it were, to crime are those whose unlawful activities spring directly from their medical calling, or depend on exploiting their medical knowledge or skill. Early in the present century, developments in plastic surgery and specifically in facial reconstruction fired the imaginations of writers of sensational fiction. In Gaston Leroux's *Wolves of the Sea* (1921) and other tales about the Devil's Island desperado Cheri-Bibi, there appears a mysterious character known simply as "the Kanaka" who has mastered some highly advanced surgical techniques. When Cheri-Bibi and his henchmen take over the prison ship that is conveying them to Devil's Island, the Kanaka isolates Cheri-Bibi and his arch rival, the Marquis de Touchais, in the ship's sick bay and surgically exchanges their faces. The author quoted a newspaper article on the pioneer experiments of Dr. Alexis Carrel in tissue grafting to lend plausibility to this nonsense.

A different treatment of the theme appears in Joseph Kesselring's classic comedy *Arsenic and Old Lace* (1941). Dr. Herman Einstein, a drunken and dissolute plastic surgeon, has changed the face of gangster Jonathan Brewster three times. On the last occasion, having attended a horror film just before operating, he made his patient look exactly like Boris Karloff.

Writers of crime fiction have not overlooked the opportunities of the psychiatrist, and particularly of the director of a mental institution, to engage with impunity in criminal activities, including illegal detention, hypnotic suggestion, and various forms of unlawful coercion. This theme was exploited in two nineteenth century novels, *Hard Cash* (1863) by Charles Reade and *The Rose and the Key* (1871) by J. Sheridan Le Fanu. With the development of psychoanalysis in the early twentieth century, the topic acquired new interest and relevance.

The title character of the gloomy, Hoffmannesque German film *The Cabinet of Dr. Caligari* (1920) is the director of a mental institution who also appears as a traveling mountebank and hypnotist. The "somnambulist" he exhibits at fairs is one of his patients, a murderer, whom he has placed in a hypnotic trance. Under Caligari's direction, the somnambulist kills anyone who happens to arouse his master's enmity or threaten his security. Hypnotism and mind-altering drugs play a role in the criminal activities of Dr. Mabuse, an evil genius who appeared in novels by Norbert Jacques and in two German films, *The Great Gambler* and *The Inferno* (both 1922), directed by Fritz Lang. (Sequels, also by Lang, appeared in 1932 and 1960.) The plot of the film *Spellbound* (1945) turns on two interwoven themes—a murder committed by the director of a sanitarium and the traumatic amnesia of another character, induced by witnessing the murder.

In these and dozens of other tales of crime and suspense on the printed page, the stage, and the small and large screens, writers have played with a paradox: that one who has devoted time and effort to the study of medicine, and has been accepted by society as a healer and comforter of the sick and a preserver of life, should act instead against the good of society by violating the rights of others, endangering their health, and even taking their lives. Looking below the surface, we can interpret this literary figure as a caricature based on the cynical lay image of the private physician as cold, inconsiderate, and selfish, a ruthless bandit who charges exorbitant fees but is always out playing golf when you need him.

A second thread woven into the fabric of the mad doctor is the fictional quack or charlatan. Quacks can be found in the literature of many countries and periods, more often as comic characters or the butts of satire than as sinister figures in serious fiction or drama. Before the present century, the itinerant mountebank hawking quack nostrums and panaceas was an integral part of Western society. In *The Play Called the Four P's* (1549) by John Heywood, a clownish apothecary retails drugs with resounding Greek and Arabic names, which, he frankly admits to his cronies, are worthless. Dulcamara in Gaetano Donizetti's opera *L'Elisir d'Amore* (1832) travels about selling love potions to gullible peasants.

The crooked druggist operating from a shop is also a familiar figure in early modern fiction. At the conclusion of William Shakespeare's *Romeo and Juliet* an apothecary breaks the law for personal gain by selling Romeo, who believes Juliet dead, a lethal draft with which to commit suicide. Jean de LaBruyère included in his *Caractères* (1688) a portrait of the quack Carri, who makes a living by selling a worthless and possibly harmful cure-all that has been handed down in his family for generations. The apothecary Lavement in *Roderick Random* (1748) by Tobias Smollett keeps down his overhead by substituting worthless materials for the ingredients called for in the prescriptions he fills.

The pompous, narrow-minded, mercenary physician who spouts Latin to impress and mystify his patients while prescribing unpleasant, expensive, and useless treatments became almost a standard character in the later comedies of Molière. Syringe, the surgeon in John Vanbrugh's comedy *The Relapse* (1696), promises to cure Lord Foppington of a trifling sword cut, provided that nobody else is permitted to inspect the wound. Dr. Sangrado in *Gil Blas* (1715) by René LeSage treats all patients with copious phlebotomy and a water diet, regardless of the diagnosis. In E.T.A. Hoffmann's tale "Signor Formica," the charlatan Accaramboni treats poor painters for nonexistent illnesses and extorts their best pictures from them in payment.

Numerous quacks appear in more contemporary literature. Memorable examples occur in the writings of physician-authors Arthur Conan Doyle—particularly Dr. Cullingworth in *The Stark Munro Letters* (1894)—and A. J. Cronin, whose novel *The Citadel* (1934) was an urbane diatribe against the fashionable society quack. In *The Autobiography of a Quack* (1899), S. Weir Mitchell traced the career of Ezra Sandcraft, who makes a comfortable living by treating his patients for diseases of his own invention. When he is told he has Addison's disease, he assumes his doctors are playing the same game with him, and refuses the treatment that might have saved his life. George Bernard Shaw portrayed some interesting specimens of the quack in his drama *The Doctor's Dilemma* (1906). Jules Romains exposed the elaborate schemes of a systematic quack in his satirical comedy *Knock, or the Triumph of Medicine* (1923).

A comparison of these fictional characters shows that the term *quack* can have any of three related meanings. It can refer to an unschooled, irregular practitioner who presents himself to the public as a healer but is really a fraud without medical training or credentials. It can also mean a duly trained and qualified practitioner who has never attained an acceptable degree of competence or who, having attained it, has lost it again through lack of diligence or failure to keep up with medical progress. In addition, the term may be applied to a physician who, although fully competent, habitually treats patients for nonexistent illnesses, performs unnecessary surgery, and charges excessive fees.

Granted that each type of quack has a basis in historical fact, and that examples of all three are currently flourishing in our midst, the fictional quack also has a deeper, symbolic meaning. Even the competent and conscientious physician may convey to the patient, by his display of superior knowledge and his use of unintelligible jargon, a threat of exploitation. The laity's impression of the doctor as a smooth-talking confident man thus finds its echo in the fictional image of the quack or mountebank, who for personal gain practices deception in purveying medical services.

The third literary prototype that has entered into the formation of the modern mad doctor is the seeker of forbidden knowledge, specifically of knowledge about human biology that will give the seeker the power to restore or perpetuate youth or to conquer disease or death. Much of the fiction and entertainment embodying this theme pertains to the genres of fantasy and science fiction.

Early fictional experimenters were modeled on the medieval alchemists, who sought the philosopher's stone (a means of transmuting base metals into gold) and the elixir of life, which would confer immortality and perpetual youth. Faust, or Faustus, the physician, alchemist, and astrologer who barters his soul to the Devil in return for unlimited gratification of both his intellect and his senses, first appeared in German popular literature in the sixteenth century. He is the subject of dramas by Christopher Marlowe and Johann Wolfgang von Goethe, of operas by Hector Berlioz, Charles Gounod, and Arrigo Boito, and of novels by Thomas Mann and others.

The misguided experimenter who is probably most familiar to the modern public is Victor Frankenstein, the protagonist of Mary Shelley's novel *Frankenstein; or, The Modern Prometheus* (1818), who is diverted from the study of chemistry by an overpowering urge to solve the mystery of life itself. Frankenstein assembles an ideal man using parts selected from various corpses and infuses his creation with artificial life. The result, as all the world knows, is an eight-foot monster whose loathsome appearance cuts it off from communion with the human race. Initially tame and benevolent, the monster becomes vicious and vindictive, committing several murders and at length destroying itself.

Some fictional researchers have sought to retard or conquer aging. Dr. Heidegger in Nathaniel Hawthorne's story "Dr. Heidegger's Experiment" (1837) administers an elixir of youth to four elderly, decrepit friends, temporarily restoring not only the beauty and vigor of youth but also its folly and intemperance. In another story by Hawthorne, "Rappaccini's Daughter" (1846), a physician prevents his beautiful daughter from marrying by feeding her an exotic poison in small doses so that her touch and even her breath become lethal. When a medical student who has fallen in love with her attempts to neutralize the poison, the antidote kills her.

The title character of H. G. Wells's novel *The Island of Dr. Moreau* (1896), a brilliant but misguided physiologist, surgically alters the bodies of wild animals so that they can walk upright and perform other human activities, including speech. In the end, the "Beast People," still savage by nature, turn on their creator and kill him. Griffin, the experimenter in Wells's fantasy-farce *The Invisible Man* (1897), discovers a means of making light rays pass undeflected through his body. Unfortunately, however, the treatment induces a delusional psychosis, which leads to Griffin's undoing.

Dr. Henry Jekyll, the central figure of Robert Louis Stevenson's novella *The Strange Case of Dr. Jekyll and Mr. Hyde* (1886), formulates an elixir by which he can separate the two opposing sides of his nature—his public image, intellectual and humanitarian, and his hidden self, full of greed, lust, and cruelty. The darker side unleashed by the potion eventually takes control and can no longer be suppressed, leading Jekyll on to self-destruction.

Faust, Frankenstein, Jekyll, and other rash experimenters of fiction have all violated, in a repetition of the sin of Adam, a divine taboo by seeking knowledge or power that is forbidden to Man, and have generally paid for their temerity and sacrilege with their lives. Like the fictional quack, the fictional pursuer of arcane, pseudoscientific research has a basis in reality. To the average unsophisticated lay person, the modern physician's methods may seem so irrational and his equipment so bizarre as to suggest that he is engaged not in rendering conventional health care but in pursuing some demented goal beyond the bounds of legitimate medical science. The notion of rash and ill-fated medical experimentation derives plausibility from the fact that physicians do experiment sometimes (if only because circumstances force them to act empirically) and that such experiments often go awry.

If, at the level of literary creation, the mad doctor of contemporary fiction is a synthesis of three established types—the criminal physician, the quack, and the misguided researcher—each of whom I have shown to have a symbolic reference to real-life aspects of the doctor-patient relationship, at the more intimate level of psychological perception this composite fictional character can be viewed as a surrealistic metamorphosis of the real-life physician. All the features I have identified as typical of the mad doctor will be found on analysis to correspond to attributes of the ordinary medical practitioner, as filtered through the distorting lenses of the layman's perceptions.

The basis for this distortion lies in two emotions that typically accompany the physician-patient interaction: fear of the consequences of disease and its treatment, including pain, disfigurement, disablement, and death (not to mention impoverishment); and anger arising from the loss of control over one's body and one's actions.

The physician's ability to comfort and heal, based on his special knowledge and skill, gives him a kind of authority over his patients. In order to obtain the physician's help in overcoming illness, the patient must expose his body, reveal his inmost secrets, and relinquish his personal freedom in a unique way. In these circumstances, the anger aroused by the fact of being sick and the fear of the consequences of illness are often redirected against the physician. Although these feelings sometimes evolve into open hostility, more often they smoulder on as a vague, subconscious indignation or sense of menace.

For most of us, the seeds of this deep-seated antagonism or resentment are probably sown early in life. Children often come to view the physician as a boogeyman, who inflicts undeserved punishment with his immunizing needles and in the course of examining and treating for illness. Forgotten encounters in childhood with one or more physicians probably underlie the so-called white coat syndrome, in which the very presence of the physician, ostensibly a helper and healer, induces irrational fears and elevates arterial blood pressure readings.

Such experiences may also explain why, in viewing a scene such as that with which this paper began, the average layman so readily identifies with the powerless, strapped-down, doomed subject—or rather victim—of the mad doctor.

In sensational fiction the modern physician's awesome knowledge, arcane jargon, and mysterious gadgetry are exalted beyond mere science to hyperscience, "science fiction," fantasy, and the supernatural. His use of methods that the patient cannot fully understand or relate to any prior knowledge or experience is translated into unorthodoxy, irrationality, and ultimately madness. His assumption of a dominant or authoritative role with respect to the patient is interpreted as evidence of an intention to deceive, exploit, hurt, maim, or kill.

At the same time, the typically catastrophic outcome of unorthodox medical experimentation in fiction seems to be validated by facts of common observation. Things often do go wrong in the course of the simplest and most commonplace medical and surgical procedures. Medical misadventures with disastrous results are a favorite topic of gossip and the theme of much nonsensical but ineradicable folklore. Thalidomide and multimillion-dollar malpractice awards, however, are the stuff of history, not folklore.

After viewing the performance of a tragedy, or reading a novel full of calamity and heartbreak, we return to the real world with our perceptions recalibrated, thankful perhaps that our genuine problems are so trivial by comparison with the ones we have just vicariously lived through. Similarly, after being exposed to a fictitious mad doctor, one may find one's real medical adviser more benevolent and less intimidating.

The emotional response of the lay person to the symbolic figure of the mad doctor can be thought of as taking place in three stages. In the first stage, the layman's innate fear and resentment of authoritarian medical figures in general finds rationalization in the context of a specific fictional plot from the fact that the medical figure in question is patently evil and fearsome. Next, the layman transfers his negative feelings from his real-life doctors to this fictitious (hence non-threatening) mad doctor, who thus becomes a kind of scapegoat. Finally, through his sense of satisfaction and relief when the villainous experimenter is ultimately exposed and punished or destroyed, the layman purges himself of those negative feelings so that in his actual dealings with doctors he can maintain his equanimity and conduct himself in a dignified and civil manner.

Nearly all fiction performs some such cathartic function. Physicians may well look with tolerance, if not appreciation, on even the most banal and distasteful escapist literature if it serves as a means of diverting patients' fear and hostility away from themselves.

LUNGS

PHILLIP J. COZZI, M.D.
(Spring 1994, p. 43)

In their impair, they have become beautiful.
I imagine bubbles rising
or falling like scraps of balloon

in the hands of a prankish child.
I consider India, legions of mouths
open and pleading. A diligent spouse

breath is scracely noticed in its presence. Yet
when the breathing tube is being placed
it looks like a gun held in the face. I noticed

life's itinerary: school, marriage, the brownstone
flat I never knew I'd love.
Would I punctuate my life with a cough?

I found my lost breath behind the cans
of paint, half empty, in the basement
of my drug-induced dream. It was deep

green stained and stiff with the paint
I'd used to cover the stairs out back.
It was a glove: my slipped hand filled

the space collapsed on itself, when something in
the lighting made me pause to see
the stiffened tissue beautifully filled with life.

THERE'S MORE TO DOYLE THAN HOLMES!

C. FREDERICK KITTLE, M.D.

(Winter 1997, pp. 17–21)

The author (AΩA, University of Chicago School of Medicine, 1945) is Professor of Surgery (cardiovascular and thoracic) Emeritus at Rush Medical College. Previously, Dr. Kittle was professor of surgery at the University of Chicago School of Medicine. He was chair of the American Board of Thoracic Surgery from 1973 to 1975. He has a continuing and committed enthusiasm for activities of the Arthur Conan Doyle Society.

SUPERLATIVES COME EASILY in describing Sherlock Holmes: the remarkable detective who entered this world in 1887 (*A Study in Scarlet*). He is unquestionably the best-known literary character and the greatest illusion of reality ever created. His popularity is progressive and continues unabated, as indicated by the variously named Baker Street Irregular Societies devoted to him and by their increasing number, 416 organizations worldwide at latest count, of which 321 are in the United States.[1]

I confess, however, that although attracted and charmed by Sherlock Holmes, I gradually began to wonder about the man himself who invented and nurtured the character of Sherlock Holmes and those sixty delightful tales of the canon. How did all this come about?

Arthur Conan Doyle, actually Arthur Igniatius Conan Doyle on his birth certificate, was born May 22, 1859, in a small flat in Edinburgh. Although his ancestry was Irish and his birthplace Scottish, he lived the major portion of his life in England and, with his manner and actions, epitomized the typical Victorian English gentleman. During adult life he was described as a big friendly man, over six feet tall, about 225 pounds, exuding energy and vitality.

His ancestry is important because of his family's devotion to Catholicism and the family's artistic ability. The grandfather John Doyle, a portrait painter and caricaturist, moved from Ireland to London in the early part of the nineteenth century. To the public, his art, under the nom de crayon "H. B.", was a welcome relief from the harsh and caustic sketches of James Gillray and Thomas Rowlandson.

Grandfather's talent passed to the next generation in his four sons—three of whom achieved notable success in the art world. James became an artist and historian. The next son, Richard, "Dicky Doyle," best known as the artist for *Punch* magazine, designed a cover for it that persisted for many years, and illustrated many children's books. Henry, another son, became director of the National Gallery of Ireland.

Success and recognition, however, were not so apparent with the fourth son, Charles Altamont Doyle, Arthur Conan Doyle's father. At the early age of nineteen he left London and moved to Edinburgh for a minor civil job at the Office of Works. He painted—but in a unique, whimsical, and penetrating manner— dainty childlike figures amidst large animals, in pastel colors. The figures were imaginative, wild-like, often supernatural, and did much to establish a new art genre of child art.

Grandfather John, the three uncles James, Richard, and Henry, and Arthur Conan Doyle gained additional and further distinction by their inclusion in the *Dictionary of National Biography*, and daughter Dame Jean is listed in *Who's Who*—six members of the same lineage so-designated in four generations!

Charles Doyle married Mary Foley, a well-educated woman of French ancestry, in 1855. There were ten children of this union, of whom seven survived; Arthur Conan Doyle was the second child.

At its best, life in the Doyle household was difficult. Doyle's father not only had a meager income, but he found it increasingly difficult to cope with the many stresses of daily living, an increasingly large family, and his self-absorbing, imaginative ideas of art. Progressively, he found solace in alcohol, and the home environment suffered accordingly. As his son wrote later: "My father, I fear, was of little help . . . , for his thoughts were always in the clouds and he had no appreciation of the realities of life. The world, not the family, gets the fruits of genius."[2, p. ll]

Doyle's mother devoted herself to the children's education, telling numerous stories about French and English history of knights and chivalry. Soon there was an offer from Doyle's uncles, "freeing" Doyle from his unhealthy home influence and sending him to the Lancashire Jesuit schools of Hodder and Stonyhurst.

Life at these schools was arduous, austere, and Spartan. "Corporal punishment was severe, and I can speak with feeling as I think few, if any, boys of my time endured more of it."[2, p. 16] It was here, however, that his literary abilities emerged, marked by his editing the college magazine and taking honors in the matriculation examination at London University. Because of his young age (sixteen), he was sent before entering college to another Jesuit school, in Feldkirch, Austria.

What should Doyle do for his career? For three generations his family had been preeminent in the art world. Should he develop these talents or start afresh in another direction? From his mother he had learned the pleasure of a well-told story, often a romantic historical account. Even in grade school he had found reward and great success in storytelling—delighting his classmates by some thrilling tale and then demanding food as a reward before finishing the story. His energy and ambition seemed limitless. Art and literature might offer success, but the poverty of his childhood and his mother's struggles were powerful images. Finally, he decided on medicine. It would be different, a new trend for the family.

Edinburgh had a great university and medical school, and it was geographically convenient. So, at the age of seventeen Doyle began to study medicine at the University of Edinburgh. It was here that he encountered Joseph Bell, a teacher in surgery and the prototype for Sherlock Holmes.

To augment his finances he worked at Sheffield, Ruyton-in-Shropshire, and Birmingham as an assistant to doctors. He also hired on for an exciting seven months as the ship's surgeon on an Arctic whaler in Greenland.

In these Edinburgh years Doyle began to have an interest in photography, due chiefly to his friendship with William K. Burton, later to become a well-known figure in the photography world. As a result, Doyle authored thirteen articles, chiefly in the *British Journal of Photography* (1881–1885). Some were devoted to the photogenic aspects of trips along the slave coast of Africa, the countryside in Southsea, the Isle of Arran, the Isle of Wight, et cetera—all viewed through his bulky Kodak and its wooden tripod—while other articles were concerned with the technical aspects of photography.

During medical school two of Doyle's short stories were published, one in Chambers's *Journal* (1879) and another in *London Society* (1880), as well as two brief medical accounts, one in *The Essentials of Materia Medica and Therapeutics* (1877), another in the *British Medical Journal* (1879).[3] The Bachelor of Medicine degree, M.B., was awarded to him in 1881, at age twenty-two.

After graduation Doyle signed on for yet another sea voyage, this one on a cargo ship along the west coast of Africa. In contrast to the previous trip to the Arctic, which he enjoyed greatly, this trip was uncomfortable, punctuated by a severe hurricane, a fire on board ship, and many tropical illnesses among the crew.

Soon after return Doyle was summoned to a family council in London. The family had reluctantly accepted his choice of a medical career rather than one of an artist; now they wished to help him start his medical practice. Many of their Catholic friends would and could be of great assistance. But at the very mention of the word Catholic, Doyle found himself rebelling, and he was adamant. He had developed an agnostic anti-Catholic feeling at Stonyhurst, reinforced further at the University of Edinburgh. To follow his relatives' proposal would be a moral fraud. "Never will I accept anything which cannot be proved to me. The evils of religion have all come from accepting things which cannot be proved."[2, p. 33]

To enter general practice Doyle joined a classmate, George Budd, who was already well established in the seacoast town of Plymouth and needed an assistant. Doyle's experiences with Budd are humorously related in *The Stark Munro Letters* (1895), a thinly disguised autobiographical account of Doyle's beginning years in medical practice. Doyle's value system, however, contrasted so sharply with that of the unscrupulous, flamboyant Budd that he soon left Budd to practice in Southsea, a suburb of Portsmouth, another seacoast town.

Doyle practiced medicine here from 1882 to 1890. His first task after arrival was to select a location for his home and office. Doyle's method was logical and businesslike, a market survey: "I bought a large shilling map of the town . . . and pinned this out upon the lodging-house table. This done, I set to work to study it, and to arrange a series of walks by which I should pass through every street of the place. . . . On my map I put a cross for every empty house and a circle for every doctor. So at the end of that time I had a complete chart of the whole place, and could see at a glance where there was a possible opening, and what opposition there was at each point."[4, pp. 224-25]

His beginnings of solo practice were slow: "In the first year the Income Tax paper arrived and I filled it up to show that I was not liable. They returned the paper with 'Most unsatisfactory' scrawled across it. I wrote 'I entirely agree' under the words and returned it once more. For this little bit of cheek I was had up before the assessors." Doyle was called before the tax people, both parties finally agreed and "parted with mutual laughter and compliments."[2, p. 70]

The Bachelor of Medicine degree had been awarded to Doyle at graduation; a thesis and examination were required to earn an M.D. degree. Doyle received this, a few weeks before his marriage, writing a thesis: "An Essay Upon the Vasomotor Changes in Tabes Dorsalis" (1885).

Outside his medical practice Doyle was an enthusiastic participant in many Southsea activities: he spoke at numerous public meetings on a variety of subjects—including antivivisection, vigorously supporting animal experimentation, hypnotism, and spiritualism. The organizations he attended included the Literary and Scientific Society, the Hampshire Psychical Society, and the Freemasons. By the third year of practice he was a well-respected member of the community, and his income had reached the comfortable amount of £300 a year. He was also satisfying his literary bent and had published several short stories, which incidentally supplemented his income.

In 1887, the first Sherlock Holmes story, written in Southseas, reached print (*Beeton's Christmas Annual*), after being turned down by several publishers. Its initial appearance did not attract much attention.

But all this was not enough. Despite a happy marriage, an increasing practice, and the publication of his stories, Doyle was restless and wanted more. His ambition, hopes, and versatility were not being satisfied.

At this time, 1890, Robert Koch of Berlin announced a cure for tuberculosis, exciting an enormous interest among the public. Doyle decided, rather precipitously, to visit Berlin and decide for himself if Koch's claims, about which Doyle was dubious, were true. On his return, he wrote several articles helping to debunk the popular conception of a cure for tuberculosis. A significant event on the way to Berlin was his encounter with Malcolm Morris, a successful dermatologist who had previously been a general practitioner. Morris urged Doyle to leave general practice, to specialize and come to London. This meeting resolved Doyle's indecisiveness about general practice; he elected to become an ophthalmologist. But first he had to go to Vienna for several months for specialty training.

After Vienna, Doyle moved to London and set up offices in Wimpole Street. There he waited for patients. But both his consulting room and his waiting room remained empty, giving him abundant time for reflection and further writing. Finally, in 1891 he gave himself completely to literary pursuits. Writing seemed to offer a better, more rewarding future for him than medicine.

Doyle's experiences in medical school and practice served him well and are reflected by many medical references in his stories, particularly those about Sherlock Holmes. More than any other author, he established and popularized the genre of medical fiction and, together with Poe, defined the short story as a literary entity. His strictly medical articles were few; the most extensive was a lecture, "The Romance of Medicine," given for the opening session of St. Mary's Hospital and Medical School in 1910.

By the early 1900s Sherlock Holmes had achieved recognition and enormous popularity, due in no small part by the serialization of his adventures in the *Strand Magazine*. Holmes seized the imagination of countless enthusiastic readers who by their interest changed Sherlock Holmes from a literary figure to a live person. They infused this character with blood and covered it with flesh. For them Sherlock Homes became a real person.

Sherlock Holmes and Dr. Watson have been analyzed and dissected in innumerable ways. It has often been stated that never has so much been written about so little. Holmes's birthday continues to be celebrated each January in New York, and, to paraphrase our Chicago author Vincent Starrett, Sherlock Holmes will never die because he never lived!

Although in popularity, Doyle's other stories, books, plays, and poems pale by comparison with Sherlock Holmes, they greatly outnumber by several times his detective fiction. He wrote many historical accounts, all meticulously researched, such as *The White Company* (1891), a novel about medieval life that he considered his best work. Its sequel, *Sir Nigel* (1906), and *Micah Clarke* (1889), further established him as the best historical writer since Sir Walter Scott. Other historical accounts followed: *The Great Shadow* (1892), about the battle of Waterloo, and the first of his novels concerned with the Napoleonic period; *The Refugees* (1893), a Franco-Canadian novel about the Huguenots; and *Uncle Bernac* (1897), another Napoleonic story. But his most entertaining and captivating novels in this group were the rollicking and humorous memoirs of an imaginary Napoleonic officer, Brigadier Etienne Gerard, *The Exploits of Brigadier Gerard* (1896) and *The Adventures of Gerard* (1903).

Doyle's historical writings continued in a more serious note with *The Great Boer War* (1900), about the conflict during which he had served as a senior physician in Langman's Hospital at Bloemfontein, and an official account of the British in World War I.[5] In 1902 Doyle was knighted, it was announced, for his services in the Boer War.

There were books and stories about Doyle's three trips to America and other travels.[6] He was a frequent correspondent to newspapers, particularly *The Times*, and poured forth opinions on many social and political subjects: divorce, women's suffrage, new weapons for World War I, a tunnel between England and France, et cetera. His convictions about fairness and human justice prompted him to contest the convictions and imprisonments of George Edalji[7] and Oscar Slater[8] to publicize the Congo atrocities, and to defend Roger Casement in his trial for treason.

In 1912, Doyle opened another genre of fiction with an imaginary story of prehistoric monsters and life in the Mato Grosse of western Brazil in *The Lost World*, developing the character of Professor George E. Challenger, later to appear in *The Land of Mist* (1925). Other science fiction followed,[9] stories that easily match or excel those of H. G. Wells.

Doyle maintained a lifelong interest in sports. The Sherlock Holmes stories contain nearly 150 references to various sports. As a child in the slums of Edinburgh Doyle learned rough-and-tumble fight, often defending the rights of the indigent children against the taunting remarks of the nearby rich children. In his school days at Stonyhurst he excelled in swimming, rugby, cricket, soccer, hockey, and ice skating.

At the University of Edinburgh Doyle became a forward on the rugby team and continued boxing. This expertise gained him respect on his Arctic whaling expedition, when he boxed with the crew.

Years later this love of boxing was manifested by several stories, the best known being *Rodney Stone* (1896) and the novella *The Croxley Master* (1907). The first is a blustering, fast-moving tale of bare-knuckled fights in the early nineteenth century. The second, *The Croxley Master*, almost autobiographical, is about a medical student in a small mining town who fights one of the "locals" only to learn after he wins that he has fought a professional fighter. These stories and Doyle's exuberant enthusiasm for sports helped to make boxing an acceptable activity, contrary to society's previous viewpoint, which Doyle viewed as "degenerate" dandyism. Doyle boxed with many of the first-rate amateurs of his day and knew many of the celebrated boxers such as John L. Sullivan and Tommy Burns. His expertise was recognized later when he was invited (1909) to the United States to referee the heavyweight championship between Jack Johnson and Jim Jeffries, an opportunity he declined.

In 1893 Doyle's wife developed tuberculosis, and the couple sought the salubrious climate of Davos in eastern Switzerland. There is a plaque today in Davos near the Hotel Belvedere indicating the sanatorium where Robert Louis Stevenson, Louise Doyle, and Thomas Mann were hospitalized in the same building but at different times.

In this mountainous area the restless Doyle began exploring winter sports as his wife rested. The Swiss relied chiefly on toboggans, sleds, and skates for their winter travel and sports. But Doyle had recently read about the explorations in Norway by Fridtjof Nansen and was intrigued by his description of skiing, essentially unknown in Europe. Together with two local townspeople, the Branger brothers, he obtained skis, and the three began exploring their use and developing techniques for climbing and descending the nearby mountains. Their most famous trip, about fourteen miles, was over the Maienfelder Furka, a mountain pass that separated Davos from Arosa, its neighbor to the north. The trip down this steep mountain was perilous, and although it was successfully managed by the Branger brothers, most of Doyle's descent was on the seat of his pants, a tribute to his English Harris tweeds, he wrote. Nonetheless, the pass had been conquered, and Doyle wrote several articles about this adventure and about skiing.[10] The interest he stimulated plus the natural advantages of Davos combined to popularize both skiing and Davos. He also developed a golf course at Davos. Today, just east of the Eisstadium there is a park dedicated to Doyle, "The Perfect Pattern of a Gentleman."

Doyle's interest in virtually every sport was sustained and active for many years, particularly in cricket (he toured with the British team), and golf. About the time of his knighthood he made a balloon ascent, drifting about twenty-five miles, and expressed an interest in parachute jumping. An early automobile enthusiast and owner of two automobiles and a motorcycle, he found road racing absorbing.

Doyle received his highest compliment in 1916 when he was asked to be chairman of the Olympic games in Berlin which was, of course, cancelled by the advent of World War I.

We now come to the final part of Doye's life and one that has aroused the most controversy—Spiritualism. Without consideration of this, no analysis of Doyle is complete. This interest surfaced first in 1880, lay dormant for many years, and finally reached overt expression in 1916 in his public adoption of this movement and his total dedication to it for the last fourteen years of his life.

Is Doyle's acceptance of Spiritualism inexplicable and irrational? Why and how should a man, so well educated, so sophisticated, and so critical believe in the supernatural? To some, his persistence in its existence, his faith, and his unwavering beliefs were illogical. They exemplify the dogma and absolute faith that he had found so objectionable about Catholicism. Of his Jesuit school he wrote: "I remember that when . . . I heard Father Murphy, a great fierce Irish priest, declare that there was sure damnation for every one outside the Church, I looked upon him with horror, and to that moment I trace the first rift which had grown into such a chasm between me and those who were my guides."[2, pp. 20-21]

Doyle's years at the University of Edinburgh stressed the scientific approach, the experimental proof, the philosophies of Thomas Huxley, John Tyndall, Herbert Spencer, and John Stuart Mill. Students felt the strong sweeping current of these thoughts, questioning old beliefs and developing new attitudes. Doyle reflected this stance in a later question: "Is religion the only domain of thought which is non-progressive, and to be referred forever to a standard set two thousand years ago?"[4, p. 21] One can speculate further that the vivid memories aroused by his parents' lives, their poverty-stricken state and his mother's unhappiness, none of which were alleviated by their faith, helped him to proclaim his agnosticism. His mother did not remonstrate: she departed from Catholicism herself in subsequent years.

Doyle attempted to build upon his repudiation of the contemporary religions and reached a new belief: that death does not end all and that the human soul survives death, that there is another world, and that some type of communication exists between these two worlds.

To enlarge his knowledge of Spiritualism, Doyle entered the arena of the supernatural—haunted houses, sepulchral voices, levitation, mysterious sounds, even spirit photography. He explored and examined all of them as carefully as he could. Many of these psychical phenomena he accepted as real. The intensity of Doyle's efforts for Spiritualism borders on the fanatic. His devotion compelled him to make converts, and he became a vigorous crusader. He gave countless lectures, attended seances, and wrote numerous books and pamphlets,[11] devoting himself without respite to this task. He and his family toured Great Britain, Australia, America, South Africa, America again, and then Europe—more than 50,000 miles.

It was inevitable that Doyle should encounter Harry Houdini, the great magician. Both of them were interested in supernatural occurrences, although each was convinced that they were produced by different methods. Houdini maintained that he could produce any "psychic" phenomenon that Doyle thought was caused by spirits, that he could duplicate and explain any of the seances reported by Doyle, and that everything claimed by Doyle was pure bunk. Doyle refused to yield—there were spirits, and as for Houdini's talents, well, they were supernatural, that's all, and thank you very much. Only Houdini's death[12,13] brought an end to the controversy.

In his seances Doyle firmly believed that he had received messages from the dead, including his mother, his brother Innes, and his first son, Kingsley. He continued his efforts despite the onset of cardiac problems. In the midst of his campaign he had a myocardial infarct and died quietly July 7, 1930. His philosophy about death had been expressed previously:

> You know what I think of death. It is the most glorious improvement upon life, a shedding of all that is troublous and painful and a gaining of grand new powers which are a supreme happiness to the individual.[14]

References

1. Blau P. Telephone conversation with author, April 1996.
2. Doyle AC. Memories and Adventures. London, Hodder & Stoughton, 1924.
3. ACD [sic]. Gelseminum as a poison, letter to the editor. Br Med J. 2:483, 1879.
4. Doyle AC. The Stark Munro Letters. London, Longmans, Green & Co., 1895.
5. Doyle AC. The British Campaign in France and Flanders 1914. London, Hodder & Stoughton, 1916. Continues with five other volumes similarly titled: 1915 (published in 1917). 1916 (1918), 1917 (1919), January to July 1918 (1919), and July to November 1918 (1920).
6. Doyle AC. The Wanderings of a Spiritualist. London, Hodder & Stoughton, 1921; Doyle, AC: Our American Adventure. London, Hodder & Stoughton, 1923; Doyle, AC: Our Second American Adventure. London, Hodder & Stoughton, 1924; Doyle, AC: Our African Winter. London, John Murray, 1929.
7. Doyle AC. The Story of George Edalji. T Harrison Roberts, 158 Fleet St., London, 1907. Also, Doyle, AC. The Story of Mr. George Edalji. Whittington-Egan, Rand M, eds. London, Grey House Books, 1985.
8. Doyle AC. The Case of Oscar Slater. London, Hodder & Stoughton, 1912.
9. Doyle AC. The Lost World. London, Hodder & Stoughton, 1912. Professor Challenger reappeared in The Poison Belt (1913), and The Land of Mist (1925), and in several short stories; Dr. Maracot was the main character in The Maracot Deep (1929).
10. Kittle CF. Down the slopes with Conan Dole at Davos: The birth of skiing. J Arthur Conan Doyle Soc 4:88–103, 1993.
11. Doyle AC. The New Revelation. London, Hodder & Stoughton, 1918; Doyle AC. The Vital Message. London, Hodder & Stoughton, 1919; Doyle AC. The Wanderings of a Spiritualist; and many pamphlets and other books.
12. Doyle AC. The Edge of the Unknown. New York, G.P. Putnam's Sons, 1930.
13. Ernst BML and Carrington H. Houdini and Conan Doyle: The Story of a Strange Friendship. New York, Albert and Charles Boni, 1932.
14. Doyle AC. Letter to Lily Loder-Symonds, May 13, 1915. In: Nordon, P: Sir Arthur Conan Doyle: L'Homme et L'Oeuvre. Paris, Didier, 1964, p. 170.

POETRY, ADOLESCENCE, AND SUICIDE

L. D. HANKOFF, M.D.

(Spring 1984, pp. 7–12)

Dr. Hankoff, now retired, most recently as Chairman of Psychiatry, Elizabeth General Medical Center, Elizabeth, New Jersey, wrote this paper as an extension of his work and interest in suicide. Following internship and psychiatric residency at Kings County Hospital Center, working in a newly developed program of emergency psychiatry, he established at the Center the first suicide prevention service in New York City. His interests in these areas led in 1968 to one of the first textbooks in the then emerging area of emergency psychiatry, and in 1979, Suicide: Theory and Clinical Aspects. *His research writings in various areas include psychopharmacology, community psychiatry, and history of medicine and psychiatry. These latter interests appear in* The Pharos *in "Poetry, Adolescence, and Suicide (Spring 1984, pp 7–12) and in a book,* Christians and Jews: The First Century. *Dr. Hankoff was elected to AΩA at the University of Maryland in 1951.*

THIS INQUIRY INTO THE SUBJECT OF adolescent creativity and suicide was stimulated by a study of the biographies and works of three poets who took their own lives: one in the eighteenth century, **Thomas Chatterton**, who took arsenic when he was seventeen years old, and two in the mid-twentieth century, **Vivienne Loomis**, who hanged herself at fourteen, and **Sylvia Plath**, who after taking a near lethal overdose at age twenty asphyxiated herself at thirty.

In his masterwork *Scienza Nuova*, Giambattista Vico argued that poetic style preceded prose in the evolution of speech, reasoning that prehistoric man was first mute and then acquired speech through grunts and rhythmic and onomatopoeic utterances. Vico might have found some support for his imaginative formulation in the talent of another eighteenth-century writer, who seems to have produced poetry before he wrote prose. Thomas Chatterton, born November 20, 1752, in his extraordinary precocity was the poetic equivalent of Mozart, born just four years later. The details of the life of Thomas Chatterton and the 600 pages of literary production that he left behind are hardly believable, and yet every detail has been verified. His remarkable abilities as a child were noticed by his family, and his older sister commented, "He had been gloomy from the time he began to learn, but we remark'd he was more cheerful after he began to write poetry."[1] vol. 2, p. 1138

In 1763 his first published poem appeared, entitled "On the Last Epiphany, or Christ Coming to Judgment," a work dating to his deep involvement with religion before age ten.[1, vol. 2, p. 688] The theme of death and resurrection was to persist throughout his short life. During his seventeenth year he composed a will and stated suicide plan in which he would die on the Feast of the Resurrection. He outlived this mock will by five months.

The prodigious output of Chatterton continued to the day of his death, and his 600 pages are apparently but a small portion of his efforts. He apparently destroyed verses constantly, tearing them into small bits and scattering them about his room.[2] He is most well known for the Rowley works, named for their pretended author, Thomas Rowley, a fifteenth-century parish priest.[3] These remarkable poems, stories, and plays were written in gothic penmanship, utilizing the language of the fifteenth century, and framed in the remnants of records and artifacts found by Chatterton as he rummaged in an abandoned church storage area. He illustrated his Rowley productions with heraldic devices and diagrams of the imagined Bristol settings of his characters. When Chatterton managed at age sixteen to acquire three patrons for his literary efforts, he extended his hoax to one of them and presented the patron with an elaborate coat of arms and lineage dating back to the Norman conquest. He even nourished the vanity of his gullible patron with a poem written by an imaginary ancestor. Among the Rowley works is a verse play of some 1365 lines entitled Ælla, the name of a Saxon chieftain who fought the Danes. This character, whose nuptials were interrupted and unconsummated as a result of the invasion by the Danes, goes on to many adventures and finally commits suicide because of the mistaken appearance of infidelity on the part of his new bride.

The unconsummated relationship appears again in a short story, "The Unfortunate Fathers," written in the last year of Chatterton's life. In it a sincere young man rejected by his beloved shoots himself, leaving a note that "suicide is sometimes a noble insanity of the soul."[1,vol. 1, p. 445] In the case of "The Unfortunate Fathers," a major factor in the unhappy outcome is the deceitful behavior on the part of the suicidal youth's father, who had cheated the father of the son's beloved. It may be noted that in both Ælla and "The Unfortunate Fathers," the deaths are a result of misunderstandings, and a large element of deceit by others contributes to the unnecessary suicides.

If Chatterton was not already preoccupied with suicide, certainly his thoughts were spurred on by the suicide of Peter Smith, the brother of a dear friend. Chatterton wrote "Elegy on Mr. Wm. Smith" (at first under the mistaken impression that it was his friend who had killed himself). The poem responds to

his sense of loss and relates William's supposed death to the attitudes of his rejecting relatives.

> Ye Callous breasted Brutes in human form
> Have you not often boldly wishd him dead?[1,vol.1, p. 353]

What was the element of deceit and rejection by the father figures in the life
of Chatterton? His own father had died before he was born, but he was continually
exposed to despotic and unsympathetic authorities. His patrons, when he was
able to obtain them, exploited and humiliated him. His earlier work as an apprentice tied him to writing ledgers for twelve hours a day and bitterly frustrated his creative needs. His efforts to obtain the interest of the famous literary
figure Horace Walpole were frustrated and left him with an impression of being exploited again. He expected fame and recognition for his works and in his
lifetime barely experienced recognition. The figures of unconsummated love in
Ælla and "The Unfortunate Fathers" may represent his own feelings regarding his strivings.

The bitterest affront to Chatterton consisted of a series of reversals in the last
few months of his life as he attempted to gain the attention and approval of influential individuals in relation to his works. Walpole rejected him. An influential
patron gave him a pittance for articles. A potential patron died suddenly. There
was little left for Chatterton, and on August 24, 1770, rather than eat the food
offered him by his charitable landlady he obtained some arsenic from the apothecary on the pretense of exterminating rats and died in his room, surrounded by
scattered bits of torn manuscripts.

Vivienne Loomis (1959–1973) never lived to acknowledge her ambition as
a poet. In *Vivienne,* a popularized presentation of her life and writings, this
young girl's account of the months leading up to her death by hanging at age fourteen years, five months, is analyzed by a psychiatrist, John E. Mack, together with
her writing teacher, Holly Hickler.[4] The youngest of three siblings, she early
presented unusual expressive talents in writing. These talents were encouraged
by her middle-class, intellectually oriented family, and the present biography
contains forty short poems, apparently just a portion of works written from
about age eleven to the time of her death. In addition, her inner world is reflected in school compositions and letters, particularly those to a favorite teacher
who left her school at the beginning of 1973. She was unambivalently attached
to the teacher and to her father, the two important older males in her life. The
first hint of suicidal ideation is to be found in her diary of November 1971
when she writes anticipating the teacher's departure:

> He is going to leave me. Forever?????
> It seems like I ought to
> die now while the going's
> good.[4, p. 34]

Her father, an embattled Unitarian minister, had more than his share of congregational tensions, which inevitably washed over into his family life. He and his stresses were the themes of several of her poems.

From Vivienne's poems, letters to her teacher, diary entries, and suicidal behavior, it is evident that she experienced painful feelings of depression from about age twelve onward. Most of her poems, letters, and some of her suicidal acts were freely communicated to those close to her. A poem written in February 1972 entitled "Patterns of My Lifetime" speaks of

> Emotional depression
> Existing, at first unobserved:
> An old forgotten sword
> Suddenly glistening and sharp! [4, p. 41]

In an application to a "new progressive, innovative high school" she was asked to discuss a book she found exciting. On Elie Wiesel's *The Accident,* she commented:

> I am drawn to death.
> Like the man in the book, this stage in my life is one of depression.
> I look forward to dying. [4, pp. 52–53]

In a school book report, ironically overdue, she elaborated on her reaction to Wiesel's work, adding, "I have often thought of death as a retreat." [4, p. 53] Her depression was obvious to herself if not to others, and her expressive ability enabled very explicit references to her feelings. For example, on April 11, 1973, she wrote in her diary, "I am worthless. . . . I need people and there aren't any who care. It takes tolerance not to give in to death." [4, p. 63] In September 1973 she read aloud in class (in her new school) a composition about suicide. [4, p. 100]

The authors of *Vivienne* have striven hard (and unconvincingly, to my mind) to account for her clinical depression in terms of psychological trauma. There were a variety of life events of negative impact: her maternal grandfather died when she was four-and-one-half, her paternal, when she was five; the family moved when she was seven; and in the second grade an orthodontist fitted her for dental appliances, following which she experienced "four or five years of pain and humiliation." [4, p. 10] Her early school experiences were reported to be unpleasant.

In searching for explanations of Vivienne's depression, the authors of her biography reach beyond the immediate interpersonal environment to broader sociocultural factors. They state, "Adolescents are daily confronted with overpowering instances of corruption in the social and political world;" [4, p. 160] and, "The failure to protect the young from bombardment with the shattering failures of our generation . . . results in lowering the threshold of vulnerability." [4, p. 186] They conclude, "The American culture in which Vivienne was growing up was particularly destructive to a child of her sensitivities and vulnerabilities, and contributed ultimately to her death." [4, p. 157] The precocious Chatterton, writing before age ten, often manifested the same kind of death preoccupations as Vivienne's, without benefit of American culture in the 1960s.

Sylvia Plath (1932–1963) left her mark as a poet who captured the disturbing imagery of her own time.[5-7] Her diaries as well as her poetic and prose works contain the anguished expressions of her periods of deep depression and the presages of her suicide. When she committed suicide at age thirty she was at the height of her career and had just completed to her own great satisfaction an outstanding book of poetry, *Ariel*.[8] She had been troubled by depression from her teens on, and was treated with electroconvulsive therapy prior to her nearly fatal suicide attempt on August 24, 1953. The attempt and subsequent psychiatric treatment are a basis for much of the content of her thinly fictionalized autobiographical novel, *The Bell Jar*.[9] At age nineteen, with ominous portent, Plath asked in her diary why Virginia Woolf, Sarah Teasdale, "or the other brilliant women," committed suicide.[10, p. 62] Her suicidal ruminations prior to the attempt, quite explicit in her diaries, were apparently unnoticed even by those very close to her. For example, on November 3, 1952 she writes in her diary about wanting to commit suicide. "I am afraid. I am not solid, but hollow. I feel behind my eyes a numb, paralyzed cavern, a pit of hell, a mimicking nothingness. . . . I want to kill myself.[10, p. 60] Writing to her mother two days later and to her brother the next day, she is breezy, solicitous of her mother's welfare, and flippant as she closes the second letter with, "Ah me, life is grim. If I live till Xmas, it will be a miracle."[11, p. 96] An entry in June 1953 speaks of "ending it all" with a razor, part of a wish "to crawl back into the womb."[10, p. 84] In that same month she writes to her mother and brother of her interests and excitement in her developing career, barely touching on her troubled state. "I have been very ecstatic, horribly depressed, shocked, elated, enlightened, and enervated—all of which goes to make up living very hard and newly."[11, p. 117]

The contrast between the facade she presented to her mother and her inner thoughts as revealed in her journals is so apparent as to suggest deliberate irony in her words to the former.[7] For example, as she was struggling with the depression leading to her 1953 serious suicide attempt, a journal entry on May 14, reads, "It was good to walk faceless and talk to myself again, to ask where I was going, and who I was, and to realize that I had no idea, that all I could tell you was my name, and not my heritage."[10, pp. 79-80] Addressing her mother in a letter dated May 13 and 15 as "Dearest Progenitor," she writes, "I never know anyone long before I start holding forth with pride about Grammy and Grampy and you and Warren . . . to affirm my rich heritage all the more!"[11, p. 114]

The poem "Suicide off Egg Rock" (1959) describes a death by drowning, a method she had unsuccessfully attempted. "The Hanging Man" (1960) a six-line poem, presents thoughts about suicide stemming from "vulturous bore-dom."[8, p. 69] "A Birthday Present" (1962) reflects her own previous unsuccess-ful suicide efforts.

> After all I am alive only by accident.
> I would have killed myself gladly that time any possible
> way.[8, p. 42]

In "Edge," possibly her last poem before suicide a week later in her kitchen, she sums up the need for surcease:

> The woman is perfected.
> Her dead
> Body wears the smile of
> accomplishment.[8, p. 84]

Most of the forty-odd poems of the volume *Ariel* were written in a burst of creative energy in the fall of 1962. Was it a hypomanic state? The last of these poems is dated just six days before February 11, 1963, when she extinguished her life by putting her head in the oven with all the gas jets on. One of the most arresting of the *Ariel* poems is "Daddy," in which the speaker addresses a Nazi father, killer of Jews, whose death she notes with satisfaction.[8, p. 49–51] Alluding in "Daddy" to her own previous suicide attempt she starkly poses the desper-ate wish to rejoin the dead parent, which is driving the daughter to suicide:

> At twenty I tried to die
> And get back, back, back to you.[8, p. 51]

Although the Nazi "Daddy" bore only the vaguest resemblance to Otto, her father, who died when she was eight, her diaries reveal a vivid connection to these same thoughts. As a Smith College freshman in 1951 she described in-tense ambivalence for her Germanic forbears and particularly her unresolved feel-ings for her "dead father who is somewhere in you."[10, p. 25] Was this an introject that her depressed self needed to attack in order to see herself "perfected"? Plath's preoccupation with the Holocaust and the other deathly images of her era may be a partial explanation for her choice of suicide (death in an oven) as her own final solution, combined with a severe affective disorder.

* * * * *

Most patients with primary or major affective disorders do not commit sui-cide. In long-term studies of patients with affective disorder, the rate of suicide for lifetime follow-up has been found to be, at most, 20 percent. In the case of our suicidal adolescent poets, even if we were able to establish clearly the ex-istence of affective disorder, we are faced with the question of why these par-ticular individuals chose suicide.

The issue of suicide in these talented expressive adolescents might be prof-itably approached from the vantage of the general issue of adolescent preoccupation with death. During puberty the abstract ability needed for the concept of death is achieved. The fact of death, which comes as a discovery to the school-age child, receives its full philosophical meaning in adolescence. In the development that follows, the adolescent struggles with values and beliefs and related issues of life's future. Inhelder and Piaget have put it very lucidly: "The adolescent differs from the child above all in that he thinks beyond the present."[13, p. 339] Adolescence is a time for the individual to look far into the future and envision a "life program."[13, p. 342] This future orientation and life planning of the adolescent brings the issue of the end of life constantly into his or her awareness. The issue of death may not be explicit in the adolescent's thinking, but its importance cannot be overlooked in his developing belief system. Kiell notes that of the more than 200 autobiographies or journals cited in *The Universal Experience of Adolescence,* over a third show meaningful concern with death or suicidal impulses.[14, p. 720]

As a solution to a personal crisis, suicide has sometimes acquired a heroic and romantic meaning for the adolescent. For example, following the 1774 publication of *The Sorrows of Young Werther,* Goethe's story of a young man who shoots himself over an unhappy love affair,[15] countless romantic suicides occurred throughout Europe. The deaths were attributed to the book's influence, and its distribution was banned in Copenhagen and Leipzig. The romantic story had definite autobiographical elements, but the suicidal outcome was modeled after a friend of Goethe and not himself. In his volume of verse *A Shropshire Lad,* A. E. Housman (1859–1936), describes the melancholy of youth.[16] In Lyric XIX, "To An Athlete Dying Young," he captures the irony, and romance, of a young man's preference for death.[16, p. 40] In Lyric XLIV we hear him address a dead youth:

> Shot? so quick, so clean an ending?
> Oh that was right, lad, that was brave:
> Yours was not an ill for mending, 'Twas best to take it to the grave.[16, p. 83]

In Lyric XLV he says:

> And if your hand or foot offend you,
> Cut it off, lad, and be whole;
> But play the man, stand up and end you,
> When your sickness is your soul.[16, p. 85]

Vivienne's last poem discovered after her death almost echoes Housman.

> When you are
> Too weary
> To go on
> And life strikes
> Such a finalizing chord,
> You have a choice.[4, p. 120]

This youthful impulse to a swift and fatal solution finds its seeming opposite in the other pole of life. In the aged, death is defied rather than romanticized as a solution. In Tennyson's "Ulysses" we have:

> Old age hath yet his honour and his toil;
> Death closes all: but something ere the end,
> Some work of noble note, may yet be done.[17]

More close to our time we have Dylan Thomas (1914–1953) speaking:

> Old age should burn and rave at close of day;
> Rage, rage against the dying of the light.[18]

Preliterate societies present the fact of death to pre-adults in the form of initiation rites, which act out the passage to adulthood through the symbolism of death and rebirth. The initiate who has arrived at the proper age undergoes a ritual first of separation and seclusion from the tribe and then of termination of childhood existence in a scene of terrifying noise and darkness symbolic of primeval chaos. The initiate is presumed destroyed during this transitional ordeal and is next magically reconstituted and resurrected. The initiate who is able to survive the ordeal passes on to rebirth and admission into full tribal membership status. The childhood self has died to make way for the emergence of a privileged adult. Closer to our own culture, this same symbolic process is to be discerned in the initiations into the classical mystery religions, for example, the cult of Isis.

Since time immemorial the adolescent has been subjected by physiology, folklore, and culture to rituals and experiences of initiation and transition. The scenario of death and resurrection is an apt metaphor for the transition to adulthood via processes of death of the profane and childhood self and rebirth as an adult, an initiate and respected participant in society.

The ritual and symbolism of initiation adumbrate the key psychological issues of modern youth: (a) the passionate need for entry into the adult world; (b) the ordeal, trial, and wounds of transition; (c) the considerable likelihood and fear of failure; (d) farewell and death to child self; and (e) entry and welcome to a new status.

Plath's thoughts on her serious suicide attempt, during which for three days she lay comatose in a crawl space where she had gone to die, evokes the symbolism of primitive initiation. In her diary on February 19, 1956 she wrote, "I feel like Lazarus. . . . Being dead, I rose up again, and even resort to the mere sensation value of being suicidal, of getting so close, of coining out of the grave with the scars and the marring mark on my cheek."[10, p. 99] She pursues this theme of ritual death and rebirth in her poem "Lady Lazarus."[8, p. 6]

Chatterton initiated his effort at preparing for an adult career as poet by a phase of seclusion and separation in the muniment room of St. Mary Redcliffe, where he literally acquired a new language and studied the ancient origins of his people. Thomas recreated this image of Saxon times from the artifacts he uncovered in the church storage room.

He emerged from his marginal phase with a new language, prepared to participate in the death of his child self and rebirth as an adult poet. Here the progression of his initiation ends. Some few individuals in preliterate societies never complete initiation and remain all their lives in the limbo status of the initiated. We know that the primitive tribal ordeal may be fatal, as is college hazing occasionally.

The career setbacks for Chatterton appear closely related to his suicide. The adult world of literary fame and accomplishment beckoned and rebuffed the proud genius who had already labeled himself a poet in his letters to his mother. Thomas was exploited and rejected by the elders, despaired of entering the circle of his literary peers, and in pride and rage ended his life.

Perhaps reflecting the mentality of another century, Chatterton associated his death with thoughts of resurrection and the recognition that eluded him in life. A lengthy suicide letter, considered a provocation by some, promised his suicide on the Feast of the Resurrection. His actual suicide was some months later. Perhaps more significant, however, is that first recorded poem of his youthful career, "On the Last Epiphany, or Christ Coming to Judgment," where he writes:

> For now the aweful Hour is come, When ev'ry Tenant of the Tomb,
> Must rise and take his everlasting
> Doom.[1 vol 2, p. 688]

In terms of transition, Sylvia Plath made her serious suicide attempt at age twenty, on the very threshold of the literary career she had fully committed herself to. Vivienne was not yet at the transition to career building but was stunned by the adult issues forced upon her. In particular, issues around sexual intimacy weighed on her, in the form of unwanted overtures from boys. Her sister, a year and a half her senior, had more casual attitudes, and differences between the two led to one of Vivienne's several suicide attempts prior to her fatal act. Vivienne expressed her fear of failure in the adult role in a poem written just before her fourteenth birthday, "Dreams of Reality." She portrayed herself mounted on a coal-black stallion, asking:

> Why is it
> That you suddenly know
> With certainty
> That you cannot stay astride?[4, p. 76]

These three young creative poets resonated to the death and rebirth themes of rites of passage. They seemed stimulated by the rich imagery and symbolism of a vital transition, their suicidal urges spurred by ritual dramas. It would be of interest to know the impact of adolescent initiation rituals on rates of adolescent suicide in preliterate societies. No empirical study clearly addresses the question of the correlation of adolescent initiation rites and suicide rates. In a phenomenon as sociologically and psychologically complex as suicidal behavior it is not anticipated that a simple answer will emerge. High rates of adolescent suicide have been reported among some preliterate tribes, for example, the Trobriand Islanders,[19] the Matako Indians of Argentina.[20] A case is cited of a Zambian Ndembu bridegroom committing suicide after failing to consummate his marriage ritual.[21] A study of sixty-nine primitive societies showed that suicide rates were consistently higher in (a) stable agricultural (versus hunting-gathering) societies, (b) societies customarily very open or restrained in emotional expression (versus moderate expression), and (c) societies emphasizing individual pride and shame.[22] In the case of the last correlate, the emphasis on negative emotional controls, it might be conjectured that intense initiatory ritual experiences would contribute to the emphasis on shame and pride and be associated with higher suicide rates among those entering the initiate age category. The issue, however, awaits further study.

Finally, there is the question of the poet's gift for self-expression, even insight, in the face of suicide. Is there no relief to be gained through the creative act of imaginative self-exploration and artistic projection? Do poetic insights spare their writers any need to live out their inner lives? Do not the poetic works that provide us the readers with catharsis and inspiration offer the same enhancing effect to their authors? All three poets considered here produced poetry nearly to their last day, providing literary equivalents of suicide notes in their final or near final works. Plath and Vivienne had contemplated suicide for years and made many plans and efforts in that direction. The ability to explore death and suicide themes does not appear to have deterred our three poets but, to the contrary, to have advanced the attraction of an early death, much like Housman's Shropshire lad. The final suicidal act seems to have been facilitated by poetic introspection.

Obviously, the artist is not immune to depression, and the creative act is not defense against the painful effects of the illness. The issue of self-expression is relevant to its value in psychotherapy, particularly in relation to suicidal patients. Plath had had considerable psychotherapy, prior to her attempt at age twenty as well as before her fatal act. In the privacy of her journal she asked:

> Fury jams the gullet and spreads poison, but, as soon as I start to write, dissipates, flows out into the figure of the letters: writing as therapy? (dated August 27, 1958).[10, p. 256]

In the searching biography, *Vivienne,* the authors suggest that psychotherapy might have been helpful.[4, p. 224] The actual description of the milieu of

Vivienne, however, her free expression through poetry and letters to those near her, the great emphasis on social awareness of her parents, and high valuation placed on creativity point up the possible negative effects of self-expression at critical periods. Perhaps the term *self-expression* is too broad to permit any simple generalization on its therapeutic value. I suggest that an ideology (or caricature) of unspecified self-expression has little to offer in correcting the desperate needs of the severely depressed patient and may even aggravate the condition, as does evocative psychotherapy sometimes in the frankly or potentially psychotic patient. In so concluding I am not denying the enormous and irreplaceable role of the creative arts in fostering growth and health. The positive impact of creative and artistic performances and participation that we experience in everyday living reflects, I believe, the regenerative and recreative power of self-expression in the normal state of mind. When a psychopathological state of mind prevails, however, and psychotherapy is instituted, the role of artistic expression becomes complicated. The potential for both good and ill exists when the artistic impulse is harnessed to a state of illness. Artistic self-expression that might afford relief for one individual may heighten the painful feelings of another. The artistic urge appears capable of aggravating the symptoms of a susceptible individual, who might be better served by a respite from self-expression.

References

1. Chatterton T. The Complete Works of Thomas Chatterton. Taylor DS, ed. Oxford, Clarendon Press, 1971, 2 vols.
2. Nevill JC. Thomas Chatterton. Port Washington, New York, Kennikat Press, 1970.
3. Chatterton T. Poems, Supposed to Have Been Written at Bristol by Thomas Rowley, 1777. Menston, England, Scolar Press, 1969 (facsimile).
4. Mack JE and Hickler H. Vivienne: The Life and Suicide of an Adolescent Girl. Boston, Little, Brown & Co., 1981.
5. Barnard CK. Sylvia Plath. Boston, Twayne Publishers, 1978.
6. Butscher E. Sylvia Plath, Method and Madness. New York, Seabury Press, 1976.
7. Lane G, ed. Sylvia Plath: New Views on the Poetry. Baltimore, Johns Hopkins University Press, 1979.
8. Plath S. Ariel. New York, Harper & Row, Publishers, 1961.
9. Plath S. The Bell Jar. New York, Harper & Row, Publishers, 1971.
10. Hughes T and Mccullough F, eds. The Journals of Sylvia Plath. New York, Dial Press, 1982.
11. Plath S. Letters Home: Correspondence 1950–1963. Plath AS, ed. New York, Harper & Row, Publishers, 1975.
12. Plath S. The Collected Poems. Hughes, T, ed., New York, Harper & Row, Publishers, 1981, p. 115.
13. Inhelder B and Piaget J. The Growth of Logical Thinking from Childhood to Adolescence: An Essay on the Construction of Formal Operational Structures. Parsons A and Milgram S, trans. New York, Basic Books, 1958.

14. Kiell N. The Universal Experience of Adolescence. New York, International Universities Press, 1964.

15. Goethe JW. The Sorrows of Young Werther. Mayer E and Bogan L, trans. New York, Random House, 1971.

16. Housman AE. A Shropshire Lad. New York, Three Sirens Press, 1932.

17. Tennyson A. Ulysses. In Scholes R, Klaus CH and Silverman M. Elements of Literature. New York, Oxford University Press, 1978, p. 609.

18. Thomas D. Do not go gentle into that good night. In Collected Poems. New York, New Directions, 1957, p. 128.

19. Malinowski B. Magic, Science and Religion: And Other Essays. Garden City, New York, Doubleday & Co., 1955.

20. Metraux A. Suicide among the Matako of the Argentine Gran Chaco, America Indigena 3:199–209, 1943.

21. Turner VW. The Drums of Affliction: A Study of Religious Processes among the Ndembu of Zambia. Oxford, Clarendon Press, 1968.

22. Smith OH and Hackathorn L. Some social and psychological factors related to suicide in primitive societies: a crosscultural comparative study. Suicide and Life Threatening Behavior 12:195–211, 1982.

o.d.

PEGGY HANSEN, M.D.
(Winter 1989, p. 43)

better to be cold
and cruelly efficient
better to calculate the dose
to ascertain oblivion
—better than the tubes,
the lights,
the shouting torment
of the life savers
and their instruments,
insistent on salvation
of a soul already relegated
to the dead zone,
already eaten through
with dry despair
and creeping weariness

better to be thorough,
quiet and cunning,
not to leave a trail
of false starts,
hints and innuendos

better not to reach out
in that last moment
of hesitant uncertainty
better not to cry
for help

HEALING AND HAVOC IN THE WORKS OF T.S. ELIOT AND WILLIAM CARLOS WILLIAMS

JONATHAN D. SCHWARTZ
(Fall 1991, pp. 35–37)

IT IS LONDON, 1917. An American in town, a Harvard man with family credentials, watches the Europe he has been reared to adore annihilate itself quickly and thoroughly. He reads of killings, witnesses social trauma, finds himself at a loss. He does not like what he sees or hears. From the hours between his work at the bank and sleep, from his voice and hands come verses. They start with an invitation.

> Let us go then, you and I,
> When the evening is spread out against the sky
> Like a patient etherised upon a table;[1]

More dirge than sonnet, *The Love Song of J. Alfred Prufrock* is T. S. Eliot's first published effort to describe the suffocation, the emotional grinding to a halt of his treasured Western culture in the face of the Great War. He writes of a dreary, stagnant world, narrated by a representative inhabitant, an individual overwhelmed by his own uncertainty, limitations, and impotence. It is significant that the writing begins with a reference to medicine and its intended beneficiaries. The form is disruptive. The first two lines are an almost glib rhyme—an older easy order (you and I, against the sky) replaced and abruptly forced to the table. One of the most important poems of the twentieth century establishes its melancholy from the stupor and precariousness of one receiving treatment for illness.

More than twenty years later, another war is raging, and Eliot, in search of salvation, draws his reader to a clearing in the woods to observe some rustic sacrament and ritual. A dance, a fire, a matrimony in the hours between midnight and dawn and the poet seems to believe we too, may observe and share in the escape. "You can hear the music," he entices, "of the weak pipe and the little drum and see them dancing around the bonfire." There is as much promise of redemption in this as in any of the devout T. S. Eliot's poetry. His offer is conditional, however, valid only

> If you do not come too close, if you do not come too close.[2, p. 24]

316

There was another, also man of letters, who sought to provide a solution, to resolve in some way the broken life he could not help but observe. To William Carlos Williams, a meaningful remedy entailed anything but keeping his distance. "Contact" was for Williams a means of establishing linkages broken in the modern age. Whether addressing relationships between individuals, between people and the physical world, between men and their machines, Williams was intent upon demolishing the plentiful examples of "divorce" in his time. His own method of initiating and sustaining "contact" involved a writing style seemingly devoid of lavish description but luxuriant in its intense, unfiltered presentation of characters and events. Making "contact" also meant a medical practice in semi-urban northern New Jersey, one that would find Williams

> . . . poking into houses
> with their gloom and smell
> in among children
> leaping around a dead dog. . . .[3]

> attempting to traverse
> . . . an impossible moat between the high
> and the low where
> the life once flourished.[4]

Primarily a poet and author of short fiction, Williams wrote the historical essays that were to comprise *In the American Grain* in order to achieve something resembling what the critic Van Wyck Brooks had called "a usable past." He wanted to write an American history that made "contact" with the present; he sought to avoid history "that portrays us in generic patterns, like effigies or the carving on sarcophagi, which say nothing save, of such and such a man, that he is dead."[5] He sought to demonstrate that the darker episodes in his usable past were ones in which the major figures (Ben Franklin, Cortez) eschewed "contact." Those "afraid to touch" became villains who prevented the life around them from thriving.[6] Dr. Williams glorified the vitality of encounter. He glorified rotten apples: "There is a basketful/of them half rotted on the half rotten/bench" he wrote. "Take up one/and bite into it. It is still good/even unusual . . . as if a taste long lost and regretted/had in the end, finally/been brought to life again."[7] Reviewing Williams's prose, D. H. Lawrence wrote:

> There are two ways of being American, and the chief, says Mr. Williams, is by recoiling into individual smallness and insentience, and gutting the great continent into frenzies of mean fear. It is the Puritan way. The other is by touch; touch America as she is; dare to touch her/And this is the heroic way.[8]

The quest for heroic touch would find Williams motoring the streets at all hours in and around the towns of Paterson, Passaic, and Rutherford. It would drive him in and away from houses perched on railroad tracks, above copper mines. It was at times more than he bargained for. Such an instance—an over-dose of contact, as it were—is described well in the short, short story "The Use of Force." In the four pages a Henry James character would require for a gulp of tea, Williams's doctor-narrator enters the home of a working-class Scandinavian family whose young daughter has a high fever and upper respiratory symptoms. The narrator immediately suspects diphtheria, but his attempts to view or culture the throat are thwarted by the beautiful, irascible child's refusal to open her mouth. A struggle ensues. The entire family becomes involved; tempers rise; and all semblances of physician-patient rapport are dashed. The child is eventually subdued, her throat examined, and a diagnosis strengthened, but not before she has clawed, scratched, exhausted both parents, sent the doctor's eyeglasses flying, and bitten clean through a wooden tongue blade.

"The Use of Force" is an account of conflict in which several power-relationships are turned on ear: adult vs. child, male vs. female, doctor vs. patient, and in all cases the ostensibly weaker constituent demonstrates a potency that cannot be submitted without violent effort. The beneficent role of the healer is challenged. Williams can rationalize all he wants, "The damned little brat must be protected against her own idiocy. . . .Others must be protected against her. It is social necessity." But in the heat of the struggle, the quest becomes less of one for diagnosis than for *success*. The frustration and potential failure create a "longing for muscular release" by the physician. Williams admits openly, "It was a pleasure to attack her."[9, p. 134] Reading the story, I could not but think of an account given by an American military officer (Peter Arnett) in the battle to reclaim Ben Tre in the aftermath of the 1968 Tet Offensive during the Vietnamese war:

"It became necessary to destroy the town to save it."[10]

It was Williams who wrote (concerning the arts, but relevant to healing) that "violence alone opens the shell of the nut."[11] Earlier in his career, again in a poem, he stated, "Chaos/feeds the tree."[12] Williams's longtime nemesis (Eliot), using language the Jersey doctor found arcane, wrote, "In order to arrive at what you are not, you must go through the way in which you are not/And what you do not know is the only thing you know."[2, p. 29] The statements drift in from different continents and decades. All suggest that to save, or even help, involves more than sympathy, more than benign feelings, more than knowledge, and that all salvations or restorations entail some degree of destruction. A destructive impulse was necessary for Williams to create the concise, unfettered poetry he loved to write. At times, it was necessary in his medical life as well. And most everyone knows of it. One does not need a weighty background in English literature to know why that etherized patient fronted Eliot's Prufrock. Eliot could further surmise:

The wounded surgeon plies the steel
That questions the distempered part;
Beneath the bleeding hands we feel
The sharp compassion of the healer's art.[2, p. 29]

The care giver is himself injured. In this role the individual can neither remain apart from the misery nor fully comprehend it. He harms and cures himself with each remedy. Williams's contemporary, Hart Crane, had written:

It is to be learned— . . .
But only by the one who spends out himself again."[13]

To provide care, to gain knowledge, and to do it well means to become consumed, spent. Dr. Williams—grappling a small blond girl, being clawed and bitten, cursing her and her parents, and enamored of it all—was consumed as few others could be.

Williams's immersion in his world, his involvement with patients, his interest in their lives, indicate a capacity for love of world and people. Like the scientific salvation he might bring, his love was not entirely benign. His love was bred of conflict, it nurtured but with sharpened edge. In the heat of battle he could remark, "I had to smile to myself. After all, I had already fallen in love with the savage brat, the parents were contemptible to me."[9, p. 133] It was not mere sympathy that allowed him to admire the child's "magnificent heights of insane fury." Like the landscape and people he treated and wrote about, his love could never be dissociated entirely from more penetrative, violent desires. Here was a man who would write:

. . . little girl with well-shaped legs
you cannot touch the thoughts

I put over and under and around
you.

This is fortunate for they would burn you to an ash otherwise. Your
petals would be quite curled
up.[14]

The short story "Old Doc Rivers," from *The Knife of the Times* anthology, reveals Williams's fascination and partial identification with Doc Rivers—an individual whose community presence was both nurturing and destructive.[15] Rivers, a local doctor of exceptional talent, provided cures in thousands of cases over his long career. But his unorthodox methods and later drug addiction led to avoidable mishaps. He is considered saint and also murderer. He is, in respects, a river, whose character and influence pervade an entire community—a nurturing force. Yet, like a river he has the capacity to rage and bring with him the pernicious effects of a deluge. I believe Dr. Williams spent much of his career in cautious awe of the character Rivers, attempting to support and protect the life around him, but never losing awareness of the potential destruction he might wreak. Perhaps this is as close a path to love that an individual—in or out of medicine—can hope for.

References

1. Eliot TS. The love song of J. Alfred Prufrock. In Selected Poems, pp. 11–16, London, Harcourt Brace Jovanovich, 1934, p. 11.
2. Eliot TS. East Coker. In Four Quartets, pp. 23-32, London, Harcourt Brace Jovanovich, 1943.
3. Williams WC. Sub terra. In The Collected Earlier Poems, pp. 117–118. New York, New Directions Books, 1966, p. 118.
4. Williams WC. Paterson. New York, New Directions Books, 1969, p. 34.
5. Williams WC. The virtue of history. In In the American Grain, pp. 188–207, New York, New Directions Books, 1956, p. 188.
6. Williams WC. Père Sebastian Rasles. In In the American Grain, pp. 105–29, New York, New Directions Books, 1956, p. 119.
7. Williams WC. At Kenneth Burke's place. In Collected Poems, vol. 2 1939-1962, MacGowan, C, ed., pp. 107–8. New York, New Directions Books, 1988.
8. Lawrence DH. American heroes. The Nation 112:413, April 14, 1926, quoted in Guimond J. The Art of William Carlos Williams. Urbana, Illinois, University of Illinois Press, 1968, p. 82.
9. Williams WC. The use of force. In The Farmers' Daughters: The Collected Stories of William Carlos Williams, pp. 131–35. New York, New Directions Books, 1961.
10. Sheehan N. A Bright Shining Lie: John Paul Vann and America in Vietnam. New York, vintage Books, 1988, p.719.
11. Williams WC. Catastrophic birth. In The Collected Later Poems, pp. 8–9, New York, New Directions Books, 1950, p. 8.
12. Williams WC. Descent. In The Collected Earlier Poems, p. 460, New York, New Directions Books, 1966.
13. Crane H. Legend. In The Complete Poems and Selected Letters and Prose, Weber, B, ed., p. 3, New York, Anchor Press, 1966.
14. Williams WC. The ogre. In The Collected Earlier Poems, p.154. New York, New Directions Books, 1966, p. 154.
15. Williams WC. Old Doc Rivers. In The Farmers' Daughters: The Collected Stories of William Carlos Williams, pp. 77–105, New York, New Directions Books, 1961.

PATRICIA

DANIEL J. McCARTY, M.D.

(Winter 1994, p. 13)

For fifteen long years the red wolf brought pain
to a beautiful bride.
Bites on her fingers, skin, kidneys, and brain;
bites in and outside.
Although drugged off, he returned once again,
again and again; he wouldn't say when.

Her husband filed; he couldn't abide
a ménage à trois
The house is for sale; sport truck set aside,
a grand mal faux pas
Substernal pain defied diagnosis—
death after discharge from drug overdoses.

Could the cause of her pain have remained unspoken?
Can an autopsy show a heart that is broken?

BETWEEN FRIENDS

FREDRIC L. COE, M.D.

(Fall 1993, p. 19)

In sway to the fixed rhythm of the strict clock,

Hollow vessels fate culled from the deep
End their miraculous sojourn, in harbor rock,
Where we through this long night their vigil keep
That we have kept each night since our vows were sworn;
The morning winds may find them at anchor, still,
The changing moon from obelisk to hunter's horn
May pass, and pass again, tulip from jonquil
Seize predominance while captive round they ride,
Tended so well as we who tend have skill,
But in this night for some who will live or die,
We shall deliberate, exchange careful views,
Speak resignedly of ways tried and untried,

And gaze, together, upon a rare few.

The wooden top thrown from the skilled hand,
The ice dancer on the tips of her narrow shoes,
The great massy world where we two stand,
In top spinning and rejoicing circles go,
In flying skirted joy; and every world
Turns upon momentum only bestowed
Once, at the moment the wooden top is hurled,
The arrowed body into a blur thrown,
Planets founded, and once supremely whirled,
Runs its ravishing course inevitably down,
Down, down to the leaning of the nodding top,
Settling of windfoil skirts like sails at the crown

Of a calmed ship, worlds tending to a stop

We attend on, near to the end of that process
Of the down-spinning approach to the long drop
When dow on our charges falls the great rest,
As calm and night upon old ships retiring
Fall in haven harbors barred from the seas
And we, who have not yielded to despairing
However unfulfillable their prayers and their entreaties,
Their dreams of again voyaging, gently rock
Like nodding tops that kiss in a friendly breeze

In sway to the fixed rhythm of the strict clock.

PART VIII

REVIEWS:
BOOKS, MOVIES,
AND A PLAY

CONFESSIONS OF A KNIFE

Richard Selzer, New York, Simon & Schuster,
1979, 223 pages
REVIEW BY FRANCIS D. MOORE, M.D.
(Winter 1980, pp. 38–39)

*There is little argument with the statement that Francis Moore
was one of the most innovative, exciting pioneers in American
surgery. For 28 years he was surgeon-in-chief at the Peter Bent
Brigham Hospital and the Moseley Professor of Surgery at Harvard
Medical School for 34 years until his retirement from the University
in 1981. During this period he defined the field of surgical me-
tabolism and gave both support and knowledgeable advice to
those beginning successful organ transplantation and open heart
surgery. He received many honors and honorary degrees. In 1990
an endowment for the Francis D. Moore Professorship of Surgery
was established. In his later years he was dogged by chronic illness, and committed suicide at age 88 on 26 November 2001.*

Is he a surgeon who writes or a writer who surges?

THE AUTHOR OF *Confessions of a Knife* is not new to the pen. He is the
author of two previous books, many magazine articles, stories, and essays, some of them award winning (we are told on the dust jacket). But
with this little volume Dr. Selzer is going to burst forth from his relatively small
world of special articles about "ritual of surgery" (that dim borderland between clinical practice and writing about it) into the full light of a wide read-
ership. With this book Selzer will move from the limbo of odd journal pieces to
the full illumination enjoyed by Lewis Thomas with *Lives of a Cell* and *The
Medusa and the Snail*.

In any event, no mere amateur starting out with a typewriter and a free day
could possibly produce what Selzer has written here.

This book of short essays displays a remarkable literary talent, an ability
to evoke scenes, sensations, emotions, excitement, depression, with a very spare
use of the English language. There is no excess verbiage here—short sentences,
one-word sentences, never any confusion as to who is speaking or to whom the
speech is made. He sweeps the reader along with his vision, be it of himself
making rounds, of an army surgeon 115 years ago chugging down the Mississippi

with a boatload of dying wounded from the Battle of Shiloh, or an old man and woman facing the despair of age alone on an island in the Irish Sea.

Yes, he trades a bit on his special medical knowledge. Yes, he likes to refer to the blood and guts aspect of medicine, surgery, wounds, disease, autopsies, as "dreadful" or to use shocking verbal images about the eye hanging out on its avulsed nerve, the dried dying tongue protruding over the coated, smelly teeth, the red tumor of the neck hanging like a red beard. To physicians who have learned to live with these aspects of human disease and, in a sense, to hide behind the spare vision of science, sometimes using circumlocution or euphemism to avoid this type of reality expression, such pseudomedical artifice may seem a little fluffy, a little soft and mushy, a little *Ladies Home Journal.*

But those are but minor faults and open to argument at best. Maybe such things are inevitable when a surgeon who perforce deals with the visual and tactile images of the realities of disease, both the inside and the outside of the human body, both living and dead, writes of his own experiences and images.

Does this book tell us anything about the soul of this surgeon or of surgeons or physicians in general? This has become an interesting question because of the recent interest in the relationship—if any—between literature *by* or *about* medicine and medical science, and the question of medical ethics. Dr. Robert Coles has raised these questions in several of his writings, summarized recently in "Medical Ethics and Living a Life" (*N. Engl. J. Med.* 301:444, 1979). Coles has been fascinated by Walker Percy, a physician who, in his older years, has taken up writing on general subjects *(Love in the Ruins)*. Coles has analyzed the lay image of medical practice provided by George Eliot in *Middlemarch,* F. Scott Fitzgerald in *Tender Is the Night,* Sinclair Lewis in *Arrowsmith.* The focus of Coles's interest is on literature as it displays the inner life of a physician or medical practice in general. It draws attention to the fact that the physician cannot demonstrate humanism and ethics in the outer world of his practice if he does not live such a life within himself. It purports a sort of neo-monasticism that seems very welcome in a world of affluent physicians and the "big business" of medical science.

Is there any of this in Selzer's book? Yes, but it is not prominent nor is it the main or simple, obvious focus. When he speaks in shocking terms or metaphors about disease, the fundamental message is one of humanism, of sensing the suffering of others, and seeking to live in his own life and picture in his own mind compassion and the trials of others, usually patients.

On the other hand, the book presents no easy moral lessons about the inner soul of a doctor as one sees in *Arrowsmith,* no easy indictment of all those terrible doctors, such as one encounters in *The Citadel* or *Not as a Stranger,* no easy spectacularisms such as one has found in *Coma,* or such Hollywood "medisoaps" in which the patient and the platitudinous message are portrayed as a strong bid to Hollywood and a cheap shot at the life and loves of young people working in hospitals. That is genre of literary work in which the author has made a trade-in, obtaining large monetary rewards in return for the special privilege of writing with intimate knowledge about the "inside" of medicine. *The Andromeda Strain* was another angle, Crichton obviously trading on his special knowledge, but not so much cheapening it as popularizing it.

But there is none of that here. There is none of the "sci-fi" of *The Andromeda Strain,* employing special knowledge of the natural to evoke an image of the supernatural.

When Selzer wants to write of something supernatural he just tells us about Pegasus with a broken wing trying to fly out of the peach orchard at Shiloh, and we accept it as a remarkable image, but without any fancy fixings or frosting.

This book contains twenty-three essays, all of them short, some autobiographical, and set in contemporary time and place. Others evoke more distant images but are equally interesting.

When I saw this title in a recent book list, my thought was, "Here is another surgeon bursting into print, making capital of his special knowledge and experience, trading on his privilege, a surgeon who writes."

Now, having read this book, I realize that we have here a remarkable author and a unique literary accomplishment—a writer who surges. And surge he does, both at the New Haven Hospital and the Yale Medical School, and through the pages of this remarkable little book.

BOOK REVIEW

E. A. STEAD, JR.: WHAT THIS PATIENT NEEDS IS A DOCTOR

By Galen S. Wagner, Bess Cebe, and Marvin P. Rozear, Durham,
Carolina Academic Press, 1978, 244 pages

REVIEW BY PAUL B. BEESON, M.D.

(October 1978, pp. 43–44)

To HAVE SERVED AS HEAD OF A MEDICAL SCHOOL department of medicine after World War II, amid the hectic swings of public favor and disenchantment, during a period of unequalled progress in biomedical science, has challenged scores of presumed able people. They met with varying degrees of success. This book is about one who did the job well.

That so many of his former students and colleagues have combined to try to describe him, and the way he worked, is a tribute that will be paid to few of his contemporaries. The book is a compilation of the sayings and writings of E. A. Stead, together with essays about him by people who worked alongside him at various times and under varying circumstances. Whether their combined effort will make him "come alive" to people who have not actually known him is difficult to say. Naturally, there is some jerkiness in a work of this sort, and undoubtedly certain chapters will be of greater interest than others to different readers. To convey the flavor of it requires that a few passages be cited.

With regard to clinical students:

> The system of evaluation changes when the student enters the clinical area. Up until that time he has made an "A" if he could answer the questions. In the clinical area, he is judged primarily by the effect of his actions on others.

To serve as one of Stead's house officers was not exactly relaxing. There is a hint of this in the subtitle of the book, and the following is a rather extreme sample—a remark to one who was having trouble recalling laboratory results: "You should become more familiar with the Arabic culture. They have developed an interesting system; it is called numbers. You may find it useful to use this system as you go through life."

In the sixties, when intern candidates seemed mainly interested in the number of nights off duty, he wrote this to prospective applicants:

The training of physicians is the purpose of the Department of Medicine at Duke University. Experience has taught us that the selection of your internship is the most important decision of your professional life. This experience will mold you more than any other. As you examine our program, you must pay primary attention to our product. The details of how we produce the product will largely have to be taken on faith and, in all honesty, our judgment here will be better than yours. Duke is not for everybody, and medicine is a demanding mistress. Experience has shown that Duke does give a very rewarding experience to intelligent graduates who wish to achieve excellence in medicine. [our] staff does believe that doctors exist to care for people.

Here are some views about choosing new members of the department:

Select those who are more interested in conveying attitudes than in transmitting facts. Select those who are more concerned with what is not known about a subject than in the transmission of current knowledge. Select those who listen well rather than those who parrot the same record each time the button is pushed.

The most effective teachers create a shadowy framework in which the student can climb. If the teacher fills in the skeleton in great detail, he will limit the learning. If he makes the form recognizable but leaves the final shape and details to the student, the student may produce a much better intellectual synthesis than the teacher.

The effectiveness of the teacher must be judged by the things which happen after the student and teacher part company.

I'm not so immune to the simple pleasures of life that I don't enjoy hearing a young man say that he has learned a lot from me but, realistically, I know it's not so. Bright men teach themselves."

Here are samples of remarks made during ward-round teaching:

Because every biological system is different from every other one and because every observer brings some bias to the scene, it is easier to learn incorrectly than correctly from the practice of medicine.

I'm sure it is natural to feel hostility toward the alcoholic. An amateur can feel any way he wants, but a doctor is a professional.

Stead's advice was eagerly sought by young people regarding training and career plans. Here are some of his guiding principles:

My answers have always reflected my belief in the importance of the present. If the program pays dividends in satisfaction and pleasure while it is being pursued, he cannot lose. No matter what happens in the future, the fun of the present belongs forever to him. I have been surprised at how rarely the young doctor, engaged in planning his career, asks the question that I judge to be of greatest importance: "How do I plan my educational program to help me gain the greatest satisfaction out of each day of my life?" His great concern is to become technically competent, and he assumes that out of this happiness will flow.

Stead's special investigative interest was cardiovascular disease, and his work had real influence on our present concepts of the pathogenesis of circulatory failure. His remarkable ability to think about clinical phenomena and to learn from observation of patients is portrayed in a chapter entitled, "When the Heart Cannot Perform Its Task."

In a chapter entitled, "Years of Growth," Robert Whalen, a former chief resident and a gifted writer, describes Stead in his various roles as administrator, educator, and clinician, with special emphasis on his remarkable relationship with the house staff. Two really moving pieces are short tributes written by Bess Cebe, his secretary, and his son, Bill.

Of the hundreds of people I have known in academic medicine, Gene Stead is one of the few about whom I would use the word *great*. He has excelled as clinician, teacher, investigator, and administrator. This book will give special pleasure to those of us who worked with him, but it is also a treasury of wisdom even for those not so fortunate. I am tempted to classify it as required reading for anyone contemplating a career in academic clinical medicine.

CATCH-30, AND OTHER PREDICTABLE CRISES OF GROWING UP ADULT

Gail Sheehy, *New York*, February 1974
REVIEWED BY CARLETON B. CHAPMAN, M.D.
(April 1974, pp. 65–66)

Carl Chapman was a distinguished scholar, physician, teacher, and dean. After his undergraduate days at Davidson College he was awarded a Rhodes Scholarship at Oxford. He earned both an M.D. and M.P.H. at Harvard. His field was preventive cardiology and was recognized for his expertise by being elected president of the American Heart Association and the American Federation for Clinical Research. As Dean of Dartmouth Medical School he led this school, third oldest in the nation, from being a two-year school whose "graduates" went on to Harvard and other schools for completion of the M.D. degree to one granting the doctorate in, at first, three years, and later, four years. During this interval he built the clinical departments into strong, productive entities. The longest paper ever published in The Pharos *was a scholarly dissertation (191 references), "The evolution of the right to health concept in the United States." Written with John M. Talmadge, A.B., this was printed in the January 1971 issue of* The Pharos. *Because of its length, it regretfully could not be included in this anthology. Before retiring back to Vermont, not far from Dartmouth, he served as President of the Commonwealth Fund in Manhattan. He died on December 10, 2000.*

WHAT'S A REVIEW OF AN ARTICLE IN A PERIODICAL doing in a Book Review section? An answer may be that some authors put their most provocative ideas in articles soon after those ideas take shape. A book may come later and, although it may place the author's ideas in a more complete and stately setting, the excitement and breathlessness of the original article is often lost. So it may be with Gail Sheehy's article in *New York,* which deals with the developmental psychology (and psychopathology) of the intermittently grueling passage from age 20 to the mid-50's when calm is, at long last, supposed to reign. Sheehy's presentation is rambling and disjointed; but her topics and her own thoughts are interesting, stimulating, and timely.

"Adults," says Sheehy provocatively and quite correctly, "have kept the experience of adulthood largely a secret—unlike child development." *Very* unlike it. Developmental psychology, in the minds of most of us, is kid-stuff, important enough for children from age one to adolescence. But after that, and certainly after the magic age of 21, adulthood becomes a void, inquiries into which are taken to be signs of personal weakness and, in the case of the beleaguered male, of unmanliness.

Sheehy turns early in the article to Erik Erikson as, indeed, she had to; there was, until fairly recently, virtually no one else. She quotes Erikson's neat division of adult passage into three phases: first, the twenties when " . . . intimacy is the key word"; second, generativity (in the forties and early fifties), a paternal and creative phase in which the need to guide and assist new generations and young associates is manifest; and finally, the stage of ego integration in the late fifties, " . . . a state of mind beyond bitterness which will allow the individual to engage in his next season with renewed vitality," or, failing to achieve it, to plunge into blank, despairing (and perhaps premature) old age. She then turns to Levinson, whose formulation recognizes no distinct phases. "A man's life structure is in constant evolution. . . . Times of crisis, of disruption or constructive change, are not only predictable but desirable. They mean growth." Sheehy seems to straddle both concepts. Her hypothesis is that we all " . . . must get into the adult world between the ages of 22 and 29, before moving through the Age Thirty Transition (29 to 32), before being ready to engage in Settling Down (32 to 39)."

It's that Age Thirty Transition (the phase of "lack of mutuality") that intrigues and distresses her; hence her title. And one of the reasons seems to be that the Catch-30 phenomenon is rougher, in her view, on the female member of a couple than on the male. With the professional confidence the male acquires as be traverses his late twenties, having now become "something more," he urges his wife to do the same. This to her is betrayal, says Sheehy. She has built a home and faithfully looks after children; but her man now wants yet more. Neither of the two, says Sheehy, is really wrong; but it's at this phase that the "Testimonial Woman" may enter the picture.

In older and more conventional parlance, the Testimonial Woman was called merely *the other woman* or possibly a *lady friend*. But that, in the context of Sheehy's argument won't do. To support her usage she resorts to astonishing etymologic argument: *testimonial* has as its root the Latin *testis* (witness). "In olden times," says Sheehy, "cupping the sexual parts of a man by another man in greeting was a 'testimonial to manhood' and the basis for the original handshake. The Testimonial Woman offers the same service—she fortifies his masculinity." That, however, is only one possibility. It may also be that for reasons having little to do with worries about his masculinity, the Catch-30 male has come to seek variety, that he feels, or thinks he feels, the need for multiple loves, which, in themselves, are not necessarily major threats to his original commitment. In any case, it seems utterly safe to say that in seeking reassurance as to his manhood, or in trying to convey the same reassurance to another man, our Catch-30 male of the nineteen-seventies is unlikely to resort to the ancient precursor of handshaking.

Somewhere along the line, a husband, ". . . skimming through his Age Thirty Transition," may leave his wife behind; she cannot, after all, make the transition from housewife to career-woman (or its equivalent) as suddenly or as soon as Sheehy thinks the Catch-30 husband wants her to do.

But, of course, he may be perfectly happy with her as she is. The Catch-30 phase has a certain reality but it does not necessarily mark the beginning of the end of a marriage. It may, however, mark the beginning of profound changes in the relationship—for better or for worse. But Sheehy's focus on the Catch-30 phenomenon seems, on balance, to be too stark. Later transitions— the gradual recognition in the late 30's and 40's that retirement, senility, and death are not mere abstractions, and unending questions about one's own Life System ("in what way are [one's] values, goals, and aspirations being invigorated or violated by [one's] present Life System")—are of equal or greater importance. One's Life System, with its external and internal components, comes under scrutiny well after the Catch-30 phase is past. Women seem to examine it from their own point of view and, perhaps, with less intensity than men. In any event, men in their late 30's and early 40's may, and often do, find that their "way of living in the world" is so unacceptable that they seek a break with their past, very often in a professional sense. This is, perhaps, less true of those who have entered the medical profession than of those in business or industry. But, even so, there is vast unrest *within* the profession: the internist or pediatrician chooses now to enter psychiatry; the successful surgeon becomes a medical missionary; a disillusioned generalist becomes an administrator. Such events are the products of the vast process that is Sheehy's primary concern. And as they run their course, most people—male and female—attribute their genesis solely to external causes. Fewer than 10 percent, says Sheehy, would (or could) say: "There is some unknown disturbance within me and even though it's painful, I feel I have to stay with it and ride it out."

In the end, and drawing on the insights of others in the field, Sheehy creates her own more-or-less logical synthesis. She starts with the age interval 16–22 *(pulling up roots)*, proceeds to the 22–29 interval *(provisional adulthood)*, then to the 29–32 *(Catch-30)* transition. Drawing heavily on Levinson, she characterizes the 32–39 phase as *rooting*, and moves on to the 39–43 interval, *mid-life transition*.

Disappointingly, she gives it short shrift although she clearly recognizes its importance:

> Nearing 40 [a man] will be struck with a simple, shattering fact: he has arrived at the mid-point of life. He has stopped growing up and begun growing old. Entering the stage of greatest fulfillment, he is simultaneously jolted by the awareness that his death lies beyond. The paradox may send him off on a magical bet. One last chance to make it big.

> And a desperate time it is. He can no longer have a real mentor, although he may be mentor to younger folk about him. And, now or later, he may be vastly disturbed by the fact that he seems to be able, in a very important sense, to serve other men's sons far better than he can serve his own.

> A man faces the gap between youthful dreams and actual fulfilment. . . . He may make a series of departures from well-established lifelong baselines. . . . The task is an awesome one: to find ways to connect parts of the self not provided for in the old Life System.

Which is fine as far as it goes. But, in dealing with *mid-life transition* so cursorily, Sheehy's total effort goes only part way toward correcting the entrenched view that developmental psychology is concerned solely with the young and very young. It may just be that the mid-life transition, for both men and women, is potentially the most disruptive, dangerous and ill-understood phase of all. Nor is it very convincing to say that if one traverses earlier phases with skill, grace, an aplomb, he (or she) is likely to cope with mid-life transition without major disturbance.

Perhaps. But every adult psychiatrist or counselor comes to know and fear, through his clients' lives or his own, the massive and major peaking of forces in mid-life that so often produces life's greatest desperation and disruption. Whatever has gone before the mid-life transition, a man or woman who has difficulty with the transition may well have Big Trouble. And counselors need badly to understand the transition much better than is now possible.

Sheehy's final phase, 43–50 (Restabilization and Flowering) is, like the preceding phase, dealt with sketchily. And one inevitably draws the inference that to Sheehy, meaningful life struggles end at 50 years of age. By that time, one supposes, a man or woman either has made it emotionally and otherwise; or there's no hope that he or she will *ever* make it.

It goes without saying that one's judgment of Sheehy's important and intriguing article will be moulded in some measure by the reader's own age. The present reviewer has traversed all her stages and has run off the scale as she defines it. Yet developments, transitions, periods of elation, and periods of anguish occur and recur as often and with as much intensity as ever. During the years of campus unrest and the drug scene, the *in* phrase was *identity crisis—*

a whole succession of them. And to those no-longer-young academics who were trying to cope, it was very clear that turbulent youth fervently believed that only youth was capable of experiencing such crises. The rest of us were out of it, comfortably ruminating and reminiscing. And, on being told that those crises, or their equivalent, recur until death or senility intervene, the reaction of youthful colleagues was almost predictable: first, disbelief; then annoyance; and finally, a measure of desperation and despair. "Do I have to go through this sort of thing *all* my life?"

Sheehy, Erikson, Levinson and others, using different labels and perspectives, all provide the same answer:

"Yes, young friend—man or woman—you do!" And Sheehy, echoing Levinson, winds up her piece with this gentle bit of irony: "With any luck at all, crises such as Catch-30 will not be our last."

Nor has she done with the topic. There's a book in progress which, hopefully, will give the anguish and struggle of the Mid-life Transition a much fuller treatment. But her *New York* article, as it stands, begins to illuminate a long neglected and distorted topic; and one that has singular significance, professionally and personally to men and women in medicine.

THE LAST TANGO IN PARIS

Directed by Bernardo Bertolucci
Starring Marlon Brando and Maria Schneider
REVIEW BY RALPH CRAWSHAW, M.D.
(October 1973, pp. 146–148, 163)

Ralph Crawshaw, still very active in Oregon as a writer and editorialist, wrote this about his stint as movie reviewer of The Pharos:

"It is safe to say that no one goes to medical school to become a movie reviewer. What moved me into that role was rage and the support of an understanding editor, Dr. Helen Glaser. The rage came with reading a review of Fellini's Satyricon in MD magazine. With an aseptic view of the social pathology of ancient Rome, the review trashed the film for its lack of redemption, presumably physicians' redemption. For me it was a gold mine of the pathology that daily straggles into hospital emergency rooms.

During the 17 years that I served as the writer of "Physician at the Movies," I developed a relationship with the reader that proved most rewarding, teaching me deepening perspective on the medical vocation: Generally, physicians are drawn to movies for entertainment, a dreadful word coming from early French, meaning to "stand between," to be uncommitted, as in "to entertain an idea." But a funny thing happens on the way to the box office: the doctor's vocation kicks in. We watch films as the doctors we are, dedicated healers. The spectacle of human suffering makes poor entertainment for caring doctors unless it leads to our compassion.

Movies stir our hearts and eyes as much as our minds and reason. Movies are windows on our culture and inadvertently challenge the caring physician to judge what appears on the screen against his/her experience. My job was to illuminate that view with words that might sharpen our sense of lifelong mission.

Ralph Crawshaw, M.D.
AΩA, New York University, 1973

The Beauty that is annexed and appended to folly, is a lamentable accident and error of the mortal and perishing life; it does but seldom happen; but with this unnatural mixture the sublime Artist can have nothing to do; it is fit for the burlesque.
— William Blake from "A Descriptive Catalogue," The Portable Blake, Viking Press, New York, 1946, page 522.

Little Orphan Annie and Daddy Warbucks Make It in Technicolor

After seeing *The Last Tango in Paris* I had an idea of writing not one, but three or more reviews of the film. Certainly, though not customary, there is no reason why a provocative book or movie might not be reviewed many times. Each reading and subsequent rereading, or reviewing, of an artistic work may stimulate new and different thoughts, just as the repeated review of an elaborate scientific work may produce an increasing depth and breath of understanding. Certainly no two views of *The Last Tango* can be the same, at least not for me.

However, more than curiosity about a complex movie drew me back to a second viewing of *The Tango*.

In fact, the primary reason for me to see it again, and partially to disqualify any conclusions in this review as well, was the circumstance of the first view. The film had opened the evening I stopped by in Washington, D.C., and as I was in town for just a brief time I made a point of calling the box office the next night. The response was expected; a recorded voice announced that the house was sold out. Undaunted, I took a cab out Connecticut Avenue early enough to arrive as the box office opened, and sure enough there was one seat: Left, first row, far right. I took it and was suddenly transported back to those dear departed Saturday afternoons when my buddies and I would line up at the local movie house to be first to run down the aisle for the front row seats where we could watch Rin Tin-Tin giant size. Federico Felleni took a similar experience from his boyhood and developed it into a delightful sequence in *Roma*. He and his parents squeeze into first row seats and watch a vastly distorted gladitorial battle gyrate, lopsided and gigantic, above them on the too-close screen. Well, that is how I saw *Last Tango,* only it was buttocks and breasts, swirling in their immensity as I craned my neck to the left and tipped by head far back. I ended up with a pain in the neck. In the vernacular of the film, my view of it was "half-arsed."

The plot is simple. A male and a female, Paul and Jeanne, happen to meet under uniquely private circumstances. They tacitly agree to rape each other, physically, mentally, morally, and religiously. Three days later, to the tempo of their tango (slow, quick, quick, hold) their anti-relationship ends as one of them breaks the implicit contract.

At least twenty trails trace out from this bare plot (no pun intended) and limited cast. The technic is superb. In contrast to *Clockwork Orange,* where garish color makes any humanness difficult to appreciate, Bernardo Bertolucci plays light and dark, warmth and cold, flesh tones and death pallor in a masterful manner, always reinforcing the human, living quality of the color against the diabolic action. The acting, particularly that of MarIon Brando, is excellent. An unbelievable person, yet a person, emerges in all his repulsive squalor of values as Brando portrays the unlikely character of Paul. He never succumbs to the potentially larger-than-life melodrama, which a lesser actor might have used. Maria Schneider is her part. Though I know nothing of her background I found Schneider so fitted for Jeanne that she may well have been living the part since age one. In perspective the difficult story, though improbable, is possible, but unlike a similar tale of deterioration, *Death of a Salesman,* it lacks immediate plausibility. So many coincidences are called for to set the slim plot moving that it must be considered a fairy tale, a dreadful one, but nevertheless a fairy tale.

Here are some of the possible trails that lead away from just one viewing of *The Last Tango:*

Violent sex as a defense against grief: Certainly, despite all the "love making," no one in his right mind is going to call this film a love story. The heroine's confusion of "war" and "whore" speaks to the use of sex as a weapon.

Failure of a tragedy to convince: A careful comparison with Arthur Miller's *Death of a Salesman* would uncover the lack of operational hubris in the nonheroic character of Paul. The consequent loss of empathy for Paul's fate could be contrasted with the genuine sorrow felt for Willie Loman.

Psychology of the dance: The complex rhythm that reverberates through the film is intense. Starting with the cliché, "It takes two to tango," the stylized, one-two-interactions of the partners might become more understandable, not in the scientific minutia of comparing their post-rotary nystagmus to the reactions of the gypsy Karogarn dancers of southern India, but in the overall sweep of the dance, the joining of two in an act of innate culture.

Religion: Any film that commences with the hero shouting to the sky, "F——king God," has a religious theme, in this case not the coming of the "anti-Christ" but the pursuit of the "non-Christ," the glorification of meaningless sacrifice.

Science fiction: The partners have a "space ship," an apartment on the Rue Jules Verne, in which they completely insulate themselves from the earth and its inhabitants. With just a bit of unwinding the tale could reveal them as twins in a womb, a fiction of science, but a tale.

Pornography: Of course, pornography is a potential review. However, most present talk of pornography is yet another rehash with a limited vocabulary, generally including "prurient," "moralistic," "art for art sake," and "freedom." The important part of this review would be an attempt to recapture a word slipping into oblivion from disuse, and that word is "vulgar."

Comparative values: Paul's attempts at dehumanization are not, despite appearances, bestial but mechanical. Paul, though he attempts to be animal, fails, for he lacks, until it is too late, the beast's instinct for perpetuation of species. A review might show how Paul's concentration on one aspect of animalization, copulation, becomes a mechanical function of his own sex drive and deprives sex of any meaning of the animal in man. It simply becomes a ritual, a mechanical value—complete and efficient motion.

Psychology of the actor: The effect of the role on the actor should make a worthwhile study. Somewhere, George Bernard Shaw points out that the occupational danger for an actor is his loss of soul, and though considering the effect of Brando on the role and of the role on Brando might be a poor mix of fact, gossip and conjecture, it has possibilities.

Medicine: A slim review on the medical problems of dissipation is possible. How a man can kill himself in the pursuit of pleasure is not of much interest in our consumer oriented world, but the review might start with obese King Farouk strangling on his filet mignon and continue to the spectacular death of President Félix Fauré of France, who exhausted himself to complete collapse and death attempting to gratify the particular perversion of the most famous courtesan of his day, Mme. Steinheil. All of this could find a medical application not only in the care of the post-myocardial infarct patient but in the soaring incidence of venereal disease throughout our nation.

Literature: There could even be a review of the reviews of *The Last Tango*. It seems that every other person with a typewriter and access to printer's ink has whipped off a review, and, oh, the high flown words and phrases! Frankly, I believe myself capable of flying a phrase as high as the next but, oh, the bore.

Actually the first review that comes naturally is *The Last Tango* as a *fairy tale*. The sub-title of Little Orphan Annie and Daddy Warbucks is not pejorative. Our mythology is as much more a product of the comic strip as it is of Thomas Bulfinch's age of fable. The basic ingredient of the American myth is the simple good guy, All-American, weak yet strong, unlettered yet wise, poor but rich, who overcomes evil by virtue. Throw in an occasional joke and you have the comic strip. Perhaps some can remember Happy Hooligan—the archetype who eventually developed through Hairbreath Harry into Superman and Dick Tracy. Good old H. Hooligan set the style for all future comic strip heroes with his indestructible innocence. All our heroes turn out to have the strength of ten because their hearts are so pure. Paul's final failure to discover this strength in his world disillusions him. Neither his heart, nor any of the people in his life, are so pure that they can summon more than the strength of one. A few of them know it, but poor Paul just never is able to accept the reality that experience teaches.

Perhaps it sounds like turning from the ridiculous to the sublime to talk of comic strips and American literature of the 20's in the same paragraph, but together they reveal the problem for Paul's generation, the "oh, so lost" generation. He is an American ex-patriot, slogging along in the fading footsteps of Ernest Hemingway, F. Scott Fitzgerald, and Gertrude Stein. They are all fugitives from the crass America that hypocritically proclaimed progress and freedom of mankind (innocence) while going about the business of exploiting everything that could be commercialized. It was too much for those "tender souls" to bear, so off they went for their extended college boy holiday in Paris. Lest I sound too harsh with some of our local folk heroes, I contrast them with William Carlos Williams, the physician poet, who knew the whole crowd on a first name basis. He stood his ground in Patterson, New Jersey, and dealt close at hand with ever present evil.

Anyway, the background painting in the opening of *The Last Tango*, against which the credits appear, might well have been a portrait of Hemingway in his Sun Valley home the morning his wife came downstairs to find him dead. As he, the figure in the film just sits there with its head blown open, "The world is too much to take," written in "innocent" blood all over the living room.

The film portrays a malevolent pursuit of innocence, a forlorn innocence, which is to be hunted down, rooted out and destroyed. Paul is intent on getting the great American myth out of his system, even if it kills him. He was cheated out of innocence by the people in his life, and he hungers for revenge. It makes you stop and wonder where Paul ever got the idea of innocence anyway. Perhaps he never heard about the Vietnam War (Oh, . . . how I wish someone would drop that other G.I. boot and admit that the U.S.A. has finally lost a war). Of course, Paul was too young ever to have heard of the Watergate Affair. Paul infers he got the idea of innocence some place in childhood watching his dog chase rabbits, but he is certain his innocence slipped away for him the night his father made him milk a cow before Paul went on a date. As a consequence of his Pa's harsh demands he went to the dance smelling of the cow manure stuck to his shoes (shades of the old body odor advertisements stuck to his psyche?).

Well, Paul's problem with the cow manure brought to mind a tale even more odoriferous, told to me in the comradeship of a residency nearing completion. It happened to one of the most illustrious psychoanalysts now practicing in (would it not be more precise to say on) Beverly Hills. It seems this worthy was reared in a small, provincial, midwestern town, not far from Paul's Ohio home. On his first date my friend hurried to pick up his choice of the high school girls, and while taking a short-cut across her front lawn he slipped and fell. With the bounce of youth he was back on his feet and up the porch steps. He rang the door bell, and was warmly welcomed by the girl's father for the ritual wait while "Daisy is getting ready." After relieving my friend of the corsage he carried, the father took but a moment to remark on the terrible odor that had suddenly filled the room. Then, to his abject embarrassment, my friend found that his slip had been on dog dung. Scarlet and speechless he tried to ignore his condition but the older man, unlettered in the niceties of generation gaps, took in the whole situation and with a few reassuring words to the effect that my friend was not the freshest lily of the season, escorted him to the basement, stripped him of his trousers, and the two of them scrubbed away the offending odor. So my friend went to his first prom in wet pants, smelling of yellow laundry soap, but he survived the wiser for the experience.

I know that Paul could counter that there was no one there to teach him how to scrape cow manure off his shoes, but, ah, that is the price of being innocent.

Yes, *The Last Tango* is supposed to be a shocker, but bear with one more recollection to see how badly out of date the film is. I cannot speak for all upstanding American boys, but I can attest that Paul's loss of innocence was long delayed. Here he is acting like Daddy Warbucks, the all powerful man, chasing around with a kid half his age, who is bereft of a father and looking for all the world like Little Orphan Annie. Frankly, the crowd I hung out with worked this through in the fifth grade. While Miss Greenfield, our long suffering teacher, was belaboring us with the plot within a plot of *Treasure Island*, Henry Wooling, Roy Anderson, and a few more of the cognoscentes of whom I was part, had as lurid a library as you could wish, stashed away under a log by the spring on the old farm.

We had all the pornographic comic strips, or at least it seemed so (John Anderson, Roy's older brother, who was two years ahead of us in school, was our literary advisor in the venture). My memories of Gasoline Alley are now a bit vague but the antics of Popeye and Olive Oyl, as I remember them, in a large wheelbarrow trundled by Wimpy, dissuaded me from any unnecessary burden of innocence. Too bad Paul did not stay in school through the fifth grade, for there were some frightfully relevant things going on there for the kiddies.

Lest he think this last example is cut from whole cloth, the doubting reader can look it all up in a four volume study of the role of multi-million dollar industry, in the pornography that flourished during the thirties.[1]

Frankly, Paul where have you been? In my consultations with a local Headstart program we deal with the ever present problems that you stumble upon in *The Last Tango*. The five and six year olds are strong on exploring the possibilities of "the pussy thing" and should you ever have the chance I would be pleased to bring you along for a lesson in mankind's eternal struggle to balance passion and reality.

The tragedy, which is Paul's, and implicitly humanity's, rests with his failure to learn from experience. His grim insistence that innocence must be regained effectively blinds him to reality. His *bête noire* prevents him from ever seeing innocence in its mature form, love, until it is too late. Only as he dies does he get it through his thick skull that innocence can be regained, but in the form of a loving family, which makes possible innocent children. He never sees through the paradox that the ultimate satisfaction of personal demands comes with the subordination to the needs of others. Oh Jerusalem! when will men learn to replace the lure of sentimentality with a respect of sentiment? Appreciated sentiment is the path to heaven on earth, while the pursuit of sentimentality will, at best, end us all up in the funny papers.

Reference

1. Gilmore DH. Sex in Comics: A History of the Eight Pagers, Greenleaf Classics, Calif., 1973.

MOVIE REVIEW

SATURDAY NIGHT FEVER

Starring John Travolta and Karen Lynn Gorney
Directed by John Badham
Produced by Robert Stigwood
REVIEW BY RALPH CRAWSHAW, M.D.
(October 1978, pp. 39–42)

*S*ATURDAY NIGHT FEVER IS A HIT AND JUSTLY SO, for the acting is outstanding, the music excellent, the dancing superb, and the retelling of the American Dream poignant. John Travolta, as the hero, Tony Manero the disco king, charms the audience. No one can fail to respond to his hard-surfaced innocence, a boy-man launching out into a world much larger than his Bay Ridge, Brooklyn turf.

The second star of *Saturday Night Fever* is the music. Unlike so many musicals, such as *Grease* and *West Side Story,* which make the music into a character, a production, complete with underlying refrain, *Saturday Night Fever* puts its music in its place as background, where it stays yet "speaks" a vernacular that is as powerful as a Greek chorus. The rock rhythm of the Bee Gees with "Stayin' Alive" and "More than a Woman" is precisely part of Tony's life and of the story. The music, dancing, and Tony are a recognizable unit. Even Beethoven's Fifth Symphony and Moussorgsky's "Night On Bald Mountain" are recognizable not as "classics" but rather the integrated expression of kids who were introduced to them by Mickey Mouse in Walt Disney's *Fantasia* and who, once they got their hands on electric guitars, integrated the music into the way they live their lives. Incidentally, the sound track has sold better than the film, with a gross exceeding $100 million.

Travolta's dancing matches or perhaps excels Fred Astaire's. Travolta has none of the engaging, perhaps tricky, "continental" quality of Astaire, yet as a working-class "kid" even his way of walking down the street has uniquely lyrical expression. His girl friend waits for him outside their dance studio rather than inside, because, "I wanted to watch you come down the street; I like the way you walk." In fact, when he steps on the dance floor the girls about him naturally fall into step with him. In the climactic Saturday night dance contest at the 2001 Odyssey Ballroom, Travolta moves with a primitive grace that sets his partner and the audience afire with an erotic blaze, in a way that Astaire never could, despite his virtuosity, and even with Cyd Charisse as a partner. Travolta's dancing has an elemental power that could send a latter-day Nietzsche down on his knees, worshiping Dionysus. He is not dancing out the American Dream on his toes, nor tapping it out with his feet; Tony expresses it with every cell in his body.

Tony is the eighteen-year-old second son of a first generation Italian-American working-class family settled in the Bay Ridge section of Brooklyn. He is a hero to his little sister but a failure to his parents, because, rather than making it like Frank, his older brother-priest, he is a stock boy at a local hardware store. He is a hero to his gang, the Faces, however, for once out of the house, particularly on Saturday nights, he is transformed into the king of the disco, every bit as much as was Clark Kent in emerging from a telephone booth as Superman.

As every king knows, however, thrones are not forever, and through a series of disillusionments Tony learns that achieving the most that adolescence can offer in Brooklyn of the 1970s is not enough. First, he learns that his father does not care that he can make more money, "A four dollar raise, what can you buy with four dollars these days. You can't even buy three dollars." His brother Frank gives up the church. Tony, with Stephanie, wins the dance contest, but he gives the prize away when he realizes that another couple was better. Finally, after being turned down sexually by Stephanie with, "You don't have a place," punctuated with a knee in the groin, he loses his friend, Bobby, a fellow member of the Faces in a fall from the Verrazano-Narrows Bridge, where they have been playing chicken over the New York bay.

Although these particular rites of passage may sound crude, they remain entirely plausible to the audience, which is drawn into Tony's life by his consummate portrayal of an adolescent, fighting with his mother, then crying for the pain he has caused; loving an unattainable girl; being the cock of the walk with his buddies yet at the same time a bewildered lad amazed and frightened at the distance to manhood. The audience is held, willingly or unwillingly, by Tony's authentic voice. Listen to the rage of this unpolished poet as he sums up his life in Bay Ridge:

> Bump, bump de bump and dump. . . . That's all we do, go around dumping, dump, dumping our load. Dumping on something, dumping on dumpers in a dump. My pa gets dumped at work, he dumps on my ma, she runs to the church to dump that and for all the rest she's got me, the dumper's dump. The spics, we dump on them, they dump on us. Dumb dumpers . . . even the humping is dumping most of the time.

Should you sit back to reflect on what a great film *Saturday Night Fever* is your thoughts might track along with mine, though I doubt it, since like Tony

I too am a Brooklyn boy. Unlike Tony, however, I am from Brooklyn's Bedford-Stuyvesant section, and all I knew of Bay Ridge were the reflections my grandparents passed on to me of nights at the Brooklyn Heights Casino, an 1890 version of the same fever that strikes Tony on the weekends. Should you doubt that Saturday Night Fever (it was Sunday Night fever back in the days of the six-day work week) is an old disease, let me cite an eminent authority of 1894, Stephen Crane, as he quotes a "stranger" on the Bay Ridge boat.

> The gayety which arises upon these Sunday night occasions is different from all other gayeties. There is an unspeakable air of recklessness and bravado and grief about it. The train load is going toward that inevitable, overhanging, devastating Monday. That singer there tomorrow will be a truckman, perhaps, and swearing ingeniously at his horses and other truck-men. He feels the approach of this implacable Monday. Two hours ago he was ingulfed in whirligigs and beer and had forgotten that there were Mondays. Now he is confronting it, and as he can't battle it, he scorns it. You can hear the undercurrent of it in that song, which is really as grievous as the cry of a child. If he had no vanity—well, it is fortunate for the world that we are not all great thinkers.

> We sat on the lower deck of the Bay Ridge boat and watched the marvelous lights of New York looming through the purple mist. The little Italian band situated up one stairway, through two doors and around three corners from us, sounded in beautiful, faint and slumberous rhythm. The breeze fluttered again in the stranger's locks. We could hear the splash of the waves against the bow. The sleepy lights looked at us with hue of red and green and orange. Overhead some dust-colored clouds scudded across the deep indigo sky. "Thunderation," said the stranger, "if I did not know of so many yesterdays and have such full knowledge of tomorrows, I should be perfectly happy at this moment, and that would create a sensation among philosophers all over the world."[1]

The "Heights" Casino may be the raw equivalent of Tony's 2001 Odyssey Ballroom. The point is not that my grandparents were among those who indulged in "an unspeakable air of recklessness and bravado" but that in some sense the Bay Ridge section of Brooklyn, the turf of the Faces, is, if not a magical area, certainly a historic one in the authentic development of the United States of America.

The film is replete with bridges, opening with a shot of positively the most famous bridge in our country, the first genuine space-leaping suspension bridge, the focus of much American painting and poetry . . . the Brooklyn Bridge. Since the film is contemporary, the bridge shown is a new bridge, the Verrazano-Narrows, some distance down the bay, connecting Brooklyn with another island, Staten, but even so bringing it closer to continental United States. This bridge lights Tony up with a flash of imagination. Tony is a poet, albeit without polish, who expresses himself largely through his body in his dancing. When his dancing fades he unsuspectingly finds himself reciting his poetry to his girl friend, every bit as fervently as did Dante to Beatrice, as they sit looking up at the bridge:

> The towers go up 690 feet. Center span is 228 feet wide. They got forty million cars going across it every year. They got 127,000 tons of steel, almost three quarter million cubic yards of concrete. Center span is 4,260 feet—total length including approach ramps—over two and a half miles. . . . I know everything about it. They've even got a guy buried in the concrete. He fell into it when they were building the bridge. Sometim—after 2001, on a Saturday night you kno—we drive up there, me and Bobby C. and the other guys. We swing from the cables. We almost fly.

> I come down here a lot, too. Look at it, get ideas.

But Tony is not the first to sit at that point on the globe, Bay Ridge, Brooklyn and find Calliope, the Muse of poetry, usurping Terpsichore, the Muse of dancing. Listen to Hart Crane, in his ode to the Brooklyn Bridge, a poet struggling with the immensity of this precise point on the globe, poised between Europe and the New World, poised between a humanistic and a technological world, linking his present with an aboriginal past of Saturday Night fevers:

> Dance, Maquokeeta! snake that lives before,

> That casts his pelt, and lives beyond! Sprout, horn!

> Spark, tooth! Medicine-man, relent, restore—Lie to us dance us back the tribal morn.[2, p. 24]

Little does Tony suspect that his erotic dance with Stephanie, to the point where he finds fulfillment, was presaged by an Indian, Maquokeeta, but the words of Hart Crane reveal the magic bond.

Yet for antecedent bridge worshipers on that shore, seeking a link to a larger world, the greatest is an early editor of the Brooklyn Eagle, Walt Whitman. Listen to him as he looks across that expanse of water to Manhattan, anticipating Tony, if not the bridge itself.

> Flood tide below me! I see you face to face!

> Clouds of the west sun there half an hour high I see you also face to face.

> Crowds of men and women attired in the usual costumes, how curious you are to me!

> On the ferry-boats the hundreds and hundreds that cross, returning home, are more curious to me than you suppose,

> And you that shall cross from shore to shore years hence are more to me, and more in my meditations, than you might suppose.[3, p. 143]

Then follows his direct salutation, it seems, to Tony:

> What is it then between us?

> What is the count of the scores or hundreds of years between us? [3, p. 145]

Granted it must be that these men, Tony, Stephen, Hart, and Walt, all feel the magic of that spot, Brooklyn's shore, where you look across the water to where the New World begins. All feel, each in his own way, the importance of crossing over. They are all men in transition, but of a special rare transition, for they all wish to carry over with them the fire of their special inspiration. Little wonder that they capture the imagination of a countless audience, for they are optimistic men in a threatening world.

Tony's struggle to move across to the promised land, disguised as it is, shadows the struggle of heroes who preceded him. He must leave behind his family, friends, job, and most important he must abandon his identify as a local person, the best dancer in Bay Ridge. He must do it all and remain a man with hope. The shock of his friend's death, more than the promise of love or fame, moves him over to the other side. He learns that transitions are not to be played with in a fearfully real way. He resists the decision to grow beyond Brooklyn, despite seeing through the empty victories at the dance contests and the subsequent rebuff of his sexual prowess by Stephanie. Perhaps he could have held on to his illusory Brooklyn world, his old world, if he had not seen the fatal travesty in his friend's playing with transitions. Bobby C. became the arrested adolescent playing chicken on the bridge with no intention of growing by the experience, only hoping to share a place in the gang by proving his "manliness." Reluctantly, Tony recognizes it as suicide, for when the patrolman asks him if Bobby jumped, he says, "No, but there are a lot of ways of committing suicide!" Now Tony must either break with the past and make it to the other side, or he too will die, suffocated by a job that is going no place, a family that is dead to him, and a gang that knows nothing but games.

The film shows Tony's transition as the modern man must make it. He is not Errol Flynn, master mariner at the prow of his river-crossing ship, nor is he Clark Gable, journeyman steel worker securing the last rivet in the girder and jumping down on the distant shore. The rites of passage are not that glamorous these days. Tony makes it across, like most of us, underground. He takes the subway. He rides all night, considering his fate much as Hart Crane describes:

> The phonographs of hades in the brain
> Are tunnels that re-wind themselves, and love
> A burnt match skating in a urinal—
> Somewhere above Fourteenth TAKE THE EXPRESS
> To brush some new presentiment of pain—

> Thunder is galvothermic here below. . . . The car
> Wheels off. The train rounds, bending to a scream,
> Taking the final level for the dive
> Under the river—
> And somewhat emptier than before,
> Demented, for a hitching second, humps; then
> Lets go. . . . Toward corners of the floor
> Newspapers wing, revolve and wing.
> Blank windows gargle signals through the roar.[2, pp. 67,68]

But Tony does make it. He finally gets off the subway the next morning in Manhattan and finds his way to Stephanie's apartment. They make up on a new basis of equality and friendship. Stephanie, realizing he is a new man, agrees, "Okay, we'll help each other. We'll be friends."

Walt puts it another way, but comes to the same conclusion, difficult as love may be for each and every one of us to understand.

> City of orgies, walks and joys,
> City whom that I have lived and sung in your midst will one day make
>   you illustrious,
> Not the pageants of you, not your shifting tableaus, your spectacles,
>   repay me,
> Not the interminable rows of your houses, nor the ships at the wharves,
> Nor the processions in the streets, nor the bright windows with goods
>   in them,
> Nor to converse with learn'd persons, or hear my share in the soiree or
>   feast;
> Not those, but as I pass O Manhattan, your frequent and swift flash of
>   eyes offering me love,
> Offering response to my own—these repay me,
> Lovers, continual lovers, only repay me.[3, p. 113]

If you have not seen *Saturday Night Fever*, do, and when you go remember that it is not just Tony up on the screen dancing his feet off in Brooklyn, but it's Stephen and Hart writing their guts out, and Walt singing his head off, and Everyman doing his level best to put meaning and love in his life, all right up there on the screen before you.

References

1. Crane S. The New York Sketches of Stephen Crane, edited by R. W. Stallman and E. R. Hagemann, New York, New York University Press, 1966, reprinted from the New York Press, 14 Oct. 1894, p. 75.
2. Crane H. The Bridge. New York, Liveright Publishing Corporation, 1970.
3. Whitman W. Leaves of Grass. Garden City, Doubleday, Doran & Co., 1940

MOVIE REVIEW

ARROWSMITH

Starring Ronald Colman, Helen Hayes, A. E. Anson, and Myrna Loy
Directed by John Ford
Based on the novel by Sinclair Lewis
REVIEW BY RALPH CRAWSHAW, M.D.
(Winter 1984, pp. 49–52)

G OING TO THE MOVIES CAN BE A MOST CURIOUS EXPERIENCE. For me
an example was in again viewing *Arrowsmith,* the film that fifty years
ago fixed in my mind the ambition to become a scientist physician, and
in now experiencing an eerie sense of closure of my own professional life, observing it from both ends simultaneously. I had a feeling stronger than *déjà vu*
and more deeply poignant than that produced by a sentimental journey to a
childhood home. Yet stranger still was how the experience opened my eyes to
a serious condition that impairs a number of physicians: uncontrolled appetite
for knowledge—"The Arrowsmith Syndrome."

Drs. Kevin Fox and Peter Dans of the Johns Hopkins Department of Medicine
had invited me to add some thoughts about medicine and movies to the Johns
Hopkins Hospital annual AΩA celebration in April, 1983. The program consisted of two days of films and seminars, starting with a one-half hour TV documentary on the life of house officers at the University of Washington, moving
to the 1971 film, *The Hospital,* starring George C. Scott as Herb Bock, the professor of medicine destroyed by his ruthless pursuit of excellence, and culminating with *Arrowsmith.* Our symposium sought perspective on physicians'
ways of life over three generations, for the movies afford a wonderful window
on generational change, and we wanted to make the most of it. Nor were we ill
advised in using *Arrowsmith* as our fulcrum for discussion. In an interesting
article in *Möbius,* "*Arrowsmith* and the History of American Medicine," Gert
Brieger underlines the importance of Sinclair Lewis's epic in understanding the
development of twentieth-century medicine in the United States. He uses it as
the central reading for a course on medicine and humanities.[2]

Certainly, the novel is richer and more detailed than the movie, but the film
adequately depicts the development of Martin Arrowsmith (Ronald Colman) from
his birth in the Midwest, through college in 1900, to medical school, intern-

351

ship, practice in rural and urban America, and participation in American medical research from 1910 until the opening of the Golden Age of Medicine in 1925. Arrowsmith's generation of physicians, the generation that is grandfather to that of our present medical students, much as Osler's generation of physicians is a great-grandfather, appears as big as life in any contemporary metropolitan hospital.

As a boy, Martin Arrowsmith is inspired to become a physician by a local general practitioner who, in his crusty way, emphasizes that the only three literary works a good physician need know are *Gray's Anatomy,* Shakespeare's plays, and the Bible. In his graduate education, however, Martin's definition of a good physician greatly expands as he studies with an outstanding scientist, Max Gottlieb (A. E. Anson), a character Sinclair Lewis, with the help of his friend Paul de Kruif, fashioned after a combination of Frederick G. Novy, a teacher of de Kruif, and Jacque Loeb, a physiologist at the Rockefeller Institute. Gottlieb is ruthless in holding to scientific method at a time when the discipline is considered by many practitioners to be just a notch above witchcraft. The quest for scientific truth becomes Arrowsmith's central belief, although on graduation he is forced by the lack of money to enter practice in the rural town of Wheatsylvania. While he delivers babies and pulls teeth, in his kitchen laboratory he simultaneously develops a serum with which to treat cattle suffering from an epidemic of black leg. Not too surprisingly, as a new doctor in town his originality earns him more enmity than respect.

The first time *Arrowsmith* flickered before my twelve-year-old eyes in 1933, I was unaware of how completely captivating Martin Arrowsmith's sense of self-sacrifice could be nor how neatly his dedication to science solved both his and my unconscious problems with mature love. Martin Arrowsmith meets his future wife, Leora Tozer (Helen Hayes), when, as a medical student, he walks on the ward of a metropolitan hospital to pick up a meningococcus sample for his mentor's laboratory. Unsure of his way, he asks directions from a probation nurse, who is down on her knees scrubbing the floor. When she fails to snap to attention, even as she apologizes, he rages at her, "*I* am Dr. Arrowsmith." This theme of unquestioned preeminence of the man/scientist over the woman/servant is slightly softened but never relinquished throughout the film; Martin and Leora marry, but it is a sometimes marriage for her. She begs, scrimps, saves, and patiently waits, while he eats, sleeps, talks, daydreams, works, and does what he wishes, all in his own good time, never acknowledging her needs. It was and is a male adolescent's ideal of the man/woman relationship, particularly when empowered with the unquestioned authority of the hero's macho self-sacrifice for science. Martin is not expected to have any responsibilities in the marriage, while Leora remains perpetually grateful that she is permitted to serve him in his pursuit of a holy grail.

The film climaxes after Arrowsmith follows Gottlieb to the "McGurk Medical Foundation," a fantasy institution fashioned after the Rockefeller Institute, where Martin develops a possible cure for plague. The foundation sends him to test his discovery during an epidemic of plague on "St. Hubert," an imaginary island in the West Indies. Reluctantly, Martin permits Leora to accompany him but without a smidgen of feeling for her, in his single-minded dedication to randomized clinical trials of his serum. Understandably, there is considerable local resistance to his treating the natives much as he treats his wife, like laboratory animals. Only after Leora dies of the plague does he began to differentiate between human beings and guinea pigs. Overwhelmed with her death through his own neglect, he asks the key question to all humanness: "Do you know that I loved you?" Mad with remorse he abandons his randomized clinical controls and administers the serum indiscriminately. The serum turns out to be effective, and he returns home a hero but bitter, more for the demands made on him by the institution than from remorse at Leora's death; and he rejects the human race for a hermit's life in a primitive laboratory in Vermont, where he will discover even greater cures for mankind.

"Hurrah, this is the life for me," said I to myself fifty years ago. Luckily, however, it did not turn out that way for me. I hope that despite Martin Arrowsmith's example of single-minded devotion to medicine, I have turned out to be a lover of science, not its slave. As I say, going to the movies can be a curious experience.

Once the lights came up at our showing of *Arrowsmith*, members of the audience moved to a nearby conference room to examine their reactions. The audience was small; not many had attended, for most of the physicians I met at the medical center had protested that though they very much wished to see the film, work made it impossible. Frankly, we did not expect many, for it is highly improbable that Martin Arrowsmith, Herb Bock, or their modern counterparts would spare time from work to look at themselves. Pragmatically, reflection is about as common in the nature of physicians as it is in the curriculum of medical schools, where like watching the movies, reflecting on oneself ranks as "subjective" amusement.

Coincidentally, our group, with a sprinkling of faculty members, was largely made up of women residents and medical students deeply involved with the question of medicine as a way of life. We began by examining the peculiarities of medical practice fifty years ago: cigarette smoking was incessant; *all* men wore felt fedoras; and the inconsequential sums of money then to be earned seemed magnificent. (Arrowsmith is tempted to give up his scientific studies so that he may earn $15,000 a year in private practice and own a mansion.)

Predictably, the discussion moved to Martin Arrowsmith's character and his hypertrophied dedication to mankind, which left him bereft of an understanding of people. Even his deep attachment to Gottlieb, his mentor, came into question when one of the faculty members suggested that such blind, single-minded teacher/student commitment leads in modern science to scandals like the Darsee situation. The discussion finally focused down on what is virtue in medicine, and what are the essential qualities to be sought in a physician, with the younger generation holding out for intelligence and the older for courage and compassion. Agreement was never reached, beyond a rejection of Martin Arrowsmith's and Herb Bock's definition of the good: work for work's sake.

At the AΩA dinner the previous evening I had been agreeably surprised by a request to say a few words and frankly disconcerted at saying them after the scholar and former Dean Thomas B. Turner had lovingly reminisced about the character shown by the men who had founded Johns Hopkins. Perhaps discordantly, I tried to summarize what the seminar was about. In comparing the generations we were attempting to discover more about ways of life that lead to physician impairment. I pointed out that we no longer find it acceptable to conceal physician impairment, as Sir William Osler had in concealing William Stewart Halsted's morphine addiction. The profession has matured to an open awareness of our occupational hazards, and with the same scientific gaze we use when studying diseases in others, we are beginning to look at ourselves. I hoped the curiosity of the AΩA members would be stimulated by the fact that during their careers 10 percent of Oregon's physicians are called before the State Board of Medical Examiners for serious personal failings in the practice of medicine, and of that group, 25 percent come from the upper 10 percent of their graduating classes. I went on, defining the major reason for physician impairment as poor appetite control, with pathological hunger for mind-altering drugs responsible for 80 percent of the nation's physician casualties. There are estimated to be 10,000 alcoholic physicians in the United States, and the rate of drug addiction runs between 30 to 100 times higher for physicians than for the general population.[3]

Half tempted to speak of another appetite, but fearful of poorly conceived thoughts, I closed by asking the students to remember that they must expect to defer pleasure in the pursuit of their education but that they should never defer virtue in that or any pursuit, for as they were students so should they expect to be physicians.

Unsatisfied, for the lack of a sense of solid closure on the seminar, I returned home to seek out a Hopkins man who I hoped would help me better understand the experience. I re-read William Osler's *A Way of Life*. He certainly would have appreciated my reaction to *Arrowsmith*, for he quotes Dr. Samuel Johnson on how trifling circumstances have influenced men's lives, "not by an ascendant planet, a predominating humour, but by the first book which they read, some early conversation which they have heard, or some accident which excited ardour and enthusiasm."[4, p. 9] Osler then gives the germinal experience for him in a quote from Thomas Carlyle: "Our main business is not to see what lies dimly at a distance, but to do what lies clearly at hand."[4, p. 10] This is that "clearly at hand," work-for-work's sake exhortation that students are continually fed, even though it may lead to "leanness of soul." Apparently we have hitched Osler's work ethic (though he only asked for four or five hours of concentration each day) to a medical education machine driven by fact-based testing, and we are spinning out casualties in unknown numbers.

I began to see how to bring closure to the seminar as I considered the need to couple the dynamics of medical education with the pathology of impaired physicians. I could hear again, as I have heard so often, the plea of medical students when privately confronted with their slave-like behavior: "How am I, as a medical student, to do anything but blurt out the answers when the chief of services starts grand rounds with, 'What are the numbers [the test results]?' " or, "Even if I think an operation is questionable, let alone unnecessary, how can I say anything?" or, "Should I say to the chief resident, 'I do not think I should work up this patient. I have not slept for seventy-two hours and I think my judgment is poor?' No. it is macho all the way."

Apparently it is as much a required rite of passage to overconsume knowledge in medicine as it is to abuse alcohol in other walks of life. The "man" proves himself in medical education by his appetite for facts. That is our system, and it becomes a part of ourselves.

Such a serious indictment of medical education needs adequate documentation to be considered seriously, and the documentation is not easy to find, for like most problems, the parameters of uncontrolled appetite are never clear. Though most people drink alcohol, most are not alcoholics. Yet alcoholism does exist as a clear syndrome of appetite impairment. But when does one become a drunk?

To make the case clear, then, we must delineate a pathologic entity that can be seen by all. A clue to just such an entity occurred to me, as I reflected back to the *Arrowsmith* discussion: the remark about the Darsee scandal. Though all that is known about the Darsee problem is derived from medical journals,[5] nothing from direct clinical observation, the accounts are full, carefully documented, uncontested, and make clear that a *number* of people exhibited extraordinary appetites for knowing, for having knowledge, and for being so recognized. Apparently, cohorts of Martin Arrowsmith and Herb Bock were willing to abandon their judgment by joining their names in a series of reports, the publication of which would easily gratify their hunger for knowing or being known as knowing. Did they never doubt the numbers? They seem to have believed that recognition as number chewers was a greater good.

To review briefly John Darsee, at the age of thirty-four, was discovered in his scientific work at a Harvard teaching hospital to have forged data in a number of his published papers.[6,7] His name appears on 116 articles listed in the Science *Citation Index* with some forty-six investigators sharing authorship, some as frequently as thirty-nine times. In the course of Dr. Darsee's activity, which subsequent investigation leads back to the time of his training at Emory University, only one Ph.D. took the trouble to check out his work carefully when he proposed that she coauthor a paper. She discovered serious discrepancies in the paper, declined coauthorship, and reported her findings to the medical authorities. Nothing came of her report. Forty-six others joined the frauds, and as one of the bilked coauthors subsequently reported, "It was a very flattering kind of thing. Purely and simple, he was trading on my name."[8]

We have here a case series, albeit lightly documented, of forty-six physician investigators who were hungry enough for recognition to act like scientists when they were simply being sycophants. Let me propose the Arrowsmith syndrome to explain this phenomenon, a syndrome that seldom surfaces in public, but that like alcoholism may be more common than we wish to believe in the actual practice of scientific medicine.

"The Arrowsmith Syndrome" is a pervasive impairment of judgment developing in medical scientists. It is characterized by a pathological overvaluation of knowledge as an end in itself, resulting in loss of social ties, progressive moral corruption, dehumanization, and, in extreme cases, personal dissolution, including suicide. The syndrome appears in two forms, one, the active or carrier form found in medical educators, research scientists, and practitioners with a patent hunger for fame. The other, the chronic or latent form, is found in physicians and medical students with an inordinate belief in facts, unexamined ambitions, and a latent vulnerability to intellectual stress.

Certainly, the lack of close clinical documentation leaves the symptoms of the Arrowsmith syndrome open to discussion, but a rather solid series of conjectures suggest them to be:

Primary symptoms:

1. Hyperintellectualization in a talented physician scientist who is competitive to the point of extravagant ambition.
2. Exaggerated scientific goals (Nobel Prize), which excuse remorseless demands on self, associates, and family.
3. A pronounced susceptibility to flattery for accomplishments in his field of choice as well as an acute sensitivity to professional dissonance with supervisors.
4. Absence of alternative life goals coupled with low or absent emotional and moral imagination.

Secondary symptoms: Inability to deal constructively with either direct intellectual challenge or loss. Under stress, recourse to rationalization, denial, projection, and lying.

Course of disease: Under pronounced confrontation a tendency either to flee, decompensate, with personal dissolution (alcoholism or suicide), or, following a period of intense remorse and disgust, to go into a period of remission with loss of hyperintellectualization. The scars are lifelong.

Arnold Relman, in his editorial, "Lessons from the Darsee Affair" makes some telling points about the continual need to judge ourselves as scientists.[9] He also clearly delineates the passive Arrowsmith syndrome sufferers for their impairment. "The two formal retraction notices . . . seem to suggest that his [Darsee's] coauthors at Emory had no responsibility at all for what happened, simply because they are honest and had no hand in the manipulation of the data. I cannot agree, and neither will most other editors."[9, p. 1417]

Dr. Relman leads us to a proper understanding of the Arrowsmith syndrome. It is not a single moral flaw in one culprit—Arrowsmith never faked his data—rather, it is the ambience of unfettered hyperintellectualization that is the cause of all the cases. In effect, there are many more alcoholic physicians than those who end up in detoxification centers, and as a profession we should be strong enough to acknowledge the strong possibility that there are many more physicians with a pathological hunger for facts than the one or two who are caught.

Dr. Relman sagely advises that "any attempt to police the system would probably create such an atmosphere of suspicion and distrust that the free spirit of scientific inquiry would be crushed."[9, p. 1415] No, we do not need a prohibition on any hunger, including the one for knowledge, but as clinicians we need to learn much more of the pathology of knowledge hunger rather than to forget the Darsee case as a single case of moral turpitude.

A detail that simply cannot leave my mind since I listened to the Johns Hopkins women physicians look at the way of life with a candor, sometime fierce, always refreshing, is that the one scientist who refused to be named on one of the fraudulent papers was a woman. Perhaps it was a coincidence, but I do not think so, for I believe women are bringing to the profession a new definition of truth, closer to our innate biology and psychology, as they take a greater role in medicine's future. Certainly, Mrs. Arrowsmith, had she lived, might have offered a different view on the truth of Dr. Arrowsmith's humanness.

We all have hungers and we all need to be reminded by those who love us—our spouses, children, mentors, and patients—that we can lose ourselves to our hungers should we fail to judge ourselves wisely, not as scientists, but as human beings. Since it is improbable that you can see *Arrowsmith*, unless some TV executive discovers it as the primordial "General Hospital" and makes a super-epic of it, read this tale of twentieth-century medicine and then read it again for the patent dehumanization our medical education and research system fosters under the guise of a new religion of science. Although the possibility grows, I hope it will never be said that we remain human in spite of being physicians.

References

1. Crawshaw R. The physician at the movies: The Hospital. Pharos. 35(4): 171–73, 1972.
2. Brieger G. Arrowsmith and the history of medicine in America. Möbius 2(3):32–38, 1982.
3. Scheiber SC and Doyle BB, eds. The Impaired Physician. New York, Plenum Medical Book Co., 1983, p. 4.
4. Osler W. A Way of Life. New York, Paul B. Hoeber, 1937.
5. Culliton BJ. Coping with Fraud: The Darsee Case. Science 220;31–35, 1983.
6. Nutter DO, Heymsfield SB and Glenn JF. Retraction. N Engl J Med 308:1400, 1983.
7. Heymsfield SB and Glenn JF. Retraction. N Engl J Med 308:1400, 1983.
8. Knox RA. Deeper problems for Darsee: Emory probe. JAMA 249:2867–76, 1983, p. 2871.
9. Relman AS. Lessons from the Darsee Affair (editorial). N Engl J Med 308:1415–17, 1983.

The Physician On Broadway:
EQUUS

A play by Peter Shaffer. New York, Atheneum, 1974. 211 Pp. $7.95.
REVIEW BY CARLETON B. CHAPMAN, M.D.
(April 1975, pp. 80–82)

A PLAY CURRENTLY ON BROADWAY wouldn't ordinarily be a fit subject for a book review for *The Pharos*. But *Equus* is no ordinary play and is likely to be of great interest to health professionals; and, for that matter, to anyone interested in the strains and stresses of adolescence.

Among the New York critics, Walter Kerr gave it top marks, especially for its ingenuity and technique. To him, it ". . . is one of the most remarkable examples of stagecraft, as well as of sustained and multifaceted sensibility, the contemporary theater has given us" *(New York Times*, Section 2, pp. 1 and 5; 3 November 1974). Brendan Gill said that "on its most accessible level, [the play] is a mystery story: somewhere in England . . ." and goes on from there to construct a very skillful estimate *(The New Yorker* 50:123–124; 4 November 1974). But these comments were only the beginning: there have been others since, and it looks as if they will keep coming for quite awhile. Which may mean simply that no one is likely to come away from the play without having been moved by it. He (or she) may dislike it intensely, or he may (like Walter Kerr) think it the greatest: but he is not likely to fail to react.

> How came Mr. Shaffer to choose such an extraordinary theme? In a brief but essential prefatory note, be offers an explanation. Several years ago a friend told him, on passing a stable, about a crime he'd heard discussed at a dinner party in London: a highly disturbed young man had deliberately blinded several horses with a metal spike. The crime had ". . . deeply shocked a local bench of magistrates.** It lacked, finally, any coherent explanation." The report also shocked Mr. Shaffer. "I knew," he says,

---

** In England and Wales there are something like 900 Magistrates' Courts served by nearly 20,000 lay Justices of the Peace. Normally, a Magistrates' Court, or Bench, will have three to seven such officials sitting together. There is no jury. The Courts handle ninety-eight per cent of all criminal offenses (and some civil ones), and have very broad powers in all but the most serious cases. The Justices are drawn from the community in which they live and are usually unpaid "very strongly that I wanted to interpret it in some entirely personal way. I had to create a mental world in which the deed could be made comprehensible."

Equus does precisely that, and does it convincingly.

Since the starting point is necessarily composed of the ingredients of the actual crime—a disturbed boy, blinded horses, and shocked magistrates—all three elements figure in the play itself. But to develop his explanation for the psychodynamics of the crime, Mr. Shaffer moves deeply into Old and New Testament imagery, Pauline Christianity, and modem psychiatric theory and practice. Superficially, the play's focus is on seventeen-year-old Alan Strang and Dr. Peter Dysart, a middle-aged psychiatrist. But to me the actual focus is on the intricate struggle between the boy and his parents, the emphasis being on son vs. mother or vice-versa. The role of the psychiatrist is little more than the vehicle by means of which the fundamental struggle is conveyed to the audience.

The story itself is not very complex. The stableboy, hardly literate but intelligent and sensitive, reared as an only child by his fanatically religious schoolteacher-mother, stabs out the eyes of six horses, including one of which he is pathologically fond, and is hauled into the local Magistrates' Court for his crime.

The play, done on a square-railed platform furnished only with benches, opens with a premonitory soliloquy by Dr. Dysart, which is quickly interrupted by a visit from Hesther Salomon, a magistrate and a long-time friend. She entreats him to take the young offender, Alan Strang, into therapy. "My bench wanted to send the boy to prison. For life, if they could manage it. It took me two hours solid arguing to get him sent to you instead."

Dysart grudgingly accepts and proceeds, through two longish acts broken by a ten-minute intermission, to extract a reenactment of his patient's emotional development from those most intimately concerned with it.

Alan's initial entrance has a dramatic quality all its own. He is small, has a blond afro-hairdo, and conveys hostility even in his lithe bodily movement. In reply to Dysart's routine questions he sings one of the most perverse tunes ever used on commercial television:

> Double your pleasure,
> Double your fun,
> etc.

This goes on, we learn from the various dialogues, for several days before anything like effective verbal communication begins between patient and therapist.

From that point things move rapidly and are conveyed by very ingenious staging techniques, especially the disposition of the actors on and around the square platform. The six horses, never totally out of sight, are played by six young men dressed in chestnut velvet, metal hooves on their feet, and towering metal horse masks mounted on their heads. The principal lines at any given moment are spoken by actors on the square platform; but others immediately off it speak lines that interweave appropriately with the focal conversations.

As the patient and therapist begin to speak to each other, several items, to become significant a bit later, are introduced. Then Dr. Dysart goes to see Dora Strang in her home. Her husband, Frank, is a printer and is still at his shop. Dora begins to explain how fond Alan has always been of animals; he has a picture of a horse over his bed; she once read him a story about a horse named Prince and said that the boy liked to imagine that horses could talk. There was yet more about horses. Then Dora gets into Biblical themes:

Dora: They're in the Bible of course. "He saith among the trumpets, Ha, ha."

Dysart: Ha, ha?

Dora: The Book of Job. Such a noble passage. *You* know—"Hast thou given the horse strength?"

Alan: [*responding offstage*] "Hast thou clothed his neck with thunder?"

Dora: [*to Alan*] "The glory of his nostrils is terrible!"

Alan: "He swallows the ground with fierceness and rage."

Dora: "He saith among the trumpets,"

Alan: [*trumpeting*] "Ha, ha!"

The actual passage is Job 39:19–25 and is part of a long section in which The Lord is, by his queries and comments about horses, emphasizing Job's weakness as a mere human being. And Job finally replies abjectly: "Wherefore I abhor myself and repent in dust and ashes" (42:6).

The brilliant Biblical imagery, conveyed to her son by Dora, is recalled later in the play when Alan, recounting an actual and traumatic early experience with a horse, literally looks up into the horse's mouth:

It was huge. There was this chain in it . . . I said 'Does it hurt?' And he said . . . the horse . . . said . . .

Alan, unable to finish, tries to remember when horses began to acquire such great meaning for him. There was the story of Prince; and the white horse in The Revelation of St. John the Divine (19:11-16):

And he that sat upon him was called Faithful and True, and in righteousness he doth judge and make war.

His eyes were as a flame of fire . . . and he had a name written, that no man knew, but he himself.

And he was clothed with a vesture dripped in blood: and his name is called the Word of God.

Alan doesn't quote the entire passage but the setting is such that he can be assumed to have known all of it—vividly; and possibly the even more terrible descriptions of the four horsemen in Revelation 6:2–8.

"God sees you Alan. God's got eyes everywhere." This from Dora to her son. And, asked by Dysart if she had told the boy anything about sex, she replies in standard Pauline terms:

> That if God willed he would fall in love one day. That his task was to pre-
> pare himself for the most important happening of his life. And after that
> . . . he might come to know a higher love still.

She never quite gets round in the play to quoting The Apostle Paul's many admonitions to the Galatians, Thessalonians, and Corinthians concerning the evils of adultery and fornication; lines that unmistakably equate sex with sin and sin with sex. Nor does she quote his famous lines from First Corinthians (7:8–9):

> I say therefore to the unmarried and widows, it is good for them if they abide
> even as I. But if they cannot contain, let them marry: for it is better to
> marry than to burn.

But the sense is there even though her mindless description of her son's task seems on the surface to be less severe than Paul's harsh statement. Yet it is no less harsh; only more subtle.

The remaining item, also not quoted directly, in what may appropriately be called *the Pauline sequence,* is Romans 6:23:

> For the wages of sin is death.

The whole is inherent in Dora's lines and in her superb portrayal of the role of the mother-still-spinster, brought up in the Victorian mould and unable to see the fatuity and inhumanity in Paul's version of the Christian legacy. Nor is she able to relate naturally or easily to her husband, whose deficient insight leads him into absurd but damaging overreaction.

Add to this Alan's early preoccupation with a lurid picture of Christ on his way to Calvary, burdened by the cross and being scourged and reviled by Roman soldiers; add also the fact that the picture (like the telly set) was angrily re-moved by his father, and the picture of the horse substituted: with all this, the ingredients of Alan's complex psychosexual maldevelopment are more or less complete. The child was the recipient of undiluted brilliance of Biblical imagery and violence, made worse by the absence of warmth and affection within the fam-ily, and somehow not mitigated by contact with other children.

Dora's greatest trial comes when she visits Alan in the hospital to which he was sent by the Magistrates' Court. She is asked to take his supper tray to him. The boy seizes it and throws it at her, whereupon she flies into a rage and slaps him. A nurse frantically intervenes. Then Dora faces Dysart on center stage. He angrily tells her never to come again. The scene that follows is perhaps the most terrible in the play: Dora, having invested much of her adult life in what she considered to be the welfare of her only child, now surveys the wreckage; and struggles desperately with her guilt:

> We're not criminals. We've done nothing wrong. We loved Alan. We gave him the best love we could.

And later:

> If you knew God, Doctor, you would know about the Devil. The Devil's there. . . . I'll go. What I did was inexcusable. I only know he was my little Alan, and then the Devil came.

One reviewer said disparagingly that Dora, though a teacher, can come up with nothing better in her distress than her comment about the Devil. Actually Dora came up with a great deal. For my part, the slap she gave Alan was not inappropriate; and neither were her words to Dysart, with their overwhelming intimations of guilt and grief at the knowledge that no second chance can ever be hers. Invoking the devil was the only way open to her in her time of utter despair. And it is a tribute to Shaffer's skill and feeling that neither the misshapen boy nor the prim, wretched mother can be hated or scorned; or even actively disliked.

It would be unfair to disclose the play's resolution in full. But there *is* a resolution, enormously dramatic and gripping and in substance, credible.

The play's denouement is preceded by an incident in which Alan and his girl, quite by accident, see his father at a skinflick. The upshot of the encounter is that father Strang lamely tries to explain his presence as official; for business reasons. And Alan, finally, begins to understand and accept his father, to a point. Then comes a much-discussed nude scene in which the girl tries to seduce Alan and thus precipitates the beginning of the play's turbulent end.

Of weakness there's a fair amount. For one thing, the psychiatrist himself is not quite real, unless English psychiatrists differ radically from the American sort, which I doubt. And the significance of Dysart's meaningless marriage, his absent sex life, and his fascination with Greek archeology (as elicited by Alan in swapping secret for secret) doesn't quite fit the play's Grand Plan. True, everyone who has been through anything like psychoanalysis must have wondered a good deal about his analyst's sex life, among other things. But whatever form such things take, they have little relevance to the evolution of one's own problems unless the analyst is a fool, or unless he believes that modern views of psychotherapy require him to have sexual relations with his patients: which may amount to the same thing. Much of this figures in a discerning but sharply negative comment on the play by Sanford Gifford, a psychoanalyst *(New York Times*, Sect. 2, pp. 1 and 5, 15 December 1974). And it may well be that the play's most serious defect (as Dr. Gifford suggests) is the implication that Alan's acting out will, by destroying his pain and interrupting his psychodynamic short circuit, bring him into "normal" society. Dr. Dysart paradoxically infers that this may be a serious *loss* for Alan. Yet need he have worried? The reality is probably something quite different. What is the prognosis for a semiliterate seventeen-year-old who has had psychotic episodes, no usual or rewarding one-to-one relationships, and who has come into therapy only after a vastly paranoid psychotic crisis?

For Alan, unlike Job, was not able to say to his Equus god-lover-tormentor:

> I abhor myself. I repent in dust and ashes.

Instead, he tumbled into rebellion and put out god's eyes, unable to bear the torment of that unrelenting and unforgiving gaze. But the wages of sin is still death. And the scene ends with Alan screaming: "Find me! Find me! Kill me! Kill me!"

READING LEAVES

AUDREY SHAFER, M.D.
(Spring 1996, p. 33)

October light slices through louvered blinds.

I listen
to pain-writ poems
A litany of misdiagnoses
repeated tests
maladroit exchanges
inexorable debility—
Finally, a disease label
patched on the illness
Names the horror.
A new stanza begins.

I squeeze between the slats
and listen to a lone vermilion maple
sing to me
of leaves too broad and useless
to last a winter's chill.

Coughs, the rustle of papers
Cue me to join the applause.

Next reader.
I am about to glide outside again
When I am grabbed by words
a child draws
hunched over her paper, crayon gripped
oh so careful not to cross the lines
careful, lest mommy's cancer return.
Tender and quiet, the scene is painted
auburn and henna in my mind.

But I take care to hide my care—
glance surreptitiously about
and hunker down.

The earth's long bow to summer sun is done—
Another year perhaps I'll share
Such plaintive notes
with tears allowed to fall.

PART IX

WOMEN...
THEIR HEALTH
AND RIGHTS

THE EARLY BIRTH CONTROL MOVEMENT: ROLE OF THE NINETEENTH-CENTURY AMERICAN PHYSICIAN

ROBERT QUINTO SCACHERI, M.D.
(Spring 1993, pp. 15–20)

THE EARLY YEARS OF THE AMERICAN BIRTH CONTROL MOVEMENT were characterized by remarkably rapid success in the face of enormous adversity. Written contraceptive information was practically nonexistent in the United States in 1800. The first significant American tract on birth control did not appear until 1831, and, almost immediately, contraception was attacked as immoral and unhealthy by religious, social, and medical leaders. Forty-two years later it was also essentially declared illegal, with the enactment of a federal law prohibiting the mailing of information on the prevention of conception. Despite these obstacles to family planning, the average number of children born to an American woman between 1800 and 1900 fell from more than seven to about three. It is appropriate to begin with an exploration of the medical community's understanding of sexuality, especially female sexuality, in order to provide a context for examination of the physician's role in the changing demographics of the nineteenth century.

The "science" of sexuality

In the nineteenth century, American society underwent several changes that made birth control desirable. Richard D. Brown has called the sum of these changes the development of the American "modern personality."[2] James Reed has pointed out that as part of this new American psyche both urban and rural Americans in all classes were "increasingly better educated, read more newspapers and books, participated more in the political process, had more faith in material progress, and were more confident than their fathers of the individual's ability to control nature and his own life."[1, p. 4] With increasing education and intellectual awareness came the desire and capability for self-determination.

But what was it about nineteenth-century society that made family planning the manifestation of this new self-determination? Carroll Smith-Rosenberg and Charles Rosenberg have pointed to three explanations. The first related to the economic motivations of families in an increasingly industrial society. Children were seen increasingly as a drain on finances, no longer being the economic asset they had been in the agricultural setting.[3] Other historians have added that children were now seen as impressionable beings who would someday take up the American banner of progress and who required more attention, more moral and intellectual training, and more physical care, none of which were possible unless couples had fewer children.[1,4] A second reason for the increased interest in contraception was that the role of women was changing. Marriage was increasingly being viewed as a mutual relationship, with husband and wife equals. She should have control over her body and her relationship with her husband. Finally, as women gained rights, they began to rebel against the pain and permanent disfigurement or death that often accompanied being pregnant many times.[3]

Despite the clear desire for contraception, the medical community as a group shirked responsibility for the construction of family planning strategies throughout the nineteenth century. Early and mid-nineteenth century medical textbooks failed to provide any information on contraception. Even in 1890, William Goodell, professor of clinical gynecology at the University of Pennsylvania, admitted in his textbook of gynecology, "It is . . . so hard a task to discuss such subjects in acceptable language, that I confess to some squeamishness, and would much rather refer you to suitable textbooks, were there any."[5]

There were several arguments against family planning that the conservative physician tended to adopt. First, nineteenth-century leaders equated sexual intercourse with procreation; intercourse as an act of love, let alone passion, without the intention of creating children, was inconceivable.[1] A second argument against birth control became especially popular late in the century. This was the fear of race suicide. As early as 1860, censuses showed that the American birthrate was rapidly declining. Even worse, it was declining much faster in native-born Americans than in foreign-born Americans. Social leaders preached that it would not be long before the country was populated primarily by aliens. Smith-Rosenberg and Rosenberg have suggested that another reason for opposition to birth control was its association with female autonomy. Social leaders feared that contraception would lead to liberation from childbearing and child raising and to the diversion of women into education and the work force.[3]

Simple articulation of these arguments by physicians did little to suppress the popular interest in contraception. What did hinder the birth control movement, however, was the use of medical and biological jargon and theories to justify the denunciation of contraception. It became common practice late in the nineteenth century for medicine to describe gender in such a way as to promote preservation of the "traditional and proper" sexual relationships. Physicians used bedside observation and autopsies to analyze the differences between men and women, but final explanations of gender were not made based on these observations alone. Rather, scientific findings were interpreted with an eye on social stereotypes. Physicians looked to anatomy and physiology to explain what they saw, or wanted to see, as the social differences between men and women.[3] The role of the nineteenth-century doctor was to "comfort and to reassure by interpreting the natural order, by explaining the sources of disease in the individual's failure to observe the laws of nature and of society."[6, p. 111] The man's greater musculature and superior skull size were seen as the foundation for his role as provider. The whole female body, on the other hand, was seen as constructed for childbearing and child rearing.[3]

Woman was portrayed as the sum of her reproductive parts. In a lecture given to a class at Jefferson Medical College in 1847, Charles D. Meigs, a prominent gynecologist, stated that the woman was "a moral, a sexual, a germiferous, gestative and parturient creature."[7] In 1870, another physician claimed that it was "as if the Almighty, in creating the female sex, had taken the uterus and built up a woman around it."[8] It was even suggested that the uterus was connected to the central nervous system, thus implying that the womb was the female brain. All of these beliefs were designed to promote the social stereotype of woman as mother.[3]

Anything that prevented a woman from fulfilling this maternal role was considered harmful to her health. Women were told that practically every known obstetrical and gynecological disease could result from birth control. In his preface to the 1870 American edition of a French work on the subject, P. de Marmon, M.D. wrote:

> On first reading the original of which I here offer a translation, I was struck by the number of diseases and moral troubles caused by that unnatural practice entitled Conjugal Onanism [sexual indulgence without the goal of procreation].[9]

Condoms and *coitus interruptus* were considered unhealthy, because without the reception of male "nervous energy" and the presence of semen in the vagina the woman could not expect true fulfillment.[3] Even if a woman seemed to escape the ill effects of birth control sooner or later, "about the fortieth year, the disease [cancer] grows as the energies fail—the cancerous fangs penetrating deeper and deeper until, after excruciating suffering, the writhing victim is yielded up to its terrible embrace."[10] As in the example above, physicians usually described the delayed health effects of contraception as occurring around the menopause. Women were led to believe that the changes they were observing at that time were pathological and the result of their earlier "crimes against nature." As Alexander J. C. Skene, a professor of gynecology at the Long Island College Hospital, noted in 1889:

> The woman who willingly tries to reverse the order of her physical being in the hope of gratifying some fancy or ambition, is almost sure to suffer sooner or later from disappointment and ill-health. Doctors make fortunes (small ones) by trying to restore health and peace of mind to those who violate the laws of morals and health in their efforts to prevent reproduction. In such cases, the relations [physiological processes] are deranged by perverted mind influence. Disease of the maltreated organ follows, and revenges their wrong by torturing the brain and the nervous system.[11]

The mentality expressed in the quotations above persisted in medicine well into the twentieth century and was devastating to the birth control movement. It can be argued that the unfortunate scientific denunciation of birth control was the nineteenth-century physician's most significant contribution to the early family planning discussion.

Medical contributions to the birth control movement

Despite the anticontraceptive atmosphere of the medical community as a group, contraceptive information did exist, and it was most often physicians who provided it. Prior to the nineteenth century, abstinence and *coitus interruptus* were basically the only forms of birth control available to American couples. By the middle of the nineteenth century this situation was changing, as discussions of contraception appeared in self-help books that dealt with sex and marriage. Some were written by physicians who advocated special devices and medicines that only they sold.[1, p. 6] They were able to run profitable businesses selling ineffective contraceptives mainly because most trained physicians were not interested enough in birth control to provide better guidance to the public.[6] Not all the advice was useless, however. Several physicians recognized the need for family planning and gave clear explanations of effective contraceptive measures.

In 1832, Charles Knowlton, M.D. (1800–1850), published the first major birth control tract written by an American physician, *Fruits of Philosophy, or, The Private Companion of Young Married People* (later changed to *Adult People).*[12] Knowlton became interested in birth control after reading an essay entitled *Moral Physiology* by Robert Dale Owen, a social scientist who advocated population control.[13] After reading Owen's essay, which briefly mentioned *coitus interruptus,* the condom, and the vaginal sponge, Knowlton became convinced of the need for an extensive, medically accurate work on the subject of birth control. Of his decision to fill the void in birth control literature, Knowlton wrote, "I could not learn that any medical man had ever directed his attention to the subject, and I was resolved to do so myself."[12, p. 86] Knowlton's work is important for two reasons. First, it was an eloquent summary of the contesting viewpoints that characterized the nineteenth-century fight for contraception. Second, it provided specific details of a method of contraception.

Because of the opposition to birth control, Knowlton devoted the first quarter of *Fruits* to proving the value of contraception. He addressed two charges made by the opponents of birth control. To the first charge, "that it will lead to illegal intercourse"[12, p. 7], Knowlton replied that premarital sexual intercourse was already prevalent and that the participants used *coitus interruptus*. He thought his book would allow unmarried lovers "to enjoy a more complete, agreeable, but not more hurtful intercourse, than they otherwise would, and this too, without risk of conception."[12, p. 8] The second charge that Knowlton considered was the claim that contraception was "against nature." His response was a brash question, "Well, what if it is?" and then another, "What is civilized life but one continual warfare against nature?"[12, p. 9] He pointed out that in a sense every comfort resulting from modern science is against nature. This manipulative view of nature was an essential part of the "modern personality" transforming America.

Knowlton next listed the many advantages of contraception. He argued that family planning would prevent overpopulation of the country and decrease the frequency of abortion and infanticide. Knowlton also pointed out that parents with hereditary diseases would be able to have sexual intercourse without fear of bearing sick children. Finally, Knowlton reminded the reader of his experience as a physician and referred to the large number of women and children who had died in childbirth despite a doctor's earlier warning that parturition could be fatal. Often, the shape of the maternal pelvis prevented the birth of a living child, and consequently, "Its head must be perforated, or it must even be dissected, and extracted in pieces."[12, p. 30]

Having provided an ample defense of birth control, Knowlton briefly discussed *coitus interruptus* and pointed out its inconvenience and its inefficiency. The best form of birth control, Knowlton concluded, was douching with spermicide. Of this method, which he termed "the syringe check," he wrote:

> [It] at length occurred to me, to add something to the water [douche] that should not hurt the woman, but yet kill the little tender animalcules, or in other words, destroy the fecundating property of the semen.[12, p. 47]

Knowlton recommended several spermicides, including hemlock bark, red rose leaves, green tea, raspberry leaves, and even very cold water. He claimed that effectiveness, safety, low cost, simplicity, and no sacrifice of pleasure, in addition to putting contraception "in the hands of the female, where for good reasons it ought to be,"[12, p. 85] were the advantages of "this check." He was correct about the efficacy of douching; although not as effective as *coitus inter-*

ruptus, douching has been shown to reduce the risk of conception by over 80 percent. Knowlton concluded his discussion of contraception by noting, "[B]eing a practicing physician, enjoying a full share of the confidence of those around me, my opportunity for acquiring information has not been small."[12, p. 88] Knowlton used his position as a doctor to question people about very private matters in order to judge the efficacy of douching. This work would be the closest that nineteenth-century physicians would get to a systematic clinical investigation of birth control.

Fruits of Philosophy sold well. In its first five years, Knowlton sold seven thousand copies. As one colleague of Knowlton lamented, *Fruits of Philosophy* could be found "in nearly every part of our wide-spread country."[14] Under Massachusetts law, Knowlton was prosecuted three times, twice successfully. Nonetheless, according to Knowlton, a juror told him he loved the book, and the judge subscribed for the next edition. Moreover, Knowlton's medical practice thrived following the publication of *Fruits*.[1]

Knowlton had taken an important step in advocating a mechanical means of contraception. He recognized that "natural things" should no longer be considered sacred. Abstinence and *coitus interruptus* could be replaced by more convenient contraceptives. Knowlton approached his subject scientifically, as opposed to many of his successors. In *Fruits* Knowlton emphasized "the caution that ought to be exercised against drawing conclusions from a too limited number of facts or cases,"[12, p. 81] and noted, "Hasty conclusions from a limited number of facts have done more to retard the progress of science than incredulity."[12, p. 73]

Eighteen years later, Frederick Hollick (1818–1900) published another work, in common language, advocating contraception.[15] Supposedly a graduate of medical school in Edinburgh (although no record of his attendance exists), Hollick had established an enormous lay following even before publication of *The Marriage Guide: or, Natural History of Generation* through a series of public lectures on female anatomy and physiology.[1] His book, "intended for the use of Married Persons and those about to Marry"[15, p. 4] added to his fame.

Hollick began his chapter "On the Prevention of Conception" by declaring that it was "the duty of every physician"[15, p. 332] to explain to his patients the advantages and disadvantages of specific contraceptive techniques. He went on to announce, "I would neither give advice nor offer an opinion on the subject [morality of birth control], as I consider that all persons should decide for themselves, and that their decision concerns themselves alone."[15, p. 333] This was a blatant declaration of the female patient's right to knowledge about her health options and her right to make her own decisions.

The Marriage Guide provided the details of all current contraceptive methods. After thorough descriptions, Hollick dismissed *coitus interruptus* and douching as dangerous to men and women, respectively. The use of a vaginal sponge was reported to interfere with both partners' pleasure. Hollick did not recommend the use of a condom because it prevented contact of the semen with the vagina, leading, in the woman, he felt, to "great nervous irritation."[15, p. 339] One method described by Hollick consisted of "forcibly compressing the Male Organ close to the Scrotum, just previous to emission, so that the Semen cannot escape."[15, p. .339] The problem with this, he said, was that the semen entered the bladder, and with time this route for ejaculation became the rule, rendering the male sterile.

At the end of the chapter Hollick recommended the rhythm method and referred the reader elsewhere in the book for a description of the safe period and menstruation.

> [T]he egg reaches the Womb some time between the second and tenth day after the Menstrual flow has stopped and . . . it then remains there from two to six days at the utmost, but after that it passes away. Consequently, Conception is possible as long as sixteen days after every monthly flow has stopped, but after that time it is impossible.[15, p. .213]

Hollick's understanding of the menstrual cycle was not perfect, but one who followed his prescription would be less likely to become pregnant than one who did nothing at all. *The Marriage Guide* is important in the history of birth control because it explained the menstrual cycle in reasonably accurate detail to lay people and because it provided a clear statement of yet another form of contraception.

While giving the condom an unfavorable review, Hollick might have added that it was too expensive. Prior to 1846, when the cold-cure process for the vulcanization of rubber was perfected, condoms were usually made from sheep cecum, a process that was prohibitively costly. One of the first people to recognize the economic advantages of rubber contraceptives was Edward Bliss Foote (1849–1906), a graduate of Pennsylvania Medical University. In 1858 he published a book written for the layman called *Medical Common Sense*.[16] As a means of checking the rate of population growth, Foote recommended the rubber condom ("the apex envelope") and the "womb veil," the forerunner of the modern cervical diaphragm. The advantage of the womb veil was that

> its application is easy and accomplished in a moment, without the aid of a light. It places conception entirely under the control of the wife, to whom it naturally belongs; for it is for her to say at what time and under what circumstances, she will become the mother, and the moral, religious, and physical instructress of offspring.[16, p. 380]

For men, he also offered for sale the "membranous envelope," a condom made of fish bladder; and, for women, he suggested his invention, the Electro-Magnetic Preventive Machine. *Medical Common Sense* was extremely popular and went through many editions and revisions. In 1876, Foote was prosecuted for distributing contraceptive information through the mails and was fined the hefty penalty of $3,000.[17]

By 1858, individual medical men had provided Americans with an impressive selection of contraceptives. In the twenty-six years since the first publication of *Fruits of Philosophy,* doctors had added five effective methods of contraception to the timeless methods of abstinence and *coitus interruptus.* Despite the accomplishments of men such as Knowlton, Hollick, and Foote, however, most physicians still viewed birth control as a threat to traditional society and opposed it, often lending the weight of false scientific claims to their denunciations of contraception.

The beginnings of change

By the 1880s, however, the "modern personality," which had first appeared seventy-five years earlier, was beginning to manifest itself in medical circles, as physicians began to debate amongst themselves the wisdom of denouncing birth control.

In 1882, one of the first medical journal articles on contraception in the United States appeared in the *Michigan Medical News* and occasioned many letters demonstrating interest in birth control.[18, p. 286]

The most articulate of the later birth control advocates was Edward Bond Foote, M.D. (1854–1912), the son of the author of *Medical Common Sense.* His essay on population control, "The Radical Remedy in Social Science," is a clear statement of the new attitude that was developing in physicians.[19] Nineteenth-century doctors were becoming more confident in the ability of medical science to improve life. As Foote said in his introduction, "In short, the scientific method is the art of civilization, and all efforts for the perfection of civilization in order to be successful must be in accordance with the scientific method."[19, p. 4] According to him, progress was due to "... thwarting Nature—evading Nature's decrees—but the scientist really takes advantage of one natural law to protect himself against another, manipulates natural forces within his control so as to make them protect him against those beyond his control."[19, p. 6]

Richard Shryock has suggested that this attitude toward nature was one of the distinguishing features of the nineteenth-century American physician. Following the medical progress of the eighteenth century, which had climaxed in the discovery of a vaccine for smallpox, science was seen as especially powerful, given to man by God to fight his evils, be they natural or not.[20] American society's eventual acceptance of these beliefs was an integral part of its decision to embrace family planning.

Despite his faith in the power of science, Foote recognized that general acceptance had not yet occurred and that law and tradition prevented many physicians from discussing birth control. He wrote:

> But among physicians themselves there is a vast amount of ignorance on the subject [contraception], and comparatively few are well enough informed about it to give such advice as is naturally expected of them. Many physicians are, like all other classes, seeking information, and are anxious to compare notes and experiences, but with the channels of interchange blockaded, each has to observe and learn for himself.[19, p. 94]

Other physicians must have agreed with Foote's assertion that it was time to begin a medical discourse on the birth control question, because, two years later, the first serious discussion of birth control in a medical journal was published.

In 1888, a discussion of contraception took place in several issues of the *Medical and Surgical Reporter.* The symposium was occasioned by an editorial that pointed out that

> there is danger that an undue dread of discussing it [contraception] frankly in medical circles may deprive medical men of the means of properly directing a disposition which cannot be ignored, and which, in the present state of human nature and civilization, it seems possible to eradicate.[21, p. 342]

The editorialist made sure that his readers were aware that if they did not act soon, medicine would lose control of birth control. The notion that "people are going to do it anyway so we might as well get in on it and regulate it" pervaded twentieth-century birth control discussions.

The writer in the *Reporter* continued, "It will not do to cover up such a state of affairs with euphemisms. Those who know what goes on in the privacy of many a home, as physicians only know it, know that the dread of pregnancy and childbearing has wrecked the peace of thousands of households."[21, p. 342] This writer recognized the advantage the physician had in analyzing the birth control debate. His job allowed him knowledge of people's inner secrets, of their private lives. The response to his call for letters was large, with most of the writers asking for the details of contraceptive technique. Demonstrating the sad state of affairs at the time, another writer confessed that he often gave his patients who asked for contraceptive information "... the old woman's advice 'to take a glass of cold water before going to bed and *nothing else.*'"[22, p. 616]

Many other medical articles on contraception followed in the 1890s. In 1898, a speaker at a symposium on "sex hygiene" in Chicago acknowledged, "Outside the medical profession it is taken for granted that the doctor knows all about these things [sex]. But within our ranks we are aware that this is not true. The text-books omit this department."[23] The Chicago symposium was an attempt to dispel myths about sexuality and place the medical study of marriage and sexuality on firm scientific footing. In this sense it was a failure. The participants continuously slipped into the sexist habits of their predecessors. For example, condoms were described as effective but unfortunately "a non-conductor of electricity" and "not the easiest thing in the world to put on."[23, pp. 188, 190] Paternalistic recommendations were made on when to give contraceptive advice and when to withhold it: "We all know perfectly the difference between the dragged-out woman on the verge of consumption. . . . and the society belle who mistakenly thinks she does not want babies when every fiber of her being is crying out for this means of bringing her back to healthy thought."[23, p. 184] Unfortunately, the Chicago physicians were unable to put the medical moralizing of their predecessors behind them. They could not approach the birth control topic objectively.

Despite the promise offered by the discussion of birth control in the medical literature, it would not be until the 1920s that any physician would undertake an objective, systematic study of birth control. Men such as Knowlton, Hollick, and Foote had recognized the need for contraception, and their writings demonstrate that the technology for family planning was available. Many physicians understood that their exclusive access to personal information on sexual relations put them in the ideal position to investigate the subject of contraception, but very few acted upon this understanding. Most physicians chose to condemn birth control as immoral and unhealthy rather than study it, let alone champion it as a social panacea. These doctors believed that part of their role in the community was to provide stability by supporting the traditional social order. With respect to birth control, the medical community operated like a conservative oligarchy and used science as a weapon against threats to the status quo. When one realizes that it was not until 1937 that the American Medical Association officially recognized birth control as a service available to patients,[1] it becomes clear just how effective and dangerous a weapon it was.

References

1. Reed J. The Birth Control Movement and American Society: From Private Vice to Public Virtue. Princeton, New Jersey, Princeton University Press, 1978.
2. Brown RD. Modernization and the modem personality in early America, 1600–1865: A sketch of a synthesis. J Interdisciplinary Hist 2 (Winter): 201–28, 1972. As cited in Reed J. The Birth Control Movement and American Society: From Private Vice to Public Virtue. Princeton, New Jersey, Princeton University Press, 1978, p. 4.
3. Smith-Rosenberg C and Rosenberg C. The female animal: Medical and biological views of woman and her role in nineteenth-century America. J Am Hist 60:332–56, 1973.
4. Kennedy DM. Birth Control in America: The Career of Margaret Sanger. New Haven, Yale University Press, 1970.
5. Goodell W. Lessons in Gynecology, 3rd ed. Philadelphia, D.G. Brinton, 1890, pp. 562–63. As quoted in Cirillo VJ. Edward Bliss Foote: Pioneer American advocate of birth control. Bull Hist Med 47:471–79, 1973, p. 471.
6. Reed J. Doctors, birth control, and social values: 1830–1970. In Vogel, MJ and Rosenberg CE, eds. The Therapeutic Revolution, Essays in the Social History of American Medicine, pp. 109–34, University of Pennsylvania Press, 1979.
7. Meigs CD. Lecture on Some of the Distinctive Characteristics of the Female. Delivered

before the class of the Jefferson Medical College, January 5, 1847, Philadelphia, 1847, p. 5. As quoted in Smith-Rosenberg C and Rosenberg C. The female animal: Medical and biological views of woman and her role in nineteenth-century America. J Am Hist 60:332–56, 1973, p. 335.

8. Holbrook ML. Parturition without Pain; A Code of Directions for Escaping from the Primal Curse. New York, Wood & Holbrook, 1873, pp. 14–15.

9. De Marmon P. Translator's preface. In Bergeret, LFE. The Preventive Obstacle, or Conjugal Onanism, transl from 3rd French ed. New York, Turner & Mignard, 1870. Reprinted in Rosenberg C and Smith-Rosenberg C, eds. Sex, Marriage and Society. New York, Arno Press, 1974.

10. Black JR. The Ten Laws of Health; or How Disease Is Produced and Can Be Prevented. Philadelphia, 1873. As quoted in Smith-Rosenberg C and Rosenberg C. The female animal: Medical and biological views of woman and her role in nineteenth-century America. J Am Hist 60:332–56, 1973, p. 349.

11. Skene AJC. Education and Culture as Related to the Health and Diseases of Women. Detroit, 1889. As quoted in Reed, J. The Birth Control Movement and American Society: From Private Vice to Public Virtue. Princeton, New Jersey, Princeton University Press, 1978, p. 41.

12. Knowlton C. Fruits of Philosophy or the Private Companion of Adult People, 4th ed. Philadelphia, FP Rogers, Printer, 1839. In Klessig KK. Microfilm, Chicago, Library Resources, Inc.

13. Owen RD. Moral Physiology; or a Brief and Plain Treatise on the Population Question. New York, Wright & Owen, 1831.

14. Alcott WA. The Physiology of Marriage. Boston, Dinsmoor & Co. 1866, p. 180. Reprinted in Rosenberg CE, ed. Medicine & Society in America. New York, Arno Press, 1972.

15. Hollick F. The Marriage Guide, or Natural History of Generation. New York, TW Strong, 1850. Reprinted in Rosenberg C and Smith-Rosenberg C, eds. Sex, Marriage and Society, New York, Arno Press, 1974.

16. Foote EB. Medical Common Sense; Applied to the Causes, Prevention and Cure of Chronic Diseases and Unhappiness in Marriage, rev. New York, Edward B Foote, 1864.

17. Cirillo VJ. Edward Foote's Medical Common Sense: An early American comment on birth control. J Hist Med Allied Sciences 25:341–45, 1970.

18. Himes, NE. Medical History of Contraception. New York, Gamut Press, 1963.

19. Foote, EB, Jr. The Radical Remedy in Social Science; or, Borning Better Babies through Regulating Reproduction by Controlling Conception. New York, Murray Hill Publishing Co., 1886. Reprinted in Rosenberg C and Smith-Rosenberg C, eds. Sex, Marriage and Society: Birth Control and Family Planning in Nineteenth-Century America. New York, Arno Press, 1974.

20. Shryock RH. Medicine and Society in America: 1660–1860. New York, New York University Press, 1960.

21. Prevention of conception, editorial. Med Surg Rep 59: 34243, 1888.

22. Peirce I. The prevention of conception. Med Surg Rep 59:614–16, 1888.

23. Editorial Staff of the Alkaloida Clinic. Sexual Hygiene. Chicago, 1902. As quoted in Reed, J. The Birth Control Movement and American Society: From Private Vice to Public Virtue. Princeton, New Jersey, Princeton University Press, 1978, pp. 42–43.

THE ROLE OF PLANNED PARENTHOOD

ALAN F. GUTTMACHER, M.D.

(July 1965, pp. 81–84)

*Dr. Guttmacher was President of Planned Parenthood-World
Population. Prior to assuming this post, he was Chief of the
Department of Obstetrics and Gynecology at the Mount Sinai
Hospital in New York and Clinical Professor of Obstetrics and
Gynecology at the Columbia University College of Physicians
and Surgeons. In 1947, he was the recipient of a Lasker Award.*

THE EPIGRAM, "THERE IS NOTHING NEW UNDER THE SUN," is given the
lie by the extravagant growth of world population. For this is a new biological phenomenon, a phenomenon which is the product of the Twentieth
Century. To be sure, history records excessive concentrations of human beings
in yesteryear, but these were localized areas of overcrowding such as imperial
Rome at the time of Trajan and Hadrian when over two million persons are said
to have lived in the Eternal City. Second century Rome had its traffic jams of
chariots and dung-carts and also its avenues of four and five-storied apartment
dwellings. Yet at the same time its provinces and most of the world were thinly
populated or populated not at all. In fact, it is stated that world census grew at
an annual rate of 0.2 per cent or less until the seventeenth century.

Even as recently as 1940 world population was increasing at the relatively
leisurely rate of one per cent per annum. In the next two decades the rate accelerated to 1.7 per cent and today the demographic division of the United
Nations estimates the rate of annual global population growth to be more than
2 per cent.

When the dissemination of birth control information first took the form of
a social action movement, there was little or no concern with the excessive rate
of population growth. The now famous contribution by the Reverend Thomas
Malthus was first written in 1798 off the top of his head as an "Essay on the
Principle of Population" and later refined under the title "A Summary View of
the Principles of Population," for the 1824 supplement to the *Encyclopaedia
Britannica*. He foresaw the fact that populations tend to grow in geometric progression while food supplies at best increase in arithmetic progression, which

interested but a few momentarily. In actuality, at the beginning of the Twentieth Century many intellectuals predicted "race suicide" through failure of population growth in several countries, notably France.

Popular birth control, not as a movement but as an individual service to the masses, was initiated in England in 1823 when Francis Place, a self-taught workingman, widely distributed handbills in London and the industrial north advocating contraception. His motivation was not the impersonal abstract of too many people too fast, but rather the hopeless plight of the individual. He advocated birth control for the prevention of pregnancy in cases of maternal illness and for its economic-social value through limitation of family size. Malthus recommended moral restraint, that is, late marriage, while Place advised either the precoital intravaginal insertion of a sponge or the technique of coitus interruptus. Curiously enough, there was no legal interference with Place or his several disciples.

In 1830 an American, Robert Dale Owen, later a U. S. Congressman, published in New York "Moral Physiology," a small booklet on birth control recommending coitus interruptus as the chief method. Himes, in his remarkable "Medical History of Contraception," writes of "Moral Physiology," "This eloquent and refined tract filled an immediate need. It went through several editions within a year and 75,000 copies were sold in America and England." "Fruits of Philosophy" by an anonymous physician was the pen work of Charles Knowlton, a respected Boston physician and a Fellow of the Massachusetts Medical Society. His book, the first medical writing on contraception since the chapter in second-century Soranus' "Gynecology," extolled the post-coital douche. The book, published in New York in 1832 and reprinted in Boston in 1833, got the "anonymous" author in trouble with the puritanical Massachusetts police and earned a respite from practice for the good doctor, for he was.

Incarcerated in the Cambridge jail for three months

Such pioneer efforts were kept alive in succeeding decades by physicians and lay people. Perhaps the two most influential from the medical profession were Abraham Jacobi (1830–1919), and Robert L. Dickinson (1860–1950). Dr. Jacobi, who was jailed for his part in the 1848 revolution in his native Germany, escaped to the United States. Among numerous accomplishments, he founded the *American Journal of Obstetrics and Diseases of Children,* and made pediatrics a specialty in the United States. Dr. Jacobi was the first president of the American Medical Association openly to espouse family planning which he did in his presidential address of 1912. Dr. Dickinson wrote brilliantly, scientifically, and indefatigably about planned pregnancy and techniques of contraception from 1924 until his death at 90 years of age in 1950. His initial contribution, "Contraception: A Medical Review of the Situation," was the first paper in the United States by a gynecologist and obstetrician of unquestioned medical stature to detail and evaluate contraceptive methods. It was written as a deliberate challenge to the Federal Postal Laws, since it was originally widely mailed as an article in a medical journal and later as a pamphlet. He proved that in some cases the eminence of an author grants immunity from repressive prosecution.

Turning back the story to 1869, we find that Anthony Comstock, a representative of the Society for the Suppression of Vice, caused contraception to be included in an obscenity law passed by the legislature of New York State. Other states soon enacted laws of this type and four years later Comstock was able to engineer passage by the United States Congress of Federal obscenity legislation including an anti-contraceptive clause. It is difficult for those of our generation to realize the impact of this statute. It became illegal to transport by mail or common carrier any information on contraception or any contraceptive. Druggists, hospitals, even doctors were afraid to use the mails for contraceptive advice or to do anything in this area that might make them susceptible to criminal prosecution.

Into this repressive environment came the feminist rebel, Margaret Higgins Sanger, born during the 1880's, the sixth child of a family of eleven in Corning, New York. After training as a nurse, marrying, producing three children. and taking the cure for tuberculosis, she commenced her epoch-making career in 1912 by publishing a series of articles in *The Call,* the leading New York Socialist paper, on "What Every Woman Should Know," followed by "What Every Girl Should Know." Her theme was contraception and the emancipation of women from sexual servitude. At this time Mrs. Sanger worked as a nurse on the Lower East Side where the death of a mother of several children from a illegally induced abortion changed her life. She resolved to cease her nursing career and to devote her immense talents and energy to freeing motherhood throughout the world from the shackles of unwanted pregnancies through the knowledge and use of contraception.

Such knowledge could not be acquired from doctors in America, so in 1913 she took her family to Paris where she talked to physicians, midwives, druggists, and the women themselves. She learned what she wanted to know and returned to the United States early in January, 1914, determined to present her knowledge of contraception to the women of America through a new monthly newspaper, *The Woman Rebel.* The first issue of 8 pages appeared in March. In it she lashed out at Comstock and forewarned him she would break the law by publishing contraceptive information. Despite the fact that her article contained no line describing contraceptive techniques, within one month the March issue was declared "unmailable" by the Post Office Department, as were the several subsequent issues. Margaret Sanger was arraigned on August 25 and was to be tried October 20, 1914, when she fled the country for Canada from whence she sailed for England, leaving her family behind. Prior to her departure she wrote and had printed *Family Limitation,* a pamphlet revealing actual techniques of contraception, an act calculated to breach widely the Comstock Law. When three days out at sea she wired her New York associates to release 100,000 copies of *Family Limitation.*

While abroad in 1914–15 amidst the Great War, Margaret Sanger studied all the literature then extant in the libraries of London on contraception and family planning and made friends of liberal leaders such as Havelock Ellis and Marie Stopes. She also coined the phrase "birth control." In her travels she went to Holland and was coached in contraceptive techniques by Dr. Rutgers who, with Dr. Jacobs, had opened the world's first contraceptive clinic in the Netherlands 35 years previously. From a multiplicity of techniques she chose the diaphragm as the best.

In October 1915 she returned to New York to see her children and to face trial. Circumstances, such as her willingness to be tried immediately following the tragic death of her only daughter, her decision to act as her own lawyer, and her fragile health and beauty, all combined to launch the birth control movement with its central figure, an indomitable, fearless American woman. When the State dropped the charges against Mrs. Sanger, the movement had won its first significant legal battle, though, of course, it did not establish conclusively the legality of disseminating contraceptive information.

The Voluntary Parenthood League, progenitor of today's Planned Parenthood Federation, had been organized in 1914 during Mrs. Sanger's absence by Mary Ware Dennett and others interested in suffragette and feminist movements.

On October 16, 1916, Mrs. Sanger opened the first birth control clinic in the United States in the Brownsville section of Brooklyn. It was raided by the police almost immediately and the three women involved in its operation were arrested. While free on bail the women reopened the clinic and were then rearrested on the charge of "maintaining a public nuisance." As a result Margaret Sanger served 30 days in the Queens County Penitentiary. On her appeal for a later conviction, the Court of Appeals in January, 1918, rendered an opinion which opened the door to the legal prescription of contraception in New York State by physicians for health reasons.

Birth Control Leagues had meanwhile been started in several cities throughout the country and in 1917 they were unified under the name of the National Birth Control League with Margaret Sanger as President. The organization soon changed its name to the American Birth Control League.

In 1923 the Clinical Research Bureau of the American Birth Control League opened in two rooms on lower Fifth Avenue. The demand for expert contraceptive advice was tremendous and the patient load of 1,655 in 1925 skyrocketed to 9,737 by 1929. In 1929 the Bureau was raided and Dr. Hannah Stone, its magnificent, madonna-like director, another physician, and three nurses were arrested. Supplies and confidential records were seized. This infraction of the confidential relationship between doctor and patient aroused such a storm of protest and such strong support for birth control by members of the medical profession and the lay public that the five defendants were discharged. Birth control became front page news throughout the country, a place it has never relinquished.

In 1931 a resolution supporting birth control was passed by the Public Health Committee of the distinguished New York Academy of Medicine. In that same period several national Protestant and Jewish denominations, and almost one hundred other national, regional, and local educational, civic, and religious groups first came out publicly in behalf of family planning. In the 15 years since 1916 one birth control clinic had grown to thirty-one.

Since 1931 contraception has been endorsed as an essential health service by many nationwide medical and health organizations. Among the most influential are the American Medical Association (1937), the American Public Health Association (1959), and the American College of Obstetricians and Gynecologists (1963).

In 1935, NBC ended radio censorship of the topic of birth control by broadcasting the address of Representative Pierce of Oregon at the "Birth Control Comes of Age" dinner in Washington, commemorating the 21st anniversary of the founding of the U.S. movement. This breakthrough was followed, during the next two decades, by continurally increasing discussion of birth control in all mass communications media: newspaper, magazines, radio, and eventually, TV.

In 1936, an important decision was rendered by the U. S. Circuit Court of Appeals for the Second Circuit, affirming the legality of importing contraceptive appliances from abroad. In order to test the Comstock restrictions on mailing of contraceptive devices and information, Dr. Hannah Stone had vaginal diaphragms shipped from Japan. She notified the Customs authorities about its arrival. They seized the package. Upholding her action in the now famous case of "The U. S. vs. one package," the Circuit Court ruled that the Federal birth control statute was not intended "to prevent the importation, sale, or carriage by mail of things which might intelligently be employed by conscientious and competent physicians for the purpose of saving life or promoting the well-being of their patients." This essentially exempted the medical profession from the Federal Comstock Law and made possible the wide dissemination of birth control information and products under medical auspices. In many states, the rationale of the Federal decision was applied, by court decision or custom, to state laws on birth control, thereby freeing doctors and medically supervised agencies to prescribe contraception. Legal difficulties in Connecticut and

Massachusetts arose when the courts in those states expressly refused to adopt the rationale of the Federal decision. There is high hope that the Massachusetts statute will be repealed by legislative action in 1965 because the U. S. Supreme Court has found the Connecticut law to be unconstitutional.

In 1942, the United States Public Health Service adopted the policy of giving requests from State Health Officers for financial support for birth control programs the same consideration and support that it gives other state medical programs. Contraceptive services were offered in the official public health programs of Virginia, North and South Carolina, Alabama, Georgia, Florida, and Mississippi. More recently other states, including Maryland, Tennessee, and California, have implemented a similar health department policy.

In the early forties the American Birth Control Federation changed its name to the Planned Parenthood Federation of America (PPFA). In 1947, a nationwide poll of American physicians revealed overwhelming approval of birth control.

During the '50s, PPFA became increasingly concerned with the population problem—local, national, and global. PPFA participated in 1952 in the founding of the International Planned Parenthood Federation, under the dual leadership of Margaret Sanger and Lady Rama Rau of India.

In 1965 the American Planned Parenthood Federation has Affiliates operating in 125 cities; they conduct more than 250 clinics. The clinics offer services in both contraception and the diagnosis and therapy of infertility. Some of the Affiliates also give marriage counseling. The clientele is drawn in most part from the most underprivileged groups in their area. The philosophic goal of the movement is: responsible parenthood—each child a planned and wanted child born into a family properly prepared to receive it.

It becomes increasingly obvious that birth control clinics isolated from other medical services are an anachronism. There is no need for special smallpox vaccination or polio vaccine clinics. Such therapy is universally recognized as a legitimate component of essential preventive medicine. It is felt by the American Public Health Association and other qualified bodies that contraception belongs in the same category. Therefore Planned Parenthood is attempting vigorously to educate the lay public, the political leaders and the medical and public health professions to accept this viewpoint. When they do, separate privately-conducted conception prevention clinics will not longer be necessary, for these public medical facilities—private physicians, hospitals, city, county and state health departments—will take over the assignment.

TWO STRIKES: THE ROLE OF BLACK WOMEN IN MEDICINE BEFORE 1920

LISA E. THOMPSON, M.D.

(Winter 1995, pp. 12–15)

The author received her M.D. degree from Case Western Reserve University in May 1994, and when writing this essay was an intern at the Henry Ford Hospital in Detroit. While a medical student, she received National Medical Fellowships in 1990 and 1991, awarded to outstanding minority students, and the Ivan E. Shalit Prize for excellence in patient care. This paper won honorable mention in the 1994 Alpha Omega Alpha Student Essay competition.

∞

BLACK WOMEN HAVE HISTORICALLY BEEN REGARDED as a group with two strikes against them: their gender and their race. Ironically, while this perception was the prevailing one in the postslavery era, black women continue to struggle against prejudice and ignorance today. Black women have made tremendous strides in medicine in spite of this false image of being doubly handicapped. In terms of numbers of black female physicians and black medical students, however, not much has changed over the past hundred years; in the United States today black women still comprise a tiny fraction of the medical profession. Unfortunately, many of the obstacles black women face today in pursuing medical careers are not terribly different from those that stood in their way in the past.

It is important, therefore, to profile the pioneer black female physicians and their struggles in the early twentieth century. The first black women physicians in this country were not only pioneers in the medical field but also role models for their communities. They possessed the special qualities necessary to overcome seemingly insurmountable obstacles with poise and dignity. While the paucity of written data on these historical figures is discouraging, it is important to chronicle whatever sketchy biographical records are available. In addition, it is frustrating that this material often fails to give any insight into the personalities of these women. Most historical records provide few if any clues about their feelings and thoughts as they faced their individual challenges. One must imagine, however, that in addition to intelligence and talent, each possessed perseverance, determination, and an indomitable spirit in order to accomplish their goals.

The aim to become a physician in the United States before 1920 was a lofty goal for a black woman. It should be noted, however, that black women were no strangers to the field of medicine. In the pre-Emancipation era many worked as apprentices and assistants to white doctors. As lay midwives, black women had been delivering both white and black babies in the deep South long before most white obstetricians began practicing.[2] Nonetheless, black women were generally barred from formal medical training. By 1920, only sixty-five black female physicians were documented in the United States.[3, p. 145]

Dr. Rebecca Lee and Dr. Rebecca J. Cole (1846–1922) were the first and second black female physicians in America to graduate from medical school, in 1864 and 1867. They became physicians at a time when the white community regarded and treated blacks and women as little more than chattel.[3, p. 145] In sharp contrast, the black community considered any educated black man or woman to be a precious commodity. There was, however, a great deal of disparity in the level of social status a professional black man could attain compared to a black woman. For instance, young black male doctors gained instant prestige in the community upon completing medical school. Young black women doctors, on the other hand, were regarded as the same as highly trained nurses, and, although they were something special in the eyes of the community, they were still a step below their male counterparts. The biographer of a black Memphis physician wrote:

> In that age and time a Negro doctor was as popular in Negro life as money is in business. With Dr. before a man's name, he immediately became the community leader, the outstanding figure that received the honor, respect, and admiration of the entire populace. Everybody looked up to him and felt complimented to pay homage to him. Negro men accepted the ideas and thoughts of the colored doctor in all things as right and final, and Negro women worshipped them. . . . The doctor lived in the best home, wore the best clothes, rode the best horse and was the unrivaled suitor of the fairest of the community's fair sex.[4]

The attitude of the black community toward black women was only one of several obstacles that prohibited the advancement of black women in medicine during the post-slavery era. Another major obstacle was the lack of medical institutions willing to train black women. There were seven medical schools established for blacks between 1868 and 1904. By 1914, only two approved schools existed: Howard and Meharry.[5, p. 18] Howard University's Medical College was chartered by the U.S. government in 1868. After its inception the college actually trained more white than black students. The first two women to graduate from the college were white. In 1873 the Medical College's alumni association made the bold move of denouncing discrimination against black women, proclaiming it as unworthy of the profession.[5, p. 15] Ironically, because of its broad-minded stand, Howard's delegation was refused a seat at the Association of Medical Colleges in 1877.

Meharry Medical College in Nashville was the first school in the South to provide for education of black doctors.[5, p. 15] It graduated a larger number of black women than any other school. Leonard Medical School (1882–1914), affiliated with Shaw University in Raleigh, North Carolina, was also founded to train black doctors, but, in contrast to Meharry, it refused to admit black women because the all-white male staff and faculty were unalterably opposed.

Flint Medical College, founded in 1889 as the medical department of New Orleans University, sought black female applicants but segregated the training between the sexes.[5] Men and women were taught in separate rooms and given lectures and demonstrations separately.

Woman's Medical College of Pennsylvania, established in 1850, was the first regular medical school for women. Like most women's colleges of the time, it provided a positive, supportive, and nurturing atmosphere with female faculty as role models to help prepare students for the male-dominated medical profession. It was a unique program, however, because it provided training to women of every race, creed, and national origin. Most white women saw all-female medical colleges existing separately only until they could achieve integration with men's medical schools. This gender integration finally began in the 1870s when schools such as the University of Michigan, University of Iowa, Boston University, Syracuse University, and the University of California opened their doors to women.[5, p. 16] By the 1890s more than 1000 women were enrolled in 64 of the country's 152 schools. This advancement was indeed a major one for white women but was no cause for celebration for black women. By 1920 only one black woman had graduated from each of the following coeducational schools: University of Michigan, Temple University, Boston University, and Chicago Hospital College of Medicine. Four black women had received medical degrees from Tufts College and two from University of Illinois. Of course, there may have been many others who simply passed for white and graduated without disclosing their true race.

The fatal blow to medical education for black women occurred when Abraham Flexner published a major study of medical education in America and Canada in 1910.[5, p. 16] The Flexner report basically stated that, besides Meharry and Howard, all other black medical colleges were underfunded, understaffed, and unsatisfactory as to the performance of their students on board exams. It strongly influenced the closing of the majority of black medical schools and demolished the availability of medical education to many black women.

Besides the difficulties black women had in obtaining admission to medical school, their tenuous position in the medical profession was further exacerbated by the introduction and adoption of mandatory hospital internships and residencies.[5, p. 16] One example of the effects of these new requirements was given by historian Virginia G. Drackman.[5, p. 16] She described the plight of Dr. Evelyn Thompson, a graduate of Woman's Medical College in Philadelphia, who, in 1911, had applied for an internship at the New England Hospital. She was accepted by the staff without the knowledge that she was black. After her arrival at the hospital the staff asked her to leave on the grounds that she had not informed them of her race when she applied. Similar episodes sent a clear message to all black women trying to attain staff positions during that era. Another compelling example is that of Dr. Lena F. Edwards, who was told by the chief of staff at Margaret Hague Maternity Hospital during the early 1920s that she was not wanted there because of two handicaps "first, that she was a woman and, second, that she was black."[5, p. 145] Her reply:

> That is quite true, but it so happens that God gave me both of those characteristics, and I don't think there's a human being who has the right to judge me for what He did. You'll find that I do my work properly, so you'll have to find a better excuse for not wanting me.[5, p. 146]

The few black women who managed to surpass the residency training barrier often could not find practice opportunities after completing their programs. Dr. Matilda Arabella Evans (1870–1935), for example, opened her medical practice in Columbia, South Carolina, where there was no hospital for blacks, so she took patients into her own home until she could establish a hospital.[6, p. 5] Dr. Susan McKinney Steward (1847–1918), the third black woman medical graduate, reportedly attributed her slow-growing practice to the fact that many patients thought women physicians were "too manly."[7] Even black patients were frequently reluctant to patronize black doctors.

> [B]lack doctors had a harder time proving themselves to their potential patients because they were black and doctors. A mistaken diagnosis or treatment, a high charge or perceived insult, a charlatan or unqualified physician, cost black physicians a much higher price than it did white physicians.[8, p. 520]

Because of professional exclusion by white physicians the task of establishing a medical practice was even harder. Blacks were seen by white physicians as their intellectual inferiors.

> White doctors in Tennessee could still say frankly to a white sociologist in 1920, "You will find that the negro mind is incapable of any considerable development, and . . . a colored man is not to be seriously regarded as a real physician. He is a good negro, but still a negro."[8, p. 522]

Dr. May E. Chinn even recalled of her black male practice partners that they were divided into three groups:

. . . those who acted as if I wasn't there; another that took the attitude "what does she think she can do that I can't do?" and the group that called themselves supporting me by sending me their night calls after midnight.[8, p. 546]

Openly racist behavior was not only used as a tactic to undercut the position of black physicians before their patients, but it often endangered patients' lives when, for example, white doctors refused to consult with or assist their black colleagues in the treatment of severely ill patients. Black physicians were also regarded by white physicians as their economic competitors. Some of the fears about competition can be explained by the state of medicine and the national economy in the late nineteenth and early twentieth centuries. Black physicians were attempting to enter medicine at a time of professional overcrowding, especially in the South. Blacks were predominantly an impoverished population, making it difficult for black doctors to earn a living caring for them exclusively.

Besides dealing with racial hostility, black women doctors could not escape the stigma of their gender. *The Brooklyn Daily Eagle*, illustrating this point, reported that in 1870, when women doctors entered the Bellevue Hospital, "male students greeted the ladies with hisses, in-decent language, paper balls, and other missiles."[7, p. 201]

Dr. Steward selected homeopathy as her preference in medical study, in spite of the perception by other M.D.s that homeopaths were "quacks," because it was easier for women to be admitted to homeopathic facilities. A teaching career definitely would have been a more "normal" pursuit for young women in the nineteenth and early twentieth centuries, but these first black female physicians were, obviously, progressive people who wanted more.

All of these barriers meant that there were sparse opportunities for black women in medicine. Many black women with medical degrees worked as nurses because they could not secure residency positions. As the doors of more black medical schools closed, middle-class black women could only pursue careers in teaching or social work. For those of lower socioeconomic background, nursing was the only pathway for escaping a life of domestic service.

Although the odds were always stacked against them, somehow the first black female physicians persevered. Perhaps they survived because of their motivation and self-reliance. Dr. Steward reportedly paid her own tuition for medical school by working full time as a teacher in a Manhattan school while still managing to graduate as class valedictorian. Dr. Lucy Hughes Brown overcame incredible odds to earn a medical degree. She was born of poor parents, and her mother died when she was a young girl, leaving her to care for seven brothers and sisters. In spite of this burden, she pursued her elementary studies at home and was capable of teaching school at an early age, prior to going to medical school. She is frequently quoted as saying that the ingredients of success included:

> "great adaptability, good judgment, the ability to hold one's tongue, and a willingness to do work outside the usual line," and finally, a willingness to "take for their services what patients can afford to pay."[9, p. 18]

Each of the remarkable black women who were pioneers in the medical field overcame the challenges of being black and female in her own way. Their careers encompassed not only important medical pursuits but also social activism. Dr. Georgia E.L. Patton Washington (1864–1900) was an ex-slave who, in 1893. became the first female graduate of Meharry Medical College.[6, p. 5] She was one of the few black physicians to practice in Liberia at a time when black emigration was a topic of intense controversy.

Dr. Caroline Still Wiley Anderson (1848–1919) graduated from Woman's Medical College of Pennsylvania in 1878. She was initially refused admission to the New England Hospital for Women and Children because of her color but later was admitted as an intern. Her major social contribution was the founding of the Philadelphia YWCA for black women.[10, p. 16]

Dr. Eliza Anna Grier graduated from Woman's Medical College of Pennsylvania in 1897.[6, p. 5] She practiced in Atlanta, Georgia, and Greenville, South Carolina. She dedicated her practice to the poor and neglected in spite of frequent financial difficulties.

Dr. Georgia Dwelle Rooks Johnson (1884–1977) established the Dwelle Infirmary in 1920. This, the first successful private hospitals for blacks in Atlanta, Georgia, operated for approximately seventeen years without one death.[6, p. 5]

Dr. Chinn, whose father was a former slave, was the first black woman graduate of the New York University/Bellevue Medical Center. In 1926 she became the first black female intern at Harlem Hospital. Her belief that her patients were victims of society as much as they were victims of disease compelled her to study for and obtain a Masters degree in public health from Columbia University. An ironic note about her illustrious career is that although she worked in cancer research at the Strong Clinic for more than twenty years, her name was never included on the roster."[3, p. 146]

Dr. Edwards, who received her medical degree from Howard University and worked at Margaret Hague Maternity Hospital in New Jersey, did outstanding work in obstetrics. Among her innovative techniques was the performance of deliveries with minimal or no anesthesia. She was associate professor of obstetrics and gynecology at Howard University for several years, but at age sixty she left teaching and established Our Lady of Guadalupe Clinic, a twenty-five-bed facility in Hereford, Texas, serving more than 5,000 migrant workers."[3, p. 146]

All of these doctors are examples to the world that black women are not

"handicapped" by their race and gender. Each of these women bravely overcame adversity to develop skills and talents that they used to serve their communities. The marks they made are powerful beacons to black women currently
attempting to pursue a medical career. Racial hostility is not as blatant today
as it was in the postslavery era. Prejudice is more subtle, and the barriers between
the races as well as between the sexes are often hidden. Misconceptions and
discriminatory acts do continue to exist. On the other hand, in today's world,
black women doctors have even more opportunities and more tools available
to them to act as role models, both to the black community and to other women.
By continuing to excel in medicine and to work for social change, black women
physicians can shatter the idea of "two strikes."

References

1. Pierson WS. Dr. Justina Ford: Honored as first black female physician in Colorado. Cob
   Med 86:60, 1989.
2. Holmes U. Louvenia Taylor Benjamin. southem lay midwife: An interview. SAGE
   2(2):51–54, Fall 1985.
3. Goodwin NJ. The black woman physician. N Y State J Med 85:145–47, 1985.
4. Johnson TJ. From the Driftwood of Bayou Pierre. Louisville, Kentucky, Dunne, 1949,
   p. 28. As quoted in Savitt TL. Entering a white profession: Black physicians in the New
   South, 1880–1920. Bull Hist Med 61:507–40, pp. 513–14, 1987.
5. Hine DC. Opportunity and fulfillment: Sex, race, and class in health care education.
   SAGE 2(2):14–19, Fall 1985.
6. SAGE Staff: Photographic essay. SAGE 2(2):4–9, Fall 1985.
7. Seraile W. Susan McKinney Steward: New York State's first African- American woman
   physician. Afro-Americans in N Y Life & History 9(2):27–43, 1985.
8. Savitt TL. Entering a white profession: Black physicians in the New South, 1880–1920.
   Bull Hist Med 61:507–40, 1987.
9. Hine DC. Black Women in White: Racial Conflict and Cooperation in the Nursing
   Profession 1890-1950. Bloomington, Indiana, Indiana University Press, 1989. As quoted
   in Martin MS. Dr. Lucy Hughes Brown (1863–1911): A pioneer African-American physician. J S C Med Assoc 89:15–19, 1993.
10. Martin MS. Dr. Lucy Hughes Brown (1863–1911): A pioneer African-American Physician.
    JSC Med Assoc 89:15–19, 1993.

PART X

DYING . . . AND DEATH

BIOLOGICAL ASPECTS
OF DEATH

LEWIS THOMAS, M.D.
(July 1974, pp. 83–89)

A summary of Dr. Thomas' contributions to science and litera-
ture prepared by Dr. Gerald Weissman is printed before the pa-
per, "The meaning of science in medicine" on page 40.

S O MANY OF OUR COLLECTIVE ATTITUDES, those beliefs that we express together as a society, have undergone such upheavals within the past half-century that the term revolution no longer serves to describe what is happening to us. Socially, culturally, we seem on our way to becoming a new species, and the changes are now occurring at an accelerated rate. It is no longer the old familiar problem that we cannot understand what our grandparents or parents were thinking in their time. A great many of us, not all that old, can no longer understand what we ourselves were thinking, ten years ago, even last week. This is true for what we used to regard as our most fundamental, fixed beliefs, about religion, manners, art, music, sex, abortion, morality, the family, even war. Just recall how we can now calculate, coolly, the effects of war on cities crowded with people, compared with what we *thought* we thought war was 50 years ago. Everything has changed for us, almost.

Except for our collective attitude about death. This remains much as it has always been, but it is safe to assume that this will change too, and soon. Perhaps, in fact, it is already changing without our recognizing the change. This could happen more easily and inapparently that the change in our beliefs about, say, sex, because we really have not had a clear recognizable structure of collective belief about death, not for a long time.

For most of us, death is still a secret, personal, private subject, not to be talked about, certainly not in public, and not much to be thought about. This is one aspect of what may become a very important change: perhaps, before long, we will talk as openly about death as we now do about sex, or money. But not yet. It is still a hidden subject, a sort of indelicacy, and we think about it evasively.

I have no doubt that we are in for a new, more open, candid, public attitude about death, and in just the next few years the whole complicated process

395

of dying will become more discussed, more analyzed, and at the same time, probably, much less of a frightening mystery. This does not necessarily mean, however, that we will develop a more rational point of view. The mere fact of talking more openly about death, and accepting it as a phenomenon of nature, is not in itself an assurance that we will come out with good answers for ourselves. Indeed, it is conceivable that we could end up rationalizing death, talking it away into insignificance, even using a new, modem, mass group-therapy approach to protect ourselves against worrying at the same time about our highest obligations as social animals. I have in mind the totally new experience of world famine, on a scale never before contemplated by human society. Famine is, to be sure, the most ancient of human problems, but it has always seemed like a transient, localized, basically soluble problem, a spontaneously reversible disease of society, one that we can always live through, or die through, without risking the ruin of the social compact that binds all of us together. What lies ahead, for all of us, unless we begin making some of the sacrifices that are needed for any sensible approach to the world food problem, is starvation and death on a truly immense scale, irreversible and progressive, involving scores of millions of people, including uncountable numbers of children. The famine now being caused with regularity, by the slight shift of the monsoon belt in an area extending from northern Africa across into Asia, is only the faintest hint of what lies ahead. Soon, despite the "green revolution," which we were all reassuring ourselves was to be the ultimate solution, the world is going to run short of food on a world scale. It is a population problem, basically, but now it is too late for us to change the population back to a more manageable size. Even if we can scale up the world's production of food by new technologies, there will have to be a redistribution of food, and if we cannot achieve this, one sector of human society will soon be watching the other sector starve to death before its very eyes—on television, by satellite relays, in newspaper photographs, spread out in all the news magazines.

I hope that we will hang onto the conviction that every individual human life is incalculably precious, and that when death occurs prematurely, and preventably—as is plainly the case for world famine—this is a totally unacceptable event. I hope that we never become so rational about death as to talk ourselves into the belief that this kind of dying is any sort of "fact of life," something "natural," to be taken for granted. But I must confess that I have a fear of this. I do not feel easy about the way the words "practical" and "pragmatic" have achieved such dominant influence in our language.

In a certain sense, death is a relatively recent invention in biology. We got along without it for at least a billion years, perhaps longer. There was no need for it until the invention of sex.[1] Prior to that evolutionary decision, the single-celled prokaryotic microbial organisms that must have comprised the total life

of the earth, up until the appearance of oxygen in our atmosphere, lived by bi-
nary fission; and when you do this there is no such thing as a natural death.
You could run out of food, of course, and die that way, or get burnt to death
by ultraviolet light if you drifted too near the surface of the water into the sun,
and naturally you could always be eaten by something else, but failing these
mischances, and given enough food and shelter, you really could go on forever.
There was no aging, and no finality. You disappeared from life, not by dying,
but by being diluted away, first by dividing into two, then into four, then eight
and so forth, until the last trace of yourself was no longer distinguishable in
the mass of new bacterial flesh. Indeed, it may not even be fair to say you van-
ished, since each of the new cells, whatever its generation number, was essentially a duplicate of your original self. I suppose the only really definitive way
to go, in that sort of life, was through mutation. When that occurred, as of
course it did, and still does, the single organism could fairly be regarded as a dead
ancestor . . . dead by pure chance.

With eukaryotic life, and especially with metazoan life, organisms incurred
the absolute requirement for death as an essential biological process. As soon
as it arrived it must have become quickly associated with new genes for resisting it, or stalling it off, and this sort of genetic information has steadily become
more and more complex, culminating in the elaborate rituals, ceremonies and
dances in resistance to death that are the special contribution of our own species.

It is interesting that animals seem to have inbred attitudes about death, quite
apart from their universal resistance to becoming involved in the process. There
are behavioral aspects to dying, perhaps genetically programmed.

There are some creatures that do not seem to die at all; they simply vanish
totally into their own progeny. The cycles of the slime mold have episodes that
seem as conclusive as death, but the withered slug, with its stalk and fruiting body,
is plainly the transient tissue of a developing animal; the free-swimming ame-
bocytes are using this organ collectively to produce more of themselves.

There are said to be a billion billion insects on the earth at any moment,
most of them with very short life expectancies by our standards. Someone has
estimated that there are 25 million assorted insects hanging in the air over every
temperate square mile, in a column extending upward for thousands of feet,
drifting through the layers of the atmosphere like plankton. They are dying
steadily, some by being eaten, some just dropping in their tracks, tons of them
around the earth, disintegrating as they die, invisibly.

You never see dead birds, in anything like the huge numbers stipulated by
the certainty of the death of all birds. A dead bird is an incongruity, more star-
tling than an unexpected live bird, sure evidence to the human mind that something has gone wrong. Birds do their dying off somewhere, behind things, under
things, never on the wing.

Animals seem to have an instinct for performing death alone, hidden. Even the largest, most conspicuous ones find ways to conceal themselves in time. If an elephant missteps and dies in an open place, the herd will not leave him there; the others will pick him up and carry the body from place to place, finally putting it down in some inexplicably suitable location. When elephants encounter the skeleton of an elephant out in the open, they methodically take up each of the bones and distribute them, in a ponderous ceremony, over neighboring acres.

It is a natural marvel. All the life of the earth dies, all the time, in the same volume as the new life that dazzles us each morning, each spring. All we see of this is the odd stump, the fly struggling on the porch floor of the summer house in October, the fragment on the highway. I have lived all my life with an embarrassment of squirrels in my backyard; they are all over the place, all year long, and I have never seen, anywhere, a dead squirrel, except those killed on the road by our cars.

In our way, we conform as best we can to the rest of nature. The obituary pages tell us the news that we are dying away, and the birth announcements in finer print, off at the side of the page, inform us of our replacements, but we get no grasp from this of the enormity of scale. There are three billion of us on the earth, and all three billion must be dead, on a schedule, within this lifetime. The vast mortality, involving something over 50 million of us each year, takes place in relative secrecy. We can only really know of the deaths in our households, or among our friends. These, detached in our minds from all the rest, we take to be unnatural events, anomalies, outrages. We speak of our own dead in low voices; struck down, we say, as though visible death can only occur for cause, by disease or violence, avoidably. We send off flowers, grieve, make ceremonies, scatter bones, unaware of the rest of the three billion on the same schedule.

Less than half a century from now, our replacements will have more than doubled the numbers. It is hard to see how we can continue to keep the secret, with such multitudes doing the dying. We will have to give up the notion that death is catastrophe, or detestable, or avoidable, or even strange. We will need to learn more about the cycling of life in the rest of the system, and about our connection to the process. Everything that comes alive seems to be in trade for something that dies, cell for cell. There might be some comfort in the recognition of synchrony—in the information that we all go down together, and in the best of company.

For the present, we must continue our ceremonies of simultaneous acknowledgment and resistance, and of all these, the modern hospital represents the ultimate metaphor, symbolizing in every conceivable way the unacceptability of death. Everything in this huge, intricate, incomprehensible institution publicly asserts man's capacity to win out over mortality, to defy death, to extend life. We apply our new technology twenty-four hours a day to reverse a biological process that, along with birth, is the most universal of all the facts of life that we know about.

We really do not do this, of course. This is the way the television and magazine stories make it seem, but we know better. It is premature death, preventable death, that we are concerned about. We know our limitations, and we know, better than most, that even if we develop new technologies to prevent or cure every one of the major diseases that now do us in, we would still be done in by aging, by wearing out, by the running down of clocks in our genomes. What we have perhaps not acknowledged with sufficient conviction, even to ourselves, is the biological necessity of this process in the scheme of things, which was stipulated for all of us, long since, by the process of evolution itself. We could only achieve immortality by going back to being single cells without nuclei, and that really seems too great a price to pay.

For a short but interesting time, we do in fact go back to being single cells, each of us, in the very process of dying. Death is itself a sort of physiological process of adjournment, involving an enormous committee of cells, with an end to all collaborative actions among them. The central administrative mechanisms are turned off; the heart stops, the brain stops, and that is the end of life for the organism, but not for the lives of the cells. Forty-eight hours after death, sheets of skin cells are still alive and can be cultivated as organ cultures almost indefinitely. Fibroblasts remain viable for even longer periods. In the earlier hours, during the first eighteen hours or so after death, large numbers of leukocytes continue to move about in the tissues. Final mortality for various populations of cells is determined by local conditions of pH, nutrients, noxious breakdown products from other, more fragile cells and the like, but it is an independent process. It is decentralization that initiates the death of the whole organism.

We might expect a major change in our attitude toward death, in the future, if we were to learn more about the physiological process itself. As things are, today, we do not have much real information, except in an incomplete and highly reductionist sense: we know, of course, that the process can be launched and carried through to completion by interference with the central nervous system, and it is also obvious that cessation of the heartbeat is a prime cause of death, but we know very little about the events that must occur, *seriatim*, in any fatal disease—especially in prolonged, chronic disease—which gradually, cumulatively, and irreversibly, lead to death.

It is partly, and probably largely, because of this extensive area of ignorance that the fear of death is such a universal apprehension. The process is itself almost totally mysterious, and therefore it is frightening to most people. There is the most widespread impression that dying simply has to be, by its very nature, an agonizing process; this is the generally accepted, literary view, even though there is no evidence that it is even a painful experience, much less agonizing, and a great deal of evidence to the contrary. William Osler, who observed in his time the dying of a great many people, and paid attention to what he saw, concluded that there was no such thing as an agony of death.

It would be rather surprising, in fact, if the act of dying were to turn out to be itself a difficult or highly distressing process. In view of its absolute universality, one would expect there to be the same provision by genetically-determined mechanisms for guidance through the various stages, each designed for the advantage of the organism, that we have long since become accustomed to finding in all the other crucial acts of living. There is a certain body of anecdotal information to support this point of view. One example is the story recorded by the British explorer, David Livingstone, concerning his own almost-death. He was on an expedition in East Africa, in lion country, and was suddenly surprised and caught by a wounded lion. He was taken across the right chest and shoulder in the animal's jaws, and bitten through with sufficient violence to crush part of his thorax and fracture his upper humerus. The lion was killed before finishing him, and he recovered from his injuries. Later, he wrote a puzzled description of the episode. There had been no pain, he said, and more surprisingly, no sense of fear or alarm. On the contrary, he had the most extraordinary sense of calm and detachment. As he recalled his sensation, it was so peaceful as to be almost pleasurable. He was deeply impressed by this experience, and subsequently elaborated the theory that all living creatures are provided by nature with a protective physiologic mechanism that is somehow switched on at the verge of death, and carries the organism through in a haze of tranquility.

We ought to be learning more about this phenomenon, if indeed it exists, from the patients with coronary disease who undergo cardiac standstill and then, thanks to modern electronic and pharmaceutical technology, have the whole process reversed and are brought back to life again. To be sure, most of these have amnesia for the whole affair, but a few have been able to remember significant parts of the experience, and their accounts appear to support David Livingstone and Osler. One man, a noted actor with coronary disease, underwent cardiac standstill in front of a Los Angeles hospital and was carried in, for all practical purposes completely dead, and was then revived by cardiac stimulation. According to his account it was a very strange experience, but the strangeness was because there seemed to be so many agitated people around him, excited for no reason that he could understand, while his own sensation, in the midst of all the surrounding, distant excitement, was only an awareness of quietude. The oddity was the contrast between what he knew to be serenity and the unaccountable behavior of the people around his stretcher.

Something like this reaction has been reported in a recent study of the process of dying in patients with chronic obstructive disease of the lungs. In contrast to the reaction on the part of most, if not all, professional observers, who agree that this must be an especially distressing way to die, the patients themselves appeared to be far less concerned. Most of them, in fact, seemed to be preparing for death with considerable equanimity, as though intuitively familiar with the business. One elderly woman, within two days of death, reported that the only distressing part of the process was in being interrupted; on several occasions she was provided with the conventional therapeutic measures to maintain oxygenation or to restore fluids and electrolytes, and each time she found the experience of coming back harrowing. She was deeply resentful at this interference with her dying.

It may be true, then, that there are sequential, programmed events in the physiology of dying, designed to complete the process in an orderly way. If so, we should be on the watch for instances of pathophysiology here, since the existence of any such mechanism, ready to be turned on, might pose certain hazards for the living, before their time.

It is conceivable that such a mechanism is involved in certain otherwise unexplainable forms of death. There is a paper by G. W. Milton, in *Lancet*,[2] describing the syndrome of unexplained death in certain patients with cancer.

Milton, whose base is the Melanoma Clinic of Sydney Hospital, points out that there is a small group of patients with cancer who are best not told the truth about their disease because of the risk that the news will kill them. He terms the reaction "the syndrome of self-willed death," and writes the following clinical description:

> The syndrome of self-willed death nearly always affects a big man proud of his virility. The patient, when first confronted with the problem of his malignant disease, appears to disregard it and be extraordinarily cheerful. Far from appearing to feel sorry for himself, the patient will laugh, joke and be facetious with all who come near him. Overnight, the patient's whole manner changes and he is physically and mentally transformed. He literally turns his face to the wall and lies inert in bed, covering his face with the bedclothes. He does not seem to be terrified but is vague, evasive and shows blank indifference.

> When questioned, his answers are minimal, and as soon as the questions stop he is silent. He eats little but does not complain of lack of appetite. Although often reported to be sleeping badly, he does not complain. In fact, he has no complaints. He does not lament his fate nor does he look abjectly miserable, rather he gives the impression of being completely indifferent.

> Blood pressure, pulse and respiration remain normal. He does not become either cachectic or dehydrated.

> Within a month of the onset of this syndrome the patient will almost cer-
> tainly be dead. At necropsy, there will often appear to be no adequate ex-
> planation for the cause of death.

Milton, an Australian, associates this syndrome with the phenomenon of unexplained death following "bone-pointing" by witch doctors among aboriginal natives, and cites several well-documented examples of this kind of death to illustrate the similarity. The cardinal feature of death from the casting of a spell also appears to be the extraordinary indifference of the victim; he seems to be detached from the rest of society, although in no evident anguish or distress, and simply dies, quite unaccountably, within the next few weeks.

If these things are true, and I suspect they really are, then we might conclude that there is such a thing as a physiological mechanism for dying, which possesses, like all other physiological devices, a pathology all its own—in the sense that if it can be inappropriately switched on, the process will proceed to disaster in an orderly and predictable fashion. If this is true, it is an aspect of dying that seems to me quite new, and of considerable biological interest, and I wish we knew a lot more about it. At the moment, it seems a complete mystery; terms like "shock" or "stress" are of no help at all in explaining the event.

It seems to be agreed, among anthropologists who have looked into it, that the process is a reversible one, and this may be extremely important. If the victim of a spell can acquire the services of a more influential witch doctor, he can be convinced that the spell was defective, and then he will then recover completely. In other primitive societies it is claimed that if a man can survive being hexed once, by having the hex cancelled out professionally, he can never again be hexed.

It has been proposed by some observers that this kind of death has its counterpart among wild animals and birds, and perhaps there are experimental models waiting to be explored with this in mind. It is a commonplace, for instance, that wild birds may die suddenly while their legs are being banded; the European wild rabbit dies with some regularity soon after being captured; there are innumerable accounts of unexplained deaths among presumably healthy animals in zoos, where it is the fact of being in the zoo that is itself lethal.

Perhaps there are such things as lethal facts. Twenty-five years ago, Curt Richter, at Johns Hopkins, was studying the behavior of wild rats placed in water and compelled to swim for long periods in order to survive. He discovered, quite by accident, that clipping the whiskers away from a rat made the animal death-prone.[3] Normal rats remained afloat for as long as three days, but a rat without his whiskers would simply give up and die within a few minutes. There was no explanation available for this kind of death, which occurred with impressive regularity. The animals did not appear to be drowning, in the medicolegal sense, nor did they go into shock, nor have arrhythmias or cardiac stand-still. They simply gave up, and stopped living.

Perhaps the most interesting of all Richter's observations was that this phe-nomenon, like the death from cancer news or bone-pointing, was completely reversible. All he had to do was to remove the dewhiskered rat from the wa-ter for a brief interval, long enough for the animal to perceive that there was the possibility of relief. Then, when put back into the bath this rat would swim on for hours, matching the performance of the whiskered controls. Somehow, having no whiskers for a rat means that you will die if you get into deep wa-ter; it is a lethal fact, and something very like a magic spell. Cancel it out with a counterspell, by lifting him out of the water, and he cannot be scared to death a second time.

There are stories something like this in all areas of the literature on cancer, and I suspect that this is the way some of the magical cures of cancer may work. I once was told about a man with advanced, terminal Hodgkin's Disease who heard about Krebiozen during the early days of the substance and became con-vinced that be would survive if only he could get Krebiozen.

He got it, and underwent a miraculous recovery, even with objective shrink-ing of the Hodgkin's nodes. Then the radio announced the discrediting of Krebiozen, and he promptly went into a profound relapse. Then, as an exper-iment, his doctor lied to him, and convinced him that the recent batch of Krebiozen, with which he was being treated, had turned out to be inactive, and this was what the radio news had been based on; now he would receive a new batch of really active material. With this, he began a new, equally dramatic re-covery, and survived well beyond the expected period. He still had Hodgkin's Disease, and eventually died from it, but, when he did, it was death from the dis-ease, not death from the spell cast by the disease.

These are some of the medical problems associated with the large puzzle of death, badly in need of further study. I have a hunch that there are perfectly straight-forward, scientific approaches to the mechanisms involved in dying, and I also have a hunch that the information would turn out to be extremely useful in the long run. It is our present state of ignorance that is, in large part, responsible for the total unacceptability of dying, and sooner or later we are going to have to change our views about this. We cannot go on indefinitely with today's attitude that death is an outrage, or that it only occurs because we have somehow blun-dered, or "caught something." It is a normal part of living, and our dilemma is that it is the part about which we have acquired the least information.

The taxonomy of human death has become just as complex and elaborate as the taxonomy of disease; indeed, we tend these days to take for granted that the two kinds of classification are superimposable. That is to say, there is no way of dying that is not explainable by at least one disease entity. There is, I believe, a major fallacy here, and it has a profound influence on contemporary public attitudes about the meaning of death. When we say, as we do, that death and disease are inextricably related to each other, and that it is always one disease or another that must be listed as the direct cause of death, we automatically exclude the ancient concept of natural death because we cannot fit it into today's taxonomy. Death certificates do not allow for natural death, and I am afraid most of us who are involved in clinical medicine don't allow for it either—or at least it is safe to say that we don't allow for it with the generosity it deserves. For there is such a thing as natural death, and there is nothing wrong with it except for the fact that we cannot find a place to list it among known causes. There is, correspondingly, such a thing as "unnatural death"; the shortest definition for this, I should think, would simply be "death before its appointed time." When the science and technology of medicine have been brought to a sufficiently high level—which I take to be a perfectly reasonable and achievable objective for modem medicine sometime during the next several decades— we will have the means to prevent or cure outright all of what we now consider to be the major diseases of human beings. I do not see anything at all starry-eyed about the forecast that this will happen. The plain record of the past seventy-five years has already proven, major disease by disease, that it can happen, and that it tends to happen as soon as scientific research has provided us with a sufficiently clear insight into the underlying mechanisms of disease. I cannot see any great difficulty about this, provided we have enough time and enough good science; I doubt that there are any human diseases whose mechanisms are genuinely and permanently impenetrable. In short, I have total faith in the technological power of the medicine of the future, given the best of possible worlds.

But I do not believe that this new power will ever enable us to change the incidence of natural death. Statistically, it stands now at 100%, and that is bound to remain the figure. We will continue to age and wear out; we may perhaps learn how to change the rate somewhat, someday, but we cannot change the drift. We cannot evade the second law of thermodynamics any more than the next creature, and all our clocks must run down sooner or later.

How can we die without a disease to cause the death? This is easy. We do it all the time. It only requires that we change our definition of disease a little bit. When we wear out and begin to come apart, all sorts of things can happen here and there in our tissues: blood vessels may become plugged or burst their walls, or defense mechanisms against ordinarily amiable microorganisms may break down, or the elaborate communication systems, involving messenger services between various cells and tissues, may go out of business, and these, or combinations of these, are the recognizable mechanism of natural death— but the actual cause of death, in these circumstances, is not disease, it is the mechanism of dying itself. When medicine reaches the point, in its evolution as scientific art, when most human beings have a fairly clear run through life and have, at the end, a chance at making use of this mechanism, we will have finally earned our keep.

I believe that the general acceptance, in our civilization, of the notion that dying is always a detestable, avoidable outrage—that whenever it occurs, at whatever age, it means failure, unsuccess, and loss—is in part responsible for a fundamental strain on our health care system. If death is assumed to represent a remedial flaw with each event interpreted as a new piece of evidence for ineptitude and bad management by the human organism, we automatically drive it into our minds that the whole animal is fundamentally fallible, badly made, always at risk of flying to pieces. In other civilizations, in which dying is taken more for granted as a natural fact of life, there is not the same anxiety about the lethal risks of plain everyday living, and there is considerable more trust in nature. It is when you regard nature as a badly run business, carelessly thought out, that you also develop a deep mistrust of your own personal arrangement, and it is not a long step from there to the notion that today's cold in the head could have you in the grave by tomorrow afternoon. We, in our western, industrialized, sophisticated, knowledgeable, mature society, are unwilling to put up with even slight physical inconveniences because they all carry, if only symbolically, the risk of dying. We cannot permit anything to go wrong, even for a few hours, without demanding intervention. Call the doctor.

A familiar television commercial, broadcast almost incessantly a year or so ago, illustrated our attitude in dramatic form; The scene opened with a young woman sitting beside her mother at a dressing table. The young women, gazing in anguish at her mother's head, spoke in hushed, horrified tones ordinarily used for the mention of cancer. She said: "You mean you used a shampoo for three days and you still have the dandruff?" Then, after a long pause, came: "Oh Mom, *see* the doctor!"

Everyone recognizes that we need a better kind of health education for people in general, and there is talk of ambitious new programs on television and radio to provide the public with more solid and rational information about disease. This is not enough, in my opinion. To be sure, it will be very helpful if people are aware of better ways of living, of some of the sensible precautions that can be taken to prevent disease (like stopping cigarette-smoking, for example, or eating a more human diet), and it would be especially useful for people to recognize more generally than they do that most illness, statistically speaking, is spontaneously reversible and automatically self-curable. However, we need more than this. Somehow, there ought to be a better way for all of us to accept the plain, open, obvious fact that human beings are, by and large, absolute marvels. Perhaps what we need is not so much public education as public celebration.

As these things are talked about today, most of the education deals with the chanciness of living and surviving. To hear us talk, you would think we would never make it through life, any of us, without the most constant, anxiety-ridden surveillance of our fragile, fallible selves. This really is not the way it works, you know, and we ought to be able to say this openly without undermining the whole structure of preventive medicine.

The human organism is, in real life, a splendid invention. For all the complexity of its working parts, and the unfathomable intricacy of their interactions with each other, the thing works, right up until the time it begins to wear out and come apart through aging. Most of us—really, *most* of us—have a perfectly clear run through most of our lives without ever developing a serious illness. We are not as fallible as we make ourselves out to be. We do not live under a constant threat of disease, nor are we always on the verge of foundering.

Now, of course, these glowing tributes cannot be paid to the human frame when human society itself is run in failure. If we are not fed adequately and, especially, if we fail in collective measures for public sanitation, or if, as most notably it has occurred in this century, we persist in blowing each other to bits of flesh, it is obvious that there will be little to celebrate. But the design itself, and its built-in potential for near perfection—the sheer power of the human organism—is something to talk about, and we have tended to overlook this aspect of ourselves throughout most of our history. It may turn out that a sophisticated scientific awareness of the splendor of life in general, and of human life in particular, will be the greatest of all the benefits we will gain from the current revolution in biology and the approaching revolution in medical science.

References

1. Jacob F. The Logic of Life. Pantheon, 1974.
2. Milton GW. Self-Willed Death or the Bone-pointing Syndrome. Lancet 1:1435–1436, 1973.
3. Richter K. The Phenomenon of Unexplained Sudden Death in Animals and Man. In The Meaning of Death, edited by Herman Feifel, Ph.D. New York, McGraw-Hill, 1959.

LEARNING CURVE

EDWARD M. McMAHON, JR., M.D.
(Fall 1992, p. 25)

Moments after birth
the infant grips offered fingers
by reflex
and can then be lifted bodily
into the air.

More slowly come the saltatory skills
of age.
Decades and pain perfect the art
of letting go.

MAN'S RIGHT TO DIE

LEON R. KASS, M.D., PH.D.
(April 1972, pp. 73–77)

Born in Chicago, Dr. Kass earned his B.S. and M.D. degrees at the University of Chicago, and then went on to take his Ph.D. in biochemistry. He was elected to AΩA in 1962. For more than 30 years, his activities have been focused upon the ethical and philosophical issues raised by advances in biomedical sciences, and more recently, with broader moral and cultural issues. His essays have dealt with in vitro fertilization, cloning, genetic screening and genetic technology, organ transplantation, aging research, euthanasia, assisted suicide, and the moral nature of the medical profession. In 2001, President George W. Bush appointed Dr. Kass to the position of Chairman of the President's Council on Bioethics. He currently is the Addie Clark Harding Professor in the Committee on Social Thought and the College at the University of Chicago.

This paper is based on a talk given at a colloquium on "Man's Right to Die," held at Cornell University, Ithaca, New York, on March 8, 1971.

∞

THERE IS TODAY MUCH CLAMOR ABOUT RIGHTS. We hear discussed claims of a right to health, a right to education, a right to clean air, a right to privacy, a right to be born, and a right not to have been born. Usually, the questions at issue concern whether and for whom such rights exist, and how they are to be protected. Sometimes, however, there is confusion, and hence, discussion and disagreement, about the very meaning of the asserted claim. A case in point is the assertion of "Man's Right to Die."

The single phrase is in fact at least three different phrases, depending upon which of the three key terms is emphasized: *MAN'S* right to die, man's *RIGHT* to die, man's right to *DIE*. Let us consider each in turn. What do we learn from emphasizing *MAN'S* right? We can dismiss the possibility that we are to consider a right of men not shared by women, or a right which women already have but which men don't yet share. The word *man* here is sexless, generic for the human species. We can also reject the possibility that the emphasis on *man's* right means to call into play the distinction between the human species and other species. Rather, what we do learn from focusing on the word *man* is that we are to consider a right ascribed to all of mankind, not limited to Americans or New Yorkers, or to bank presidents or welfare mothers. We are supposed to think and talk about a universal right of man as man, i.e., a *natural* right and not merely a *civil* or *legal* one.

What can we learn from the second phrase, man's *RIGHT* to die? What is meant by saying someone has a *right* to something? A *right* is not identical to a desire or an interest or a capacity. We may have a desire for and an interest in the possessions of another, and the power to take them by force or stealth—yet we can hardly be said to have a *right* to them. Neither can we be said to have a right to be loved by those we hope will love us, or a right to become wise. There are many good things that we may rightfully possess and enjoy, but to which we have no claim if they are lacking. Having a right means having a justified claim which can be asserted (or claimed) against another to act in a fitting manner or to deliver what is justly owed. We need also distinguish *making* claims from *having* claims. To *make* a claim or demand for something is not sufficient to establish that one *has a claim*, i.e., a right, to it. (Conversely, some rights may be said to exist, even if no claims are made.) In considering man's *RIGHT* to die, we must take care to establish that we are talking about a *right*, and not merely a desire, interest, power, or demand.

Duties are the correlatives of rights: one man's right necessarily implies another man's duty. The obligations of others entailed by a right to die I shall consider later. For the moment, we should note that there are some people who might rather have us discuss "man's *duty* to die." Consider Nietzsche's famous assertion: "In certain cases, it is indecent to go on living." Or consider the exhortation to duty in this passage from Pericles's Funeral Oration, as reported by Thucydides:

> Thus choosing to die resisting, rather than to live submitting, they fled only from dishonor, but met danger face to face, and after one brief moment, while at the summit of their fortune, escaped, not from their fear, but from their glory. So died these men as became Athenians. You, their survivors, must determine to have as unaltering a resolution in the field, though you may pray that it may have a happier issue.

We should also note that there are some people who speak about *rights* but who really mean *duties*. By attending to the distinction between right and duty, we can be on our guard against those who disingenuously demand that people be given certain rights *only because* this is the best means for getting them to perform certain alleged obligations. For example, *some* people who argue for a woman's right to have an abortion really don't care about women's rights, but hope thereby to get women—especially the poor, the unmarried, and the nonwhite—to do "their duty" toward limiting population growth. Similarly, some who now argue for a right to die, really mean for people not only to have it, but to exercise it with dispatch, so as to decrease the mounting social costs of caring for the irreversibly ill and dying. We should consider whether the assertion of a human *right* to die has attached to it the string of a human *duty* to die.

Before going on to the third reading of our title phrase, let me pause momentarily to consider some important questions that emerge from the first two renditions taken together. We have seen that we are here considering an alleged universal right of man, a natural human right. But where would such a natural right to die come from? How is it granted? On what is it grounded? How would we know we have it? How many of us are prepared to hold with Thomas Jefferson as a self-evident truth, that all men "are endowed by their Creator with certain inalienable Rights"? Are we in the embarrassing position of asserting a natural right of man, while rejecting both the notions of Nature and of Nature's God on which such a natural right could be grounded?

We come to the third, and I think intended, formulation, "man's right to DIE." Even assuming that men have natural rights, this is indeed a strange right; taken literally, it denotes merely a right to the inevitable. In fact, the certainty of death has long served as a paradigm for the term "inevitable," as in "death and taxes." And the name for human beings commonly used in ancient times, *mortals,* makes our inevitable death our defining characteristic, thus distinguishing us from the immortal gods. Why need we claim a right to the inevitable? Is death in danger of losing its inevitability? Are we in danger of bodily immortality? Or is "man's right to die" merely a dramatic phrase, not to be taken literally, and therefore one whose meaning we have yet to uncover?

Whatever its meaning, the claim of this peculiar right to die is a new claim. Usually, new and peculiar claims are signs of new and peculiar circumstances. Why has this question of a right to die arisen now? Perhaps by exploring the context we can gain some clues to the meaning.

The claim of a human right to die is voiced largely if not exclusively in the technological West. No such claim appeared in times when medicine was and in places where medicine still is impotent to combat disease and preserve life. Its birth is almost certainly tied to modern medicine's acquisition of enormous powers to sustain and prolong life. Improved sanitation, immunizations, and antibiotics have virtually eradicated large numbers of lethal infectious diseases, including diphtheria, smallpox, typhoid fever, poliomyelitis, pneumococcal pneumonia. Powerful drugs prevent death from shock; hormones, e.g., insulin or steroids, prevent deaths due to endocrine deficiencies. Recent years have seen the perfection of mechanical devices—such as cardiac pacemakers, respirators, and machines for renal dialysis—to sustain vital functions, and the development of transplantation and artificial devices to replace defective vital organs. The results add up to a large increase in the average life expectancy, plus improved chances for young and old alike to escape from seemingly certain death, thanks to the new "heroic" powers.

Yet we have paid a high price for these successes. Ironically, the success of the mechanical devices in forestalling death has introduced confusion in determining that death has in fact occurred, since the traditional signs of life—heartbeat and respiration—can now be maintained entirely by machines. The serious and unfortunate consequences of blurring the distinction between a man alive and a man dead have yet to be fully appreciated, but that is a subject for another occasion.

Other costs of our greater power to prolong life have been widely recognized. The heroic efforts to "save" the severely-ill and injured are sometimes only partly successful; they sometimes succeed only in salvaging individuals with severe brain damage, capable of only a less-than-human vegetating existence. Such patients are increasingly found in the intensive care units of teaching hospitals; some are sustained in this condition for several years.

Yet even the ordinary methods of treating disease and prolonging life have tended to impoverish the context in which men die. Fewer and fewer people die in the familiar surroundings of home or in the company of family and friends. At that time of life when there is perhaps the greatest need for human warmth and comfort, the dying patient is kept company by cardiac-pacemakers and defibrillators, respirators, aspirators, oxygenators, catheters, and his intravenous drip. Ties to the community of men are replaced by attachments to a community of machines.

We must also consider the growing number of old people still alive thanks to medical progress. As a group, the elderly are the most alienated members of our society: not yet ready for the world of the dead, not deemed fit for the world of the living, they are shunted aside. More and more of them spend the extra years medicine has given them in "homes for senior citizens," in chronic disease hospitals, in nursing homes—waiting for the end. Ironically, penicillin, which has helped to carry them to the antechamber, now bars the door to death-delivering pneumonia, once called "the old man's friend." We have indeed learned how to increase their years, but we have not learned how to help them enjoy their days.

With increasing technological power has come decreasing personal contact between doctor and patient, and greater dependence on hospitalization and institutional care. The growth of knowledge has brought specialization, and specialization (along with increased patient loads) has helped to undermine the general practice of medicine through which a physician could get to know his patient as a person, and thus serve him in an individualized way right up to his death.

Medicine has indeed helped us to stay alive, but often only at the cost of keeping us alive beyond our time, and of preventing us from having a good death. Adept at uterine curettage and cardiac massage, medicine now sits, like Cerberus, at both portals, making it harder to get in and harder to get out. It is therefore understandable that some people should exaggerate their fears in complaining, "When my time comes, they are not going to let me die."

Even this brief look at the circumstances which have fostered the assertion of a new and confusing right helps us better understand its meaning. What is really being claimed is a *right to die with dignity*. Thus understood, it is not a right to something certain and inevitable, but to something which has become precarious and increasingly rare.

But has our discussion really made any progress? Unless we can specify the ingredients of a death with dignity, we will have produced little more than a high-sounding cliche of little practical value. Let me attempt some specification.

A death with dignity means a death of one's own, an individualized death somehow appropriate to one's individualized life. But a death of one's own is impossible unless one knows that one is dying. The first specification is therefore that the patient has a right to know what is the matter with him, and also, his prognosis. The truth about his condition belongs first of all to him. He needs to know the truth if he is to have any chance of being ready or prepared to die, of making his death timely. He may have accounts to settle, arrangements to make, projects to complete, religious duties to perform, promises to keep, and loved ones to bid farewell. He needs to know the truth if he is to have a share in the decisions concerning the nature of his terminal care. He needs to know the truth if he is to work through his feelings with respect to dying, and to have a chance of experiencing this part of his life. To keep the truth from the patient is to treat him as if he were already dead.

There are, of course, many ways of communicating the truth to the patient, some of them inappropriate, some insensitive or even gratuitously cruel. I will never forget my shock and anger when, as a medical student on morning rounds, I witnessed the following exchange between a timid, very frightened, middle-aged patient and his surgeon, the morning after surgery:

> Patient: Doctor, please, it wasn't cancer, was it?
> Surgeon: Mr. —, you bet your life it was!

There are different things that might be said, and different ways of saying them. As both Dr. Elisabeth Kubler-Ross and Prof. William May[2] have pointed out, the choice is not confined to the blunt delivery of brute facts, on the one hand, and a dissembling cheerfulness or silence, on the other; often, an indirect approach is preferable. There are perhaps exceptional cases in which the patient might be better off not knowing; in all cases, the manner of conveying the truth must be particularized to the individual patient and the specific circumstances. But the basic presupposition must be to convey the truth, the exception, to withhold it—not the other way around.

The right to human company and care is a second ingredient of a death with dignity.[8] Those who live on will lose a friend or loved one; he who dies loses *all* friends and loved ones. He is thus entitled to more than the usual amount of company and care, *especially* when the possibility for cure or recovery vanishes. The notion of care includes, of course, relief of pain, as well as the relief of hunger and thirst, and the maintenance of pleasant surroundings free of obnoxious stimuli. But *human* company and caring is even more important, if the patient is not to feel prematurely abandoned. This duty to keep company and to care when he can no longer cure falls no less upon the physician, than upon family and friends. His patient is the person, not just his disease. There will be times when the patient will want to be alone, to meditate, to pray, to rest. These wishes need to be known and honored. We should heed the old Hebrew injunction, "Don't set up a clatter outside the window of a dying patient," which warns us against distracting him, against insensitively drawing his attention back to the busy world he is about to leave. But the usual problem is not too much company and care, but too little.

Perhaps this abstract account would benefit from my relating one of my own first experiences in caring for the dying. As an intern in medicine, I was assigned as a patient a middle-aged woman suffering from acute leukemia. On previous hospital admissions, she had bounced back remarkably following drug and x-ray therapy. Even while taking her history, I took a strong liking to her, and was deeply moved by her spiritedness in the face of such adversity. I let my wishful thinking get the better of my judgment, and convinced myself that we would again be able to knock her disease into remission. I spent several hours talking with her on subsequent days, mostly listening to her reminisce about her family and her life. On each visit, I offered reassurance and optimism, though I suspect that I needed them more than she. After several weeks it became clear that she was slipping. Her disease did not respond to drugs; in addition, she developed a painful and uncomfortable fungal infection in her mouth, which we treated by painting her mouth with Gentian violet. Partly because of the purple dye, partly because of her weakened condition, her face took on the appearance of a mask which seemed to mock our efforts and to announce in advance their failure. I found it harder and harder to visit her. At last, I stopped entirely. After all, I rationalized, her private physician was still looking after her, and I had many other patients to attend to. After a few days, her private physician told me that she had asked about me, and wondered if I were well. Guiltily, I promised to visit, but did not do so. After a full week had passed, the head nurse on the floor cornered me and chastised me severely for my negligence. That evening, after dinner, I went back to the patient's room. Though greatly weakened and drowsy, she took my hand and was obviously pleased to see me. We talked for fifteen minutes or so, and I then went on to make evening rounds, only to be called in less than an hour to learn that she had died quietly in sleep. She had long been reconciled to the impossibility of cure, and had wanted only company and signs of caring. I had failed her far more in the latter than in the former; were it not for the nurse's admonition, I would have failed her completely.

After a right to know the truth and a right to human company and caring, both rather general claims not unique to the dying patient, we come to a third ingredient which is somewhat specialized: the right to be allowed to die unmolested by meddlesome procedures. The dying patient should be free to refuse the use of extraordinary measures of prolonging life, where "extraordinary" is a term relative to the patient and not just to his disease. He should not be obliged to undergo or continue even ordinary treatments, no matter how customary in medical practice, once these are deemed useless in his particular case. Under some circumstances, hospitalization itself may be a meddlesome intervention. There is no good reason why people should be sent to hospitals to die, or why they should be kept there once it is clear that the dying process is irreversible. The dying patient himself should have a share in deciding how vigorously he is to be treated and where he is to die, a decisive share if possible. This point again emphasizes the need for him to know the truth.

What about the question of having one's death hastened? Does the dying patient have the right to be mercifully killed, a right to assisted suicide? Both the Judeo-Christian tradition and the traditional ethic of medical practice have always clearly distinguished between allowing to die and deliberately killing, endorsing the former and condemning the latter. Indeed, the Hippocratic Oath states, "I will give no deadly medicine to anyone if asked, nor suggest any such counsel." However, in recent years, some people have questioned the validity of the distinction between allowing to die and deliberately killing, pointing out that both discontinuing the antibiotics and administering deadly poison equally result in the death of the patient. That the outcome is the same is not to be denied. But the two acts are descriptively and morally different. First of all, the intention is different. In the one case, the intent is to desist from engaging in useless "treatments" precisely because they are no longer treatments, and to engage instead in the positive acts of giving comfort to and keeping company with the dying patient. In the other case, the intent is indeed to directly hasten the patient's death. Secondly, the agent of death in the first case is the patient's disease, in the second case, his physician. The distinction seems to me to be valuable and worth preserving.

Nevertheless, it may be true that the notion of a death with dignity encompasses under some conditions (e.g., protracted untreatable pain) a direct hastening of one's death. It may be an extreme act of love on the part of a spouse or friend to administer a death-dealing drug to a loved one so in agony. But this is indeed a delicate matter, if we wish to insure that the hastening of the end is never undertaken for anyone's benefit but the dying patient's. Indeed, we should insist that he would have to spontaneously demand such assistance while of sound mind, or, if he were incapable of communication at the terminal stage, that he would have made previous and very explicit arrangements for such contingencies. We might also wish to insist upon a second qualification, that the physician not participate in the hastening. As one doctor put it, if mercy-killings were legalized tomorrow, doctors must not do them. Doctors must not kill.

But even if these qualifications were met, and if mercy-killing were permitted, I doubt if we could establish the *right* to be mercifully killed. To repeat, rights imply duties, and I doubt that we can make killing the *duty* of a friend or loved one.

Recent reference to patients incapable of communication points to a serious question which has not yet been treated. What are the rights of and our duties toward a person who can not help us decide, who is comatose or senile, or without speech? The physician unfortunately sees many such patients. I would suggest the following guiding principle: under these circumstances, the physician should act in the name of the patient as a proxy, judging as best he can, based upon what he knows and can learn about the patient's own wishes. Ideally, a patient and his physician will have discussed such contingencies at an earlier date. Yet because of the changing nature of medical practice, with a decline in the frequency and depth of long-term doctor-patient relationships, and because of a general reluctance on both sides to speak about death, such anticipatory discussions rarely occur. Because of the lack of doctor-patient communication, an increasing number of people are leaving written instructions on what they wish done. Another source of knowledge concerning the patient's desires is the family, although guilt or malice could enter their counsel. It should be the physician's burden to serve to the end as the loyal agent of his patient; he should neither force nor permit the family to make the final decision.

I have filled in some of the ingredients which I think are included in the notion of a right to a dignified death: a right to the truth, to human company and caring, to share in the decisions, to be unmolested, if that is one's wish. The practical import of these rights is clear, since correlative duties fall to doctors and families. But having explored the meaning of man's right to die with dignity, we still have not settled whether such a right exists. Repeated assertion will not, by itself, turn a concept into a reality. We have already hinted at some of the problems in establishing or defending claims to universal natural rights, and we are all too well aware of the difficulties in securing and protecting any such rights once their existence is established in theory. I leave these questions for another time.

One final point. There is perhaps a sense in which we should consider the phrase *man's right to die* literally. Far from being a curse, mortality may indeed be a necessary condition of a worthy life for individuals and of a decent human community.

Recall the words of the Psalmist: "So teach us to number our days, that we may get us a heart of wisdom." And consider these remarks by the philosopher, Hans Jonas:

> Contemporary biology holds out the promise of indefinite prolongation of individual life. . . . But if we abolish death, we must abolish procreation as well, the birth of new life, for the latter is life's answer to the former; and so we would have a world of old age with no youth. But youth is our hope, the eternal promise of life's retaining its spontaneity. With their ever new beginning, with all their foolishness and fumbling, it is the young that ever renew and thus keep alive the sense of wonder, of relevance, of the unconditional, of ultimate commitment, which (let us be frank) goes to sleep in us as we grow older and tired. It is the young, not the old, that are ready to give their life, to die for a cause.[4]

If these reflections are correct, and I think they are, our title taken literally points to perhaps another universal human right, namely, man's right to be mortal. Let us keep this in mind in thinking about proposals, now being voiced, that we proceed to conquer biological aging *en route* to bodily immortality.

References

1. Kubler-Ross E. On Death and Dying, Macmillan, New York, 1969.
2. May WF. The sacral power of death in contemporary culture. Presented at a symposium on Problems in the Meaning of Death at the annual meeting of the American Assoc. for the Advancement of Science, Chicago, 29 Dec., 1970.
3. Ramsey P. On (only) caring for the dying. Chapter 3, in The Patient as Person, Yale, New Haven, 1970. (My discussion here owes much to Professor Ramsey's much more thorough and illuminating inquiry into the ethics of caring for the dying.)
4. Jonas H. Contemporary problems in ethics from a Jewish perspective. Journal of Central Conference of American Rabbis, January, 1968, pp. 27–39; reprinted in Silver DJ, ed., Judaism and Ethics, Ktav Publ. Co., New York, 1970.

BIRTH, DEATH, AND THE LAW

GUIDO CALABRESI, LL.B.

(April 1974, pp. 39–41)

This paper is based on an addressed delivered at the banquet hon-
oring new members of AΩA at Duke University Medical Center
in November 1973. Since this article was written, I have contin-
ued to teach at the Yale Law School, served nine years as Dean
there, and then, in 1994, became a judge on the United States
Court of Appeals for the 2nd Circuit. While I am serving full time
as a federal judge, I continue to teach three courses a year at the
Yale Law School. As part of my teaching, a few years ago, I gave
a university-wide course open to the public on "Life, Death, and
the Law." In addition, I frequently teach a course in the law school
called "Tragic Choices." My interests in the topic of this article
have continued unabated.

— *Guido Calabresi. LL.B.*

WHEN IS A PERSON DEAD, WHEN IS HE FIRST ALIVE? The last few years have seen extraordinary interest in these two questions. Yet much of that interest, it seems to me, has been misdirected. The moments in which the soul enters and leaves the body are, obviously, of great significance to theologians, but they are rather hard for lawyers and doctors to determine. And, even if lawyers and doctors could know when these transcendental moments occur, they would, I suggest, be only occasionally concerned with them in making many of the decisions that they must make. This statement may seem obvious, yet the most sophisticated doctors and lawyers frequently fall into an analogous trap, the trap of wanting "birth" and "death" to be unitary instead of functional concepts.

We tend, like the theologian, to ask if a person is alive or if he is dead, as if there were only one answer to that question when instead there are many answers, each of which may be valid depending on the purpose for which we asked the question in the first place. Recognition of this fact was important even in the past when medical technology gave us little control over peoples' bodies; it is essential today when medicine gives us any number of diverse reasons for asking the questions and any number of ways of controlling the possible answers.

Let me present a frivolous example and follow it with a more serious one. The tax law frequently requires higher taxes on gifts made within three years

417

of death than on gifts made earlier. Yet it would be absurd to have a definition of death, for purposes of this section of the tax law, which induced the Internal Revenue Service to urge a physician, against the fervent pleas of putative heirs, to turn off a heart-lung machine because the three years since a gift had been made were nearly up. And this would be no less absurd even if for other purposes, like burial, someone kept "alive" by a heart-lung machine might well be properly considered still living. Similarly, there is little reason why the events that would justify a physician, whose principal role is that of treating a patient, in abandoning further efforts at keeping a patient "alive" should be the same events that would justify approval of the taking of that patient's organs for transplants. Where the consequences, both in terms of the patient's and society's interests and the possibilities of abuse, differ there is no *a priori* reason why the same events should control, simply because we have grown accustomed to using a unitary concept, "death" to determine many results.

The same is true for the beginning of life. It is hard to see why either conception or parturition should determine all the widely different situations in which we are apt to ask whether there is life. Yet much of the rhetoric that has abounded recently would suggest just that—with some pointing to conception and others to parturition as if it didn't matter why we were asking the question, and as if the law had not always to some extent acted on the assumption that birth, like death, was a process, and that what was allowable or appropriate for certain reasons at one point in that process might not be allowable or appropriate at other times or for other reasons.

If examples are needed, these three might serve. The first is the early property law rule that allowed an unborn child *en ventre sa mère* to inherit real property, if he were later born alive, even though the general law required continuous ownership of property by a live person. The inconsistency of this rule with other definitions of "life" then current gave rise to the celebrated toast, honoring the judge in the case, Baron Turton, and scoffing at the professor whose field this was, Charles Fearne. It goes, "So lift the cup to Baron Turton, who though the law was clear and certain, preferred to help a little fetus, than round out Charlie Fearne's dull treatise." The second is the long debate on whether and when damages could accrue to a fetus injured through someone's negligence. The third is the proviso, included, I believe, in virtually all anti-abortion laws, that permitted abortion (but not infanticide) to save the mother's life. For the first, life began at conception, for the second, somewhere during pregnancy, for the third, not until parturition. Yet all definitions co-existed, and all served rational purposes.

I cannot here go into great detail as to what ought to constitute life for what purposes. But I would like to consider how many different points in time we might identify were we not accustomed to using words like birth, life, and death, which sound so unitary. Were we not limited to those terms we might well ask the following questions: At what point in time and with what safeguards should a society that forbids suicide nonetheless permit a person to demand not to be kept alive any longer? What additional safeguards or facts should be present to permit such a person to make vital organs available for transplant, by sale or by gift? Or should the utility of his organs cause us to permit him to give up the ghost more easily? What more is needed before a family can say, regardless of what the patient has stated, that it is time to call this person dead? At what point should a physician be entitled to make that decision, regardless of the family or the patient? What additional safeguards would be needed if the patient's organs were desired for transplant, or should that enable the physician's decision to come earlier? At what point, if ever, can we say that a person's organs are sufficiently removed even from any memory of personality so that if some of them, e.g., skin, are still "alive" and useful for transplants, society should be able to use them regardless of family or deceased? Finally, do any of these moments bear any relation to moments that are relevant for issues of estate and gift taxation, or inheritance law?

Similarly we might ask, what is sufficiently unborn so that either possible parent can be permitted without any reason to prevent life occurring? What requires at least that both possible parents concur? Are the times up to which abortions may seem justified in cases of rape the same as those that may justify abortion in cases of possible deformity or where the mother's health is genuinely in danger?

If we value life not just for the individual concerned but for society as well— that is, if we think that those values that depend on a concept that life is terribly important, should be preserved, and encroachments made on them only when supported by powerful reasons—then the degree to which we appear to be destroying life and the existence of alternative ways of dealing with the particular problem, which could be solved by destroying life, ought to affect whether we consider acceptable a decision that to some degree undermines those values. Viewed this way it is easy to see why most states permitted abortions to save a mother's life at any stage of pregnancy. The fetus even though nearly born is generally viewed as less a person than the mother. It is less aware of itself, its destruction is less visibly a destruction of life than permitting the mother to die, and no alternative seems possible. But can the same be said for late abortions on the ground of possible deformity, when most deformity causing events occur in the first trimester, when occasionally a late abortion will yield a "live" no-longer-fetus, which, if it is not deformed, we would all strive to keep alive, and when alternatives for easing the plight of those born deformed (and the plight of their families) could be made available if we were willing to spend money to create them? Similarly, if we value life and dislike what would seem to cheapen it, what grounds are there for permitting any but extremely early abortions in cases of rape (except perhaps in the most unusual cases of ignorance)?

Once again, the transcendentalists on both sides of the question will object and at a transcendental level I may well agree with them. If "life" is one and it begins at conception then that undoubtedly affects matters; the same is true if life is simply not there until parturition. But we should all recognize that both viewpoints are purely religious, and as such are only an appropriate basis for laws to the extent that the religion is very broadly shared. It is no accident that Catholic doctrine opposes abortions even to save a mother's life, nor is it an accident that most states permitted such abortions. Similarly, unless one shares the metaphysical view of those who deny that anything related to life occurs between conception and birth, abortion at any stage must justify itself, in terms of the harms it does and the benefits it claims in the specific situation. And that justification must always answer to whether if it is accepted it would not also justify infanticide except for those who accept the metaphysic that would make of parturition a moment of ensoulment—that is, the justification must not prove too much.

All this may seem a long way from my starting point, but it is not. I am not arguing for or against abortions or for or against organ donations at a given level of senility. Rather, I am suggesting that too often there has been no argument because there has only been a clash of conflicting metaphysics. Where the parties involved truly believe in different faiths and where they also believe that their faith should govern, then discussion is, in fact, useless. But I would contend that often the parties, whatever their faiths, would be willing to allow law and medicine to act to accomplish more down to earth purposes, were they not confused by words like birth and death into thinking that what holds for one situation must hold for all. I am sufficiently optimistic to believe that at a functional level, and in examining the benefits and harms that would result from one or another rule, we may find a measure of agreement even among those whose religions differ, so long as they agree not to stand or fall on their transcendental stance. Even if agreement did not occur we would at least have a meaningful debate—which is more than we have had to date.

I do not mean by all this to say that there are no advantages to trying to make "birth" and "death" unitary concepts. Far from it, indeed it was the utility of having a fixed point (even if fictitious), which explains why for so many years these concepts have had a basically unitary definition, deviation from which did occur but only with great difficulty. What I am saying is that today the reasons for deviations from a single definition seem to have become so great that attempts at adhering to a unitary notion of birth and death may well be counterproductive.

Obviously the dropping of hard and fast definitions entails problems for both doctors and lawyers. At the very least it would require us to think a lot harder about what is permissible and what is not in real and human terms rather than in terms of the pre-determined and untouchable categories. And when people begin to think that way the danger of cynicism and, even more, of megalomania are very great indeed.

These dangers are, of course, the best arguments for adhering to strict rules and all-encompassing definitions even when such definitions are in a real sense arbitrary. The best argument for the strict gold standard is not that it was a rational control over quantity of money (in fact, catastrophic depressions and inflations were caused by it). It was, rather, that "rational" man would do worse than any arbitrary standard would.

I am sufficiently an optimist, however, to believe that we can do better through a rational examination of the consequences of a series of differing notions of life and death, than through adhering to one gold-plated definition. I hope so, at least, because I think we all now know too much to make a unitary definition of birth and death any barrier against abuse. No longer does the single concept of life protect whatever is alive in a fetus from being snuffed out for the benefit of others; no longer can it serve to protect the old and weak from being discarded when others view them as too great a burden. That being so, it is inevitably up to medicine and law to face the fact that something, which in some cases should be viewed as life and protected, must in other cases be viewed as something less. If we do face this fact we may yet come up with safeguards that would enable us properly to view ourselves as humane. If we don't we may do in other areas what we may have done in that of abortions and go from a definition of "life" so strict that we could not adhere to it to one that is more destructive of life and of the values that depend on its preservation than is absolutely necessary and hence that is more destructive of life than a humane society can tolerate.

tommy

PEGGY HANSEN, M.D.
(Winter 1989, p. 43)

hushed and small,
impatient sleep holds you,
poor shadow of former selves
fading from a hospital bed,

slipping from the prison
this disease becomes,
as friends and neighbors
melt into frightened night,
wary of contagion.

and now the cancer
spreads its blue rose
over your pale limbs,
a hungry lover
claiming every rise and hollow

while the virus waits,
silent hatchling cuckoo
planted in a fated gift
of urgent blood

and the fevers come,
the chills, the gasping,
and most terrible
the slow erosion
into witless dreams.

A SURVIVOR'S TALE

SARAH B. CUTLER

(Spring 1996, pp. 37–40)

The author received her undergraduate education at Smith College. She is the niece of a distinguished American physician who is a member of Alpha Omega Alpha. We learned from him that she had prepared an account of her experience during her husband's terminal illness, and we invited her to submit the manuscript for publication in The Pharos.

—*Robert J. Glaser, M.D.*

The response in the form of letters to the editor that Dr. Glaser received after publication of "A survivor's tale" was enormous, more than for any previously published essay in The Pharos. *Many of these letters were published in the Fall 1996 issue.*

IN OCTOBER 1993, MY HUSBAND WAS ADMITTED to a major teaching hospital with a preliminary diagnosis of glioma. A biopsy revealed an inoperable grade-4 astrocytoma buried deep in the midbrain. Following intensive radiation treatment, he returned home in December and remained under hospice care until he died on May 21, 1994, not quite eight months after the first symptom was detected. He was forty-six.

Because it pertains to the understanding of what follows, the reader should know that Mike was thirteen years younger than I, and that we were married only after his discharge from the hospital.

He was the love of my life.

* * * * *

On the second of October 1993, Mike and I left our home in the Northeast for a sixteen-day trip to Asia. The company he had helped found in 1987 was on the verge of going public. The two of us had discovered happiness together after failed marriages. Our future seemed full of promise.

An ominous shadow appeared as we touched down in Seoul. Mike remarked that his right leg felt weak. We reassured ourselves that the long flight was probably the villain, though I felt watchful and uneasy. His gait became noticeably more halting in days to follow, but we maintained our travel schedule. Flying home, Mike spoke of tingling in the fingers of his right hand.

At noon on Monday, October 18, we arrived back in the states and imme-

diately sought medical opinion. An MRI was scheduled for Wednesday afternoon, then cancelled when the machine broke down. Mike was told they would
reschedule when the machine was repaired.

Minutes after hearing this news Mike called me at a lunch party next door.
"I want you to come home now," he said. For the first time, I detected anxiety
in his voice. I hurried back. I found Mike sitting on the couch amidst stacks of
papers and file folders. "Sally," he said, "I don't know what this is, but it's coming down on me very fast and there are things you need to know."

I telephoned a physician friend up the street. After talking with us for about
ten minutes, he offered to arrange a CT scan at our local hospital that afternoon. As soon as the hospital called, we left the house. Mike would not come
home again until December 6th.

We were married on December 8.

The scan performed that afternoon showed the mass. Sounding what seemed
to us a triumphant note, the ER physician pronounced his verdict. "We know
exactly what your problem is! You have a glioma!"

In two hours we were en route by ambulance to one of America's premier
teaching hospitals. Our nightmare had begun.

Eight o'clock on the evening of October 20, we enter the emergency room.
A nearby friend who has answered my urgent appeal for a place to stay that
night and a way of getting there soon joins us. Hers is a place where I will spend
many troubled nights ahead since our house is more than an hour away from
the hospital. By 2:00 on the morning of the twenty-first Mike is settled in a
semiprivate room. Later that day he moves to a private room.

A biopsy is scheduled for Friday, cancelled, and rescheduled for Monday.
Shocked and terrified, we wait for answers behind our closed door. The hours
crawl. Events occur in slow motion. From time to time a nurse checks Mike's
blood pressure. With a flash of gallows humor, he jokes that the concern for
his blood pressure is misplaced since he *knows* what he's dying of! Our nerves
are jangled by the incessant clamor of a call bell located just outside our door.
At wits end and with an edge in my voice, I ask a man at the nursing station
about the disturbance. "Nothing *you* need to worry about," he snarls. His
reply is intended to set my boundaries. It also sets a tone. We resume our
dreary vigil.

Thursday melts seamlessly into Friday into Saturday into Sunday. The sun
sets and rises and sets again. Time has stopped, but the beat goes on. The bell
splinters the silence. Meal trays come and go. Blood pressures are taken. Flowers
are delivered. A housekeeper mops the floor and empties the wastebaskets. We
pretend to read the Sunday *Times*. Mike telephones his mother in New York
as he does every Sunday, telling her he's fine, not telling her he's in the hospital.
I leave the room while they talk. It's more than I can bear.

That evening a nurse reveals that the biopsy might again be postponed. In the meantime, an examining physician has suggested that the mass might be an infection rather than a tumor. Only a biopsy will tell. Teased by hope and starved of information, we have, by Sunday night, endured a lifetime of suspense.

The nurse's warning of further postponement sends me to the phone to call the chief of a hospital service, a childhood acquaintance. I do this reluctantly, but our tension has reached fever pitch. *Something must be done!*

I will never know whether it was that call that produced the desired result, but the biopsy is performed on Monday, as scheduled.

Days later, in a chance encounter in the hallway, the physician whose Sunday evening I had disturbed tells me my call had come just after he had learned of the death of his "best friend." I express regret for his loss, about which I could not have known when I made the call, and apologize for my intrusion. Apologies are expected of patients and those who love them when they cross the line or cause inconvenience to busy people.

Monday morning the nursing supervisor returns after a four-day absence to reports of my distress. She asks to speak with me. "Sally," she begins, "I want you to know that I, too, have grown children." Momentarily unbalanced, I quickly realize she thinks I'm Mike's mother! I laugh.

Later on, the radiation oncologist, for reasons unclear to me, remarks twice during a consultation, "At least we know Mike has *some sort* of family out there."

"How's the girl friend today?" asks a primary nurse. Our unconventional relationship seems to excite speculation and gratuitous comment laced with disapproval. I feel slightly defensive for the first time in our years together.

To nearly everyone we are "Mike" and "Sally." Despite his MIT doctorate in physics and a long resumé of professional achievements, Mike is degraded and infantilized. While residents younger than my children stand over his helpless body, Mike stoically endures their mock-cheerful greetings. "Good morning, Mike. I'm Dr. Smith. How are you feeling today?" (The eminent physician Paul Beeson has recalled to me his experience at Atlanta's Grady Memorial Hospital forty years ago when the segregated black patients were called by their first names while the white patients were respectfully addressed as "Mr." and "Mrs." Forty years later *all* patients are second-class citizens.)

Two or three days after the biopsy confirms our darkest fears, Mike begins twice-daily radiation therapy.

To reach the radiation laboratory he will journey by wheelchair, later by gurney, down several floors and through a building complex to the basement of another. There he will wait his turn among other miserable human beings in various stages of debilitation. Some speak in hushed tones with relatives whose faces are creased with worry. Others, more dead than alive, lie mute and hollow-eyed on gurneys.

On one particular day, the grotesque "Halloween" masks molded to the features of those receiving brain irradiation are stacked on the floor against the concrete walls. These masks are fitted to the patient's face and screwed into the table upon which he or she lies during radiation so that the head remains stationary. Each symbolizes a family's tragedy, a grim reminder, should one be needed, that ours is shared suffering.

To arrive at this scene of desolation we rely on the round-trip services of "transportation," the name given those who trundle patients around the hospital. Since demand for these services exceeds supply, patients ready to return to their rooms sometimes sit or lie wretchedly in the radiation lab waiting room for as long as an hour before they are rescued. As Mike's condition swiftly deteriorates, these delays cost him nearly unbearable physical and emotional torment.

A friend and I wait in the living room on Mike's floor for his arrival from radiation. Suddenly, my friend begins to wave at someone in the corridor. All I see at first glance is a stranger in a red windbreaker with a thick folder tucked under his arm. Looking more closely, I see he is pushing Mike's wheelchair. I hurry over. The stranger explains. "I brought my father in for radiation therapy today. I felt so sorry for this man," he says, gesturing at Mike slumped in his chair, "that I asked if I could take him back to his room. They said 'Yes,' and handed me his file."

I thank him warmly and unburden him of Mike and his medical history. With Mike settled in his room, I go to the nursing manager to protest handing a patient over to a stranger. Thereafter, I become "transportation."

On Mike's last day of radiation, I search in vain for a wheelchair. Finally, I ask the man at the desk to find one for us. Twenty minutes pass and no wheelchair appears. I return to him to suggest that he telephone the radiation laboratory to explain our delay. "By the way," I say, "is the wheelchair on its way?" The man who had told me to mind my own business the first time we met fires back. "I've *ordered* a wheelchair and it will *be* here when it *gets* here!"

On the day of our final departure, a messenger delivers a legal document to the hospital to accompany Mike home. When the document fails to appear in Mike's room, I inquire at the desk. The document is there, but the man at the desk does not consider it his job to carry it twenty yards down the hall or even to report its arrival. Nor, as he makes clear to a caller a week earlier, is it his job to transfer patients' calls from the desk to their rooms. My complaints to the nursing manager about this employee's discourteous and unhelpful manner are met with, "I hear you." As far as I know, he is still there.

About a week after he enters the hospital, Mike suffers a brain bleed. In the absence of available beds in the ICU the attending physician prescribes private nursing care around the clock.

The first of the private nurses comes on at 11:00 p.m. I have gone home for the night. The next morning Mike says, in a barely audible voice, "All she talked about last night, Sally, was where she should leave her bill and who was going to pay it." My outrage seals my reputation as a whistle blower.

Later on, when I seem poised to modify a decision made at an earlier conference I had not attended, the nurse who knows me as "the girl friend" says with contempt, "I was right there when you and Mike made that decision! You'll have to get your priorities straight!" Her memory, not mine, is at fault. The scolding is not deserved.

This unprofessional behavior is not the sole property of the staff supervised by the nursing manager. Early one morning I find her engaged in a discussion with Mike about the possibility of a day at home. She makes a point of ignoring my arrival in the room. Mike is clearly confused by her rapid-fire questions about stairs, railings, accessible bathrooms in our house. I interject that I am better able to answer her questions than Mike is. (Since Mike was hospitalized I have had ramps and railings installed at home.) She bristles. "You sound stressed this morning! I'll talk to you when you calm down!" Before I can respond, she turns on her heel and leaves the room.

She's right! I *am* stressed! But disrespect directed at a family member in the presence of a dying person is inexcusable. Later that day she volunteers an apology. It's too late. The damage is done. The apology belongs to Mike, who never receives it.

On another occasion, the nursing manager summons me to her office to confide importantly that a night nurse has reported Mike is afraid I will leave him. I'm floored! Is the nursing staff prepared to believe that because we're not married, I will abandon Mike when he needs me most? Can Mike believe that? My confidence in our mutual trust is shaken.

Subsequently, he tells me that what he actually said is he's afraid I'll find him repulsive. Some reflective listening by the attending nurse and her supervisor would have clarified his concern and spared me unnecessary heartache.

The door opens and two men pushing a gurney enter the room. "We're here to take you down for your MRI," they explain to Mike. "Oh?" I respond. "I thought it had been canceled." With a glance at their clipboard, they nod agreement and go away.

Around Thanksgiving, Mike is transferred to a rehabilitation facility in the hope that he might learn to compensate for some of the disabilities arising from the tumor. Six days later he is readmitted through the hospital emergency room with a fever of 103 and an angry, full-body rash resulting from an allergic reaction to anti-seizure medication.

During Mike's brief stay in "rehab," I go home for the day to check the mail and get some clean clothes. I arrive back after a trip prolonged by heavy rain and a trucking strike to find Mike propped up in bed with a tray of spaghetti

in front of him. By now he has lost the use of his right side and much of his
ability to communicate verbally. Attempts to feed himself with his left hand
have created a mess. "I spilled my spaghetti," he says, crestfallen. A battery of
equipment—walker, wheelchair, commode—is crammed into his small room. It
was not there when I left that morning. Mike lies on what looks like a pile of
dirty laundry. His lunch tray, untouched, rests across the arms of the chair.

I can hardly imagine a more pitiful sight. I report what I have found to the
nursing supervisor, who takes full responsibility. The attending physician stops
by to apologize and promise that steps will be taken to see that this does not happen again. But despite the goodwill of the staff on this and every occasion, one
of our most distressing experiences occurs here.

Early one morning I find Mike's door closed. A nurse in the hall asks me to
wait outside while Mike uses the commode. Moments later she peers through
the window in the door and exclaims with evident dismay. "Oh, my goodness!
He's fallen on the floor!" The odds of serious injury in such crowded conditions are substantial. Far worse is the profound humiliation Mike must feel at
finding himself naked on the floor and powerless to recover. We have reached
a very low point.

Afterwards, the nurse says, "Well, now we know he can't be left unattended."

It is mid-November. I request a private meeting with Mike's primary physician to question whether the radiation treatments, which are clearly com-
pounding Mike's distress, should continue. He persuades me to proceed.

In retrospect, I rue that decision. Knowing what I do now about the prognosis of inoperable astrocytomas, I believe the outlook was hopeless from the
beginning. I am aware of no significant breakthroughs in the treatment of this
condition in the past two decades.

But our need for truth competes unsuccessfully with the physician's need to
battle the cancer and control decisions, however hopeless the odds and at whatever the costs—physical, emotional, and financial—to the patient. He woos me
with graphs and hypotheses. Foolishly, I allow myself to be seduced.

Our physician's inability to accept defeat gracefully is dramatized in our
last meeting, which has all the earmarks of a hit-and-run accident. Shortly before noon on a day in early December he comes to Mike's room to speak with
me. Leading me to the elevator area where there is no place to sit, he delivers
his message. "We're stopping radiation. It's not doing any good. I have a meeting to go to." Without another word, he vanishes into a waiting elevator. We
will never see or hear from him again.

We pack up and come home to the welcoming embrace of our local hospice
organization. We have seen the last of hospitals.

Aphasic, hemiplegic, unable to read or write, yet fully comprehending, Mike
lay in a hospital bed in our room at home surrounded by loving friends and

family and attended by nursing assistants fine-tuned to his every need and wish. Hospice staff brought with them an understanding the hospital personnel, for the most part, had not reached: that Mike's disease was, in a way, mine; that his tumor would forever change our lives in real and threatening ways; that what we both needed most was support and comfort and information. What a difference their humane and compassionate approach made to the last six months of Mike's life.

Since Mike died, I have struggled to discern the reasons so many teaching hospitals earn dismal marks in patient care. One answer may be that the medical community believes it has cornered the market on wisdom, that they understand our needs better than we understand them ourselves, that their services are a privilege to be accepted without question or complaint, and that we need to know only as much as will affirm the decisions they make for us. We are left only with the responsibility to incorporate their priorities and conform to their practices. In this environment the patient and family become abstractions, mute props in the drama of their own living and dying.

Another answer may be that technology has displaced the old-fashioned therapy called comfort. On a statue of Edward L. Trudeau, pioneer in the treatment of tuberculosis, is inscribed the fifteenth-century folk saying that the business of medicine is "to cure sometimes, to relieve often, *to comfort always* (italics added)." This time-honored *sine qua non* has become the missing component in the care rendered the dying in today's teaching hospitals. Many physicians and nurses who were drawn to medicine for humanitarian as well as scientific reasons appear to have lost sight of their original purpose. Comfort has dropped out of the march of progress in medical science and technology.

People facing death thirst for comfort that medications and technology alone cannot provide. Most fear physical suffering. Others fear financial ruin or the loss of significant relationships. Almost all, to a greater or lesser extent, fear nonbeing. Great medical practitioners will treat those fears with compassion and insight born of understanding. Others, perhaps not having resolved their own fears surrounding death, will bring only technology and pharmacology to the bedside and park their common humanity at the door. This is not enough.

To be sure, sick and dying people and their family members can be difficult and demanding and angry, but time and effort must be expended to uncover the roots of these emotions and behaviors and to treat them as carefully as one treats the patient's medical condition.

In a perfect world, a stay as a patient in a teaching hospital would be a prerequisite for entering the medical profession. How else is empathy learned? How better to understand the daily assaults on dignity and intelligence than to experience their sting firsthand? To see through my eyes, you must walk in my shoes.

Unfortunately, I am not optimistic that much improvement will occur in my lifetime. Old habits die hard. An elitist approach to the treatment of mortally ill patients has a long history. Members at the head of the medical profession transmit their values to those who come after them. A self-important, callous attitude towards patients and those who love them is contagious, as our experience proved. Add to it the growing disregard for common courtesies in everyday life and you have the formula for comfort denied.

On a more positive note, the hospice movement gathers strength. In increasing numbers, people are choosing to place themselves under hospice care when their time comes to die. As one with intimate, painful experience of the dying process, I am eternally grateful we had that choice and that we made it.

* * * * *

Years ago, I accompanied Mike to a conference in Vermont. The time was midsummer, August, I think. Late one evening while we stood gazing at a sky filled with stars, Mike's voice suddenly broke the spell. "You know, Sally," he mused, "I often think how marvelous it is that all the elements in our bodies were once part of the stars."

On every clear night since he died I am consoled by the thought that Mike is, again, part of the stars.

Postscript . . . June, 2003

With my 69th birthday on the horizon, I have traded a career for volunteer work that includes, among others, a day a week in the emergency room of the local community hospital and service on the board of directors of Advocates for Youth. I am still hoping to impart the lessons distilled from the experience I described in my article to medical and nursing students, but so far there have been no takers.

In May I traveled to New Haven where my uncle, Paul Beeson, was honored with his portrait, which now hangs over the podium in the auditorium of the Yale Medical School. I am delighted to say that at age 94 he is still the handsome and humble man I've loved all my life—a hero to me as he is to so many others.

The memory of Mike's last days is still cruelly painful, but I am fortunate to have two wonderful sons and four lively grandchildren. I'm sad that they will never know firsthand what an extraordinary person he was.

— Sarah B. Cutler, M.D.

Part XI

THE REALITIES
OF HEALTH CARE
IN THE
UNITED STATES

SOME THOUGHTS ON MEDICAL CENTER GOVERNANCE

ROBERT G. PETERSDORF, M.D.

(Fall 1987, pp. 13–18)

Bob Petersdorf earned his M.D. at Yale in 1952, where he was elected to AΩA in 1951. Only 12 years later he was named Chairman of the Department of Medicine at the University of Washington School of Medicine. In 1979 he left to become President of Brigham and Women's Hospital in Boston. Rounding out academic medical positions (see his article, below) he served as Vice Chancellor and Dean of the School of Medicine at UC San Diego. This was followed by his 8-year appointment as the President of the Association of American Medical Colleges, and he continues to write and speak with an active and articulate pen and voice about issues of medical academe.

Introduction

I HOPE I WILL BE PARDONED FOR MAKING THIS TALE somewhat autobiographical. In my somewhat checkered career, I have been a department chairman, a hospital director, a vice-president for health sciences, and a dean. And, for whatever reason, I have now graduated to the position of guru, devoid of the stresses and strains of line command.

Six years ago I presented the first Robert H. Williams Lecture to the Association of Professors of Medicine. This lecture was entitled "*The Four Horsemen of the Apocalypse.*"[1] In it I described the four major actors in the governance of the medical center: the horseman on a white horse with a bow and crown—the dean; the rider on a red horse with sword drawn to do battle—the department chairman; the horseman on a black horse holding a pair of balances—the vice-president for health affairs; and the horseman on a pale horse ridden by death and followed by hell—the hospital director. In that presentation I characterized the roles of these players along the following lines:

The dean as the leader of the medical school faculty, as the major manager of the medical center, and clearly as the white knight.

The vice-president as the arbiter of disputes between the deans of the several health science schools, and between the dean and the hospital director. I pointed out the inherent conflict between deans and vice-presidents and admonished the V.P.s that conflict could be avoided only if they, the V.P.s, stayed out of the internal management of the medical school.

The chairman of medicine as the champion of quality, riding with drawn sword to slay the dragon of mediocrity.

The hospital director, in my allegory of six years ago, as the heavy—the downer who transformed the ivory tower of academe into the snake pit of practice and bottom lines.

In reading that piece over recently, I had to remind myself that I wrote it at the conclusion of my brief and not altogether salubrious tenure as a hospital director, and just before I accepted a deanship. But after five years in the latter post I have drawn some new and different conclusions about who governs whom or who should do so.

What has become clear to me after five years of decanal duty, and a new perspective of chairmen, hospital directors, and vice-presidents from my present post of neutrality, is that some of the riders need to change horses.

The enlarging scope of academic medicine

Although the academic establishment underwent its greatest period of growth between the early 1960s and 1980, in point of fact, growth of the academic medical center has continued. Between the early 1960s and 1980s forty, and now forty-one, medical schools have come on-line. The number of medical schools has definitely plateaued, but the cost of running them has doubled. Relatively, they are no more expensive compared to the rest of health care, but we are now talking about a $10 billion per year business. As an aside, I note that there are three fewer university-owned hospitals now than there were six years ago—a consequence of divestiture of hospitals by their parent universities.

The magnitude of growth during the past twenty years can be seen in better perspective when it is realized that first-year and total medical school enrollments have doubled; the number of interns and residents has nearly doubled; and the number of graduate students in the basic medical sciences has tripled. An even greater increase in size has taken place in our faculties. The faculty of clinical departments has increased some 625 percent in the past 20 years. Basic science faculty has tripled, although it has lost in size relative to clinicians. The thought I want to leave is that although we have produced enormous diversity in the size and scope of our 127 medical schools, we have created a colossus whose administration poses both significant problems and significant challenges.

Academic medical center governance structures

Given the size and complexity of academic medical centers, it should come as no surprise that various mechanisms of governance have been devised. There are four basic types of system structures. In the first, the consortium model, the organization is governed by a coordinating body, a relatively weak mechanism. Each institution has its own board and management. In the second model, the holding company, there is a central board, a corporate manager, multiple institutional boards, and independent managers of individual institutions. A situation in which several boards are joined is exemplified by the overlapping board model. Finally, there is the corporate, and, in many ways, the simplest, model, which is typified by the state university and its board of regents, central management through a vice-president or vice-chancellor for health affairs, and management of the hospital or hospitals by the hospital director, and of the medical school by the dean.

One can legitimately ask why I am offering this mini-course in Management I, particularly when the models I have described are both relatively simplistic, and perhaps even illusory. In point of fact, an academic medical center organization is usually more complex than those described above. The point I am trying to make is that virtually all of these models have as the chief executive officer (CEO) of the medical center: a president, chancellor, vice-president or vice-chancellor for health affairs or health sciences. What is happening in the real world is that more and more academic medical centers have separated the position of vice-president from that of dean of the school of medicine, and in every instance in which there is both a vice-president and a dean, the vice-president is in charge. What are the reasons for the emergence of the vice-president as the primary manager of the medical center?

Firstly, most university presidents wish to deal with only one person, who is in charge of all of the health sciences.

Secondly, hospital directors do not like to report to deans of schools of medicine. In fact, they do not even like to report to the hybrid of the species—the vice-president/dean.

Thirdly, deans of health science schools other than medicine like to report to deans of medical schools even less. Even though they admit that the school of medicine has between 80 and 90 percent of the action among the several health science schools, they like to consider themselves the *de jure,* if not *de facto,* equals of the dean of the school of medicine.

Six years ago I pleaded for the primacy of the dean of the school of medicine. I am not sure that this view is any longer realistic, perhaps even for individuals who hold the dual title of vice-president/dean, a circumstance that pertains to about 15 percent of medical center CEOs who are also the deans of their medical school. An argument can be made for a combined vice-president/dean in an academic medical center that consists only of a medical school *cum* hospital. But even here, the recalcitrance of hospital directors to report to the dean must be taken into consideration when organizing (or reorganizing) an academic medical center.

The vice-president/dean school of medicine interface

In my previous presentation, I pointed out the inherent turf battles between the vice-president and the dean. I believe that many of these turf battles could be eliminated if two points were recognized.

The first is that the vice-president is at least one layer removed from the faculty. Put differently, the major difference between the vice-president and the dean is that the dean is both a member of and the leader of the faculty.

The second point is that we would be better served, I believe, if we left the managing to the vice-president and his/her staff, while recognizing the dean as being primarily the academic leader of the faculty. We have made a mistake, perhaps exacerbated by the AAMC's emphasis on management training for deans, by insisting for a decade and a half that deans be managers, rather than academic leaders. In defining who should ride what horse, we should make clear that whatever managerial authority the dean exerts should be at the academic level, leaving the overview of the hospital and the medical center, including their budgets, to the vice-president. A corollary of this formulation is that the vice-president might have under his aegis certain staff functions, such as development, that is, fund raising, planning that should encompass the entire medical center, public relations and, where appropriate, governmental affairs.

Does this mean that the dean would be emasculated? I hardly think so. As the acknowledged leader of the faculty the dean is the individual primarily responsible for recruiting, reviewing, and removing department chairs; for oversight of the curriculum; for the admission and care and feeding of medical students; for organization of the alumni; for relationships with the practicing community; for instituting and maintaining academic relationships with community hospitals; and for many other functions. As a manager, the dean would remain responsible for the medical school budget. To the extent that most medical schools budgets are fixed, however, the managerial functions of the dean's office would be curtailed. The academic functions of the dean, however, clearly would be upgraded. In fact, it would be preferable, both from the point of view of his present and future function, for the dean to look and act more like a faculty member than a manager. After all, all deans are tenured members of the faculty and are expected to rejoin the faculty more actively at the conclusion of their deanship. The best advice that I can give to deans is to keep a hand in teaching, rounding, and even working in the laboratory—they may well need these skills in the future.

Because I am advocating less rather than more management for deans, I favor more rather than less management for the vice-president. I have already indicated that he/she should have managerial responsibility for the medical center's finances. Secondly, a number of functions that are now carried out separately by the vice-president, the dean, and the hospital director, such as development, planning, and public relations, should be consolidated in the office of the vice-president. This shift would result in the pooling and saving of resources, and eliminate duplication and turf battles.

The hospital director's role redefined

The era of cost containment and competition has made the director of a teaching hospital a very different being than was the case ten, or even five years ago. In order to assure fiscal survival of their teaching hospitals, hospital directors have entered the world of competition with both hands and both feet. They have contracted, joint ventured, satellited, and competed with the best of them. Equally important, they have managed to survive—indeed, some have thrived in this competitive environment. What this means, however, is that the hospital director has more and more become a businessman and less and less an academician or a quasi-dean. This is probably as it should be.

On this note, let us send the vice-president and hospital director riding off into the sunset, the former managing the academic medical center, the latter laughing all the way to the bank. Both are riding black horses.

The deanship redefined

I am afraid that in the past the dean tried to be too many things to too many people. As a consequence, he has asked too much of himself, and people ask too much of him. When he could not perform all of the duties expected of him or deliver on all of the promises he had made, he became the target of a variety of groups in his constituency. This constant state of dissatisfaction, both external and internal, has played a major causative role in the continuing turnover of deans. Having the dean be the academic leader would eliminate at least some of this pot shooting because it would constrict his constituency, as well as his managerial functions.

The department chairmanship redefined

Perhaps the department chairman has a sufficiently small venue so that he can provide both academic and managerial leadership to his department. But just as is the case with the dean, whether he can do so successfully is doubtful. Chairmen of relatively small, clinically active departments are likely to spend a good deal of time personally in the operating or consulting room, sometimes to the neglect of teaching, usually to the neglect of research, and almost always to the neglect of administration. The business acumen of the chairman of a small clinical department is likely to be similar to that of a leader of a specialty practice group or partnership. This type of chairman is unlikely to be a big player in the institutional arena.

A much more difficult job is being chairman of a large, research-intensive department, particularly one that also has substantial clinical responsibilities. Departments of medicine, pediatrics, psychiatry, and neurology are typical examples. Chairmen of these departments generally follow one of two patterns. Either they continue to be active in research to the neglect of the clinical scene, or they do the clinical and business end of the job while neglecting the department's research agenda. This biphasic nature of clinical departments has led me to conclude that some schools would do better if the chairman tried to emphasize one side of the equation while neglecting the other, or vice versa. Specifically, I would not be disappointed if some of our clinical departments concentrated on teaching, training, and clinical service. So long as the medical school built upon such a department turns out competent, concerned, compassionate professionals, it is, in my view, fulfilling its major obligation. It is foolhardy in this time of constrained resources and technically sophisticated research to have every department of medicine, pediatrics, or psychiatry be a mini-research institute.

For the large, diversified clinical department, such as most departments of medicine, the chairman, unfortunately, is coming to look more and more like a dean. He is expected to be a manager, an entrepreneur, an academic leader, a faculty rep, a curricular innovator, an investigator, and more. As a consequence of his multiple responsibilities—real or expected—the chairman is often perceived to be wanting. Perhaps the best piece of evidence that deans and chairmen of medicine are offspring of the same clone is the difficulty that is being encountered in filling these positions, and the time that is required to fill them. Among the sixteen medical schools in the West, three deanships are now vacant, and four new deans have just been appointed. Two chairs of medicine are now vacant. The national figures show that in the 127 medical schools, twelve deanships are now filled by acting deans, and among the chairmanships of medicine, sixteen are filled by acting chairmen. Moreover, the searches to fill these positions are now being measured in generations. Some searches in the West have been going on for more than two and one-half years. The administrative profile of a chairman of a large clinical department is looking more and more like that of a dean.

Why do deans and chairmen of medicine seem to have so much administrative dyspareunia? There are several reasons:

- The expectations of their respective constituencies are entirely too great and cannot be fulfilled.
- They are expected to be responsive to students, housestaffs, faculties, university administrators, boards of trustees, associate deans, division heads, hospital directors, practice plan managers, local, state, and federal agencies, patients and patient interest groups, alumni, medical societies, the

media, specialty boards and societies, potential faculty recruits, journal editors, and animal rights groups, to mention just some.

- They do not have the time or have not taken the time to maintain an intellectual life of their own, whether this takes the form of a modest size laboratory, a clinical practice, involvement in teaching and training of housestaff, or even textbook editing. A diastole for intellectual pursuits is essential, not only to keep the dean or chairman sane, but as an academic asset held in escrow for the time when either the dean or the chairman gets tired or gets fired—events that seem to be the inevitable end to the chairmanly or deanly career.

A dean or chair often does not have the authority to go with his/her responsibility. This dichotomy takes two forms: material and professional. On the material side, from the point of view of the dean, most of the resources are in the departments, and from the point of view of the chairman, most of the resources are with the divisions. In fact, in my dotage, I have come to the conclusion that the best job in the department of medicine is that of division head. His term seems to be the longest and the most secure; his performance is rarely, if ever, reviewed. Division heads can and usually do tell the chairman how much clinical service they want to render and when and how they want to render it; they tell the chairman just whom, and when they want to teach. They have become masters of the end run and often negotiate quite separately with the hospital director—the substance of these negotiations being unbeknownst to the chairman. Their space is sacrosanct. While chairmen of departments come and go, division heads seem to stay forever—much like the rulers of the ancient Hanseatic city-states: proudly autonomous and accountable to no one.

A major cause of unhappiness among deans and chairmen is the second-guessing, backbiting, and often just plain bitching by the faculty, an activity euphemistically called faculty governance. I do not deny for one minute the faculty's right to decision making in academic matters—student admission and curriculum among them, but I seriously wonder whether such knotty problems as assignment of research space, recruitment of new faculty, priority setting for new programs, and other such matters can be readily settled by a consensus of voting faculty. In fact, what is lacking in many faculty groups is mutual trust within the group and trust of those who have been selected for positions of leadership.

How can we make being chair or dean more attractive? I am genuinely concerned about the failure of deanships and chairmanships of medicine to fill and to fill rapidly. The inability to fill these key positions in medical schools seems to have at least three root causes:

First outside recruitments for these positions are often unrealistic. I have found over the years that it is very difficult, indeed nearly impossible, to persuade happy and/or productive people to move, even though far too many are willing to spend everyone's time and money, including their own, in exercising academic brinksmanship, to look at jobs that they know they will not take.

Second talented inside people are being regularly overlooked or denigrated. Apparently, the house poodle never shows quite as well as the outside contender, although often he is much easier to live with.

Third the job of dean and/or chairman may have become genuinely unattractive. This thesis is the most worrisome, because it indicates that the way in which we have structured the job is flawed. I can address only the third of these possibilities and will refrain from commenting on the first two, except to point out that failures to recruit deans or chairmen successfully can often be laid squarely at the door of the search committee members, whose esteem of the job being offered is exceeded only by the esteem they have for themselves and who seem to want to recruit only candidates who can walk on water. To my knowledge, there has only been one of these in recorded history.

How can we improve the job of chairman and dean?

I would like to suggest that we look at football for a model. I have argued elsewhere for two-platoon faculties—clinicians/teachers and investigators/teachers with emphasis on the proper balance between the two platoons and appropriate rewards for both.[2] I would now like to extend this analogy to the coaching staff. Most football teams have a head coach, an offensive coordinator, and a defensive coordinator, not to mention coaches for smaller groupings—a backfield coach, a wide-receiver coach, an interior-line coach, et cetera. I would like to have us base departmental and even institutional organization on such a model. For example, the chair of a large department of medicine would have two deputy chairs, one for clinical affairs and one for academic affairs. The first would deal primarily with clinical services and academic functions carried out in the clinical setting, including student teaching, housestaff affairs, patient care matters, and clinical practice. The other deputy chair would deal with academic matters, including research, graduate training, academic space, and industrial relationships. The departmental organization would comprise one side of a matrix, while the division heads would comprise the other. Institutions that do not have a vice-president for health affairs or where the dean and vice-president is the same person, might need to have a third deputy dean or assistant vice-president to deal with planning, development, and public and governmental relations. As I indicated above, however, where a vice-president exists I would assign those functions to his office. Reporting to the deputy deans would be assistant deans for clinical matters, such as practice-plan directors, medical directors, chiefs of service at various affiliated hospitals, et cetera. On the academic side there would be assistant or associate deans dealing with faculty appointments, student admissions, curriculum, and space. There can be a number of permutations on the schemes. Whatever the model, a successful dean or chairman of a large department must have the ability to delegate. Only if the chair or dean has or cultivates this ability will he/she get the time to make the job attractive.

Chairs and deans also need to be rewarded materially. It should not be necessary to take a pay cut to take these executive jobs or to see a lot of patients to make ends meet. At the same time the premium for doing these jobs should not be set so high as to lead to deprivation at the conclusion of the dean's or chair's term.

There should be some degree of job security for chairs and deans. I would suggest a minimun five-year term, with a five-year renewal, subject to review, as being routine, and a third five-year term constituting the maximum. This would permit the chairman or dean to count on a life after, and to plan accordingly. Among the cadre of present deans only a handful have exceeded the fifteen-year maximum, and most are below the five-year minimum.

There should be a mandatory period of rest, relaxation, and retooling for all major chairs and deans at the conclusion of their tours of duty. I would suggest six months for one term, a year for two terms, and eighteen months for three—all at full pay. If we permit the chairs or dean more time for professional activities during his chairmanship or deanship, these retooling leaves should permit the chair or dean to return to the ranks of the faculty better than ever.

Finally, the institution should work out a reasonable system of rotations so that not all major chairmen's terms end at once. The reviews should be staggered and be predictable, and they should extend to all levels of the administration, including division heads, for whom the number of terms should also be restricted. To a large extent, the leadership of a medical school would need to come from within, and a substantial segment of the faculty should expect to take its turn in the administration. The intensive, interminable, and inordinately expensive recruitments, which all too often are nothing more than exercises in academic brinksmanship, eventually must cease. Think of how much lower our collective cholesterols would be if we did not have to go to all of those recruiting dinners! And think how much more sensibly our resources would be spent if we did not have to use them to match the inflated shopping lists of putative candidates. And think of how nice it would be to have a faculty made up of individuals who would be familiar with a school's culture, its strengths, its weaknesses, and its problems, and who were willing to solve the institution's problems, not only their own.

Biomedical administration is not the monster that we have made it out to be. One can be just as creative in approaching administrative tasks as in the laboratory. Using one's administrative talents in recruiting, organizing, and facilitating can be rewarding and fun. My thesis is that it does not involve having to mount a black horse, and certainly not riding the pale horse followed by death. In fact, all administrators can ride the white horse. All they need to learn is how to get on the horse, not to fall off, and to dismount at the right time and in the right place.

ACKNOWLEDGEMENT: I am grateful to Dr. Steven Ruma for suggestions concerning this presentation.

References

1. Petersdorf RG and Wilson MP. The four horsemen of the Apocalypse: Study of academic medical center governance. JAMA 247:1153–61, 1982.
2. Petersdorf RG. Is the establishment defensible? N Engl J Med 309:1053–57, 1983.

Postscript: A reassessment in 2003

Most of the 1987 article dealt with reporting relationships. It described various models including one where the dean reported to the vice-president for health affairs, where the dean and the vice-president were the same person and reported to the president of the university or the provost. I also discussed methods by which to make the deanship or chairmanship of the large department less burdensome. I emphasized that even fifteen years ago, the hospital director was moving toward a business model. Fewer hospital CEOs were physicians than in the past.

What has changed? In general, the titles of the leaders of the academic medical center have not changed. There is a tendency for the dean of a medical school and the vice-president for health affairs to be the same person. The hospital directors continue to be relatively autonomous, although, in some academic medical centers, they report to the vice-president for health affairs or to a vice-president/dean. The bureaucracy has increased rather strikingly. There are more and more associate deans, more associate and assistant vice-presidents, and many more associate hospital directors. Aside from the personnel, however, the structure of the academic medical center has changed only modestly.

The merger movement

A number of community hospitals, and several major teaching hospitals, have attempted to merge. Most of these attempts at merger have taken place since 1995. They have enjoyed varying success. Community hospitals of similar size and with similar missions have generally merged relatively smoothly. The merger of academic medical centers has generally been more difficult and more traumatic. John Kastor's book, *Mergers of Teaching Hospitals in Boston, New York, and Northern California*, describes in some detail the merger of the Brigham and Women's and Massachusetts General Hospital in Boston (Partners), which has gone pretty well; the merger of Stanford and the University of California, San Francisco, ended in divorce; and the merger between Presbyterian Hospital and

New York Hospital in New York is much more complex. The resulting governance structure of these merged entities has been more complicated, has involved diverse academic cultures, and has usually resulted in significant turnover of academic and administrative leadership. They have not been rousing successes.

Finding the answers

All segments of the academic medical center have become more time-oriented. There has been an increasing tendency to report financial results more frequently, certainly as often as quarterly. The sources of funding have changed. Subventions have steadily decreased for state-sponsored medical schools and teaching hospitals. In private institutions, where hospitals have characteristically been separate from medical schools, philanthropy, grants, and patient care revenues have played an even larger role than in the past. All medical schools and their affiliated hospitals have, in the past several years, been hurt by diminishing reimbursements from Medicare, Medicaid, and third-party payers.

The climate in academe

When I wrote my article for *The Pharos* 15 years ago, academic medicine was a relatively pleasant, carefree existence. This is no longer the case. The pleasures of academe have been replaced by the stresses of academe. These stresses have resulted in more lawsuits, and less satisfaction of patients with the care that they receive. A significant number of citizens cannot pay their hospital or physicians' bills and there has been an inexorable increase in the number of uninsured or underinsured. The bottom line is that there is a lot in the American health care system that needs fixing, irrespective of medical center governance.

— Robert G. Petersdorf, M.D.

AN EARLY CALL FOR HEALTH CARE REFORM: THE COMMITTEE OF 430 PHYSICIANS

PAUL B. BEESON, M.D.

(Winter 1993, pp. 22–24)

With his warm intelligence and sensitivity, Paul Beeson has affected in positive ways all those students, residents, faculty, and family who have known and worked with him over many years. It has been said that he exemplifies the word "physician," accomplishing it by mastery of the art of healing and treatment of diseases. He was elected to AΩA at McGill in 1946. He served as chairman of medicine at two universities, Emory and Yale. He was selected to be the Nuffield Professor at Oxford University and after his formal retirement he joined the VA hospital at the University of Washington as a Distinguished Physician. Beeson has been a champion for the health and well-being of the elderly. In 1978 he chaired the first Institute of Medicine study on "Aging in Medical Education," and as the editor of the Journal of the American Geriatrics Society *he fused the areas of practice, academia, and teaching.*

∞

THE *NEW YORK TIMES*, SUNDAY, NOVEMBER 7, 1937, featured a front-page article: "National Policy on Health Asked by 430 Doctors." The signatories, listed under the heading, "Signers of the Statement on Social Medicine," included several medical school deans and many highly regarded clinical teachers. The changes they advocated were radical, but in retrospect appear farsighted, and are of special interest today, in connection with the debates going on about health care reform, involving physicians, hospital administrators, executives of large businesses and insurance companies, government officials (including candidates for election), and members of the public.

The Committee of Physicians had formed after publication of a survey of doctors' views by the American Foundation, a philanthropic organization established by Edward Bok. A questionnaire had been addressed to several thousand American practitioners, asking:

Has your experience led you to believe that a radical reorganization of medical care in this country is indicated? If so, in what direction?

444

If you do not believe that radical reorganization is indicated, what, if any, changes or revisions in the present system would you like to see made? What evolutionary possibilities would you stress?[1]

Two thousand replies had been received, and they were published, more or less *verbatim* in two thick volumes.[2]

The committee's statement opened with four principles:

1. That the health of the people is a direct concern of the government.
2. That national public health policy, directed towards all groups of the population, should be formulated.
3. That the problem of economic need and the problem of providing adequate medical care are not identical and may require different approaches for their solution.
4. That in the provision of adequate medical care for the population four agencies are concerned: voluntary agencies, local, state, and federal governments.[3] These principles were accompanied by specific proposals:
   - to minimize risk of illness by prevention;
   - to provide adequate care for the medically indigent (the cost to be met from public funds);
   - to support medical education by public funds;
   - to use public funds for medical research;
   - to use public funds to pay the costs of hospitals caring for the medically indigent;
   - to allocate public funds, as far as possible, to private institutions;
   - to extend public health services (federal, state, and local) by evolutionary process;
   - to assign experts to plan and direct the measures proposed;
   - and to consolidate all health functions of the government, preferably under a separate department.[3]

The committee added the opinion that health insurance alone does not offer a satisfactory solution to the problems addressed. Not surprisingly, the committee's views and recommendations, sure to alter medical practice radically, provoked controversy. The leading spokesman in opposition was Morris Fishbein, editor of the *Journal of the American Medical Association (JAMA)*.[3-5] Responses for the committee came from its secretary, John P. Peters, professor of medicine at Yale.[6-9]

My purpose in recounting the episode of the Committee of 430 Physicians is to recall some of the language used in support of, and in opposition to, the committee's proposals.

Fishbein's arguments

Fishbein had seen the committee's statement in advance of its appearance in newspapers, and he attacked it before the official release, along this line: The committee was "self-appointed" and lacked any organizational backing. The signatories tended to have special interests, in that so many were faculty members or deans of medical schools. They must have signed in order to get government money for clinics and dispensaries. Some signers were unthinking; they must have signed because it looked like a "good" list. Some of the signers had done so under the impression that the recommendations had the backing of the American Medical Association (AMA), and later regretted having signed. It would be hazardous to hand over to the federal government the control and standardization of medical education and medical science; this would put the government right into the practice of medicine. The danger of putting the government in the dominant position in relation to medical research was "apparent." The tender of government funds to the nonprofit voluntary hospitals, the pride of American philanthropy, would put them into the practice of medicine. In order to give complete care to the medically indigent 500 additional hospitals might be needed. What would then happen to all the fine nonprofit church hospitals? The House of Delegates of the AMA was opposed to compulsory sickness insurance, which "deteriorates the nation" as it has deteriorated every country in the world where it exists. No country had as high a standard of medical service as the United States. Change in the present system would enslave the medical profession and be the first step toward totalitarianism. Group practice plans, that is, prepaid health insurance, give inadequate or no care for certain diseases. The government was already investing large sums in the control of venereal diseases, and in gaining better knowledge of the cause of cancer. The federal government was already spending $125 million on various medical activities: the military services, the Public Health Services, Bureau of Mines, the Food and Drug Administration, the Department of Agriculture, and the Department of Labor (maternal health). With regard to preventive medicine, we could not with present knowledge prevent a single case of infantile paralysis. The committee's suggestion that the ultimate direction of medical care should be in the hands of experts did not define who or what experts are. The AMA had long tried to keep politics and politicians out of the practice of medicine. The AMA's House of Delegates had authorized spending every cent possessed by the AMA to oppose these changes, because maintenance of a free medical profession is fundamental to the life of the American people, and to American democracy.[3-5] One article concluded: "It was Abraham Lincoln who said: 'A people cannot exist, half-slave and half-free.' I tell you no people can exist with a medical profession enslaved to make a politician's holiday."[5, p. 504]

Responses by Peters

Following are excerpts from an address before the American College of Physicians in 1938:

The social responsibility of medicine, as I see it, is to provide to all classes of the population medical care of the highest quality.

The most distinctive feature of our era is the enormous technological advances that have come from the rapid development and exploitation of scientific discoveries. One of the inevitable consequences of this has been the substitution for individualistic enterprise of large organizations which can assemble and coordinate the skills and facilities necessary for production under the new system. . . .

To provide the highest quality of medical care for every person, modern facilities for diagnosis and treatment . . . must be universally available. The cost of such a program under the present system would have to be borne by the patients as individuals. It is self-evident that none of these costs can be met by the poorest members of the population. . . . It is forever to the honor of the medical profession that its members have uniquely recognized their responsibility to serve gratuitously those who cannot afford to pay. . . . Proper care consists no longer of purely personal services; it involves purchase and maintenance of expensive equipment. . . . The burden of caring for the indigent must be distributed so that it falls equitably upon the whole population. I believe this is possible only if transferred to the government.

In those countries in which compulsory health insurance has been introduced it has vindicated itself inasmuch as it has insured wider distribution of existing medical services to the class to which it applies with more certain compensation to physicians who practice under its provisions. . . . The productive services of medicine have been largely taken over by educational and research institutes and hospitals. No program for the improvement of medical care that considers only the distributors to the neglect of these productive services can be satisfactory. . . .

It is unnecessary to linger long upon the enormous physical plant which the modern medical school must possess and maintain. . . . The chief laboratories of the clinical departments of a medical school are hospitals. Without them no school can possibly survive. . . .

The productive investigations which advance medical knowledge are conducted chiefly in the medical schools and hospitals of this country. . . .

Evidently, if reorganization for the improvement of medical care is contemplated, production must be considered quite as much as distribution and consumption, because it is production that ultimately determines the quantity and quality of supply. . . .

It is my impression that the government alone can assume the burden of providing, maintaining and correlating the necessary medical resources. . . .

[T]he public health services of this country have been free from corruption and politics. . . .

It is rather amusing to reflect that at the present time most of the advances in medicine which the rich enjoy are developed in hospitals and institutions through the instrumentality of indigent patients. . . .

The most pressing present problem of government is the discovery of the formula that will assure proper allocation of responsibility and expert control. This is more likely to be obtained, in my opinion, if the initiative is taken by those who are expertly trained. In any reorganization of medicine this means primarily physicians.[7]

Comment

I find no information about the Committee of Physicians after 1944. Probably, the onset of World War II diverted attention, and the loosely knit organization unravelled. But many of the measures called for did come about. Federal agencies, especially the National Institutes of Health, now support medical research with about $10 billion annually. Medicare, Medicaid, and an augmented Veterans Hospital system are providing medical care for some portions of the population. Medical schools have been able to expand, and to engage in research at a level scarcely imaginable in 1937. This research effort has substantially improved our capacity to prevent, cure, or palliate diseases.

The Committee of 430 Physicians was of course not the only agency to call for reform of the American health care system before World War II. Daniel S. Hirschfield has described efforts by national legislators, and even by the AMA, dating back to 1912.[10] President Franklin D. Roosevelt had an interest in better health care, and considered ways to couple this with Social Security.

Now, decades later, one finds reason to hope that fairer and less costly medical care will come about. Respected physicians, for example Arnold Relman (the modern John Peters), along with public health authorities, elected officials, and medical economists, are suggesting measures to mitigate existing difficulties. Some professional societies, for example, the American College of Physicians, have proposed concrete plans. No longer does the American Medical Association flatly oppose change, as in the days of Morris Fishbein (who was relieved as editor of *JAMA* in 1949). In 1991 the AMA published a collection of articles from its various journals, describing the problems and suggesting means of alleviation.[11] A recent editorial by George D. Lundgren, editor of *JAMA,* stands in sharp contrast to Fishbein's style. Here is his concluding paragraph:

An aura of inevitability is upon us. It is no longer acceptable morally, ethically, or economically for so many of our people to be medically uninsured or seriously underinsured. We can solve this problem. We have the knowledge and the resources, the skills, the time, and the moral prescience. We need only clear-cut objectives and proper organization of our resources. Have we now the national will and leadership?[12]

I think the answer to his question is **yes**, though not by means of one comprehensive act. Again, to quote Peters in 1938:

A sweeping program suddenly imposed on this country as a whole, out of the head of any Jove, would undoubtedly create confusion if not chaos. Thoughtful investigation and experiment promise more than grandiose projects born of emotional preconceptions. The program must be built in an evolutionary manner, step by step.[7, p. 543]

References

1. Schnabel TG. Introduction. In American Medicine: Expert Testimony out of Court, vol. 1, pp. xxxix-xlvii. New York, American Foundation, 1937.

2. American Medicine: Expert Testimony out of Court, 2 vols. New York, American Foundation, 1937, p. xliii.

3. The American Foundation proposals for medical care, editorial. JAMA 109:1280–81, 1937.

4. Principles and proposals of the Committee of Physicians, editorial. JAMA 109:1816–17, 1937.

5. Fishbein M. American medicine and the National Health Program. N Engl J Med 220:495–504, 1939.

6. Peters JP. The story of the principles and proposals for the improvement of medical care. N Engl J Med 217:887–90, 1937.

7. Peters JP. The social responsibilities of medicine. Ann Int Med 12:536–43, 1938.

8. Peters JP. Medicine and the public. N Engl J Med 220:504–10, 1939.

9. Peters JP. Medical care for veterans and civilians. Med Ann District Columbia 13:43943, 1944.

10. Hirschfield DS. The Lost Reform: The Campaign for Compulsory Health Insurance in the United States from 1932 to 1943. Cambridge, Massachusetts, Harvard University Press, 1970.

11. Caring for the Uninsured and Underinsured: A Compendium from JAMA and the Specialty Journals of the American Medical Association. Chicago, American Medical Association, 1991.

12. Lundberg GD. National health care reform: An aura of inevitability is upon us. JAMA 265:2566–67, 1991. p. 2567.

PRIVATE HEALTH AND PUBLIC MEDICINE

LESTER BRESLOW, M.D., M.P.H.
(April 1969, pp. 44–47)

Lester Breslow is Professor Emeritus of Health Services and Dean Emeritus, School of Public Health at UCLA. He received both advanced degrees from the University of Minnesota. Consistent with his job as Director of Public Health of California, he has been President of the American Public Health Association and the Association of Schools of Public Health. He is a member of the Institute of Medicine of the National Academy of Sciences. Among other honors, he has received the Lasker, Dana, Healthtrac, and Lienhard (IOM) awards. This paper is based on a lecture delivered in May 1968 to the Alpha Omega Alpha chapter at the University of California School of Medicine in San Francisco.

W E HAVE GROWN SO ACCUSTOMED TO THE EXPRESSIONS "public health" and "private medicine," and to the perceptions they represent, that it has become difficult to see the reality of the health world on any other framework. A switch of wording may encourage exploration of some different views.

The common perceptions of public health and private medicine are probably associated with their historical roles.

Public Health

Public health in the modern sense grew out of the social necessity of controlling epidemic disease in cities during the early days of the Industrial Revolution. In those days people flocked from the land to work in the developing factories. However, the conditions of life and the inability of the people to cope with these conditions resulted in tremendous epidemics of intestinal and respiratory diseases. To maintain a stable labor force and protect life in the new, industrial cities, these vast epidemics of a century or so ago had to be controlled. The organized community effort to accomplish this task became known as "public health." Subsequently, the same type of organized community effort proved useful in attacking other health problems such as tuberculosis, venereal disease, infant deaths, nutritional deficiencies, and more recently, the chronic diseases.

450

In the advent of public health, it should be noted that an enlightened public frequently was ahead of the prevailing theories and practices of the medical profession. For example, the big clean-up campaigns directed against the filth of the mid-19th century were led to a considerable extent by social reformers. Their campaigns actually preceded the germ theory of disease; only later did this theory become the scientific base for control of communicable disease. It may be more correct to say that medical science responded to, rather than was responsible for, the great 19th century idea of hygiene. Science tended to follow, not lead social action.

Social action in concert with medical science has led mankind out of the period of mass tragedy due to uncontrolled communicable disease. In fact, we have proceeded so far in reducing communicable diseases that their very rarity now leads to some ironic small tragedies. These occur as a result of the failure of physicians to recognize diseases that were once common but are now rare. For example, during World War II, several young soldiers from the South Pacific died of laryngo-tracheal diphtheria acquired on board ship while returning home. The disease spread on shipboard from diphtheric skin infections and was unfortunately not recognized by physicians who had no experience with diphtheria.

Even though occasional events such as these emphasize the necessity for continuing vigilance, it is clear that medical science has transformed our lives. It has exerted its influence both through public health and private medicine as we have understood them.

Private Medicine

During this same time that public health was developing, roughly 1830–1930, the individual practice of private medicine was the predominant pattern of physician care. This pattern of medical practice prevailed because, apart from means for the control of communicable disease, the technology of medicine was meager and only minimally effective. Even though progress in surgery and other branches of medicine was taking place and creating the base for current advances, the individual physician by himself or with an assistant could still do most of what it was possible to do. This included as a large element providing comfort for the sick. Surgery and the pharmacopoeia were only beginning to show their potential.

In the period when the individual practice of medicine was the almost exclusive pattern, the physician was essentially a private entrepreneur. He regarded himself as beholden to no one and as working only for his patients. This manner of work fostered independence. The social role of the doctor was quite similar to that of the small businessman. He provided through his own individual efforts and not "working for somebody else" something that people wanted and were willing to pay for. This experience may account for the fact that the physician's social outlook was very similar to that of the small businessman.

This sketchy and simplified account may indicate how the common ideas and the corresponding expressions "public health" and "private medicine" came into being. Physicians and public health workers, as well as others in our society, still carry the perceptions that are related to these historical roots of "public health" and "private medicine."

But suppose we try to look at the present health world through a different perspective, epitomized by the words "private health" and "public medicine." Concepts and expressions for them that seemingly contradict common views can sometimes lead to new insights.

The value of contradiction in viewpoint was illustrated recently in a paper by a University of California (San Francisco) medical student concerning the sickle cell trait.[1] He traced the establishment of this biological variation among a large group of people to a form of agriculture introduced into central Africa, which led to proliferation of malaria-bearing mosquitos. Sickling of red cells became a biologically adaptive trait because of the resistance it afforded to malaria. It is common to say that "man's biologic nature determines his social nature, his culture." Thus, we still hear people say that war is inevitable because of man's biologically determined aggressiveness. In the case of red-cell sickling it appears that "culture determined biology." A form of social endeavor, agriculture, led to establishing a biological variation among people engaged in the endeavor. The thesis advanced by Wiesenfeld may be much more generalizable. For example, we commonly regard human longevity, reproduction, and pathology as aspects of man's biology; yet, these are increasingly affected by the culture that man has created. The social conditions of life profoundly influence how long man lives, his pattern of reproduction, and the diseases that affect him. Thus, contradictory notions, like "culture determines biology" rather than "biology determines culture," may be useful.

So let us explore briefly the ideas of private health and public medicine.

Private Health

In the past, health was largely determined (and still is determined in many parts of the world) by the external conditions of life: extremes of heat or cold, food supply, exposure to insects and micro-organisms, and demand for exhausting work as a condition of survival. These were the circumstances that resulted in the pattern of disease and influenced his culture, including where and how he lived. The uncontrolled physical environment was largely responsible for the pathology that made man sick or killed him. Personal behavior had relatively little influence on his health.

Suddenly in the second half of the 20th century the situation is radically different, at least in many countries of the world. Man has very largely overcome those forces of the external world that induced the diseases of the past. Now, man's own behavior determines the pattern of disease affecting him. This behavior is both social and personal.

In his social behavior, man is rapidly extending the physical and chemical pollution of air, water, and soil with as yet only dimly understood adverse effects on health. What man does through social organization—in war-making, in certain industrial activities and in other ways—obviously profoundly affect his well-being. However, circumstances do not permit elaboration of this point here.

In the realm of modern personal behavior, serious deleterious effects on health are all too evident. Consider what is known about some of the current major causes of death.

The lung cancer epidemic, which will soon account for one-fourth of all cancer deaths in the United States, is due to cigarette smoking.

Fatal accidents, another major cause of death, result largely from automobile driving under the influence of alcohol and possibly other drugs.

Cirrhosis of the liver is also associated with the abuse of alcohol.

Suicide constitutes the most direct personal action.

Coronary heart disease, the largest single cause of death in the United States and responsible for about one-fourth of all male deaths, reflects to a considerable extent individual choice of food, cigarettes, and exercise.

Overeating as a factor in diabetes and cigarettes in emphysema should also be noted.

It is clear that personal behavior, that is, how people use the readily available food, alcohol, cigarettes, and automobiles, accounts for the current pattern of mortality. Morbidity, too, is largely a reflection of the style of life. Health has become a private affair in the sense that an individual's behavior influences to a considerable extent when he dies and what his illness will be. This fact gives meaning to the expression "private health."

Great advances will occur when people fully realize that the external physical environment has been replaced by personal behavior as the major influence on health.

Of course, this fact is not yet widely accepted by the American people. They still tend to hand responsibility for health over to doctors, clinics, and hospitals. The increasing ability of medicine to cope with illness and increasing ability of people to pay for this means of coping with illness has perhaps encouraged excessive dependence on it. Moreover, it is easier to attribute responsibility for one's health to someone else.

Reluctance to accept the notion of "private health," i.e. personal action as a major factor in one's own health, apparently stems from several aspects of modern life. Among these I would include the social demoralization that is now spreading in the wake of our finally realizing the horrendous nature of some of our past national policies, both those of a decade or so in duration and those of a century. Hopefully, out of this crisis will come a new commitment to our nation's original ideals and greater personal effort toward achieving them— including healthful behavior.

Public Medicine

In the meantime, medical science has produced the means for dealing much more definitively with illness than was possible even a couple of decades ago. Medicine is now remarkably able to prolong life and minimize disability. Many forms of heart disease, cancer, stroke, kidney disease, and other current major health problems are yielding to advances in many fields in which medical science is pushing rapidly ahead.

As a consequence of this advancing technology, however, it is no longer true that the individual physician by himself or with an assistant can do most of what it is possible to do. Medical service has become more complex. While most of the actual visits of patients to doctors concern conditions that can be handled by a single doctor, the fact is that application of medical science to significant live-saving and morbidity-reducing goals increasingly requires extensive medical organization.

Rather suddenly in the mid-20th century, just as health has changed, medicine has also changed.

This change in the technological, and therefore in the organizational, aspects of medicine has brought a number of consequences which some physicians tend to resist. As noted by Victor Fuchs, "The medical profession, or at least a significant portion of it, seems to believe that there can be rapid and far-reaching technical change without disturbing the traditional organization of medical practice. This belief is irrational. One clear lesson from economic history is that technical innovation means organization change."[2]

The young physician, however, no longer views himself only as an individual entrepreneur. He sees himself increasingly as a member of a health team involving various types of nurses, laboratory and radiation technicians, physical therapists, social workers—a whole array of medical and allied specialists. Physician care is less and less the isolated endeavor of a single practitioner. It is a part of a larger endeavor involving other personnel as well as facilities, equipment, and organization.

The public sees this development, too, and notes its significant features: greater effectiveness (it really does save lives and prevent disability); need for organization of service in the interest of efficiency; and higher cost. These features have led to increasing public involvement in medicine, in short, "public medicine."

This expression unfortunately still carries a "bad" connotation to many physicians and others. In the present context it means that medicine no longer consists exclusively of individual physicians making individual arrangements with their patients. The cost of using hospital and other complex medical facilities has led to various forms of public participation in the payment process. The strong trend toward prepayment or insurance involving both non-governmental and governmental endeavor is one aspect of public medicine in the sense the term is used here. Group arrangements for payment are becoming increasingly public as they extend to cover a larger portion of medical care—public as distinguished from individual, private arrangements for care.

Moreover, medicine is becoming more public in that ownership and control of the technical resources for medical practice are largely passing from the hands of individual physicians. Hospital and related facilities for care of the sick are coming increasingly under public, including but not limited to governmental, surveillance and ownership.

These trends spring from the technological advance and greater effectiveness of medicine. They do not reflect, as has been unfortunately so often alleged, some foreign ideology. They reflect the growing American conviction that just as "war is too important to leave to the generals," so "medicine is too important to leave to the doctors."

This idea may not be to everyone's liking, but it does appear to represent the real world. Public medicine, in this sense of greater public involvement in the development and management of health facilities and in the process of payment for health care, now is rapidly expanding. It will probably take the form of more and more governmental participation in these matters since, in a democracy, government does tend to assume representation of the public interest.

New Responsibilities for Physicians

Private health and public medicine imply new responsibilities for physicians.

The first is to teach individuals who seek care that health is now largely a private affair. One's health depends to a considerable extent on his personal behavior. The physician's work with his patients is incomplete unless he assists them all to adjust their personal behavior with a view toward its health effects. Most physicians will encourage patients with chronic obstructive pulmonary disease to give up cigarette smoking. It is necessary to go beyond this and encourage patients to quit cigarette smoking whether or not they have current disease attributable to it.

The second is to join in the leadership of public medicine, to teach the public that quality is the essential ingredient in medical care. In the concern about and effort to control the cost of medical care, many of us in medicine as well as elsewhere have lost sight of the goal: it is not dollars, whether viewed by the government budget officer or by the private entrepreneur physician. The time has come for physicians to tackle seriously the problem of improving the quality of medical care, i.e. improving its ability to be effective. We must learn ourselves and teach the public how to achieve the desirable goals of public medicine.

To help prepare physicians of the present generation as well as the next for these new responsibilities, medical schools are assuming an expanded role. In addition to advancing medical science and technology, and educating the profession in these aspects of health care, medical schools are responding to the demands for attention to the social application of medicine. Responsibility of the physician for guiding his patients to health, rather than merely diagnosing and treating their diseases, will undoubtedly influence the medical curriculum to a greater extent in the future than in the recent past. Medical schools will also be expanding the traditional notion that medical care consists exclusively of a one-to-one, patient-physician relationship. While that is certainly a relevant system, it is not the only one. Another relevant system is the relationship of medical care as a whole to the community, sometimes called social medicine. In this social arena of medicine physician responsibility is urgently needed and medical schools must help prepare the profession for it.

The immediate future is bewildering. As we are bounced around by the large social forces unleashed at the present time, the tendency to feel sorry for ourselves naturally arises. Some members of the profession suffer from nostalgia for times now passed; but social pressures inevitably bring the new. Let's appreciate the opportunity of being physicians at a time when service to people can be so important to them and rewarding to us.

References

1. Wiesenfeld SL. Sickle Cell Trait in Human Biological and Cultural Evolution. Prize Essay, presented at California Academy of Preventive Medicine, March 25, 1968, San Francisco.
2. Fuchs VR. The Basic Forces Influencing Costs of Medical Care. Report of the National Conference on Medical Costs. Washington, D.C., June 27–28, 1967. U.S. Government Printing Office, pp. 16-31.

THE SOCIAL CONSCIENCE AND THE PRIMARY FUNCTION OF THE HOSPITAL VIEWED IN HISTORICAL PERSPECTIVE

JOHN H. KNOWLES, M.D.

(July 1963, pp. 67–74)

John Knowles was a tragic victim of pancreatic cancer at the age of 53, but his legacy as pulmonologist, educator, administrator, and medical historian is extraordinary. As general director of the Massachusetts General Hospital from 1962–71 he presided over this superb institution through very important years of growth linked closely with the Harvard Medical School. Then, until the year of his death in 1979, he took on international problems of sickness and need as president of the Rockefeller Foundation. Many of his colleagues and friends remember his failed bid to become assistant secretary of the Department of Health, Education, and Welfare. The Rockefeller Foundation has arranged a collection of his writings from 1944 to 1979.

T HE CONTEMPORARY HOSPITAL HAS REACHED A CENTRAL AND UNIQUE position as a social instrument of society in its eternal battle with disease and suffering. Its present form has been moulded and shaped by the needs of society as well as its beliefs, values, and attitudes. It is a mirror of society and reflects not only its culture, but its economy. In just the past half century, science has contributed so heavily to the knowledge, treatment, and prevention of disease that the present science and technology of medicine can no longer be mastered by the individual. The resultant necessary specialization in all areas of medicine and the massive technology contained within the walls of the urban teaching hospital have been of pronounced benefit to mankind. The steadily mounting benefits have created the social problem of rising expectations in a rapidly expanding, longer-lived population, progressively less able *individually* to afford the steadily rising cost of medical care.

The problems of medicine and hospitals today demand a more effective social technology for their solution. Society's potency increases with the increasing division of labor while the individual's decreases. In the case of the hospital, social action by the total institution becomes mandatory if effective solution of some of the social, political, and economic problems of medicine is to be found. A strong, institutional social conscience leads to social action for the benefit of the community. As Titmuss has said . . . "progress in medical science in psychological theories and in the specialized division of medical skill has converted medicine from an individual intuitive enterprise into a social service."[1]

Historical Perspective

Historical perspective is necessary as we view the evolution of the hospital to its present central position in the provision of health services and its unique role as a social instrument. The earliest hospitals were the healing temples of ancient Egypt, the public hospitals of Buddhist India and the Mohammedan East, and the sick houses (Beth Holem) of Israel. The earliest physicians were both priests and magicians. Disease represented the work of evil spirits and could be induced by infractions of religious codes. The ancient Oriental custom of hospitality for guests and travelers pervaded the Levant and houses were built where weary travelers and strangers could stop for food and lodging, and if sick, nursing care.

Indeed the very derivation of the word hospital shows what an important part these travelers and their hosts played in the evolution of the hospital. Hospital comes from the Latin, *hospes,* meaning host or guest. The English word *hospital* comes from the Old French "hospitale" as do the words "hostel" and "hotel" and all were originally derived from the Latin. These three words, hospital, hostel, and hotel, although of different meaning today, were at one time used interchangeably.

In Greek mythology, Aesculapius, the pupil of the centaur, Chiron, became the son of Apollo and the god of medicine. The cult of Aesculapius was centered at the Temple of Epidaurus where the priest-physicians received the sick with their votive offerings and practiced their magic, mainly using ritual and hypnotic suggestion. The temple at Kos was one of the most famous sanctuaries of Aesculapius; it was here that Hippocrates was born about 460 B.C.

The evolution of the modern hospital is usually associated with the advent of Christianity. The Christian ethic of faith, humanitarianism, and charity resulted in the creation of a vast hospital system. At the Council of Nicea in A.D. 325, the bishops were instructed to establish hospitals in every cathedral city. Emperor Constantine, the first of the Roman emperors to embrace Christianity, ordered the closing of all pagan temples of healing in 335 A.D. The pagan practices of Greco-Roman medicine were discarded and the authority of the church in medical practice was complete.

The great Crusades between 1096 and 1291 established numerous hostels for the sick which dotted the way to the Holy Land. In England, St. Bartholomew's and St. Thomas' Hospitals were founded by monks in 1123 and 1215. Medicine was practiced by monks and priests in the hostels adjacent to or in designated areas of the monasteries. Peripatetic apothecaries and blood-letting surgeons plied their trade in the houses of their patients and only the destitute, the weary traveler, and those with diseases regarded as hopeless found their way to the hospitals. Special hospitals were founded during this period for the halt, the blind, the aged infirm, lepers, and orphans.

With the arrival of the Renaissance in the late 1200s and the Reformation in the 1500s, the Middle Ages which had seen the great development of the Christian hospital system came to a close and the age of individualism and humanism began. The fetters of religious dogma and scholasticism were loosed, new medical curricula were established from the experience at Salerno, Bologna, Montpellier, and Oxford, and the practice of medicine became an important way to make one's living as an individual, intuitive enterprise.

The Reformation Parliament of Henry VIII dissolved the monastery system of England between 1536 and 1539 and the hospital system disappeared with it. Thousands of impoverished and homeless citizens along with the halt, the blind, the aged infirm, and lepers were cast adrift to roam the countryside. Out of this chaotic and bleak situation arose the voluntary private, nonprofit hospital system of England, the direct forebear of the major part of our American hospital system. First, however, the Royal hospital system came into being when Henry VIII refounded by Royal Charter St. Bartholomew's in 1546 and St. Thomas' in 1552 on a secular basis, the latter named, "The King's Hospital in Southwark."

These two hospitals cared for the entire sick population of London for the next 170 years. Whereas the monastery system had cared for incurables, the sick poor, and those with specific disabilities, the burden shared by these two hospitals forced them to limit their work to the *curable* sick and in 1700, it is recorded in the orders, "No incurables are to be received"[2] at St. Thomas'. This accelerated the development of the workhouse for the able-bodied ne'er-do-well, and the almshouse for the care of incurables.

With the growth of individualism and the Protestant ethic which found its expression in hard work, laissez-faire, and self-reliance, coupled with the forces of mercantilism, urbanization, and the Industrial Revolution, the merchant prince developed and was able to amass a large fortune. A social conscience matured and was to find its expression in private philanthropic work. Sir Thomas Guy, a wealthy London merchant founded Guy's Hospital in 1724, one of the first voluntary, privately endowed hospitals of modern times.

The new age saw further development of the profession into three main guilds, the Physicians, Barber-Surgeons, and Apothecaries. There were rules for apprenticeship training and licensing, designed to set standards and protect the members from outside domination and unfair competition. The apprentice system of training held sway and the honorary physicians and surgeons of the

London hospitals were paid by the apprentice for their training. No longer peripatetic merchants, the physicians gave freely of their time to the care of the sick poor, and imbued with enquiring minds, added to the knowledge of clinical medicine. To provide free medicine for the impoverished, the College of Physicians of London founded the first dispensary in 1696.

The 18th and particularly the 19th century in England saw the founding of *special hospitals* because of the social, financial, and medical restrictions for admission to the "general" hospitals, the necessity for segregation of infectious diseases and lunatics, and the desire of the profession to group patients with similar diseases for observation and study. Thus, smallpox and venereal disease hospitals in 1746, obstetrical in 1750, and mental in 1751 were followed by fever (1802) and eye (1804) specialty hospitals in London, frequently situated on Harley Street, hence the term, "Harley Street specialist."

It is important to emphasize that during the 18th century most of the care given in hospitals was nursing and the hospital remained an institution for the sick poor. The Hotel Dieu, founded in A.D. 651 by the Bishop of Paris and the oldest hospital in existence today, contained some 2,000 beds. In 1788 the death rate amongst patients was nearly 25 per cent and frequently two and sometimes eight patients occupied one bed. Attendants living in the hospital were noted to have an increased death rate of 6 to 12 per cent per year. It wasn't until 1793 that the Convention of the French Revolution ruled that there should be only one patient to a bed and the beds should be separated by at least three feet.[3]

It was the prototype of the British voluntary teaching hospitals of London that ultimately arose in America, but only after more than a century following the first settlements in colonial America. As Shyrock has noted, "In Spanish and French colonies the church set up such institutions more promptly. But the Anglican and non-conformist English churches had given up the hospital tradition, and state or 'voluntary' agencies acted only under the cumulative pressures of public need, secular humanitarianism, and professional initiative."[4]

I shall confine my comments to the Massachusetts Bay Colony and Boston in the evolution of the institutions that housed the sick. I am also primarily concerned here with the development of the university-affiliated teaching hospital and shall therefore finally focus on the Massachusetts General Hospital. Of the roughly 7,000 hospitals that exist in the United States today, there are 140 with university affiliation, 1,000 accredited as teaching institutions, and over 5,000 that are not classified or accredited as teaching institutions. It should also be noted that we are a nation of small hospitals (under 200 beds) and not large ones.

The most powerful stimulus to the founding of the American hospital was the process of urbanization and indeed, the history of the city is the history of social progress (or social decline, I might add) in any civilization. Urbanization concentrated the need for care in a small area and provided the tools for the solution of the problems. Public health measures for the segregation of infectious disease in quarantine hospitals very early fell under the jurisdiction of the General Court of Massachusetts, establishing the State's responsibility in these matters. The city produced the merchant prince with the social conscience who was to devote his fortune to private philanthropic work for the good of his fellow man. Intellectual activity abounded and flourished in the City. Educational institutions were founded and finally, schools of medicine which needed institutions where they could teach and learn from first-hand experience.

Urbanization

The progressive urbanization of Boston was slow, initially, and gained rapidly only with the arrival of the 19th century. The population grew from 4,500 in 1680 to 11,000 in 1720[5] and to 32,896 in 1810[6]. As late as 1845 "Boston remained . . . a town of small traders, of petty artisans and handicraftsmen, and of great merchant princes who built fortunes out of their 'enterprise, intelligence, and frugality.'"[7] The merchant princes amassed their fortunes from entrepreneurial triangular traffic between Boston, Oregon, and Canton; Southern ports and Liverpool; and the West Indies and Russia. The town lacked a fertile back country, had no large source of labor, and lacked the power of a good water supply. Entrepreneurial activity was the only answer. The resultant wealth was wisely invested and Boston became a great center of finance and banking, supplying the money for the first railroads in this country and gaining a firm hold on the development of the textile and shoe industries in Massachusetts. The home of the merchant prince and the petty artisan contained favorable social conditions and in 1790 it was said that poverty and pauperism were declining relative to the total population[8] and well they might, for "Boston offered few opportunities to those who lacked the twin advantages of birth and capital."[9] Most immigrants, until the Irish hegira of the 1840s, passed through Boston on their way West or went directly to Philadelphia or New York.

Institutions For the Care of the Sick

What of the state of the public's health during this time and the provisions for the care of the sick? The original colonial practice of "outdoor relief" whereby local citizens were paid to take the sick into their homes was soon outmoded as the burden increased and infectious diseases became the main public health problem.

Smallpox was the chief public health problem of the 17th and 18th centuries. Major epidemics hit Boston at least four times between 1644 and 1689 and seven times in the 18th century beginning in 1721 with the last great epidemic in 1792. The General Court had taken measures in 1699 and 1700 to provide for the isolation of townsfolk and quarantine of ships' crews known to have "the plague, smallpox, pestilential or malignant feaver, or other contagious sickness, the infection whereof may probably be communicated to others."[10] The earlier "pest-house" was replaced by the quarantine hospital built on Spectacle Island by the order of the General Court in 1717. Later abandoned and replaced by one on Rainsford Island in 1737, it was managed by the Town Selectmen.

Some idea of the seriousness and magnitude of the smallpox epidemic can be gained from the figures in 1721 when the disease was introduced by the infected crew of a British ship newly arrived from the West Indies. With a total population of 10,700 in the town, 5,759 contracted the disease and 842 died, nearly 8 per cent of the total population. It was during this epidemic that Cotton Mather had written to Dr. Zabdiel Boylston, urging him to try the inoculation method developed by Timoni of Constantinople. Subsequently, he inoculated 242 persons in nearby towns with only 6 deaths. After much prolonged controversy, inoculation hospitals for the practice of inoculation and segregation of infected patients were approved and set up by the General Court as well as private physicians between 1764 and 1790. The "Grand Inoculation Hospital" was Dr. William Aspinwall's which had 150 beds. Games, music, and parades were arranged for the inmates. The inoculation hospital disappeared with the introduction of Jenner's vaccination by Prof. Benjamin Waterhouse in 1800.

So much for the early quarantine and inoculation hospitals. The first almshouse in Boston opened its doors in 1665. It was consumed by fire and a new one was built in 1686, which by 1790 had 300 occupants.[11] A bridewell for the disorderly and the insane in the early 1700s and a workhouse for the able-bodied, ne'er-do-wells built in 1735 were immediately adjacent. It was stated that ". . . the earlier almshouses of Massachusetts were indicative of all that is evil in the eyes of social service. They admitted of slight if any separation of the sexes. They afforded no classification according to age. They housed little children with the prostitute, the vagrant, the drunkard, the idiot and the maniac . . . they were schools for crime—breeders of immorality and chronic pauperism"[12] and, I might add, the easy transmission of infectious disease among the impoverished sick.

In 1800, a new almshouse, designed by Charles Bulfinch, was built on the north side of Leverett Street in the West End which was to stand until 1825. The Reverend John Bartlett was its Chaplain, a fortunate assignment as we shall see.

Meanwhile another institution, the forerunner of the present day ambulatory medical clinic, was established through the efforts of the Massachusetts Humane Society which had been founded in 1780. The Boston Dispensary was founded in 1796 for two reasons: 1) so that the sick could be cared for in their own houses and 2) they could be assisted at a less expense to the public than in a hospital or the almshouse.[13] Although described as a drug store with a physician for ambulatory patients,[14] it served both the humanitarian and the economical reason for its existence.

A final institution for the care of the sick was established at the turn of the 19th century. Agitation for the construction of a hospital had been voiced by the Boston Marine Society at their meeting of October 1790. Its purpose was to care for merchant mariners, frequently far from home, where most medical care was being given for those fortunate enough to avoid the "pesthouses." A Congressional Bill entitled, "An Act for the Relief of Sick and Disabled Seamen" was signed by President John Adams on July 16, 1798 and established a form of governmental compulsory sickness and accident insurance to provide medical care and hospitalization for seamen by the collection of 20c per month per mariner on every American merchant ship coming from a foreign port.[15] In 1803 a Marine Hospital was completed in Charlestown for the Port of Boston, and in 1804 it moved to its new quarters from its first location in 1799 in the barracks buildings at Fort Independence on Castle Island. It housed an average of 30 patients.

The medical profession and medical education

Finally, the medical profession and the founding of the Harvard Medical School in 1782 must be considered as they played a crucial role in the founding of the Massachusetts General Hospital. Colonial America, whether for praise or blame, was traditionally English. The middle classes emigrated to America and the first physicians were "ships' surgeons" or apprentices from London hospitals, and not English physicians who were enjoying high social prestige and good incomes in London. Most of the early practitioners were peripatetic surgeon-apothecaries, and commonly, ministers doubling as physicians. Medical education consisted of the indentured apprentice system. On the eve of the Revolution, only 5 per cent of the 3,500 established medical practitioners held degrees, and scarcely 10 per cent had had any formal training.[16]

Harvard College had been founded in 1636 on a strongly puritanical and theological basis and its first two presidents, in keeping with the times, were minister-physicians. Its second and third presidents were graduates in medicine of Cambridge, England. By 1700, there were said to be 26 graduates of Harvard College who had practiced medicine in New England, although none had a medical degree.[17] The indentured apprentice system remained the main form of medical education.

In 1772 Dr. Ezekiel Hersey of Hingham left 1,000 pounds to Harvard College to support a resident professor of anatomy and surgery. Edward Augustus Holyoke of Salem, a graduate of Harvard College in 1746, had amongst his many apprentices, John Warren. On September 19, 1782 the Harvard Corporation adopted some 22 articles (probably written by John Warren) which established the Harvard Medical School. John Warren in Anatomy and Surgery, Benjamin Waterhouse (a Quaker, M.D. Leiden 1780) in Physic, and Aaron Dexter in Chemistry and Materia Medica were appointed the first three professors. The first lectures were given in the basement of Harvard Hall in the fall of 1784 and thence the quarters were shifted to the Holden Chapel.

This new method of teaching was not universally applauded as is shown by the several public clashes of the Massachusetts Medical Society with the new medical school in Cambridge. The Society, founded in 1781, demanded the right to examine and license all physicians,[18] prevented the faculty from using the Boston Almshouse for the teaching of medical students in 1784, and defeated a proposal by the Harvard Corporation to the General Court for the establishment of a "public infirmary" in Cambridge for the care of the sick and the teaching of medical students.[19] The Boston Medical Society wrote that "the scheme of annexing a Medical Establishment in this Town to the College in Cambridge is not only impractical, but nugatory."[20] Fortunately for the democratic concepts of our young nation, it was not discovered until later how wrong this "majority vote" would prove to be.

In 1782 John Warren was appointed to care for the sick in the almshouse (on Park Street) and, although he took his apprentices there, it was not until 1810 that Harvard medical students were allowed to enter the new almshouse on Leverett Street for clinical training. At this time the alms-house had approximately 350 occupants, of which about 50 were sick and infirm. At this time medical education at Harvard consisted of two winters of lectures and a third year as apprentice to a practitioner before the student could qualify for his degree in medicine. Benjamin Waterhouse urged the use of the new Boston Marine Hospital for teaching medical students and was Chief Physician there in 1807. Professor Waterhouse was to be succeeded by James Jackson on September 15, 1812 at the Harvard Medical School. In 1810 the medical school had moved from Cambridge to Boston. In 1816 it was to move to Mason Street and thence to the head of North Grove Street adjacent to the M.G.H. in 1847. Thirty-six years later it was to make another move to larger quarters in the newly developed Back Bay almost equidistant between the M.G.H. and the rapidly growing Boston City Hospital in the South End. The Boston City Hospital had opened its doors in 1864 to meet the growing needs of a rapidly expanding immigrant population, drawn from Ireland by the great potato famines.

The founding of the MGH

We have attempted to describe the various factors that were to result in the founding of the Massachusetts General Hospital in 1811—the advent of Christianity with its humanitarian spirit; the age of individualism with its development of the merchant prince with a social conscience, indulging in benevolent philanthropic work; the process of urbanization with its resultant concentration of misery and social need, as well as with its concentration of energy, intellect, and resource which could provide for social needs; the relative inadequacy of the existing institutions for the care of the sick; and finally, the rise of the enquiring medical mind, scientific thought, and the new concern for an improvement in medical education requiring that a hospital be available for teaching.

The well-to-do were cared for in their homes—a situation which was to prevail until the turn of the 20th century. Philadelphia and New York had already established their hospitals under almost identical but better developed circumstances and the Boston philanthropists and doctors were equally anxious to have such a humanitarian institution grace their city.

The stage was set and the sequences of events seems totally rational. All the factors and forces for the creation of such an institution were present and in person. A minister, the Rev. John Bartlett, the Chaplain of the Boston Almshouse, called the meeting spurred on by the Christian ethic and the inhumane conditions in the almshouse. James Jackson and John Collins Warren were present representing the profession and the needs for medical education. The merchant princes were represented by John Phillips and Peter Brooks.[21] The letter that Warren and Jackson were to compose to the wealthy and influential citizens of Boston, and the subsequent report of the Legislative Committee recommending the State's approval of the hospital's charter summarize beautifully the social need for such an institution and the responsibility with which it would be charged.

The Legislative report stated:

> The Hospital, thus established, is intended to be a receptacle for patients from all parts of the Commonwealth, afflicted with diseases of a peculiar nature, requiring the most skilful treatment, and presenting cases for instruction in the study and practice of surgery and physic. Among the unfortunate objects of this charitable project, particular provision is to be made for such as the wisdom of Providence may have seen fit to visit with the most terrible of all human maladies—a deprivation of reason. . . . [22]

On February 25, 1811 the General Court granted a charter for the incorporation of the Massachusetts General Hospital to James Bowdoin and 55 other prominent Bostonians. Active interest and participation by the State in the conduct and maintenance of the Hospital was assured from the outset, not only through repeated financial aid, but by the practice which continues to this day of the Governor's appointment of 4 of the 12 Trustees.

The War of 1812 interfered with the raising of funds, but by 1817 enough private money was available so that final aid from the State in the form of prison labor and granite allowed the construction to begin. The great Charles Bulfinch was the architect. James Jackson was appointed Physician and John C. Warren,

Surgeon to the M.G.H. On September 3, 1821 the first patient was admitted, and no other application was made until September 20.[23] The first "Annual Report" printed in March 1822 contained what today would be regarded as direct advertising. It began "We entreat all those into whose hands this address may fall, to reflect well upon the advantages which this Institution offers . . ." and then listed the comforts and advantages of hospital care.[24] The public was slow to forget their experiences in the pesthouse and almshouse and as late as 1849 the hospital was yet to be completely filled.[25]

By 1823, the West wing of the Bulfinch Building was completed and there was a total of 93 beds. In 1824 the Trustees ordered that medical students and doctors attending operations should be admitted free of charge, rather than be charged by the Staff.

In the early years (as well as today), the most pressing problem was the discrepancy between expense of running the hospital and the income from patients, friends, and endowment. The free bed subscription idea was instituted by the Massachusetts Humane Society in 1824 when it gave the hospital enough money to support 6 free beds for 5 years. Subsequent annual drives were conducted for gifts for the support of free beds and in 1826 "23 beds were occupied . . . at an average expense of $3.52 per week for an average stay of 5.5 weeks."[26]

Four contributions of the hospital as a social instrument

I would like now to narrow our historical view to four examples of the hospital's role as a social instrument—that combined or total institutional effort which enabled the hospital to contribute solutions to the social problems of the times. There are 1) the founding and development of the McLean Hospital, 2) Medical Social Service, 3) the Baker Memorial Plan, and 4) the Emergency Ward, examples of the social conscience of the hospital and a total institutional effort to fulfill the needs of the community in its primary function of the care of the patient.

McLean Hospital

We have reviewed the conditions that resulted in the State's Charter of the hospital designating the humane treatment of the mentally ill as one of its prime functions. These conditions were the shackling of lunatics in the almshouse, the extreme financial and emotional expense of caring for such patients, and the necessity for their segregation from the community as well as the other occupants of the almshouse. In England, the inhumane treatment of the insane was slowly being rectified through the efforts of John Howard and William Tuke, both Quakers. In 1792, the York Retreat was founded by Tuke—stressing kindness, no restraints, and a favorable environment as regarded food, lodging, occupational work, fresh air, and exercise. In the same year Philippe Pinel, the great advocate of "moral treatment" was placed in charge of the large Paris institution, the Bicetre, for insane men. His success in "striking off the chains" of the insane here and later at the Salpetriere Hospital for women was perhaps the turning point in the humane and moral treatment of the insane.[21] Up to that time the insane had been total social outcasts. The public paid an admission fee to watch the bizarre activity at Bethlehem in England, more popularly known as "Bedlam."

* * * * *

The Trustees of the M.G.H. proceeded with dispatch and by 1818 the first patient was admitted to what was then called the Asylum in Charlestown, a mansion redesigned by Bulfinch. In 1833, Dr. Rufus Wyman, the first Super-intendent, wrote, "chains or strait jackets have never been used or provided in this asylum."[28] Dr. Luther Bell, appointed in 1836, gave considerable support to the efforts of Dorothea Dix by his professional statements on the treatment of the mentally ill, and therefore at least indirectly aided Miss Dix's efforts to correct the squalor, crowding and heartless indifference that she found in the State asylums.[29] By 1847, in contrast with the General Hospital, the Asylum was full, with 173 patients, and only two-thirds of all who applied could be admitted.

In 1882, the new Superintendent, Dr. Edward Cowles established the *first* training school in a mental hospital for psychiatric nurses in America. At the turn of the century he also established the importance of biological research in mental illness with the addition of Otto Folin and Philip Schaeffer to the Staff.

Social Service

The second example of an institutional social conscience arose in 1905, after Dr. Richard Cabot had been appointed physician to the Out-Patient Department in the new outpatient building. As Washburn stated,

> From its very earliest days the General Hospital has shown an interest in its patients' problems and a humane attempt to lighten their burdens. When the Hospital was a small affair, the Trustees themselves visited the patients regularly. In many instances they saw to it that relief over and above medical care was provided. As doctors and patients and Hospital officers were a small family, the troubles of the patients and the underlying causes of their disease, their disposition upon discharge were considered, and often remedied and alleviated . . . the Resident Physician (Director) or his assistant took great pains to see to it that discharged patients were properly escorted to their homes, that patients left on the doorstep were suitably placed, and that allied administrative problems were handled as humanely and efficiently as the means and facilities at their disposal would permit. The problems were not so difficult when New England had a homogeneous, uncrowded population, with a good standard of living.

With the tremendous unrestricted immigration of the latter part of the
19th and the early part of the 20th century, the difficulties became greater
and more complex.[30]

It was Dr. Richard Cabot who recognized the necessity for a more coordinated and formalized program of social help when he employed two full-time
workers in 1905, whose sole function was service for problems relating to the
care of the patient. Their report in 1906 listed their work which included hygiene teaching, infant feeding and care, "vacations and country outings" where
it seemed a necessary part of treatment, help in finding jobs or changing jobs according to the medical need, provision for patients "dumped" at the hospital,
and "assistance to patients needing treatment after discharge from the hospital
wards. The report for 1918 added utilization of "all the sanataria, convalescent homes, vacation funds, employment agencies and charitable agencies that
may . . . help the patient or his family to pay for the medicine, apparatus, or
vacation that may assure recovery."

By 1935, Dr. Washburn could write, "No hospital in the United States, of
any size worthy of the name, is without such a department, and in many other
countries the example has been followed."[31]

Expensive? Yes—very much so. In 1918 the expenses of the Department
were roughly $25,000. Today (1961) the expenses exceed $250,000. The value
of the contributions cannot be priced however, and continues as a vital example of the social conscience of the hospital and its determination to fulfill its
primary function.

The Baker Memorial Hospital and Fee Plan of 1930

In 1917 the Phillips House was opened and for the first time provided completely private rooms for the well-to-do, a milestone of great significance as we
shall see later. This left a large segment of the population unable to afford completely private care and unable to qualify for admission to the general hospital
and its wards. As Washburn said in 1914, "This group in the community must
often be ill in their homes, dependent upon physicians who cannot provide the
necessary laboratory tests and scientific examinations which are readily available in a general hospital."[32]

Sixteen years later on February 27, 1930, the Baker Memorial Hospital for
patients of moderate means was opened. Patients were admitted if they fell
within certain income limits. The average income of the patients admitted during the first year of operation was $2,101.74. Hospital charges were $6.50 per
day for a single room and $4.50 for a four bedded room. The Staff had agreed
to a set of fees regulated by the hospital, with a maximum of $150 no matter
how long the patient stayed or how complicated the condition. As Dr. Washburn

wrote: "The Massachusetts General Hospital is blessed with a medical and sur-gical staff which is public spirited and desires to cooperate with the Hospital in any progressive movement for the good of the community. Of its own volition the staff has agreed to accept at the Baker Memorial a small regulated fee for its professional services."[33]

In this first year, the average all inclusive charge was $158.94. The average length of stay was 13 days. Fifteen per cent of the patients needed special nurs-ing care with an average additional charge of $121.40 demonstrating vividly how important and costly special nursing care was even in those days.

The experiment was a success and the patient of moderate means was indeed protected from excessive hospital costs and professional fees. Here stands a shining example of a cooperative institutional effort to solve a pressing social and economic problem of medicine—doctors, administration, and trustees working together to utilize the maximum potential of the hospital as a social in-strument.

The Emergency Ward

Today one of the most useful measures of a hospital's ability and willingness to serve its community is the functioning of its emergency department. Are its fa-cilities open 24 hours a day, seven days a week? Does it accept alcoholic patients? Is its service predicated by need and not determined by the ability of the patient to pay? In short has it become the sanctuary for the fulfillment of human need in time of suffering, anxiety, distress, or disaster? If any of these questions are an-swered negatively, it has not optimally fulfilled what the community wants and needs today, indeed what it expects from this department of the hospital.

On November 28, 1942 the hospital rose to the disaster of the Cocoanut Grove fire. On May 23, 1962 Everett Knowles' completely severed arm was reattached to his body. In 1950 the E.W. saw 18,000 patients—this year, 1963, the figures will exceed 44,000. Disaster planning continues within its walls as well as in conjunction with the Massachusetts Port Authority at the Logan Airport. The Trustees have rearranged the space and expanded the Staff as the community's needs and demands have constantly increased. The social con-science of the institution has been translated into action for the benefit of its community of patients as well as doctors who want and need the ready avail-ability of men and machines—which are no longer available in the office and which are too expensive to house in every hospital.

Conclusion

This brief review has traced the historical foundations of the American teach-ing hospital. It has stressed the role of the hospital as a social instrument. The hospital has now emerged as the "health center" and provides the platform where the profession meets the public. Its tremendous responsibility is matched by an equally great opportunity as an organized, coordinated social instrument for the study and solution of the social and economic problems that beset medicine and the community today. Medical schools and the Staffs of many hospitals have not turned their faces readily to these problems. Health has now become a birthright and the benefits of medical science must be available to all. The public looks with rising expectations to the medical profession and the political profession, and the hospital finds itself squarely in the middle providing the center stage where all the forces meet. Better understanding of the hospital, its historical evolution, its present problems and its obligatory role as a social instrument, is necessary if the profession wishes to keep the use of this instrument in its own hands.

References

1. Titmuss RM. Essays on the Welfare State. New Haven:Yale University Press, 1959, p. 135.
2. Ives AGL. British Hospitals. London: Collins, 1948, p. 17.
3. Rosen G. A History of Public Health. New York: MD Publications, 1958, p. 151.
4. Shyrock RH. Medicine and Society in America: 1660–1860. New York: New York Univers, 1948, p.9.
5. Shattuck L. Census of Boston for the Year 1845. City of Boston, 1846, p. 5.
6. Handlin O. Boston's Immigrants. Cambridge: Harvard University Press, 1959, p. 239.
7. Handlin O. Boston's Immigrants, p. 11.
8. Shattuck L. Census of Boston for the Year 1845, p. 113.
9. Handlin O. Boston's Immigrants, p. 12.
10. Blake JB. Public Health in the Town of Boston, 1630–1822. Cambridge: Harvard University Press, 1959, p. 33.
11. Lawrence RM. Old Park Street and Its Vicinity. Boston: Houghton Mifflin Co., 1922, pp. 33-35.
12. Kelso RW. The History of Public Poor Relief in Massachusetts. Boston: Houghton Mifflin Co., 1922, p. 112.
13. Lawrence WR. History of the Boston Dispensary. Boston, 1859, p. 14.
14. Davis MD and Warner AR. Dispensaries: Their Management and Development. New York: Macmillan Co., 1918, p. 6.
15. Trask IW. The United States Marine Hospital, Port of Boston. U. S. Public Health Service, 1940, pp. 11-12.
16. Shyrock RH. Medicine and Society in America: 1660–1860, pp. 7–9.
17. Viets HR. A Brief History of Medicine in Massachusetts. Boston: Houghton Mifflin Co., 1930, p. 42.
18. Moore TE. The early years of the Harvard Medical School. Bulletin of the History of Medicine 27: 530–561 (see p. 535), 1953.
19. Moore TE. The early years of the Harvard Medical School. Bulletin of the History of Medicine 27, p. 555, 1953.
20. Harrington TF. The Harvard Medical School: A History, Narrative and Documentary. New York, 1905, pp. 274–278.

21. Eaton LK. New England Hospitals: 1790–1833. Ann Arbor: University of Michigan Press, 1957, pp. 34–36.
22. As quoted in Garland JE. Every Man Our Neighbor. Boston: Little, Brown and Co., 1961, p. 5.
23. Bowditch N I. History of the Massachusetts General Hospital. Boston, 1851, p. 55.
24. Address of the Trustees of the Massachusetts General Hospital to the Subscribers and to the Public. Boston, 1822, p. 16.
25. MGH. Annual Report, 1849, p. 5.
26. Eaton LK. New England Hospitals, p. 105.
27. Shyrock RH. In One Hundred Years of American Psychiatry. J. K. Hall, ed. New York: Columbia Univ. Press, 1944, p. 15.
28. Washburn FA. The Massachusetts General Hospital: Its Development, 1900–1935. Boston: Houghton Mifflin Co., 1939, p. 268.
29. Deutsch A. The Mentally Ill in America. Ed. 2. New York: Columbia Univ. Press, 1949, pp. 158–185, 197–198.
30. Washburn FA. Massachusetts General Hospital, p. 459.
31. Washburn FA. Massachusetts General Hospital, p. 467.
32. MGH. Annual Report, 1914, pp. 61–62.
33. Washburn FA. Massachusetts General Hospital, pp. 249–250.

PREPARING FOR A BALANCED-STATE SOCIETY

DAVID B. ROGERS, M.D.
(October 1976, 136–138)

Dr. Rogers (AΩA, Cornell, 1946) was president of the Robert Wood Johnson Foundation of Princeton, New Jersey. He previously held posts as dean and professor of medicine at the Johns Hopkins University School of Medicine and as professor and chairman of the Department of Medicine at Vanderbilt University. This paper is based on an address he delivered at the Baylor College of Medicine commencement, May 1976.

David Rogers had a meteoric career in medicine. He was a respected investigator in infectious disease, recognized as a gifted clinician, the youngest chair of medicine when appointed at age 32 at Vanderbilt University, dean of Johns Hopkins University School of Medicine, and in 1972 the founding president of the Robert Wood Johnson Foundation. In later years as the Walsh McDermott University Professor at Cornell, he helped early on to bring national focus to the problems of patients with AIDS.

Throughout his professional life, perhaps Dr. Rogers's greatest contribution was as a medical statesman. With eloquence and clarity he spoke to issues of health care for all, particularly the poor and minorities; the problems of training too many specialists; the high cost and unevenness in the delivery of health services; and the sometimes misplaced substitution of technology for caring. In his writings and talks, Dr. Rogers brought an intense personal compassion. The underserved and the unheard were his constituency. He believed it was the responsibility of the medical profession to do its part to relieve their misery.

This article could easily have been written today. It certainly needs to be read today. The answers to current problems faced by academic health centers are not simply realized by growth, intense competitiveness, and the generation of more revenue. Dr. Rogers cautions about the inevitability of resource limitations and the approach of an institutional steady state, but, he emphasizes, not a stationary one. Getting bigger, getting richer cannot be the only measures of success. How can our medical schools, hospitals, and research institutions continue to improve and prosper as they move toward what Dr. Rogers calls a "balanced states society"?

The brilliance of his essay is that it is still so timely, nearly three decades later. The sadness is that it remains so.

— RICHARD C. REYNOLDS, M.D.
AΩA, Johns Hopkins University, 1953
Professor of Medicine, University of Florida

Today's medical school graduates are emerging during a period of considerable social ferment. As a nation, we are going through an intense period of self-deprecation and doubts about our abilities to cope with a multitude of social problems. This attitude about ourselves is not new; it has been a characteristic of Americans during many periods of our history. Indeed, voicing and facing such dissatisfactions has often led to taking important new steps toward a better period in this country. But at present the intensity of the doubts about our collective abilities to improve our lives and those of others is more severe than in times past. The present litanies about our failure significantly to improve relationships between peoples of different colors or cultures, our inability to halt the disintegration of our inner cities, our failure to educate young people properly, or to conserve energy, or to preserve our environment, are not too different from the rhetoric of the past. But today our trust and confidence in leadership at all levels has hit a distressing low, and the feeling that there is nothing we humans can do to halt the plunge toward an impersonal and unpleasant world seems more pervasive.

As one might anticipate, medicine—and how we handle our affairs and our responsibilities—has not escaped this despairing view of our present abilities to cope. Criticism has been leveled at the process by which we select young men and women for medical careers, at the lack of balance between the kinds of physician specialists we turn out and the actual health needs of our population, at the inequities in the geographic distribution of health professionals, the increasing hospital orientation of physicians, the alarming escalation of medical costs, and the apparent decline in the human or caring qualities of doctors. Thus, simply living in current society, or reading the paper, or conversing with those outside of medicine, daily brings to our awareness the fact that we physicians and the services we deliver are held in less esteem than in the past.

What has happened to make so many people so anxious and doubting of our capacities to improve the human condition? Although the problems we face are complex and contentious, a nation with the 200-year track record we possess should be able to roll up its sleeves and go to work on them. But today we seem to be flailing about more and enjoying it less than in the past.

I have a thesis about why we are going through all these contortions. It is that this period represents the "warm-up" for some profound adjustments in what we want out of life. People are recognizing, dimly but instinctively, that solutions to many of today's problems will require more sweeping changes in what we value and how we live than we feel comfortable about. There is an increasing feeling on the part of many that previous ways of approaching problems will not prove as satisfactory in improving our future world as in times past. It is the recognition that we have spent our natural and human resources too wastefully and that we must begin to prepare for a plateauing world of limited growth that most troubles us.

Although we would prefer to ignore it, we face an increasing awareness that the Western world is on a course destined to cause us to run out of many of the resources that we believed were infinite. Not tomorrow—perhaps not in this century—but run out of them we shall. We have used our natural resources with imagination and enthusiasm in creating our country and our culture. But it is now clear that there are limits to the abilities of this planet to produce food, energy, or other natural commodities. We have by no means reached that limit— but for the first time we recognize that a limit is out there. At the same time, we have created powerful technologies with the potential for destroying much of our world, if misapplied. So, in some quarters, people are reluctantly beginning to suggest that our life-style and our consuming habits and our ways of dealing with each other must be modified if clean air, clean water, woodlands, wildlife, or even humans, are to be preserved for the future. There is increasing recognition that if we overspend some resource today, or deal carelessly or insensitively with other individuals or peoples, even for the sake of a 30- or even 50-year boom or short-term national advantage, we may be miscalculating. Unless some remarkable new technology appears on the scene that can permit us to continue "progress" as we have known it in the past, we shall need to find ways of living productively and happily in a world that can clearly become better, but where most enterprises probably cannot become much bigger. Girding to prepare for living and spending more conservatively than in the past will require significant modification of the traditional American views of "progress" and fulfillment and success.

At first blush, this prediction does not sound like such a world-shaking revelation. "Slowing the pace" is an oft-stated desire of many, and it would seem that adjustments to a decelerated world would be relatively easy and perhaps result in downright relief. Nevertheless I think otherwise, for I believe adaptation to such a world will require profound changes in what we decide we value most highly, and in the ways we manage our lives, our resources, and our technologies. Because it will be so different, we are, quite humanly, struggling as hard as possible to avoid facing that more contained future.

The ways in which all living systems start, develop, and plateau is surprisingly uniform. All living things grow by rules that contain them. The development of bacteria, or cell cultures, or seagulls, or people can be plotted along a biologic growth curve familiar to all of us. All contained life-systems start slowly. But as replication starts, the system enters a logarithmically accelerating growth phase that proceeds for differing periods of time. This phase may be measured in hours or in centuries, but eventually it slows and plateaus. It reaches a steady state, one that may be short or long or may proceed indefinitely. It is active and evolving; it is not stationary, but it is steady. The leveling off may be due to pressures of space, or food, or other events, but it always happens. I know of no exceptions to this biologic phenomenon. We are now seeing signs of its approach in one particularly significant dimension—the almost zero population growth of our Western world.

Genetics has taught us that creatures with the same parents, be they fruit flies or mice or men, have similar if not identical characteristics. But one cannot help but wonder whether living creatures born during the rapid phase of multiplication, where there are no limits on space or food supplies, may not be subtly different than their descendants born when crowding or limitations on nutrients begin to be felt. Those qualities that make for successful adaptation to a world of infinite resources may not be those of advantage in a nonexpanding world, and we need to consider what these qualities should be—for the success of our profession and the health of our patients.

The kinds of approaches that opened up the West, built our cities, created our giant industrial complexes, our academic medical centers, and the technologic world of today—may not be the kinds of ways of doing business that will make for a better or happier or healthier America of tomorrow. True, there are still many frontiers to open up—particularly in underdeveloped parts of the world—but no longer can we ignore the fact that there are limits to growth as we have previously defined it. Our world has a ceiling on it, and we are approaching it.

To an important degree, the satisfactions of individuals generally viewed as successful in our society have come from an expansionist role—from building a bigger or more comprehensive department, a larger research effort, or a larger institution. A deep-seated part of the American dream and ethos has been the tenet that each of us can go as fast and as far as his or her intellect, energy, and creativity will permit. The future may require a different orientation—or a redefinition of what represents growth or progress or a meaningful life.

It is my own belief that we can prepare for such a world if we reorient our thinking a bit. I am convinced that rather than viewing a steady state future with foreboding we can see it as an even more exciting opportunity to use our talents effectively, if we approach it properly. Clearly, we have one remarkably renewable resource—and that is the creativity that resides in the human animal. By utilizing our human creativeness we can add significantly to human services and the enrichment of life, and more than offset the drain on our far from infinite natural resources.

I am, by avocation, a sculptor of wood. Within this particular facet of my life I am quite comfortable in working within certain very rigid limits. As I approach a block of wood, I recognize from the outset that it will never, never become a bigger block than the one with which I started. My challenge is to carve a more powerful or more effective piece than I have been capable of before within a similar constraint. In the process I hope that I do not discard pieces that I will subsequently need, or split the block from lack of care, or forget proportions of the figure that I am attempting with the result that a leg is too short or a head too small. The final outcome is never quite what I had hoped for, but I get a little closer to it each time. Obviously, similar constraints surround the composer, who has only a limited number of musical notes with which to work, or the painter, with a finite spectrum of colors to place on his canvas.

Perhaps the flower children of the 1960s were telling us something we should have listened to more carefully. They may have been saying—do better with what you now have. Make it more effective or beautiful but don't ask for more. We need to consider whether that injunction may not have important satisfaction and survival value for the future.

How does all of this apply to medicine—to the careers we pursue or the roles we play as doctors? Perhaps quite directly.

First, we shall have to consider much more carefully than did those who preceded us the costs of the application of our medical interventions and what our patients will gain from them. There is much to suggest that our American society is spending as much of our monies as we can logically allocate to health and medical affairs. I would guess that the day is not far off when those who guide major academic medical centers will have to recognize that they will never have more money or more faculty or more resources to utilize than they have at that moment. Their task will then become how to make their particular medical center, its biomedical research effort, and the care it dispenses increasingly effective without acquiring more resources. They will have to face a difficult series of priority decisions. How much of the institution's efforts and resources should be devoted to new science? How many procedures can the EMI scanner replace in order that its acquisition be justified, and how many lives will its use improve? How many cardiac surgeons should the center train each year?

Obviously, a steady state need not and should not be stationary. It should be just as busy as a stable state, and even more challenging and demanding of human resourcefulness and ingenuity. But medicine will find such a balanced state difficult to reach. The process will require shedding some things to gain some things. Workers in industry, agriculture, and other fields utilizing natural resources have had considerable experience in making priority decisions, but we in medicine are coming late to this discipline. The introduction of new technologies will require that outmoded ones be eliminated. A much tougher critique of what represents advancement of medical science or medical care or medical education will be required than has been true in the past.

Second, I believe that we are close to the end of an era in which it has been reasonable to follow the route of the technologic imperative. As we have developed new technologies that improve diagnosis or management of illness, we have promptly added them to our armamentarium, even if the benefits can be applied to only a few individuals, and regardless of expense. In the steady state I see us approaching, more restraint will be required. We shall need to give more consideration to the value of information acquired or the quality of life extended.

We have sometimes pursued the technologic imperative to do all that we are trained to do beyond what makes sense; we must instead sensibly guide and restrain it. We should use our heads more and the laboratory and our technologies less—or more selectively. Today we are sometimes going too far, and medicine, and our patients, are losing something in the process.

Third, we shall need to be more imaginative about how we can extend the radius of our influence to make our contributions available to more people. Physicians are expensive and valuable products of our society and are among the finite resources we must use more wisely and effectively. Can other less costly health professionals take over some of the tasks that now occupy our time, but represent less important use of our skills? Are there new ways of organizing—new groupings of health professionals and facilities? Can we devise better ways to reach those who need our services but who now do not find their way to us? Can we involve our patients more in responsibilities for their own health?

Last, we need to give more thought and attention to how we can strengthen and expand the human caring function of medicine. We live in an anxious world, in which many of the traditional sources of human support—family, church, fraternal groups—are faltering. Medicine, while it cannot replace those support systems or handle all of the fears and doubts that beset people, needs to play a more effective role in working with these problems. Can physicians—or more precisely, can we—help people have more confidence in themselves and help them learn to adapt to life in a plateauing economy when all of our training and experience has suggested that whatever is not growing bigger is dying? Can growth be viewed and defined very differently?

Preparing for a world approaching a steady, but not stationary, state—or deciding where medicine will fit in the order of things, or how we best help people deal with the illnesses that we cannot cure, will be an important part of our new mission. Medicine is a coping, healing force. Most of us have a deep sense of commitment to people and their problems. Our own capacities to look at problems in fresh ways or work within constraints, be they biological or financial or technological, can play an important role in helping people to adapt to and prosper in a quite different world than we have known to date. I hope we can make full use of the skills and special privileges we have acquired as physicians to help people have productive and fulfilling lives in that better but not bigger world.

PART XII

THE PATIENT, STUDENT, AND DOCTOR . . . INSPIRATION

THE PATIENT AS ART

JOHN H. STONE, III, M.D.

(January 1974, pp. 9–10, 31)

Dr. Stone (AΩA, Emory University, 1974), when writing this piece, was Associate Professor of Medicine (Cardiology) and Director of the Division of Ambulatory Medicine at Emory University School of Medicine. This paper is based on the Valediction Address delivered at the Medical School's graduation ceremonies in June 1973. A first book of his poems, The Smell of Matches, *was published in 1972 by Rutgers University Press. His book,* On Doctoring, *coauthored with Richard C. Reynolds, is an inspiring book given to matriculating medical students at many medical schools. They are distributed free by the Robert Wood Johnson Foundation.*

Students give many reasons why they enter medicine. If a common denominator is to be found among their reasons, perhaps it is the patient. At least for many of us in our earliest thinking about the medical profession, it was the relationship between the helper and the helped that attracted us most. Along the way toward medical education, we are immersed in the science and, hopefully, the art of medicine. John Ciardi, the American poet and translator, in a poem entitled, "Lines From the Beating End of the Stethoscope," wrote, "Where science touches man it turns to art." A good line of poetry, and a goal devoutly to be wished for. In medical school, the science of medicine is presented in a disease-oriented fashion that proceeds from the basic sciences to a given patient. As we come face to face with that patient, we begin to learn first-hand what it is to bring science and art together. Let me describe what I feel it is possible to find in this encounter with the patient, in addition to systole, diastole, and split second sounds.

William Carlos Williams, the New Jersey physician and Pulitzer Prize-winning poet, who almost singlehandedly changed the face of American poetry while carrying on a very busy practice, summarized the point that I wish to make. Dr. Williams wrote in his autobiography,

> And my medicine was the thing which gained me entrance to these secret gardens of the self. It lay there, another world, in the self. I was permitted by my medical badge to follow the poor, defeated body into those gulfs and grottos. And the astonishing thing is that at such times and in such

places—foul as they may be with the stinking ischiorectal abscesses of our comings and goings—just there, the thing, in all its greatest beauty, may for a moment be freed to fly for a moment guiltily about the room. In illness, in the permission I as a physician have had to be present at deaths and births, at the tormented battles between daughter and diabolic mother, shattered by a gone brain—just there—for a split second—from one side or the other, it has fluttered before me for a moment, a phrase which I quickly write down on anything at hand, any piece of paper I can grab.[2]

Let me suggest that there is some kind of lesson here for all of us, whether or not we write it down. I would submit to you that in addition to bringing his art and science to the patient, William Carlos Williams discovered art there already. In other words, the patient *is* art, *found* art, if you like, but art nevertheless. In what ways, we might ask, is the patient art?

First of all, the patient is rhythm. He is rhythm as recorded by his electrocardiogram, his electroencephalogram; rhythm as manifested by the motility of his gut, the surges of his blood pressure, the motions of his breathing, the periodicity of his hormones, even his walking. He is a rhythmic animal as surely as Bach is rhythm. And what is Bach if not, first, a magnificent heartbeat? Some observers feel that the converse is also true: that human rhythms are in fact the basis for art. The rhythm of music is clear in this regard, but it has been suggested that there may even be a physiologic basis for poetry. Iambic pentameter, the mainstay of English poetry, is a series of weak and strong stresses for a total of five beats to the line—and what is that but a series of five heartbeats: lup dup, lup dup, lup dup, lup dup, lup dup.

The patient, as art, is paradoxical and unpredictable and ambiguous. Given half a chance, his illness will mean two or three things rather than only one. But what art is profound that leaves the viewer nothing to do? We must enter into it and ask our questions in the middle of it. Robert Frost speaks to this point in one of my favorite couplets:

> We dance round in a ring and suppose,
> but the Secret sits in the middle and knows.[3]

The patient, like art, will confuse and elate us and help us understand what we were born for, and to.

Furthermore, the patient occurs in a setting that is uniquely his and that is crucial to our viewing of him. In short, the patient occurs against a background, a backdrop, an accompaniment, a left-hand bass for the right-hand melody. His art is unlikely to be understood unless it is viewed in the context of this setting.

The patient is a microcosm. He is a "particular" that can lead to the "general." He is a continuing reminder of the air-blown penicillin-producing mold on Sir Alexander Fleming's agar plates.

He comes in all shapes and forms to fit all tastes and fancies—from rustic to pop art, from the Baroque elderly woman to the twelve-tone cacophonic high school dropout. Which is to say, he is unique and idiosyncratic.

Like art, he does not tell all that he has to say at the first sitting. The more we look, the more we see. The more we listen, the more we hear. And beyond even this, the more we see and hear, we discover, the more there *is* to see and hear.

The patient, like art, is bigger than we are. He will have the last word. He will outlast us. His pain will be ours, and his terror, and his hopes, and finally, perhaps, his illness. For what are we *all,* ultimately, but patients!

Like art, the older the patient is, the more majestic and complete-in-himself he may become. One need look no further than the last quartets of Beethoven for confirmation of the beneficial effects of aging.

Once we see and recognize the art in a given patient, we can more easily forgive his or her shortcomings and inadequacies, which we, as patients, share, of course. The corollary of this is that the older *we* are, the better we become at recognizing his art, for having seen it before and missed it the first several hundred times. You will not find the art in the patient unless you look for it. You will not, I suggest, be able to properly manage the patient until you find the art within him.

I say to you, then, the patient is his *own* art. When we bring to him the art and science of medicine, only good can come of it. And there are other dividends: viewed in this light, and when we *expect* to find art, there is *no such being* as a routine or uninteresting patient (I might ask, parenthetically, under *what* Bill of *whose* Rights need a patient *be* interesting, anyway, and *to whom?*) If the patient *is* art, and I believe he is, we must train our eyes and ears and fingers to find the art that is there. Alexander Pope said, "The proper study of mankind is man."[4] I say to you, then, from now on, *the patient is the curriculum.* You have the tools with which to continue your study. Study his art and it will enhance yours.

The other prerogative—advice—I cannot resist. I have a few final thoughts, which are directed toward the prevention of medical thrombosis. Now you are young; your cardiac output is high and your blood flow turbulent. But thrombosis is a danger and recurrent problem for us all. I would suggest several areas of preventive attack:

I hope you will keep a view of medicine that is larger than your practice. Keep in touch with the needs of the wider community: the indigent, the wealthy, and the politicians.

Continue learning, of course. There is much we have not taught you because there is much we do not know. In science, as in other human learning, there is a pattern on the way, hopefully, to truth. First we name. Then we find facts to put around the names. Syndromes follow. And, finally, some insights into pathophysiology and therapeutics. When I think objectively about the present state of medicine, I think of a broad tapestry—someone has started a corner here, additional weaving there, but no one knows what the final design will look like. And even since you started medical school, some of the thread has had to be unraveled and begun again.

As I have stressed already, from now on the patient *is* the curriculum. A few words, then, about the ceremony of seeing patients: I should like to encourage you when taking medical histories, to include for the patient the question, "What did *you* think was wrong?" Often, the patient knows and is waiting only for the opportunity to tell us. But, in addition, this single simple question allows the patient to tell us what he was afraid was wrong, which may be just as important. Such a question opens up the entire interview and will allow you, for example, to identify out of all the young women with headaches, the one whose friend recently died of an intracerebral hemorrhage.

With respect to the physical examination, need I do more than emphasize, "Look at the patient." Don't touch, at first. Look the first time you see a new patient. You will never again see him or her in quite the same light. Other data will take precedence: lab tests, x-rays, etc. And the chance for certain insights will have passed. In such activity, I think, is the answer to the question Charcot posed about muscular dystrophy, "How is it that, one fine morning, Duchenne discovered a disease which probably existed in the time of Hippocrates?"[5]

Be humble. One of the best ways to stay humble is to find out when we are wrong. You will have the opportunity to learn much over the next several years concerning the natural history of disease. In your residency training, I recommend that you write names and hospital numbers on cards or in notebooks and that you come back six months or a year later and find out what has happened to those patients. Without such an exercise, you will make the mistake of assuming that your diagnoses were always correct, and you will never learn the full depth of the patient's mysterious art.

And finally, I hope that you will teach. The word doctor comes from the Latin "docere" which means to teach. We are all pupils and teachers: teachers of physicians, of students, of allied health personnel, and of that great nameless student, the Public. Unless we teach the Public, you and I, the major problems that confront society—hypertension, atherosclerosis, drugs, alcoholism, air pollution, chronic obstructive pulmonary disease, will not be solved.

It was Hippocrates, after all, who said, "Life is short, the art long." He added that "opportunity is fleeting, experience treacherous, judgment difficult."[6] Let us all remember this—and keep remembering.

To commence is to begin—says my dictionary— from the vulgar Latin through the Middle French and Middle English to whatever it is that we speak now. Some of you, I hope many of you, will make creative contributions to the art and science of medicine. This is the proper time to congratulate you on having arrived at a new beginning. Never before, except perhaps tomorrow, has there been such a great feast of ideas upon which to feed. I wish you continually hungry for that food, and with the mental dietetics to choose food wisely. Moreover, I wish you good speed and God speed toward the education that *is* civilization; toward the humanity and wisdom that no one ever has been or ever will be able to give you, but which you must recognize and claim for yourselves, in the name of all of us. Whereupon, of course, you must teach someone else. And someone else. And someone else. That, I believe, is in large measure what the past several years have been all about. If that sounds rather like a benediction, may it stand to bless you, whatever the commencement, and in all your beginnings.

References

1. Ciardi J. Lines From the Beating End of the Stethoscope (poem). Saturday Review, Nov. 18, 1967, p. 12.
2. Williams WC. The Autobiography from The William Carlos Williams Reader. New York: New Directions, 1966, pp. 307–308.
3. Frost R. The Secret Sits (poem) from The Poems of Robert Frost, The Modern Library. New York: Random House, 1946, p. 422.
4. Pope A. An Essay on Man, Epistle IL.
5. Charcot J-M. Quoted in The History of Medicine by Fielding H. Garrison. Philadelphia: W. B. Saunders Company, 1929, p. 15.
6. Hippocrates. From the Aphorisms, quoted in Home Book of Quotations, Burton Stevenson, Editor. New York: Dodd, Mead & Co., 1967, p. 104.

JOHN SNOW TAKES THE WATERS

MANUEL MARTINEZ-MALDONADO, M.D.
(Spring 1994, p. 10)

Immersed in his tub, steam rising above the brow,
he thought of the possible explanation:
beneath the stones worms crawled.
Animistes shuddered at the impending
scourge of gods bent on retribution.
They all had drunk from the well.
In the crystalline flow of shared dew,
hidden like a missed comma,
poisonously poised, choleric in its simplicity,
it had reached an invaded the dark crypts,
destroyed villi, turned on switches
in cells by yet innominate proteins.
The swift losses, the scornful cascade
of vital fluids, the ebbing inner sea,
the shrivelling cells resembling coral.
And then: quivering pulse, darkness in the sky,
heavy, vibrating lids over
the empty eyes—
the overt coma, the camphor-lined,
recalcitrant, unmarked grave.
The well, the horror of the well.

TEACHING THE
MEDICAL STUDENT

FAITH T. FITZGERALD, M.D.

(Summer 1979, pp. 17–19)

Among all others, Faith Fitzgerald is the most appropriate to write about teaching and learning in medical school. She earned her B.A. at UC Santa Barbara and her M.D. at UCSF (AΩA, University of California, San Francisco, 1969) After her residency at UCSF she began her growth as an academician there and at the University of Michigan. Since 1980 she has been active as a program director in internal medicine, and many duties in the dean's office. Her mission in medicine has been to teach, and she has succeeded admirably. In 1996 she was elected as a Master of the American College of Physicians, and served as governor of the northern California chapter. She won the California Medical Association Golden Apple Award in 1992, the ACP Distinguished Teacher Award in 1996, and the 2002 Centennial Distinguished Teacher Award by AΩA/AAMC. She is a teacher!

As a teacher of general internal medicine in a university hospital, I am the recipient of much well-intentioned advice. Everyone, it seems, is an educational philosopher. This interest is laudable, because it attests to the profound concern so many have for the future of our profession, but it also is a source of confusion. Medical educators and analysts, teachers, ethicists, faculty, the laity, and the students themselves—all have their schemes for the training of the ideal physician.

Mine is not a trade school: we teach more than simply a selection of skills, more than a body of knowledge. Being a physician is not just what one does; it is what one is. Therefore, I expect medical students to approach their chosen profession not as an avocation but as a dedication. Students should begin with the conviction that an aspiration to be average is inadequate. If they, every single one of them, do not secretly or openly determine to be the best doctor ever born, they are aiming too low.

In the years of their training some of the characteristics that help students get into medical school will continue to serve them well. These are industriousness, curiosity, honesty, humor, and caring. Other attributes, functional but ignoble, should be discarded upon entry. These are cunning, inclination to political machinations, hedonism, self-aggrandizement, and deceit.

My students almost invariably fear that the intensity of their medical studies will abridge their Renaissance humanity. While it is true that currency of an
immense body of information is essential, it is not the case that each student
must be immediately and intimately conversant with the data contained in each
of twenty-five monthly medical journals. The compulsion to do only medicine
to the exclusion of all else generally arises from a sense of guilt we all share. It
may be overcome by simply expanding the definition of medicine, as is proper,
to encompass all human experience. Indeed, students betray their trust if in
frantic pursuit of microcosmic medical minutiae they neglect the macrocosm
in which these things have relevance. Besides, they become stuffy and dull and
no fun to be with.

This is not an exchange, not a relief of the students' obligate mastery of
medical science. I expect them to know that, and more.

As a corollary to the anxiety of the loss of humanism, students entering
medical schools not infrequently anticipate in themselves an almost monstrous
transformation from idealistic, warm, loving people into cold, cynical technicians. I am quite sure that students emerge from training as the intrinsic doctors that they are. Medical school does not create meanness, pettiness, cruelty,
or greed. What it may do is provide the skills and the setting within which these
traits can be made most dramatically manifest, be the individual so inclined.
The same opportunity is provided for students to be magnificent, if they are
good enough.

The first years in medical school often require an agonized acquisition of
endless, ever-changing, sometimes ponderous data. It is, I think, important to
remind our students that what they are doing in their preclinical years is learning the language of basic science, that language with which we ask of all subsequent clinical experience the fundamental question, Why? What I encourage
them to do is to concentrate upon the intellectual discipline, which is the scientific
method. They may then work out what they cannot recall and, more importantly, what is not yet known. The scientific method alone stands between modern medicine and magic. Students, faculty, and the public must beware of the
concept that scientific competence and physicianly kindness are mutually exclusive
or antagonistic. They are not. One cannot be a good doctor without both.

In the clinical years, most of one's learning comes from the day-to-day association with the patients and house staff on the wards. The principle of self-
education, upon which we in internal medicine work, implies that the clerkships
are designed to allow the student to maximize their potential for learning, compulsive logic, and honesty. We, as faculty, obviously cannot teach these; what
we can do is provide for our students the opportunities to expand and apply
their individual talents. It may seem trite, but it is clearly true that each student
gets out of a clerkship what he or she puts into it. We try as a faculty to provide

for the student the environment within which that student may grow to maximum excellence.

The clinical years, to paraphrase Osler, begin with the patient, continue with the patient, and end with the patient. But we have, often, many more students than patients. Clinical clerks complain to me that their circumscribed experience will compromise their education. This anxiety is even more intense for the clerks who are, by the luck of the draw, assigned to the subspecialty wards for their core rotations. Since the types of patients one sees will obviously vary from ward to ward and from hospital to hospital, it is essential for a student on any clinical clerkship to recognize that it remains his or her job to harvest as much as possible from each individual patient. Since it is obvious that no one can observe firsthand all possible diseases in medicine, each student must make a concerted effort to en-tend learning beyond the immediate case. It is in fact true that the well-motivated student can learn all of medicine from just a single patient. I am not training students who will emerge from medical school as paraphysicians. I want to teach physicians the approach to perpetual self-improvement. This means that my major emphasis will not be to encourage my students to devote large amounts of time learning to do procedures and developing laboratory skills that give the external appearance of competence. The feeling of finally being "a real doctor" and "necessary to the ward team" can bring immediate gratification, but this pleasure should come from reading or attending conferences rather than from doing procedures. Those students who opt for procedures will, unfortunately, have technique without understanding—both a transient and a somewhat dangerous facade. While I shall encourage my students to perform those procedures that are necessary for the best care of their patients and that give them mastery of new techniques, I shall ask them each to exercise judgment and shall proscribe the house staff from using the students for "scut."

While I do want the students to be participants on the wards, I do not want to deceive them into thinking that they are, or should be treated as, full-fledged physicians. There is a sort of protected status to the clinical clerkship, which is insulting to some students. They lament their separation from "the ward team" and the fact that they are treated differently than the house officers. In truth, the only disadvantage to being treated like a student is that someone might realize that you are a student and not be fooled into thinking that you are not. In the era of candor, it seems to me a reasonably good thing that people know that you are what you are. Medical school clerkships are the last opportunities for students to be "different" in a way that is to their advantage. After graduation, one is not perceived differently than others and has no protected time for lectures or reading. I encourage clinical clerks to embrace this "separate" status, rather than struggle against it.

A major complaint of my medical students on the medical wards is that there are too many conferences. These conferences, they say, are not always relevant. Surely, relevance is entirely retrospective. Whenever I am asked whether this or that issue is "relevant," I answer, "Maybe." Nothing is rare to the patient who has it; nothing is irrelevant to the person to whom it occurs. The history of medicine is quite clear on the point that the esoteric has not infrequently emerged into prominence, the theoretical into actuality, in short months or years. What I hope to do is to teach students, not just for the present, but for the future. The facts presented at conferences, the manner of their acquisition, and a critical analysis of their meaning are important. Maybe not now, maybe later—but I want physicians for both now and later.

The question of special lectures for clinical clerks has repeatedly come up. What people seem to be asking for is a set of talks on *"the* workup of anemia" or *"the* workup of hypertension." In my opinion, these rarely are useful. Moreover, they are deceptive, in that they imply that there is such a thing as *"the* workup" for anything. Cookbook formulae are more suitable to the training of paramedics than to the education of physicians. The latter must be directed by a basic understanding that allows him or her to modify any evaluation or therapy to the individual patient.

This stance creates uncertainty, of course, and opens the abyss of the awful recognition that no established pattern holds for more than a few patients, and generally for more than a short time. This knowledge is unfortunate for those who like certainty. The truth is that there is no certainty in the practice of medicine beyond the certainty of change. Teachers would be lying to students if they tried to make it seem otherwise.

My students complain that the requirement for them to do write-ups is too much: they are too long, or there are too many of them. Yet the written workup (the history and physical) is the basic tool of the physician. Ninety-five percent of all diagnosis resides in the history and the physical examination, principally the former. One gets the rest from the laboratory, and that residual should get smaller as one gets better at taking histories and doing physicals. The written workup, properly done, is our major mode of communication. It should not be a mindless exercise in secretarial work, nor a cryptographic aggregation of the latest in jargonistic abbreviations. It should be a carefully constructed, cogent, synthetic, and thoughtful assay of the information gathered from the patient. It is only by compulsive attention to this information, as embodied in the written work-up, that one may begin to solve the patient's problems. It is because the history and physical are the pivotal point of our art that we place so much emphasis upon it.

My students always complain that they have too little time to read. Of course! May they always have too little time to find out everything they want to know. If they are satisfied with the amount they are learning, happy with what they know, content that they have conquered the literature on any particular point in medicine, they have ceased to grow.

Medical students recently have been expressing to me concern about the demands that medicine places upon them. The very perceptive amongst them realize that medicine makes no demands of them. They make demands of themselves; the pressures that drive them are generated internally and born of their sense of compulsion. We expect no more of our students than what they expect of themselves—and that is the problem for those of them who have high expectations.

It has been suggested that clinical clerks have a designated day off every week. My answer to that is that any clerk may have off as many days as he or she may take without compromising either education or patient care. The converse also obtains: if there is work to be done, patients to be taken care of, and things to be learned, it is the student's obligation to do that. Medical students are adult graduate students and know themselves what sort of physicians they want to be. The decisions are entirely up to them.

No single teacher or department can control the idiosyncrasies of the students, the house staff with whom they work, or the faculty. Some students will want more conferences, some less. Some students will want to stay long hours; some will want to go home early. Some will want more experience, others more structure. Some house staff will use students; some will teach them; some will ignore them. Faculty will underestimate a student's skills, as others will overestimate them. Students are, in fact, a mixed group of highly variant individuals with different needs, talents, and backgrounds. Uniformity is hardly to be expected from them or towards them.

Students now, as in the past, construct their physicianhood by taking bits and pieces of the characteristics of people whom they most admire and putting them together to make themselves. My job, as a teacher, is to provide for them a clinical milieu in which they may accomplish this with the least inhibition, and to make available to them the best possible set of paradigms as best I can. Consequently I constantly ask of faculty and house staff that they conduct themselves as if studentry was watching and taking example from them—because it is.

In advising my students as to what field or subspecialty they should enter, I try to remind them, and myself, that there is no intrinsic virtue to any particular area of medicine. What one chooses to do in medicine matters less than that one does it very, very well. A superb primary-care physician is no more nor less noble than an excellent research virologist. They both apply themselves where they serve best.

One of the most important tasks given the teacher of medical students, I think, is to convey to them the immense joy that comes from a job well done. My goals are simple: to stimulate students of medicine to want to know more, and to do more, and to do it better than it has ever been done before. My greatest satisfaction as a teacher of clinical medicine ultimately will be to deliver the care of my patients and of my profession into the hands of those who are clearly superior to me in the art, my students.

Postscript—2003

Since I wrote this much has changed: I still teach students and housestaff in a university medical school, but I am envious of the authority I had as a teacher 23 years ago. Today I seem far less able to control curricular content or "the classrooms"—the wards and clinics and offices in which patients are seen. The frenetic pace of patient care ("triage and turf," the housestaff say), economic restrictions of diagnostic and therapeutic options, even the very language of our chart notes is mandated by managed care rather than individual patient needs or educational goals. Students have too many patients, passing through too quickly. Written workups are shorter as time and efficiency are valued above meticulous completeness: histories and physical examinations may be done by groups (faculty and resident and student at the same time) in cacophonous circumstances, and student examinations may consequently be derivative. Faculty struggle with increased patient numbers and paperwork and they have less time for teaching. Because education at the bedside or in an ambulatory setting is neither efficient nor remunerative in cash, and because real patients are not predictable, we paradoxically teach students patient evaluation and management "sans" patients, using simulations: computers, CDs, videos, models, and actors. We place more reliance on "guidelines," less on contemplation. The message to students and housestaff is clear: no longer apprentices to craftsmen, they are junior workers in the health-cares factory "the industrial revolution" of medicine. The human riches of student-patient contact are diminished: the quirky social histories, quiet moments of shared emotion, the generation of affection born of time and familiarity with one another, the pursuit of incidentals both in history and in physical examination not immediately germane to the instant but of importance both to the patient and to the satiation of the curiosity of the student . . . things I thought valuable in 1979, and still do today.

Still, I am optimistic: students, residents and faculty even in their despair, remain committed to education and individual patient care circumnavigating all obstacles. Patients are still generous to students. Because of them, and in spite of inhospitable circumstance, human centered medical education will continue.

— FAITH T. FITZGERALD, M.D.
AΩA, University of California, San Francisco, 1969
Professor of Internal Medicine and Assistant Dean of Bioethics and Humanities
University of California, Davis

COMPETENCY

DAVID L. SCHIEDERMAYER, M.D.

(Fall 1991, p. 37)

After all, it comes down to this:
The doctor and patient,
door closed, curtain drawn.
Here the ancient art begins;
history unfolds in
spoken word,
ritual touch,
poultice and purge,
a foretaste of
the blade itself.
What have we taught them?
What shall we teach them?
This and nothing less:
the gentle gaze,
the discerning heart,
the healing spirit,
the love that begins
with science and ends
in this room, for all our sakes.

LIVING, LEARNING, AND LOOPHOLES

FAIRFIELD GOODALE, M.D.
(Summer 1985, pp. 12–14)

Dr. Goodale writes, in July 2003:

Two years at Bowman Gray convinced me to retire to a small town on the coast of Maine where my wife and I raised miniature donkeys, pigmy goats, bantam hens, Norwegian horses, and red factor canaries. I was also town selectman, volunteer fireman, chairman of the clam commission, and board chairman of the local hospital.

Five years ago, on the spur of the moment, we moved to California where we thrive on considerable acreage with horses and other livestock, and look forward to periodic visits from our 5 children and 15 grandchildren.

— FAIRFIELD GOODALE, M.D.

WHEN I ARRIVED AS DEAN AT THE MEDICAL COLLEGE of Georgia on April Fools Day, 1976, I found that, even after a number of years in academic medicine, I still had a great deal to learn. During the past eight years the faculty and students of this institution have taught me much about education, hospitals, people, and myself.

At this time I feel no need to address problems of this school. Instead, I would like now to concentrate quite selfishly on what I believe I have learned about myself and about the groves of Academe.

I find that when I try to apply what I have learned about myself or about education to circumstances of the real world, I am often unsuccessful. Moving from the ideal to the practical, in trying to implement what one is convinced should be done, often leads along treacherous pathways. Sometimes one simply makes mistakes through ignorance in the mechanics of this transposition; sometimes one does not foresee the obstacles that will prevent success. Also, acting on one conviction may necessitate putting aside or suppressing another, thereby often producing an ethical dilemma of distressing proportions.

Of great help in my decanal education has been some wise advice contained in a delightful article sent to me by a friend shortly after my arrival here. This

amusing allegory, written by a professor whose colleague had just accepted a deanship at their university, is entitled, "Letter to a New Dean," and part of the professor's advice to his friend reads:

> Beware . . . the illusion that the deanship involves a subtle, special ex-
> pertise, the mastery of a craft whose dark secrets are unknown to your
> faculty colleagues, a solitary struggle with esoteric problems we cannot
> understand. This view of the deanship is poppycock. . . . A qualified aca-
> demic administrator is only a professor who answers his mail.[1]

Although tongue-in-cheek, he speaks thoughtfully. Also, Henry Miller offers
encouragement to administrators. "Our destination is never a place but rather
a new way of looking at things."[2]

While answering my mail I have discovered new ways of looking at things.
First, I've learned that sometimes one must be unreasonable. The unreasonable
man, as George Bernard Shaw reminds us, persists in trying to shape the world
to himself and therefore frequently effects desirable change.[3] Too often, however, this attitude requires the courage to be heard, the courage to take a stand,
the courage to avoid the role of bystander, though the issue be unpopular, though
appeasement is easy, though silence be expedient. Often, the appearance of
courage is as important as the substance of courage.

I have also learned to make no small plans. They will stir no one, least of all
oneself, and one's work will be diminished accordingly. Far better it is to form
big plans, exciting plans, plans with a vision. Although one who dares splendid
things will certainly run risk of failure, how much better it is to take that risk
than to dwell in a twilight that knows neither victory nor defeat.

I have come to know that while equality is frequently not possible, equity, or
fairness, is always possible and forms one of the strongest bases of trust. Trust,
in turn, is unquestionably the foundation of success for any organization.

I have found that academic organizations are fascinating collections of people, ideas, and ambitions, where faculty expectations are often difficult to meet,
especially when each of two opponents expects the dean to have his rival sum-
marily dispatched by the firing squad. At the same time, of real challenge and
usually of particular satisfaction and fun is the unraveling of problems raised
by faculty colleagues who are delightfully collegial most of the time but who
may, in the twinkling of an eye, become stubbornly resistant to even the suggestion
of change. This opposition to needed change, as, for example, in the area of
curriculum, brings out any faculty's least charming attributes. Clearly, no one
wants his or her own cage rattled.

It is not surprising to find that in our medical school, as in virtually every medical school with which I am familiar, the curriculum is stressful and overcrowded
with more details than all the microchips in Silicon Valley could possibly han-

dle. Whenever I think of curricula and information overload, I think first of a kitchen compactor compressing its contents into an unattractive and indigestible mass. Then, I think of my grandmother cheerfully telling her pregnant daughter that having a baby is like pushing a grand piano through a transom!

It seems to me that most curricula are so powerfully compacted that, even while delivering apparently healthy offspring, they still create painful and often damaging learning experiences. Medical students must be protected against faculty Vandals and Visigoths who ignore the fact that too much information may rot the mind and shrink the soul. I would hope, as I have suggested in years past, that this country's medical curricula will be overhauled with the objective of a far greater emphasis on humanism and creativity than is currently the vogue.

I have learned that the governance of a medical school depends, in part, on the same two talents that John Buchan deemed necessary for statesmanship, namely "the conception of wise ends and the perception of adequate means." This faculty has both of these talents in large supply and needs only the chance to use them. It has yet another talent: it has managed to avoid the cerebral ossification so often brought on by the academic aloofness so aptly described in Leonard Bacon's quatrain.

> This was decreed by superior powers
> In a moment of wisdom sidereal
> That those who dwell upon ivory towers
> Shall have heads of the same material.[5]

The faculty has shown me, in various ways, how important it is to be a futurist. Living each day as it comes is grand, so long as it includes planning for tomorrow. Surprises tend to be unpleasant and often counterproductive, and their shock can only be avoided or lessened by anticipation. When you deploy your troops on the front side of the mountain and the enemy attacks the rear, you will do well to have an alternate plan of action. Change, uncertainty, and planning for the future make uneasy bed fellows, but one must become comfortable with making decisions in the face of ambiguity and, frequently, with insufficient information. In these circumstances the words of a Chinese poet have been helpful.

> [H]e who wants to have right without wrong,
> Order without disorder,
> Does not understand the principles
> Of heaven and earth.
> He does not know how
> Things hang together.
> Understanding how things hang together is of pressing importance to each
> of us.[6]

Faculty and students alike have taught me to listen more and to talk less. One learns nothing by talking, and only those who have listened well have something worthwhile to say. At the same time, it seems sensible to be sparing with advice; the wise do not need it, others often resent it.

I have also learned to tolerate, even to welcome, quandaries and uncertainties, remembering that no sailor ever distinguished himself on a smooth sea. The faculty has taught me that the person best able to solve a problem is usually the person who is closest to it, not necessarily someone who wears three more stripes on his sleeve, or who breathes air more rarified. I have noticed that good problem solvers seem to be those who, in their personal lives, establish goals and expectations that are not impossible to realize but are difficult and lofty enough to challenge their abilities.

I have become convinced, particularly in the last several years, that alumni, under able leadership, are as important to a school as any board of trustees. They not only help the school financially, but they serve as role models for students, and, equally important, they can be gadflies to the faculty and administration, goading them to seek excellence.

I have been impressed that each of us must carefully avoid the anti-leadership vaccine that, as John Gardner points out, society tends to administer to our young people today.[7] A person recognized as a "me-firster," a status seeker or compromiser corrupted by power, will rarely become, and certainly not long remain, a leader. The person who is willing to accept responsibility for establishing goals, expressing values, defining priorities, and providing hope, however, will find the role of leader thrust upon him. Our world needs leaders badly.

I have discovered how important it is to understand the implications of one's knowledge. Through knowledge, a person can move from hypothesis to consequence, from discipline to achievement, from process to content.

I have learned too that at times the capacity to enjoy one's own company beyond that of others is essential. Nowhere will you find a quieter or more untroubled haven than within yourself. Appreciation of oneself is the only real wealth there is, and from it comes strength and peace and self-confidence.

The faculty has taught me how crucial it is not to take oneself too seriously. A few drops daily of a tincture of self-ridicule and a few anti-smugness tablets help keep a proper balance. These, coupled with a sense of humor, make a splendid combination, without which life is simply a series of nasty bumps and misunderstandings.

I have had proven to me the value of friendship—with its openness, warmth, and trust. A person's capacity for friendship can be measured by the size of the circles he draws to take in the world. Some of us make our circles very little bigger than ourselves; but others of us, wiser and stronger, build enormous circles that are filled with light and warmth and love and all manner of friends.

Lastly, I have come to appreciate that human life is a brief, golden span between two oblivions, starting as a miracle, ending in mystery. In between are varying degrees of happiness and frustration, of gratification and anxiety, of joy and pain. Acceptance of each lies at the heart of all personal fulfillment.

I would like to close with this anecdote. Shortly before W. C. Fields's death, a friend visited him in the hospital.

On entering the room, he caught Fields, a well-known agnostic, poring over a Bible. Amazed, the friend asked him what he was doing. Fields closed the book, and smiling slyly, replied, "I'm looking for loopholes."

It is human nature, of course, to look often for loopholes in order to avoid ethical dilemmas and unpleasant decisions; but it is also human nature to reach for the best, which means rejecting the option of loopholes. Few of us attain the levels of excellence of which we are capable. So much there is to see and do along the way, so much applause for second- and third-rate achievements, that to settle for loopholes and mediocrity is all too easy. But Richard W. Livingstone's words ring true:

> Always, soon or late, humanity turns to excellence as naturally as a flower turns to the sun: mankind crucifies Christ and executes Socrates, and they die amid derision and hatred; but in the end they receive the homage of the world.

So now, as I leave the Medical College of Georgia, the most valuable knowledge that I carry with me is that excellence is our most important renewable option; it must be the conscious choice of each organization and each individual if excellence is to be realized.

I thank the faculty for that insight.

References

1. Rosenheim E, Jr. Letter to a New Dean. AAUP Bulletin 49(31):226–31, 1963, p. 226.
2. Miller H. Quoted in Moon, WLH. Blue Highways: A Journey into America. New York, Fawcett Crest, 1984, p. 370.
3. Shaw GB. In Peter, LJ. Peter's Quotations: Ideas for Our Time. New York, William Morrow & Co., 1977, p. 411.
4. Buchan J. Montrose. London, Oxford University Press, 1957, p. 413.
5. Bacon L. Quoted in the Western Reserve University School of Medicine Alumni Bulletin, First Quarter, 1959, p. 5.
6. Merton T. The Way of Chuang Tzu, New York, New Directions Publishing Co., 1965, p. 88.
7. Gardner JW. No Easy Victories. New York, Harper & Row Publishers, 1968, p.129.
8. Livingstone RW. Some Tasks for Education. London, Oxford University Press, 1946, pp. 47–48.

PART XIII

NOW . . .
THE FUTURE,
VIEWED FROM
THE
20TH CENTURY

Prudence: The guide for perplexed physicians
in the third millennium.

PRUDENCE: THE GUIDE FOR PERPLEXED PHYSICIANS IN THE THIRD MILLENNIUM

CYNTHIA M. A. GEPPERT, M.D.
(Summer 1995, pp. 2–7)

In addition to her other activities as a psychiatrist, Cynthia Geppert is a Research Fellow with the Empirical Ethics Group at the University of New Mexico School of Medicine. She received her M.D. from the University of Texas Science Center at San Antonio in 1997 and, subsequently, a Ph.D. in philosophy, with a dissertation in the ethical and religious aspects of psychiatric genetics. She also holds and M.A. in Religious Ethics from Vanderbilt University. Her research interests are in clinical ethics, medical education, genetics, religion, spirituality, and consultation liaison psychiatry. Recently, she was awarded the Association for Academic Psychiatry fellowship and the Webb Fellowship from the Academy for Psychosomatic Medicine for her clinical service.

One thing hastens into being, another hastens out of it. Even while a thing is in the act of coming into existence, some part of it has already ceased to be. Flux and change are for ever renewing the fabric of the universe, just as the ceaseless sweep of time is for ever renewing the face of eternity. In such a running river, where there is no firm foothold, what is there for a man to value among all the many things that are racing past him?

— Meditations, Marcus Aurelius1, [p. 93]

THESE WORDS OF THE EMPEROR AND PHILOSOPHER MARCUS AURELIUS were written at a time when the Roman Empire was fading and the new Christian world had not yet come into being. His book *Meditations* contains the thoughts of a reflective and disciplined man living in what the scholar E.R. Dodds—borrowing a phrase from the poet W.H. Auden—called an "Age of Anxiety." Dodds saw such a period of history as an age in which there were "both material and . . . moral insecurity."[2]

Today, physicians are educated and practice in an age similar to the Age of Anxiety, and many of them would probably express feelings similar to those of Marcus Aurelius. The sources of modern world flux moving medicine toward the twenty-first century are numerous, powerful, and seemingly irreversible. The profession of medicine stands at a unique moment in its history, for at no other point has medical science and technology so outstripped and overwhelmed the cognitive paradigms and ethical structures of its professionals.

The title of this essay is an allusion to the medieval philosophical classic *The Guide for the Perplexed,* written by the Jewish physician Maimonides. His intention was to assist the thinking men of his day to discover true wisdom amidst the many conflicting intellectual currents that influenced their moral and professional life.

Before Louis Pasteur and the discovery of microbes, the advent of antibiotics and diagnostic machinery, the physician could, in the famous phrase, "comfort always, relieve often, and cure sometimes." A thorough history, a good physical exam, a pleasant bedside manner, excellent diagnostic skills, and the willingness to be of service were the best tools any physician could bring to a patient. With a limited pharmacological armamentarium, surgical techniques dependent on speed in the absence of anesthesia, and a scientific base for therapeutics extremely narrow in scope, medical intervention had as its goal, in most instances, to relieve symptoms; comfort was always appropriate.

The discovery of penicillin and effective anesthesia, the institution of the clinical trial, and the rapid development of surgery, radiology, and laboratory techniques in the wake of World War II forever changed the face of medicine. To "cure often" seemed possible; perhaps even in the optimistic days of the magic bullet, physicians dreamed someday of curing always. But perhaps in pursuit of the dream of curing, they forgot the reality of comfort care. Now, ironically it appears time has moved backwards, and, on several fronts, medicine is hard pressed by change. Perhaps nothing did so much to shake the collective confidence of the medical profession as a disease identified in 1981, which, by the year 2000, is predicted to reach the epidemic proportions of 1 million cases: acquired immunodeficiency disease (AIDS). It is foreseeable in the not too distant future that primary care physicians will confront a microbial menace for which they no longer have an effective defense. Even healthy people may once again die from streptococcal or staphylococcal infections as they did at the turn of the century. In *TIME* magazine, Michael D. Lemonick wrote:

> Humanity once had the hubris to think it could control or even conquer all these microbes. But anyone who reads today's headlines knows how vain that hope turned out to be. New scourges are emerging—AIDS is not the only one—and older diseases like tuberculosis are rapidly evolving into forms that are resistant to antibiotics, the main weapon in the doctor's arsenal. The danger is greatest, of course, in the underdeveloped world, where epidemics of cholera, dysentery and malaria are spawned by war, poverty, overcrowding and poor sanitation. But the microbial world knows no

boundaries. For all the vaunted power of modern medicine, deadly infections are a growing threat to everyone, everywhere.[3, pp. 62–63]

The very drugs that now are useless against the cunning of microbial resistance have also betrayed physicians. Diethylstilbestrol (DES), thalidomide—these resulted in only the most infamous scandals. Almost more disturbing are the continuous reports in journal after journal of untoward side effects of what were considered beneficial medications. Technology, too, is not immune to this unmasking. As a recent study on back surgery determined, operations were overused and in many cases dangerous and ineffective.[4] Most new medications, particularly those for mental illness, may take years to show toxicity. As funds are cut for basic research, it may not be feasible to evaluate the efficacy and safety of many drugs and therapies that physicians accept and patients expect. The faster the pace of pharmaceutical research and technological development, the wider the epistemological gap grows.

Nowhere is this gap wider than in the protean realm of genetics. According to *U.S. News and World Report:*

> The rate of change is unlike anything medicine has witnessed before, as researchers fish genes out of cells at a dizzying rate. Last year saw the discovery of more than a dozen mutations responsible for diseases ranging from Alzheimer's to hyperactivity to colon cancer. Almost as soon as a gene is discovered, commercial laboratories are ready to offer a genetic test—a pace that threatens to outstrip both physicians' and patients' abilities to make sense of the information.[5, p. 60]

The genetics revolution has raised questions that will take years for legislators, scientists, ethicists, and society at large to debate and attempt to resolve, and, yet, physicians must incorporate genetics, with all its ambiguities, into their practice. Of all the challenges that physicians will confront after the year 2000, none is more daunting and carries more potential for peril than medical genetics. Neither their education nor training will have prepared them, nor will the law or ethics provide many guidelines, at least immediately, to help doctors play what is truly a Promethean role.

The genetics revolution is the quintessential example of a cultural phenomenon that underlies and unites these developments in microbiology, pharmacology, and molecular biology—the information explosion. Facts and theories grow exponentially; scientific information has long since moved beyond the capacity of a single human mind to encompass. Medical education in the wake of the Flexner report has been founded on these basic scientific data, and medical schools attempt to teach an expanding universe of facts to their students.

Medical schools influenced by educational theorists and psychologists have designed curricula that emphasize the regurgitation of massive amounts of isolated facts. Medical students are insufficiently trained to analyze or integrate these data so that information would be transformed into knowledge. It is no wonder that most efforts at medical education reform have been directed toward teaching problem solving, as it is one of the only rational means of coping with this vast body of changing scientific discovery.

Faced with such an explosion of medical knowledge on the one hand, and extreme lacunae in practical knowledge on the other, physicians have been caught between the demands of patients and the fear of the lawyers whom those patients will hire if the treatments their physicians administer should prove harmful. Nothing has done more to damage the physician-patient relationship than the intrusion of the legal profession into what has always been a sacred bond of mutual trust. Threatened with lawsuits, many young physicians avoid risky specialties, such as obstetrics, retire early, work for corporations that bear the cost of malpractice, order extensive and unnecessary tests to protect themselves, and, finally, strive more avidly for monetary gain both as a defensive measure and as a means of compensating themselves for the apprehensive and adversarial climate in which they must work.

Lawyers are not the only third parties interfering in the practice of medicine. Physicians are increasingly subject to government regulation and the dictates of insurance companies. Doctors must currently explain and justify, usually to non-physicians, almost every minute of time they spend with a patient. Such big brother scrutiny places physicians in a defensive posture; suspicious and fearful, they again must let economic and legal concerns influence their clinical judgment if they are to remain in practice. Over all these political trends looms the specter of health care reform. Plan after competing plan is proposed and discussed, rendering the physician's future even more insecure. The resident and medical student, even the established practitioner, must ask: Shall I be able to enter the specialty of my choice, make a decent living, have liberty to treat my patients as I see fit?

The scientific, educational, and political movements outlined here constitute an Age of Anxiety, a period of "material and moral uncertainty." Physicians cannot obviously reverse these trends, but must continue to practice medicine in an era of doubt, suspicion, and litigiousness. The question then becomes, *What is the best way to practice medicine in an Age of Anxiety?*

The beginnings of an answer may be found again in the writing of Marcus Aurelius.

> In short, all that is of the body is as coursing waters, all that is of the soul as dreams and vapors; like a warfare, a brief sojourning in an alien land; and after repute, oblivion. Where then can man find the power to guide and guard his steps? In one thing and one alone: Philosophy. To be a philosopher is to keep unsullied and unscathed the divine spirit within him, so

that it may transcend all pleasure and all pain, take nothing in hand without purpose and nothing falsely or with dissimulation, depend not on another's actions or inactions, accept each and every dispensation as coming
from the same Source as itself.[1, p. 51]

The physicians of the twenty-first century will be forced by the logic of the
events we have described to become philosophers or no longer be professionals. Western philosophy's origins in the Greek city-state were practical and
moral, and it is to this tradition of community-based medicine that physicians
must return. There is, of course, a long and distinguished legacy of physician-
philosophers from Hippocrates to Albert Schweitzer. The writings of nearly all
of these men give a privileged position to the cornerstone of practical philosophy, the virtue of prudence. Prudence, what the Greeks called *phronesis,* is the
most important quality a physician practicing in the Age of Anxiety can possess.
In a recent work on medical ethics the title of the chapter "The Moral Conversion
of the Physician and the Centrality of Prudence" profoundly sums up the vital
role of this often misunderstood virtue.[6]

Historians of philosophy trace the idea of *phronesis* back to Aristotle, who discussed the notion of practical wisdom in his *Nicomachean Ethics.* His ideas were
reinterpreted from a Christian perspective by the scholastic theologian Thomas
Aquinas, who transformed *phronesis* into the concept of *prudentia,* the moral
virtue of prudence. Prudence survived in the Christian moral tradition and has recently been revived in the writings of moral philosophers and medical ethicists
belonging to the virtue school. Founding members of this philosophical school
Edmund D. Pellegrino and David C. Thomasma defined the virtue:

> Phronesis is the term Aristotle used for the virtue of practical wisdom, the
> capacity for moral insight, the capacity, in a given set of circumstances,
> to discern what moral choice or course of action is most conducive to the
> good of the agent or the activity in which the agent is engaged.[7]

Phronesis does not seek to avoid doubt and uncertainty; rather it is the attribute that enables one to make a decision amidst such confusion. As Miguel
A. Bedolla has stated:

> The truth of existence is reached in concrete action. But the truth is not a
> given, what is given is only the experience. Thus humans must deliberate
> in order to decide. Phronesis, or Prudence, is a virtue of deliberation about
> what is good and useful for man. The possessor of Phronesis is the ma-
> ture human. The prudent human realizes that deliberation with a view to
> possible action can neither concern things that are not capable of being
> changed nor goals that cannot be realized. Phronesis is not about the un-
> changeable order of the world; it concerns only human affairs and, among
> them, only those which can be objects of meaningful deliberation.[8]

Prudence is the necessary virtue when one cannot know yet one must still do.

The cultivation of the virtue of prudence will enable a physician to fulfill the medical duty that will become paramount in the Age of Anxiety: do no harm. As *Epidemics I* in the Hippocratic corpus admonishes, "As to diseases, make a habit of two things—to help, or at least to do no harm."[9] There has never been a period in the history of medicine in which there was such great potential to "do harm," and though awareness of this fact may be only implicit in the consciousness of physicians, it is clearly a source of intense anxiety. Who can foresee the consequences of fetal tissue implants on patients with Parkinson's, on the mothers of the fetuses, on society as a whole? When physicists were developing atomic energy, few of them foresaw the horrors of Hiroshima or the plague of nuclear waste. Now, it is the biological sciences that are at the cutting edge of discovery; yet, it is often physicians who must prescribe the new drugs, employ the new technologies, and cope with the medical, moral, and social aftermath, fallout, as it were, for themselves and their patients.

The virtue of prudence will enable a physician to keep focused on the traditional goals of medicine and to interpret them in the rapidly changing context of modem medicine. A widely used clinical ethics manual lists the basic goals:

(a) Promotion of health and prevention of disease,

(b) Relief of symptoms, pain and suffering,

(c) Cure of disease,

(d) Preventing untimely death,

(e) Improvement of functional status or maintenance of compromised status,

(f) Education and counseling of patients regarding their condition and its prognosis,

(g) Avoiding harm to the patient in the course of care.[10]

Achieving these goals in the Age of Anxiety will become increasingly difficult, complicated, and ambiguous precisely because of the epistemological gap in pharmaceutical and technological progress. American medicine is active and interventive as a reflection and expression of the mainstream pragmatism in which it is embedded. Americans as a people have built their society on a conquest of nature, capitalist economics, individual liberty, and the Protestant work ethic. Yet, at this critical watershed, what is needed are exactly the opposite attitudes and behaviors—the moral virtues of temperance, fortitude, and justice. Like spokes in a wheel, these virtues are connected to one another through a single hub, prudence—which is the *central* virtue.

The physician today is like someone driving a car very fast when fog rolls in suddenly, blurring the horizon; only a fool will keep going at the same speed, perhaps to tumble over a cliff that he or she cannot see one hundred feet ahead. The wise driver will slow down, paying careful attention to every landmark of a scene where visibility is so radically diminished. In many ways, medicine has reached a point where it must prudently order the pace of science or proceed at its own risk. Patience and discernment—these are not skills that come easily to physicians, but they are the watchwords of this troubled Age of Anxiety. Albert R. Jonsen has written:

> In conclusion, it may appear that dwelling on the negative apodosis of the maxim, "do no harm," rather than upon the positive protasis, "be of benefit," creates the impression of a minimalist morality. This may be. But, if we recall the version of the maxim, "at least do no harm," we may see it not so much as a morality of lower limits, but as an admonition to humility. When good persons possess great powers and wield them on behalf of others, they sometimes fail to recognize the harm done as they ply their beneficent craft. The medical profession has such power and its practitioners usually intend to use it well. They must become sensitive to its shadow side.[11, p. 832]

The Age of Anxiety has thrust upon physicians the uncomfortable and painful task of confronting this shadow side. Even the virtues of light: truthfulness, compassion, benevolence, may result in the propagation of darkness. For example, does a physician tell a person that he or she carries the gene for breast cancer or Huntington's chorea when the doctor has no assurance that the patient will develop the condition or, more importantly has no treatment to offer? It is beyond the scope of this paper to explore the issues of confidentiality and patient autonomy, but I should note that what would seem a straightforward fulfillment of the goals of prevention of disease and counseling of a patient has now become a much more muddled morass.

Let us, for instance, apply the goals of relief of symptoms, pain, and suffering, and of improvement of functional status or maintenance of compromised status to psychiatric patients. The new drug Prozac, a member of the class of serotonin re-uptake inhibitors, was so startlingly effective in the treatment of depression that a book about it made the bestseller list; yet, its very success triggered a backlash. First, a tendency towards suicide was touted as a side effect, and though this concern has been largely dismissed in the scientific literature, a more serious question lingers. Prozac, it seems, is a mood elevator and personality enhancer like none seen before, and many thoughtful writers have raised the specter of a *Brave New World*. Psychiatrist Peter D. Kramer, author of the book *Listening to Prozac*, has written:

> None of the ethical concerns about Prozac—its influence on affect tolerance, autonomy and coercion, cultural expectations, evolutionary fitness, transcendence—has disappeared. But once we have lived with Prozac for a while, once we have taken the measure of the drug, once it has worked on us, those worries may seem less urgent. Our worst fear—Walker Percy's

fear, the fear of the medical ethicists and evolutionary biologists, my own
fear when I first saw patients respond to Prozac—was that medication
would rob us of what is uniquely human: anxiety, guilt, shame, grief, self-
consciousness. Instead, medication may have convinced us that those affects are not uniquely human, although how we use or respond to them
surely is.[12]

It seems obvious that people would not want to suffer the misery and isolation of depressive symptoms, but it is less clear if they would like traits like
shyness, hyperactivity, introversion, or melancholy to be labeled symptoms of
mental illness, amenable to treatment. The brilliant and tormented Virginia
Woolf walked into a river rather than suffer another episode of bipolar affective disorder; today she could be managed with lithium and Tegretol and probably live on to write more great novels. Yet, the possibilities, even probabilities,
given human nature, for exploitation remain. Identity, personality, the nature
of humankind—these are the classic problems of philosophy. Yet, every physician in the near future will be forced by the tenor of the times to make such
philosophical decisions about patient care.

The goal of preventing untimely death may be the biggest conundrum medicine and society face in the coming millennium. Euthanasia is only the most
dramatic of the moral dilemmas that await a world where the majority of persons are elderly and resources are dwindling. Who will be the object of the injunction to "do no harm"? Will it be the patient, his or her overburdened family,
the debt-ridden government, or the exhausted physician?

Insurance companies, the government, families, and their own economic
and professional pressure will subtly and insidiously push the physician towards a kind of tacit eugenics. Only the physician may stand in the way of a movement designed to remake the population in the image of financial and political
interests. Shannon Brownlee has written in *U.S. News & World Report*:

> The coercive practice in eugenics has a habit of creeping in from unex-
> pected quarters. A recent federal report found that dozens of Americans
> had lost their jobs and health insurance after taking a genetic test. . . .

> Such heavy-handedness may be shocking, but geneticists worry more about
> what Francis Collins calls "homemade eugenics —the decision parents
> themselves now (and will increasingly) make on the basis of prenatal tests.
> In a recent poll, a quarter of Americans thought genetic engineering should
> be used to improve physical appearance; 34 percent found it acceptable for
> boosting intelligence. . . . Our definition of what's normal becomes narrower
> and narrower as we fix what once wasn't broken.[13]

These are clearly questions that should be tentatively answered after long de-
liberation; and yet, it is physicians at the bedside front lines who must almost

instantaneously struggle for feasible solutions for their patients. Prudence, more than any technical skill or scientific knowledge, will guide a physician through these challenges and will guard him or her from the many temptations to act without due consideration of the uncertainty of the consequences.

A prudent physician will realize that to prescribe another antibiotic to a child with the flu because the mother requests medication may one day result in that child dying from an infected skinned knee. Rather than to allow himself or herself to be controlled by the dictates of insurers and bureaucrats to order more tests or conversely not to perform a procedure a physician believes to be required, a prudent physician will communicate to the patient the risks and benefits of his or her recommended course, making him or her an ally rather than a current consumer and potential litigant.

American physicians have been trained to act; the prescription pad, the scalpel, and the MRI are the modern physician's response to the pain and hope, suffering, and trust that patients bring to their offices. As American society becomes more secular, physicians become the new saviors; science produces the new miracles; and a healthy, seemingly endless life on this earth replaces the aspiration for a better life beyond. Yet, life is not endless, nor, as we are swiftly and catastrophically discovering, are our financial and cultural resources limitless. The moment in history has come when doctors should not do all they can do or even all patients might want.

The end of the first millennium was a similar period, when the populace was filled with dread and dreams, fears and expectations, and when the predominant historical reality was unprecedented change. Today, as I have argued, we have precisely such a climate, in which distorted visions of scientific utopia and doom have generated enormous ill-informed trepidation and fantasy surrounding the promise and peril of medicine in the third millennium.

Physicians must seek the humility and wisdom to refuse to be either divinized by patients' projections or cowed by their demands. Prudence can give the physician the confidence he or she needs to reassert a right too often usurped in recent decades by corporations and consumerism, to practice medicine with benevolent responsibility. Courage and maturity will be needed to arrive empirically at the existential definitions of the traditional medical duties of compassion, fidelity, and truthfulness in such radically new clinical situations.

It may well be, as the postmodern era of medical practice dawns, that the virtues of a simpler time will once again be needed. The scientific mind and the skilled hand have accomplished great works in the last century, but viewed from a prudent perspective, their limitations and flaws emerge, and the possibilities and values of the gentle touch and the listening heart reemerge as equally powerful healing arts.

The physician who, foreseeing the chaos of events in the third millennium, practices in accordance with the virtue of prudence, develops thereby a moral self-possession amidst uncertainty, and spiritual integrity to endure duress without compromising principle. Prudence truly accomplishes in the mind of such a physician the goal of Maimonides to serve as a "guide through the most perplexing of times." Sir William Osler, himself a disciple of Marcus Aurelius, described the character of such a prudent physician working in an age of anxiety with the word *aequanimitas:*

> Imperturbability means coolness and presence of mind under all circumstances, calmness amid storm, clearness of judgment in moments of grave peril, immobility, impassiveness, or, to use an old and expressive word, phlegm. It is the quality which is most appreciated by the laity though often misunderstood by them; and the physician who has the misfortune to be without it, who betrays indecision and worry, and who shows that he is flustered and flurried in ordinary emergencies, loses rapidly the confidence of his patients.[14]

References

1. Marcus Aurelius: Mediations, Staniforth, M, trans. New York, Penguin Books, 1964.
2. Dodds ER. Pagan and Christian in an Age of Anxiety. London, Cambridge University Press, 1965; New York, W.W. Norton & Co., 1970, p. 3.
3. Lemonick MD. The killers all around. TIME, September 12, 1994, pp. 62–69.
4. Understanding Acute Low Back Problems. U.S. Dept. of Health & Human Services, Public Health Service, Agency for Health Care Policy and Research, AHCPR Publ. No. 95-0644, Rockville, Maryland, December 1994.
5. Brownlee S, Cook GC and Hardigg V. Tinkering with destiny. U.S. News and World Report, August 22, 1994, pp. 61–67.
6. Bedolla M and Geppert C. The Foundations of Medical Ethics: A New Perspective on an Old Tradition. Manuscript prepared for a course in medical ethics, St. Mary's University, San Antonio, Texas, Spring 1994, p. 139, unpublished.
7. Pellegrino ED and Thomasma DC. The Virtues in Medical Practice. New York, Oxford University Press, 1993, p. 84.
8. Bedolla M. Nature, History and Genetics: Solon or Prometheus? Paper presented at St. Mary's University, San Antonio, Texas, September 29, 1994, unpublished.
9. Hippocrates. Epidemics I and III. In Hippocrates, vol. 1, Bk 13. Jones, WHS, trans, pp. 139–288. Cambridge, Massachusetts, Harvard University Press, 1962, p. 165.
10. Jonsen AR, Siegler M, and Winslade WI. A Practical Approach to Ethical Decisions in Clinical Medicine, 3rd ed. New York, McGraw-Hill, 1992, p. 17.
11. Jonsen AR. Do no harm. Ann Intern Med 88:827–32, 1978.
12. Kramer PR. Listening to Prozac. New York, Penguin Books, 1993, p. 299.
13. Brownlee S. A new eugenics? The narrowing of normality. U.S. News & World Report, August 22, 1994, p. 67.
14. Osler W. Aequanimitas. In Aequanimitas: With Other Addresses to Medical Students, Nurses and Practitioners of Medicine, 3rd ed., pp. 3–11. Philadelphia, Blakiston Co., 1943, pp. 3–4.

MEDICAL PRACTICE: PAST, PRESENT, FUTURE

DENTON A. COOLEY, M.D.

(Winter 1997, pp. 13–16)

There is no better way to conclude this anthology than from sage words about the course that medicine should take in the decades of the 2000ᵗʰ years. Denton Cooley (AΩA, Johns Hopkins University School of Medicine, 1944) is President and Surgeon-in-Chief of the Texas Heart Institute in Houston that he founded in 1962. After undergraduate education at the University of Texas, he earned his medical degree at Johns Hopkins where he was elected to AΩA. Hopkins and London were the sites of his cardiac surgery training. After many years at Baylor University School of Medicine, he began another portion of his career at UC Texas at Houston. In 1968, he (and Norman Shumway at Stanford) performed the first heart transplant operations, and a year later, he implanted an artificial heart in man. He has received the Medal of Freedom and the National Medal of Technology.

Dr. Cooley is clinical professor of surgery at the University of Texas Medical School, Houston. As an Alpha Omega Alpha visiting professor, he presented this paper at the Medical University of South Carolina in March 1996.

THE 1990S HAVE BEEN A TIME OF TRANSITION, a bridge not only between two centuries, but also between two millennia. The currents of time are swirling furiously around, pushing us further away from the past and closer to the future. Medicine can no more escape the effect of these currents than we can escape our own mortality. In the fall of 1996, medical schools around the country matriculated the Class of 2000, the first crop of twenty-first-century physicians. At this portentous moment, the end of one era and the dawn of another, it is fitting that we consider the past, the present, and the future of medical practice.

Medicine comes of age

Not until the end of the nineteenth century did our profession gain the public's trust and respect. After a series of important advances in pathology, anatomy, and microbiology, medicine at last became regarded as a truly *scientific* discipline. As stated by Edward Shorter, in the 1920s and 1930s, this perception was used by pharmacology companies for advertisements "featuring, not various prescription drugs. . .but clean-shaven, lantern-jawed physicians reading the latest pathology journals at a time of night when the rest of the population was at play."[1, p. 790] Perhaps even more important in gaining the public's respect, however, was the physician-patient relationship. During this era, the physician was considered "a demi-god possessed of boundless authority over patients."[1, p. 790] Patients trusted their personal doctors implicitly; thus, even though they had few real tools, physicians were often able to heal their patients through somatic means. Patients suffering from such ailments as "hysteria" and "neurasthenia" were comforted just by their physician's familiarity and presence. In 1849 a physician wrote:

> If he has been the physician of the family for any length of time, . . . this feeling of affectionate reliance is deep and ardent; so much so, that it is a severe trial to the sensitive mind to be obliged to consult a stranger.[2]

Much of this familiarity was due to the preeminence of history taking and of the exhaustive physical examination. Physicians regularly took lengthy histories, allowing their patients "to tell . . . their stories at their own pace."[1, p. 792] Familiarity was also engendered by close physical contact between physician and patient. This tactile approach to diagnosis helped the patient feel that the doctor was personally invested in his or her welfare. Throughout this era, however, medicine remained more a prognostic discipline than a therapeutic one. Although great advances had been made in identifying illnesses, little means were available to cure these ailments.

World War II and beyond

I graduated from Johns Hopkins Medical School in 1944, not long before the end of World War II. With that war came a new era of therapeutic advances. The introduction of antibiotic drugs such as Prontosil (1935) and penicillin (1945) allowed physicians to treat successfully illnesses that were once thought untreatable.[1] When I began my surgical practice fifty years ago, only one-tenth of the operations we now perform routinely had even been conceived of. Our operating rooms were primitive compared with those of today. We had not heard of heart lasers, stents, or angioplasty balloons. Then, in 1953, John H. Gibbon, Jr., introduced the first heart-lung machine. Shortly thereafter, we designed our own device, and constructed it with materials procured at a kitchen supply company.[3] Suddenly, a whole new world of surgical possibilities opened before us. Operations that only ten years before would have been thought of as impossible became almost commonplace. This exciting period of development culminated in 1967, when Christiaan Barnard performed the world's first heart transplant.[4] At that moment, there seemed no limit to how far medicine could go.

Unfortunately, these technological and surgical advances came with a price: sacrifice of the physician-patient relationship. Because diagnoses could be made more accurately in the hospital or in the office, physicians stopped making house calls. New diagnostic techniques also diminished the need for physical contact between physician and patient, and made taking long histories unnecessary. As a consequence, physicians began to concentrate more on identifying and treating patients' ailments than on forming connections with the patients.

Thus, the very technology that had been designed to aid both the physician and the patient caused a rift to form between its benefactors. Patients began to resent the high cost and increasingly impersonal nature of medical treatment.[5] They were alienated by the rising economic and social status of physicians.[6] When cardiac transplantation failed to fulfill its potential as a treatment for end-stage heart disease, this rift grew wider. Today, malpractice suits, unheard of in the early part of the century, are common occurrences, and physicians must carry insurance to protect themselves against the inevitable judgment.

In fifty years, the image of the physician has come full circle. The public now often sees doctors as in-different technicians, interested more in buying new cars than in listening to patients' problems. John A. Owen, Jr., wrote that "the appellation 'greedy doctor' has become increasingly popular and nowadays ranks right up there with 'sleazy lawyer' and 'crooked politician.'"[6, p. 2] Do we deserve such resentment? In part, yes. A few doctors place their fees above the best interests of their patients. Many of us know of physicians who perform unnecessary tests, not to protect themselves against lawsuits, but to make more money. A few even refuse to treat patients in the emergency room unless a large deposit is made. The number of doctors who practice in such a dissolute manner is small, but when faced with such blatant abuse of power (which is often reported in the media), how can the public help but react negatively?

In the last half of this century, we have become more technicians than caregivers. When we want information, we look to the chart instead of to the patient; when we want to diagnose a patient's illness, we look at X-rays or laboratory results instead of examining the body. In our defense, these changes in medical practice were made with the best of intentions; today's technology *has* allowed physicians to make definitive diagnoses instead of educated guesses. Rarely, if ever, have medical innovations been made with financial gain, rather than patients' welfare, in mind. Even so, in the last half century something very precious has been lost—medicine's humanity.

Managed care umbrella

To protect the public from a few unscrupulous physicians, we are in danger of destroying our profession as a whole. The proposed panacea to cure the ills of the health care system is managed care. In this system, physicians become members of such groups as independent practice associations (IPAs), health maintenance organizations (HMOs), and preferred provider organizations (PPOs).[7] In 1993, 75 percent of physicians had at least one managed-care contract;[8] in 1994, 50 million people were enrolled in approximately 574 managed care organizations.[9] I was an early proponent of managed care, or the "bundling" of services at a set price. Through bundling, we could provide quality care at reasonable prices.

Some managed care organizations, however, are concerned less with quality care and more with maximizing their profits. While managed care was designed to protect patients from receiving too much care, some types of managed care may actually be launching an era of "undercare." Physicians with managed care contracts are given incentives to lower costs by reducing care. If they order expensive treatments, their salaries may be adversely affected. Thus, primary care physicians or "gatekeepers" may delay referring their patients for specialized treatment, sometimes with serious, or even fatal consequences. In an issue of the *American Medical News,* a physician tells the story of a woman whose primary care physician chose to examine the lump in her breast himself for months until he finally ordered a breast biopsy, which revealed cancer. He asks the question,

> Have health insurance executives forgotten that they or their relatives . . . may wind up in the hands of a stranger who, in a 10-minute evaluation, will decide that the pain in their back or abdomen or chest doesn't justify the expense of an MRI study or an echocardiogram—and who will send them home with their metastatic spine cancer, dissecting aortic aneurysm or pneumothorax?[10]

Even worse than the retreat of specialists may be the preeminence of administrators in making medical decisions. Here's what one Fort Worth surgeon had to say:

> You're talking to somebody who doesn't know a whole lot about medicine, who doesn't understand what it's all about, and you have to convince them to let you do something. . . . When that happens, you either end up with some uninformed, untrained person telling a doctor that he can't do something or with the doctor convincing them that he should do it. You don't reach an intellectual decision.[11, p. 44]

Administrators have the power to tell doctors how much time they can spend with a patient, and "many allow only 10 minutes for a returning patient and no more than 20 minutes for a new patient."[10] Perhaps laws should be enacted to hold the administrators of health care organizations accountable for such "undercare" of patients: "[Cost cuts] must not be accomplished by transforming the doctor from a caring friend who has the final say about patient care into a hired hand marching to the tune of a corporate business plan."[10]

Ironically, managed care may not fulfill its ultimate purpose to decrease health care costs. Many HMOs follow a policy of shadow-pricing: their charges "shadow" those of traditional insurance plans, increasing steadily at a slightly lower rate.[12] These organizations are cutting internal costs, not to benefit the taxpayers, but to increase their own profits; these "for-profit" companies are often more interested in increasing revenue than in ensuring quality of care. In 1994, the CEOs of managed care organizations made 35 percent more in direct compensation than CEOs of other businesses with comparable revenues; in base salary and bonuses, managed care CEOs made 62 percent more. The executives of two managed care companies made more than $10 million in salary, bonuses, and stock incentives.[13] Thus, before plunging head first into drastic reform measures, we must determine whether such reform will merely exchange our few "greedy doctors" for a plethora of "greedy executives."

The issue of outcomes

The rise of managed care has precipitated public disclosure of outcomes rates, particularly in cardiac surgery.[18] Public disclosure has been called "the third revolution in medical care," or "the Era of Assessment and Accountability."[14] Increasingly, patients are demanding to know more about the care they will receive. In the past, the public regarded the physician with unquestioning confidence; today, patients have begun to regard providers with the same suspicion they formerly reserved for large corporations. No longer will patients blindly put their health (and, many times, their lives) in the hands of caregivers—they now demand an assurance of quality.[15]

Managed care organizations also rely on outcomes data to make health care decisions. In order to choose among providers competing for managed care contracts, health organizations need an accurate method of evaluating the quality and cost-efficiency of medical services. Unfortunately, these statistics do not always tell the full story.

The arrival of "scorecard medicine" has also signaled the arrival of an entirely new breed of medical problems.[16] In a February 1996 issue of the *New England Journal of Medicine*, Brent Weston and Marie Lauria tell the story of an infant girl referred to them with acute lymphoblastic leukemia.[17] When they recommended that she undergo an allogeneic bone marrow transplant operation, her HMO referred her to a "center of quality" in another state. Even though treatment at this center would cause the parents tremendous emotional and economic hardship, the referral was made. Despite numerous appeals by her physician and family, the HMO refused to refer the girl to another center closer to her home. After studying the outcomes of various transplant centers, the

HMO had decided to refer all of its patients only to this center. The center that had been selected had "no particular expertise in acute lymphoblastic leukemia in infants or in the preparative regimen or transplantation procedure."[17, p. 543]

In the end, the girl was sent to the center; her mother was demoted; and her father lost his job. When the child had a relapse some months later, the HMO referred her to a different transplant center: the one where she had previously been treated was no longer considered a "center of quality."[17]

Anecdotes like this one are only too common. As a means of measuring quality, outcomes rates are imprecise, at best. As we saw in the above example, they often do not take into account psychosocial factors, such as family dynamics and the patient-physician relationship. In addition, an accurate means of adjusting outcomes data according to risk has not yet been developed. Although the Society of Thoracic Surgeons of New Jersey,[19] New York,[20] and Pennsylvania[21] are developing outcomes databases that include risk stratification, the method each uses is different, making the outcomes from these databases difficult to compare.

Toward the future

Change is inevitable; public disclosure *will* become a fixture of the health care system. Thus, to protect themselves and their patients, physicians must become involved in establishing a national database with an accurate method of risk adjustment. If physicians take control, outcomes data could be used to enhance the quality of care that patients receive. Since public disclosure of outcomes rates was initiated in New York State, there has been a 41 percent decrease in risk-adjusted mortality associated with coronary artery bypass grafting. The largest decrease in mortality occurred among physicians who had had the highest mortality rates before public disclosure was initiated.[20] Thus, fear of high mortality rates had little effect on already conscientious physicians, but it may have motivated other providers to raise their standards of care. Used appropriately, outcomes pinpoint inefficiencies and reduce the number of preventable deaths. As I have written elsewhere, "While public disclosure may help prevent wanton medical abuses, we must not become dependent on statistics to determine excellence of care."[15, p. 2]

There is no doubt that problems exist in today's health care system and that these problems must be solved; many of these flaws, however, are rooted in American cultural attitudes. The United States is a nation addicted to "quick-fixes." Instead of preventing problems, we react only when faced with disaster. In health care, this approach causes costs to skyrocket and our health as a nation to suffer.

In the twentieth century, our knowledge of disease has expanded dramatically. For example, we now know that many cases of heart disease and cancer could be forestalled, or even prevented if people would avoid certain deleterious practices (such as cigarette smoking) and adhere to a strict, nutritious diet. Still, every year more Americans die of heart disease than died in all of this century's wars combined.[22] Increasing rates of violence, drug abuse, and teen pregnancy have also contributed to the rising costs of health care. Such misfortunes might be avoided if young people were better educated. Thus, newer, more technologically advanced, *more expensive* methods are developed every day to treat patients who should never have needed them.

If we truly want to save money and improve the quality of American life, the solution is not managed care; it is preventive medicine. We must rid ourselves of our dependence on expensive BandAids and learn to prevent medical problems before they start. To play its part, medicine must return to the community. For too long, we have isolated ourselves in scientific cloisters; to practice preventive medicine, we must reclaim our relationship with our patients.

Change must also come from the public. As citizens of a wealthy nation, we are not preoccupied with the same issues as people in the past. Survival is rarely an issue; today we are more concerned with the quality than with the uncertainty of our existence. While the Greeks believed that health was a state of balance,[23] Americans believe that health is a state of perfection. Aches and pains that I accept as a normal consequence of aging cause in others inordinate alarm. Our society's preoccupation with beauty has made our plastic surgeons rich and our young girls sick with eating disorders. Length of life has become more important than quality of life. Consistently, the lives of terminally ill patients are extended by ventilators or other measures of extraordinary care. Our society lives in denial of death, as if, with enough knowledge and technology, it were possible to stave it off somehow. We need to remember the wisdom of Ben Franklin: "In this world, nothing is certain but death and taxes."[24]

What should medical practice in the twenty-first century be like? I believe that the future of medicine is ours to create. Radical measures of reform are not the answer—they would only distract us from the fundamental causes of our medical discontent. Instead, our young physicians must lead both a charge and a retreat: they must combine the scientific knowledge we have gathered in the last fifty years with the ancient compassion and nobility that distinguishes our profession. Medical schools must find room in their overburdened curricula to teach their students that the humanity of the patient is as important as his or her ailment. We must renew our dedication to our patients and our profession, and adapt to the changing medical climate. We must build on our accomplishments, not raze them. Physicians must become proactive: if we allow ourselves to be swept helplessly away by the tide of reform, we shall not be able to stand up for our patients.

There are no limits to what we can accomplish in the next millennium, the next century, or even the next decade. Never believe that there is a limit to medical progress. In the 1880s, Theodor Billroth declared, "Any surgeon who wishes to preserve the respect of his colleagues would never attempt to suture the heart."[25] In less than a century (and within a fifteen-year period), we had developed the heart-lung machine, bypassed blockages in the coronary arteries, transplanted the native heart, and implanted an artificial heart. To paraphrase Otto von Bismarck, *medicine* is the art of the *impossible*.[26]

No doubt, the next century will see the development of such medical marvels as the artificial heart and gene therapy. However medicine evolves, though, it is the responsibility of both the old and new guard to uphold the compassion and nobility that forms the core of our profession.

> There are men and classes of men that stand above the common herd: the soldier, the sailor, and the shepherd not infrequently; the artist rarely; more rare, the clergyman; the physician almost as a rule. He is the flower (such as it is) of our civilization; and when that stage of man is done with, and only remembered to be marvelled at in history, he will be thought to have shared as little as any in the defects of the period, and most notably exhibited the virtues of the race. Generosity he has, such as is possible to those who practice an art, never to those who drive a trade; discretion, tested by a hundred secrets; tact, tried in a thousand embarrassments; and what are more important, Heraclean cheerfulness and courage. So it is that he brings air and cheer into the sickroom, and often enough, though not so often as he wishes, brings healing.
>
> — Robert Louis Stevenson[27]

Let me assure young physicians that if they are motivated to provide compassionate service and to focus on the welfare of their patients, their rewards will justify their dedication to this honorable profession.

References

1. Shorter E. The history of the doctor-patient relationship. In Bynum WF and Porter R, eds. Companion Encyclopedia of the History of Medicine, vol. 2, pp. 783–800. London, Routledge, 1993.
2. Hooker W. Physician and Patient, or A Practical View of the Mutual Duties, Relations and Interests of the Medical Profession and the Community. New York, Baker & Scribner, 1849, p. 384.
3. Gibbon JH, Jr. Application of a mechanical heart and lung apparatus to cardiac surgery. Minn Med 37:171–80,1954.
4. Barnard CN. The operation: A human cardiac transplant: An interim report of a successful operation performed at Groote Schuur Hospital, Cape Town S Afr Med J 41:1271–74, 1967.
5. Kovner AR. Futures. In Kovner, AR, ed. Jonas's Health Care Delivery in the United States, 5th ed, pp. 532–53. New York, Springer Publishing Co., 1995, p. 544.
6. Owen JA, Jr. Doctors and dollars: Hippocrates revisited. Pharos 57(1):2–5, Winter 1994.
7. Cooley DA. Health and medicine. In Templeton, JM, ed. Looking Forward: The Next Forty Years, pp. 106–27. New York, Harper Collins Publ., 1993.

8. Eisenberg JM. Economics. JAMA 273:1670–71, 1995.

9. Grover FL. The bright future of cardiovascular surgery in the era of changing health-care delivery. Ann Thorac Surg 61:499–510, 1996, p. 502.

10. Laster L. Managed care translates to 'Let the patient beware.' Am Med News, February 19, 1996, p. 18.

11. Lamensdorf H. Quoted in Richardson, M:. Can managed care control costs without controlling you? Tex Med 88(10):36–44, 1992.

12. Freudenheim M. For Xerox, HMOs failing to provide complete cure. Houston Chronicle, February 16, 1993, Business Section, p. 4.

13. Mitka M. HMO executives claim fat paychecks. Am Med News, February 5, 1996, pp. 3, 23.

14. Relman AS. Assessment and accountability: The third revolution in medical care. N EngI J Med 319:1220–22, 1988.

15. Cooley DA. Building shelters: Safeguards in public disclosure of outcomes data. Circulation 93:1–3, 1996.

16. Topol EJ and Califf RM. Scorecard cardiovascular medicine: Its impact and future directions. Ann Intern Med 120:65–70, 1994.

17. Weston B and Lauria M. Patient advocacy in the 1990s. N Engl J Med 334:543–44, 1996.

18. Clark RE. The 515 Cardiac Surgery National Database: An update. Ann Thorac Surg 59:1376–81, 1995.

19. Parsonnet V, Bernstein AD, and Gera M. Clinical usefulness of risk-stratified outcome analysis in cardiac surgery in New Jersey. Ann Thorac Surg 61:S8–11, 1996.

20. Hannan EL, Kilburn H, Jr., Racz M, et al. Improving the outcomes of coronary artery bypass surgery in New York State. JAMA 271:761–66, 1994.

21. Griffith BP, Hattler BG, Hardesty RL, et al. The need for accurate risk-adjusted measures of outcome in surgery: Lessons learned through coronary artery bypass. Ann Surg 222:593–99, 1995.

22. Academic American Encyclopedia, s.v. World War I, World War II, Korean War, Vietnam War.

23. Banta HD and Jonas S. Health and health care. In Kovner AR, ed. Jonas' Health Care Delivery in the United States, 5th ed., pp. 11–33. New York, Springer Publishing Co, 1995.

24. Bartlett's Familiar Quotations, 15th and 125th anniversary ed., s.v. Benjamin Franklin.

25. Richardson RG. The Surgeon's Heart: A History of Cardiac Surgery. London, William Heinemann Medical Books, 1969, p. 28.

26. Bartlett's Familiar Quotations, s.v. Otto von Bismarck.

27. Stevenson RL. Dedication. In Underwoods: A Child's Garden of Verses, vol. 15 of The Works of Robert Louis Stevenson, p. 9. New York, Peter Fenelon Collier, Publ., not dated.

INDEX

521